The Lion And The Lily:
Nova Scotia Between 1600-1760

Volume I

Peter Landry

www.blupete.com

To "Margo"

Report errors: errata@blupete.com

Order this book online at www.trafford.com/07-2430
or email orders@trafford.com

Most Trafford titles are also available at major online book retailers.

Note for Librarians: A cataloguing record for this book is available from Library
and Archives Canada at www.collectionscanada.ca/amicus/index-e.html

Printed in Victoria, BC, Canada.

ISBN: 978-1-4251-5450-9
Volume I

*We at Trafford believe that it is the responsibility of us all, as both individuals
and corporations, to make choices that are environmentally and socially sound.
You, in turn, are supporting this responsible conduct each time you purchase a
Trafford book, or make use of our publishing services. To find out how you are
helping, please visit www.trafford.com/responsiblepublishing.html*

*Our mission is to efficiently provide the world's finest, most comprehensive
book publishing service, enabling every author to experience success.
To find out how to publish your book, your way, and have it available
worldwide, visit us online at www.trafford.com/10510*

 www.trafford.com

North America & international
toll-free: 1 888 232 4444 (USA & Canada)
phone: 250 383 6864 ♦ fax: 250 383 6804 ♦ email: info@trafford.com

The United Kingdom & Europe
phone: +44 (0)1865 722 113 ♦ local rate: 0845 230 9601
facsimile: +44 (0)1865 722 868 ♦ email: info.uk@trafford.com

10 9 8 7 6 5 4 3 2 1

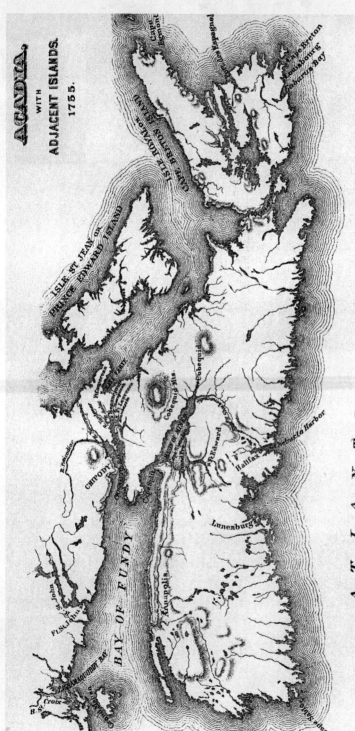

The Lion And The Lily:
Nova Scotia Between 1600-1760

Table Of Contents

vii

Table Of Contents xi

Annapolis Royal and in addition determined to extend the English presence by sending an additional 500 under Arthur Noble who took up a position at Grand Pré. The English went into winter quarters figuring they would get a start in the early spring and surprise the French military who had stationed themselves at Chignecto. The tables were reversed when the French caught wind of the English intentions and immediately set off on a winter march, overland.

not pursue the matter and the Acadians were pretty much left alone by the local English authority, represented, as it was, by one small and incapacitated English garrison located at Annapolis Royal. This situation was to dramatically change through a six year period beginning in 1749.

The Acadian oath (1729/30) as was secured by Governor Philipps was unconditional, at least on paper it was. It seems, however, that the Acadians were talked into signing the oath on the basis of "verbal promises" made. They were told at the time that they would be exempt from the necessity of bearing arms in the event of a conflict with the French. This compromise — and it seems there was not much doubt that it was made — was to haunt the masters of Nova Scotia for the next 25 years and contribute significantly to the tragic developments that were to culminate with the deportation of 1755.

The decision to deport the Acadians was one that was taken at the local level (Governor Lawrence and his Council). Even if he felt he had to clear the intended deportation with England — there was no time for it in these days of sail. Here was an opportunity to be seized upon. The Acadians boldly refused to take an oath of loyalty. Nothing new. They had done this in the past, and with no consequences. The difference this time was that Lawrence had 2,000 troops under his command and who were but a couple of days away.

In comparing the backgrounds and personalities of these two (Winslow and Monckton), one might better understand why the relationship, as between the 52 year old colonial gentleman and the 29 year old army officer from England to whom Winslow was obliged to report, was, to say the least, strained. Winslow, though he gave little notice of it, must have wanted to get out from under Monckton's command as soon as possible. Winslow was relieved when the orders came up from Governor Lawrence personally asking for him to head the detachment which was ordered to the Minas area.

On August the 19th, we would have seen Winslow and his detachment, on the first tide, slip over to Grand Pré, but a dozen miles from Fort Edward. He entered the River Gaspereau and landed his forces. Winslow and his men were in anticipation that "it is likely shall soon have our hands full of disagreeable business to remove people from their ancient habitations." He took up his quarters "between the Church and the Chapel yard, having the priest house for my own accommodation and the church for a place of arms."

Having paid a visit to Captain Murrray at Fort Edward, Winslow and his small party was sailing back to Grand Pré. He had in his pouch a good copy of the citation translated into the French. He arrived at his camp at two o'clock in the afternoon on September the 2nd. Winslow was to immediately call for his officers: copies of the citation were to go out, to be posted in all conspicuous places. The Acadian men were ordered to attend at the church in Grand Pré on Friday, the fifth, at three o'clock in the afternoon, no excuses.

Table Of Contents

Volume II

Table Of Contents   xvii

180 warships and transports. It had been hoped by the British prime minister, Pitt, that this tremendous invasion force could have done double duty in 1758: first Louisbourg and then Quebec. With the capitulation of Louisbourg on July 26th, the immediate question before the British commanders was whether they should push on to Quebec?

Pitt's resolution was that all the works and defenses of Louisbourg's Harbor, "be most effectually and most entirely demolished." It was intended that the materials be so "thoroughly destroyed, as that no use may, hereafter, be ever made of the same."

Maps & Plans

Introduction

"Oh dream of Empire! 'plauded in gilded courts,
For thee long vigils pass in these shattered forts;
For thee that mighty camp whitens yonder hill,
And two nations bleed as their monarchs will;
Gold wrung from patient toil wastes in foreign war,
And devastating armies roam the Red Man's shore."
— Charles Ochiltree Macdonald.

History, in a perfect world, should occupy a pure place on the larger canvas of literature: to take its place amongst all forms of literature — unadulterated. The brilliant English writer, Macaulay,[1] contrasted the following notions: poetry and philosophy, imagination and truth, and romantic literature and history. He observed that each element in the pair is hostile to the another, each, having an exclusive right to the territory occupied. Good histories, in the proper sense of the word — we have not. But we have good historical romances[2] and good historical essays. My goal was to write a series of good historical essays on the early history of Nova Scotia which might turn, metamorphic like, into a whole history. It will, however, never be a pure history. The people, the dates, the places: they are all as accurate as I possibly could make them after much research carried out over many years amongst the published materials on Nova Scotia, of which we have a wealth.[3] The persons to whom I refer are in fact real people who made indelible marks on Nova Scotia. These people, however, including the historical characters who kept contemporaneous notes, were each, like everyone else in the human race, tinged with romance and subject to the uncontrollable events in which they turned: this is the stuff of which "true romance" is made. These romantic events glisten like diamonds in the pages of Nova Scotian history.

The province, or geographical area of the world which attracts our attention, was from an early date to present day known, to the English as Nova Scotia, to the French as Acadia. The present day eastern-Canadian province of Nova Scotia is, except for a short connecting peninsula, surrounded by the sea. It extends out into the northwestern Atlantic Ocean, a part of the northeastern seaboard of North America. To its north is the entranceway to the great water highway leading into the heartland of North America: the mighty St. Lawrence.

The St. Lawrence River led Europeans, mainly the French, beginning four centuries ago, into the interior of the North American continent, and on, out into the Great Lakes and down the Mississippi River. The English pretty much restricted themselves to the American eastern seaboard south of Nova Scotia. This English territory had a natural western border, the Appalachian Mountains with its continuous ridge from north to south, from Mount Katahdin in the present day State of Maine to Mount Springer in the present day State of Georgia. By 1700 the English felt hemmed in and those brave English traders who found their way into the Ohio valley ran smack into the French and their allies with whom they had a unique relationship, the native Indians. Throughout the 17th century and the first half of the 18th, the northern part of the North American continent was a battle field for two European powers: the French and the English. It is these historic battles of which I write. We pick up with the very first explorations as the 17th century opens and continue along in our narrative, through to a point just past the mid-18th century, when French rule in North America came to an end. The end, of course, being heralded when Wolfe appeared before the walls of Quebec in 1759, the beginnings of which event we but touch on as we end this book. This work is restricted in time (1600 to 1760) and also geographically, to the province of Nova Scotia. I will touch on the larger events in the world only as is necessary to bring the events under review into perspective. My work is the story of Old Acadia.[4]

Part One

Early Settlement & Baronial Battles:

1605-90

Chapter 1

Fish And Furs

What I write here is but a very brief sketch of the earlest times of the north-western Atlantic fishery. If a book were to be written then it would be by and large a historical accounting of past facts. The book however would of necessity, open and end in speculation.[1]

Further along in this work, we will consider the early explorers, of which there is a written record; but, for now, we write of the fishermen of old, who, coming from western Europe, made their living in the waters and the shores of northeastern North America. No thought was made by these early fisherman to write of their experiences, nor was there any need for it. No one back in the old ports of western Europe was looking for written reports; what was looked for were the products contained in the holds of the returning vessels. On the docks, in season, would be found: the ivory and hides of the walrus; the long horn of the narwhal, the down of eider ducks; the skins of the beaver, the otter, the fisher, the martin, the mink, the muskrat and the bear (brown, black and white); and, of course, barrels and barrels of salted fish. No captain, owner, or investor was much interested in writing down where the vessel had been or how to get there; it served no commercial purpose to do so (indeed it would be the telling of a commercial secret), assuming in the first place that any of them could write.

We cannot now count or name[2] the persons who preceded the Cabots. These unnamed men, well after the earlier voyages of the Norsemen, from the western ports of Europe came to the northeastern shores of North America for some considerable period of time before the traditional dates which can be found in history books. These unnamed men followed the traditions of a long line of fathers. The interest that these earlier seafarers had in the new world was something that was decidedly fishy. For you see, there were many hungry people back in Europe, and the waters off the coast of "new-found-land" teemed with great schools of cod, such that one could fill his boat with them, even if using the crudest of equipment; this was tempting news to any fisherman who had been plying his trade in the fished-out waters off the shores of France and England. Even though the stories of fishermen are notoriously untrustworthy, they nonetheless became the dreams of the young men who frequented the public places in such ports as Bristol in England and St. Malo in France. It was these dreams of these young men, like the dreams of young men in all times, that drove western European men to the far off shores of North America. The dangers of any long sail over the ocean was evident to all fishermen, but there are always risks when one sets out to make a living on the sea, whether a few miles off or a few thousand. So what if it's a long sail and you will not see your family for months — that's what "fishin' s'all about": and the promise that you could fill your boat with a short stay, drove many illiterate fisherman to the northern shores of America.

What is for sure, is that, by the opening of the 16th century, men were becoming aware of the huge catches of fish that could be had off the northeastern coast of North America:

This intelligence ran like wildfire through Europe, second only in importance to the finding of a previously unknown continent. Codfish were gold-fish in those spiced meat-eating days. Fleets flocked to this piscatorial eldorado. In 1504 probably 100 schooners, large and small, were on the Banks. As early as 1530 it has been stated 500 sail English, French and Portuguese, a few Dutch and Spanish, carrying 6,000 men, annually visited 'Baccalaos,' cod-land, in the spring, returning with cargoes in the fall. The home-coming was a gala event in maritime communities. It is possible women and clergymen occasionally accompanied the ships to Acadia and Newfoundland. ...

The market was Europe. There was no temptation for families to migrate, and American winters were dreaded, the air being thought to cause sickness. From year to year the same harbours were usually resorted to for curing, without any conflict between groups.[3]

For the French and the Portuguese salt was abundant and they brought it out to the fishing grounds with them. In England, however, salt is not so readily available, indeed the English fishermen had to purchase it from their competitors. Back in the early days one either had a fresh fish or a rotten fish, unless it was pickled within a day or two of it being caught. It was a great boon to saltless countries when during "the third quarter of the 16th century the English developed a 'dry' method of preserving fish: cod was cleaned, lightly salted, and dried in the sun."[4]

With the shift to the "dry" fishery, came more shore exploration. The dry fishery "involved more prolonged contacts with the natives and even some certainty of return to a specific spot."[5] However, up to the time of the founding of Port Royal, men rarely wintered over. Indeed, no one wanted to come and live year-round on these barren shores, which through the winter would often freeze up solid.[6]

It is easy to switch from fish to fur, for there is a connection. The fisherman who made their way from Europe would bring back with them in the fall a few furs which brought some immediate cash directly they landed at their home ports. These fishermen managed to get these few fur pelts right off the backs of the native Indians. As for the Indians, they were happy to make these spring trades as winter was coming to an end and kettles and knives were needed. But, initially, this trade was but a part time activity for the fishermen, one that went on for a number of years, but gradually full time fur traders came. These full time traders would have to get an early start in the spring if they were to make the best deals. The way to get a real early start in the spring, is, of course, to winter over; and so, there came into being year round settlements such as that which the French set up at Port Royal, to which we shall refer. Within a generation or two, as the 17th century progressed, the fur trade on the east coast dried up; not so much because the populations of the fur bearing animals sunk (I imagine they did) but more because the traders went further and further inland to seek out the Indian traders and their supplies. This chase for furs led the white man right across the continent. Thus, it was the northern fur bearing animals that were responsible for opening up the northern territories; indeed, the full extent of Canada became known before that of the western United States. In this context, one will have to consider the inland explorations as they expanded the western horizons of America. One might begin with Radisson and Groseilliers (1660); and then to continue on with Henry Kelsey (1690), La Vérendrye (1730), Samuel Hearne (1770); and so many, many, others, most of whose names have now been lost to us. Though I am out of my current time frame, I should add that the long push west ended, of course, with Alexander Mackenzie as he paddled down Dean's Channel on the western coast on the 22nd of July, 1793. Initially, however it was the European fishermen who started the fur trade and it began on the east coast. Professor Brebner makes the point:

After 1543 the fisherman who resorted to Newfoundland and the Gulf saw the fur trade gradually develop. In the courts of Europe there was an eager demand for the princely marten-skins. Other furs and the hides of elk, deer and bears satisfied a less discriminating taste. Specifically, however, it was the hat-makers who became the stimulators in Europe of a demand for beaver-skins for which the first time came at all near to reciprocating the Indian demand for European goods. The precise requirements of the hat manufacture were somewhat technical, but the basic consideration was that the downy hairs of beaver fur possessed in unrivalled fashion the gift of natural coherence into an extremely durable felt.

The beaver meadows nearest the coast suffered first, but northern North America with its wealth of water-ways provided relatively untouched areas farther on. Thus the hat-makers of Europe were transformed into the prime movers of an exchange in America which sucked into the interior the men who followed the ever-retreating 'beaver frontier' across the continent.[7]

As the native traps yielded fewer and fewer pelts the native trappers turned themselves into traders and went inland. The Europeans, following the age old custom of cutting out the middle man, "began to send their vessels up the river either to tap virgin sources of furs or to intercept the flow of them from the interior which the Gulf barter had already brought into being." This process started when in 1534 the merchants of St. Malo financed and sent Cartier off and continued beyond 1793 when, finally, MacKenzie, popped his nose out of the bushes and peered out into an arm of the Pacific ocean. And thus, America proceeded in its development; almost exclusively through private enterprise.

I finish this part with a sad note on Walruses, a quote from John Quinpool:

In 1534 Jacques Cartier was the first to report an extensive walrus fishery in 'Acadian' waters in the Gulf of St. Lawrence, which has practically become extinct, south of Greenland. The St. Malo navigator stated the Magdalen islands were surrounded with "many great beasts, like huge oxen, with teeth (tusks) like an elephant, that go in the sea." This is the first walrus or seacow record in America. Colonel Richard Gridley, Boston, was at the siege of Louisburg and at the fall of Quebec in 1759. He received a grant of the walrus fishery which the French had conserved.

One of the earliest executive acts following erection of Prince Edward Island into a separate government in 1770 was an attempt to check destruction of the walrus fishery, which nevertheless, was finally ruined during the succeeding half-century. None have been taken for 100 [170] years. These animals weighed up to 4,000 pounds. Oil from the blubber was fine quality, a little of the flesh was eaten, the rest thrown away or some used for fertilizer, while the skins were accounted valuable for harness and similar uses. After the War of Independence in 1783, Governor Patterson of St. John's Island (Prince Edward Island) advised British authorities: "New England vessels are in a fair way to destroy the sea-cow fisheries, if there are not some steps taken to prevent them. The chief resort of these fish is about this island and the Magdalen islands.

Colonel Gridley, Magdalen islands, admitted killing 5,000 principally females, in a summer. The young were little value and were abandoned. Gridley's slaughter was mainly on land and out of season. He fled to Boston, when an order was issued for his arrest. Females, in the spring calving season, frequented shallow water or established themselves at sunny places on land. Relatively few males were taken, as they usually kept in deep water. If a calf was captured or killed, the mother would not leave the spot and became an easy victim. Fishing captains generally kept a calf on board and caused it to make noise to attract females.

Chapter 2

Early European Explorers

Norwegians—though there be very little record of it—visited the most northern parts of eastern North America over a thousand years ago. Indeed, maybe before the Norwegians, the Irish paid a visit; or maybe, in classic times, the Greeks.[1] However, what we do know, pretty well for sure, is that the Norsemen first came to Iceland, then as the decades and centuries unfolded they traveled beyond Iceland, to Greenland; then again, beyond Greenland to the shores of Baffin Island and Labrador; then again, swinging south, in their frail vessels, down they came along the upper coast of eastern North America.[2] Whatever motivated these northern Europeans to keep extending their northern voyages, and exactly when[3] they might have made them, are further matters on which we are obliged to speculate. Was it for timber? Was it new lands for splintered clans? Whatever the extent of their explorations and the timing of them, it is believed that any settlements of the Norsemen were but of a temporary kind and that they made no great impact or contribution to the exploration of North America.

Before we deal with such known explorers as Cabot and Cartier, we must acknowledge the thousands of seafaring men, who, in the process of making a living, came to the shores of America, especially those that are washed by the waters that flow over the great fishing banks of the northwestern Atlantic. Discovery, like everything else in life, is an evolutionary process and one voyage by one family was built upon the knowledge gained on a previous voyage of another family member; only slowly did the Europeans become aware of their courses and their objectives that lie to the west over the ocean.[4]

The earliest explorers, as we have seen, were the unknown and unsung fisherman of western Europe who likely came to the shores of North America in an earlier millennium; these brave seafarers continued their family traditions up to and beyond 1500s. It is with the 1500s, that one can begin to examine our written history. Among those spunky Frenchmen who first wintered over on the forbidding north-eastern shores of America and in particular on the ironbound shores of Nova Scotia, were to be found leaders and local managers who were obliged (and, for this, historians will be forever grateful) to file reports to their backers back home. As we will see, the original European explorers of this country were little supported by their respective governments. It was not in the charter of any government back in those days to go forth and to explore or to bring "the light of civilization" to other persons of the world. There were no fine ideals that were put into group action; nor was there to be until the English colonies revolted, in 1776, a time which extends beyond that under review. Nonetheless, in these early years of exploration, great expense was incurred to outfit long lasting and self-sustaining expeditions. Those who financed these expeditions naturally expected to get their capital back with a profit. The greater the risk (and ocean crossings were very risky) then the greater the expected return. What were these expected returns? It was trade that drove the exploration of the Americas.[5]

Bear in mind that there was still no thought of America being a vast continent; no greater conception existed than that it was a chain of islands, and that along this direction there would be found a short cut to Cathay instead of going south, round the coast of Africa. What, in the minds of the financing merchants, was heartily to be desired may be summed up in one brief formula: a secret path to Oriental riches, north-about, obviating any collision with Portuguese or Spaniards.[6]

At first, and for many years after, it was Oriental trade, or rather the prospect of it, which drove so many marine explorers west over the vast Atlantic. And then, having fetched up on blocking shores, to sniff up and down the seacoasts like expectant mice, frustrated, but sure that there did exist a way to the spiced cheese westward and beyond. The way had to be there, if only it could be found. All land is surrounded by water, any land on the earth was but an island, and the Americas, it was figured, could not be an exception. So sure that a passage was to be had through the islands of America that they already had a name for it, "The Straight of Anian." But who could have imagined such an island stretching, practically speaking, from one end of the earth to the other? Looking back on history, we now know, that while Columbus "discovered" the Americas, the configuration of this half of the world was not to be fully understood for yet another 300 years. It was only with the expeditions of James Cook (1728-79), George Vancouver (c.1758-98) and Sir Alexander Mackenzie (c.1755-1820) was any geographer able to put a fix on America at its thickest part.

It is June 24th, 1497, a dozen miles or so, east, off the northern part of Cape Breton Island. The alert seaman, while hanging off the shroud of a small sailing vessel, at daybreak, sees something that might well appear to be, to the unobservant, just another line of low lying dark clouds; it lies flat on the western horizon in the reflection of the rising sun; it is of the darkest misty green. For the last few days the seamen aboard the *Matthew* had observed the tell-tale signs of land: soaring gulls, the poking heads of seal mammals, bits of floating material, and a western horizon which looked different.

The *Matthew* was one of two small English sailing vessels which had been "wandering fifty-two days" across the vast Atlantic.[7] In the captain's cabin of the *Matthew*, in a long oaken chart chest, fitted against the bulkhead, with its brass fittings, would be found in one of its slender, long and wide drawers — a Royal declaration, with its lines of black ink swirled upon the dry and whiten sheep skin (slit, smooth and indentured at its edges), with great gobs of red wax with ribbon bound up in it at its bottom; and, too, at its bottom: the Royal Signature, Henry VII of England. The mission of the men aboard these two small English sailing vessels, in 1497: "to subdue, occupy, and possesse ... to be holden and bounden to Henry of all the fruits, profits, gaines, and commodities to pay unto him in wares or money a fifth part of the capital gaine so gotten."[8]

In anticipation of fresh water and fresh food, the crew begin to douse their sails and lay out their anchors. A new land had been "discovered," which we have come to call Nova Scotia. John Cabot (1425-c.1500),[9] his sons and a small band of English sailors came ashore, it is figured, at the foot of Sugarloaf Mountain[10] on the northeastern tip of Cape Breton Island; there they built and erected a cross and unfurled the British Royal Standard. Shortly thereafter, these explorers gathered up their anchors, set sail, and steered a course for home.

Time passed. Only Spain was to immediately follow up with her discovery of the Americas to the south. Within years Spanish conquistadors hacked their way through the jungle and the people of central and south America. Spain for most of the 16th century was to have an exclusive on America. The French and the English at first were blissfully ignorant of the riches to be obtained over the western horizons. In 1522, however, a French corsair off the cape of St. Vincent took a Spanish ship which was sailing home from New Spain. The French captain was amazed at what he found in the holds of the Spanish treasure ship. Soon, the leaders of both France and England were to know of the riches that were to be had in the Americas, to be found either through piracy or exploration.

In 1524, two explorers came to the shores of Acadia: Gómez and Verrazzano. Esteban Gómez (c.1483-1538) was a Portuguese sailor. He, together with his 29 crew members, in 1524, in his 75 ton caravel, *Anunciada*, sailed up the coast and into the Bay of Fundy.[11] It is reported he arrived back in Europe and had with him, 58 live natives, captured somewhere on the coasts of either Maine or Nova Scotia.

It was Verrazzano (1485-1528) who named Acadia, "Arcadia." Verrazzano, in 1524, sailed under a French flag in his tiny caravel, the *Dauphine*, together with a Norman crew of 50. He cruised a vast area, from Virginia and then north along a stretch of land that now covers the northeastern part of United States and the Canadian provinces of Nova Scotia, New Brunswick, Prince Edward Island, and the southern parts of Quebec.

After this date, 1524, I should say, European navigators depicted America as far south and as far north as one might go (as opposed to so many islands) — one huge mass of land, seemingly impenetrable. But hope persisted for many, many years thereafter that there was a way through, to the riches of the orient.

The Voyages Of Jacques Cartier:

Jacques Cartier (1491-1557), in 1534 received a royal commission from the French king "to discover certain islands and lands where it is said that a great quantity of gold, and other precious things, are to be found."[12] Cartier had two ships and 61 men. During the month of June, having crossed the north Atlantic in twenty days, Cartier entered the Strait of Belle Île from the north; by July he was off Prince Edward Island; and by August he and his men were headed home to St. Malo. In the spring of the next year, Cartier was back, this time sailing up the highway into Canada, the St. Lawrence River, there to visit the site of present day Quebec. In October of 1535, Cartier and his men left their sea-going ships behind at Quebec and travelled to Hochelaga (Montreal), there to observe the communal huts of the Iroquois. Cartier and his men were the first organized group of Europeans to spend a winter in Canada. By the spring of the following year, 1536, these intrepid French explorers were making their way down the St. Lawrence; and, by summer, they were back, snug in their home port, St. Malo.

Five years passed before Cartier returned to Canada. He was to spend another winter (1541-2) at Quebec, a hard one for him and his men. In the spring, Cartier returned to France leaving de Roberval, his "co-adventurer," behind to spend the winter (1542-3) at Quebec.

The principal point to be made of Cartier's voyages is that Cartier had claimed the explored lands for the King of France; and, at least around the mouth of the St. Lawrence, this was the same territory which Cabot had ceremoniously claimed for England, 40 odd years earlier. With this fact in mind, it is easy to see why the English always thought the French in their northern settlements were but claim jumpers. However, while it may well have been the English who first stuck a flag pole into the soil, it was the French who first overwintered. So too, they established, outside of Florida, the very first permanent settlement in North America, Port Royal; but I run ahead of myself.

As for the English, we left off in 1497 with Cabot. The next noteworthy voyage of an Englishman was that taken by Sir Humphrey Gilbert (1537-83) in 1583 when he headed west to America under the directions of an English company, the Muscovy Company. Gilbert was an educated and well connected man; he set his sights and turned his mind to the finding of the Northwest Passage. During the month of August, 1583, after bucking head winds for seven weeks, Gilbert landed on the island of Newfoundland. At the expense of his own and his family's fortune, Gilbert had set out with five ships (he was to loose three during his adventure). After a brief period of discovery, Gilbert, and his brave followers, set out later that summer for home in the two ships remaining to him, the *Squirrel* and the *Golden Hind*. The *Squirrel*, during a storm, when down into the Atlantic depths; her occupants, including Gilbert, never to be heard from again.

It was in 1584, if we would have been in one of the anti-chambers of the Elizabethan court, that we would have seen Sir Walter Raleigh giving dispatches to Captain Philip Amidas and Captain Arthur Barlow, dispatches which contained orders to go to America. Sailing from the Thames, on 27th April, 1584, they sighted the Canary Islands on the 10th of May and then the West Indies on the 10th of June; from there they sailed north up the eastern coast of America until they came to Cape Hatteras, and, in behind, to drop anchor in Pamlico Sound. Amidas and Barlow were back safely in England by September of 1584. Virginia, named after the virgin queen, and which covered a wide stretch in those days, had been "discovered" by the English.

Next, on 9th April, 1585, we have the expedition commanded by Sir Richard Grenville, a cousin of Raleigh's, and, once again,

Captain! ... Oh! Excuse me — Admiral Philip Amidas sailing from Plymouth after resting over at Porto Rico with his fleet, sailed back into the Pamlico Sound region, however, not before Amidas' flag ship was wrecked somewhere along that treacherous shore that has Cape Lookout at one end and Cape Hatteras at the other. Grenville dropped 108 people off on Roanoke Island and left them to their fate; as for himself — he went back to the comforts of England. These first English settlers wintered over on the island under the governorship of Ralph Lane. (Incidentally, before 1585, Europeans knew nothing of tobacco. Its introduction into Europe was entirely owing to this expedition.) Things did not go well for the Roanoke Island settlers. They had, throughout the winter, fought amongst themselves and with the Indians to such an extent that they were unable to secure food for themselves; by the spring of 1586 they were existing on roots and oysters. Who knows what might have happened to them, if they had not been picked up and brought back to England by none other than Sir Francis Drake, himself. Drake was checking in on them with his 23 ship fleet; he had just completed his main task. In the previous year Drake's fleet had been sent out by Elizabeth to raid the Spaniards in the West Indies. The Roanoke Island settlers begged Drake to bring them back with him to England; he did; and thus the first English settlement on Roanoke Island was left to the natives.

Another group of 117 settlers arrived at Roanoke Island in May of 1587; at least 17 of them were women. The governor this time was a man by the name of White. He had a daughter named Eleanor who came out to the new world with him, she and her young husband, Ananias Dare. Indeed, the first English child in America was born to Eleanor on 18th August, 1587, a little girl named Virginia Dare. This 1587 party soon came to realize they would not last long without additional supplies, so their leader, White, sailed off to England for supplies. White got back to England alright, but, another historical event delayed him getting back to Virginia: the Spanish Armada. Two years were to pass before White went ashore at Roanoke Island and not a soul could be found. There was no sign of a struggle and no bodies were found. It is supposed they went off as a group to locate better quarters — not a word was ever heard from them: "ninety-one men, seventeen women and nine boys."

The entire eastern coast of America, before 1584, was known as Florida, but, within a few years of having entered into the 17th century (1600), we see that it could be divided up into three geographical districts: Florida, Virginia, and Acadia. No one was capable of defining the western borders of any of these three large geographical areas. Acadia, in the north, "belonged" to the French; Florida, in the south, "belonged" to the Spaniards. The northern borders of Florida were somewhere in the Carolinas, so Virginia, to which the English laid claim, fitted itself in between Florida and Acadia.[13]

In 1599, Elizabeth gave to a number of influential persons, a charter which incorporated the East India Company with Sir Thomas Smith to be its first governor. In April of 1601, ships of the East India Company sailed south, south by the Canaries, and south down the long coast of Africa; and then around the cape and across the Indian ocean to Sumatra; there to arrive in June of 1602. By September, the ships had returned to England filled with "cinnamon, pepper and cloves ... a great commerce had been initiated which was to raise England from a poor to a wealthy nation, and eventually establish the British Empire."[14]

From Falmouth, on the 26th of March, 1602, two ships, the *Concord* and *Dartmouth*, with noble men aboard, including Captains Bartholomew Gosnold and Bartholomew Gilbert, set sail for the Americas. Gosnold was to make "an effort to find a short, quick way across the Atlantic and get a hold of this vaguely-conceived territory without going by the 'unneedful' southerly Canaries-West Indies route." They went north of Roanoke Island into another part of "Virginia" to a place we now know as Martha's Vineyard. By June, 1602, we would have seen sailors on the shores of Elizabeth Île (Cuttyhunk Island) dividing up the remaining victuals between the crew, who were to sail back to England, and those that were to be left behind. When those who were to stay behind surveyed the small pile of supplies that was to be left to them, a discussion broke out and a few days later they all went back to England. Further reference is to be made to the voyage a Captain Martin Pring, who, in a two ship English expedition, the *Discovery* and the *Speedwell*, explored the Long Island Sound area during the year of 1603. By October the *Discovery* and the *Speedwell* were back at their home port, Bristol. So, still, as of 1602, there was no permanent settlement of Englishmen on the east coast of America. And their experiences in the settlement business was indeed sad.

Though no settlements came about as a result of the voyages of Captain Gosnold and of Captain Pring, regardless of what their intentions might have been, their voyages could be described as positive, in that a shorter route to Virginia had been worked out. Generally, however, England's experiences in America were mostly negative:

One disaster after another; the accumulated toll of missing men and wasted voyages; the struggles against bad weather, hunger, thirst, disease and wretched discomfort; the quarrels and mutinies, the failure to give merchants a tangible reward for the capital risked; the continuous series of disappointments — all these were the preliminaries and conditions before England was to come in active possession of northern America.[15]

If people are inclined to learn at all from their experiences, they can just as easily, and some times more effectively, learn from their negative experiences: England did. What was needed was more complete preparation and a greater knowledge. We will see that with its increasing experiences, England would eventually establish a beachhead on the eastern coast of North America.

———————

Chapter 3

The Founding Of Port Royal

Today one can stand on the grassy slopes covering the ramparts of old Fort Anne, at Annapolis Royal, and look out beyond the mouth of the Annapolis River to a widening tidal basin. The Annapolis basin is in the shape of a stubby carrot thirteen miles long and four miles at its widest; and off from its northwestern shoulder, tides of sea water ebb and flow through a narrow two mile cut, Digby Gut, a portal through the North Mountain range to the Bay of Fundy, one of the largest bays of the Atlantic ocean. The North Mountain range forms a backbone on which, it seems, the larger peninsula of Nova Scotia hangs. The cold north winds meet this sweeping range and are veered up, sheltering the southeastern valley beyond. This ensconcing hump of land extends itself northeastward, covering the continuing valley below, until it dazzlingly drops itself off from the precipitous purple heads of Cape Blomidon, down, out of sight, through the jeweled shores of the Minas Channel. This capturing hollow, the Annapolis Valley, is filled with something not much of which is to be found in the rocky northeast coast of the Atlantic, sweet alluvial soil. Meandering along its hundred mile length, and splitting its ten mile width, are its two main rivers, the one flowing southwest, the other northeast: the Annapolis and the Cornwallis. Standing there today on the grassy slopes of the mouth of the Annapolis River, with the full length of the fertile valley behind, one can imagine a small wooden ship, having passed through the gateway of Digby Gut into the calm expanse of the Annapolis Basin. Let us go back to 1604 and see the sight: a small sailing vessel ghosting along this amphitheater of woody hills, to slowly come up to a spot, not far off, just west of the present day ramparts of Old Fort Anne; to a place back then which was but a head of land marking where the fresh water coming west intermingles with the salt water of the Atlantic. Here we see our intrepid French explorers, led by de Monts,[1] looking over the rails of their small boat at, what appears to be, unoccupied land; here, they see a place much to their liking. A year later, there on the northern shore of the Annapolis Basin, tucked under the North Mountain range, this group of Frenchmen were to establish one of the first permanent European settlements in North America.[2]

Given that there was a sufficient attraction to come to the general area, that present day area of eastern Canada, it is easy, for one with some climactic and geological knowledge of the area, to see why the site of Port Royal was specifically picked for the first settlement. The attraction for the French in 1604, one that has driven all people in every age, was commercial. By the beginning of the 1600s it was appreciated that America was quite separate from the spice lands to be found in the orient; only as the years unfolded did these European seamen come to realize how extensive a block America was to be. Only with a thorough acquaintance of the Americas would the western route to the orient be found. This increasing knowledge brought about a corresponding increase in the awareness of the richness of the Americas, as the Spanish demonstrated during the 16th century. In the south, it was gold and silver[3]; in the north, it was to be food and clothing: fish from the northwestern Atlantic and the pelts of the northern fur bearing animals. The French, having established themselves at Port Royal, Samuel de Champlain[4] among them, had a pretty good hunch that the Saint John River, just across the Bay, would be a wilderness highway down which the Indians might come in the interests of trade with their canoes full of animal pelts.[5]

With the founding of Port Royal, the French had staked out their lands in Acadia by right of possession. The French were not the only European country attempting to colonized North America; the English were there too. It was, as we will see, a struggle for these new European arrivals; it was, for them, a strange land occupied in part by strange people; the elements were severe; and they were far from home. They brought with them their old habits, and, unfortunately, their old prejudices.

The position of the wretched little colony [Port Royal] may well provoke reflection. Here lay the shaggy continent, from Florida to the Pole, outstretched in savage slumber along the sea, the stern domain of Nature, — or, to adopt the ready solution of the Jesuits, a realm of the powers of night, blasted beneath the sceptre of hell. On the banks of James River was a nest of woe-begone Englishmen, a handful of Dutch fur-traders at the mouth of the Hudson, and a few shivering Frenchmen among the snow-drifts of Acadia; while deep within the wild monotony of desolation, on the icy verge of the great northern river, the hand of Champlain upheld the fleur-de-lis on the rock of Quebec. These were the advance guard, the forlorn hope of civilization, messengers of promise to a desert continent. Yet, unconscious of their high function, not content with inevitable woes, they were rent by petty jealousies and miserable feuds; while each of these detached fragments of rival nationalities, scarcely able to maintain its own wretched existence on a new square miles, begrudged to the others the smallest share in a domain which all the nations of Europe could hardly have sufficed to fill.[6]

De Monts:

On December 18th, 1603, royal letters patent was received by Monsieur de Monts, whereby de Monts was given "rights" to territory between 40° (on a line which today sits Philadelphia) and 46° (on a line which is just north of peninsular Nova Scotia). On March 7th, 1604, de Monts sailed from La Heve, France, in "two vessels, one of 120 and the other of 150 tons"; on board were 120 men. After a voyage of one month's duration[7] these two ocean-going sailing vessels made landfall; the smaller of the two at Canso,[8] and the other, with the leaders aboard, came to shore some 160 miles south of Canso at Cape LaHave. De Monts cautiously made his way down this foreign coast a further 40 miles or so, until they reached Port Mouton[9] where their ocean-going sailing vessel was put at anchor. It seems that de Monts was very conscious of what it would mean if he and his explorers should be shipwrecked on this foreign shore, so, the vessel was to stay in the Port Mouton area for about a month while Champlain[10] and Jean Ralleau[11] (de Monts' secretary) were sent further down the coast with a view to locating an appropriate place at which the explorers might set up their quarters on land. They were concerned about the natives (though as things turned out they had nothing to be too much worried about, at least not of the natives of Nova Scotia); thus, they thought it necessary to find a position which might be easily defended.

Leaving de Monts, together with the larger part of the expedition behind, Champlain and Ralleau together with a crew of about ten, to man the longboat, set out westward. Eventually rounding the end of the large peninsula we know today as Nova Scotia, they came up around its back-end, northeast, and they were soon caught up in a bay, which they named Baie Sainte Marie (today, St. Mary's Bay). It would not appear that Champlain and Ralleau went much further, but rather, returned to the mother ship to report to de Monts.

Now, shortly after de Monts first arrived on the coast of Acadia, he discovered another French vessel on the coast illegally engaged in trading with the natives. This vessel was the *Levrette*, either owned or captained (could be both) by a Jean Rossignol. The *Levrette* and her cargo of pelts were seized by de Monts, and she and her crew were brought under the command of de Monts.[12]

Having received Champlain's report, de Mont determined to relocate. The de Monts' ship and the *Levrette* went in company to St. Mary's Bay, and both were put at anchor (I suspect at Weymouth). De Mont, leaving most all of his men behind,[13] now joined Champlain in the long boat and explorations continued.[14] They found their way out of St. Mary's Bay likely proceeding through the gut at Tiverton and into a much larger bay they called "Baie Française" (Bay of Fundy), whose limits were not determinable upon entry. They sailed northeast keeping the land to their right; when, after 30 miles or so, another gut made its presence known, a narrow entrance which can only be discovered when it is more or less directly abeam. Taking an abrupt turn to the right, this small group of Frenchman of about a dozen sailed through this narrow passage with its high ridges left and right and into a revealed and beautiful basin which opened to their left: they named the entire area, Port Royal. This was to be de Monts' first sight of the place at which eventually he was to settle; it was during the month of June, 1604: June, a time when freshness and beauty reign in Acadia.

The beauty and safety of Port Royal — to be called Annapolis Basin by the English many years later — plainly registered on de Monts' mind. He did not, however, on this first visit, spend much time at the place as he was determined to continue with his explorations and wanted to do so before the good seasonal weather ended.[15] Back out through the gut they went and into the broad expanse of the Bay of Fundy (Baie Française). They sailed up to the head of the bay and then south along the coast of present day New Brunswick arriving at the mouth of the Saint John River on June 24th, 1604.

These dozen men were obviously more concerned about making winter quarters for themselves than to spend too much time on exploration. They quickly departed the mouth of the Saint John, dismissing it as a candidate, likely because its mouth can be treacherous when the tide is flowing. This little intrepid group of Frenchman in their little wooden sail boat carried on down the coast of present day New Brunswick; until they reached, on June 26th, Passamaquoddy Bay. It naturally drew them in, through the islands and up the St. Croix River until they reached a small island which we know today as Dochet Island; it was here they determined that they would fix their winter quarters. This island, which they named Île Sainte Croix (the island of the Holy Cross) — now long deserted and sitting lonely in the middle of the St. Croix River — is situated not far up from the mouth of the river, a river which today forms part of the Canadian (New Brunswick) and American (Maine State) border.

Having made their decision, they dispatched the long boat to St. Mary's Bay with instructions to move the larger vessels, the men and the supplies to St. Croix. De Monts, Champlain and a couple of men were left behind to consider the defences of the chosen site. And so, the two larger vessels were soon riding in the river alongside St. Croix Island, and these brave Frenchmen turned to the necessary construction of their first home on the continent, and it was no mean establishment. There on St. Croix, they built an oven building, a blacksmith shop, as well a little chapel and a cemetery (which, by the spring, as it turned out, was to contain a number of them).[16]

The snow first fell as early as the 6th of October and came in such profusion that it was from three to four feet deep as late as the end of April. On the 3rd of December ice was floating in the river, and it later increased to such an extent that it became difficult and dangerous, and even at times impossible, to leave the island. The cold was extreme in its severity and duration, to such a degree that, as Champlain says, 'all our liquors froze, except the Spanish wine. Cider was dispensed by the pound.' ... The food was mostly salt and nourished them badly... As a result of such conditions some of the men fell ill, then others and yet others, until there developed among them that disease most dreaded of all by those wintering in cold countries, the scurvy, which soon got so far beyond control that of the seventy-nine men composing the company, fifty-nine were afflicted with the disease and thirty-four miserably perished.[17]

After pointing out that around "our habitation there is at low tide a large number of shell fish, such as cockles, mussels, sea-urchins and sea-snails, which were a great boon to all"; Champlain continued and wrote of his impressions on his first winter in Acadia:

During the winter, many of our company were attached by a certain malady called the *mal de la terre*; otherwise scurvy, as I have since heard from learned men. There were produced in the mouths of those who had it, great pieces of superfluous and drivelling flesh (causing extensive putrefaction), which got the upper hand to such an extent that scarcely anything but liquid could be taken. Their teeth became very loose, and could be pulled out with the fingers without its causing them pain. The superfluous flesh was often cut out, which caused them to eject much blood through the mouth. Afterwards a violent pain seized their arms and legs, which remained swollen and very hard, all spotted as if with flea bites; and they could not walk on account of the contraction of the muscles so that they were almost without strength and suffered intolerable pains. They experienced pain also in the loins, stomach and bowels, had a very bad cough and short breath. In a word, they were in such a condition that the majority of them could not rise nor move and could not even be raised up on their feet without falling down in a swoon. So that out of seventy-nine, who composed our party, thirty-five died, and more than twenty were on the point of death. The majority of those who remained well also complained of slight pains and short breath. We were unable to find any remedy for these maladies. A post-mortem examination was made of several to investigate the cause of their malady. ...

Those who continued sick were healed by Spring, which commenced in this country in May. That led us to believe that the change of season restored their health, rather than the remedies prescribed. ...

It would be very difficult to ascertain the character of this region without spending a winter in it; for, on arriving here in the summer, everything is very agreeable, in consequence of the woods, fine country, and many varieties of good fish are found here. There are six months of winter in this country. [18]

The spring (1605) brought considerable relief to those that had wintered over at St. Croix. With the churned up ice now gone from around their island holdout, water, food and fuel become obtainable. With the freshness of the new season, the physical strength of these first Frenchmen soon returned; and, so too, their spirits when Pontgravé[19] appeared coming up the river in a shallop (small boat) on June 15th. (Champlain reported that Pontgravé had anchored his sea-going vessel 18 miles away from the settlement.) I should note that Pontgravé, together with Ralleau had been sent back with the returning vessels the previous autumn; and, now, they had returned with supplies and 40 fresh men. Having just spent such a dreadful winter — it should not be surprising to learn — de Monts determined to move the colony. Champlain tells us of this decision:

Sieur de Monts determined to change his location, and make another settlement, in order to avoid the severe cold and the bad winter which we had in the Island of Ste. Croix. As we had not up to that time found any suitable harbour, and in view of the short time we had for building houses in which to establish ourselves, we fitted out two barques, and loaded them with the framework taken from the houses at St. Croix, in order to transport it to Port Royal, twenty-five leagues distant, where we thought the climate was much more temperate and agreeable. Pontgravé and I set out for that place; and, having arrived, we looked for a site favourable for our residence, under shelter from the northwest wind, which we dreaded, having been very much harassed by it.[20]

In September of 1604, before they experienced their miserable winter on the St. Croix, Champlain had sailed further down the coast of the present day State of Maine. They were proceeding into territory which was known to French fishermen and traders as Norembega, a fabled country. Whatever the extent of this territory, Champlain did not appear to get much further down in his coasting explorations than that of Mount Desert Island and

the mouth of the Penobscot River (called by Champlain, Pem-
etigoet), at least on that first voyage in the autumn on 1604. The
following year, after these adventurous Frenchmen had regained
their health, they continued their exploring activities. In an
armed pinnace, "a bark of fifteen tons, with de Monts, several
gentlemen, twenty sailors, and an Indian with his squaw, ... set
forth on the eighteenth of June on a second voyage of discovery."
Passing down the coast, they went beyond the point where they
had left off the year before. The 9th of July brought them to
Saco Bay and into the territory of the Armouchiquois (later to
be called the Massachusetts). The principal difference between
the Armouchiquois and the tribes to the north of them was that
the Armouchiquois tilled the soil and raised "maize, beans,
pumpkins, squashes, tobacco and the ... Jerusalem artichoke."
They carried on down into Massachusetts Bay and called into a
harbour which, when the Pilgrims stepped ashore 15 years later,
became known as Plymouth Harbor. According to Parkman,
"Indian wigwams and garden patches lined the shore."

Of the human tenants of the New England coast he [Champlain] has
also left the first precise and trustworthy account. They were clearly more
numerous than when the Puritans landed at Plymouth, since in the interval a
pestilence made great havoc among them.

Parenthetically, I add, that the Massachusetts tribe and
this small band of Frenchman got off to a very bad start. This
bad start between the French and the Massachusetts tribe was
not indicative, leaving out the Iroquois nation, of the overall
relations which the French, versus the English, were to generally
have with the original occupiers of the North American woods.
It seems a party of French sailors went ashore below Cape Cod,
"Nausett Harbor," to get water, when an argument broke out
between the sailors and a group of natives over the ownership of
a certain kettle. At any rate, there was soon one dead Frenchman
lying on the beach, and with that the ships guns were put into
play; well, I will let Parkman tell of it:

The French in the vessel opened fire. Champlain's arquebuse burst, and was near killing him, while the Indians, swift as deer, quickly gained the woods. Several of the tribe chanced to be on board the vessel, but flung themselves with such alacrity into the water that only one was caught. They bound him hand and foot, but soon after humanely set him at liberty.

The experience that the French had with the Armouchiquois was unlike the experience they had with the MicMacs. The French found the MicMac to be friendly and eager to trade, whereas the further south these Frenchmen went, they found the "savages were numerous, unfriendly and thievish." This experience only served to confirm their decision that the best place for the French colony was to be that place which they returned to found: Port Royal. As it turned out, like so many minor events in history, the theft of a kettle was to have a great effect of the French English configuration in North America. At any rate, the confrontation with the Cape Cod Indians brought to an end any further exploration by the French of what was to become known as the New England coast. The French under de Monts determined to leave the place to the natives, and effectively to the British when English colonists (the Pilgrim Fathers expedition) stepped ashore at Plymouth in November of 1621.

So it is, that we would have seen a small group of Frenchmen industriously piling up their possessions and moving them across the bay from St. Croix.[21] There, at the head of Port Royal (which today we call the Annapolis Basin), under the shelter of the north mountains they built their habitation, a closed quadrilateral dwelling, which has generally been accepted by historians as being the first European settlement, aside from Florida, to be established on the continent of North America.[22]

In the fall of 1605, de Monts, leaving a holding company behind at Port Royal under the command of Pontgravé, sailed for France.[23] The second winter in Acadia was not as hard on the Frenchmen as was the first winter; but still, 12 more men died of scurvy. Spring arrived and there was no sign of French ships with the necessary supplies. Time passed; and soon, Pontgravé and his men began to despair that de Monts would return with provisions. In order to save themselves, they turned to the business of building a sea coasting vessel. The work was most likely carried out under the direction of Champdoré, an accomplished boat builder. In this boat, the Frenchmen intended to set out for Canso where they knew they would find ocean going sailing vessels of French origin. Such vessels had come into that port with their seasonal fishermen for years. It was to be their chance to get back home to France rather than to spend another cold and hard winter in Acadia, especially without supplies.

Not that anybody should be critical, but Pontgravé, in his plans to desert Port Royal, jumped the gun. Help was on the way. On May 13th, 1606, the ship *Jonas* had set sail from France. The expedition was under the overall command of Jean de Poutrincourt[24] and was sent to re-provision Port Royal. De Mont, this time, is not aboard, having determined he might best serve by staying in France to continue to shore up the company's financial problems. Aboard, however, was Poutrincourt, Charles de Biencourt,[25] and a French lawyer by the name of Marc Lescarbot.[26] The *Jonas*[27] did not reach Port Royal until the end of July and suffered a "long and tedious voyage."[28] The *Jonas*, with men and supplies, arrived just after the overwintering occupants of Port Royal (Pontgravé, Champlain, et al.) had left for Canso; indeed, they had missed each another by just a few miles. Pontgravé, however, was to find out from a passing ship that the *Jonas* had arrived on the coast; and so, on hearing this, Pontgravé hurried back to Port Royal to join up with his fellow countrymen who had arrived at Port Royal on July 31st. "The *Jonas* brought out a number of new immigrants and considerable fresh supplies."[29] After an appropriate celebration during which the two meeting parties caught up on the news, plans were soon made for another coastal exploration. Leaving Lescarbot behind, Poutrincourt and Pontgravé set sail in the *Jonas* and made their way, once again, down the American coast; they returned to Port Royal on the 14th of November.

During the summer and fall of 1606, while their friends were on their cruise south, Port Royal was under the direction of

Lescarbot and Louis Hebert,[30] and they and the men under them make a number of improvements to the living arrangements at the habitation. On November 14th (1606) the exploring Frenchmen returned to Port Royal and soon after, the *Jonas* returned to France, no doubt with bales of furs in her hold. The intrepid Frenchmen left behind, with their spirits much buoyed, settled in to spend a third winter in Acadia. It was at this time we see the *ordre de bon temps* (the order of good times) was brought into being; it was an eating club whose sole object was to bring good cheer to those who would otherwise be obliged just to wait as the cold and dreary winter passed by. And while the *ordre de bon temps* was to keep these Frenchmen entertained — still they died; but, only seven this time.[31] The prominent members of the French company who were at the habitation during the winter of 1606/07 were: Poutrincourt (Lord of the Manor), Champlain, Biencourt, Lescarbot (the lawyer), Louis Hébert (the apothecary), Pontgravé, Champdoré, and Daniel Hay (surgeon).

With the arrival of spring, in the year 1607, the French continued, with great expectations, to improve their settlement. Their buildings and grounds around the habitation were improved upon; a grist-mill was built. This grist-mill was built on the Allain River, situated near by the present day Annapolis Royal. So too in this year, farming activities (much of it on an experimental basis) were carried on in the natural fields surrounding the lower part of the Annapolis River and their explorations of the area were extended.

In the meantime, back in France, things were not going well for de Monts and his company. The plain fact is that while the company's revenues were high, the expenses were higher; and the loss of de Monts' monopoly position was imminent. Thus, it was, in 1607, with the return of the company's ship, in the spring, that Poutrincourt received word that Port Royal was to be abandoned. And so, sadly, in the fall of 1607, this brave group of Frenchmen — Poutrincourt, Champlain, et al. — departed[32] Port Royal: "the desertion of the colony was complete; not a European was left in the hamlet or the fort, or in the vicinity."[33]

The group — after exchanging sad farewells with their friends, the MicMac — made their way around the end of peninsular Nova Scotia and up the eastern coast to Canso where the *Jonas* awaited them.[34] For the next two years Port Royal remained without white inhabitants.

———————

Chapter 4

Poutrincourt's Second Settlement
(1610-13)

It was the 26th day of February, 1610, when at Dieppe, France, men on a small wooden sailing vessel climbed the rigging to set sail, to shape them so to catch the breezes to Acadia. Poutrincourt was aboard and with him were a number of converts: a second attempt was to be made to occupy Port Royal.

Having secured the backing of a French merchant by the name of Robin, Poutrincourt was back at Port Royal by June. Among this small group were two boys: Charles LaTour, age 14 years; and Biencourt, age 19; they traveled with their fathers, Claude LaTour and Poutrincourt.[1]

The local natives were delighted that their French friends had returned, as their conversions demonstrated. Among the new arrivals was a French priest by the name of Flesché. Father Flesché baptized a number of MicMac Indians, including, on June 24th, 1610, at Port Royal, Chief Membertou.[2]

The ship that brought these returning Frenchmen was immediately despatched back to France, with young Biencourt aboard. An effort was made to get a second lot of supplies over within the season. Biencourt made record time in getting back to France, arriving on August the 21st, 1610. He arrived, however, at a bad time. France was in political turmoil arising in the wake of the assassination of Henry IV by a fanatic named Ravaillac, a tool, it was said, of the Jesuits. Henry's son, nine year old Louis XIII, took the throne and the power was held by the Queen Mother, Mary de Medicis, who was wholly controlled by Italian favourites. The queen received Biencourt but forced upon him a number of conditions before she would allow him to set out once again. The principal condition was that he take with him two Jesuit missionaries. This condition was completely unacceptable to Poutrincourt's backers, certain channel merchants who were

Huguenot Protestants. Ultimately, after considerable man-euvering, friends of the queen bought out Poutrincourt's backers and his son, Biencourt, finally set sail from Dieppe on the 26th of January, 1611.

Though it was expected that Poutrincourt's son, Biencourt, would get back before winter set in, we see that he did not. By developing their hunting and fishing skills (no doubt with the help of their MicMac friends), Poutrincourt and his 23 charges survived the winter (1610/11) proving that Acadians could get by in the new land through the worst of its seasons without help from the home country. At any rate Poutrincourt and his small band got through the winter without loss of life.

During the month of May, 1611, Beincourt and 36 others, having set out more than three months earlier, in a small vessel, *Grace de Dieu*, arrived midst much fanfare at Port Royal. They had had a long and arduous voyage from France. They touched land at Canso on the 5th, then Port Royal on the 22nd. Beincourt had brought with him, in addition to much needed supplies, the two Jesuits: Biard and Massé.[3] Beincourt barely tolerated these courtly priests and there was to be "a series of disputes between the Jesuits and the young governor."

By July, the French supply ship, *Grace de Dieu*, was set for its return trip to France.[4] Poutrincourt himself was returning with furs to trade in France for more supplies and trading goods. Left behind at Port Royal was 19 year old Biencourt and 22 others. Among this group were the two Jesuit missionaries. Conflict soon broke out.

Some six months later, in the middle of the Acadian winter, on January 23rd, 1612, Poutrincourt arrived with supplies from France. With him is yet another Jesuit, Gilbert Du Thet, bringing the number during this time to three Jesuit missionaries: Énemond Massé,[5] Pierre Biard (c.1567-1622) and Gilbert Du Thet,[6] These missionaries did not reside with the French inhabitants. Rather, it would appear that they lived among the native people. Father Massé moved across the bay to take up residence with those living at the mouth of the Saint John River and Father Biard ministered to the natives in and around Port Royal. These priests were working the natives in order to accomplish a mission of the French royal crown and those that guided it: save souls for the Christian God. The natives were, it was thought by these religious people of the time, rich fishing grounds for souls: it was but necessary to get them baptized and see that they die in a state of grace.

It was Madame de Guercherville, a favourite of the queen mother, who was of the view that in the new world, souls might be saved by the wholesale lot. Having bought the rights which de Monts had to Acadia, de Guercherville sent a vessel out to Port Royal under the command of M. de La Saussaye. La Saussaye set sail on the 13th of March, 1613, with "48 persons, including her crew, together with horses and goats and a year's allowance ..."[7] He arrived at Port Royal towards the end of May having first come ashore at Cape LaHave, there to ceremoniously take possession of the country for his mistress. At Port Royal he found but five Frenchmen, the others being absent on account of their exploring activities. La Saussaye's intention, it would seem, was to extract Madame de Guercherville's Jesuits and to move on to a new site. This new site was to be at Mount Desert Island in the current day State of Maine.[8]

Argall:

Meanwhile, at Virginia, plans were being laid to snuff out the lights of the budding French colonies both at Mount Desert and Port Royal. On the 28th of June, 1613, Captain Samuel Argall (1572-?)[9] sailed from Virginia in the *Treasurer* ("equipped with fourteen guns"). Argall first went to Mount Desert. Returning with French prisoners, the governor of Virginia, Sir Thomas Gates, ordered Argall back to Acadia to do a more thorough job of it. Within a few weeks Argall was back at Mount Desert destroying the buildings and fortifications, from there he went to do the same at both St. Croix and Port Royal.

The first shots in 150 years' war in America between France and England, were fired from Virginia to Acadia in 1613, seven years before the Pilgrim Fathers, which is evidence there was plenty of elbow room and that the initial clash was not a border affair. Practically 500 miles of wilderness intervened between Jamestown, Virginia and Port Royal, Acadia and in between there was a small subsidiary French settlement recently located at Saint Sauveur, Mount Desert, Maine.

Captain Samuel Argall, soldier of fortune, captor of beautiful Pocahontas by a trick afterward Deputy Governor of the 'old Dominion' and later knighted for service in Algiers, was in northern waters with an armed schooner to protect a fleet of Virginia vessels engaged in the fisheries. Piracy was rampant at the time and Indians were hostile.

Without warning, Argall bombarded French settlements at Saint Sauveur and Port Royal, killed several including a priest, took others prisoners, burned buildings, carried off portable belongings, pulled down crosses and even erased stone carvings containing French emblems. The attacks were made in a prolonged peace between the two countries and were ostensibly based on a charge of trespass and prior British title, dating from Cabot's Discovery of North America 116 years earlier.[10]

James Hannay describes the sacking of Port Royal, 1613:

At Port Royal he [Argall] found no person in the fort, all the inhabitants being at work in the fields five miles away. The first intimation they had of the presence of strangers was the smoke of their burning dwellings, which, together with the fort, in which a great quantity of goods was stored, he completely destroyed.

Having set sail in France on 31st December, 1613, Poutrincourt arrived at Port Royal on March 27th, 1614 to find the fort in ruins and the inhabitants starving. Poutrincourt had no choice but to return to France with most all of the colonists; his son, Biencourt, however, chose to stay behind in Acadia. "For several years after the destruction of Port Royal by Argal, there is a blank in the history of Acadia, and one which it is now impossible to fill. Biencourt still remained in the country, and occasionally resided at Port Royal, and it does not appear that any considerable number returned to France. A languid possession of Acadia was still maintained ..." Hannay added as a footnote: "Louis Hébert, who had been the apothecary at Port Royal, appears to have returned to France, for he took his family to Quebec in 1617."

And thus it was, that in 1613, the second French attempt to colonize Port Royal ended with the return of the adventurers to France. However, two young men, Charles Biencourt and Charles La Tour, appear to have continued on in Acadia, living off the land just as their friends the MicMacs did.

Penobscot:

In time, the La Tour family "erected a fort and trading house at the mouth of the Penobscot River" (located in the current day state of Maine). In 1626, La Tour was dispossessed of his establishment at Penobscot by the English who again came up from the Plymouth colony. Presumably, then, after his family was expelled from Penobscot, La Tour came to Port Royal and allied himself with Biencourt until Biencourt's death.

During the years, 1613-29, there was but a "languid possession of Acadia,"[11] a time when La Tour and Biencourt ran the woods with their Indian friends. France was in political turmoil and could not see to her internal needs, let alone the needs of a few Frenchmen in America.

Chapter 5

The First Scots In Acadia

While France may have been in languid possession of Acadia, the English, as we shall see, were taking steps to assert their rights. It was during September of 1621 that James the First of England granted a sizable part of the north-eastern coast of North America to a Scottish nobleman, Sir William Alexander of Menstrie, Earl of Stirling.[1] The royal charters, like all important state documents of the time, were in Latin. Thus it was that the words "Nova Scotia" were first used to identify it as a British province.

The crown only gave rights: for funds, it was necessary for Sir William to look to others. In his efforts to raise general interest in New Scotland, Sir William, in 1624, published a pamphlet entitled "An Encouragement to Colonies." In this pamphlet he set forth, in eloquent terms, the advantages offered to settlers in New Scotland. "It contained a map of the country, in which Scottish river and place names supplanted those given by the French, as the Tweed for the Ste. Croix, the Clyde for the St. John, and so on over the whole region."[2]

A few years passed before, in 1629, Sir William's son (another Sir William), "having been knighted and made Knight Admiral, started with a fleet of four vessels containing seventy men and two women," reached Port Royal.[3]

De Monts and his men, in 1604, given the dreadful experience during their first winter in Acadia, were more concerned about the weather then they were of attacks by other men and tucked in under the sheltering North Mountain range.[4] The Scots, on the other hand, were looking for a defensible position; they were wary of the Indians, the French, and ship borne pirates that made their rounds. Just such a position was found not far from the first French habitation. It had a full array of natural defences. There was a bluff of land stuck at the point of a peninsula located between the juncture of two rivers; such a place would leave the defenders but a small front exposed to hostile land forces. Thus, in 1629, New Scotland established its community at a place we now known as Annapolis Royal. A small wooden fort, Fort Charles (after Charles of England) was built; a commanding position in a pretty place.

Little is known about this early Scottish settlement. During the first winter, according to one account, so ill prepared were these Scottish settlers that thirty out of seventy perished due to "scurvy and other diseases"; and those that survived were then forced that spring to face the Indians and their scalping knives.[5]

Having gone home the previous autumn, Sir William Alexander, Jr. came over in company with the Kirke brothers and likely went as far as the Gaspé, where they arrived on June 15th. Alexander had explored the area the year before and had left an overwintering band of Scots at Gaspé. While the Kirkes went on to Quebec, Alexander, together with those he picked up at Gaspé returned back to the eastern coast of Cape Breton, and, during July, established a settlement (known as Lord Ochiltree's settlement) at Port aux Baleines, not far and just north of present day Louisburg. On this 1629 trip, Sir William had Claude La Tour with him. La Tour had been captured by the Kirke brothers the year before,[6] and had since shifted his allegiance to the English. Sir William, after having seen to the Baleines settlement, seemingly under the senior La Tour's direction, sailed directly for Port Royal.

In the meantime, on June 26, 1629, Captain Charles Daniel left France in command of two vessels with the object of provisioning Champlain at Quebec. Separated from his companion ship and being driven to shore by a storm, Daniel sought refuge at St. Anns Bay, Cape Breton (the French called it by its Indian name, Cibou). Daniel soon learned from his Indian friends that the Scots had made a settlement on the eastern side of northern Cape Breton.

Though England and France had entered into the *Treaty of Susa* on April 23rd, 1629, Daniel attacked Lord Ochiltree's

Cape Breton settlement on September 8th, capturing the fort and taking the colonists prisoners.

In the fall of the year, Claude de La Tour, who had come over with Sir William Alexander (leaving Sir William to spend the winter at Port Royal), sailed back to England with a view to coming back out the following spring with provisions. Aboard the returning English ship, in addition to La Tour, were the Indian Chief Segipt, his wife and son. Contained in one of the reports that La Tour bore for the English authorities, was a recommendation that both La Tour and his son Charles should be granted baronies covering the southeastern shore of Nova Scotia from present day Yarmouth to the mouth of the Laheve.

An English Lady:

In 1630, Claude La Tour, having been appointed an English baron by royal decree, arrived in Acadia (Port La Tour) with a bride, an impressive woman, a royal maid of honour. An altercation broke out between father and son. The senior La Tour was obliged to back down and he took refuge at the Scottish fort at Port Royal.

In the same year, two French vessels, having set sail from Bordeaux, arrived late in the season with supplies, arms, and ammunition for the new fort at Grand Cibou (Cape Breton) and for Fort Louis at Port La Tour. They had been sent out by a merchant by the name of Jean Tuffet (Company of New France) and the expedition was under the command of Captain Marot. The ships were freighted with "food, building supplies, munitions and tradesmen to construct a new fort; also, three Recollet missionaries disembarked to provide services which had been missing in Acadia for the previous four years.[7] (It was shortly after this that an invitation was extended by the son to the father for the elder La Tour to leave the Scottish fort at Port Royal and to come to Cape Sable to live. The senior La Tour was only to happy to make up and come live with his son; he did so and lived out the rest of his life in a rather aristocratic style in a house built nearby the fort where Claude La Tour and his lady lived with their two maids and their two menservants they had brought to Acadia.)

The son was not around to entertain or be entertained by his illustrious father; he had business which needed attending, the peltry business. Charles La Tour had determined that while a continuing presence in the Cape Sable area was good; the best furs, in volume, were to be had at the mouth of the Saint John River. So it was that Charles La Tour "concluded to erect a strong fort at the mouth of the Saint John River, where there was a powerful tribe of Indians, which would serve the double purpose of repelling the intrusions of the English in that direction, and would give the French at the same time command of the whole peltry trade of that vast wilderness, which extended to the River St. Lawrence."[8]

Meanwhile, the Scots carried on at Port Royal. In the autumn of 1630, Sir William (the younger) returned to England leaving Sir George Home in charge of the Scottish settlement.

During April, 1631, a "well stocked" vessel was sent from France to supply both Fort St. Louis and the fort at Cape Breton. The vessel also brought news that Charles La Tour was the recipient of a royal commission as the "King's lieutenant-general in Acadia."

By the *Treaty of Susa* (April, 1629) the English had agreed to the return of conquered territory in America. The English had argued that the Alexander settlements in Nova Scotia were not conquered territories. The English, however, on the promise by the French that Queen Henrietta's dowry (due from the French crown to the English crown) would be paid, gave up the Alexander settlements. Thus, on July 11th, 1631, the English king informed Sir William that the arrangement in respect to his ownership of Nova Scotia would have to come to an end, as the English king had returned Acadia to the French king. A message was sent out by Sir William Alexander to Sir George Home at Port Royal, to remove "all the people, goods, ordnance, ammunition, cattle and other things belonging to the colony, and to leave the bounds thereof altogether waste and unpeopled as it was when his son first landed there."[9] Savary reports that the "majority of the Scottish settlers probably returned to Scotland, but some joined the Puritan colony in Boston, and some joined the French at the site of the present town [Port Royal] and at LaHave." This short lived Scottish colony left its mark on the Acadian culture as at least one Scotsman, a Melanson, eventually took a French wife.[10]

Fort Charles:

Fort Charles remained operational under its commander, Andrew Forrester, until in 1632, when, with the arrival of de Razilly, it was surrendered up. M. A. MacDonald reported that 46 colonists were taken aboard Razilly's *St. Jehan* and were carried back to the shores of England and put off considerably south of their desired destination. The wily Scots had arrived back in England with money in their pockets, for de Razilly had — being the aristocratic gentleman that he was — paid the Scottish for the food and munitions that had been left behind at Fort Charles.

Thus, the short lived Scottish colony in Acadia came to an end after a tenuous four years of existence; more than a hundred and fifty years were to pass before Scottish emigration to Nova Scotia was to occur again and then in considerable numbers. By 1831, this influx significantly contributed to the Nova Scotian base from which the present day population grew.

Chapter 6

The de Razilly Settlement

Isaac de Razilly was born among the French nobility at the Château d'Oiseaumelle in the Touraine country of France (which could be starkly compared to the scene of his death 48 years later at LaHave in Acadia).[1] His mother, a de Valliers, had a brother, Claude, who was a commodore in the French navy. At the age of 18, Isaac was appointed a knight of the order of Saint John of Jerusalem[2] and a member of the French navy. He distinguished himself in the naval service. At one point he was in command of a thirteen ship squadron. In one of his battles off the coast of La Rochele he lost an eye when a vessel blew up. By 1626, de Razilly had made such a name for himself that he was consulted by Cardinal Richlieu himself.[3] It was with Richlieu that our hero worked out a plan for the buildup of Acadia, so "to block any English encroachment north of the 36th parallel."[4] The result was the founding of the *Compagnie de La Nouvelle-France*, or the *Compagnie des Cent-Associés* (the Company of 100 Associates, as it came to be known). The associates included Richlieu, Samuel Champlain and de Razilly (the naval commander for the company).

Thus, by 1627, there was a French trading company with capital and power, and a goal of establishing themselves in Acadia by recruiting, supporting and sending out the first true group of French settlers to Acadia. Its first efforts, ones of substantial proportion, came in the form of four ships loaded, in the spring of 1628, with "settlers, cattle, food, and other supplies" (for both Champlain at Quebec and La Tour at Cape Sable). An English squadron got at them and it is questionable whether any of the French ships got through to New France, in 1628.

Naval fighter that he was, de Razilly, after conferring with Richlieu, determined that in the following year (1629), he would convoy the French supply vessels to America. As it turned out, peace broke out between England and France, so he and his war ships were sent against the Moorish pirates who were raiding the French shipping in the Mediterranean.

Company of 100 Associates:

Though the Company of 100 Associates had been started up with much enthusiasm, certain "investors" were getting concerned, for five years had passed and not much of an establishment had been made in Acadia. It was agreed that efforts should be renewed, but the money chest was all but empty; a further investment of funds was required. To achieve this, the Company of 100 Associates carved up their territories and sold them off to a number of smaller private companies. De Razilly and some of his friends formed one of these private companies that became known as Razilly-Condonnier Company. This company was set up with an equipped vessel and the sum of 10,000 livres. Thus, we come to de Razilly's first expedition to Acadia.

Isaac de Razilly, described as "Knight Commander of the Order of Malta, a distinguished naval veteran and an enthusiastic proponent of French colonial development" accompanied by his cousin Charles de Menou d'Aulnay,[5] his nephew, Claude de Razilly, and by Nicholas Denys[6] (a native of Tours) came to reclaim Acadia for France.[7] De Razilly's choice for his headquarters was to be LaHave. Having left France during July, this founding group disembarked at LaHave on September 8th, 1632.

One might wonder at this hero of the sea, this connected politician, this aging bachelor; yet, apparently, as Deny writes, "he had no other desire than to people this land, and every year he had brought here as many people as he could for those purposes." The historians observe that de Razilly approached his projects with zeal, and his aptitude for getting things done, and getting them done correctly, was well known. His influence, given that he had such a friend as Richlieu, stretched far and wide.

Treaty of St. Germain-en-Laye, 1632:

By the *Treaty of St. Germain-en-Laye*, Port Royal, with the whole of Acadie, passed again into the hands of France (March, 1632), and Isaac de Razilly was sent out to take formal possession of the country from the English. With him came the Recollet missionaries, who had been banished from the Province by the English during their occupancy, and resumed their cures. With him also came Charles de Menou, seigneur d'Aulnay de Charnisay, as one of his lieutenants, Charles Amador de La Tour, of Cape Sable, being the other, each for a separate section of Acadie, D'Aulnay's the western and La Tour's the eastern. De Razilly, who acted as governor, or lieutenant-general for the French king made his headquarters at La Have, where he settled forty families, but after his death, which occurred in 1633 or 1634, D'Aulnay removed these settlers to Port Royal, located them with twenty more whom he brought from France on the site of the present town [Annapolis Royal], and built a new fort for their protection. In 1634, Claude de Razilly, the brother of Isaac, received a grant of Port Royal from the company of New France. In 1635 the same company granted the fort and habitation of La Tour,' on the Saint John River, to Charles La Tour. This fort was situated where the town of Carleton now stands, and became the theatre of stirring events subsequently. Isaac de Razilly had left all his rights and property in Acadie to his brother Claude, who, in 1642, conveyed them to D'Aulnay.[8]

De Razilly's position to both d'Aulnay and La Tour was somewhat that of a royal overseer. They both appear to have been subordinate to de Razilly, but in different senses. La Tour was in possession of prior rights to at least part of the territory and it was up to de Razilly to keep La Tour happy while de Razilly and his backers cut themselves in on the action. De Razilly, as we have seen, was a powerful and persuasive man who determined he could live with La Tour, if La Tour could live with him, basically on a 50-50 basis.[9] D'Aulnay, to de Razilly, was more like a gentleman's servant, or as Calnek put it "one of his lieutenants."[10] At any rate, de Razilly saw to it that d'Aulnay and La Tour were to be equals, for each had "a separate section of Acadie, d'Aulnay's the western and La Tour's the eastern. De Razilly, who acted as governor, or lieutenant-general for the French king made his headquarters at LaHave."

Hannay wrote that de Razilly, "in the first year of his settlement at LaHave brought to Acadia forty families," however, it was not at LaHave that these French colonizers, the seedlings of the French Acadian population and culture, were to take root; as we will see they moved to the farming lands of the present day Annapolis Valley.[11] Further, Hannay wrote, that upon the death of de Razilly (December, 1635) and upon effectively taking de Razilly's power, d'Aulnay moved the LaHave colonists to Port Royal so to establish himself there, closer to his growing enemy, La Tour who had established himself at the mouth of the Saint John. So too, I should add, putting farmers on the fertile lands surrounding the Annapolis River would mean that d'Aulnay could supply food to the outlying posts of his expanding empire. Indeed, once he was relocated at Port Royal, he arranged for some "twenty additional families" to come out from France.[12]

During de Razilly's command, Acadia got a very good and quick start. In the summers, French ships came to LaHave with men and supplies. Soon, this truly first French Acadian colony, was well established with subsidiary establishments at Port Rossignol (Liverpool; fishing) and Mirligueche (Lunenburg; lumbering). Up the Petite Rivière, some of the first farms in Nova Scotia were established.

By 1635 the colony at LaHave and its surrounding areas in Acadia were so well established, that de Razilly sent d'Aulnay and La Tour down the coast to oust the English at Penobscot. The English had dispossessed the French (La Tour) back in 1626; de Razilly wished to return the compliment, and, it would appear, he was within his legal rights to do so, due to the *Treaty of St. Germain-en-Laye*. After the takeover of Penobscot (in the current day state of Maine) d'Aulnay was left in charge, likely a move that upset La Tour, since it was he and his father who had originally set up the place. We can mark the year, 1635, as the year when d'Aulnay and La Tour, these two feudal barons of Old Acadia, became mortal enemies of one another — no matter that they were both Frenchmen located in an inexhaustible land consisting of thousands of unpeopled square miles. The prime difficulty was this: an agreement had been entered into between de Razilly and Charles La Tour. Now, Charles La Tour was nobody's fool; he sailed to Paris and hired himself a well connected Parisian lawyer. And after the interviews and hearings, the necessary negotiations were pursued and La Tour had a deal. He was to keep absolute power (short of a royal decree) over his own little pockets in the wilderness: At Cape Sable and on the mouth of the great Saint John River (current day New Brunswick). Further he was to get half of the entire profits of the pelt trade from "Canso to New Holland"; de Razilly the rest. The critical clause that some smart lawyer in Paris dreamt up gave each party absolute rights to the others warehouses and books of account; as M. A. MacDonald put it "each man had been set as a watchdog over the other." Incidentally, that deal was struck in a very formal setting with clerks and lawyers all about, in a building on rue Quincampoix, in the heart of the French financial district of Paris: it was a deal that was going to stick. It would have probably all worked out, except —

De Razilly died suddenly at La Hève in December 1635. History tells us little of his death, other than he was active and well-motivated right up to the last.[13] Likely he died, as so many of us will, by an embolism to the heart or brain. De Razilly, however, though he had but three years (1632-35) in the colony, left a legacy which impacted on America. On account of his colonization effort, the Acadian culture came about; a root culture of the Canadian people, and of a number of people in the United States especially, those living in Louisiana, "Cajuns."[14]

———————

Chapter 7

The Battling Barons Of Acadia

De Razilly's brother[1], Claude de Launay-Razilly, was as much the entrepreneur as his brother was, if not more so; Claude not only had an interest in the Razilly-Condonnier Company, he also had two private companies operating in the St. Lawrence region. With his brother's death, Claude, being a busy man, authorized d'Aulnay to act for him in America: so it was that d'Aulnay carried on in de Razilly's footsteps.

While d'Aulnay covered the front lines, his boss, Claude de Launay-Razilly, covered the home market back in France. This arrangement seem to work very well and the second stage of the LaHave colony's growth got off in a prosperous manner, with strong leadership from d'Aulnay on the ground in Acadia and strong connections back in France.

From LaHave To Port Royal:

As events unfolded, d'Aulnay and his French followers left LaHave to set up new homesteads on ideal marshland around Port Royal.[2] In making the move, d'Aulnay could have been as much motivated by fear of the company's creditors as anything else; it seems clear, however, that d'Aulnay was anxious as well to position himself up against his competitor. La Tour, at the mouth of the Saint John River just across the waters of Baie Française (Bay of Fundy), had strategically positioned himself on the Saint John, and his title was good. In the spring, like maple sap, animal pelts spilled down the Saint John on the bottoms of bark canoes with wild men keen to trade for hatchets, knives, flintlocks, pots, and clothing.

With the de Razilly estate having given its nod, d'Aulnay's superior position in Acadia was assured. For insurance, d'Aulnay married the daughter of one of the bosses of the Razilly-Condonnier Company, Jeanne Motin. D'Aulnay's legal power stemmed from the rights which the de Razilly company had been granted by no less a personage than Richilieu. There was too, the contract between de Razilly and LaTour. The good will extending between de Razilly and LaTour was one thing: between d'Aulnay v. LaTour, it was quite another. Acadia broke out into war.

Under the terms of a legal contract, d'Aulnay and La Tour were to share power; each with his separate section of Acadia. The adversaries positioned themselves, more or less, on the shores of Baie Française, across from one another: about fifty miles of open water separated them. Port Royal, as we have seen, was given up by the Scottish in 1632. Its advantages were that it possessed good farming land and it is within reasonable sailing distance to the largest rivers in the northeast. Now, it may have been that d'Aulnay could have located himself at the mouth of one of the rivers south of the St. John that drain the present day State of Maine, but that would have left himself open to English raids. Possibly the winning argument for d'Aulnay was that one would have to go as far down as Virginia to find better food growing conditions than those found, and by then proven to exist, around the lands of Port Royal.

And so it passed that d'Aulnay re-built on the foundations the Scottish fort at Port Royal.[3] The Acadians had found their capital and sunk their roots that were to last at Port Royal.

Though the vacuum created by de Razilly's death was to be felt in 1636, La Tour and d'Aulnay did not immediately lock horns. No direct conflict can be seen from a reading of the historical accountings, until after d'Aulnay laid charges against La Tour in the French courts in 1641.

During this five year period, 1636-1641, we see that both adversaries had fortified their positions. Certainly they put all their men to work to build ever stronger fortifications.[4] In addition, they both returned it seems yearly to France to recruit more friends and more backers. Both La Tour and d'Aulnay were successful in this regard, to a degree. Settlers were recruited and brought out, though not many. Also, each of these Acadian barons contracted for an influential wife: La Tour for Françoise Jacquelin; and, as we have seen, d'Aulnay for Jeanne Motin.

On the 26th of March, 1640, La Tour and Françoise had set sail for Acadia aboard the *L'Amitye de la Rochelle*; she carried eight passengers and a crew of 20. La Tour had entered into a formal contract at Paris for his wife. As for d'Aulnay and his Jeanne Motin: well, she was a young and available French girl (a scarce commodity in the early years) who was already in the colony having come out in 1636. She came out with her married sister, who was the wife of the Sieur du Breuil, Razilly's lieutenant at Canso. At some point a romance blossomed between d'Aulnay and Motin, and, undoubtedly, proper arrangements would have been made with her father, Louis Motin, Sieur de Courcelles, who in addition to owning shares in the Razilly-Condonnier Company, was the controller of salt stores located at one of France's colonies, perhaps in the Caribbean.[5]

It will be remembered that there was an agreement struck back around 1632 between La Tour and de Razilly that they were each to share in the peltry trade of Acadia. Each was to get a special percentage of their own particular area (La Tour, for example, Cape Sable and the Saint John) and both were to get a percentage of the whole. By this French contract, each was made the policeman of the other. Each had the keys to all storage or warehouses in Acadia no matter to whom they belonged. Each had the right to inspect the books of the other. This French contract was struck between La Tour and de Razilly, who both apparently figured they could live with it. There is nothing in the published historical material to the effect that there was ever any trouble between La Tour and de Razilly. This, likely, because de Razilly was a powerful gentleman who knew La Tour and treated him with respect; and throughout, it would appear, La Tour recognized de Razilly as his senior. Upon the death of de Razilly and the succession of d'Aulnay, friendly contractual relations ceased. Now, it seems plain that these two French gentlemen of the 17th century could not see eye to eye on anything except for the lovely Jeanne Motin, who, in succession, each was to marry.

Neither La Tour nor d'Aulnay could give any accommodation to the other. It was clear at some point in time a fight would break out; and it was just as clear that the place of this fight was to be in front of a warehouse at either at Saint John or at Port Royal (you will recall each had rights to inspect the operation of the other). As it happened, the fight broke out at Port Royal: "La Tour went to Port-Royal in 1640 to check the furs and supplies there, he was refused permission and it appears that he and d'Aulnay came to blows."[6] D'Aulnay, as opposed to La Tour, would not press for a show down until after he pursued his legal channels, which apparently were pretty good. D'Aulnay succeeded in taking out an order, dated February 13th, 1641, granted in France upon an ex-parte application.[7] This order was delivered in August to La Tour who by then was safely ensconced in his wooden fort on the Saint John. La Tour treated the order with scorn, saying it was obtained by the misrepresentations of d'Aulnay. He did not feel compelled to go to France to answer these trumped up charges. Why, it would take him away for upwards to two years during which time d'Aulnay would swoop in and help himself.

With the opening up of the new year we can see that a deed had been executed conveying all of Claude de Razilly's interests and title in the Razilly-Condonnier company to d'Aulnay. In the meantime, d'Aulnay's continued court activity was bringing him success. On February 21st, 1642, an order was granted empowering d'Aulnay "to seize La Tour's forts and his person, and send him to France as a rebel and traitor to the King."[8] It would appear that everything was going d'Aulnay's way: back home in France, d'Aulnay's friends were winning over La Tour's friends.

In the spring of that year, La Tour's agents managed to get supplies and recruits through to him, in spite of a royal embargo against him. Twenty-six tradesmen were transported from France to his fort, including: a baker, a cook, an apothecary, an armourer, an upholsterer, a tailor, a cobbler, a salt-maker, a slate-layer, and a ship's carpenter.[9]

D'Aulnay's increasing power in France is due to a French financier by the name of Emmanuel Le Borgne. Le Borgne had advanced sums of money to d'Aulnay against d'Aulnay's ability to get animal pelts back to the French market. D'Aulnay spent the funds in chartering vessels, buying arms, and hiring soldiers, all designed to unseat La Tour.[10]

We see that just before winter set in, during October of 1642, La Tour sent his lieutenant, Rochette to Boston "with a shallop and fourteen men" seeking help from Governor John Winthrop; or, more particularly, the Boston merchants.

Up to the spring of 1643, there was apparently no direct conflict between d'Aulnay and La Tour. D'Aulnay, being a Catholic supporter, had an advantage over La Tour; Catholics versus Protestants (Huguenots) had the upper political hand in France. Remember that at this time, France was in a state of more than normal political turmoil, due to the deaths of both Richelieu (December, 1642) and Louis XIII (April, 1643). Political power was shifting and it wasn't clear which way things were going to go since but a five year old was to take the French throne. (In 1642, Louis XIV would succeed his father with Queen Anne of Austria as regent and Mazarin as chief minister.)

The *Clement*, a large armed French vessel loaded with ammunition and supplies and armed men (140), was sent out in the spring of 1643 by the Huguenot merchants of Rochelle; they were coming to the aid of their man, La Tour. The crew of the *Clement*, on the approaches of the Bay of Fundy, having kept a wary eye out, spoted the d'Aulnay's blockading fleet. The captain of the *Clement* made a smart move. The vessel ran down wind and out to sea, she then shaped a course for Boston. On the deck of the *Clement*, we would have seen Françoise Jacquelin, La Tour's wife, being one of those keeping an anxious eye out, positioned not far from the captain. Françoise had originally come to Acadia with the spring sailing of 1640. Françoise, during the years 1640-43, had returned back home to France with each autumn sailing, likely to get clear of the bad weather and see to the spring provisions. At any rate, here we have Lady La Tour returning and carrying goods to her husband's seigniory in the new world, in the spring of 1643, aboard the *Clement*. However, the *Clement* could not make a direct run to the mouth of the Saint John. After waiting out a period of time at Boston, Françoise came up the coast, once again, to relieve her husband who continued to be bottled up on account of d'Aulnay's blockade. In the early part of the summer a message gets through to Fort Latour, overland from a landing further south along the coast. How surprised and pleased Charles La Tour must have been to hear that Françoise, his wife, who he had not seen since the previous September, was but a few miles away. After a few anxious days, under the cover of darkness and thus evading d'Aulnay's patrolling fleet, La Tour managed in a shallap to venture out of the mouth of the Saint John to meet the *Clement* at her mooring in a secluded cove down the coast. Imagine the scene as La Tour swung himself aboard the deck of the *Clement* there to participate in an emotional reunion with his wife and his fellow countrymen.

With just the *Clement* and the few forces he had at the fort, La Tour knew that he had to get reinforcements and he figured he might be able to buy the ships and hire the men he needed from the people of Boston, fellow protestants who were not averse to a little adventure, especially if there was to be some money in it. The *Clement* made sail for Boston, where La Tour managed to charter four vessels armed with "thirty-eight pieces of ordnance." He also enlisted 92 soldiers to compliment the 140 which were aboard the *Clement*. This fleet then left Boston on the 14th of July, 1643, and proceeded up to the Bay of Fundy. D'Aulnay was chased back to his stronghold at Port Royal. After a short altercation at the mill, La Tour's fleet went back across the bay to his fort on the Saint John. The Bostonians were then paid off and returned to their home port.

That September, 1643, Lady La Tour, as was her routine, boarded the *Clement* for the return trip so to winter over in France.

Lady La Tour And The *Gillyflower*:

Through the winter of 1643/44 both d'Aulnay (personally)
and La Tour (or rather his wife) went off to France in order to
secure additional supplies, so to keep the war going between
the two feuding barons in Acadia. While d'Aulnay's political
connections continued to remain in good order, La Tour,
through his wife, could not convince the merchants to continue
their support. The cards were against the La Tours; they were
protestants; and protestants were just then becoming a much
persecuted group in France. Madame La Tour, on her arrival in
France, became aware that her presence might be reported to
the authorities. Without getting the sought after help from her
previous backers, she fled, in disguise, to England where this
charming woman succeeded, in little time, "in freighting a ship
from London with provisions and munitions of war for Fort La
Tour." So, Madame La Tour sailed back to Acadia. However,
we need to be reminded that sailing across an ocean takes time;
months, and sometimes, months again, especially if the captain
of the vessel wishes to trade and take on supplies in the islands.

In the meantime, far away in Acadia, La Tour became more
than just anxious that his wife might not be able to return; he
went to see his Boston friends, arriving there in July, 1644. La
Tour, however, was not as successful as he had been in the past
in securing the needed help. He set sail on the 9th of September,
1644, "in company with the ketch *Mountjoy*, engaged to carry
supplies to his fort." Just as his sails disappeared over the northern
horizon, another set took its place, more to the east; it was the
Gillyflower from England; Madame La Tour was aboard with
her people and supplies. It seems the vessel had made its way
into the Bay of Fundy, but was obliged to give up getting into
Fort La Tour, as d'Aulnay — having that spring just come from
France with reenforcements — was once again blockading the
mouth of the Saint John. D'Aulnay was in his sailing ship, the
Grand Cardinal and she apparently outclassed the *Gillyflower*.
Gillyflower's master, as the *Grand Cardinal* heaved alongside,
was forced to conceal Lady La Tour and her people in the hold

and to conceal the identity of his ship, which he pretended was bound direct for Boston. D'Aulnay believed the captain and the *Gillyflower* was set free: she made a beeline for Boston.

While thankful to arrive safely at Boston, Lady La Tour was however upset, as she was being delayed; her object in setting out from France with supplies was to get to Fort La Tour, not Boston. Upon her arrival at Boston, this indefatigable lady immediately sought the help of the courts: she took an action under the charter party and won her suit. An order was taken out to seize the cargo of the vessel which the captain had been picking up; maybe Madeira wine, or sugar cane from the islands, but whatever it was, it was sold for a good price. Lady La Tour then hired three vessels in Boston (likely through La Tour's principal creditor at Boston, one, John Paris) to convoy her home and "at length arrived safely at Fort La Tour, to the indescribable relief of her husband, who had almost despaired of her safety. She had been absent from him for more than a year."

It would appear this was the first winter that the couple spent at their seigniory on the Saint John. They no doubt delighted themselves with one another's company, but there was business to be done. At some point in the ensuing winter, 1644/5, an agreement was executed, likely at Saint John, between John Paris of Boston and La Tour: the La Tours, it would appear, put up all their worldly goods in exchange for the use of Paris' ships. In February of 1645, they set sail to return to Boston with La Tour aboard. Madame La Tour had been designated to stay behind to mind the fort.

La Tour's Defeat (1645):

It was during this time, in the early spring of 1645, that while La Tour was absent in Boston, one of the saddest scenes to behold in Canadian history unfolded. D'Aulnay launched an attack on Fort La Tour. It was Easter, and no doubt all on both sides were praying to their particular God before similar looking altars; it was April 13th, 1645. D'Aulnay intercepted a Boston vessel and was to learn Lady La Tour was alone in her manor and her husband away at Boston. Through trickery d'Aulnay took Fort La Tour. (The Recollets were tipped off and reminded of Lady La Tour's Protestantism. Then at a critical moment a bribe, which undoubtedly came with a special dispensation, was passed to the outposted guards.) When the alarm went up, Lady La Tour inspired her small garrison and personally directed the successful repulsive efforts from one of the bastions of the fort. "Twenty of the besiegers were killed and thirteen wounded in this affair ..."[11] Nonetheless, d'Aulnay succeeded in gaining entry; it is suspected that that one of the Recollets slid the bolt. Shortly after gaining entry and bringing the last of the La Tour forces to their knees, d'Aulnay hung every man in the garrison, right there, in front of the eyes of the brave Lady La Tour while she stood with a rope around her neck. As it turned out, Lady La Tour was not hung; however, she did not live for long after.

Lady La Tour fell ill (it is said from "sadness and resentment") and she died within days. She was interred, with solemn ceremony "so that she should be recognized" somewhere behind the fort in the same general area as the soldiers' graves, it is reported that d'Aulnay sent her son, (apparently she gave birth to one at some point in time) back to France in the care of the late Madame La Tour's waiting ladies. I should say, for the sake of preserved history that there is no evidence that the brave Lady La Tour or her female attendants were harmed by d'Aulnay or his men.

After his success in completely wiping out La Tour in Acadia in the spring of 1644, d'Aulnay sailed back to France that winter, 1644/45. He likely got a quite a reception back in France; a hero, a French hero. On the larger scene, the long war, *The Thirty Year War*, had finally came to an end: the French nation, in support of conservatism, as represented by the Holy Roman Church, ruled as it was by the all powerful Richelieu, had managed to keep the forces of Calvinism out of France.

His encouraging news that peace was restored between the European forces, and that in Acadia La Tour had been effectively put down, had a great effect on getting families signed up for the New World. It was that spring, in 1645, that d'Aulnay brought more families over from his mother's seigneury, headquartered at the Château de Charnisay, located near Loudon, in the province of Vienne. At that time he transported some 20 families, the largest group of family settlers that Port Royal would see for many years to come.[12]

Nicholas & Simon Denys:

It will be recalled that Nicholas Denys and his brother Simon came over with de Razilly, in 1632. They should not be forgotten as they are as every bit as illustrious as our feuding friends, d'Aulnay and La Tour. In the beginning, 1632-35, the Deny brothers stuck pretty close to their commander, de Razilly. During this period, they industriously set up a "wood working plant" near present day Riverport. So too, at some point, the Denys set up a fishing station at Port Rossignol (Liverpool).[13]

At the time of de Razilly's death at LaHave, Denys was wintering over in France, charged with the duty of "recruiting settlers."[14] D'Aulnay and LaTour, however were there at LaHave with de Razilly at the time of his death, or soon hurried there upon hearing of the death; and, thereafter, to declare their Acadian real estate claims to any who would listen.

In the 1640's and '50s, when Acadia was turned into a medieval battleground, the Denys brothers, it is likely, thought it best to just let d'Aulnay and La Tour waste one another out.

With the joining of the two houses (d'Aulnay and LaTour), in 1653, Denys established settlements at Ste. Pierre, Ste. Anne's and Nipisiquit.[15] Nicholas Denys was not long to be left alone though, for d'Aulnay arrived at Denys doorstep and presented what he thought was a more superior set of papers from the king; d'Aulnay promptly "captured Denys' forts, seized his goods, broke up his fishing establishments, and ruined his settlers."[16]

With the death of d'Aulnay in 1650 (more about that to come), Nicholas Denys returned to Acadia, once again; and, by 1654, Denys is at St. Pierre with his fears of being surprised and being mauled by a superior force lessened. He didn't bargain, however, for the feisty women these Acadian feudal barons had married.

Mrs. d'Aulnay took a page from her late husband's book and despatched a party of armed men from Port Royal to visit Denys at St. Peter's. D'Aulnay's forces seemingly had little difficulty overpowering Denys. Both of the Denys brothers were brought back in irons to Port Royal.

The Denys brothers were soon released, and they quickly cleared out of Port Royal and sailed for Quebec. Simon Denys had had enough of it and determined to remain at Quebec, but Nicholas returned to his home at St. Peter's and build it up again. Again, Denys was raided by a superior force. This time, in 1653, it was Emmanuel Le Borgne. Le Borgne, it will be recalled, was a creditor of the d'Aulnay estate and had sailed over from France to liquidate and take in payment whatever he might get his hands on that was even remotely connected to the now dead d'Aulnay. St. Peter's, Le Borgne believed, was but another piece of real estate that belonged to d'Aulnay; Le Borgne cared not about the claims of Denys. Le Borgne and his 60 men caught Denys away on a visit to his establishment at St. Anns (some 40 miles by sail over the great Bras D'Or Lake). Without much opposition, St. Peter's was pillaged and plundered once again. A few days later they ambushed the unsuspecting Denys who was making his way back over the short neck of land which today is spanned by a canal and a water lift. Once again, Denys was brought back to Port Royal and "placed in irons and confined in a dungeon." Before departing for Port Royal, Le Borgne's men burnt the establishment at St. Peter's down to the ground. As for Denys: he was released by the end of the year and directly headed off to France with a list of grievances. No sooner had Le Borgne arrived back at Port Royal with his booty and prisoners when he, in turn, was taken prisoner because of the forces of the English general, Robert Sedgwick, which had been assembled to clean out both the French and the Dutch which had located themselves along the eastern coast of North America.

General Robert Sedgwick:

In international matters, the Dutch were fighting the English in the first *Anglo-Dutch War* (1652-54). In 1654, Cromwell sent to Boston four armed vessels with instruction to root out the Dutch who had established themselves on Manhattan Island. Before General Robert Sedgwick was to get under way for his raid on the Dutch, he received word that a peace had been concluded between England and Holland. "Those who had the expedition in charge thought that it would be a pity to let so fine an armament go to waste for want of employment."[17] Sedgwick sailed during July of 1654 and saw to the capture of Pentagoet, Port Royal, and LaHave.

La Giraudiere & Denys:

The English seemed to have let Denys alone, and from his rebuilt establishment at St. Peter's, he continued to administer his far flung establishments at Chedabucto, St. Anns and Nipisiquit (Bathhurst). While it is not my purpose to list the travails of Nicholas Denys, I do wish to add one more before we come to 1669. At some point, and I have yet to determine when, another French trader by the name of La Giraudiere, whose association with Acadia must have been short, arrived in Denys' territory with a view to grabbing a piece of the action (La Giraudiere, it is more likely, was one of the 120 armed men which Denys had earlier brought over with him). At about this time Denys was concentrating his forces at Chedabucto, feeling it was exposed. While Denys and his loyal men were building a fort at Chedabucto, La Giraudiere picked St. Peter's as his point of attack and was successful. What La Giraudiere really wanted was to establish himself at Chedabucto; he achieved this goal through a trade with Denys. La Giraudiere made some very good opening moves in his efforts at conquest. He, however, made a mistake which was to unseat him within the year; he agreed as part of the swap (St. Peter's for Chedabucto) to submit himself to a French court for a determination as to who owed what. Denys was a litigator whereas La Giraudiere was not. It was determined, after a hearing back in France, that La Giraudiere was in the wrong and he was ordered to give up Chedabucto in favour of Denys. A new grant was issued to Denys on the 9th November, 1667.

In 1669, another misfortune visited Denys: his home and his buildings located at St. Peter's were completely destroyed by fire. It is here, with him and his family sailing off to his second home at Nipisiquit (Bathurst, New Brunswick) that I end my references to Nicholas Denys as he relates to Nova Scotia; though, I should say, that he continued on and lived to the ripe old age of 90 years. During his last years at Nipisiquit he turned writer. He wrote his *Historique des l'Amérique*, published in 1672. It is an invaluable source to the historian. Nicholas Denys died, in 1688, at Nipisiquit.

Epilogue To The Baronial Times:

It remains for me, before concluding this chapter, to finish up my loose ends in respect to our two principal characters: d'Aulnay and La Tour.

As for La Tour: having heard in August of 1646 of his utter defeat and the death of his wife, he made his way from Boston to Quebec. During the next four years La Tour was absent from Acadia. Two of which years, at least, he spent fighting the Iroquois and engaging in the fur trade (in his travels, he visited the shores of Hudson Bay).

As for d'Aulnay: after his success in completely wiping out La Tour in Acadia, as of 1645, he was the absolute ruler in most all of Acadia with establishments at Port Royal, Penobscot and Saint John. Denys, as we have seen, was restricted to a narrow strip along the northern shores of what we now know as Nova Scotia and New Brunswick.

For the next five year period, 1645-1650, there took place the most substantial development in the root stock of the Acadia people. This early growth occurred at Port Royal, due, undoubtedly, to the foresight and industry of d'Aulnay. During this five year period, it may be safely concluded, the nucleus of the Acadian population was formed.[18]

When out on the River at Port Royal, d'Aulnay or maybe one his friends made a sudden lurch in their small boat; maybe one was responding to a joke, or a fish on the line — who knows?

In any event, d'Aulnay was thrown into the cold water and died as a result. The loss of their leader, d'Aulnay, had to be a huge blow to this first French Acadian community. It seems, in these early days, struggling settlers (no matter French or English) were struck by one blow after another, and another, and another: some from nature, some from man.

Madame d'Aulnay, the invincible Jeanne Motin, like so many wives on the frontier, simply filled in for her husband and picked up his traces: she had eight children of her own and a French colony which needed leadership.

The Marriage Of The Two Houses:

Upon hearing of the death of his nemesis, La Tour likely took little time in catching a sailing ship for France. In France, he apparently got the right kind of reception, for on February 25th, 1651, Letters Patent were given by the King of France to Charles La Tour by which he was made governor and lieutenant-general of Acadia.

There then occurred what had to be a most interesting courtship, a courtship based on Love? Necessity? Political Expediency? — likely for all these reasons. On February 24th, 1653, Charles La Tour, for the "peace and tranquillity of the country, and concord and union between the two families," married Madame d'Aulnay. And, by this union, Jeanne Motin and Charles La Tour brought about peace in Acadia and made a contribution to the Acadian population: they had five children, three girls and two boys.[19]

Le Borgne at this period of time (c.1654) was in charge at Port Royal. La Tour, his new wife, the d'Aulnay retainers and, undoubtedly, all the d'Aulnay moveables of Port Royal were safely tucked away at the foot of the Saint John River, in behind the wooden walls of Fort La Tour. Le Borgne proceeded on the basis that he neither had a claim against La Tour nor the assets on the Saint John. As for Denys: he had once again re-installed himself at St. Peter's and had legal papers which he had his lieutenant deliver to Le Borgne at Port Royal. Le Borgne was disdainful of Denys' lieutenant. Indeed, he was just in the midst of laying plans, during July of 1654, to go up and teach Denys a further lesson when he was suddenly interrupted by the English general, Robert Sedgwick, an event to which we have already referred.

Le Borgne, in the midst of his plans for the recapture of Denys, was suddenly startled by the appearance of the English fleet in Port Royal Basin. To a real soldier the prospect of an encounter with an enemy, however superior in strength, is seldom unwelcome, but to a man like Le Borgne, who was waging war by writs and ejectments, and undertaking the capture of fortresses on commercial principles, such a sight was sufficiently alarming. Still, when summoned to surrender, he replied with a boldness which he could scarcely have felt, and placed the English under the necessity of attacking him. The men that he sent out against them were repulsed and put to flight, and Le Borgne, finding that his vocation was not that of a soldier, resolved to capitulate. Advances to that end were made on the 15th August; on the 16th the articles were completed and signed on board the Admiral's ship, *Auguste*, and on the following day Port Royal was surrendered.[20]

The English, as of 1654, due to Sedgwick's military conquest, were now in charge of Nova Scotia from Canso to Penobscot. Captain John Leverett was left at Port Royal "as governor and commander of the forts of Saint John, Port Royal and Penobscot; this English possession continued from 1654 to 1667.

While La Tour, in his fort across the bay, at the mouth of the Saint John River, likely felt comfortable in his abilities to defend himself against Le Borgne, he was not so sure he could hold out against English armed forces, should they arrive. La Tour then sailed for London to see if he could renew his old English connections. He was successful in this regard, for, during 1656, Cromwell granted Acadia to Thomas Temple, William Alexander and Charles La Tour. Thus, we see that a vast area was encompassed by a merchant's agreement: from the shore at Merliguesche (Lunenburg) around the southern tip of peninsular Nova Scotia and up to the head of the Bay of Fundy; and then, south, along the shores to a point located by the mouth of the River St. George in the present day state of Maine, three hundred miles inland ("one hundred leagues").[21]

We close this scene that same year, 1656. Two Frenchmen (Radisson and Groseilliers) arrived at Quebec from beyond the Lake Michigan and the Wisconsin country, with fifty canoes laden with pelts. The focus on Acadia as the center of the peltry trade if it had not shifted to Quebec by 1656, certainly did then, when, the authorities looked out onto the St. Lawrence to bear witness to this sight of a train of large birch bark canoes, roped and operated by wild looking maneuverers. It is, too, in the year 1656, that La Tour sells his interest out to Temple and Alexander, and, goes into retirement at Cape Sable.

Chapter 8

The English

North America was divided up by the first European adventurers into three geographical districts: Acadia, Virginia and Florida. Florida was part of New Spain which was to be found to the west and south of Virginia; Acadia was in the north. Between the northern boundary of Florida (somewhere in the Carolinas) and the southern boundary of Acadia (undefined and which was to cause trouble for two centuries), lies Virginia. New Spain and New France were open-ended at the back and a massive land continent stretched west; New England was hemmed in by the Alleghenies.

The first permanent English settlement arose as a result of legal rights granted by James the First, on April 10th, 1606. Two Virginian companies (the London Company and the West of England Company) received through these grants rights to the east coast of America. It was quite a wide swath of land from 34º, Cape Fear, North Carolina; to 45º, Nova Scotia. With sensible and practical instructions, the Virginia settlers came by way of the West Indies in three sailing vessels: the *Susan Constant* (100 ton) with Captain Christopher Newport in charge, the *God Speed* (40 tons) with Captain Bartholomew Gosnold, and the *Discovery* (quite small at 20 tons) with Captain John Ratcliffe. During 1607, after having set out from England four months earlier, these small wooden sailing vessels, with their expectant occupants, sailed into Chesapeake Bay; the first vital germ of English colonization on the continent was thereby established. On the shores of the Powhatatan River, forty miles up, on the north side, thousands of miles away from their beloved England these English adventurers tied their vessels to trees and unloaded a number of their possessions ashore: Jamestown was founded. It was to be the first permanent English colony in America. To go into the infancy years of Jamestown would indeed be an interesting story in itself, but is beyond the scope of this work.[1] The story of Jamestown is the story of Spanish spies and men who mutiny. It is the story of discord and death. At the same time, it is the story of bravery as Captains Newport and Smith extended, through explorations, England's knowledge of the surrounding shores — not only of the ocean, but also of the inland rivers and lakes. It is the story of love and loyalty and inter-racial relationships, such as that of Captain Smith and Pocahontas. It is the story of fish, oysters, bread, deer, turkeys, corn and tobacco. It is the story of pigs and the founding of Bermuda by the British. It is the story of making pitch, tar, glass, ashes and soap. It is the story of disillusioned and disgruntled men.[2]

Samuel Argall:

While on the subject of Jamestown, I should mention Samuel Argall, the first persecutor of the Acadians. He was a man with no particular credentials other than he was a captain of "an illicit trading-vessel." Argall was "a man of ability and force ... unscrupulous and grasping." The English Governor of Virginia, Sir Thomas Dale, saw in Samuel Argall an ideal person to deal with the neighboring French. It was of no matter that there existed practically 500 miles of wilderness between Jamestown and Port Royal, English "rights" were to be enforced, and, I might add, booty to be had. Argall was set to the task of clearing out the French to be found somewhere north, up the coast. Arriving off the coastline of Maine, Argall tricked the Indians (normally the Indians had a distinct fondness for the French and a dislike for the English) and was soon led to his quarry. By this time, 1613, the French had made three establishments in the area: Mount Desert, St. Croix and Port Royal.[3] In short order, Argall, with lawless violence, ransacked and plundered all three; and, so he thought, Acadia was to be "effectually blotted out."[4]

It was in Acadia where the first shots in America were exchanged between the English and French, these ancient European enemies. These bloody exchanges — of which Acadia was to have more than its share — kept up for over a century and a half and continually shook the struggling communities of North America until accounts were permanently settled between the years 1758 and 1760. But we have much territory to cover before we come to the concluding events.

The Massachusetts Colony:

Before passing on and back to Acadia I will give a quick accounting of the founding of the earliest New England colonies. There was of course the colony which was established in 1630 north of the existing colony of Virginia. It was John Winthrop (1588-1649), a forty-two-year-old Puritan magistrate who lead his colonists ashore and founded the Massachusetts colony.

When they landed, there were already some two thousand people in New England, among them the separatists of the Plymouth colony who had emigrated a decade earlier and had by now established a network of small trading outposts as far north as Maine. The influx of English continued, so that ten years after Winthrop's bay colonists arrived there were nine thousand people in Massachusetts alone, more than thirteen thousand in New England, and nearly twenty-seven thousand English in America. What's more, these settlers had financed themselves. By comparison, the three hundred colonists of Razilly's state-supported expedition seemed almost insignificant.[5]

In 1633, the Dutch settled at a spot which now marks Hartford on the Connecticut River. In 1634, Lord Baltimore founded Maryland. And, in 1635, New Hampshire was granted to Captain John Mason.

―――――――――――

Chapter 9

Acadia
(1654-84)

It was in 1660 that Chouart Des Groseilliers (1618-c.1696) and his younger companion, brother-in-law Pierre-Esprit Radisson (c.1640-1710) — superb woodsmen and traders, both — arrived at Montreal with a flotilla of canoes "so great a number of boats that did almost cover the whole River." The first significant tap had been placed into a huge north American territory drained by the Great Lakes: a drainage system which included countless lakes and rivers over which trading goods flowed. European goods were much valued and were traded as much by the redmen as they were by the whitemen — maybe more, as they went from hand to hand generally westward through countless tribes. In went knives, hatchets, pots and cloth: out came furs in exchange.[1]

State Control (1663):

With private companies or persons such as Radisson and Groseilliers hauling in such riches; well, it just didn't seem right. Courtiers, like all politicians through the ages, thought they should cut themselves in and spend it on the "business of the state," thinking, it seems, that those who legally earned the money did not know how to spend it. In 1663, at the urging of Governor d'Avaugour, the French territories in North America passed from under the control of trading corporations to the direct control of the French government: the furs of Radisson and Groseilliers played no little role.[2] This was accomplished by a royal decree dissolving the Company of New France. In the process, the Company was to lose title to its lands not actually worked or cleared, or done so within the ensuing six months of the date of the degree.

Le Borgne Occupies LaHave (1658):

In these years, Acadia was English territory, having been captured by Sedgwick in 1654. But the conquest did nothing to change the situation of the budding Acadian colony at Port Royal. They continued to express themselves in their French tongue, in their French habits, and in their French religion. Indeed, in parts of Acadia, the French took charge. Le Borgne's son, together with fifty men, in 1658, occupied LaHave and rebuilt the fort that de Razilly had established there in 1632 and abandoned after his death, c. 1640. In 1664, notwithstanding that the territory was conquered English territory, France had granted Emmanuael Le Borgne (Bourge) Du Coudray a seigneury at LaHave. Thus, Le Borgne thought himself legitimately in charge at LaHave; Thomas Temple, the English Governor, likely considered him but a mere tenant at will.

Temple, *2nd Anglo-dutch War* & Marquis De Tracy:

Thomas Temple was in charge of Acadia for a nine-year period, which extended from the time he bought his rights from La Tour in 1656, to the time that he was ordered by the British crown to hand over his rights to the French by the *Treaty of Breda* in 1667. Temple made his headquarters at Penobscot. From there he maintained garrisons at Port Royal and at Saint John. It was during this time that the La Tour fort at the mouth of the Saint John River was abandoned in favour of a new fort at Jemseg, fifty miles or so up the Saint John River. There, at Jemseg, the occupiers were tucked out of the way of marauding, seagoing pirates; and, likely too, it was a better place at which to trade with the descending river Indians.

In 1664, the English — *The Second Anglo-Dutch War* having broken out — conquered the settlements that had been established by the Dutch within the areas that we now know as New York and New Jersey, which, by the *Treaty of Breda* (1667), was retained by England. This would put the English in charge of most all of the North American eastern coast, including Acadia. It must be remembered that the center of French influence in North America was Quebec: it never was to be Acadia.

In the meantime, a high level French military officer, Marquis de Tracy, was sent out from France with a substantial contingent in order to shore up its position at Quebec. The French at Quebec were safe enough from an overland attack by the New Englanders, for between them stood an effective barrier, the Alleghenies. What was required was to smash the Iroquois threat. Tracy and his troops, veterans of the Turkish wars, advanced into Mohawk territory and "the savages fled before this great European engine of war, leaving to Tracy their wooden villages, their stores of food and the crops standing in the fields. The French burned them all ..." By this action, the French, centered at Quebec, were finally and completely rid of the menace which had been a continuing threat to their very existence since their arrival fifty years earlier. Thus, at Quebec, new times were to arrive for the French settler and the French trader.[3]

Acadia Passed Back To The French:

In 1667, by *The Treaty of Breda*, Acadia was transferred to France.[4] While the treaty was signed on July 31st, 1667, the formal hand over did not take place until 1670. The English colonial governor, Thomas Temple at Penobscot, was not about to just simply hand over his command without double-checking with his masters back in England, a process, in the days of sailing ships, which could take many months. Nonetheless, the French were clear in their own minds that Acadia was once more to be under the French flag and did not think that there should be too much delay about the matter.

In 1668, Alexander Le Borgne, who assumed his father's (Emanmanuel Le Borgne), noble title of Belleîle, was of course delighted with the news that Acadia was to be in "French hands," once again. That year, Le Borgne sailed the entire coast of Acadia with the news. History is unclear in this, but Le Borgne arrived at Boston late in October of 1668. He intended to show his papers to Governor Temple, who was apparently temporarily away from his command post at Penobscot entertaining himself with his friends at Boston. Temple himself was not at all impressed and had some indication from his own sources that King Charles of England was not yet ready to give up Acadia. Temple dismissed Le Borgne and sailed for Acadia and immediately took the place back by going to the town square at Port Royal and unceremoniously tearing down the French flag and running up the English one.[5]

The Governorship Of Grandfontaine (1670-73):

There now comes to the historical stage of Acadia, Hector Andigné De Grandfontaine (1672-96); he was the French governor of Acadia between 1670-73. He had strict orders from Colbert[6] that he was not to act on his own; he was to take his orders from the intendant at Quebec. This "subordination to multiple authorities, in France and in Canada, made action on his part difficult." Overall, however, the historical conclusion seems to be, that, though hampered, Grandfontaine did much for Acadia during the three years he was in charge, 1670-73. During this period we have the first new French settlers to come to Acadia since d'Aulnay brought settlers over from his mother's seigneury, *circa* 1640.[7] Further, in 1671, it was under Grandfontaine that the first census in Acadia was carried out.

To the extent that Grandfontaine spent anytime in Acadia, it seems he spent it at Penobscot.[8] "The fort which he had made his residence was a paltry work, incapable of resisting any serious attack, and only fit to be used as an Indian trading station." But even at that, it was likely that Penobscot was the best defended position in all of Acadia. The fort at Jemseg, as Hannay pointed out, was in a worst state than the fort at Penobscot. Fort Latour at the mouth of the St. John "had been long abandoned, the fortifications at Port Royal had crumbled away, Fort St. Louis, at Port Latour, had degenerated into a mere fishing station ..." As for the fort at LaHave, where Le Borgne had been but a few short years ago, it "had no other tenants but the wild beasts from the forest which surrounded it."[9]

During the month of August, 1669, a French naval vessel, the *Saint-Sebasten*, under the command of Pierre de Joibert, together with a British officer aboard, sailed from one Acadian place to another and in turn accepted each on behalf of the French: Acadia by the terms of the *Treaty of Breda* was officially to be French territory. Penobscot was handed over on August the 5th; Jemseg, on the 27th; and Port Royal on September 2nd, 1670.

Grandfontaine appointed his deputies. Pierre de Joibert was in charge at Jemseg. At Pentagoet, the Baron Saint-Castin[10] was to establish himself. Le Borgne, the most senior Frenchman at Port Royal, was initially put in charge at that place. Le Borgne, however, was not long to survive in a position of leadership. He was, it seems, a hard master. In concert with the resident priest, Molin, he "caused a negro to be hung without any trial, killed an Indian, and banished three inhabitants."[11] Grandfontaine, therefore, had good reason to dismiss Le Borgne; he probably would have liked to have gotten rid of his officer at Jemseg too, as they (Joibert and Grandfontaine) did not get along.

The years between 1670 and 1673 were good growing years for Acadia. Its population showed buds of growth well up in the Baie de Française, at the western end of the Minas Basin and the far reaches of Cumberland Basin (Beaubassin). This important growth can now be noted because Grandfontaine had a census taken. It was due to Grandfontaine that, during this period, a significant number of settlers from France were landed and a bad administration was cleaned up. Direct assistance was supplied to the settlers, such as the bringing in and the giving out of spinning looms. Notwithstanding this progress, the authorities at Quebec decided to move Grandfontaine as they were apparently tired of the complaints, particularly from the officer at Jemseg, Pierre de Joibert.

While being appointed during May, the new governor of Acadia, Jacques de Chambly (d.1687) did not arrive at Pentagoet until the autumn of 1673, presumably to relieve Grandfontaine of his duties. De Chambly was not to be there at Pentagoet for long.

The Dutch Take Acadia (1674):

During 1674, the French governor, de Chambly, was surprised by a Dutch force under Captain Juriaen Aernouts and after a brief fight, the fort at Penobscot was given up. The Dutch raider then continued up the coast and entered the Saint John River, where, and in like manner, he put an end to the French operations at Jemseg which was under the command of Joibert. Aernouts declared all that he had conquered to be New Holland, and, promptly sailed away with his French prisoners (Chambly and Joibert among them). At Boston the prisoners were ransomed back to the French at Quebec. When Captain Aernouts sailed away from Acadia he left no Dutchman behind. The forts, from what I can determine, at both Jemseg and Penobscot, were left to stand unoccupied for the next couple of years. In 1676, Castin reoccupied Pentagoet; and, in 1677, Joibert (who succeeded Chambly as the administrator of Acadia), established himself once again at Jemseg, which was then to become the seat of French power and the capital of Acadia.[12]

Beaubassin & Bergier (1678-84):

Joibert died[13] in the year following his appointment and Michael Leneuf de Beaubassin (1640-1705, the elder) was then named as governor. Beaubassin was the first of an unusually large number of French naval heros who were to take land posts as governors of Acadia. Beaubassin earned his reputation in 1676, when he and his brother-in-law, the son of Nicholas Denys, Sieur Richard Denys as second in command, in their French war vessel, seized three English ketches from Boston that were taking on coal at Cape Breton. Frontenac[14] was that pleased with Beaubassin's accomplishments that he granted a large piece of land at the Isthmus of Chignecto which became known as the Beaubassin seigneury.

While Beaubassin was establishing French rights on the ground, there came a certain merchant from La Rochelle, one Bergier, to take charge of the waters off of Acadia. He laid a plan before the French king, Louis XIV, who, on the 14th of April,

1684, appointed Bergier as "lieutenant for us in the government of the country and coasts of Acadia."[15] In the summer of 1684, Bergier cruised the waters of Acadia enforcing the rights of French fishermen as against those of New England.[16] Two ships, the *St. Louis* and the *Mariann*, set out for their cruise in Acadian waters, on May 11, 1684; by October they were back at France having successfully impressed a number of fishing captains from New England that fishing in Acadian waters, for Englishmen, was a dangerous business.

So, the year 1684 is reached and we see two strong men in Acadia: Bergier and Beaubassin. Things were looking up for Acadia. However, she was shortly to receive a fatal blow.

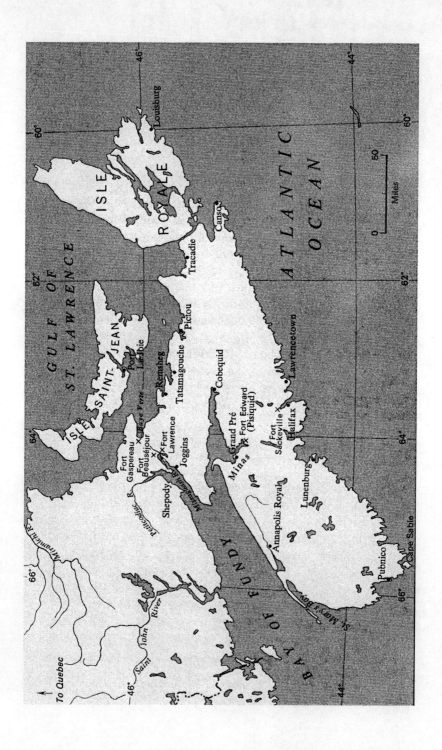

Part Two

The English Takeover:

1660-1712

Chapter 1

Introduction

In the first part of our book on Acadia, we confined ourselves to the early 1600s, a time when the eastern edges of North America were being first opened up to Europeans. In Acadia, we saw how the French, on account of fishes and furs, came in their small and frail sailing ships on their southwestern courses and set themselves up as feudal barons in the wilderness. During these early years, we saw how the French precariously perched themselves at Port Royal, which was really but another outpost on an ill-defined boundary between the lands in North America claimed by the French and the English. It is historically apparent that these claims disregarded the notion of possessory rights.

In 1710, Port Royal exchanged hands for the last time, as British forces attacked and captured it. The neutrality of the some 2,000 Acadians that made their home in Acadia in the year 1710 was not much questioned then, or thereafter, as the dramatic events unfolded in the ensuing fifty years. The Acadians continued to raise their families and, in behind their hand-made dikes, to farm their lands that stretched east from the newly named capital, Annapolis Royal, to the shores of the Minas Basin and beyond towards the Isthmus of Chignecto.

On the turn of the century, 1700, Acadia's population was almost exclusively French. The population of Port Royal, though captured by the English in 1710, continued to be French. There were only a few English families and those that did exist were structured with an English soldier and a French Acadian girl at its head. So it was that the only Englishmen to be found in Nova Scotia were the English soldiers. Of those, there were altogether but a few hundred located at Annapolis Royal and at Canso. This situation was not to change until Cornwallis arrived with his settlers in 1749.[1]

The *War of the Spanish Succession* (the British colonies called it *Queen Anne's War*), began in 1701, and ended in 1713 with the *Treaty of Utrecht*. Louis XIV was too anxious to see that one of his relatives took the Spanish throne and the result was that England, in 1713, made "an advantageous peace." France was to give away to her successful rival three sections of her holdings in North America: Hudson Bay, Newfoundland, and Acadia ("according to its ancient limits").[2] Canada with its stronghold at Quebec, a possession to be retained by the French, was to be preserved by the sentinel islands at the mouth of the mighty St. Lawrence. These islands included Île St. Jean and Île Royale (the present day islands of Prince Edward Island and Cape Breton).

Much of the reign (1643-1715) of Louis XIV, the "Sun King," occurred before the historical times with which we are about to deal; Louis XIV died in 1715. (His grandson, age fifteen, was to succeed him with the Duke of Orleans to act as regent.) So, France was under a new royal regime when Acadia came into English hands; and, interestingly enough, so too was England. Queen Anne died in 1714 and the first of the Hanoverians, George I, took the throne. One might have thought that new rulers on both sides would make for a better relationship between the two nations; but there is no discounting the bloody and bitter competition which had existed for centuries between these two European nations. War, declared or not, was to continue between France and England throughout the next century with, up to 1760, one of its principal battle fields being Acadia. Such is the international and political landscape as our story opens in a geographically unique peninsula located high on the northeastern coast of North America: Nova Scotia.

_____

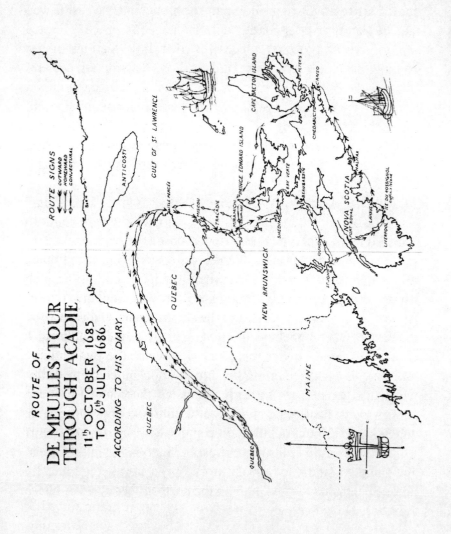

ROUTE OF
DE MEULLES' TOUR
THROUGH ACADIE
11ᵗʰ OCTOBER 1685
TO 6ᵗʰ JULY 1686.

ACCORDING TO HIS DIARY.

ROUTE SIGNS
OUTWARD
HOMEWARD
CONJECTURAL

GULF OF Sᵗ LAWRENCE

ANTICOSTI

CAPE BRETON ISLAND

PRINCE EDWARD ISLAND

PETER'S I.

CANSO

CHEDABUCTO

QUEBEC

ILE PERCÉE

MISCOU

TRACADIE

MIRAMICHI

BAY VERTE

BEAUBASSIN

SHEDIAC

NOVA SCOTIA

PORT ROYAL

LAHAVE

LIVERPOOL

ILE DU POSSIGNOL

NEW BRUNSWICK

ST JOHN

MAINE

QUEBEC

QUEBEC

Chapter 2

Intendant De Meulles' Visit
(1685)

On February 6th, 1685, Charles II of England died with all his court around him: "brave, witty, cynical, even in the presence of death"; and for his mistress, Nell Gwynn, he had his last words, "Do not let poor Nelly starve." James, the dead king's brother, took the throne of England.

> His mind was dull and narrow, though orderly and methodical; his temper dogged and arbitrary, but sincere. ... [James II] cherished an entire belief in the royal authority and a hatred for parliament. His main desire was for the establishment of Catholicism as the only means of insuring the obedience of his people; and his old love of France was quickened by the firm reliance which he placed on the aid of Louis in bringing about that establishment.[1]

In spite of his views, however, James vowed to the people, a vow the whole country welcomed with enthusiasm: "I will preserve this government both in church and state as it is established." What in the mind of James had been established, and what was in the collective mind of the population, was, I am afraid, two different sets of establishments. James thought that Catholicism and monarchy had been established with his Ascension, the people thought otherwise. England possessed a state sponsored religion, the Church of England, and — as the next few dramatic years would show — it was to remain that way: not by royal authority, but by a government driven by popular demand.

During these three years (1685 to 1688) there was much turmoil in England, at all levels, as James attempted to force his Catholic views on the people. ("Catholics were admitted into civil and military offices without stint ...") Englishmen in large numbers were hung, whipped, imprisoned, and "sold into slavery beyond the sea."[2] James was to stand "utterly alone in his realm.

The peerage, the gentry, the bishops, the clergy, the universities, every lawyer, every trader, stood aloof from him." And soon, even his soldiers would leave him. The *Glorious Revolution* of 1688 came about; and by it England was to turn permanently Protestant; and by it the English people had important civil rights enshrined.[3]

In what almost seems like a reaction to the political occurrences in England, Louis XIV in 1685 revoked a treaty (*Edict of Nantes*) which, in 1598, had provided for religion tolerance and a guarantee to protestants that they could practice their religion in France without fear. After its revocation in 1685, there then followed the destruction of a people, which came about because of the merciless persecution and resultant dispersal of about a million French Protestants, known as Huguenots.

Both France and England extended their holdings in North America: La Salle, in 1682, reached the mouth of the Mississippi and in the same year a group of Quakers followed William Penn (1644-1718) across the Delaware River into the wilderness and established Pennsylvania.[4]

In the meantime the French in North America were making a wide sweep through the vast wildernesses of North America. The number of Frenchmen on the ground, however, were very thin. In 1686, in Acadia, there were about 885 French people. The population centers (if we can call them that) were located at Port Royal (592), Minas (57), and Beaubassin (127).

At Port Royal there were but 30 soldiers, and that is all we seem to know of the French military establishment of Acadia. These 30 men were quartered on the inhabitants, a fact which supports the proposition that there was a lack of fortifications at Port Royal in 1686. The civilian population occupied the marsh lands ascending up the rivers away from Port Royal, mainly on Rivière Dauphin (the Annapolis River of today). Despite the setbacks brought on by both nature and man, the Acadians had survived their first 50 years and had, though small and simple, a prosperous base.

A Visit By The Intendant And Bishop:

Jacques de Meulles,[5] the Intendant at Quebec, visited all of the Acadian settlements during the years 1685-6. At the same time, Bishop St. Vallier (Quebec) made a pastoral visit; so, there being both the Intendant and the Bishop, there must have been quite a entourage.

We can see from the history of things that a number of important matters were attended to at this time in Acadia; undoubtedly this was on account of de Meulles. A census was conducted, which as I have already pointed out, amounted to a total count, for all of Acadia, 885 persons. In addition to the 592 at Port Royal, there was 127 at Beaubassin, 57 at Minas, 19 at LaHave and Mirliguaiche (modern day Lunenburg), 15 at Cape Sable, 16 for all of the Maine coast (mostly at Pentagoet [Castine]), 6 at Miramichi (Richard Denys family), 6 at Nepisiguit (Bathhurst; Philips Esnault family), 26 at Île Percée and 15-20 at Chedabucto (the town of Guysboro); on the Saint John there were to be found the three Damour brothers, M. Martignon (his wife Jeanne LaTour (age 60) and their daughter, Marianne, aged 24.

A map (see page 76), doubtlessly in connection with his visit to Acadia, was issued by "Jacques de Meulles, Intendant of New France," and drawn by "Jean-Baptiste-Franquelin, King's hydrographer." The original of this map is yet in France (*Service Hydrographique de la Marine*, Paris), and a copy is to be found at the Public Archives at Ottawa.[6]

Generally through the years France paid little attention to Acadian affairs. However, during the years, 1685-88, she paid some attention.

The visit of Jacques de Meulles, in 1685, was an example of an increased interest during this three year period. Hannay wrote: "The French Government had sent two war vessels to the coast of Acadia in the Autumn of 1688, which captured six English ketches and a brigantine, which were engaged in fishing." Webster wrote: "In 1688, the King sent the frigate, *La Friponne*, commanded by M. Beauregard, to guard the coasts, and enforce order. On July 14, 1688, a ship of 250 tons, the *St Louis of la Rochelle*, arrived at Chedabucto Bay with supplies for the fishing company that had earlier established themselves there."[7]

Prior to 1686 there was not much of a settlement to be found at Minas, this because of the uncertainty of title. As is the case today, no one was interested in settling on and improving lands if there was a risk of being displaced by another with a better right to title. Two influential Acadians, Bellîle (LeBorgne) and Beaubassin (Michael Leneuf de la Valliè), were at odds with one another, both asserting seigniorial rights to the lands at Minas. Thus, there were to be found only 57 people at Minas (1686 census); none at Pisiquid (Windsor) or Cobequid (Truro). Hitherto, this land dispute held development back. Intendant Meulles, being on site, brought the dispute to an end by giving the nod to Bellîle, who was then to be the seignior at both Port Royal and Minas; there was, therefore and thereafter, to be a significant transfer of population from Port Royal to the Minas area. Also at this time, in 1689, at Cobiquid, Matthieu Martin (b.1636), a life long bachelor, having received one of the few signeuries ever given out in old Acadia, planted a settlement on the River Wecobequitk.

Further, in his effort to bring legal stability to Acadia, de Meulles appointed a local resident, Michel Broudrot, in 1686, as *"étatit lieutenant-général à Port Royal et juge du lieu."* Broudrot had come to Port Royal with his family in 1642; he is a direct ancestor of a great number of people of Acadian descent.

Fort St. Louis At Chedabucto:

In 1686, a company headed up by Gabriel Gautier was granted a 20 year right to the fisheries at Cape Breton, Île St. Jean (P.E.I.) and the Magdalens. On territory which was previously granted to another Company, Gautier, erected a small fort and fishing establishment at the head of Chedabucto Bay, on the site of the present day Guysborough. The establishment at Chedabucto, known as Fort St. Louis, consisted, in 1687, of two buildings, 60 X 20 feet each, defended by four cannon.

"There were 150 residents, of whom 80 were fishermen. The Company owned a barque of 30 tons and a number of fishing shallops. Later, a detachment of regular troops was stationed at the fort acting under the Governor of Port Royal."

The Meneval Report:

Before coming to the milestone year of 1690, we should introduce into our history, Louis-Alexandre Desfriches, chevalier, Sieur De Meneval[8], the governor of Acadia at the time it was attacked by the English in 1690. He arrived to take up his duties in October of 1687. Upon taking a measure of the place, he reported to the French authorities. This report discloses the tough conditions which presented: shortage of flour and workers, 19 muskets between 30 soldiers and a surgeon who was a drunkard. Further, as a practical matter, there were no fortifications behind which the French might hold out if attacked by the English. In this report we also see where it is suggested that the soldiers be encouraged to marry into the existing French population. It is also reported that Les Mines was developing. Further, in closing off his report of 1688, Governor Meneval pointed out that the English coveted Acadia.

The Meneval report, together with that which was likely filed by de Meulles as a result of his official visit in 1685/6 motivated the French military hierarchy back in France to put in place a building program. With the arrival of Governor de Meneval, in 1687, there also arrived a French military engineer, one Pasquine. Pasquine also reported to his superiors and laid out specific plans for a fort at Port Royal. On the first of October, 1689, a French military Engineer by the name of Vincent de Saccardy was sent out from France. First calling in on Chedabucto (Guysborough), de Saccardy arrived at Port Royal in the frigate *L'Embuscade*. His orders, apparently, were to build a fort at Port Royal. He barely got started, when, on November 1st, 1689, he headed back to France for further instructions. Apparently he left the project in such an unfinished state that the palisades were left open, a situation which continued to exist, when the English arrived under Phips, the following spring.[9]

Chapter 3

The Taking Of Port Royal
(1690)

On December 17th, 1689, at Boston, war between France and England was declared. The matter had been brewing for some time. On February 13th, 1689, James (VII of Scotland and II of England) was defeated in Ireland at the *Battle of the Boyne*, on the very date that the reign of William and Mary began.[1] With the election of William and Mary, the claim of divine right or hereditary right, independent of law, was formally brought to an end. Further, the British Empire was to be Protestant, just as sure as the French empire was to be Roman Catholic. William, due to the help which the French king had extended to James, declared war on France.

Today, one can stand on the grassy slopes covering the ramparts of old Fort Anne (Annapolis Royal) and look out into Annapolis Basin (Port Royal). This historic spot is located at a point just at the mouth of the Annapolis River and marks the eastern end of this tidal basin. The Annapolis Basin is in the shape of a stubby carrot thirteen miles long and four miles wide. Off from its southwestern shoulder, tides of sea water ebb and flow through a narrow two mile cut, Digby Gut, a portal through the North Mountain range from the greatest bay of the northwestern Atlantic ocean, the Bay of Fundy. This range, a mere echo of an eastern mountain range, forms the backbone on which the larger part of peninsular Nova Scotia hangs. The cold north winds meet this sweeping range and are veered up, sheltering the southeastern valley beyond. This ensconcing hump of land extends itself northeastward, covering the continuing valley below, until it dazzlingly drops itself off from the precipitous purple heads of Cape Blomidon — down, out of sight, through the jeweled shores of the Minas Channel. This capturing hollow, the Annapolis Valley, is filled with something, not much of which is to be found along the rocky northwest coast of the Atlantic: sweet alluvial soil. Meandering along the valley's hundred mile length, and splitting its ten mile width, are two principal rivers; the one flowing southwest, the other northeast: today we know them as the Annapolis (previously known as the Rivière Dauphin by the French) and the Cornwallis (the Antoine).

Port Royal, being a harbourage to French cruisers and a place from which hostile Indians drew supplies, in 1689, was a place marked by New Englanders to be destroyed. New Englanders were driven to action by: the Abenakis raids on their New England outposts, the confiscation of English fishing boats off the Acadian coast, and the raids which Frontenac was launching. In 1690, Frontenac sent three war parties out from Canada: from Montreal, Three Rivers, and Quebec. Their destinations, respectively: New York, New Hampshire and Maine. The blood of English settlers along the western and northern borders of New England flowed. This business simply horrified New Englanders and something just had to be done about it.[2] It was limp, but it was reason enough to destroy Acadia. Throughout her history, we see, again and again, how Acadia was to answer for the decisions taken at Quebec. It was simply easier to get at Acadia, than ever it was to get at fortress Quebec, safe as it generally was behind the Alleghenies to be got at only through two dangerous funnels of access: one being that over a treacherous land march via Lake Champlain, the other a treacherous sea journey up the St. Lawrence. Much easier, just to go up and kick the stuffing out of Acadia.

Sir William Phips was a most interesting and colourful character of history.[3] He was supported by subscriptions taken by the merchants of Salem and Boston. Phips was outfitted with "7 ships, armed with 78 cannon and carrying 736 men, 446 of them being militiamen."[4] Arriving off of Digby Gut on the 19th of May, 1690, the New England fleet proceeded through the portal and into the Basin of Port Royal. The French garrison consisted of around 80 men,[5] the fortifications, as we have seen, were in an unsatisfactory state and no cannons were mounted: it should not be surprising therefore, to read, that the French, after having made an assessment of the English forces, capitulated in short order.

The terms of capitulation were that the French governor and his soldiers should leave the fort with arms and baggage and be sent to Quebec by sea; the inhabitants should remain in peaceful possession of their property, and the females should not be molested; and that the inhabitants should not be interfered with in their religion and that the church should not be touched.[6] In spite of these promises made before the capitulation, the New Englanders spent, after the surrender of the French, twelve days pillaging the community. They removed the cannon and leveled anything that looked like a fortification (they cut the palisades in two). After doing all of that, Sir William called the peasant Acadian farmers together and had them take an oath of allegiance to William and Mary of England, which they did without demur. Phips then determined to obliterate all existing authority (religious, civil and military) by taking away with him to Boston the two priests (Petit and Trouvé), Governor Meneval, and 58 soldiers. Before leaving Port Royal (not an Englishman was left behind) Phips attempted to organize a provisional government by appointing selected French Acadian leaders to form a council.[7]

In addition to capturing Port Royal, Phips dispatched certain of his officers and ships to seize the posts at Castine, LaHave, Chedabucto[8] and all those settlements at the head of the Bay of Fundy. "Massachusetts had made an easy conquest of all Acadia; a conquest, however, which she had neither the men nor the money to secure by sufficient garrisons." By the end of May, 1690, Phips was back in Boston basking in his glory.[9]

Chapter 4

French Flag On The Saint John
(1690-98)

Villebon On The Saint John:

Joseph Robineau de Villebon,[1] a French military officer, though of the new world, had spent the winter of 1689/90 at Paris. His orders for the spring were to return to Port Royal with reinforcements.[2] Villebon set out from La Rochelle on May 4, 1690, sailing on the *Union*, a ship owned by the Company of Acadia. After a favorable crossing, the *Union* fetched up just off of Port Mouton and there the newly arrived Frenchmen pounced on a coastal fishing vessel which had come up from New England to make a living. After taking his time with the English prisoners (it would appear he let them go after questioning) Villebon sailed on to Port Royal arriving there on June 14th. To his surprise he found Port Royal had been under attack but days before. The fort was under an English flag; the church and other buildings had been destroyed; the town plundered; and its military, civil and religious leaders — so he was to hear — carried away to Boston as prisoners of Sir William Phips. Not an Englishman was to be found at Port Royal; but, nonetheless, Villebon felt obliged to set new plans for himself, on the spot. With Meneval captured, Villebon assumed the position as acting governor of Acadia. After taking charge, Villebon quickly determined that Port Royal was too vulnerable and open to further attack; he therefore elected to take those military forces under his command and head for the Saint John across the Bay of François (Fundy) where he thought there would be greater safety up-river.[3] Before doing so, he determined to shore up what was left of Port Royal, as best he could.

He immediately summoned the inhabitants from the out-settlements, in whose presence he soon afterwards took formal possession of the place and fort, and, indeed, of all Acadie, in the name of the French king. Mathieu de Goutin resumed the exercise of his duties as judge and commissary, and exhumed the 1,300 livres which he had buried on the approach of Phipps in the spring. Thus was the capital of Acadie once more in the possession of France.[4]

Sensing danger, Villebon crossed over to the mouth of the Saint John River on June 18th, a sail of but a few hours. In the *Union*, he passed into the harbour of Saint John (a dangerous business that needs the right winds, tides and visibility). Once in the harbour Villebon's men unloaded provisions[5] brought from France into two smaller boats, pinnaces or long boats, which were likely uncrated and assembled on the spot. These two smaller vessels, much better at navigating the river than their mother boat, departing on the 27th, then proceeded up the Saint John to cover the distance to Jemseg, 40 miles or so up the river where Grand Lake meets the Saint John. In fact, because the pinnaces moved so slowly in their tracks, at some point on route, Villebon moved out ahead in a flotilla of canoes. At some waypoint or other, after waiting a longer time than he had expected to do, he, Villebon, with a renewed sense of danger, retraced his track in the canoes all the way back down the Saint John. At the mouth, inside the harbour, he surreptitiously observed the *Union* and the two missing pinnaces in the company of English ships, one with 18 guns and the other with 8. It might be presumed that the *Union*, with the best of her crew busy elsewhere, was no match for the 190 pirates that had arrived in two ships to take her. She was now flying an English flag. Perrot (the ex-governor) and de Saccardy[6] were among those left behind on the *Union*; they had been made prisoners (Perrot was badly treated). These freebooters had followed Villebon by a few days, having picked up his scent at Port Royal, maybe earlier. These villains had arrived at Port Royal just after Villebon had left and squeezed information out of the struggling settlers by the simple expedient of hanging two of them and burning down their buildings — in one of which, an entire family was "roasted." Having lost the *Union* and his supplies — the pirates sailed away with the works — Villebon quit his plans for the Saint John and traveled up river and overland to get to Quebec.[7]

Bonaventure:

Villebon, apparently having returned to France on Frontenac's instructions in the fall of the previous year, would have been seen, in the spring of 1691, aboard the *Soleil d'Afrique* a naval French cruiser under the command of Simon-Pierre Denys de Bonaventure.[8] The *Soleil d'Afrique* first arrived at Quebec in the summer of 1691 and there she stayed until Frontenac was satisfied she was no longer needed for the protection of Quebec. In the fall of 1691, she was permitted to descend the St Lawrence in order to go to Acadia, having aboard her the Acadian governor, Villebon, and supplies necessary to set up the governor's new headquarters on the Saint John. The *Soleil d'Afrique* arrived at the mouth of the Saint John River mid-October, 1691.

Col. Edward Tyng:

While Villebon and Bonaventure were unloading the *Soleil d'Afrique*, an English merchant ship with Col. Edward Tyng (b.1636) aboard stumbled upon them. Tyng was appointed by the English to be the English Governor of Acadia and was on a little tour in an under-armed merchant ship.[9] He was on his return to Boston when he thought to poke his nose into the mouth of the Saint John River to see if there were any Frenchmen about. (I remind the reader that while this is a good port, a safe entry into or safe exit out of Saint John Harbor can only be made mid-tide, during a period of slack water.) The *Soleil d'Afrique*, having unloaded her cargo, was lying in the stream and was out of sight to Tyng and his crew of New Englanders as they shot the narrows on the slack tide: they were surprised by the presence of such a French force and were immediately captured and made prisoners of the French.

After Villebon got himself squared away at Jemseg he came back down the Saint John in order to make arrangements in respect to Tyng, his vessel and her captured New England crew. Captain Bonaventure, it would appear, was soon under way to return to France before bad weather set in. Villebon sent his river boat down to Boston with Tyng and his captured crew with a view to trading English prisoners for French prisoners, those that Phips had taken at Port Royal in the previous year. [It is interesting to note that Villebon also sent a young girl down to Boston which the Indians had ransomed to a French lady, who, at this time was living on the Saint John River, Madame Damours (Guyon).]

Baptiste:

Though there was some illegal trading going on with Boston, a substantial amount of the supplies needed by those at Port Royal and at Jemseg were supplied by French privateers operating out of the mouth of the Saint John and at Port Royal (a long time haven). For example, we see that on January 5th, 1692, as cold as it was and with ice on the rails, where Baptiste called into the Saint John with a prize in tow, taken off the coast of New England. Outfitting himself at Port Royal, Baptiste, from December 1691 through to May 1692, captured eight English ships one of which was laden with salt, a valuable cargo back in the days of salted fish.[10]

The Chevalier Of Port Royal:

As for Port Royal: after its sack, in 1690, and after its governor, the 58 soldiers that had been stationed there, and the community's two priests had been carried off to be placed in Boston prisons — Phips swore in, on an English flag, a few key Frenchmen to govern Port Royal.[11] It is at this juncture, that a curious little development is observed (history is full of curious little developments). The history books thereafter refer not to La Tour as the central authority, though Phips had sworn him in as the council's president, but rather to someone dubbed

"M. Chevalier." In English that would be like calling somebody "Mr. Gentleman." We are therefore left wondering who this "M. Chevalier" really was. There is some suggestion that it was just a French Sergeant to whom Phips took a shine: a point not to be easily determined. "M. Chevalier" did a good job of running the fine line of keeping both the English and the French authorities content with his performance at Port Royal. While generally Baptiste and his operations were winked at, Baptiste was held somewhat in check; certainly Chevalier required Baptiste not to be too obvious about his piratical activities.[12] As for the local population, Chevalier seemed to have their complete confidence. Importantly, for the English, and for the exposed people at Port Royal, Chevalier was able to deliver on his promise to the English that no Acadian (at Port Royal, at least) would raise any arms against the English.[13] During these times, Port Royal was a free port, full of intrigue with both the French and the English coming and going, both learning the secrets of the other. During this period, 1690-98, it would appear that the French flag was pretty much restricted to the Saint John River. "The settlers of Port Royal do almost no trade with the French of the Saint John River because of their fear that if the English learned of it, they would be burned out."[14]

> ... the post at Port Royal would be as advantageous and even more so for the welfare of the garrison and for the king's subjects living in the settlements on the Bay of Fundy, provided that it were safeguarded from attacks by enemies; help could be given easily to the settlers of Minas and Beaubassin, and obtained from them, as well, in case of need; the garrison could secure food more easily; navigation is open all season, and, moreover, vessels coming to this country would have safe retreat. I have been assured that the Company's trade would be much larger than it is here [up the Saint John River], even the trade in pelts."[15]

Attacks On New England:

During these years the snow turned red on the outlying settlements of New England. Particularly beginning in February, 1692, when the French and their allies sprung their surprise attacks on exposed English settlers. People at York were massacred, their homesteads burned and the countryside laid waste. In April, the Kennebecs arrived on the Saint John to tell of their news to Villebon. Villebon threw a party, "presents ... followed by a magnificent feast ... broached a barrel of wine which did not last more than a quarter of an hour."[16] I might add here, as we learn from Villebon, that a missionary from Beaubassin, Abbé Baudoin, had led a group of MicMacs down along the coast to join in with their brothers located close to the New England border. Disagreements, however, broke out, after which Baudoin led his MicMacs back home before the raids got under way.[17]

Jemseg And Beaubassin:

While Villebon during his governorship, 1690-1700, made Jemseg his headquarters, he treated the place seemingly as a potential hole to be scrambled into in the event of another major invasion from New England. The French fort at Jemseg, some 60 miles inland, while relatively safe from attack, especially in the winter with the Saint John frozen over, would not have been a position from which one could keep in communication with the other parts of Acadia. What was necessary, if Villebon was to keep up with his intelligence, was for him to travel about. We see that on November 29th, 1692, Villebon, after having been there for a short gubernatorial visit, sailed up the coast from Mount Desert in a small boat with a view to spending the winter at Beaubassin. From Beaubassin, Villebon could travel by sailing vessel to either Minas or Port Royal. At any rate, Villebon was under Frontenac's orders to meet Iberville and Bonaventure who had been sent down in the French ships, the *Poli* and the *Envieux*, from Quebec to spend their time on the open coast over the winter to see what they might do to get at English shipping. Villebon was to meet them at Baie Verte (though he preferred if they had come to the Saint John) and there he was to give them as much intelligence as possible. Villebon, however, made his temporary headquarters at Beaubassin which was a four-hour hike across the isthmus to Baie Verte; at Beaubassin, Villebon could spend the winter amongst an established Acadian population.[18]

Desperate Situation At Quebec (1692):

During 1692, we see Frontenac writing of the desperate situation the French find themselves in at Quebec. "What with fighting and hardship, our troops and militia are wasting away. ... The enemy is upon us by sea and land. ... Send us a thousand men next spring, if you want the colony to be saved. ... We are perishing by inches; the people are in the depths of poverty; the war has doubled prices so that nobody can live. ... Many families are without bread. The inhabitants desert the country, and crowd into the towns."[19] But help could not be sent by mother France as she had suffered greatly at the hands of the English navy. Off the coast of France, during May of 1692, a much superior (90 to 50) Anglo-Dutch fleet engaged the French fleet under Admiral Tourville, and the *Battle of Barfleur* ensued (La Hogue). With hardly a loss on the allied side, the French fleet was scattered and many were burned, including transports which were being assembled to take the French army to England. In the result, to the great relief of most everyone in England, William's throne was saved; but, more than that, the French fleet was practically destroyed and "France ceased from that moment to exist as a great naval power; for though her fleet was soon recruited to its former strength, the confidence of her sailors was lost ..."[20]

Chapter 5

French Privateers &
Assaults Overland

French Privateers Swarm The Sea Like Locusts:

The French are come to a new way of fighting, they set out no Fleet, but their Privateers swarm and cover the Sea like Locusts, they hang on our Trade like Horse-Leeches, and draw from it more Blood than it is well able to spare, whilst we go on as we did, without new Methods to counterman them; the French King breeds up a Nursery of Seamen at our Charge, whilst his Subjects are made Rich by our Losses ..."[1]

In the busy French port of La Rochelle, on April 8th, 1694, we would have seen well-armed French naval vessels: *La Bonne* (Baptiste) and the *Bretonne* (Bonaventure). It may be they first headed for Quebec, but by the beginning of the summer, *La Bonne* and the *Bretonne* were in Acadian waters to assist in a significant French military effort which in 1694 unfolded in Acadia. While it seems by the first of the summer plans had been laid to sail to Placentia, a little cruise first to the south was in order. Natives were supplied to assist; 30 aboard *Bretonne* and 15 aboard the French corvette, *La Bonne*. Within a couple of weeks prizes were being brought back to Acadia. One brought into Saint John had particularly valuable cargo aboard. She had been headed to Boston from Barbados and had the misfortune to run into Baptiste. Thus it was, that Acadia was to be awash in rum and molasses in this season, while Boston was running dry. At one point while Baptiste was on the high sea with a number of prizes in tow he was come upon by two armed English vessels. The English had the best of the ensuing sea battle and Baptiste was soon the prisoner of the English. The following day Baptiste however made his escape when all these vessels (the count seems to be six, all together some likely roped together) were countered attacked by yet another French privateer (La Ronde) who just happened to have come upon the scene.

After escaping the English, Baptiste in the *La Bonne*, in July of 1694,

... left for Minas, where he has a substantial credit to revictual for another raiding expedition. I sent letters by him to the leading settlers whom I can trust, telling them to make it appear that provisions were only given him under duress, in order to relieve them of responsibility if the English should learn of it; if they do what I suggest, as I believe they will, Baptiste will take two aboard and will hold them as prisoners until he has been provided with what he requires in the way of supplies. He has taken to them all the goods which they might need.[2]

After having revictualled at Minas, on September 2nd, Baptiste was back at Saint John, but he ran into trouble, as Villebon describes it: "he struck a squall, and had much difficulty in saving his corvette, which ran aground; he is putting her in order so that he may go back to his raiding at the end of the month." These early sailors were very ingenious and were able to get their wooden sailing vessel back in trim without having much in the way of equipment and supplies. By November 3rd, 1694, Baptiste "set out in his corvette with a crew of 45 men."[3]

British Losses:

The losses, for the year 1695, were over one hundred British vessels to French Privateers. This most likely took place in the English channel, but certainly there were losses along the coast of New England. French privateers worked out of Acadian ports in the late 17th and early part of the 18th centuries. It best be stated, however, that not all Acadians who owned a sea going vessel are to be categorized as privateers. Some simply ran trading vessels. For example, there was Abraham Boudrot of Port Royal. Boudrot was a mariner like Baptiste, but, unlike Baptiste, earned his living in a legitimate way; he was a trader running back and forth from Boston under licences from both the English and the French authorities.[4]

These privateers did not restrict themselves to fairweather sailing. We saw Baptiste set out fresh in the face of an Acadian winter, in November of 1694; and where he came in with prizes (more sugar, more rum) during January and in March, 1695. In May, he was still bringing prizes in; but he knew himself to be a marked man and suspected that English gun boats would soon be off the coast looking for him. He did not leave his corvette at the mouth of the Saint John, as apparently was his practise,[5] but rather, ran her down to a harbour "three leagues from the Saint John River." If the aim of Baptiste was to hide his vessel from the British gun boats, he missed; as towards the end of May, 1695, he was bottled up in Musquash Harbor by two English battle ships. To avoid capture Baptiste ran *La Bonne* up on shore, and he and his crew deserted her.[6] This was during the month of May, 1695, when we would have seen Baptiste and his crew running up the beach and then to disappear in the adjacent woods. In the background, in Musquash Harbour, we might have seen, too, the English busy lowering their longboats in order to give chase — to no avail. Historical detail is missing, but it certainly seems that it did not take long for Baptiste to be under sail again. In February of 1696 he had in his command a sloop, *Deux Frères*.[7]

Baptiste, for the balance of 1695, seems to disappear from the historical record. We do see, however, references to Bonaventure and of François Guyon.[8] By August, 1695, Guyon had relieved Bonaventure in respect to a regular run that had been established between Minas and the Saint John. Previously, on July 12th, we see Bonaventure at the harbor at Saint John. His ship had been "entirely stripped of its rigging and its masts were much damaged." Apparently, Bonaventure, was in a fight and Villebon was of the view that the English must have received the worst of it. Within ten days Bonaventure had re-rigged and had slipped her moorings at Saint John. By August 1st, Bonaventure was at Baie Verte; the next day he was off, up the St. Lawrence to Quebec.

With the opening of the new year, on January 15th, 1694, Governor Villebon dispatched his brother, M. de Neuvillette "over the snow to Quebec" to see if he might get Frontenac interested in sending him 50 soldiers for a spring and summer offensive. In his despatch he indicated that the French had the full support of the local natives; further, he explained to Frontenac, "I am still without a single soldier for active service ..." We can see by the activities that unfolded that year, that Neuvillette's plea did not fall on deaf ears.

By May 16th, 1694, Neuvillette was back from Quebec. By June, we see des Groutins ferrying supplies across to the Saint John from Minas: a French offensive was being staged.

Oyster Pond:

New England, as we have seen, suffered cargo losses at sea; on land, New England was to lose settlers. On July 27, 1694, with the encouragement of the French governor, Villebon, and under the direct leadership of their priests and a French military man, Villieu, a united force of 230 Indians attacked a small English settlement at Oyster Pond (now Durham, twelve miles from Portsmouth, New Hampshire). "... the attack was made on the sleeping people, 104 of whom were ruthlessly slaughtered, the majority being women and children; twenty-seven were taken prisoners and more than 60 homesteads were burnt." Webster, in his short sketch on Father Thury, reported that this priest was among those who led the Indians and "said Mass in the midst of smoking houses and the bodies of the slain."

On June, 1695, Governor Villebon reported: "The Indians of Kennebec, Pentagoet, Meductic and Madazasia[9] arrived here with the leading chiefs from all their lodges." Feasts and presents followed. In all, there were 14 chiefs; Father Thury acted as the interpreter. The MicMacs of Richibucto (their chief was known as Hiarim) were not at this grand meeting; they had gone to Cape Sable to prey on English fishermen (Cape Sable, it should be noted, on the south eastern part of peninsular Nova Scotia, was a good deal further away from Richibucto than is the Saint John River). Villebon, while he was thus entertaining his native allies[10] and convincing them of the virtues of fighting the English, kept open for himself certain valuable English connections. A quantity of Beaver skins were moved from Governor Villebon's store house, up the Saint John River, through Port Royal (a free port); and then down to New York on a trading vessel; flour was exchanged in addition to money.

Fort William Henry (February, 1696):

It now becomes necessary to make reference to an event which was to bring on repercussions which were felt well into the following century. Fort William Henry, the most northern outpost of New England, was situated at Pemaquid (present day State of Maine). It has been described (Webster) as the strongest fortress in New England, at the time. It was built in 1694 by Phips with his influence and money. During February of 1696, a group of natives approached the gates of Fort William Henry. Among the group were two chiefs, Egeremet and Taxous. The natives were there to request an exchange of prisoners.[11] The commandant of the English fort went out with his group apparently to parley but suddenly the English raised their guns and fired. After the smoke cleared Egeremet and two of his sons lay on the ground shot to death. Taxous managed to escape.

A Sea Battle:

Last we saw of Bonaventure he was headed for Quebec in August of 1695. It must be that he was assigned to convoy protection and returned to France in the fall of 1695. Parkman wrote of Bonaventure's return in 1696:

Early in 1696 two ships of war [likely July], the *Envieux* and the *Profound*, one commanded by Iberville and the other by Bonaventure, sailed from Rochefort to Quebec, where they took on board eighty troops and Canadians; then proceeded to Cape Breton, embarked thirty MicMac Indians, and steered for the St. John. Here they meet two British frigates [the *Newport* and the *Sorlings*] and a provincial tender belonging to Massachusetts. A fight ensued. The forces were very unequal. The *Newport*, of twenty-four guns, was dismasted and taken; but her companion frigate along with the tender escaped in the fog.[12]

July 15, 1696: Just a day after their battle with the English, the French vessels entered Saint John Harbor. After discharging stores for Fort Nashwaak, the French, on August 2, 1696, set sail for Pentagoet. I now turn to Hannay:

At St. John the *Profound* and the *Envieux* took on board fifty more MicMacs and father Simon, the Recollect Missionary of the St. John. At Penobscot, where they arrived August 7th, they found Villieu and Montigny with twenty-five Canadians, Thury [Father], St. Castin [Sr.] and three hundred savages waiting for them. On the 14th August the whole party commenced the investment of Fort William Henry, at Pemaquid, by land and sea.

Fort William Henry (August, 1696):

Fort William Henry fell to the French. The English officer in charge, Captain Chubb, and his garrison were sent to Boston. The fort was burnt to the ground.[13] Iberville and Bonaventure, in the *Envieux* and the *Profound*, left Acadian waters, after their success at Fort William Henry; they sailed for Placentia.[14]

Church's Raid on Beaubassin (September, 1696):

Because the French had done their business at Fort William Henry, a certain captain from Boston, Benjamin Church[15] was promoted and advanced as the man to take revenge on Acadia. In short order, Englishmen were proceeding up the coast in "open sloops and whale boats." Church and his four hundred men (50 to 150 of whom were Indians, likely Iroquois) came up to the head of the Bay of Fundy. They arrived off of Beaubassin on September 20th. They managed to get ashore and surprised the local inhabitants. Most of the terrified inhabitants fled into the woods. The braver came forth to confront Church with papers which had been drawn by Phips in 1690 showing that they had sworn fidelity to the English king. Church was not much impressed, particularly since he just finished reading a proclamation heralding the success of French arms, a proclamation which had been posted to the church door, and which inadvertently the hurried Acadians had forgotten to take down. Church immediately set fire to the church with its French proclamation on the door, and then stated that every other deserted building would be set afire. Knowledge of this forced many of the Acadians out of hiding. Nonetheless, a number of buildings were subsequently burned down at Beaubassin, to the ground. According to Governor Villebon: "The English stayed at Beaubassin nine whole days without drawing any supplies from their vessels, and even those settlers to whom they had shown a pretence of mercy were left with empty houses and barns and nothing else except the clothes on their backs."[16] After this, on September 29th, Church and his men proceeded back down the bay arriving on the same day at the mouth of the Saint John; plans were put in place to go up the St John, 60 miles, in boats with their war supplies to attack the fort situated where the Nashwaak enters into the Saint John, Fort St. Joseph. The English attack fell apart and Church's men were soon itching to get back down-river and sail back to their homes and farms in New England.[17]

A Shaky Peace:

While Governor Villebon was expecting that the New Englanders were going to descend on Acadia in force during 1697, the English did not arrive. Any major plans for New England boys to go up to Acadia to teach these "Frenchies" some more lessons were likely set aside by the authorities on the European news of "peace" developments.[18] Nevertheless, some battling activity both at sea and on land continued. Baptiste was captured and made a prisoner of the English in the Spring of 1697. Further, on November 15th, 1697, Villebon reported that French fishing vessels were being overpowered on the Grand Banks by a "brigantine fitted out at Boston, with six guns and eighty men" with the French fishermen being taken as prisoners to Boston. Villebon spent the year getting his defences ready. He made feasts for the Indians and repositioned what few forces he had under his command. Villebon wrote in his report that there was a "war-party of English and their Indians of Kennebec and Pentagoet" which had been sent to Acadia. As to where and when this English party hit, the reviewed records do not reveal.

For the winter of 1697-98, Villebon, holding out at Fort Nashwaak up on the Saint John, kept his men busy in domestic projects. He divided his soldiers into doing the two principal tasks of the winter: "sawing boards ... and cutting and hauling fire wood." With certain of these trees, Villebon was most impressed: "We have had a pine three feet in diameter cut for a mast ... which I intend to send to France as a specimen." Villebon wrote about other trees, too: elms ("suitable for pumps and guns mounts") and ash ("for pulleys"). Further, in his report, we see: "... I asked the settlers of Minas to grind as much flour as they could for which I would send when the ice melted. We have wintered all our boats at Nashwaak for greater security, knowing well that very little was to be found at Port Royal."

On April 21st, 1698, a ship from Boston arrived at the mouth of the Saint John and a runner was sent to Governor Villebon with a pack of official looking letters. Villebon was informed by Lt.-Governor William Stoughton that peace had come to the nations of France and England by the terms of the *Treaty of Ryswick*, signed the previous autumn: doubtlessly this was news to Villebon. The letter from the governor of Massachusetts to the Acadian governor was dated at Boston on March 3rd. Stoughton had released all prisoners at Boston and expected that Governor Villebon would do likewise. Lt.-Governor Stoughton recited the steps he had taken to make sure that all hostilities stopped and trusted that "you will issue and enforce the same orders as I have put into effect here; that none of the enemy, Indian or otherwise, shall be encouraged or assisted in any way ... that you will prevent and restrain these barbarous savages from further shedding of Christian blood ... that you will do your utmost to live like a good neighbour ...."

There was, however, one prisoner which Lt.-Governor Stoughton was not immediately ready to release: Baptiste. He was more than a prisoner of war; he was, the English thought, a common criminal. We saw earlier that Baptiste was made a prisoner of the English, in the Spring of 1697.[19]

Within the week, on April 28th, 1698, Villebon made out an official reply to Stoughton. In an equally official looking letter (elaborate ink markings on parchment with ribbons and seals pasted and strung to the bottom), Villebon, in his French manner, expressed his concern that Baptiste was not being treated as a prisoner of war. Villebon also warned Stoughton that the English best keep a good outlook for Indians, as it was unlikely that the message that peace had been achieved between England and France had gotten through to these French allies, indeed it was likely that war-parties had already left Quebec. Villebon concluded: "When I shall have received news from France, and the commands of the King, my master, in regard to the declaration of Peace, I shall not fail to inform you. In the meantime, you should give orders to your fishermen not to come to the shores of Acadia to fish; nor should your private merchants trade at the French settlements until the King has sent me instructions covering these matters." This reply was sent back down the river and delivered to the Master of the English vessel who was waiting.

Some time was to pass before Villebon, on June 1st, 1698, received independent word of peace through fishermen from Quebec. It was at this point, with the coming of peace, that it became safe for French Acadian administrators to travel. Within a few weeks, on August 2nd, Villebon crossed over to Port Royal, the old capital of Acadia, which since 1690, was a "free port."[20] Port Royal was now clearly to be back once again under the French flag. Villebon put the straps of government on and declared that trade with the English without his permission would be a crime and the criminal's goods would become goods of the state. The people of Port Royal did not take to kindly to this assertion of the state: "people murmuring about the interdiction of trade with the English." State pomp and ceremony was used to quell any adverse emotions: on the 3rd, Villebon "ordered a salute to be fired in honour of peace and instructed the settlers in the line of conduct they were to follow."[21]

Next, the French governor and his entourage,[22] after leaving Port Royal, carried on to the only other two centers of Acadia: Minas (August 15th) and Beaubassin[23] (August 21st). At each place, the ceremony and lectures as conducted and given at Port Royal, were repeated. Villebon, having made his flag tour of Acadia, arrived back at the Saint John on August 25th, 1698.[24]

In Acadia and New England, the declared peace of 1696 was to take hold a year later. The French and English may not have been at war with one another, but these people, foreign to one another as they most certainly were, were not to be friends. Villebon did not want to see English ships in Acadian waters: he wrote the authorities at Boston: "Bonaventure ... who is this year Commandant of the King's ship, *Envieux*, has confirmed by sending back to you several of your fishing boats which he captured on his arrival on these shores, informing you, on the King's behalf, that if they should again return to fish or trade they would be considered as lawful prizes." While so establishing French rights at sea, seemingly having no faith in the declared peace, Villebon built his defenses on land. With the help of Bonaventure and his crew ("with 25 sailors to cut palisades") Villebon built his new headquarters at the mouth of the Saint John, which he was to move into that fall (1698) "leaving Fort Nashwakk in the care of two soldiers."[25]

The Death Of Governor Villebon:

In the fall of 1699, Villebon, this rough colonial diamond, made one of his last entries into his ongoing report to Pontchartrain. He was pleading for his men: "It would be better, Sir, another year, not to send biscuits as rations for the carpenters; flour would be more convenient... and brandy instead of wine would please them better." Further, he reported "only 77 soldiers in all" and suggested that "several of the soldiers, who have been here seven years, would be very suitable as settlers." And, further, suggested that "soldiers should be sent over from France, 40 would be a good number, and if some artisans could be included among the recruits, it would contribute greatly to the development of this country."

On July 5, 1700: Villebon died at Fort Saint John and with his death the French capital of Acadia reverted, having had no government for ten years, back to Port Royal. Without a military presence on the Saint John River, a "vast territory was left to the Indians and for more than a generation no white man was seen there save those who travelled by way of the river in making the long journey between Quebec and the peninsular portion of Acadia."[26]

Chapter 6

Dièreville

(1700)

Not much is known about Dièreville. He was a French surgeon who, after coming to Port Royal in 1699, stayed for a year. He was apparently hired by certain La Rochelle merchants to establish trading connections in Acadia and then to report back to them. Once back home, in a curious mixture of prose and verse, he wrote of his Acadian adventure: recounting his travels and his experiences; describing the local flora and fauna; telling of the state of the beaver trade; and setting forth an invaluable record of the life and customs of the native inhabitants of Acadia. Dièreville's book, for historians, has become one of the première contemporary descriptions of Acadia in the dawn of its second century, the year of 1700.

Dièreville had departed La Rochelle on August 20, 1699 in the vessel *Royale-Paix* (a Merchantman which had 14 cannon in ballast with a capable captain that smoked a pipe "with two clerks and a consignment of merchandise to be used in trading at Port Royal."[1]

It is interesting to read that at the beginning of Dièreville's overseas trip to Acadia and at its end were punctuated with life threatening events. The first of these events I tell now, the second I tell of later on. It concerns the tricky business of getting aboard a high-sided ocean going sailing vessel, such as that being boarded by Dièreville and his friends at La Rochelle, during August of 1699. It was windy and he had to climb up a rope that had been dropped down to the long boat that had been rowed from the jetty to the side of the large sailing vessel held to the harbour bottom by a heavy-duty cable. There, the "six stout Sailors" held the long boat to the large vessel as best they could, while the young doctor awkwardly shinnied from protrusion to protrusion, dangerously, up the heaving side, in the spray and in the wind. He made it aboard, however, and later "had the satisfaction of seeing that even the most agile of them (the 22 crew members of the *Royale-Paix*) were as much troubled in climbing the ladders of the shrouds, as I had been in ascending a simple rope."

Chebucto:

After about a 42 day run westward over the broad Atlantic,[2] the *Royale-Paix*, likely around October 1st, ran into what we now call Halifax Harbor and which, then, was known as Bay Senne, or Bay Saint, as named by Champlain. The *Royale-Paix* was low on water and wood, and had just come in from quite a blow. In the vicinity of the Grand Banks, Dièreville had spotted 10 English fishing vessels. So we would have seen, in 1699, during a beautiful time of the year for these parts, October, the French sailing vessel, *Royale-Paix*, travelling down the full length of the harbor (Halifax) and coming into what is now called Bedford Basin.[3] Coming back up the harbor, where Halifax City stands today, Dièreville saw "a pleasant prospect; at its edge a building used for drying cod. ... It was half as long, & quite as wide as the Mall in Paris, built on a fine beach along the River, at a distance which permitted the water to pass under it at high tide & carry away the refuse of the Cod." This was a French fishing station (*dégras*) which by this date, October, 1699, was deserted.[4] But there came to the wind blown sailors (Dièreville and company), as they surveyed their surroundings, a group of Indians, a few quietly at first, more and boisterous later. Some had "little bark canoes." This was Father Thury's flock which could be found along the Shubenacadie system.[5] Father Thury was a missionary from Quebec, who, back in 1685, had come to Acadia. More recently, 1698 and 1699, Thury was busy trying to draw all the Indians together at one place (Halifax in the winter and Shubenacadie in the summer). At the age of 48, Thury died on June 5th, 1699, with his faithful native followers about him. Dièreville observed that the Indians were very gentle people, though "armed with Musket & hatchet." "I gave them a good breakfast of Meat & Fish & they munched Biscuit with the best appetite in the world, & drank Brandy with relish & less moderation than we do; ... on sitting down to table, they said their prayers devoutly & made the sign of the Cross, &, when they had finished, they gave thanks with the same piety. Each had a Rosary around their neck." It would appear that Dièreville stayed but a couple of days, but he was there long enough for the Indians to take him to a "Wood nearby," there Father Thury had been buried but four months before; "A Tomb of stakes, covered with bark."

Dièreville spent a number of days with his new found native friends after which he set off for Port Royal. On October 13th, Dièreville arrived at Port Royal. The *Royale-Paix* was anchored well off the shore and the captain and a few hands headed to the village in a long boat. Everybody on shore was scurrying; the initial belief of the inhabitants was that pirates were making another visit to Port Royal (a regular event for these deserted people). "The Settlers had, in the meantime, taken their most valuable possessions to hiding places in the Forest. When we landed & they knew that we were their friends, we saw the Carts coming back all loaded."

Arrival At Port Royal:

The crew of the *Royale-Paix*, of course were anxious to spend, finally, some time on shore; but first there was important work to be done. Certain of the *Royale-Paix* auxiliary vessels had to be unlashed and lowered over the sides; deck covers had to be unnailed and unlatched; and holds to be gotten into. These unloading jobs were well under way and smaller boats had been lashed to the sides of the mother ship; it does not take too much of an imagination to see pulleys, ropes and sailors doing their job as great quantities of trading goods are heaved up and about. Before much of it got to shore, nightfall arrived; and tired men took to their bunks after a good meal, a few pipes and a grog or two. An unexpected storm of hurricane proportions came up in the night and before long very severe winds tried their best to pry the bower anchors of the *Royale-Paix* free from the muck of the holding ground. The ropes which held the smaller vessels to the larger, all in various states of being loaded, were soon worn through. That night the howling winds grabbed all loose things, both from the top and sides of the *Royale-Paix* and tore the works asunder and spread the pieces to the nearby shores of Port Royal. This upset was to have a great effect on Dièreville's trading plans. He reported that one of the smaller boats, into which most all of his precious goods had been carefully transferred, went to the bottom with all of its newly acquired cargo. Next day, in the twilight of the storm, the shores were littered with barrels and crates; tossed and broken; contents everywhere and all of it very wet. To dry the merchandise, which first had to be rinsed in fresh water, all of it was spread out in the fresh air and turned, over and over: Port Royal must have been quite a sight.

Thus, Dièreville was to be in very poor spirits during his first days at Port Royal. He wrote in his journal, "How can one live in such a place?" he exclaimed, "nothing but huts and hovels, woods and streams!" The warm greetings from all the inhabitants, however, soon revived his spirits. The inhabitants cared enough, too, for Dièreville, to put him in occupation of the largest house in town; it consisted of three rooms with an attic and a part of a cellar made of "masonry."

Description Of Acadians At Port Royal (1700):

The parish priest was in the leading line of the Acadian greeters.[6] The priest escorted Dièreville to the small church (presumably having been rebuilt since Phips and his New Englanders had burnt it down in 1690). There, in this simple church the two men knelt and said their prayers "& then Monsieur le Curé took me to his room, which was ill-furnished, &, contrary to the rules concerning Presbyteries, at one end of the Church & adjoining it." On looking around Dièreville observed "Across the marshes oxen draw the plough." The Annapolis River back then was called the Rivière Dauphin and had dwellings on each side of it running above Port Royal for a number of miles.[7] "The other river called the Mill River [Allain's River] ... is not more than a league in length & much narrower. There are three Mills upon it, one for Wheat & two for Lumber, with three or four houses." There were approximately 500 people at Port Royal, a number which represented about half of the entire population of Acadia which consisted, at that time only of three communities: Port Royal, Minas, and Beaubassin. Acadian clothing was made of wool, and, they still wore "Hooded Capes" (the France of fifty years back). Their shoes were made of Elk and seal skin and are flat soled. There was no fishery in existence, though Dièreville did attempt during the year of his stay to establish a "green fishery." Seal hunting went on and in addition to the skins of which they made use, the seals were a source of oil for burning and kegs of it became trading commodities. In the pastures there was sheep and cattle; in the fields cabbages & turnips. As to cabbages & turnips: "neither of these vegetables goes into the pot without the other, & nourishing soups are made of them, with a large slice of pork." At the beginning of the winter a number of their animals (pigs more often than cows) were killed, salted and put into barrels.

The Missions:

I did mention the le Curé at Port Royal, which leads me to say a word or two about the priests at Acadia. From a reading of Governor Villebon's reports, we see that both the priest at Port Royal and at Minas were Recollects (the mission at Minas had been established as a "Foreign Mission" in 1699). At this date (1699), there were no priests to be found at Beaubassin or at Villebon's post at the mouth of the Saint John.[8] The MicMac Mission was a mission which was separate from those established for the Acadians, both in kind and in place. Father Thury, to whom I earlier referred, had attended to the spiritual needs of the Acadian MicMacs. Thury died at Chebucto (Halifax) during 1699. He had been at Chebucto since the previous year, likely though, in season, traveling back and forth on the Shubenacadie lake and river system. Thury was replaced by Father Maudoux. Villebon was not much impressed with Thury's replacement. The two had met at another post; they did not get on with one another. Villebon thought that Maudoux was not up to the job of gathering all the Indians into one place — a French scheme struck upon just prior to Father Thury's death. Maudoux, Villebon pointed out, did not speak the language, and, at any rate, being the hunting and gathering people that they were, the Indians could not possibly live all gathered up in one place. Webster wrote that Father Maudoux succeeded Father Petit in 1693 and continued on there at Port Royal until its capture in 1710.

Dièreville's stay continued through all the Acadian seasons to the following fall, 1700. The king's ship, *l'Avenant*, 45 guns, which had been sent to replenish the forts both at Plaissance and at the mouth of the Saint John, called in on Port Royal. Dièreville had made plans to return to France on a smaller company vessel and was glad to see he could return on the *l'Avenant*, which, on account of its size would make for a faster and easier passage; besides, he would have the "courtesy & affability" to be found in "every Naval Officer." One of the reasons *l'Avenant* arrived at Port Royal was so she might pick up a cargo of "30 or 40 fine masts" which the people at Port Royal had prepared for shipping, and which was added to those shipped at Saint John. Only Dièreville was invited to come aboard the French navy ship. His two clerks were left behind to finish up their affairs and to follow along three weeks later in the smaller frigate which the company had sent from France.

Dièreville departed Port Royal on October 6th, 1700, and arrived back home in France a month later, on November 9th. Thus, we see the end of Dièreville's one year stay at Acadia.

Chapter 7

The Last Years Of French Port Royal

On November 1, 1700, Charles II of Spain died. Philip, the Duke of Anjou, grandson of Louis XIV and of Maria Teresa (daughter of Philip IV) succeeded to the Spanish throne as Philip V. With the opening of 1701, the Duke of Anjou entered Madrid to take the throne of an intact Spain and "Louis proudly boasted that henceforth there were no Pyrenees."[1] England became more nervous than normal and wondered what the French empire would be up to next: in anticipation, the English fleet was increased to 30,000 men and the army to 10,000.

The powerful in England were conscious that a childless King William would soon be dead and the Stuart line at an end. A new act of succession was laid before the House which allowed for no king or queen unless he or she be in communion with the Church of England. It was at this time, incidentally, that the independence of the judiciary was to be secured: no judge should be removed from office save on an address from parliament to the crown. Further, two important principles were established; first, the king acts only through his ministers; and, second, that these ministers are responsible to parliament. In the meantime, Louis XIV's reign in France continued in its despotic fashion.

On the 21st of February, 1702, William III fell from his horse, a fall which would prove to be fatal to the frail and sick man; he died two weeks later. "During his reign (1688-1702) the National Debt was commenced, the Bank of England established, the modern system of finance established, ministerial responsibility recognized, the standing army transferred to the control of parliament, the liberty of the press secured, and the British constitution established on a firm basis."

On March 8th, 1702, Queen Anne took the throne of England. How Anne found herself to be on the throne of England; and how she and the lives of the historical characters around her became intertwined, is one of history's more interesting stories; but, it cannot form part of mine.[2]

Acadia As The New Century Begins:

I now turn to Acadia and the developments there, as a new century got under way.

While Port Royal had been the seat of Acadian government pretty much from the beginning, its importance slipped from 1670 with the seat of government being at either Pentagoet (Castine, State of Maine) or from one of the forts on the Saint John. It was determined by the French authorities, at some point after its official handback, by the *Treaty of Ryswick* (1697), that Port Royal should once again be the capital of Acadia. In addition, with the death of Governor Villebon, in 1700, the French governor at Placentia, Newfoundland, Joseph de Brouillan,[3] was ordered to take over at Port Royal.

In 1702, via Chebuctou and Grande Pré, Brouillan made his way to Port Royal. It was during this time that Broullian made his first observations of the Acadians. While he admired the prosperity of the French Acadian village he found at Grand Pré, he was bothered by their independent spirit, something that was to become the hallmark of the Acadians. "It seems to me," says Broullian in one of his reports back to France, "that these people live like true republicans, acknowledging neither royal authority nor courts of law."[4]

Port Royal, as Brouillan found it, consisted of a fort of sodded earthwork, and to the right looking west "was the Acadian village, consisting of seventy or eighty small houses of one story and an attic, built of planks, boards, or logs, simple and rude, but tolerable. It also had a small, new wooden church ... The ruling class, civil and military, formed a group apart, living in or near the fort, in complete independence of public opinion ..." The inhabitants had plenty of cattle, a lot of hemp, and it was gorged with beaver-skins; it lacked pots, scythes, sickles, knives, hatchets, kettles for the Indians, nor salt for themselves."[5]

Brouillan's immediate task was to rebuild the fortifications at Port Royal (mostly from materials coming from the French fort at Saint John which he had torn down and floated across the Bay of Fundy.) His next task was to get the French inhabitants in the area back into a productive mode. Farming on these fertile lands was to continue, but, in addition, Brouillan was keen on getting the Acadians into the business of building boats and fishing fish (an industry that, due to his experiences at Placentia, Brouillan knew about). To get the inhabitants of Port Royal to work together, however, was to be a challenge, for, as Brouillan observed, they had a "detestable custom" of squabbling over any and all detail, for example, where to put the church and where to put the public market. Under Brouillan's directions the settlers were formed up into militia groups (to go along with the 200 French regular troops, or so, then stationed at Port Royal); further he saw to the building of a lime kiln, a mill, and ships were built.[6] Most importantly the fortifications of Port Royal were rebuilt: and just in time, too, for shortly after the arrival of Brouillan another attack was made by the New Englanders, once again under Benjamin Church.

Scandal At Port Royal:

It was during 1701 that we see Simon-Pierre Denys de Bonaventure, the French naval officer, coming to Port Royal; he had been appointed by the authorities[7] to be second in command under Governor Brouillan. And, so too, we see how the lives of Louise Guyon and Bonaventure became entwined at Port Royal; a most interesting, romantic and true story.[8] As it turned out, Bonaventure's sexual involvement with Guyon cost him his promotion as the Commander at Port Royal — such were the mores of the time. The affairs of these French officers (Brouillan and his successor, Subercase also had affairs) kept the French tongues at Port Royal and at Quebec a-wagging.

Butchery On The New England Frontier:

We had seen earlier where Benjamin Church, in 1696, had come up the coast and caused much trouble laying waste to the small Acadian settlements. A one sided view would make out these New Englanders, such as those under Church, as nothing but a bunch of brigands intent on making life miserable for those they descended upon. Indeed, when these armed Englishmen arrived, life was made to be miserable for the Acadians; not only during the raids, but for the seasons thereafter, as crops were torched and animals killed. The Acadians bore the brunt of the fury of the New Englanders' revenge throughout this historical period; and this due mainly to geography.

The New Englanders had a right to their revengeful feelings. The French and their Indian allies, throughout the period, looted and killed English settlers along the frontier as it then existed, in the wilds of current day Maine, New Hampshire and Massachusettes. These attacks were usually launched from Quebec, usually in the winter. (The French were much better with the help of their Indian allies, of traveling over mountains, over frozen lakes and down frozen rivers: the English never seem to get the knack of it.)

I Quote Francis Parkman:

> That morning, [August 10th, 1703] several parties of Indians had stolen out of the dismal woods behind the houses and farms of Wells, and approached different dwellings of the far-extended settlement at about the same time. They entered the cabin of Thomas Wells, where his wife lay in the pains of childbirth, and murdered her and her two small children. At the same time they killed Joseph Sayer, a neighbour of Wells, with all his family.

This raid was only part of a larger combined attack up and down the New England border including a settlement at the falls at Saco, Spurwink, Cape Porpoise, Winter Harbor, Purpooduck Point (a spot near the present city of Portland) "... the Indians burst into the hamlet, butchered twenty-five women and children and carried off eight." The murders and burnings continued with little variety and little interruption during a ten year period.

Scarcely a hamlet of the Massachusetts and New Hampshire borders escaped a visit from the nimble enemy. Groton, Lancaster, Exeter, Dover, Kittery, Casco, Kingston, York, Berwick, Wells, Winter Harbour, Brookfield, Amesbury, Marlborough, were all more or less invested, usually by small scalping parties, hiding in the outskirts, waylaying stragglers, or shooting men at work in the fields, and disappearing as soon as their blow was struck. These swift and intangible persecutors found a far surer and more effectual means of annoyance than larger bodies. As all the warriors were converts of the Canadian missions, and as prisoners were an article of value, cases of torture were not very common; though now and then, as at Exeter, they would roast some poor wretch alive, or bite off his fingers and sear the stumps with red-hot tobacco pipes.

Colonel Benjamin Church's Raid On Acadia, 1704:

And so we see, in 1704, the forces of New England under Benjamin Church (now raised to the rank of Colonel) spending the spring and summer attacking and looting along the Acadian coasts. "He was furnished with a force of five hundred and fifty men, besides officers, and provided with fourteen transports, thirty-six whale boats and a shallop, and he was convoyed from Boston by three war vessels of forty-two, thirty-two and twelve guns respectively."[9] It would appear, once again, that Beaubassin was the principal objective of the forces of Benjamin Church. The French at Port Royal, due to Bruillian's foresight, remaining safe behind the rebuilt earthen walls.

Colonel John March's Raid On Acadia, 1707:

During the summer of 1707, the English, led by Colonel John March, laid siege to Port Royal on two separate occasions. Both, as it turned out were abortive efforts. This was due mainly — in comparison to so many other French Acadian commanders — to the superior abilities of Governor Subercase who by then was in charge of Port Royal; supported, as is so often the case in successful military operations, by a measure of good fortune.

Between the two attacks of John March (the first in June and the second in August of 1707), Morpain ("a Privateer from San Domingo") had just happened to sail into Port Royal with two prizes in tow, one a slave-ship and the other ladened with foodstuffs including: 340 barrels of flour, bacon, ham, and butter.

These supplies were a godsend and arrived just days before the English sailed into the Port Royal basin for the second time in 1707. The English had 22 ships, including a two war ships (54 guns and the other, 45), 5 frigates (from 18 to 30 guns), 8 brigantines and 7 transports. The English landed their forces (1600 besides ships' crews) on August the 22nd. Subercase did not stay behind his walls, but aggressively went out and met the enemy with cannon at both the east and west sides of the Annapolis River (then known as Rivière Dauphin). During this fight, the French had working for them a number of exceptionally brave fighters, including; the experienced governor, Subercase; the young Baron Castin; and another young French officer by the name of Antoine de Saillant. (De Saillant's life, as one of an 18th century soldier, makes for a sad and short story; the young officer married a local girl, Anne Mius de Poubomcou, just weeks before, on the 18th of July; he died of his battle wounds on September 8th, 1707.)

The New Englanders failed on their two attempts to subdue Port Royal in 1707, but the rest of the Acadian countryside, undefended as it was, from along the coast of Maine to the head of the Bay of Fundy, was ravished. I should add, however, the people of these districts were not butchered, as, so many were along the New England border.

So it is, with the bloody raids along the frontier borders, one might better understand why New Englanders organized seasonal counterattacks against the French. Quebec was the nest to be got at, however, getting sufficient forces before the walls at Quebec and sustaining them for the time required to lay siege was not within their means. For the seafarers of New England, the object of their attention was to be Acadia, simply because they could more easily get at Acadia. And while it might be argued that there is little evidence that the Frenchmen at Acadia initiated the raids at the border, Acadia did harbour pirates which preyed on New England shipping.

Chapter 8

Prelude To English Acadia
(1709)

Governor Brouillan died on September 22nd, 1705, at sea while returning to Acadia from France. Subercase,[1] who had up to then been the French governor at Placentia, was appointed to take Brouillan's place. Subercase arrived at Port Royal during October of 1706. During that summer, Subercase attended to the first order of business, the building of a "bomb-proof powder magazine ... and a large building part of which was to be used as a chapel ..." Subercase wrote home: "The land is good and fertile, and produces everything that France does except olives. There is abundance of grain and an inexhaustible supply of wood of all sizes for building. ... The people here are excellent workmen with the axe and the adze."[2] The activities continued in the following years: "During the whole summer of 1708 he [Subercase] thus employed two hundred and fifty extra hands, and greatly improved the defences of the place, finishing the barracks, erecting a bomb proof magazine, and building a chapel and quarters for some of the officers."[3]

This increased defence activity at Port Royal under the leadership of Subercase, incidently, seemed to have made the local Acadian population uneasy. The fear of further English attack, the call of the military for unpaid labour and disputes over property lines — a combination of all, I suggest — led a number of Acadians to head north-east up the valley. For instance, in 1708, Martin Benoist (at this point 65 years of age) and his son (27) together with other family members, struck out for the Minas Basin area, then onwards to Piziquid, and then onwards to Cobequid; seemingly only stopping after a suitable and unoccupied track of land, sufficiently far enough from Port Royal, had been located.

Affirmation of Acadian fears was soon to be had. On the 28th April, 1709, Vetch[4] and Nicholson[5] entered Boston harbour in HMS *Dragon*, both ambitious with plans struck in England for an attack on Canada. Colonel Nicholson was to head the attack overland by way of the Hudson River and Lake Champlain. All of New England was thrown into a feverish pitch of activity as the news of the great plan was carried throughout New England. Men gathered at all points and waited for the promised ships and supplies. Months passed: spring turned into summer: summer passed. No ships? Where were the ships? On October, 11th a vessel arrived from England and the frustrated remnants of the gathered forces of New England heard the news: the expected ships, supplies and soldiers had been sent to Portugal instead. The governors of the English colonies then convened and resolved to immediately send Vetch and Nicholson back to England in order to revive the plans for an attack the following year.

The French :

Acadia, through its entire 150 years existence, between 1605 and 1755, was a continuing source of aggravation to the New Englanders. The incursions of the Indian raiding parties led by French officers with the resulting death and property damage were bad enough; but the shipping merchants of New England were upset on a separate count. Too many of their ocean cargoes coming over from Europe and up from the Caribbean were being taken on the high seas by French "sea wolves." "For certainly we are in a state of war with the pirates ... Those great rogues and enemies to all mankind ..."[6] This situation was aggravated in that the authorities in the English colonies had no legal power to deal with these pirates; after capture they had to be transported to England for trial. Governor Nicholson of Virginia sent 97 over, and, of those, only 26 in England were put to death.

The lack of support which France gave to her colonies drove the Acadians to support these French Privateers, these "sea-wolves." There were only three communities of any size in peninsular Nova Scotia at this time (c.1700) and these three contained most all of the population of Acadia, they were: Port Royal (Annapolis Royal), Les Mines (Grand Pré), and Beaubassin (Chignecto). All three of these places were havens for privateers (pirates to the English) who cruised down along the New England coast. The French authorities at Port Royal, due to France's neglect, were only too willing to make these sea-going desperadoes into patriots, and were only too willing to act as a fence and pay for the ill-begotten goods carried in the holds of these privateers. The three most famous French privateers at the time were Morpain,[7] Castin,[8] and Baptiste.[9] In the year 1692, Baptiste is recorded to have taken nine vessels in six months. In 1694, Baptiste, in a big, bright fighting vessel, which he had brought back with him from a visit to France, took five prizes off the coast of New England. In 1695, another lesser known privateer, François Guion,[10] took three vessels in June when their escorting frigate went up on "a rock south of Grand Manan." With the *Treaty of Ryswick* signed in 1702, privateering became less wide-spread. This lull, more a truce than a peace, lasted only to 1709. The French privateers who had been pent up and ready to go back to business, in 1709, sank 35 New England bound merchant ships! No wonder we see in the official correspondence of New England, "Port Royall, that Nest of Spoilers so near to us."[11]

Vicarious Atonement:

And, so we might see why the New Englanders were so intent on bringing Nova Scotia under the British flag (both in 1710 and in 1745). Whether the individuals composing the invading forces were driven by loyalty to the British flag or their relish for rapine, the political objective of the whole was to put a stop to the losses of New England both upon the sea and at the borders. The New Englanders were driven to take to their boats and sail up the coast and discourage the French by looting and burning Acadian villages; and hoping, in so doing, to put pressure on the real culprits at Quebec.[12]

When war-parties from Canada struck the English borders reprisal was difficult against those who had provoked it. Canada was made almost inaccessible by a hundred leagues of pathless forest, prowled by her Indian allies, who were sure to give the alarm of an approaching foe; while, on the other hand, the New Englanders could easily reach Acadia by their familiar element, the sea; and hence that unfortunate colony often made vicarious atonement for the sins of her northern sister. It was from French privateers and fishing-vessels on the Acadian seas that Massachusetts drew most of the prisoners whom she exchanged for her own people held captive in Canada.[13]

The French And English Systems:

The French and English upset one another — and it was not just that they were ancient enemies; and it was not just because they spoke, to what was to the other, a language foreign: these two people were different for these reasons, and, just as much, because they were governed differently. England and her colonies were to benefit from its enlightened ideas about government,[14] which, while still evolving, was essentially in place by 1700. On the other hand, throughout the entire time of our story (1700-1763) France was yet labouring under a political system that had not evolved much from medieval times,[15] a system of privileges, a system to which the country stubbornly hung onto until overturned by a bloody revolution late in the 18th century, a time beyond that which is under review. Thus, the French inhabitants of North America did not have their democratic assemblies as did each of the English colonies. They received their direction from the king and his representatives, the governor and the intendant.[16] New France was therefore run as if it were a province of France, and, like the provinces back home, things were run on feudal principles. In Canada, prior to 1763, absolutism and centralization were the principles on which government was conducted. Parkman treated the subject:

The English colonies were separate, jealous of the Crown and of one another, and incapable as yet of acting in concert. Living by agriculture and trade, they could prosper within limited areas, and had no present need of spreading beyond the Alleghenies. Each of them was an aggregate of persons, busied with their own affairs, and giving little heed to matters which did not immediately concern them. Their rulers, whether chosen by themselves or appointed in England, could not compel them to become the instruments of enterprises in which the sacrifice was present and the advantage remote. The neglect in which the English court left them, though wholesome in most respects, made them unfit for aggressive action; for they had neither troops, commanders, political union, military organization, nor military habits. ...

In Canada all was different. Living by the fur trade, she needed free range and indefinite space. Her geographical position determined the nature of her pursuits; and her pursuits developed the roving and adventurous character of her people, who, living under a military rule, could be directed at will to such ends as their rulers saw fit. ... The rival colonies had two different laws of growth. The one increased by slow extension, rooting firmly as it spread; the other shot offshoots, with few or no roots, far out into the wilderness. It was the nature of French colonization to seize upon detached strategic points, and hold them by the bayonet, forming no agriculture basis, but attracting the Indians by trade, and holding them by conversion. A musket, a rosary, and a pack of beaverskins may serve to represent it, and in fact it consisted of little else.[17]

Chapter 9

The Taking Of Port Royal
(1710)

It is a September day on Annapolis Basin, it is 1710. We see French soldiers, ragged in appearance. Some are having an easier time of it standing guard on the earthen ramparts of the fort while others are hard at work piling up the ready building material hereabouts, alluvium; and while readily moveable by both man, and by nature: dirt, it should be pointed out, is not good fort building material. Suddenly, one yells out excitedly and points southwesterly, towards the gut, the narrow opening that lets the ocean waters into the basin. Ships are entering: a couple at first, then a couple more, and soon the basin is straddled with, with — English ships! And, *"Mon Dieu"* — they are coming at us again.[1] There appears "36 transports, 4 ships of 60 guns each, 2 of 40 guns, 1 of 36 guns and two bomb galleys ... besides a number of open sloops for carrying of lumber and other utensils for the cannon."[2] Imagine the terror of the French population as they run to the shore, to look out and to see such a crowd of sailing vessels; to see them, all in turn, rounding up and dropping anchors; then, to see, regiment after regiment of armed men streaming on to the shores in their "flat bottomed whale boats" newly built the year before: men from Massachusetts, New Hampshire, Connecticut and Rhode Island had come to do in the French. Of the 2,000 soldiers,[3] 400 hundred are of the regular English army, the rest colonial militia. The sight unfolding before the French gave every indication that a well planned military affair was underway.

The Commanders:

The 1710 British campaign against Port Royal was under the command of the 55 year old Englishman, Francis Nicholson. The two other prominent officers in this campaign was a 42 year old gentleman from Edinburgh, Colonel Samuel Vetch and the

Boston born Sir Charles Hobby, a 45 year old who had been knighted by the queen in 1705. The French, for their part, had one of their most capable leaders that they had ever sent to America, Daniel d'Auger de Subercase; but, the odds for Subercase this time around were too long: 2,000 well supplied English troops[4] versus his 300 (ill-equipped, tired, and discouraged); the French garrison gave up within ten days.

Unlike those of 1704 and 1707, the attack on Port Royal in 1710 had "royal support." This support, which consisted of ships-o-war and British regulars, accounted for its success in no small measure. This kind of direct military support was not only of considerable advantage when the invading forces came under enemy fire (regular forces were always steadier in the field than were militiamen) but served as a considerable inducement to the colonials to raise their forces to a higher level of discipline. A militia man was promised "a month's pay in advance, together with a coat worth thirty shillings ... and a Queen's musket ... which he might keep as his own forever." The officers, while on campaign, were to be kept in style: "... it was voted that a pipe of wine, twenty sheep, five pigs, and one hundred fowls be presented to the Honorable General Nicholson for his table during the expedition."[5]

By the 25th of September all the British were ashore.[6] Several days were to pass before the British artillery and stores were landed; and, all along, cannons roared from both the French fort and the English bomb-ketch. By the 29th the English were ready to get down to their siege business. Within 24 hours, the French sent out a white flag of truce and the guns fell silent. Within 24 hours of that, terms were worked out and Port Royal capitulated. This is the short version of the taking of Port Royal in 1710. I now proceed to give some details.

The Queen's Warrant:

Port Royal had been taken before, indeed twice before, and both times by men from New England: under Major Robert Sedgwick in August of 1654 and under Sir William Phips in May of 1690: in each case it had been restored to France by treaty. The taking of Port Royal in 1710 is particularly important to our story, for, with its capture came England's claims to all of Acadia. This is the time to acquaint ourselves with Francis Nicholson. This Yorkshireman had made powerful friends both in London and in the colonies. During the winter of 1709\10 Nicholson had befriended the Queen, herself. She became anxious (and thus so became everyone) to appease Nicholson for his great disappointment of the year before when a colonial effort to conquer Canada had to go by the boards because her majesty's senior military officers had determined to divert the forces intended for America, at the last moment, to the continent. Queen Anne, however, made up for things in her royal fashion: a warrant was given over her signature:

> Instructions for our trusty and well beloved Colonel Francis Nicholson Whom we have appointed to be Commander in Chief of out forces to be employ'd in the reduction of Port Royal and other places in Nova Scotia Given at our Court att St. James's the 18th of March ... In the 9th year of Our Reign [1710].

Any review of the military expedition to take Nova Scotia in 1710 would include a look at the career of not only that of Nicholson, but also that of Vetch. The comparison of the characters of these two — Francis Nicholson, the standoffish, bachelor Yorkshireman; and Samuel Vetch, the gregarious Scot — would make for an interesting story in itself. Nicholson's commanding position, *vis-a-vis* Vetch, in 1710, it would appear, was just exactly reversed from that which was intended the year before. While Nicholson had by royal warrant the command of the invading forces this time around, directly the French capital was taken, then, by the same royal warrant, Vetch was to take charge of the conquered territory: it was a formula that was bound to cause problems. Among the corps of English officers there was a 26 year old junior officer by the name of Paul Mascarene[7] of whom we will hear more as this history unfolds. This young French speaking officer (a very great asset to the English forces), mainly because of his affability, was to bring considerable relief to the strained relationship at the top of the English command.[8]

The Fleet Sets Sail:

The fleet of fifty or sixty sailing vessels, having set sail on Wednesday, September 18th, 1710, made their way up the coast from Boston. On Thursday, the 21st, the fleet, in order to weather a storm, came to anchor at Passamquoddy Bay in behind Campobello and Deer Islands, approximately 60 miles or so from their objective just across the Bay of Fundy. On Saturday, the 23rd, they "arrived at Port Royal River and entering in at the Gutt, a parcel of Indians fired several volleys of small shot at them." A few blasts of the big cannon from the ships, however, sent the Indians scurrying for cover. The whole fleet came to anchor above Goat Island west of the town and the fort. One of the ships, the *Caesar* ran aground in the process and "the wind rising with a violent swelling sea bulg'd the ship." The captain of the *Caesar*, her pilot, a sailor and 23 soldiers were drown.

The Landing:

The fort was strategically built on a small point of land sticking out into the south side of the river. Just opposite on the north side is a smaller point of land. The points of land come together throttling the Rivière Dauphin[9] at its mouth; at this point the shores of the river are but a shot away. The invading troops landed on both sides of the river, well below and away from the guns of the fort. Each column advanced up their respective shores, using the cover which the trees would have provided. On the south side was General Nicholson and his forces. On the north, Colonel Vetch. Vetch was faced with the challenge of getting his troops across the river under the guns of the French so to meet up with Nicholson on the other side; and thus to be all assembled before the fort. As Nicholson explained in his diary, he "marched up near to brick-kilns in a single file, the way was so bad that in many places they were forc'd to cut their way, and in the evening we encamped in the adjoining woods ..." Next day, Tuesday, the 26th, the two forces met up "in sight of the Fort with Drums beating, and Colours flying" and when "the rest of the Army came up, and we dined." The French and their Indian allies kept up their efforts with small arms especially against the posted sentries; but the French and their Indian allies were far less in number than the English and their Indian allies. Nicholson determined to clean out the snipers and ordered a regiment to attack and force the French to go in behind their walls. A "hot skirmish" developed as the French forces fired "from their Houses, Fences and Gardens with their small arms." Soon the French were locked up behind their fort walls; the task being accomplished without too much of a loss on either side. A proper siege was now to commence.

By Friday the 29th, the British had unloaded the needed "stores of War" and the English cannons were unlimbered, set up on their emplacements, leveled and aimed at the fort. But these big guns were not heard from; by having been thus set up they had served their purpose. "After Diner two French officers[10] an Ensign and Sergeant with a Drummer came out of the Fort with a flag of truce, and brought our General a letter from Monsieur Subercase ..." The letter read as follows:

Sir,
Although I have not the Honour of knowing you I do notwithstanding address you with a full assurance that you will grant me one favour, since especially it is in behalf of our women, some of which are noble; Sire they did all along Flatter themselves that they could hear and bear the noise of your bombs without fear, but they now find themselves a little mistaken. One is our Major's Lady, the others are our officers Wives, who have two maiden servants to follow them; my prayer is that you grant them your Protection in your camp, and that you order that nothing that is uncivil or abusive be offer'd to them. Farther, as you have the Character of being a most Gallant and very honest Gentleman. I still presume to crave your farther favour for a few more of our Lady's who are gone into the Woods, our Lieutenant Governor's Lady is one of them, so that as its possible they may come into your camp or be taken by some of your out Scouts. You'l please to protect them in some place or other where you shall judge fit, and I shall be extremely obliged to you as being really,
    Sir, your most
    humble and obedient servant, Subercase.

Nicholson Detects A Ruse:

The etiquette of such proceedings required that the officer coming from one camp to another under a flag of truce is to be announced by a peculiar drum roll (a *chamade*) and come but half way and hold up, there to be met by an officer of the other camp. The officer who came to treat would then be blindfolded and led into camp. Nicholson returned a letter but kept the French officer. "I had just now the honour of receiving yours of this day and am concerned that you did not take the proper methods, for as I conceive before your officers came out of your Garrison you should have caused a Chamad to have been beat upon the ramparts to know if it were agreeable to me or not, such methods being observed amongst Soldiers, it should have been so done if you had anything to ask of me."[11] Numerous letters were passed between the commanders, each trying to out-psyche the other. Subercase was trying to get the release of his officer, but Nicholson sent one of his own into the fort, the French officer which was initially sent to Nicholson was kept by Nicholson, and he observed that he found the French officer was quite versatile being able to converse in English, though initially he pretended not to know the language. Subercase was aghast at the accusation that he had sent a spy and maintained he but wanted to save the French ladies from the horrors of war and meant only to put them under the protection of an honourable English general, and, indeed, one of them was with child. To which Nicholson replied that he was only too willing to keep the French ladies safe, "the Queen my royal Mistress hath not sent me hither to make War with Woman, especially in their condition. ... I leave it to your choice to send them or not, ... but I cannot part with your officer, believing you would imagine me but little experienced in War, should I send him to inform you what he has discovered he coming into the body of our encampment before he was blinded, I am also more inclined to believe him a spy, because you are more desirous of his discharge than the Lady's ... You have one of my Officers and I've one of yours, so that now we are equal." With that Subercase threw in his hand.[12]

French Ladies Up The River:

Incidentally, it is interesting to report, that certain of the ladies were not apparently in the fort but rather had already been sent up the river upon the sighting of the English fleet, to a place some four or five leagues up the river, 25 to 35 miles, to be in hiding somewhere around the present day village of Middleton. After the capitulation Nicholson sent two boats up the river "to fetch in the French Ladies that escaped for fear of our bombs." On Tuesday, the 3rd of October, "the French Ladies came down the River in the Boats which, the General sent for them, and came to our Camp, where they Breakfasted with the General, and were conducted into the Fort; Sir Charles Hobby led in Madam Bonaventure, and the rest were led in by other Officers."

The officers on both sides during this affair treated one another with considerable courtesy, as was generally the case in the 18th century: the turnover went smoothly. On October 6th, two hundred New England soldiers marched to the fort gate and formed in two lines on the right and left. Nicholson and his entourage advanced between the ranks, with Vetch on one hand and Hobby on the other, followed by all the field-officers. Subercase came to meet them, and gave up the keys, with a few words of compliment.

> Sir, I'm very sorry for the misfortune of the King my master in losing such a brave fort, and the territories adjoyning; but count myself happy in falling into the hands of so noble and generous a General, and now deliver up the keys of the Fort, and all the magazines into your hands, hoping to give you a visit next Spring ..."

The garrison, made up of about 200 hundred Frenchmen,[13] then advanced out of the fort with drums beating and flags flying, and dragging a small mortar.[14] They were proud but starving soldiers in rags and tatters, many of whom were no more than adolescents, a sight which sadden even the victors. Each saluted the English commander as they passed; then the English troops, in turn, marched in, raised the union flag, and drank the Queen's health amid a general firing of cannon from the fort and ships.

Nicholson changed the name of Port Royal to Annapolis Royal; and Vetch, already commissioned as governor, took command of the new garrison, which consisted of two hundred British marines, and two hundred and fifty provincials who had offered themselves for the service.

The French Garrison Sent Home In Style:

On Friday the 13th and Sunday the 15th of October, 1710, the first deportation of the Acadians took place at Port Royal (though this deportation did not apparently include any settlers, but only the military and administrative types found behind the walls of the fort at Port Royal). The defeated French were taken aboard three English transports: the *Frigot* (a total of 118 including Subercase, Bonaventure, Goutin, and their respective families), the *Four Friends* (71) and the *John and Anne* (69). A grand total of 258 Frenchmen were shipped out and over to France, an obligation the English created for themselves by the terms of the capitulation.[15] The English did what they could to make the voyage as comfortable as they might for their friends, the French officers.

Besides the Ship Provision on Board the Transports for France, General Nicholson ordered to be put on Board 4. Pipes of Wine, 4. Casks of Jamaica Sugar, and several sorts of spice for the women and children, and a hogshead of rum instead of beer. The General also gave to Monsieur Subercase out of his own store of all sorts of Liquor, besides wine and beer and other provisions to a considerable value, both for himself and others, to be disposed of as he thought proper.[16]

For the loss of Port Royal to the English, History does not blame Subercase, a veteran of more than thirty years' service and who "borne fair repute as a soldier."[17] There was, as we have seen no comparison between the forces of the defending French and the attacking English; further, some of the soldiers and many of the armed inhabitants deserted during the siege. The capitulation was signed on October 13th, 1710. Colonel Vetch, a man who was to play a considerable role in the first years of

Nova Scotia as an English colony, was left behind at Annapolis Royal together with a "heterogeneous garrison of four hundred and fifty men"[18] left in a fort in a ruinous state.

Chapter 10

Annapolis Royal
(1711-12)

And thus, in 1710, Acadia by conquest was passed to England, a fact confirmed by the *Treaty of Utrecht* (1713). The Acadian lands were to be English grounds but the hearts and tongues of the occupants remained French. The center of Acadia ran northeasterly up along the Annapolis Valley to the forked and muddy headwaters of the Bay of Fundy, the shores of Minas Basin and Chignecto Bay. At the time, 1710, the French population resided principally in only three communities, Annapolis, Minas, and Beaubassin. Both Annapolis and Minas had approximately 600 French inhabitants, Beaubassin at the isthmus, 300, and Cobequid had 80; a total of 1,500.[1] The closest community, Minas (Grand Pré) was 70 miles from the fort at Annapolis Royal and the others were more distant still. There were no roads. To get anywhere, for the natives, it was by forest-path and canoe. As for the white man, he travelled relatively less dangerously by small sail boat up and down and around the seacoasts. The distant guns at Annapolis Royal and the little garrison located there had little effect on the Acadians; they continued to farm their lands and raise their black cattle, sheep and hogs[2] behind their dykes undisturbed by outside authority as they had been doing for the previous hundred years.

Québecois at Acadia:

What must now be mentioned, and to which we will return in greater detail as our story progresses, is the involvement of the Quebec authorities in Acadian affairs. French military personal were clandestinely sent to Acadia from Quebec. These patriotic fellows were more interested in guns and the forests rather than in plows and the fields, as were the Acadians. They infiltrated the Acadians and represented themselves as priests sent to shepherd the Roman Catholic flocks of Acadia. Some came dressed as Indians and lived among them.[3] The Québecois amongst them wished to see the Acadians rise up and retake Acadia for the French king, but the Acadians, while intimidated with threats of excommunication and Indian reprisals, had little stomach for doing battle with the English.

The first intrusion upon the Acadians, by the English, at their center around the Minas Basin, was to occur shortly after the capitulation of Annapolis Royal, in November of 1710. On the 8th, Mascarene, together with about 75 men, went aboard the Brigantine, *Betty*. The *Betty*, having sailed up the Fundy, dropped her anchor on the 13th in the "Manis Road," and from her 42 Englishmen rowed ashore in a flat-bottomed boat. They were received by about "150 of the inhabitants with demonstrations of joy." Having appointed eight deputies or representatives (tax collectors) the English party left the French Acadian community at Minas after a seven day visit. I note that Mascarene paid "sixteen Livres for the Lodging and Diet ..." Mascarene and his contingent were back at Annapolis Royal by the 20th of November; with them went one of the deputies, John Landry, who bore a gift for Governor Vetch, "a parcel of Furr."

The First Winter:

The first winter for the English soldiers in their captured fort at Annapolis Royal was to be a struggle, a struggle which was indeed to be continued for the first forty years of English rule in Nova Scotia.[4] To begin with, the fort was not set up to accommodate 450 soldiers.

The accommodation was increased by turning the greater part of the chapel into barracks, but still the troops had but poor lodgings all winter. The frost having hindered the building of the chimneys, they suffered from want of fire. Fuel was also obtained with great labour, risk and expense. There was none in store in the fort, and all they obtained had to be cut on the opposite side of the river, then transported across, for which three flat-bottomed boats were kept continually going and coming, and then hauled to the fort.

They also began to feel other wants, that of bread especially, 'nothing but pease and beefe and little or no porke,' he [Vetch] says, being served out to them. An attempt to obtain supplies of grain from the inhabitants up the river led to a collision with some of them.[5]

In addition to being without supplies, the fort itself was in a very bad state of repair. This small English troop was without food, clothing, and shelter; and a northern winter was coming on. Having just come through a siege and thus being in dire straits themselves, the shortages at the fort could hardly be made up by the locals; indeed, the Acadians looked to their new masters for support.

At the time of the English takeover, the town just below the fort held the largest population of Frenchmen in all of Acadia. At Port Royal (now named by the English Annapolis Royal) the residents made their living by serving the needs of the port. While some farming was carried out at Port Royal, by 1710, the community was depending on those farmers who were then at Minas. A number of the sons and daughters had relocated, circa 1690, to Minas, located north-east of Port Royal some seventy miles as the crow flies.[6] The sloops which would normally run down the Bay to the market at Port Royal did not risk bringing their cargoes, the grains of Minas, to a place that was under siege by the English, and by the time the English had installed themselves, winter weather was setting in. Starvation before the arrival of spring, both for the English and the French inhabitants at Annapolis was a real prospect until in January of 1711 when there arrived a sloop from Boston with supplies. This was likely the same sloop on which Vetch returned home for a couple of months. He left Sir Charles Hobby (1665-1715) in charge until April when Vetch returned to his duties at Annapolis Royal. The promise of April caused Vetch to do an accounting. He had found, that of the 450 men that he had started with the previous spring, he had lost 116 through death and desertion. In May, Vetch wrote:

The inhabitants in general, as well French as Indians, continue still in a great ferment, and uneasiness. Those within the Banlieue, (who are but few), that have taken the oath of allegiance to Her Majesty, are threatened and made uneasy by all the others, who call them traitors, and make them believe the French will soon recover the place and then they will be ruined. The Priests likewise, who are numerous among them, and whom I cannot catch, (save one sent to Boston), threaten with their ecclesiastical vengeance for their subjection to heretics, so that until her Majesty shall be pleased both to give an order and afford me a sufficient force to reduce the whole country to such terms as she shall see meet to give them, we can expect no peaceable possession of the country. We have been much alarmed all winter with designs of the Indians, and the French from Canada making an attempt upon us, while the fortifications were so ruinous.[7]

The immediate project for the spring of 1711, now that the prospect of starvation was not before them,[8] was to fix up the fort which was in a dilapidated condition. Its previous occupants had received no supplies from France for three years. The earthen works were loose and in a number of places had come tumbling down. The plan was to pile the dirt up once again and to face the ramparts with logs, which, it was figured, could be got from the French inhabitants. The Acadians up the Annapolis River were apparently ready enough to do the work of chopping and floating the logs down to the fort, especially since they were to be paid for their efforts, however, it was not to be that easy. The woods were "infested" with an unseen enemy, the Indians.[9] So it was necessary when any woodworking party ventured forth from the fort, to have a considerable armed guard located nearby. The Indians had apparently threatened the inhabitants up the river, who were cutting lumber and plank for the repair of the fort, and these native agitators cut loose rafts that had been prepared to be sent down the river.

First Battle Of Bloody Creek:

To combat the Indian problem up river, a detachment of 70 English soldiers was sent from Annapolis Royal on June 10th, 1711, "to harass a nearby Indian settlement and restore the transportation of wood to the fort."[10] It was, however, their misfortune to run into a large number of French and their Indian allies who had just taken up their position in the province. The unsuspecting English party proceeded up the river in three boats: two flat-bottomed boats and one whaleboat. The whaleboat moved faster through the water and soon left the other two behind. This lead boat was ambushed while passing through "a narrow part of the river." These Indians, by and large, were not local[11]; they were Penobscots and had come from some distance, "having crossed the Bay of Fundy in birch bark canoes, and only arrived the day before." Some 30 British soldiers lost their lives and the rest were taken prisoner.[12] Those that survived the attack and who had been taken prisoner were soon traded back to the fort for supplies and money. It is interesting to note that Annapolis Royal at this time had a spy, her name was Louise Guyon. Guyon was a most interesting French lady who had returned to the English fort with a request to live there. She had been at the fort before its fall and was well-liked by the French officers, indeed, she was bedded by the top ones. She had been in Quebec for a couple of years before she presented herself at the gates of Annapolis Royal just before the ambush at Bloody Creek and charmed the British officers into letting her stay. Mascarene, the second in command of the British garrison, did not trust her and was convinced she was a spy, but his betters thought otherwise; as Mascarene says, she was "received Very Kindly by Sir Chas. Hobby." It was said two of her grown up sons led the attack at Bloody Creek, and the very next night Madame Guyon was spirited out of Annapolis Royal, not to be seen or heard of again.

Knowing that the success at Bloody Creek would give heart to the French inhabitants in the area, within days, the regular French forces which lurked about coalesced and gathered the Indians and the Acadians to their aid and a crowd of 600, having received military supplies came from Placentia, swept up to the walls of Annapolis Royal with the intention to invest the fort. For a while it looked like Annapolis Royal was to have the *fleur de lis* flying over it once again; but, overall, the numbers of men and supplies were insufficient for a successful siege and Vetch and his men were determined to dig in. Eventually the besiegers dispersed.

Admiral Hovenden Walker:

During the summer of 1711 Vetch was called away to go with the ill-fated Walker expedition (Admiral Hovenden Walker), which, at great expense to England, had been formed to go up the St Lawrence and take Quebec. Vetch was to take command of a division of the 5,300 troops which were under Brigadier-General John Hill. What happened to the Walker expedition after it left Boston on July 13th, 1711, is not germane to our story; sufficient for our purposes to point out that the French rule in North America would likely have ended in 1711, and not as it in fact did in 1759, if it had not been for the ineptitude of the leadership (both Hill and Walker) of this powerful English expedition of 1711. Several English ships were wrecked and hundreds of men lost on the shores of St Lawrence, after which Hill and Walker left North America, with its yet substantial invasion force, having not fired a shot at the enemy. It has been described as "perhaps the most inglorious naval and military expedition that ever left British shores."[13]

Vetch, while off with Hill and Walker, left Annapolis Royal, once again, under the command of Hobby. In the fall of that year, 1711, Vetch brought back one of the remnants of General Hill's army to fill the ranks of the garrison at Annapolis Royal. (This remnant consisted of 250 men and included a hotheaded Irishman by the name of Lawrence Armstrong (1664-1739), a military man who was to have a long and sad connection with Nova Scotia.) I do not know that we can conclude that the 250 new soldiers[14] were added to the existing 300 or so at the garrison, likely some were sent off to other postings. I know, at least, that Hobby was relieved in October of that year, 1711, being replaced by the English born Thomas Caulfeild (1685-1717).[15] (Both Hobby and Caulfeild were with Nicholson in 1710 when Port Royal was captured.) Vetch was not to spend the winter of 1711/12 at

Annapolis; he went to Boston, arriving there on October 20th, to be there with his family and to dismiss and pay off the provincial troops which had been under his command in the aborted expedition up the St Lawrence.

Iroquois In Nova Scotia (1711-12):

Vetch came back to Annapolis Royal in the spring of 1712. During the winter he had managed to convince the authorities that it would be a good idea to bring with him a band of Iroquois (100), under the control of his brother-in-law Major John Livingston (1680-1720) and to put a show on for their cousins in Nova Scotia. The summer of 1711, it will be recalled, was one that was full of threat and worry for the English garrison at Annapolis Royal mainly because of the MicMacs and the Penobscots.[16] Livingston had the confidence of the Iroquois and the Iroquois, having "their own technique and weapons," were feared by the natives who frequented the forests of Nova Scotia. It is interesting to note that a special issue of light muskets was given to them as "our muskets are too heavy for them." The Iroquois operated as a separate unit in Nova Scotia. Initially it was thought they might be put up in regular housing within the town, but that apparently didn't suit anyone, least of all, the Iroquois. Within weeks of their arrival, by June of 1712, the Iroquois built themselves their own fort about a quarter of a mile from the main English fort. With a great deal of their own labour and with little expense to the crown they had built "... a long square, composed of a dry stone wall of a reasonable thickness, about six feet high, heaped with sods, with a ditch before it about four feet deep, and between five and six feet high, having at each angle the form of a bastion, except towards the river, where it is in a direct line, having a breastwork or parapet of sods, with embrasure for cannon, capable to be made use of for a battery and commands the river very well thereabouts. At one point Livingston brought a number of his native charges (50) with him to Cape Breton with the objective to salvage what they could of the four British ships of the Walker expedition which had been lost off the northern coasts of this French territory in the previous year. The English knew, generally, the kind of mischief which the Iroquois could get up to, and therefore controlled them, usually by having an officer be with them at all times, often Livingston himself.[17] These native visitors to Nova Scotia stayed for a year, they left in May of 1713 to return to their native lands (around the finger lakes in present day New York). It does not appear that there was any direct conflict with the MicMacs during this period; the mere presence of the Iroquois was enough to keep the peace.

French Gold And English Paper:

That which stands out, over these first years, indeed, right up to Cornwallis' arrival in 1749, is the fact that the English garrison at Annapolis Royal was utterly deserted by their masters back home. The English authorities, having spent the money to capture the place, sent hardly anything by way of men or supplies to keep it. The historical record shows pitiful plea after pitiful plea for help. These lonely and brave English soldiers seemed to have understood the importance of keeping Nova Scotia for the English, but the authorities in their comfortable headquarters at London seemingly did not care. The needed supplies to keep the fort functioning, and just barely functioning, were for the most part brought up from Boston, usually on the credit of the commanding officer at Annapolis Royal. The local Acadians could, and did, supply some food, fuel, and basic building supplies, however, no matter the source, things had to be paid for.[18]

Unlike the French, the English did not ship gold and silver to pay for the expense of maintaining their troops overseas.[19] Thus, Annapolis Royal had no ready money to pay for supplies. Orders were made out for supplies with cooperative merchants who understood that they would have to accept "bills" signed by the commander at Annapolis Royal in payment. The Boston merchant would then usually sign them over to pay certain of his accounts in London. Ultimately the Annapolis Royal bill would wind itself through the system and come to rest on the desk of some government bureaucrat at London who would be responsible to see that the holder of the bill was paid with real money. Such a system was attended with some doubt as to whether the bills would ever be honoured by the government. The question to come into the mind of the creditor, would be — Did the officers have the authority to issue such bills? What was certain, that under such a system, is that it took an age to get paid. Thus, assuming he would take a bill drawn on London, at all, the merchant would never take it at face value; such bills were discounted. For example, a Boston merchant who did accept a bill drawn on London in payment of a £100 invoice, failing its payment in legal tender, might take a £200 bill — a discount of 50%. Such a bill, when it ultimately got paid in London by the government, would get paid at face value: the difference was necessary to make up for the waiting and the risk which was experienced by the middle men. Thus, a significant share of the money that the government in London spent on the English outpost at Annapolis Royal — never made it to Annapolis Royal: and this on account of the antiquated method of payment which, in those days, the English government employed to pay its overseas accounts.

... the bills for the pay and victualling of the garrison of Annapolis were left unpaid. The public credit was sunk so low that government bills were worth twenty per cent less than private; the government agents had advanced money till they were on the verge of ruin, and officers and men had suffered much loss and inconvenience.

The system to which I referred eventually broke down and the merchants would not ship, at all. This led to great problems for the garrison at Annapolis Royal. That it was able to continue and keep the British presence going in Nova Scotia, as was represented by a flying union jack at Annapolis Royal, is to the sole credit of those brave English soldiers who stood there at the earthen ramparts at Annapolis Royal, alone and without help.

I have wrote your Lordship so often relating to the garrison and the payment of the bills for its support, without being honoured with the least return or directions with relations to the same, that I now almost write in despair, and as the agent, who hath launched out all the money he was capable to raise for Her Majesty's service and the support of this garrison, having as yet received no reimbursement, is necessitate to abandon us, so that I cannot get any person whatsomever who will, upon the public account, advance either money or provisions for the support of the garrison, nor have we provisions for more than a month longer, a necessity to abandon the place, for the inhabitants have not provisions to maintain themselves, so that we are reduced to the last extremity, especially considering that the garrison is composed of all the mutineers and refuse of the seven regiments from which they were detached, as their own officers affirm.

This situation, as was explained by Vetch, was one that pretty well continued throughout the first 30 to 40 years of the British at Annapolis Royal; it would appear, however, that the first few years were the worst. As Vetch wrote, "Never any garrison was left in so abandoned condition as this hath been ever since its reduction [capture], during all which time I have the honour to command, there having been neither pay, nor provisions ..." Thus the garrison faced its second winter "nearly naked for want of clothing," without bedding and no food. Starvation and death was a real prospect, and in the face of these troubles, the officers faced the real risk of a mutiny of crazed soldiers. Winter set in, one of the worst seen in some time: all was going to be lost. The Governor and Council at Massachusetts were not unaware of the sad blight of the garrison at Annapolis Royal, nor of the strategic importance of the place; and just in the nick of time supplies arrived from Boston in January of 1712: a new lease was to be had for another year.

Part Three

Annapolis Royal & Louisbourg:

1713-1744

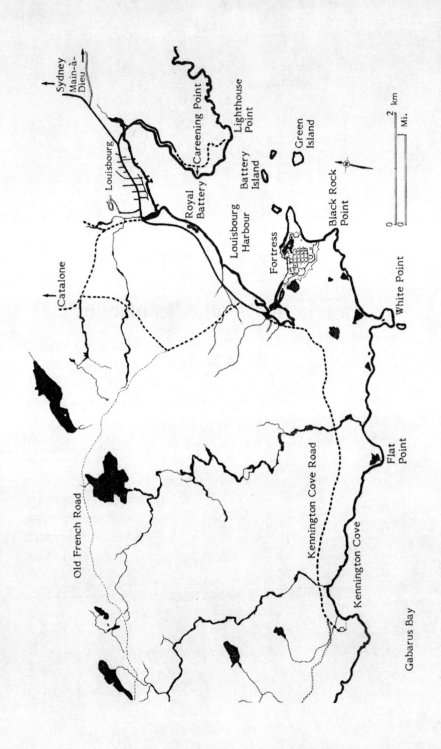

Chapter 1

Louisbourg: Its Founding

The war had pitted the "Grand Alliance" of England, Holland and certain of the German states up against France and Spain. It had come about because of the old and modern day concern of European states of seeing too many of their number come under the control of any one of them. In 1702, of course, the concern was centered on the ambitions of Louis XIV of France, the House of Bourbon. Charles II of Spain, in 1700, died childless. He had, in his last days, in the midst of court intrigue, executed his Last Will and Testament: he devised the Spanish throne to Philip, the Duke of Anjou, and the grandson of Louis XIV. In the days succeeding Charles' death, Louis was to become boastful ("... no longer was there a Pyrenees"): the world waited and wondered.

In those days, though her light was considerably faded, the Spanish empire extended beyond the Iberian peninsula, to Italy and to an area that we now know as Belgium, the Spanish Netherlands. Louis XIV felt obliged to make sure that the succession of Philip V went smoothly, and thus, sent his troops to all the various parts of the Spanish empire; simply on the basis of the request a her "friendly" ally, Spain. By 1702, the French had strategically positioned themselves throughout Europe. Holland became upset seeing the French pressing up against her southern borders. England became more nervous than normal; mostly because she did not want to lose her access to the Spanish markets. In anticipation, England's fleet was increased to 30,000 men and the army to 10,000.[1]

I cannot, in the context of this particular history, deal with the war as it unfolded on the European continent. Suffice it, that the war raged on through the early part of the century until 1709, when, in May of that year, preliminary peace articles were signed by Austria and Great Britain and presented to France as an ultimatum. Louis could not deliver on article 37 which called for the Bourbon of Spain, Philip, the grandson of Louis, to give up the throne to the nominee of the allies, the Austrian, Charles. The problem, not one that Louis could now cure, was that the Spanish people, while likely at odds with their dead king's wishes at the first of it, now wanted Philip as their king. The belligerents, therefore, in 1709, returned to the field. While France was in no shape to continue with the war: she did. The French people, as has been demonstrated so many times throughout history, proceeded to make the sacrifices needed to save themselves from foreign oppression. The "peasants starved, the rich ate black bread and sold their plate, that the soldiers might live." The French general, Villars, gave rations to a regiment on the days when it marched; on days of repose it fasted. It was in this fashion they weathered that year. Villars was in command of the last army of France and was obliged to face the armies of the allies, 120,000 strong, well equipped and supplied and knowing nothing but victory since the beginning of the war. History shows, however, that Villars and his 90,000 men were to stop the allied advance on Paris. "The French spirit, sometimes so blind and overbearing, now appeared in its pure and legitimate shape." By the end of the fighting season, the valiant French, at Malplaquet, had shown what they were made of. The English were diverted and Paris was saved. With the fighting of 1709 then concluded, France, still holding up, went to the peace negotiation table, once again. Louis XIV would give up Alsace. He would pay a subsidy to help the Allied armies to dethrone his grandson. Further, he demonstrated his good will, by, beforehand, recalling all his regiments from Spain, leaving the Spaniards to their own resources. But one thing he could not do was to undertake to fight Philip and the Spanish people with French troops. The allies understood that this was the very best offer they were going to get, and, financially exhausted, as they were, determined to accept it. On October 8th (September 27th, OS), 1711, the articles leading to the *Treaty of Utrecht* were signed at London by the French and the English. It was a good bargain for England: "A monopoly of slave trade to Spanish-America for thirty years; Gibraltar and Minorca; St. Kitts Island and Acadia; Newfoundland and Hudson's Bay; Queen Anne's title and the Protestant Succession under the *Act of Settlement* acknowledged by Louis. The fact that the Spanish Netherlands, Italy and Sicily all passed out of the power of France was also of immense advantage to the security and the trade of England."[2]

Thus it was, that by the *Treaty of Utrecht* France was to lose much, including, to come to our principal topic, all of Acadia, defined by its "ancient boundaries." Gone was this North American territory which the French had fought to hold on to for over one hundred years. The Acadians who occupied these lands were specifically dealt with by the peace makers in London and in Paris: they were to have liberty "to remove themselves within a year to any other place, as they shall think fit, together with all their moveable effects," and those who remained, were "to be subject to the Kingdom of Great Britain" and "to enjoy the free exercise of their religion, according to the usage of the Church of Rome, as far as the laws of Great Britain do allow the same." Newfoundland, too, which in part had been occupied by the French since the earliest times, including her base at Placentia, by the terms of this historical treaty, was to be given up and evacuated.[3] But, France was to retain the islands of the St. Lawrence and in particular, the island of Cape Breton. Cape Breton was to serve as an outlying eastern sentinel to Canada (Quebec).

The Choice Of Louisbourg:

Given the restrictions of the *Treaty of Utrecht*, the island of Cape Breton was the only choice for France's new Atlantic stronghold; but the question arises why Louisbourg, shrouded in fog at times and permanently bound by its granite shores — was, of all the harbors of Cape Breton, chosen? There were two other harbors which had long been known to the French: Ste. Anns and Ste. Pierre.[4] The soil, certainly at Ste. Anns, was considerably better than that found at Louisbourg; and, at Ste.

Anns, the topographics were such that a position might be found that could easily be fortified. However, the harbor at Louisbourg had more to offer. It is about three miles long and three-quarters of a mile wide and has the advantage of open waters, not ordinarily available in these northern parts during the winter months. So too, its nearness to the fishing grounds would allow her fishermen to get out in relatively smaller boats and keep her fishing industry going most all of the year through.

Actually, St. Peter's, or, Port Toulouse[5] as it was then named in 1713, came close to being the chief establishment of Île Royale, and it continued to be in the running even after Louisbourg was established, but because of the expense of intended fortifications a choice of one spot had to be made. Louisbourg eventually won out. However, as Louisbourg became more established and increasingly fortified, Port Toulouse grew in importance, and was to be a collection place for French fishermen and French lumbermen. The chief attraction of Port Toulouse was its short land connection between the Bras d'Or Lakes and the Atlantic ocean.

France had no particular root of title to the sheltered harbor we now know as Louisbourg, indeed, up to the arrival of the French settlers in 1713 the place was known as *Havre à l'Anglois*. While we read in the history books of the first literate explorers such as Cartier and the Cabots, it is now accepted that European fisherman for centuries had fished off the Grand Banks on a seasonal basis and sought refuge in the sheltering harbors to be found at Newfoundland and, of course, at Cape Breton. All three European countries — France, Spain and England — had equal claims to the fish of the north Atlantic and to the shores to which their fishermen resorted. When on shore, as might be expected, fellow countrymen congregated with fellow countrymen. At Ste. Anns, where now we find the beginning of the famous Cabot Trail, would be found the French; at Spanish Bay (present day Sydney), the Spanish; and at English Harbor, the English.[6]

The Founding Of Louisbourg:

Our scene opens on the wild and wonderful shores on the Atlantic side of Cape Breton Island, much of it now as it was in 1713. Imagine yourself a soaring gull, beginning your flight at the southern corner of this intriguing island, from Red Island to Red Head, along the quiet reaches of the Grand River and out to the Atlantic shores again. See the brilliant waters, the rocks, the sands, the dunes, the bogs and your fellow gulls. See the rugged beauty, the bird islands such as Esprit and Guyon, and the blinding beaches such as may be found along Framboise Cove; see the swelling Atlantic fetch up on Bull Rock with a low rumble, with stunning sprays reaching up and then down into the sea foam; pass with your fellow gulls over the headlands of Bull Hill and Cape Gabarus and descend down along the waters of Gabarus Bay and along into the quiet waters of what was to be named, Louisbourg Harbor. This long gliding shot of several minutes finishes up with the scene of a band of Indians gazing out over their meager summer settlement, looking somewhat puzzled as a French sailing ship, the *Semslack* glides into the safety of the harbor.

The *Semslack* had set out from France early in the season. Joseph de St. Ovide,[7] who was in charge of the expedition, was under orders to first call on Placentia and from there to transport the community found at that place — their personal possessions, furniture, tools and animals — to *Havre à l'Anglois* (to be named Louisbourg); and there, on Île Royale, to establish the French presence at a new spot on the northeastern coast. Of the twenty persons or so[8] which had embarked at France, likely most were familiar with the new world[9]: St. Ovide their leader, certainly was. For, as a military man, in 1691, he had been sent out to Newfoundland and had taken part in the defences and attacks of the local war until 1710. Costebelle, incidently, was named the governor of Île Royale; he, however, did not arrive at Louisbourg until September of 1714.[10]

Setting sail from Placentia on July 23, 1713, the *Semslack* was in company with a supply vessel from Quebec which carried a band of picked men, "40 or 50 of the best workers" under the command of Hertel.[11] The Quebec supply vessel had been chartered from a retired naval officer by the name of Boularderie.[12] And so, 116 men, 10 women and 23 children stepped ashore with their supplies[13] and Louisbourg came into being. The harbor was already occupied and the new arrivals were greeted by "one French inhabitant and twenty-five or thirty families of Indians."

"The year ... was spent in feverish activity to get the new colony started: they had to transport cannon, erect forts and dwellings, re-establish the fisheries, parcel out the beaches, build flakes and stages, explore the shores, and mark out the fairways."[14] In the earlier years, it was not at all clear that Louisbourg was to be the capital of Île Royale. Indeed, Governor Costebelle,[15] on his arrival in 1714, first established himself at Port Dauphin (Englishtown these days); Hertel at Port Toulouse.[16] There was, you see, "indecision of the court at Versailles as to the site of new colony's chief town; after approving the choice of Louisbourg, a sudden decision was made in 1715 in favour of Port Dauphin, to which the administration, the garrison, and the principal services of the colony had to be transferred. In 1718, however, the order was given to bring the capital back to Louisbourg."

The French that were to locate to Île Royale made their living by the sea; that was what they had done in Newfoundland from where they initially had come and that was what they were to do at Cape Breton. These simple French folk had built their humble abodes on the shores of the sheltering harbours closest to the fishing banks. On the small stoned beeches would be found their drying flakes; their small sailing vessels, when not at sea, bobbing at their moorings in the background. The Acadians of peninsular Nova Scotia had an entirely different experience and were unwilling, unlike their cousins of Newfoundland, to take up residence on Île Royale. There are a number of reasons for this, as we will see; but the first and principal reason was that they were farmers, not fishermen. As farmers, the Acadians around the Fundy Basin were less dependent[17] on the mother country and were also more skeptical, preferring their farms which were cleared (mostly by nature) and under cultivation rather than the unworked and uncleared land (and as it turned out, not near as fertile) as was to be found on Île Royale.[18]

Out On The Mira:

One of the first things that the Louisbourg settlers were to do was to cut out a road[19] to the nearby Mira River (to the French known as the Miré). A party might pierce into the interior some distance by going up the Salmon River and then continue west from lake to lake, and with light weight canoes would soon find themselves on the eastern shores of the Bras d'Or Lakes, and from there in a larger boat all of Cape Breton opens up.

The Mira was a source of fresh water, large straight trees and wild game. The banks of the Mira also had something else that is generally scarce in Nova Scotia, particularly in Cape Breton, — fertile soil. As time went by, farms were established on the Mira, owned and operated by the rich and powerful from Louisbourg. The raiders from New England in 1745 found them there.

> We found two fine farms upon a neck of land that extended near seven miles in length. The first we came to was a very handsome house, and had two large barns, well finished, that lay contiguous to it. Here, likewise, were two very large gardens; as also some fields of corn of a considerable height, and other good lands thereto belonging, besides plenty of beach wood and fresh water.... The other house was a fine stone edifice, consisting of six rooms on a floor, all well finished. There was a fine wall before it, and two fine barns contiguous to it, with fine gardens and other appurtenances, besides several fine fields of wheat. In one of the barns there were fifteen loads of hay, and room sufficient for three score horses and other cattle.[20]

Though Louisbourg had an abundant sea to her front and comparatively good soil of the Miré but twenty-five miles or so away to her back, it was to be the Acadians in peninsular Nova Scotia that supplied most of Louisbourg's fresh meat and grain. These Acadians were but a few days sail away. One need only a seaworthy sailing vessel and then to sail down the Atlantic coast of Cape Breton (70 miles) and through the Canso Strait (20 miles) and clearing Cape George (25 miles) to travel along the Northumberland Strait (125 miles). (Both these straits, I should note, are waters that separated English territory from French territory, the islands of Île Royale and Île St. Jean.) A landing would then be made on the shores of Baie Verte, just at the isthmus which acts as the modern day border between Nova Scotia and New Brunswick. From there, the party would go overland. After traveling over the flat marshy land by foot and canoe, the traveling party would, after some fifteen to twenty miles, come out onto the muddy shores of the Baie Française (Bay of Fundy). Once on the bay, then any part of the Acadian farming lands might be reached by sail. This trip, just described, had to be made many times between Louisbourg and the lands of the original Acadians and it surely started in the spring of 1714; it became an established Acadian trade route by which people and goods relocated themselves.[21]

Some adventurers did travel to Louisbourg in order to earn some ready cash, but few Acadians were willing to leave their farmsteads located on peninsular Nova Scotia. The fact is there never was a serious drain of mainland Acadians to the rocky shores around Louisbourg. While the French authorities encouraged the Acadians to leave and to take up their living on Île Royale, many preferred to stay put and to continue to work their fertile farms located in Acadia, as they had for generations. The Acadians who did go to Louisbourg were not farmers; but rather they were "carpenters, boat-builders, longshoremen, and tavern-keepers, who found in the activities of Louisbourg more profitable employment than Nova Scotia afforded them." [22]

The strength of Louisbourg, unlike so many new settlements in North America, was, that those who did come to Louisbourg were experienced pioneers. An English governor of the time, Colonel Vetch of Annapolis, made his point with the home office in pointing to the virtues of having a population fitted to the climate and the jobs at hand. Such a population was to be found at Louisbourg, and the resulting development of this French citadel, Vetch was to write, was a danger to the English colonies south of it.

> ... it is to be considered that one hundred of the French, who were born upon that continent, and are perfectly known in the woods, can march upon snowshoes, and understand the use of Birch Canoes, are of more value and service than five times their number of raw men, newly come from Europe. So their skill in the Fishery, as well as the cultivating of the soil, must inevitably make that Island, by such an accession of people, and French, at once the most powerful colony the French have in America, and of the greatest danger and damage to all the British Colony's as well as the universal trade of Great Britain.[23]

Whatever the reasons might be for the impressive growth of Louisbourg, as was observed by Vetch, it did not come about easily. This growth most certainly came about by the industrious Frenchmen at that place, but more critically, because high ranking Frenchmen were pleading the cause at the Court of King Louis the XIV: what was needed, to protect the French possessions in America, was fortification funds for Louisbourg.

> The English are well aware of the importance of this post, and are already taking umbrage in the matter. They see that it will be prejudicial to their trade, and that in time of war it will be a menace to their shipping, and on the first outbreak of trouble they will be sure to use every means to get possession of it. It is therefore necessary to fortify it thoroughly. If France were to lose this Island the loss would be an irreparable one, and it would involve the loss of all her [France's] holdings in North America.[24]

We will in due course come to a description of the stone fort at Louisbourg. It took time to build, and until built, during these first years, the residents had "miserable quarters" surrounded by upright pickets in the ground and batteries of guns; the population lived in simple huts built on the beaches next to their curing fish.

_____

Chapter 2

Louisbourg: Soldiers & Fortifications

The purpose of Louisbourg was military. Thus, it should not be surprising to see that its population consisted of those from the military class and those necessary to support them: civil administrators and merchants. There were no farmers about, though undoubtedly each family attempted to supplement their means of subsistence with a small vegetable garden, in season; a few chickens, a sow, and maybe a cow. The garden was located in the owner's yard. As for the domesticated animals, they were allowed to run loose throughout the town much to the chagrin of the town officials.[1]

We shall shortly be moving into a discussion about the unique (at least to North America) stone fortifications which the French erected at Louisbourg, but it is necessary to consider, in a preliminary sort of way, how the contracting arrangements for the construction of the fort impacted on the lives of the regular soldiers. As we will shortly develop, the building of forts was not, strictly speaking, a military affair. A stone fortress was a major governmental project. The work was handled by private companies under the direction of the highest of military officials. Able men, as were available, were hired by the contractors to do the back breaking work. In Louisbourg the only able bodied men who had the time, as it turned out, were the regular soldiers. So, by and large, the digging, the hauling and the placement of stone was, while under the supervision of the experts brought out from France, carried out by the soldiers themselves. The military authorities did not mind that the private contractors should pay the soldiers for their work; it kept them fit and supplemented their poor military pay.

The pay for a soldier was very, very little; and usually it only came to him twice a year. The thought was they didn't need much, since they got, with the compliments of the king, their food lodging and clothing (at least, the plan was that they should). As a practical matter, however, a single soldier could hardly make out on military pay, thus, unless there was an independent source of money (often the case for the military officers, but not the regular men), it was necessary to earn a little additional money. This, the regular soldier did by working for the locals such as they might do at harvest time; or, as was the case at Louisbourg, to work on the fortifications. As for the married military man: well, he had to be extra diligent and often kept a number of jobs going, all at the same time. A married man often got a few extra privileges. As for example, for a cut to the allowing officers, the man was allowed to keep a tavern of which Louisbourg had many.[2]

By 1738 the fortifications were just about complete. There were 580 troops at Louisbourg, 100 of whom were Swiss. Their duties extended beyond the walls of Louisbourg, as there were garrisons at both "The Royal Battery" (across the harbor on the western shore facing the entrance of the harbor) and at the battery located on *Île Royale de l'Entrée* (so positioned as to blast any unfriendly ship that should try to make her way in); and at those garrisons many miles away: Port-la-Joye (near Charlottetown, P.E.I.), Port Toulouse (St. Peter's, N.S.), and Port Dauphin (Englishtown, N.S.). Bachelor soldiers, the majority, were put up in barracks.[3] The few that were married had "civilian accommodations" within Louisbourg. The two external batteries, the Royal Battery and that at *Île Royale de l'Entrée*, had barracks to accommodate the posted soldiers, except the gun crews who lived next to their big black masters. The conditions for the troops were generally bad. The soldiers, certainly not the officers, slept two to a bunk and the hay on which they slept got changed but once a year. It should be no surprise, therefore, to see that many during the milder weather preferred to sleep outside the ramparts. These forlorn and lonely men turned to alcohol, readily available at the canteens run by the officers.

Despite severe measures that were adopted to discourage the practice, desertions were not uncommon. Not only, as we might well be able to now understand, were conditions as such as to make any sane person want to quit the army, a lot of these men never wanted to be in the army in the first place. Many were convicts who chose to go into the army for service in New France rather than spend the balance of their lives in a dank French prison.[4] This desertion problem, incidently, was not peculiar to Louisbourg. There were, in 1738, several desertions at the English garrison at Annapolis Royal. The English commander there, Lawrence Armstrong, thought, "by the help and connivance of the inhabitants."[5] There were deserters at Canso, too; the first few tried to find harborage at Louisbourg but upon discovery the French authorities sent the deserters back to the English. As for the governor at Louisbourg, he was to keep tight control over the colony so as to prevent desertions: "Nobody can leave the colony without the Governor's leave, and of his only." It was, however, common to sell "leaves of absence."

Gun drill took place every Sunday and likely it was then that the drummer boys lined up for practice:

Sleeves of the drummers' skirted coats, blue like their caps, were decorated with stripes in the link design of the royal livery, testifying service to the King. Only collars and inner linings were artillery scarlet like the boars of the cannoneers, since colors were reversed for musicians. Small hands trembled a little when they poised sticks over the heads of drums whose cases were painted scarlet and ornamented in yellow with a flaming bomb, insignia of their arm of the service, and with the same legend that adorned the caps. But the boys steadily rattled out the signals for loading, beats that would cut through the din of combat better than shouted orders.[6]

Two more points I need to touch upon before passing on to the fortifications of Louisbourg. First, the military uniforms of the age; and second, the fighting style. One might wonder about the colour of the French military jacket (*justacorps*). As impractical as it must have been, the colour was an off white (dyes were expensive) with red (artillery) or blue (infantry) facings. I must say, as an aside, that the dress of most French military men allowed them to blend into the background much better than the British regular ever could; but bright colors for military dress was entirely normal for the day. That a military man stood out in the battle field was entirely in keeping with the strict rules of organized fighting of the 18th century. Each side before actually coming to blows put on great dazzling displays in an effort to intimidate the other. There, before each other, and often before a crowd of spectators, the opposing armies would be seen: maneuvering their lines and their ranked squares; dressed in the brightest of colours, accented with glistening metal and shiny leather; with the margins being defined by arrayed artillery and horsemen just waiting for their commander's nod. This was how things evolved after centuries of battling on the fields of Europe. This, as you might imagine, was a most impractical way to go about matters in America. Military tactics, European style, by and large did not work in America, neither for the French nor the English; though always the newly arrived officer thought that it should. When it came to fighting wars in America, Europeans were inept, this because they never seemed to meet one another in an open field. However, it was gradually learned, (the French seem to catch on faster) that if one wanted to have the better of his enemy he would have to learn to fight, Indian style. The trick was to travel light and long; catch your enemy off guard; strike hard and fast; and then, while your enemy was bloodied and dazed, run away. It was, in fact, the only way that worked in the dense woods of the American frontier.

Fortress Louisbourg:

I now turn to one of the centre-pieces of our story, the mighty fortress of Louisbourg.

The French, in their determination to found Louisbourg, were settled in their object to make a place so fortified that it could withstand all but the most determined and sustained force. Such a place required careful, advanced planning. Site selection was to be, as it has always been, extremely important and the French took their time on this very important aspect of fort building. During the summers of 1713 through to 1717, in more than just one harbor, small boats with French officers were to be seen casting their lead lines into the waters and aiming their angled navigational instruments at the Shore. Data was needed: the selection of Louisbourg was not to be a casual affair. It was understood that a fort's chief strength was to come from nature; man's art was needed only for enhancement. The ultimate selection of Louisbourg was to be a perfect example of this philosophy. Outside of Quebec and Gibraltar there was no better natural setting for a fort. Fortress Louisbourg was located on a bulbous peninsula with a boggy isthmus; water to three sides and a northern swamp to the forth.

Work on the fortifications of Louisbourg began in 1717. A lot of the stone work, from what I can make of the records[7], was fitted into place through the 1720s such that by 1732, the Royal battery and the barracks, at least, were completed, though it would appear that the work on the great bastions continued through the 1730s. More generally, the work on Fortress Louisbourg continued during all of its 40 odd years of existence. Stones and artisans, both from France, were brought together on the rocky windswept shores of Louisbourg: new work went up where there had been but wild shrub: new work went up where old work had been torn out because of inherent defects or damage due to winter frosts. Year after year the work continued. Huge sums were being spent seemingly to put stone upon stone. At one point, King Louis XV (1715-74), the man who authorized the expenditures, wondered out loud to his ministers if he should one day be able to see Louisbourg rising over the horizon from his palace balcony at Versaille.[8]

On the docks of Louisbourg, in 1732, we would have seen being swung in the air a large white stone which had just been off-loaded from a newly arrived sailing vessel, it could have been *Le Rubis*. Picture it, as it swung around when there came into view, in the glistening summer sunlight, the King's Coat of Arms cut into the white stone. The on-site engineers had been waiting for this piece, for it was to give the finishing touch to one of the entrances of the fort. Also on the dock, likely being unwrapped, if the weather was dry and clear as I imagine it was this day, and being much admired by a gathering crowd, was "a painting representing St. John's baptism for the chapel of the Royal Battery." By this year, 1732, the Royal battery was complete, the platforms of the King's bastion were in place and the barracks were roofed with slate, shipped over from France. All the principal chimney flues were erected and the covered way of the Dauphin bastion was complete, as well as the bridge at the gate.

France had an international reputation for building fortifications, due mainly to her famous fort builder, Vauban.[9] It was built of stone, and though there was no lack of stone about Louisbourg, it was generally but unworkable granite: proper building stone would have to be brought in from France. Earthen work, I should note, was also used. Louisbourg like all "Vauban forts" was star shaped and the fortifications were to be pierced by embrasures for 148 cannon, though not more than 90 were ever actually mounted.

While Fortress Louisbourg was made of stone, common enough in Europe, stone fortresses were not to be found in North America.[10] As a general rule, fort builders in America used Earthen work and wooden palisades. The American Fort of the wild west, as we might all easily imagine, was found in great numbers on the leading edges of the advancing European powers as they made their western assault on North America. Wood had its advantages, in that the material came ready to hand and men of past centuries knew how to work with it; a simple wooden fort could be constructed with a good team of axe wielding men within a matter of days, though a more complex one might take a couple of weeks. The trouble, however, with unprotected wood is that it couldn't last but only a winter or two; provided, of course, that the enemy didn't burn it down before hand. With dirt, of course, the defenders were likely to see portions of their bastions being sluiced away with the rain (this, for example, was a continuing problem at the English "stronghold" at Annapolis

Royal). While immensely more expensive (masons and material had to be brought over from Europe), stone was thought to be more permanent. What these early builders did not figure on, and which every gardener in Canada now knows, is that northern winters shatter stone walls, unless, in the first place, their bases are laid deep into well drained ground with all joints well sealed. It is usual in Canada, come spring, to find shoddy masonry work heaved up and splayed out and away from its original position.

The Engineers:

The engineers, under whom the impressive fortifications at Louisbourg took form, were Jean-François de Verville[11] and Etienne Verrier.[12] Verville had had a considerable amount of continental experience; and, it's principally to him — though others obviously had their say — we owe the selection of Louisbourg as the site on which the main fortifications on Île Royale were to rise. Verville arrived at Louisbourg in 1716 to carry out reconnaissance and in the next year, on July 3rd, 1717, the work on Louisbourg was begun. It is reported that Verville had differences "frequent and varied" with his fellow officers, but as an "expert" his views usually prevailed. He "reputedly was quick tempered, [and] condoned no interference with his direction of the construction (which he considered his private preserve) ..."[13] Verville supervised the work until 1724 at which time he was transferred back to France; it was then that Verrier took over. During the next 20 years, Verrier worked towards the completion of the Louisbourg complex, consisting of: the fortifications, the Royal and Island batteries, the chief public buildings, the harbor front and the lighthouse. In addition to all of these works at Louisbourg Verrier oversaw, during this period of time, the buildings and fortifications at Port-Dauphin (Englishtown), Port-Toulouse (St Peters), and Port-La-Joie (Fort Amherst, P.E.I.). The third engineering officer to follow along in the footsteps of Verville and Verrier was Louis Franquet.[14] Franquet, in 1750, arrived with a group of French officers whose duty it was, as was agreed to by the terms of the *Treaty of*

Aix-la-Chapelle, to receive the fort back from the English, who, we will see, mainly through the determined efforts of a well-led militia from New England, had captured the place in 1745 (an immense surprise to the authorities back in French and, for that matter, in England too). After the French took their fort back, during this third and last period, Franquet oversaw an expensive fix-up, a fix-up which could not withstand General Jeffery Amherst's test of 1758. Franquet, after Louisbourg's second fall, returned to France.

Of course, one should not conclude that Louisbourg was to consist just only of walls, guns and men. Certainly it consisted of all of that, but the principal purpose of Louisbourg was to support French fisherman. It was, incidentally, to be an entrepôt (the Trade at Louisbourg is dealt with in the next chapter). Fishing and trading, in centuries past, meant sailing ships and sailing ships needed safe harbors. For safe harbors, lighthouses were needed.

It was thought to be important, early on in the evolution of Louisbourg, to build a beacon which might be lit at a prominent spot near the mouth of Louisbourg Harbor so that mariners would be able to make their way in through the dark, avoiding the treacherous rocks both to their left and to their right. We see that the lighthouse at the entrance of Louisbourg Harbor was started in 1733, though not lit until 1734. It was round and 90 feet in circumference and near 100 feet high, as one New Englander described it in 1745. It was built using cement mixed at Île Royale, the limestone having been burnt in kilns and slacked for twelve months. The Louisbourg lighthouse had an impressive display of glass at its top; glass windows, as our observer reported, "12 feet long 6 wide, the sashes are all of iron." The glass was all brought in from France:

400 panes of glass of 10 inches by 8, destined for the light-house which the King has caused to be constructed on the tower built at the entrance of Louisbourg port. One will not be surprised at the size of this glazing when ... learned that the light is seen for over twenty leagues at sea, which is exceedingly necessary for the safety of the ships. Besides, these lights are kept up with cod oil.[15]

The magnified light emanated from thirty lamps contained in a large copper pan. The source of the fire, though we see reference to "cod oil," was likely coal[16] from a mine located but a short sail away. A tax was levied on vessels arriving to pay for the upkeep of the lighthouse.

This lighthouse was simply a diamond off to one side of this impressive 18th century establishment, Louisbourg. The French engineers also built, with the same impressive results: military barracks, officer quarters, a whole harbor front, warehouses, churches, a hospital and an educational facility for the children of the well-to-do.

The Hospital:

The hospital at Louisbourg was run by the Brothers Hospitallers of St. John of God, Brothers of Charity (four had come out in 1716). The structure, occupying a city block, of solid masonry, had two stories on the upper street (Rue d'orleans) and a basement on the lower street (Rue royale). "In the centre there was a spire forty feet high, which was surmounted by a cross ..." Well, let us go to Angus Johnston's description of it:

> The hospital had four main wards, with a total capacity of one hundred and four beds, besides a number of private rooms with one bed in each. The main chapel [there were a number of chapels spread throughout Louisbourg] was located at the juncture of two main wards and was partitioned off by a curtain which, when drawn aside, allowed the patients and other citizens to hear mass from the two wards, whose combined length was about two hundred fifty feet. There was also a smaller chapel which opened off the main corridor in the rear of the building. Outside the wall of the left wing, and within the hospital yard, hung the 'Institution Bell', which served as a call-bell to announce services, orders, times of meals and of work, and extraordinary events.

The Convent:

During May, 1727, Sister de la Conception[17] came to Louisbourg to open a convent. By December she was running a convent which had 22 boarding pupils. During the autumn of 1733, three more nuns arrived. The convent was a "frame house" on

Rue d'orleans just across from the hospital. The convent's financial situation was always precarious: "the governor granted the sisters one-half of the fines paid for infringements of the fishery laws and others relative to the sale of strong liquors." By 1734, apparently, there were six nuns to be seen herding their little charges about Louisbourg.

As we have seen, there were three chief engineers who succeeded one another at Louisbourg: Verville, Verrier and Franquet. In addition, there were two junior engineering officers of import: Pierre-Jérême Boucher and Jean-Baptiste de Couagne. Boucher came out with Verville in 1717 and was to be at Louisbourg, except for the 1745 intermission, until its final downfall in 1758. (If Boucher were alive to tell his story, he could tell us more about the 32 year history of Louisbourg, first hand, than anyone else that I can think of.) Couagne come down from Montreal and arrived at Île Royale earlier than Verville and Boucher, for we see that in August 1715 he was busy at Port Toulouse helping in the building of its fortifications. Earlier, Couagne had carried out surveys around the Great Bras d'Or (a huge lake forming the watery interior of Cape Breton) and around the northern shores of Cape Breton. During these times the 28 year old Couagne made his way through the forest paths and over pristine lakes and rivers with the help of two old experienced hands: the 47 year old Indian fighter, Hertel and the 40 year old privateer, La Ronde.[18] Couagne, like his fellow officer, Boucher, had a long association with Louisbourg, continuing with his duties at that place for 25 years until his death there, in 1740. The on-site supervising engineers, Boucher and Couagne, during the construction season (May to December) were usually out in the open, working with their men; during the winter they went inside the stone interior of Louisbourg and worked as draftsmen (they both married while at Louisbourg; Couagne in 1720, and Boucher in 1733). Their superior, the chief engineer, like so many of the upper-crust of New France, usually would return to the mild climate of France and the comforts of chateau and family.

The Contractors:

The contractors of Louisbourg were Michel-Philippe Isabeau and Francois Ganet. Isabeau was the first to come to Louisbourg; it was in 1717 when he came to carry out an inspection of the site. Isabeau signed an agreement with the crown on March 7th, 1719. His job was to build the King's Bastion and Chateau Saint-Louis according to the engineering plans of Verville. As a contractor, of course, he was necessarily involved with suppliers and, it was said[19] that he took advantage of his position and traded merchandise for his own account, particularly, alcoholic beverages.[20] On November 20th, 1724, Isabeau embarked on the Victoire, so to return to France for the winter: he died while at sea. And so Ganet came on the scene and took over where Isabeau left off. Ganet, like the new broom that he was, found that, in certain aspects of the fortification work, it was necessary to start over again. It was not until 1731, that Isabeau's family was to get an adjusted payment for the work Isabeau had done. It is estimated that the French government spent 1,700,000 livres on construction work while Ganet was at Louisbourg. In 1737 (and by this time the fort was substantially completed), Ganet lost out on further work, as he was underbid by another French contractor by the name of David-Bernard Muiron.

While in years past, for those interested in the configurations of the fortification at Louisbourg, one had to rely on written descriptions, certain of the important parts of the fortifications can now be seen, rebuilt, as they have been, by the Canadian government some 200 years after their destruction — Louisbourg stands today like a military Brigadoon, occupants and all. I leave off this chapter by quoting from the monumental work of John Stewart McLennan, *Louisbourg*. McLennan, more than any other person in Canada, was responsible for the restructured works of modern-day Fortress Louisbourg.

The Citadel contained, on the southern side, the apartments of the Governor and the King's Chapel, which served as parish church; the other half was occupied by barracks. The whole work was the Bastion du Roy, the centre of the system of fortification. Between this and the sea coast were the Queen's Bastion and the Prince's half-bastion. These works by 1735 were in an advanced state, although but a few guns were mounted, for at this time the defence of the town depended on the island battery, protecting the mouth of the harbour with a battery of twenty guns broadside to the narrow entrance, and on the shore of the harbour, facing its entrance, the Royal battery completed with its towers and with its guns mounted.

... The houses were built for the most part in wood on stone foundations, and were from eight to eleven feet in height; but some of them had the first story in stone, and the upper in wood. ... there seems to have been in all the British colonies no buildings so imposing as those which the French government thought suitable for this little establishment.

———————

Chapter 3

Louisbourg: Its Trade

There were a number of reasons for the founding of Louisbourg. First off, and probably the most important, France wanted a stronghold to secure its holdings on the eastern coast of North America, holdings which had been dramatically reduced as a result of the recent war.[1] Another reason is that the French wanted a fortified place to which her fishermen might resort in the prosecution of the fishery, an industry which had long been pursued and which supplied food for French tables. A third reason, was the requirement for an entrepôt which could hold and redistribute goods to the other colonies which France continued to hold in North America, particularly Quebec and her islands in the Caribbean. A fourth, which is really just an extension of this last reason, and which was not to be a stated reason, was the provision of a safe harbour for privateers who preyed on the sailing ships of New England. This last reason, or result, as we will see in due course — spelt the doom of Louisbourg.

Not much is available to us to make any determination about the content and makeup of Louisbourg's trade prior to the 1730s. Enough to say that during the 1720s and early 1730s that Louisbourg was abuilding. I note that there was, however, a significant expansion of trade between the years 1739-44, indeed, by nearly 50%; and this undoubtedly was due to the endeavours of François Bigot[2] the notorious but hard working financial commissary at Louisbourg. During the year 1739, for example, though a bit down from the previous year, there was shipped from Louisbourg, "143,660 quintals [a hundred weight] of cod, and 1,711 barrels of oil." Dried cod[3] was what was being run down into the islands so to fuel the slave labor employed in the cane fields.[4]

During 1737, imports at Louisbourg were measured at 1,427,451 livres; exports at 1,499,446. Thus there was, as economists love to say, at least for 1737, a favourable balance of trade.[5] Dried cod, was by far and away the single biggest commodity going out of Louisbourg; what came in, as we will see, was a varied and interesting mix. During the late 1730s: the goods imported amounted to a total of 1,277,881 livres of which 770,209 came from France, 288,870 from the West Indies, 142,452 from Canada, 25,865 from Acadia, and 50,478 from New England. The officials of the time, however, expressed the view that the imports from Acadia and New England were too high. People in Canada (Quebec) complained of this. An analysis of McLennan's tables reveals: that most of the tonnage was coming in from Quebec though there was a greater number of vessels coming up from Boston. The tonnage was very large from Quebec and no ships were shown which came directly in from France.[6] One conclusion might be that the French people and French supplies must be coming in *via* Quebec. In total, there are more ships and tonnage coming in from the West Indies than from Boston, but I suppose this is to be expected: trade is reciprocal, and, as we have seen most of the goods coming out of Louisbourg was being transported to the Caribbean islands. Coming in from the West Indies, in 1740, there was rum, molasses, coffee, sugar. From Quebec: flour, biscuit, peas, tobacco, wood, nails, candles, iron. From New England: live stock, bricks, planks, pork, furniture. From Acadia: live stock, pelts, flour. By 1752 we do not see any imports from New England listed, but great quantities of goods directly from France: salt, anchors, ham, fishing nets, sail cloth, olive oil, butter, shoes, wine (1,300 casks of Bordeaux), squares of window glass, and on and on; what went back to France for this, as we have seen, was wood, animal furs, and fish; to the West Indies went wood and fish. An examination of the records reveal that a lot of the incoming goods from France and the West Indies after a short resting period on the docks of Louisbourg was then shipped into New England. The tobacco, incidently, that was smoked at Acadia, Louisbourg and Quebec — and a lot of it was smoked — most likely came through trading with the English, who, of course, got it from the Virginia farmers.

Guinea Trade:

The general description of the larger western trade routes would apply to all of the trading nations of western Europe which had access to the northeastern Atlantic. This, of course, would include both France and England. Merchantmen would first load up with trading goods, usually in Holland. These large sailing vessels would then head south and eventually down along the African coast. "Goods from Europe, largely manufactures, were taken to stations on the West African coast, and exchanged for slaves, ivory and gold. These cargoes were carried across to America and the West Indies. There the slaves were sold, and in their place sugar, rum, mahogany, logwood[7], tobacco and cotton" were taken on board for the vessel's return to European ports.

To effect a trade in foreign ports one would resort to the ancient system of barter.[8] The ship's captain would value things by a "unit value." "A number of units of value was assigned to certain quantities of each kind of goods to be exchanged: a basin, a piece of cloth, a gun, or a dozen knives." A slave, as Gill points out, was valued at around 16 units.[9]

The larger scheme of the triangular trading route, as has been just described, did not impact in any direct way on the relatively few Englishmen found during these early days within the confines of peninsular Nova Scotia. What trade existed, did so strictly as a spur off the larger Boston market. Small sailing vessels would come up the coast operated by adventurous English traders. The English at Annapolis Royal and at Canso were supplied, and, more generally too, the scattered Acadian families located well up the rivers and creeks that flowed into the Minas (Grand Pré, Piziquid and Cobequid) and Cumberland (Beaubassin) Basins. Annapolis Royal, it is to be remembered, consisted of but a small English garrison forlorn and forgotten. Certainly the English were at Canso, but Canso was but a seasonal camp for the fishermen of New England.[10] The product of their efforts, dried and salted fish, was put aboard their small working vessels and brought to the Boston market. There were no warehouses at Canso, just beach huts and fish flakes. More generally, Lawrence Armstrong, the English governor at Annapolis Royal, reported on the state of trade within the province: "Very little trade: all done by four or five coasters from Boston which supply the French with European and West Indian goods and take away grain, a few fish, but chiefly furs."

Louisbourg was busy; its character was metropolitan and cosmopolitan. How impressed the newly arriving mariner[11] must have been as he first caught sight of Louisbourg from the sea. Stone walls concealing spiraling structures within, and then, as his sailing vessel closed with the land, the scene grew larger, guns and ramparts were made out in detail. This impressive scene, like no other on the North American continent, clears off to his left as he sails through the channel with the island battery bristling with crowning cannon, and then, all before him, with the wind out of the east, the full spectacle, as his fishing or trading vessel rounds and fetches up against her anchor rode. The skyline of the interior is now fully exposed, ensconced within the stone walls and bastions of Louisbourg, and speared through with the spires of the hospital and the Chateau St. Louis. All around beneath are the squared houses and fenced gardens, the docks with their arches and sheds, and the dories, and the coils of rope, the mounds of hay, racks of fish, and everywhere: boxes and contrivances; all of it, animated by soaring gulls, roaming animals and busy people.

So why did the French put so much into the building of Louisbourg? Was all of this on account of one product, namely, King Cod? Likely, yes. The north Atlantic fishery was of extreme importance to the European power, but, as it turned out, Louisbourg became a center of trade; a source of French goods for the New England Market and a northern terminus for privateers who ranged the Atlantic seaboard from the islands of the West Indies and back again. The French were bent on the existence of Louisbourg for the same reasons that New Englanders were, ultimately, so bent on her destruction. An unknown contributor to Ben Franklin's *Philadelphia Gazette*, in 1745, made the case:

From the situation of the island, it commands the Navigation up the great River St. Lawrence, and so cuts off all Communication with Quebec, by which means the whole Country of Canada must in a little Time fall into the Hands of the English, if they are once master of Cape Breton. Some of the many Consequences of which are as follows.

The French Sugar Islands would lose the chief Vent for their Rum and Molasses, and the Supply of Lumber and Provisions, they now have from Canada; and the English Islands would gain both. Great Britain must have a boundless Vent for all Kinds of their Manufactures, and command the valuable trade in Fur, with all the Indian Nations — And those, of them who live near the English Settlements, will have no French Missionaries to stir them up to a mischievous and expensive War.

While on the other Hand, so long as the French keep Possession of that Place, all the British Plantations in North America, will be liable to perpetual Annoyance from their Parties and Indians by land; and all the British Navigation to and in America, from their Privateers and Men of War, as we have sufficiently experienced the last Summer.

The first "merchant ships" arrived at Louisbourg from France on the 10th of April, 1716. From then on she was to have a steady number coming from the ports as were located on the western coast of France. It should be noted that the French government had placed strict controls on vessels working out of her ports. If a vessel was to sail to the colonies she had to be cleared first. Bonds were required to be given and forfeitures of large sums would come about if the vessel so cleared did not return and bear proof of where she dropped her cargo. This, it seems, would have had a beneficial effect on Louisbourg as she then could truly act as an entrepôt. The French cargoes which came directly in from France would be broken up and jobbed up and down the coast in the smaller vessels coming out of Louisbourg. In 1738 seventy-three vessels came from France, forty-two from New England and Acadia, and twenty-nine from Canada and the West Indies. At the latter date some fifty-four vessels of the inhabitants were engaged in coasting and trading, besides sixty odd schooners and one hundred fishing-boats which pursued the staple industry of the coast, cod-fishing.

In season, ships from Quebec, France, and New England could be found along side or riding on their moorings in the large holding harbor of Louisbourg. Trading goods of all kind could be found on the docks along with produce from the Acadian farms, especially during the months of August through to October.

The cost of food stuffs from France was very high, the supply in Canada was uncertain, from both the voyage was difficult, and the cost of transportation therefore high; intercourse with Acadia was dependent on the inaction of its English administration, who complained at a later date that there was often scarcity in Annapolis when Louisbourg was abundently supplied. The local officials therefore found themselves hampered by the prohibition of commercial intercourse with its most advantageous source of supply.[12]

The mere presence of such a volume of sea going vessels, in itself, created activities. Ships which had been weeks at sea needed more than just provisions. Equipment needed to be fixed and replaced: "Scarcely a vessel came out which did not require a mast or spar, the supplying of which gave employment to the habitant."

Much of the incoming cargo was salt, fishing implements, boots, clothing, spirits, and the like; the principal outgoing cargo was that of dried cod — a lot of it — going down into the islands, but a substantial proportion destined for the mainly Catholic populations of France and Italy, with Marseille being the principal distribution center. The value of the incoming cargo, considering the bulk factor, was much higher than that of the outgoing cargo. This simple fact led to the development of Louisbourg as a major trading center.

More shipping capacity was required to export the fish of Louisbourg than to carry thither the imports of the place. The owners loaded the vessels to their capacity, and this surplus had to find an outlet. Thus Louisbourg became a trading centre, as it were, a clearing-house, where France, Canada, New England, and the West Indies mutually exchanged the commodities their vessels had brought, to avoid making an unprofitable round voyage, which would have unduly enhanced, the cost of its fish. The tobacco, rum, and sugar of the West Indies, the cloths of Carcassone, the wines of Provence, sailcloths and linens, came to Louisbourg, far in excess of the possibilities of local use, and were sent out again. The permitted trades with Canada and the French islands could not absorb them, so the thrifty Acadian housewife bought from Louisbourg the few luxuries of her frugal life. The more prosperous New England trader, who supplied Louisbourg with building materials, with food, with planks and oaken staves, thence exported to the sugar islands, took in exchange the commodities of France and the rum-stuff of these islands. The towns of France furnished part at least of the sailcloth for his many vessels engaged in freighting and trade from Newfoundland to the West Indies. Much of this trade was illicit.[13]

McLennan reminds us that the trade numbers that might be had from the historical records can hardly, due the illegality of it, be trusted as a true reflection of the trade going on at Louisbourg. Indeed, the sad accounts of want among the people of Louisbourg, which the Louisbourg governors had sent with their pleas for money to the home authorities, should be taken with a grain of salt. For one year, into Louisbourg, according to the accounts, came livestock (many times more sheep than cows or pigs), oxen (18), corn, rice, pickled pork, pears, apples, furniture, building materials (tar, pitch, bricks, planks, shingles), axes (1,122 of them), and, of course, tobacco (316 pipes); out went rum (715 barrels) molasses, brandy (by the keg), iron, sailcloth, cordage, and Cape Breton coal.[14]

To an industrious trader at Louisbourg, opportunity presented itself from all sides. For a good example of this, one need only consider the life of Michel Daccarrette (1690-1745). Michel came to seek his fortune in the New World when but a boy. We first discover him, at the age fourteen, working at the French fishing station at Plaisance (Placentia, Newfoundland). This was during the year 1704, nine years before the place was handed over to the British by the terms of the *Treaty of Utrecht* (1713). Daccarrette, his young wife, Jeanne, and their little daughter, Catherine, came from Plaisance to Louisbourg with one of the founding groups in 1714. Daccarrette's activities at Louisbourg would have awed any casual observer. Michel Daccarrette must have been a charming trader; for, by 1726, we see that he owned fishing operations at Louisbourg (his home) and at several other outposts, including Niganiche (Ingonish), Fouchu, and Petit-de-Grat. By this date he was operating thirty-four fishing boats (shallops). Not content to just get the fish out of the water, Daccarrette traded fish, on his own account, in both France and in the West Indies. He became "one of Île Royale's largest fishing entrepreneurs and this trade provided the basis for numerous ventures." He brought back from Saint-Malo: salt, foodstuffs, clothing, hardware and marine supplies. He also was into ship building. Between 1720 and 1740 Daccarrette sold at least 17 vessels between 30 and 50 tons, valued at about 3,500 livres apiece; these sales took place, apparently, on both sides of the Atlantic. Many of these ships seem to have been built at Île Royale. It is interesting to note that Michel Daccarrette was killed during the 1745 siege; and his son, Michel, Jr. (1730-1767), returned to Louisbourg in the 1749 takeover and carried on in his father's footsteps. During the 1750s, Michel, Jr. ran at least two privateers out of Louisbourg, the *Heureux* and *Revanche*. Michel, like his father, was very much involved in the defence of Louisbourg. He headed up, in 1758, a company of militia, which was formed by the merchants of the town.[15]

As we can see from the activities of Daccarrette, shipbuilding was carried on at Louisbourg.[16] If the ship builders ran a little low on supplies, why then, they just went into English territory and got more. As one British authority complained: "In the fall, after the British guard-ship has left Canso, the French go to Pictou, build vessels, and cut some of the finest mast timber in the world and take it to Louisbourg in the early spring."[17]

The English, as far as trade went, plainly thought that they were being out-hustled. An English pamphleteer wrote in 1746:

These advantages gain'd by the French are conspicuous from the immense Sums which they drew annually from other Countries, and which enable them to maintain powerful Armies, and afford such plentiful Subsidies and Pensions to several Powers and People in Europe: From hence they build their Ships of War, and maintain Seamen to supply them. ...
     It is computed that they draw from two to three Millions of Pounds Sterling per annum from foreign Countries, in return only for Sugar, Indigo, Coffee, Ginger, Beaver manufactured into Hats, Salt-Fish and other American

Products, and near one Million more from Great Britain and Ireland only, in Wool and Cash, in return for Cambricks[18], Tea, Brandy and Wine, and thereby fight us in Trade, as well as at War, with our own Weapons. But it is to be hoped that the Measures lately taken by the British Legislature to prevent the Importation of foreign Cambricks and Tea, and taking and keeping of Cape Breton, will be attended with considerable national Advantages.[19]

And now a few words on the relationship of the Acadians with their French cousins at Louisbourg. The relationship was ultimately one as trading partners. Upon peninsular Nova Scotia being ceded by the French to the English in 1713, it was initially thought (though the treaty was short on specifics) that the Acadians would relocate to French territory.[20] However, for reasons which will in time be more fully developed, the Acadians were loath to leave their fertile lands which they had occupied for generations at Annapolis and along the upper reaches of the Fundy Basin. That the Acadians remained on their lands for forty-five years after the English captured Port Royal by force of arms is just a matter of happenstance, but as it turned out for those years, a happy one for all. The Acadians, as they had so well learned to do, continued to farm their lands — fertile lands, the likes of which are in short supply in northeastern America and which did not exist at all in the French held territory of Cape Breton Island. The Acadians continued to live on their lands, and, as is evidenced by the population levels, prospered on their own right up to that fateful year in 1755; and for this period both the English (through legal trade) and the French at Louisbourg (through illicit trade) continued to have a local food source.

With all this reference to trade at Louisbourg, one might conclude that the general population was likely well off, or, at least, well fed. But — and many will not be surprised — while trade might bring prosperity to the traders, there are always people on the margins which miss out. If traders are but running goods in and out of the port, and where there is no local food production — then the population can go hungry, indeed, famine may set in. We see that a fear of famine caused Governor St. Ovide, in 1733, to send a ship to New York in order to buy grain. In a dispatch dated May 4th, 1734, two ships were "chartered" and put under the command Gannes[21] and Bonaventure and commissioned to go to New York "in order to get provisions." It would appear, that while these two officers picked up their cargoes, these cargoes were sold off before getting back to Louisbourg.[22] One of the reasons that shortages were occurring at Louisbourg was because traders would come in and buy up supplies on the cheap (presumably because of price controls) with the result that Louisbourg was drained. Then, with the all too common short vision of bureaucrats, ordered that no "purchase in bulk be allowed until after these ships have remained at least three weeks in port, in order that the inhabitants may have the advantage of buying first."[23] The authorities were to regret such a regulation, for the number of traders coming to Louisbourg in their vessels seriously decreased. As the President of the Navy Board was to observe to the Intendant at Louisbourg, LeNormant: The captains of these vessels "did not want to return to the colony because they had been forced to stay in Louisbourg until their cargoes were completely sold. Must leave the merchants of Canada completely free, except in cases of exceptional circumstances. It is just that these traders should take advantage to a certain extent, of the scarcity of food, inasmuch as they are obliged to bear the low prices when there is plenty of it. These are the necessary changes of commerce."

Of course, not to be forgotten are the fertile lands of the French possession, Île St. Jean (Prince Edward Island, as we know it today). The authorities recognized early, the importance of this island in the upkeep of Louisbourg. "This island produces all that is needed ["wheat and cattle"] to feed Île Royale and so render this colony independent from Acadia." Certainly, if the French could have gotten farms into production on Île St. Jean, they would most certainly have done so. By 1733, there was, at Île St. Jean, a military detachment of 30 men. The difficulty was that there was no one to work the land.[24] Try as they might, the French could not induce the farmers of Acadia to come over from the English held mainland (the current day Annapolis Valley and Chignecto). The Acadians, it seems plain, did not want to leave their well-worked and productive farms, and they no more trusted the French authorities (maybe less so) then they trusted the English. Oh! The French made promises of help in the way of stock and transportation, but the first Acadian families (and these were not many) who went over to Île St. Jean sent reports back to their cousins on the mainland that the French authorities delivered only promises.

———————

Chapter 4

Annapolis Royal (1712-20)

Where the French flag, the *fleur de lis*, had flown for so many years, we now see the union jack flying over the earthen ramparts of Fort Anne at Annapolis Royal. By international law (*Treaty of Utrecht*, 1713) Fort Anne now looked over English soil. The *War of the Spanish Succession*, however, while giving England victory, had left her financially exhausted, such that she was unable to maintain her newly acquired possessions. Those who held her far away possessions, whether at Minorca or Nova Scotia, were "ragged and unpaid." "A weight of debt lay heavy on the nation, the legacy of the long war. Everywhere, at home and abroad, the soldiers and sailors and public servants were going unpaid."[1]

The blight of the garrison at Annapolis Royal might have been relieved, if only they had someone to champion their cause. Vetch and the officers thought they had the support of Nicholson, the one who, in the first place, had led them to their victorious capture of Annapolis Royal in 1710. But, no — Nicholson, while in a position to intercede,[2] not only left the garrison to completely fend for itself, but complained to the English authorities that Vetch was getting a cut of the supply contracts for the garrison — a charge which was never substantiated. It can only be concluded that, at great expense to the young British colony of Nova Scotia, Nicholson was out to get Vetch for an insult, real or imagined, which Nicholson figured he had received from Vetch. Vetch, on the other hand, did not seem to understand that the great difficulties his administration encountered in the affairs of Annapolis Royal were traceable to Nicholson and the poison which he spread about.

In autumn he [Vetch] left, for we find him in Boston in December [1713], and now, if not before, his eyes were opened to one source of his difficulties with the British Government. When he was in extremity, besieging the ministry of relief in every form of urgency, he frequently refers them to Nicholson as able to give information and to satisfy them as to the justice of his demands; he directs his agent to endeavour to secure Nicholson's influence with those in power, and he writes to Nicholson himself, seeking his aid. But there is reason to believe that the man who he was thus trusting as his friend, was all the time his enemy and doing him all the injury in his power; that he was, in fact, the 'malicious slanderer' from whose influence he had been so long suffering.[3]

With a view to repairing his damaged reputation, Vetch, leaving Caulfeild[4] behind in charge, sailed for England in April of 1714. Nicholson — though not having been at the place since its capture, and who had done nothing but attempt to destroy it in the interim, and likely knowing that Vetch was not there — arrived at Annapolis Royal in the summer of 1714. During Nicholson's short stay he assured the officers of his continuing support for them; but he fooled no one, least of all Caulfeild:

> In August, nearly two years after his appointment as Governor of Nova Scotia, Nicholson visited Annapolis. His stay was short, but long enough to bring matters into a worse muddle than ever. Caulfeild thus describes his proceeding;
> 'At his arrival he assured the garrison of his favour and interest, tho' at the same time he stopt our pay at home, injured our credit at Boston by his orders, obliged some of the French inhabitants to quit the country, shut the gates of the garrison against those that remained and declared them traitors, though he was convinced we must subsist that winter by them or perish, for by the measures he took when he returned to Boston he left us entirely unprovided in all respects.
> My Lords, were I to relate the means and methods he took when here it would be too troublesome, there never having been anything proposed by him for either the service of the country or garrison, but a continued scene of unprecedented methods taken to ruin Mr. Vetch or any other person who interposed on that head.'
> According to Caulfield not only did he neglect to provide for the wants of the garrison, but he acted as if he designed its ruin, giving as a reason that it was useless and the country not worth retaining. Indeed his conduct was such in the other colonies, that the Governor of New York deliberately described him as a madman.[5]

Though Vetch was vindicated by a titular appointment as the Governor of Nova Scotia in January of 1715, he was never again to return to North America. The thirty year old Caulfeild carried on in charge at Annapolis Royal until his death in 1717. Though fighting great odds, in the tradition established by Vetch, Caulfeild was to keep England's outpost in Nova Scotia going; this he did by spending, as so many of the English officers did in the early days, his own money and credit. But, with Nicholson gone, and Vetch in place in England — things began to change. Supplies, in the summer of 1715, for the first time, were received at Annapolis Royal, directly "from the victualling office, London, a supply of provisions sufficient to last the garrison nine months."

The garrison lived, as shipped up from Boston, on hogsheads of molasses and barrels of salted pork. Desperate as they were for essential supplies, Caulfeild pleaded with his agent at Boston for something a little special for the officers:

> ... one Pipe best Fyall Wine one Hogshead Barbados Rum one Do best Virginia leaf tobacco two ffirkins [a cask smaller than a barrel] butter one barrel of best Musquevado Sugar ten Gallons Lime Juice two boxes of Candles one box Castile Soap two pound of pepper halfe pound of Nutmeggs to ye Value of Twenty Shillings in cinnamon Cloves Mace and all Spice, I must likewise desire you will pay ye freight for there is no such thing as money here. ... [and if the agent] can meet with any good olive oil, to send 2 galls. for governor's own use.[6]

In spite of this impressive list, it appears that the garrison received, and subsisted on pork and molasses. (I suspect that the molasses was converted to an alcoholic drink, one that Nova Scotia has long been famous for — rum.) The call for victuals would come late in winter and in early spring. The soil of the Annapolis Valley, however, was fertile; and once the ground warmed up in the spring, fresh produce was not long in the coming. This fresh produce was to come, of course, from the farmers thereabouts: the Acadians.[7]

Governor Caulfeild described the three main French communities which existed in Acadia, in 1715: "Annapolis Royal, Minis, and Checanectou," as follows:

> Annapolis the 'Metropolis" has rich sound soil, produces 10,000 bushels grain, chiefly wheat, some rye, oats and barley oxen and cows, about 2000, sheep about 2000, hogs about 1000. Masting can be had with difficulty;

pitch has been frequently made. Forty thousand weight of furs have been taken out each season since the reduction of this place. "Mines none." ...

"Minis" is 30 leagues N.E. from this place: much the best improved part of the colony: plain country, fertile soil, produces over 20,000 bushels, mostly wheat with pease, rye and barley, which is their principal branch of trade. They have at present, oxen and cows about 3,000, sheep about 4000, hogs about 2000. No masting; pitch is made there and sold at cheaper rates than what is get from New England. Considerable quantity of furs brought in by the Indians and sold by the French to our traders. Copper mines there of which the inhabitants make spoons, candlesticks and other necessities. They have between 30 and 40 sail of vessels, built by themselves, which they employ in fishing. Their harbors are but indifferent: there are about 500 men, of which 200 are settled inhabitants.

"Checanectou" is situate N. about 30 leagues away; a low country, used mostly for raising black and white cattle. Were supplied from C. in out necessity with about 70 bbls. of extraordinary good beef. The greatest resort for the Penobscot and St. John's Indians, who barter to the French great quantities of furs and feathers for provisions. Oxen and cows about 1,000, sheep about 1,000, hogs about 800, corn to support their families (about 50), computed to be 6,000 bushels. Very good coal mines there, which have formerly been used by this garrison.[8]

Chapter 5

Annapolis Royal (1720-39)

The years following the *Treaty of Utrecht*, were for both England and France, by and large, peaceful. France, financially exhausted, simply had to stay out of trouble. England's direction was pretty much under the influence of the policies of Robert Walpole (1676-1745). Walpole was a Whig, a squire, one of those turn of the century country gentlemen: rough and influential. His good fortunes rose with the ascension[1] of George I in 1714. Walpole became what might be described as England's very first prime minister (1721-42). He hung tenaciously to the belief that England's best role was that of a peacemaker. With his resignation, as we will see, in 1742, England was soon involved in war, one which was to extend over a 20 year period and have its greatest impact on large stretches of the North American continent. In England during these years, the active Jacobites[2] were few, and the Tories were broken and dispirited.

Since its armed takeover in 1710, British rule in Nova Scotia was asserted simply through military fiat; though, by 1720, a more formal looking governmental apparatus came into being when the first Council was appointed at Annapolis Royal.[3] The government, however, was still, and was to continue to be until 1758, in the hands of the chief military officer in the province, dubbed the governor or lieutenant-governor. As for the governing Council set up by Governor Philipps in 1720: he might well have been inclined to put civilians on Council, except there were no English civilians about to serve in such a capacity. As for the French inhabitants, the Acadians: they were to be governed by the English Council at Annapolis Royal through appointed deputies.[4]

By 1720, there were plans afoot in Britain to pay better attention to her holdings in North America. The Board of Trade[5] was working on a report which caused it to send out orders to its various governors in America to make surveys of the "location, trade, and structure of government" of each of the colonies from Nova Scotia to South Carolina. It was to be "a catalogue of the resources which those colonies could muster against the French."[6] One such order was given to Mascarene: he was to travel throughout Nova Scotia and gather up information, particularly on its inhabitants, the Acadians. Mascarene, a French Huguenot was well suited to this job as he was completely fluent in the French language. Mascarene's report was to be transmitted by Governor Philipps to the Lords of Trade. In his report we can see Mascarene describing Annapolis Royal and its river (the British River); 'Les Mines', "a kind of scattering town"; the 50 French families at Cobequid being a hub with connections to Chebucto (which in 1749 was to become known as Halifax) and Bay Verte; Chignecto, "abounds in more cattle than any other"; and, Canso and its value as a place "so convenient and advantageous for catching and Curing Cod Fish." Further quotes may be had from Mascarene's report concerning the inhabitants, particularly those at some distance from the English fort at Annapolis Royal: "all the orders sent to them if not suiting to their humors, are scoffed and laughed at, and they put themselves upon the footing of obeying no government. It will not be an easy matter to oblige these Inhabitants to submit to any terms which do not entirely square to their humours."[7]

We have seen, during the first years of the English at Annapolis Royal, its leadership swung between William Vetch and Francis Nicholson. By 1717, however, Nova Scotia was under the wing of Governor Richard Philipps.[8] It was to be a few years before Philipps got around, in 1720, to come to inspect his command at Annapolis Royal.[9] A contemporary report on Philipps' first observations exists and reads in part as follows:

> Intrigues with the Indians. Chief of the River Indians (a small tribe) has come in, and been satisfied with my [Phillipps'] replies to his questions. Has not sent for other chiefs, as presents have not arrived. Inhabitants clearing a road to Minas, in order to retreat thither. Forbidden to do so. Deputies returned from Minas. Council resolved to send them away with smooth words,

in order to gain time, and obtain instructions from England. Situation difficult. People cannot be made English, and will not remain quiet if the peace is broken. Believe only their priests, who are opposed to the Regent: danger also from the Indians. Two hundred Mohocks should be brought from New York to operate against them. Land at Minas very productive; but may be drowned by cutting dykes.

Philipps observed that quarrels between the officers were frequent, due "to idleness, want of discipline, and strong liquors." Thus, we see where Philipps moved to get rid of the troublemakers and put his own people in place. With a letter to the Secretary of War at London he enclosed a list of "useless officers" to be either reprimanded or removed. In April, 1720, Gilliam Phillips, a relative, was sworn in as a councilor. Further, the governor arranged for his brother-in-law, Alexander Cosby,[10] to come out and assume an important civil position at Annapolis Royal.

Philipps, on his arrival, also took steps to take control of the civilian population. In April of 1720, he nominated four Acadians ("oldest and richest") to act as deputies for the troublesome inhabitants at Minas.[11] Deputies, as we have seen, had been appointed for the Annapolis area; but, this area, being less remote, was more easily controlled by direct intervention, intervention which was new to the Acadians and naturally not liked. Indeed, the Acadians saw an advantage in distancing themselves from the British and determined to build a road over which they might haul their possessions to the more remote areas of Mines or Beaubassin. "The Acadians of the Annapolis River began to cut a road through the woods to Minas and were ordered to stop."[12]

Another of the steps taken by Philipps was to put in place administrative procedures (he arrived with a copy of "His Majesty's Instructions to his Governor in Virginia"). In April of 1721, imitating Virginia, Philipps set up a general court at Annapolis Royal with the Council to act as a judicial panel (many of Council's minutes were taken up with the hearing of cases brought before them by the French inhabitants of all the districts, especially land disputes). Before the arrival of the British at Nova

Scotia there was, practically speaking, no authority to which the inhabitants could turn in order to settle disputes.[13] Thus, to have an authority in place which would settle disputes was new to the Acadians, and equally new was the mode of British punishment: I speak of the pillory and the whip which in those times throughout England and her colonies was a common enough sight. One was liable to even more severe punishment, as for example, being "Whipt at the carts tail." Examples can be readily had of the punishment meted out at Annapolis Royal during the years under review.[14]

In addition to putting in place a court, Governor Philipps took steps to increase the English presence in Nova Scotia. Though he was woefully short of them, he sent troops to Canso. Canso[15] was a natural choice to establish a garrison and to build a small fort. It was at the other end of the province and very handy to the French strongholds on Cape Breton; and handy, too, to the Acadian route used to run produce into Louisbourg, a trade which the British sought to interdict. As it happened, the English fishermen — who, oblivious to international politics, had long since established themselves there, at Canso — were "plundered" by Indians on August 8th, 1720. In the fall of the year 1720, Philipps sent a company of men[16] to hold Canso until the return of the fishermen in the spring. At that time, Armstrong had just come back to Annapolis Royal from England where he had spent four years' leave. Phillips, likely not caring for Armstrong, an irascible Irishman, was only too happy to send him off to take the Canso command.

Philipps further observes of the Indians — though only infrequently to be found around Annapolis Royal — that their minds have been poisoned by their masters: the French. The Indians, mainly because of their limited numbers,[17] in fact did not prove to be a constant problem; but the defenceless who were working in the field or on the shore just could never tell when a roving band would show up and do its worst. The result was that a work party had to always go with an armed guard, which put pressure on the limited resources of the English. We can see from the record that Canso suffered from a number of Indian raids; and this, I suppose, because they could retire to a nearby retreat, Louisbourg. Annapolis Royal suffered less from these sorts of Indian excursions; this, likely because the locals at Annapolis Royal, who gave aid to the Indians, were promptly clamped into irons. The larger Indian raids against Annapolis Royal — as for example, the one that took place in July, 1724 — involved contingents from the larger Abenaki confederacy which would have come up the coast and across the Bay of Fundy. The English fisherman who worked away from the main fortifications at Canso, during this period (1710-1724), were at the greatest risk of Indian raids. However, the Indian war, that had been going on between the English from Canso straight through and along the present day coast of Maine, was eventually brought to an end through negotiations in 1726. In November of that year, there was a great gathering of Indians at Boston. "After discussions which lasted more than a month an agreement was arrived at, the Indians engaging to abstain from further hostilities, and to give up their prisoners. They acknowledged the sovereignty of King George to the Province of Nova Scotia or Acadia. This treaty was ratified at Annapolis Royal by the chiefs of Cape Sable and Saint John, and at Falmouth in the following August, where it was signed by twenty-six chiefs, Paul Mascarene being present to represent Nova Scotia."[18]

With the coming of George II to the throne of England, it became the duty of all officers in command to make the appropriate proclamation. Armstrong, during September of 1726, was to make such a proclamation throughout Nova Scotia. We see where instructions were given to Ensign Robert Wroth to embark on the schooner *Success*, John Underwood, Master, and "by the first fair wind to proceed on your voyage to proclaim his Majesty King George the Second." Wroth was to display as much "Ceremony & Solemnity" as he could muster in these proclamations to the Acadians. This display, as was spelled out for Wroth, was to be made in order to get the Acadians finally swung over, "Promise them that they will have a free Exercise of their Religion and title to their lands." The route laid out for Ensign Wroth was to first go to the Indians of the St. John and then to Mines, Cobequid, Piziquid, and, then, afterwards, to Checanectoo. It is recommended that he consult in all these matters with Capt. Edward How.[19] Further, in all his dealings, Ensign Wroth was to keep in mind "his Majesty's Honour & Service." He was to show "all manner of Civility to the Indians who you are likewise to entertain ..."[20] Ensign Wroth departed Annapolis Royal on September 28th. On the 4th of October he was on the Saint John River, where he met with Chief Mepomoit. All of the Indians were duly impressed with the proclamation that there was a new English king and gave their assurances they wished to be friends of the English and had always suspected that the French told them lies. The very next day, with the winds being fair, he left for Chegnecto and was there met enthusiastically by the Acadian deputies. From there, Ensign Wroth sailed to Minas arriving on the 17th. While the inhabitants of Minas were considering their position, Wroth carried on to Piziquid. (He seem to deal with Cobequid in a remote fashion.) The Acadians in all places responded in the same manner, as if orchestrated. Certainly, word could not have gotten to all the communities, just in advance of Wroth and his group; they were on a fast sailing schooner. It seems without exception, all the French Inhabitants were happy with the proclamation that there was a new king in England. Indeed, there was much partying and rejoicing. They seemed to have all signed the proclamation, but would not sign the oath as proffered unless a change was made: from the words "*seray fidéle et obeiray*," "*obeiray*" was to be struck. Wroth apparently was of the view that the oath was not going to be signed unless he adjusted the wording, so he did just that. In the result, Ensign Wroth reported considerable success in that he signed up a number of the French inhabitants throughout Acadia, who, in so doing, declared their allegiance to the English crown. However, in addition to giving way on the question of obedience to the crown (the Acadians were to consistently maintain, thereafter, that they owed no obedience in respect to taking up arms against the French), Wroth granted certain concessions in respect to trade. There was to be debate about Wroth's authority to grant such concessions; though, it seems clear, that without them, the Acadians would not have signed the oaths — as in fact they did during 1726. We see, however, where Armstrong reported to the Secretary of State that he (Armstrong) vetoed it as he thought that Wroth had "fallen into very great errors by making some unwarrantable concessions which I have refused to ratify ..."

The frustrations of Governor Armstrong extended much beyond those that he had with his subordinate officers, as we see it did with, for example, Ensign Wroth. His frustrations were many, and included: the "Boston antimonarchical traders"; the French missionary priests; the Indians; the Acadians[21]; and, probably most frustrating of all, getting some simple directions from the authorities back home.[22]

Armstrong's life and death in Nova Scotia is but representative of the desperate and lonely struggle of those British soldiers stationed there during the first 40 years of British presence in Nova Scotia. A sad testimonial to this effect is to be had by looking to a dispatch sent off from Annapolis Royal and dated December 8th, 1739: "Lieutenant-Governor Lawrence Armstrong, the commanding officer at Annapolis Royal, has taken his life."

It hath been observ'd that Governor Armstrong has been for a long time frequently afflicted with melancholy fitts, the consequences of which none ever suspected till they found him dead on Thursday 6th Instant. On whose body, Maj. Cosby Lieut. Gov of the Garrison, having ordered the officers to sitt, they brought in their Verdict Lunacy.[23]

With the death of Armstrong, Mascarene, long connected with the province, came to its command as the acting Governor. Changes in the administration of the province were immediately observable, as can be seen from the governor's correspondence. Vessels over five tons (this pretty well included all except open boats) of which a number were being built along the shores of Minas Basin (Grand Pré) "must take out a Register for them before they go a trading" and make oath that no stranger or foreigner has directly or indirectly any share in them, and that the sails, cables, cordage and other tackle are of British manufacture.

Trade with Louisbourg was to grow through the years of the fort's development. Among the traders were Acadians, as well as certain "antimonarchical" traders from Boston. From the Acadian farms to the tables of Louisbourg (and at Annapolis Royal) came foodstuffs. The commanders at Annapolis Royal took steps to prohibit such trade. At Annapolis on November 30th, 1734, an order was made by Lieutenat-Governor Armstrong:

> Certain inhabitants of 'Menis, Cobaquid, Chignectou and other places' for their 'own Private Interests & Selfish views' do, in contempt of this proclamation [Phillips' order of 1731], export annually great quantities of cattle both slaughtered and alive to Cape Breton, to the detriment of British subjects 'all manner of provisions being thereby enhanced and the Stocks are Impaired and greatly diminished by such pernicious proceedings, in violations of the Laws of nations which direct all Governments and Societys of men to Defend and provide for themselves the necessaries of Life.' Prohibition renewed 'strictly and Expressly.' No cattle to be taken out of the province except at Annapolis or Canso. Even driving cattle to any other point but A. and C., as named, in order to ship them out of the province is an offence. Penalty, one year's imprisonment, and fine [£50], which may be levied by distress upon the goods of the guilty person. Half to go to the informer, 'who shall sue for the Same.

But passing laws and the enforcement of laws are very different things. The fact of the matter is that the small British garrison of a couple of hundred men located in the south end of the province, and another contingent, smaller yet, at the north end (Canso) could hardly be expected to enforce laws over the larger territory of Nova Scotia, over a territory by and large occupied by people possessing different tongues and different cultures; it made no difference that these few British officers thought their laws should apply. Enforcement called for a much larger military presence that then existed and which, as a matter of fact, did not exist until Cornwallis arrived in 1749; up to this point, British law in Nova Scotia was written on the wind.[24]

Blissfully oblivious to the rules written in English at a small and far away garrison, the French farmers at the head of the Fundy drove their cattle[25] over pathways leading to the north side of the isthmus, to Baie Verte; and there, either to board ships or to drive along the shores of Northumberland Strait until they arrived to the land of similar tongued traders from Île Royale. French silver was flowing into Louisbourg and being spent on massive fortifications and this is what drew the Acadians and their produce. Silver coin, something that could not be found at Annapolis Royal,[26] was what the Acadians wanted; and silver coin was good currency at Boston.

Chapter 6

The Lead-Up, Canso & War
(1740-44)

Canso stands out when viewed by the mariner from sea; its waters are sheltered by the surrounding islands; and, the islands have wide beaches of small stone. It is for these reasons, for more years than have been recorded, that Canso had been a rendezvous point for European fisherman.[1] They came in the spring and left in the fall. They all knew it from its Indian name, "Gamsog", and Indians were always there in the spring to greet them and to trade.[2]

Level beaches were what the fishermen were after and the Canso islands were edged with them. Raw fish had to be immediately preserved, and the two ways to do it were either to pickle it or dry it. (The "green" or "wet" preservation process could be done at sea and consisted of salting the freshly caught fish down into large barrels.) The preferred approach during the time of our story was for the fishermen to dry their catch. They made the fish as thin as they could by gutting and splitting them and then laying them out under the sun on racks built of stripped sapling poles. The poles were spread vertically, a hand span apart, and raised off the ground waist level like a large stove rack. Running towards the waters edge, the racks were as long as the beach would permit. They were two arm reaches in width and walking aisles as wide as the width of man were in between. The men would lay the fish out for the sun and the wind to do their work; flesh side up at first and then within a short time the men would walk the aisles turning the fish over, and then over again, and again, until it was hard and could be stacked like kindling wood: cured, preserved and ready for the market. The Canso islands, being so close to the great northwest fishing banks of the Atlantic, were a natural place for this activity and provided the most amount of naturally cleared and leveled areas and simply to be had by stepping off a beached vessel. That these drying beaches were situated on islands was a bonus; wary Europeans preferred islands as they gave a natural protection from animals and Indians, which might, at any time, jump out of the endless woods stretching away from the mainland shores.

By the *Treaty of Utrecht*, as we have seen, France, in 1713, was to lose Acadia. She was allowed, however, with the exception of Newfoundland, to retain the islands of the St. Lawrence, including the islands of Cape Breton and St Jean (present day Prince Edward Island). There were to be a number of French fishermen, if not French authorities, who were of the view that the islands of the St. Lawrence would include any island north of the peninsular mainland of Acadia. Thus, under this belief, a French fisherman thought he had a continuing right to resort to the small islands of Canso. The fishermen of Massachusetts, on the other hand, were of a different view — the terms of the 1713 treaty were plain and to be enforced; let the French stick to Île Royale (Cape Breton). No matter these nice international distinctions, there were to be French fishermen who continued to use parts of the shores around Canso. Skirmishes would break out. And the native MicMac, in support of their French allies, would make hit and run raids. It became a continuing sore point to the seasonable fishermen of New England: gear and catches were being lost, boats stolen, and blood spilt. Something had to be done! Thus, it is not surprising to see that during the month of August in 1717, Captain Thomas Smart, a British naval officer, in the frigate *Squirrel* (a sixth-rate frigate of 20-22 guns, carrying 100-115 men), sailed from Massachusetts for Canso. Arriving on September 6th, at Canso, Captain Smart investigated conditions and the next day he sailed off to Louisbourg to confer with Governor St. Ovide. One cannot be sure of what transpired between the two, but by the 14th of September, Smart was back in Canso where he "seized every French vessel and all French property he could find."[3] By October 4th, he was back at Boston.

The English at Canso were but 10 miles away from the French held island of Cape Breton (Petit-de-Grat); 20 miles from Port Toulouse (St. Peter's) and 70 miles away (a half day's sail with the right wind) from the French capital of Louisbourg. Captain Smart's exercise at Canso is but one of any number of examples which could be given to demonstrate, that, while there was a long 31 year "peace" (1713-44) between England and France, it was an uneasy one for those in command of the North American outposts, French or English. These two nations, no matter that peace had been declared, simply had no love for one another; and, in North America, this lack of love manifested itself into outright hostilities. The native Indians (all of them except for the Iroquois, who a good many times were the friends of no one) — and this is but a simple and governing fact — for historical reasons were friends of the French and therefore enemies of the English. Thus, during this 31 year peace, the English had always to be cautious; the Indians, being put up to it by the French, as they were, were ready to raid any undefended English position. For example, the record discloses that on August 8th, 1720, fishermen from New England were "plundered" by Indians at Canso. It was this event that caused the English authorities, in the fall of that year (1720), to send a company of men, headed up by Captain Armstrong, to hold Canso safe for English fishermen. This was the first time that English troops had wintered over at Canso. Canso was thus to be the second English garrison established in Nova Scotia since the capture of Port Royal in 1710.[4] The military presence at Canso encouraged the New Englanders to come up and rebuild facilities for the prosecution of the fishery.

It was during this time that the historical presence of Edward How comes into focus. Edward How played a significant role in the early development of Nova Scotia. From New England, How came to Nova Scotia to take advantage of the new opportunities then available to the English at Canso. He brought his family up with him and worked hard not only at catching and processing fish (apparently he ran several vessels) but also as a merchant, running fish down the coast and supplies back up. During the 1720s, Canso was to become a busy place:

At Canso there were some fifty fishing 'rooms', or shore allotments for the erection of racks for drying fish for Europe. ... At Canso in June, 1729, he [Philipps] found 250 vessels and between 1500 and 2000 men employed in catching and curing fish ...[5]

However, as the 1730s arrived, the English traders and fishermen became very conscious of the looming fortifications of Louisbourg, but a short sail away, and investment in Canso dropped off. Edward How, however, could be seen doing his best to strengthen the place (certainly the English put little or no money into the place and in the result the soldiers on garrison duty lived a tough life; the same may be said for the garrison at Annapolis Royal). In 1735, Edward How financed construction of a blockhouse, and, in 1737, he was responsible for the building of two store houses for the king's provisions; and, in 1739, he repaired the barracks. But, notwithstanding these private contributions to strengthen the place, the Canso fishery began to decline after 1735; and by 1738 the population had greatly diminished, with fewer than ten families remaining. The English garrison at Canso had, in 1734, amounted to 160 men (this is to be compared with 200 at Annapolis Royal), but by 1744 the Canso garrison consisted of only about 80 British soldiers who then were under the command of Captain Patrick Heron. Its defences consisted of a block house made of timber. It could not be expected that these English defences could withstand a concerted French effort mounted at Louisbourg.

As for Louisbourg, putting aside Quebec, by 1739, it was the most fortified place in all of America. France had spent great sums of money and continued to do so on Louisbourg almost most exclusively on fortifications.[6] In 1738, Governor St Ovide, who had taken Louisbourg through it's first 25 years of growth, was called back to France in a cloud of suspicion, the charge being that he was in a conflict of interest. In 1739, Isaac Louis de Forant had been appointed the new governor of Île Royale. At that time, too, Louisbourg was to receive a new financial commissary, the infamous François Bigot. Before coming out,

Forant had been briefed: "The difficulties between Spain and England are becoming more and more grave, and war seems inevitable."[7] The royal ministers at Versailles thought that France may be drawn in and instructed Forant to put Louisbourg in a condition to repel an attack. Every indication is that Forant would have carried out his duties enthusiastically, but, unfortunately, he was dead within the year and buried in the military chapel of the citadel. Before 1740 was out, Louisbourg had a new governor, Jean-Baptiste-Louis Duquesnel, Le Prévost.[8]

Having just been appointed on September 1st, on the 3rd of November, 1740, Prévost, this one legged naval officer stepped, ashore at Louisbourg. This ailing 55 year old, after a quick appointment and a quick sail, had come to take over the command of Louisbourg. He was in bad spirits, and not much impressed with the officers and men whom he was to command. The appointing authorities did not see fit to name Prévost governor; he was to be but only the "Commander" of Louisbourg. This contemptuous indifference — to be named commander and not governor — undoubtedly goaded Prévost; this slight was to be just another irritant to effect Prévost's state of mind.

Upon his appointment, Prévost had been given a brief history of Louisbourg: "Work has been done on the fortifications of Louisbourg since 1718. A battery of 31 twenty-four pounders has been set up at Île Royale de l'Entrée. The Royal battery, at the side of the town, 16 twenty-fours. The town must be surrounded by a wall with bastions. In its present state, it is safe from attack. The primary object of this colony is fishing, and a considerable trade is, in fact, carried on there." It is interesting and germane to the development of the events of 1744 to see that the French expressed the view that although "the island of Canceau clearly belongs to France by the terms of the *Treaty of Utrecht*, you [Prévost] are to take no steps to regain possession of it."[9]

On March 18th, 1744, a state of war was declared to exist between France and England.[10] The causes of this war, which historians have labeled *The War of The Austrian Succession*, may be briefly stated: Emperor Charles VI died and bequeathed his personal dominions of the House of Austria to his daughter, Maria Theresa. Most all of the European rulers, objecting to this bequest, took to the battle field so "to share the spoil, and parcel out the motley heritage of the young queen."

> Frederic of Prussia led the way, invaded her province of Silesia, seized it, and kept it. The Elector of Bavaria and the King of Spain claimed their share, and the Elector of Saxony and the King of Sardinia prepared to follow the example. France took part with Bavaria, and intrigued to set the imperial crown on the head of the Elector, thinking to ruin her old enemy, the House of Austria, and rule Germany through an emperor too weak to dispense with her support. England, jealous of her designs, trembling for the balance of power, and anxious for the Hanoverian possessions of her King, threw herself into the strife on the side of Austria.[11]

It will be remembered that since 1713, a year that marked the end of the previous war between England and France, the Province of Nova Scotia, as we know it today, was divided in ownership with France possessing Cape Breton Island and the British holding the peninsular part. On the peninsula there was, as we have seen, but two raggedy and forgotten garrisons: Canso and Annapolis Royal. Annapolis was then the English capital of Nova Scotia and situated at a well established civilian community of farming inhabitants. However, these civilians, with but just a couple of exceptions, were French Acadians. This pitiful English presence is to be compared to the French presence at Louisbourg with its impressive stone fortifications, complete with a French population.

This new war, as far as the New England colonists were concerned, was one which concerned European interests. They were soon to refer to it as "King George's War." William Shirley,[12] who had become the Royal Governor of Massachusetts in 1741, saw this new war as a capital opportunity to advance his own personal interests in things military; and was, as we will see, keen on mustering the colonial militias and attacking the French situated to the north, both in Acadia and in Quebec. The other colonial governors and the common man on whom the burdens would fall, however, were not so easily convinced; thus, this new war was also to be known as "Governor Shirley's War."

We can only imagine what went through Prévost's mind as he greeted the ship captain fresh in from St. Malo on that early May day, in 1744. The news was hastily blurted out: "France and England are at war!" Upon being convinced (maybe because of the short passage time[13] the French captain experienced) that the English in America had yet to receive the news, Prévost thought, if he were to act fast he would have an advantage.[14] As it was, the French could not afford to mount a large force, however, Prévost calculated that a large force was not needed because he would have the element of surprise on his side, further, the intelligence was that the English at Canso were few and had little in the way of defensive work in place.[15]

So it was that Le Prévost, the commandant at Louisbourg, felt the need to involve himself and the Louisbourg garrison in a little warfare. Some at Louisbourg thought it to be a "foolish enterprise" and "tried in vain to dissuade him"[16]; but Prévost had his way and the decision was taken to send an expedition to Canso, but a short sail down the coast. Prévost put a locally born officer in charge, one whose family goes back to the earliest times of Acadia, a 37 year old captain by the name of Joseph Du Pont Duvivier.[17] Thus, in the greening month of May, 1744, Louisbourg was busy with men and supplies spilling down the streets to the docks and out onto the waiting vessels. For the first time since its founding in 1713, Louisbourg was mustering its forces for the real thing; this great defensive fortress was now to involve itself in an offensive effort. Canso was to be French, as the French thought it ought to be; and so too soon, if these enthusiastic Frenchmen were to have their way — all of Acadia. Louisbourg, for the most part, was in high spirits as a sizable number of her military men sailed off.

On 13 May 1744, a force of 357 French soldiers[18] were carried in a flotilla of small boats to Canso.[19] In preparation for the French landing, two Louisbourg privateers began to bombard the English blockhouse with cannon-shot. When the first shot sailed through the thin blockhouse walls, the English commander, Heron, rushed out with a flag of truce, thinking "it advisable to capitulate in time to obtain the better terms." The place was then taken over by the French and they burnt all the wooden works[21] to the ground; the English prisoners were brought back to Louisbourg. Correspondence was then carried on between the governors: Prévost at Louisbourg and Shirley at Boston. This correspondence was courteous and was usually accompanied with gifts (for example, a cask of white wine from Prévost and a cask of beer from Shirley). Eventually, it was arranged to send the prisoners[20] to Boston with a promise that they would not take up arms again for a period of one year. (It is questionable, as we will see, whether Shirley kept his promise.) It was also agreed that the combatants would not intentionally interfere with one another's fishing activities.

During the course of these discussions, in respect to sending the Canso soldiers to Boston, the French were entertaining thoughts of paying an immediate visit to the only other "stronghold" in English Acadia.

Chapter 7

The Lead-Up, Annapolis & War
(1740-44)

We have seen where the English captured Port Royal in 1710. They renamed the place Annapolis Royal and established a garrison there. So too we have seen were the English authorities, the Board of Trade at London, as part of a larger exercise, took an inventory of the English holdings in America. Thus it was that in 1720, the English carried out a "survey of the location, trade, and structure of government" of each of the colonies from Nova Scotia to South Carolina. Attention was focused on French expansion. South Carolina, New York and Nova Scotia were identified as frontier colonies: Nova Scotia was to receive special attention. The Board wanted four regiments to be stationed in Nova Scotia. Further, it wanted the French residents of Nova Scotia, Acadians, evicted, and, in turn, to transport the English inhabitants of Newfoundland to occupy the agricultural lands of Acadia. However, not one of these suggested courses of action were to be implemented, at least, not for another thirty years.

We will remember too, at Annapolis Royal, during December of 1739, where the English governor, Lawrence Armstrong, "in a fit of despondency," committed suicide by running himself through with his own sword. Because of this event, during March of 1740, Jean Paul Mascarene took over the duties as Acting Governor of Nova Scotia. In this position Mascarene was to remain, until Edward Cornwallis arrived in 1749. Through the early 1740s, leading up to the outbreak of hostilities with the French in 1744, this vigorous and diplomatic[1] man, Mascarene, who had such a long standing connection to 18th century Nova Scotia, involved himself fully in the administration of English Nova Scotia. One of the first steps which he took was to make key appointments at "Grand Pré and the places adjacent within the Gut of Mines." In connection with these appointments he gave specific directions in regards to keeping registers, records, books, minutes, etc. It is to be remembered that there was no English (Protestant) civilian population during these times, only with the arrival of Cornwallis were there to be any significant number of "English" settlers. Mascarene observed, during November of 1740, that there were only "two or three English families [at Annapolis Royal] besides those of the garrison."[2] Overall, the English presence in Nova Scotia was a military one, though there were seasonal visits from traders and fishermen from New England. We see from a contemporaneous report to Whitehall, that in 1743 there were 360 British soldiers in Nova Scotia which would have been found only at two places: Annapolis Royal and Canso: approximately 200 at Annapolis Royal and 160 at Canso ("for the defense of the fishery").

... these two bodies [the garrisons at Canso and at Annapolis Royal] are so far separated, that one of them cannot possibly support the other, nor can they even communicate their distresses for want of a small Vessel to carry Intelligence. Whereas ... the French at Cape Breton are very strong ... they have several Forts and Batteries ... [and] about 700 regular troops, besides Civil inhabitants. .. this province is entirely flanked on another side by Canada and the River of St. Lawrence, in all probability upon a Rupture with France, the French would be able to possess themselves of it, without any great Difficulty, unless some fortifications were built there in proper places, and a more powerful land & sea Force sent thither to protect the Country.[3]

Further, we see where Mascarene wrote the Secretary of State on December 1st, 1743, from Annapolis Royal: "These Inhabitants [the Acadians] cannot be depended on for assistance in case of a Rupture with France ... this Province in the meantime is in a worse condition for defence than the other American Plantations who have inhabitants to defend them whilst far from having any dependence on ours we are obliged to guard against them." Mascarene continued to point out that they have only two holds on the province: Annapolis Royal and Canso. Canso "has no other defence than a Block house built of Timber by the Contribution of the Fishermen who resort there and a few inhabitants settled in that place ..." The soldiers at Canso,

Mascarene observed, were quartered in huts. As for Annapolis Royal: "the Fort being built of earth of a sandy nature is apt to tumble down in heavy rains or in thaws after frosty weather. ... the town consists of two streets, the one extending along the river side and the other along the neck of land the extremities whereof are at a quarter of a miles distant from the Fort, has no defence against a surprize from the Indians." Several of the "families belonging to the garrison" were obliged to live on this last described street as there was no room within the fort.

When word of Canso's collapse reached the small garrison at Annapolis Royal, there was panic. While they had yet to receive official word of the outbreak of war; they soon figured it out: it had come. Rumours came through the local French Acadians that there was a mass of French soldiers and their Indian cohorts gathering together at the head of the Annapolis River, 50 miles away. The English garrison at Annapolis under Mascarene was weak and small; and the English officers, aging and tiring, knew their peril was great. Soldiers and civilians, together with their families, could be seen moving carts and baggage into the confines of the fort. Cramped as they were, they were to feel better behind the protective walls of Fort Anne. As it happened, there were three ships in the basin and they were made ready to sail; a number of children and women were placed aboard and sent off to the safety of Boston, though about 70 remained behind. Another reason for getting the ships under way was, of course, to keep them out the hands of the invaders, but importantly it was to send a special plea to the Royal Governor of Massachusetts — Send Help! Expecting an onslaught, great activity ensued as the English "engineers and artificers" together with the help of the local Acadians busied themselves; timber was cut and the fort hastily patched up.[4] "The hundred soldiers began to realize that they must at least practise their profession, and discovered to their alarm that many of their muskets would not fire. The black-smith and armourers thereupon also ceased to be civilians." Days passed, and only cautiously did any one leave the fort in an effort to supplement their meagre supplies of food and fuel. Nights passed, and sentries looked out beyond the fort walls to see starry skies and the familiar lights of the local Acadians situated in the town below the fort. Time passed. The month of May went, and so did June! Where were the invaders? The first reports received in May that the French were assembling at the head of the river were false; the English were relieved. However, on the first of July the local Acadians, who up to this point had extended their helpful services to the fort, suddenly withdrew. These Acadians just disappeared; they evaporated into the sheltering woods. This disappearance and ensuing silence "signalized the arrival of three hundred Indians sent down from Louisbourg."[5]

The easy victory at Canso spurred the French at Louisbourg to implement more ambitious plans. Though 34 years had passed, the French continued to relish the idea of pushing the English intruders off of the "Acadian" peninsula. A new war! The time had arrived! It was time for the French to take back their ancient rights; it was time to turn things back to the way they were before the English had taken Port Royal, in 1710. It should have been easy enough, for the French were then acting from a base of considerable strength — Fortress Louisbourg.

In 1739, the new French governor, Isaac Forant[6], on his arrival — observing the rundown condition of Louisbourg and subscribing, I suppose, to the notion that the best defense is an offense — set in motion plans for going on the attack. John Stewart McLennan:

> Forant wrote to urge the Minister to begin the war by attacking Acadia. With two frigates, two hundred regular troops, two thousand muskets for the Acadians, whom the English would probably disarm, the expedition under his command, he would answer for the result. Acadia joined to Île Royale would make a flourishing colony, and desiring secrecy he wrote in his own hand a letter, displaying his eagerness to attack: 'I have the honour to say only, that in the situation in which we find ourselves we require fewer forts and less outlay to attack than to defend ourselves'.

Our one-legged French commander, Prévost, having arrived at Louisbourg in 1740, embraced the plans of his predecessor, and he added details. The regulars would carry 800 muskets, two hundred haversacks and 40,000 livres in cash into the Acadian lands. Further, the raid would be pulled off during the winter when the English would be ill-exercised and low on both morale and on supplies.[7]

The French knew they had the advantage because the neutral, if not friendly, local population could move without much suspicion right up to the crumbling earthen walls of Fort Anne. Further, the English defenders were few in number and poorly provided for. Their quick, enthusiastic and successful raid on Canso, notwithstanding, the commanders at Louisbourg were slow to press their advantage. Instead of directly and immediately moving on from Canso to Annapolis Royal, the only other English place in Nova Scotia, Duvivier, who was in charge of the French forces which captured Canso in May of 1744, returned to Louisbourg to accept glory and deliver his English prisoners. Discussions at Louisbourg ensued: Prévost, as we have seen, had already settled on plans which if they had been followed would have led to a quick seizure and a return of Acadia to the French. The French plans however were not carried out. The principal reason for this, likely, is because official approval from France was not forthcoming. But also, doubtless, because Commander Prévost was faced with considerable pressure from nervous civilian leaders who did not want to see Louisbourg — poorly equipped and poorly manned as it was — reduced in strength and thus further exposed to an English attack.

Though late and not universally supported, an attack, finally, was launched from Louisbourg with the objective to take Annapolis Royal. So confident were the French that they would be able to pick up hundreds of supporters (French Acadian farmers) as they proceeded towards Annapolis Royal, that they thought all that was needed was a seeding force of 50 regulars under Duvivier. Thirty French regulars embarked at Louisbourg on two vessels (the schooner *Succés* being one of them). They then called by at the French fort, Port LaJoie on Île St. Jean (Prince Edward Island) for an additional twenty more French soldiers.[8]

Having left Louisbourg during July, Duvivier and his forces landed, on August 8th, 1744, on the northern shores of peninsular Nova Scotia (Northumberland Strait, as we know it today). This could have been at Baie Verte, but in my view it was more likely at Tatamagouche (another long since established French landing place) which would have given the invaders the shortest marching route, through the Chiganois pass, to Cobequid. Messengers would have been immediately sent to the Acadian communities (especially Beaubassin). Duvivier's best chance to pick up additional help on the mainland for the attack on Annapolis would have been at Beaubassin.[9] However, as seems clear now from history, the Acadians had little liking for outwardly attacking anyone, including the English. Only a dozen or so[10] went along with Duvivier for the attack. Generally, it would appear, Duvivier's approach in handling the Acadians was lacking: to their refusals for help, all he could do was to retaliate with threats.[11]

Duvivier did not apparently spend much time in any of the Acadian communities; he and his men pushed on over the Cobequids (a mountainous range), passing through the community of Cobequid and then, fording rivers, he would have passed through Piziquid to arrive at Minas, the place of rendezvous. It was here at Minas where he was to pick up expected supplies from the Acadians. This Duvivier did toward the end of August, 1744.

It would appear that the allies of the French, the Indians, had enthusiastically embraced the French plans to attack Acadia. They were there with Duvivier when Canso was taken during May of 1744. I surmise: that they were told, after the successful capture of Canso, to push ahead and to gather up more of their friends both on the Saint John River (the Malicites) and at Stewiacke on the Shubenachdie River (the MicMacs, whose native ancestral home was Stewiacke, a place the French priest, Le Loutre[12] had picked for his headquarters in 1738). Duvivier had to deliver English prisoners to Louisbourg and arrange for additional support, especially naval support, for the intended attack on Annapolis Royal. His Indian allies would have been told to gather their forces, and, though it may be a few weeks, they were to wait for him and his regulars. I think the likely rendezvous point for the Indians would have been Stewiacke. It is an ancient fording place and a place to which, being on foot, Duvivier would have had to come.

The Indian contingent consisted of Malicites and MicMacs. This native detachment was under the guidance of "two or three white men," Abbé Le Loutre most certainly being one of them. These fired-up warriors were under instructions to hold-up until Duvivier arrived from Louisbourg with his regular soldiers. However, impatience got the best of this native force and their leaders. A decision was made to strike out on their own to take both the fort at Annapolis Royal and the glory that would come with such a feat.

Previously we had observed that on the first of July, 1744, the Acadians around and about Annapolis Royal suddenly withdrew and evaporated into the sheltering woods. This disappearance and ensuing silence signaled the arrival of a few hundred Indians. As they emerged from the woods surrounding Annapolis Royal, they caught a couple of soldiers who were outside the fort doing some gardening. These unsuspecting soldiers were dispatched in a shower of musket balls. The Indians advanced bravely up to the walls of the fort but were immediately discouraged with discharging cannon ("the mother of the musket"). Then, out of the range of the fort guns, the Indians started to lay siege to a small block-house situated in the lower town. There were but two soldiers in the block-house and it appeared to those behind the walls of Fort Anne that they would not long be able to hold out; they needed help. Also, it was recognized by the English that a force should be sent out to tear down certain of the surrounding structures which were giving cover to the invaders. A bold plan was struck upon.

They [the attacking indians] retreated towards a small blockhouse in the middle of the street in the lower town, about a quarter of a mile from the fort.

There they amused themselves by setting fire to several houses. The blockhouse was manned only by a small guard in charge of a serjeant. Realizing the peril of his position, the serjeant asked leave to withdraw to the fort. Permission was granted by Mascarene, since he was unable to relieve him. Before this could be effected however, the Fort Engineer made the proposal that Mr. How, with a party of Artificers be placed on board the Ordnance tender to strengthen the crew, and fall down opposite to where the Indians were located in the town, and scour the street with gunfire. This was done immediately and was successful. The Indians were driven back, the guard was replaced and several buildings and fences which gave cover to the enemy were either burned or pulled down. The party returned to the fort in very high spirits.[13]

And Hannay's version:

Mr. How and a party of workmen, with a detachment of soldiers, dropped down the river in the ordnance tender, and, supported by her cannon, drove off the Indians, replaced the guard, and tore down the houses and fences which threatened the block-house with destruction. They then pulled down all the houses that obstructed the fire of the fort, and the Indians, not being able to approach within the distance of a mile, gave no further trouble, except by stealing some sheep and cattle. On the 5th July, the Massachusetts galley arrived with seventy auxiliaries, which Governor Shirley had promptly sent to strengthen the garrison. The Indians immediately became disgusted with the siege, and the very same day marched off towards Minas.

As an aside I write of Edward How, the hero of the 1744 siege of Annapolis Royal. He had been, as we have seen, instrumental in the build up of the English presence at Canso. He was not at Canso when the French in May of 1744 captured and destroyed the place. At this time when the French were putting the torch to Canso and to Edward How's personal property, he was rendering a service to the English at Annapolis Royal. He had gone to reconnoiter the French establishments on the Saint John River. By June, however, the 42 year old How was back at Annapolis Royal attending a wedding — his own. His first wife had been with him earlier at Canso, but had returned to Boston where she died. His new bride was one of the Winniett girls, 29 year old Marie-Madeleine. The attacks on Annapolis Royal during 1744 is yet another point in our history during which Edward How was to play a significant role. In addition to his earlier important commercial activities at Canso, Edward How was to play critical roles in other events at Annapolis Royal, Grand Pré (1747) and negotiations at the Isthmus of Chignecto (1750). All of which we shall come to describe in a future part of this work.

So we see, that Annapolis Royal was first attacked by the Indians of Acadia in July of 1744. They had given the matter their best effort; it is just that they came to the realization that when it came to the capturing of a whiteman's fort, both technique and cannon were needed. The Indians retreated to Minas and it was there that they met the advancing French forces, numbering, I think, about 75. With new resolve they all advanced together down the valley. They soon made camp within a mile of Fort Anne and invested the British fort for the second time that year, on the 7th of September, 1744.

The first attack by the Indians did not much effect the British forces at Annapolis Royal. Indeed, in the testing of the defences, the English were better prepared to deal with the full French force which arrived before the walls some weeks later. As it was, Duvivier marched right up to the fort with colors flying together with his seventy-five French soldiers and his allies of 450 Indians.[14] All was silent at the fort, when, suddenly a cannon roared out sending a cannon ball whistling by Duvivier's ear, an event which unnerved him considerably. The French broke ranks and made a hasty retreat to their encampment about a mile back. "His Indians made disquieting attacks, night after night, on the little garrison, the commander of which had no intention of troubling the Acadians, who were left to gather in their harvests, which Prévost feared they would not be permitted to do."[15]

Duvivier figured that if the fort could not fall by the exterior pressure of fighting forces,[16] then maybe it would fall if the forces within could be broken up and turned on one another. In the days of sieges and forts, frequently during the contest, time was called out for a parley. So it was with the siege of Fort Anne in 1744. During one of the very early parleys, Duvivier told Mascarene that he expected ships, cannon and more men, urging him to conditionally surrender so that both sides could quit fighting.

If these additional forces did not arrive, why then, the English, staying alone behind their fort walls, would lose nothing until the expectant French naval forces were to arrive. If these additional forces did not arrive, why then, nothing would be lost by the English. Mascarene suspected a ruse and did not want his hands tied, though his officers thought it to be a good deal. Arguments broke out among certain of the English officers and the regular English soldiers became disgusted and impatient with their leadership.[17] Duvivier's plan almost worked, when during one of the parleys a French officer[18] started screaming at the English officers, the effect of which, was only to reunite the English officers. The guns of war were soon booming once again.

The fighting renewed and carried on for about three weeks, when, much to the delight of the penned up English and to the disappointment of the besieging French forces, there arrived further proof of the concern which the people of Massachusetts had for their outpost. Two ships, "an armed brigantine and a small sloop," sailed into the Basin from Boston under the command of Captain Edward Tyng.[19] There now arrived badly needed supplies together with seventy or eighty newly-raised volunteers and "fifty Indian rangers." The garrison at Annapolis Royal was thus to be at a strength which probably it had not been at for a long time. The arrivals from Boston in July and then again in September brought the number of fighting men up to 270. The most important addition, however, was an eager captain by the name of John Gorham[20] and a group of full blooded Mohawks which Gorham had under his charge. Gorham's Rangers put matters on an entirely different footing than what had been established over the 34 year holding position of the British in Nova Scotia. Gorham's Rangers were an offensive bunch who knew exactly how to apply frontier techniques to their benefit.[21]

With the arrival of a second load of English re-enforcements the spirits of the attacking French forces went quickly downhill. Duvivier had expected naval support but it had yet to arrive. This was his second big disappointment in the campaign (the first being the almost total lack of Acadian fighting men at his side). It was in this state of disappointment that de Gannes, one of Duvivier's fellow officers at Louisbourg, showed up at Annapolis Royal. It was likely at the very end of September that de Gannes arrived, fresh in from Louisbourg. He produced papers which effectively required Duvivier to hand over command of the expedition to de Gannes. I shouldn't think that Duvivier was too happy with this development. (De Gannes and Duvivier had spent their entire army careers at Louisbourg. They were in strict competition with one another and could barely tolerate one another's company.) Now, I don't know why it was that de Gannes was sent to relieve Duvivier. It was not because he was to take a more effective approach in the siege, because a couple of days after de Gannes' arrival the French retired from the field altogether.[22]

And so, we would have seen at the first of October, 1744, these disappointed Frenchmen and their Indian allies, in turns, paddling and marching up the Annapolis River, tracing her alluvial meanderings, the cool fall breezes pushing a light rain which rustled the golden grasses and the brilliant hardwoods behind; memories of home and hearth on the mind of every trudging individual.

As it happened, three French war vessels arrived in the Basin of Annapolis Royal on the night of October 25th. In addition to the standard crews there were on board 50 French soldiers to assist in the taking of Fort Anne. The French naval commanders were not to see a sign of their land forces.

Bonaventure [a captain of one of the French war vessels] went ashore. He, to find out the situation, aroused an inhabitant and brought him and a companion on board the frigate, and from him hears the astonishing story that de Gannes had remained only two days at the camp. The Acadians said that the fort, which contained only provisions for eight days, was ready to surrender, and that the women and children were prepared to fly to the head of the river, at the time the situation was relieved by the departure of the French. After a stay of three days the expedition returned to Louisbourg, taking with them their captures, two small vessels with supplies from Boston. The deputies of the Acadians promptly made their peace with Mascarene.[23]

Why did the French not support their land forces at Annapolis in a more timely and determined fashion? There were armed French ships at Louisbourg that summer and they simply were not deployed.[24] Presumably, the French at Louisbourg were awaiting a French man-of-war to arrive. Indeed, the *Ardent*, an impressive sixty-four-gun ship was on her way, but she was to do double duty. The *Ardent* was to first shepherd a convoy of twenty-six vessels to the West Indies and Canada. While her departure was planned for April she never got under way with her charges until June 18th. After seeing to the safe delivery of the merchant ships she arrived at Louisbourg on August 18th with a broken bowsprit, the result of having encountered a gale. By September, however, the *Ardent* was ready to take up her station off of Annapolis Royal, but she was held back by governor Prévost to "protect" Louisbourg.[25] The *Ardent* then went hunting English privateers[26] along the Cape Breton coast; she took one into Louisbourg. Finally, on October 11th, the governor was content to let her go to Annapolis Royal, rather late in the season, but the Captain of the *Ardent* was willing. The *Ardent*, however, did not go to Annapolis Royal. Apparently, at this time, there were at Louisbourg, numerous vessels of the *Compagnie des Indies* which, with the outbreak of war, had scurried into the safety of the French port of Louisbourg. The captains of these vessels implored the officials that they should be properly escorted out of Louisbourg, back to safety, back home, back to France. "It was decided that he should take them [the merchant fleet] to France, but, as the voyage turned out, he [the Captain of the *Ardent*] might as well have gone to Acadia, for the fleet of fifty-two sail which had left Louisbourg under his convoy became dispersed, and he arrived toward the end of December without any of them."[27]

As for Duvivier and de Gannes, they and their forces, being of the belief that the promised naval forces were not to come, as of October 1st, were on their northeastern retreat up the valley. By October 9th, they were at Minas, by the 19th they were handy their embarkation point on the shores of the Northumberland

Strait (so-called today). There seemed to be some intention to winter over at Minas with the "neutral" Acadians and thus be in a position to get an early spring start on another attempt to take Fort Anne. The Acadians, upon seeing the retiring French attackers in their midst, on October the 10th spoke as plainly as they could. Supplies were insufficient and wintering over would, as a fair prospect, bring on starvation for all.[28] The French commanders therefore spent little time in these Acadian farming communities and moved their men along.

We have seen where Louisbourg, at this time, had a one-legged French commander, Prévost. He was a tired sea officer suffering from ill health and one who was always of "uncertain temper." He was waiting for Duvivier's return from Annapolis Royal. Duvivier was bound to wonder as he marched along with his men, as to what kind of a reception he would meet once back at Louisbourg. He must have been turning over in his mind what he would say to his superior. What were the reasons for the failure to take Annapolis Royal. It was, he formulated in his mind, the lack of Acadian support[29] and the lack of promised naval support. He need not have wondered or worried about what Prévost might say about the matter, for you see, Prévost was beyond caring — he had died on October 9th. Duvivier arrived back to a Louisbourg which was now under the command of Louis Du Pont Duchambon,[30] Duvivier's uncle. Prévost's death did not stop the questions from coming about the aborted affair. Discussions undoubtedly continued into the long winter nights which were now to set in. There would be time enough to discuss the events of 1744 and to make plans for 1745, as the French officers puffed on their long white clay pipes and stared into the fire-places before them. The ruminating officers reflected on the mixed results of their military efforts during 1744; on their bad luck; on their short supplies; on their mutinous troops; on their cold and damp quarters; on the lack of support and direction from home.

Back at Annapolis Royal a winter's quiet descended along with a light blanket of snow now covering the denuded countryside and the roofs of the little Acadian village and those of Fort Anne. All the chimneys have smoke curling away from them. Inside Fort Anne, the English soldiers have settled in for their long winter's nap, now that the disturbances and tumults of the season had passed. It is December, and one would have seen, in Mascarene's small and dimly lit quarters within this early 18th century fort, the dancing flickers coming from the fireplace, and, off to one side, Mascarene at his small table thoughtfully dipping his plumed pen in the nearby inkwell and writing out his report to Governor Shirley.[31]

Louisbourg and Annapolis Royal were experiencing, as Shelly put it, but a smooth spot "Of glassy quiet mid battling tides."

Part Four

First Siege of Louisbourg:
(1745)

Chapter 1

Introduction: Siege of Louisbourg
(1745)

We have now seen where France's hold on North America first started to slip in 1710 when the English captured Port Royal. From that time onward, the English held Port Royal as their own and renamed it, Annapolis Royal. *The Treaty of Utrecht* (1713) was to establish England as the sovereign power in Acadia, within its "ancient boundaries." What was excluded from the territory were the islands of the St. Lawrence which included the island of Cape Breton. Cape Breton was to serve as an outlying eastern sentinel for France to its territory broadly defined as Canada with its citadel at Quebec. What was needed, as we have seen from our previous part, was a new stronghold on the northeastern coast of North America. Louisbourg was chosen. The French court then proceeded during a period that nearly extended over a half a century to spend large sums on the fortifications at Louisbourg.

From its very beginning, Louisbourg was a dangling axe over the heads of New Englanders. It was a base from which the French might stage, during a period of war, an offensive strike to the growing and vulnerable English population along the eastern Atlantic seaboard. It was, too, a harbor for French privateers during both times of war and peace. The story I have now to tell is truly amazing. It is the story of a "band of untrained artisans and husbandmen, commanded by a merchant"[1] who captured a fortress like no other on the American continent, one that had taken thirty years to build, and one that was commanded by regular French army officers and garrisoned by seasoned troops. It was to be the first feat of arms of the budding United States.[2]

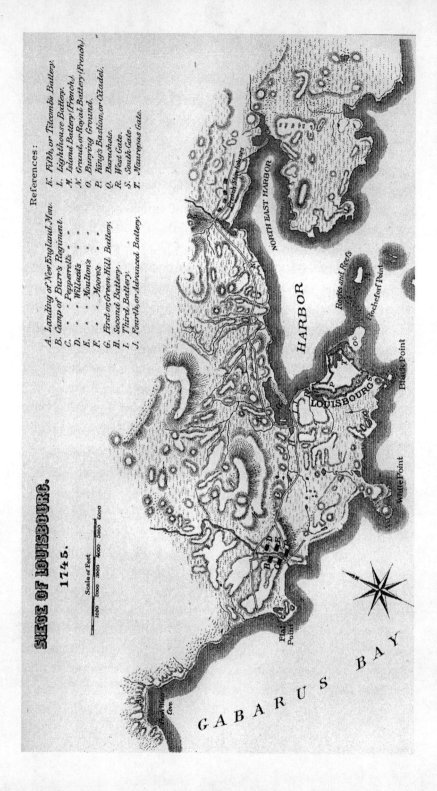

SIEGE OF LOUISBOURG.
1745.

Scale of Feet

1000 2000 3000 4000 5000 6000

References:

A. Landing of New England Men.
B. Camp of Burr's Regiment.
C.   "   " Pepperell's   "   "
D.   "   " Willard's   "   "
E.   "   " Moulton's   "   "
F.   "   " Moore's   "   "
G. First or Green Hill Battery.
H. Second Battery.
I. Third Battery.
J. Fourth, or Advanced Battery.
K. Fifth, or Titcomb's Battery.
L. Lighthouse Battery.
M. Island Battery (French).
N. Grand, or Royal Battery (French).
O. Burying Ground.
P. King's Bastion, or Citadel.
Q. Barachois.
R. West Gate.
S. South Gate.
T. Maurepas Gate.

NORTH EAST HARBOR

HARBOR

French Store houses

LOUISBOURG

Rocks and Reefs

Rochefort Point

Black Point

White Point

Flat Point

GABARUS BAY

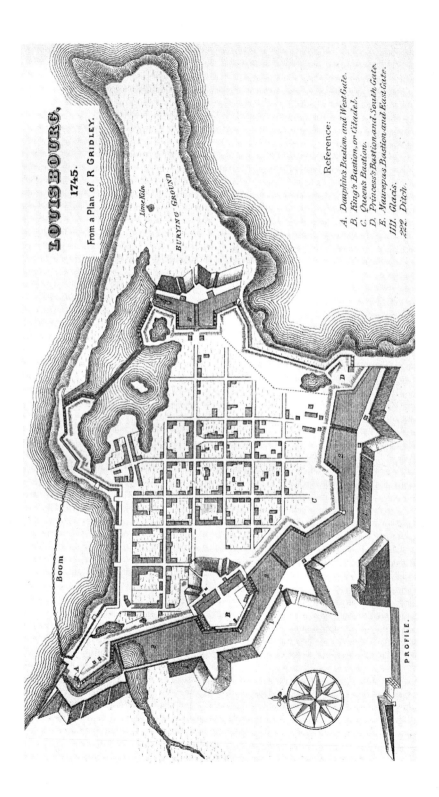

LOUISBOURG,
1745.

From a Plan of R. GRIDLEY.

Reference:

A. Dauphin's Bastion and West Gate.
B. King's Bastion or citadel.
C. Queens Bastion.
D. Princess's Bastion and South Gate.
E. Maurepas Bastion and East Gate.
HH. Glacis.
222. Ditch.

Lime Kiln

BURYING GROUND

Boom

PROFILE.

Chapter 2

Louisbourg
(1745)

St. Ovide's Prediction:

St. Ovide, the longest serving Governor of Île Royale, 1717-1739, had long predicted that an attack on Louisbourg was some day to come. He predicted that it would come early in the year, that it would be made by New England militia, and that the landing would be at Gabarus Bay.

As we have seen from an earlier part of our story, a French force in the spring of 1744 attacked Canso and forced the English to capitulate. The French burnt the place to the ground and brought their English prisoners back with them to Louisbourg. Correspondence was then carried on between the French and English governors: Prévost at Louisbourg and Shirley at Boston. This courteous correspondence (typical of the day) led to the release of the prisoners. The Canso garrison (which, incidently, included a young John Bradstreet), now released, arrived at Boston during the month of September 1744. They had stories to tell of their summer at Louisbourg. As impressive as the walls of Louisbourg must have seemed to these liberated English soldiers, they could see the weaknesses of Louisbourg and they told of them to Governor Shirley. Shirley was then to turn his long brewing plans into action.

Louisbourg Is Ill-Prepared:

Indeed, on the eve of the first conquest of Louisbourg, in 1745, we find that this fabled French Fortress was ill-prepared.

The condition of Louisbourg was in the highest degree unsatisfactory. ... it was inadequately supplied with provisions and munitions of war; its garrison was not only inadequate, but of poor quality; its artillery required an increase of seventy-seven guns to make all its fortifications effective....

This was based on the reports of the Canso prisoners, and other persons who had visited Louisbourg. In New England there must have been many scores of sea-faring people who knew Louisbourg as well as any but their native towns, all of which confirmed the news that the garrison was small, all of it discontented, the Swiss on the verge of mutiny, and the inhabitants suffering from a scarcity of provisions, the result of Shirley's own policy.[1]

Mutiny At Louisbourg:

It is time now to make a note of the mutinous difficulties at Louisbourg, difficulties which were to play such a significant role in its downfall. Certain individuals were given by the French crown the privilege of raising their own small army. Louis-Ignaz Karrer was such an individual. In 1719, Colonel Karrer raised a regiment in Switzerland.[2] It was called the Karrer's Swiss Regiment. The "owner" of such a regiment would put them out to hire, so to earn their keep. The French authorities had sent[3] Swiss troops over to Louisbourg in 1721-2. Certainly, it was Karrer's regiment that was there in 1732 when François-Joseph Cailly (1700-60c.) was posted to Louisbourg. Cailly (he was married to Karrer's niece) had arrived from Hispaniola in the West Indies to take up his new duties at Louisbourg as the commander of the Swiss troops. Now, apparently, there was always problems to some degree with the Swiss troops, mainly, I suppose, because they were not regular army and were not prepared, at times, to take orders from a regular army officer; they felt themselves to be special. Further, by and large, unlike the majority of the population, they were Protestant. So, the arrival of a new Swiss officer would hardly be an occasion for rejoicing as far as the regulars were concerned, but for Cailly, when he arrived in 1732 to take over his Swiss troops, there was extra trouble, especially as far as Governor St. Ovide was concerned. St. Ovide had heard about Cailly and was ready for him. It seems, while at Hispaniola, in 1730, Cailly was involved in a quarrel which resulted in the death of a fellow officer. While Cailly had been acquitted of murder, the family of the dead officer still held ill feelings and St. Ovide was a cousin of the dead officer. "Almost immediately there was a clash between Cailly and Saint-Ovide; the issue was

the drum roll to be used when the Swiss were on guard duty."⁴
However, it seems that Cailly and St. Ovide were shortly thereafter
to come to terms and things were soon back to their normal
state of quiet uneasiness, until, in 1740, a new commandant for
Louisbourg arrived to take the position that had been occupied
by St. Ovide. This new man was the one legged naval officer
to whom we have previously referred, Jean-Baptiste-Louis
Le Prévost Duquesnel. Directly Prévost took up his duties at
Louisbourg new conflicts arose. The fact is that Cailly and Le
Prévost could not see eye to eye, and worse, no compromise
could be worked out. At one point, in October of 1741, Cailly
defied Le Prévost in front of all and refused to assemble his
Swiss soldiers. When asked by Le Prévost to put his refusal in
writing, Cailly did so. Le Prévost made his case to the authorities
back in France with the result that Cailly was recalled to France.
He was dismissed by the authorities and pensioned off. His wife
(Anne-Marie) had been with him at Louisbourg and — likely
because her husband was obliged to take the first ship back to
France — she remained behind at Louisbourg, presumably to
settle the family's affairs. She pleaded with Prévost to put in a
good word for her husband and apparently Prévost did, as Cailly
was allowed to re-enter the service, though he never returned to
Louisbourg.

It is thought that Cailly's "vigorous defence of Swiss rights
at Louisbourg" was extreme and served to set an example of
disobedience for his men. It all came to a head just after Christmas
as the new year of 1745 dawned. As an eye witness described,
"... the Swiss revolted and had the insolence to come without
officers, drums beating, bayonets fixed, and swords in hand."⁵
Those officers who attempted to restrain them "nearly lost their
lives." The regular French soldiers were quick to join in. The
whole town became alarmed. Finally, those in charge quelled
the riot by promising the mutineers that their grievances would
be addressed. There were a number of grievances, including the
favorite of all soldiers, the food; "but their greatest grievance
was about the codfish, taken as booty at Canso" which had been

promised to them and which "the officers had appropriated to themselves, for a low price and long credit."[6]

Fortunately, the matter was brought to an end without bloodshed. The mutineers were induced to lay down their arms. They were bought off. The commissary was opened up and some seven to eight thousand livres of the king's money was paid out. At the time, no punishment was meted out; the authorities, it seems, were simply happy to see the mutinous soldiers return to their barracks. The town soon fell back into its sleepy winter mode to await the spring.

Chapter 3

The Colonial Call

As we can see from the earlier part of our history, the people of New England and of New France were constant enemies of one another. The suspicion and dislike between these two European peoples came about as a natural consequence of centuries of fighting with another; it could not be expected that it should be any different for their sons in America.

Though the directing heads of the French forces located in America were at Quebec, and while it was recognized that the taking of Quebec would be the taking of French America, in practical terms, in the days of forest paths and sailing vessels, the French at Acadia were much easier to get at than those located at Quebec. Whether, as a first step in the total elimination of the French in America, or as a step worthwhile in itself, the removal of the overhanging threat of Louisbourg, it is clear, was for the New Englanders a worthwhile objective. It made no difference to them whether this was to be a primary objective or a secondary one. The outbreak of war between France and England, for New Englanders, simply meant that it was high time to capture Louisbourg and burn out this nest of French pirates, this nest of "papists." It will be remembered that no such pretense had existed since early in the 18th century when indeed the English had successfully wrested Port Royal away from the French. But the *Treaty of Utrecht*, 1713, ended any opportunity for either the French or the English to make a direct attack on one another in North America (though the French through their Indian allies continued to attack them along the English frontier, westwardly advancing, as it was, into what the French considered was their territory). With the outbreak of war (*The War of the Austrian Succession*, 1744) both the people of New England and New France had the excuse they both had been waiting for; and, as we have seen, it was the French forces at Louisbourg who got in the first licks with raids on both Canso and Annapolis Royal in 1744.[1]

An official call to arms was made in the form of a proclamation by "His Excellency William Shirley, Esqr. Captain General and Governor in Chief in and over His Majesty's Province of Massachusetts Bay in New England." An able bodied man was to receive twenty-five shillings per month, one month's pay in advance, and a blanket was to be allowed to him. It was to be short term service (so optimistic they were) and then the volunteers were to be released so to go back to their families and regular occupations. To further entice these men, it was announced that, should a man serve in the Louisbourg campaign, he would not be pressed into His Majesty's service for two years following.[2] A further plus, and only spoken about in the ranks and amongst themselves, is the plan to have some good old fashion fun that such an outing should provide: camping with the boys; the taking of loot; and, of course, the ladies, the French ladies.[3] The New England boy proved to be no different than any other boy who is going off to war; what was missing, as we will see, was some military training and discipline.

At this time, and really right up to the outbreak of the American Revolution, there were few regular British officers and men stationed in America; some navy ships would come in during the spring and disappear in the fall of the year, like geese heading south. The militia existed — as it has always existed in any domestic community since time immemorial. It arose spontaneously among the people throughout the New England colonies; a development encouraged by the central authorities. Now, one cannot secretly call up the militia, on the contrary, the proclamation, copied and recopied on vellum paper, had to be spread by horse and sail and then turned into loud words by literate men standing on boxes in town squares. My point is: the people of Louisbourg were soon to know, most likely before the month of February was out, and most certainly by the time the spring trading ships came in with the March melts, that the *Messieurs les Bastonnais* were up to no good. While they knew they ought to brace themselves, the French took courage (and maybe too much ease) because of feelings of satisfaction and security in behind their impressive stone walls.

During 1744, with the outbreak of war and the raids against Canso and Annapolis Royal, the hot topic for discussion in the influential households of New England was whether a colonial expedition might be gotten together and sent to Louisbourg. Through the winter of 1744/45 the discussions turned from if, to how it might be done. An army was needed. However, none was to be immediately found in the American colonies. One was to be formed out of the existing colonial structure: farmers and fishermen, for soldiers; merchants and lawyers, for officers. Such an ambitious project, the taking of fortress Louisbourg, provoked much laughter in Boston. The few officers and men of the regular British forces who could be found in the colonies, snickered to themselves.[4] The colonial office back in London became increasingly more amused as the tardy and scanty reports of these organizing activities came ashore from newly arrived sailing vessels from America.

Generally, it is a difficult proposition to get independent people to move with a common purpose, particularly when it comes to political questions. The sense of independence which led to the American revolution did not spring suddenly from the collective American mind in 1776. The sense of political independence which fueled the rebellion in the New England colonies was rooted in the very nature of an Englishman's heart whether he lived in England or was re-rooted in foreign lands. Each of the English colonies were to take full benefit of the political freedom which bloodlessly came to all Englishmen and which was reaffirmed with the *Glorious Revolution of 1688*. A great number of English people came to North America to avoid religious persecution and were certainly varied in their creeds. They all carried the same ideas about popular government and how political power was to properly belong to the people and not exclusively to those with royal connections. Each of the English colonies in America had its own legislature in which would be found the people's representatives. These legislative assemblies were known by different names, for example, the popular assembly in Massachusetts was known as the "General Court," in Virginia the "House of Burgesses." The executive officer in an English colony was the royal governor as appointed by the ministers of the crown back in England.[5]

While it was principally the leaders of Massachusetts who promoted the plan to attack Louisbourg, "the response of the other Northern Colonies was considerable and prompt."[6] New Hampshire promised 500 men, Connecticut an equal number. Rhode Island authorized her sloop *Tartar* (Capt. Fones) to assist in the expedition and the raising of 150 men.[7] New York loaned guns to Shirley and voted £5,000. New Jersey, £2,000. Pennsylvania, £4,000.

After getting legislative authority[8] for the attack on Louisbourg, recruitment was soon underway. In a short time, 3,250 had signed up. One of the recruits of the 4th Massachusetts keep a diary. He wrote:

> The news of our Government's raising an army, (together with the help of the other neighbouring Governments) in order to the reduction of Cape Breton, (viz.) Louisbourg, which was like to prove detrimental if not destroying to our Country. So affected the minds of many (together with the expectation of seeing great things, etc.) — As to incline many, yea, very many to venture themselves and Enlist into the Service. Among whom, I was one, which was the, 14th of March, 1745. I, and having the consent of my friends, (and asking their prayers), (which was a great Comfort to me even all the time of my being absent.) I set out for Boston, Tuesday, March 19th. We was well entertained upon the road, and arrived, the Friday following. On Saturday we all appeared before Col. Pollard, to be viewed, both our persons and arms, Those that found their own, and those that had none, were ordered to Mr. Wheelwright's (Commissary General) to get equipment. That being done, we received our blankets at the same time, and returned to our lodging.[9]

Optimism ran high. For example, somebody discovered cannon balls in an old ordinance shed which were much too large for the portable cannon[10] — no matter, it was determined to take them. For, you see, as their intelligence revealed, these huge cannon balls would just fit certain of the big French guns — why they would just have to storm one of the batteries and turn the captured guns, back on the French — why, these balls will prove to be useful! (More surprising than this piece of optimism in regards to how these colonial cannon balls might be used, was, that they were indeed used, as we will see, just exactly as the optimistic colonials thought they might!)

The colonials convinced one another that Louisbourg would cave in directly they arrived; they passed sublime assurances back and forth to one and other.[11] One wag was of the view that these campaign planners were like novice bear hunters, busy making arrangements to sell the bear's skin before one was even spotted. Benjamin Franklin was to sound a note of reality when in a letter to his brother he wrote: "Fortified towns are hard nuts to crack [especially when] your teeth are not accustomed to it; but some seem to think that forts are as easy taken as snuff."[12] The enthusiastic military amateurs, however, were not deterred: they continued with their plans to take Louisbourg.

———————————

Chapter 4

Warren's Fleet

As it turned out the colonial expeditionary forces gathered together were to be pretty much on their own in their effort to take Louisbourg, though Governor William Shirley, at the last moment, did get significant help from the British navy, and this due to the initiative of the commander of the North American station, Commodore Peter Warren.

Shirley did not expect any direct help from England. He knew that regular British forces were needed for engagements closer to England. In any event, it seems clear, the authorities had little faith in their colonial cousins when it came to matters of a military nature. Further, it was thought unlikely, in a country with such a short season, that the fortifications of Louisbourg would give way so easily, and certainly not if the attacking army was but a scratch force lacking in cohesion and control.

Warren[1] was a naval officer with connections both back in London, and at Boston and New York. At this time, spring of 1745, his fleet was stationed in the West Indies.[2] Warren was "fully alive to the importance of reducing the French power"[3] and his views would have been known to Shirley. It was after hearing of Shirley's plans that Warren wrote London.[4] London advised that, as the commander of the naval forces in North America, the decision to go to Louisbourg, or not, was to be his. What Shirley had asked of Warren was that he should free up "two fifty or forty gun ships" to be ready by March to go with the colonial forces to Louisbourg. Shirley, it should be pointed out, was prepared to go ahead with his plans whether he got British military help, or not. Indeed, at the time he sent his colonials off on this northern adventure he had no commitment from Warren.

It is plain that Warren wanted to help his colonial friends. This Irish naval officer had charmed his way deep into the colonial aristocracy. New York was as much his home as any other place in the world. He had "a familiarity with colonial politics." So too, we learn, that from his father-in-law, Étienne (Stephen) DeLancey, a very rich merchant of New York, that Warren had developed an "appetite for investments."[5] While Warren would like to help Shirley, it was ultimately thoughts of French treasure that drove Warren to become involved. In 1744, just months before Warren heard of Shirley's plan, another navy man, George Anson, had just returned home to England, a hero, from an around the world cruise, the hold of his ship, the *Centurion*, full of Spanish treasure taken off of the *Nuestra Señora de Covadonga*.[6] Warren knew (as indeed did every captain of a British naval ship) of Anson's success and of how Anson's naval adventure had led to personal riches, fame, and promotion. Anson was an example for any naval man to follow, a man possessed of a "rational calm which no adverse circumstance could shake."[7] War between France and England was but less than a year old and prize law was in effect. Louisbourg was a destination for both commericial ships out bound and a stopover for in bound French treasure ships, and Warren knew it.[8] Warren wanted to go to Louisbourg.

After getting clearance from London the next chore was to convince his captains that they should undertake this northern cruise. His captains were convened. They were not enthusiastic. Sending a spring run of two men-of-war up the coast, one to New York and the other to Boston, would be in order; but England would be better served if the ships of the fleet stuck to their regular routes which included a continuing presence in the West Indies. Besides, his officers[9] pointed out, there's no anchorage off the hard coasts of Louisbourg. At any rate, the overall plan was fuzzy, made up by men inexperienced in military matters! Doomed it was! And, no self respecting naval officer should get himself involved in such a colonial adventure! Warren was not convinced by these arguments; his mind was made up; he announced he was going. In the exercise of his authority and proceeding under the instructions received from the Admiralty (they were not definite and Warren "interpreted them in the widest sense"[10]) Warren saw to the fitting out of three British men-of-war:

the *Superbe* (60 guns), the *Launceston* (40 guns) and the *Mermaid* (40 guns). On March 13, 1745, these three splendid ships-of-war in company with two small armed vessels and ten sail of merchantmen proceeded up the coast to Boston.

———————————

Chapter 5

Colonials At Canso

Shirley's colonial fleet left Boston on March 24th, 1745, and arrived at Canso on the 4th of April. Over three thousand men stepped ashore at Canso.[1] At that time the place was deserted, having been burnt to the ground the year before by the French. The decision had been taken to not send the colonial fleet directly to Louisbourg but rather to first stop by at Canso on the northern tip of peninsular Nova Scotia. Canso was British territory and it was there that they would gather and regroup before they made the final run up the east side of the French island of Île Royale (Cape Breton). Their objective, Louisbourg, in the right conditions, was just a half day's sail away from Canso.

It was a mixed fleet,[2] crammed full of siege supplies[3] and eager men. The voyage up from Boston took approximately two weeks, so when the men arrived they were only too happy to wade ashore to the stony beaches of the islands at Canso. Many of the sailing vessels were working boats, I imagine, normally employed by the owners in the fishery. These transporting vessels, therefore, would have been impregnated with the juices and parts of long since dead fish and thus were giving off an unmistakable odor. During their voyage, these men would have been very uncomfortable: the motion of the ocean, the smell of fish, the crammed quarters, the wet clothes, the cold food: sure, they were glad to come ashore.[4]

Seth Pomeroy lost no time in getting a letter off to his wife, Mary:

Canso, April the 6th,1745.
My Dear Wife:
    It is with great satisfaction and pleasure [that I seize] every opportunity to inform you of my welfare. I, yesterday, arrived safe at Canso which was the 14th day since we embarked. Thirteen days of being seasick, in the highest degree. Twenty four hours often without a drop or mouth full to eat or drink,

once 48 hours without. [For] days together without one mouthful of meat or anything to pass through me. The smell was more than I could bear. I do not know if a body can die of seasickness [in any event] I believed I would [and might have preferred it if the voyage] had continued a little longer. We are now in a good harbour and I feel much better. How long we shall stay here I cannot tell. Our fleet are not all yet arrived but I counted 68 sail of vessels at anchor. ... The Connecticut forces are not yet come, they are — and Warren with his men-of-war from Antigua, daily expected. ... If you should write to me, send it to Mr. Caleb Lyman at Boston. There will be opportunity by vessel that will pass and repass from the fleet to Boston every week. ... My company are all with good appetite and our provisions are good and very plenty and the daily allowance is sufficient for each man so that no body can complain ... My dear wife, my hearty love to you and the children and am your loving husband.
Seth Pomeroy.

An interesting side story concerning the transport of the troops can now be told. The colonial leaders courted risk by sending transports up the coast; not only the risk of bad weather (something to which these New Englanders who made their living on the sea could likely readily adjust) but also of the risk of running into big French gun ships that might just be lurking about (it was after all a time of war). However, since generally war ships were called to their European ports for the winter, it was thought that there was no great risk of running afoul French war ships so early in the season. In fact, the colonials did send, to assist in the military task of convoying the transports, "eleven armed privateers from 12 to 30 guns." Apparently the fleet of transports bearing the Connecticut men[5] had not far from them, but out of sight, a gun vessel, (a colonial gun vessel, generally, it should be stated, was no match for a man-o-war). The point of my side story is that the Connecticut boys might have been all shot out of the water like so many ducks had it not been for the quick thinking of a certain Captain Fones of the Rhode Island gun vessel, *Tartar*. It just so happened that a French naval cruiser, the *Renommée*, getting an early start on the season, had just come over from France. She could not get into ice bound Louisbourg harbor, so, she determined to kill a little time by cruising down the coast to see what she could see. Its a big ocean, and certainly history will show that massive fleets can sail right by each other without any knowledge of one another; but, in this case, the *Renommée* fell in with the *Tartar*. The *Tartar*, while being a vessel equipped with "fourteen cannon and twelve swivels,"[6] was no match and spent no time engaging the more powerful French man-of-war; however, the *Tartar* proved to be a most enticing decoy and led the *Renommée* away from the provincial invasion fleet, and, later, in the dark of night, slipped herself away from the guns of the *Renommée*.[7]

Once the fleet of transports were safely in at Canso[8] and likely after Captain Fones had an opportunity to tell his fellow captains of his adventure: certain of the captains of the colonial gun ships, determined to go chase the *Renommée*. As Pomeroy was to write:

> She was chased by Sneling, Tyng, Rouse and Smithers which were 16: 18: & 20 guns several more smaller ones & some hundreds of cannon fired at her yet got away from them all. The chase continued upward of 30 hours. She was about 30 gun ship, a smart sailor.[9]

The build-up of men and supplies at Canso continued throughout the month of April. The weather for the first couple of weeks of their arrival did not lend itself to camping out in the wild. By the 15th, however, the weather seemed to break and it became "pleasant and warm which seems very delightful to us all." There sprung up at Canso during the month of April a camping community consisting of over 3,000 men.[10] Families of men were to gather nightly around their respective fires; and larger groups came together at times throughout the week as was required for organizational matters. On Sundays, all the men would come together to hear their preachers.[11] On the 13th, a "block house" was erected, one that had been precut and ready to go up in the course of a day or two; it was armed with eight-pounders[12]; and, when finished, christened Fort Cumberland. Sailing vessels of all kinds kept coming in to Canso; and, a regular run was established so that there was to be continuing contact with the administrators back in Boston and missed supplies could be ordered or reordered. The arrival of any vessel from back home was always welcomed and when a "prize" was towed in the news rippled through the encampment and a large crowd gathered at the shore ever so ready to lend a hand in getting the goods ashore.[13]

Fighting, in the main, was to take place at Louisbourg, but there was some excitement to be had at Canso. Indians were lurking about, just waiting for their chance. On the 14th of April, Capt. David Donahew "came in with eight Indians; one of them a king, one of them a Queen."[14] On April, the 21st, Sunday, four New Englanders while ashore gathering wood were ambushed by an Indian and two Frenchmen. Pomeroy writes that these men were unarmed and one was shot at by a Frenchman, the ball having grazed one finger and carried through his coat sleeve. They gave themselves up to the French group and were then force-marched through the woods. After having traveled about ten miles they stopped for a rest and during this stop the New Englanders overpowered their capturers. Of the three, the Indian made his escape. The best that the New Englanders could do with the seized French muskets was to get off a couple of shots at their running target. The New Englanders, and their two French prisoners, were of the belief that the Indian was hit and likely died in the bush. The next day there was discovered "their canoe that they [the two Frenchmen and the Indian] came in and a bottle of rum in it."

Another source of excitement for the New Englanders was when they attacked the small village of St. Peter's, just a few miles away across the open water. On the 21st, "Two sloops with 70 men sent to St. Peter's. ... The sloops return from St. Peter's, they did nothing but burnt a few houses and brought away a small sloop, there being more French and Indians than expected." Talk was then obviously had about how they ought to go back and do a proper job of it. On the 29th of April, the same day that the main invasion fleet had set out for Louisbourg, a significant number of vessels made St. Peter's their objective. "This morning the fleet sailed from Canso to Louisbourg, Colonel [Jeremiah] Moulton with a detachment of about 400 men were ordered to St. Peter's to demolish it under convoy of Capt. [John] Furnell in the New Hampshire sloop."[15]

Having left Antigua in the West Indies on March 13th, as mentioned earlier, Warren's fleet made its way up the Atlantic coast from the Caribbean, and, on April 10th, fell in with a schooner from Marblehead. The Captain of the Marblehead schooner was to inform Warren "that a Fleet of 63 Sail had sailed 14 days on Sunday last with 5,000 Men for Canso under the Command of Generall Pepperrell."[16] Being unfamiliar with the waters, Warren took the schooner master on board the *Superbe* to act as a pilot; and, leaving his accompanying merchantmen to go into Boston harbor, took his fleet to Canso. Warren's fleet was to arrive off Canso on the 23rd of April.

Warren's fleet laid off shore and did not come into the harbor, though it undoubtedly was spotted by any number of the gawking colonials on the shores at Canso. Warren determined not to spend any time getting into Canso but rather kept his crews at their sailing quarters with a view to reaching his objective as soon as possible, now but just a few miles up the coast. Warren was keen to cut off access into Louisbourg Harbor so as to prevent any French war ships from getting in (in this objective he was to be entirely successful). He was also interested in preventing any supply vessels from getting in (in that regard he was not successful, but mostly so). From my reading of the accounts, the first English man-of-war to arrive was the *Eltham* under the command of Phillip Durell. The *Eltham* "had wintered in Boston and now returning after acting as convoy to 'mast ships' from Piscataqua."[17] Warren had gotten a message through to her, in care of Boston, that directly she was properly provisioned and made ready for sea, she was to join him off the coast of Louisbourg. Durell, in fact, arrived at Canso, just a day before Warren's fleet arrived. Durell in the *Eltham* came but "to the mouth of the harbour." Our journalist confirmed this with his entry of April 23rd that "Admiral Warren with three ships came by the harbour bound to the Cape he lay to one night for to speak with us."[18] So, we see, ready to do their important blockading work, four of England's finest men-of-war, of whom we shall hear more: *Superbe* (415 men, 60 guns), *Eltham* (250 men, 44 guns), *Mermaid* (250 men, 40 guns) and the *Launceston* (250 men, 40 guns). With the arrival of these powerful armed vessels, you might imagine all the colonials were further pumped and primed. As Seth Pomeroy wrote on the 23rd: "this was a fair day."[19]

This was April in Nova Scotia and many of the inlets and harbors around Canso (though Canso itself was clear) were still iced in. Our colonial evaders were keen and anxious, and all wondered what the conditions were like at Louisbourg but fifty miles further up the coast. On the 21st, a New England sloop was sent up the coast and she put her nose into Louisbourg Harbor and found it "full of ice." On the 24th, into Canso came the Connecticut men, 500 in number.[20] This latest contingent were to be met by the some 3,500 that had been there since the first of the month. All, at this point, were resolved to go to Louisbourg, surely the ice must be melted by now; all that was now needed was the right wind. Within a few days the right time arrived. On April 29th, with a 100 vessels[21] transporting them, this enthusiastic crowd headed up the coast and then into Gabarus Bay.[22]

Chapter 6

Colonials On The Beaches

The garrison at Louisbourg at this time had "only about 1,350 militia and 560 regulars."[1] They were under the command of the acting governor, Duchambon.[2] Louisbourg, it's governor, and most of its men had never been tested in battle.[3] The French, however, felt comfortable and reasonably confident behind their big stone walls.[4]

In 1734, in one of his reports to the authorities back in France, St. Ovide the French governor at the time predicted the events of 1745:

> ... if England made an attack on Louisbourg it would be by New England militiamen, of whom he had not a high opinion; that they would be supported by English men-of-war, and that they would come very early in the year in order to prevent the fishermen from France, or vessels of force from entering Louisbourg; ... [and] that the landing would be made in Gabarus or Miré bays.[5]

Now, much of North America in 1745 was a wilderness; there were no roads over which carts might be hauled. Interestingly enough, however, Cape Breton was ahead of the times: it did have roads. The French during the 1730s built them. Indeed, the locals were so busy building roads that the authorities in France expressed concern, mainly because it tied up men who otherwise might be fishing. The two principal roads brought into being at this time was the one leading inland to the farming lands of the *Miré*, and the other up the coast to *Havre de la baleine*.[6] The French were of the view that such roads were needed for communications. Besides, the road "will help to create some good settlements and will facilitate the carrying of lumber." The authorities back in France were concerned that the building of roads would — should Louisbourg come under siege — assist the besiegers. The local authority countered that the road to the

Miré "is more than a league distant from gabory Baie, this being the way by which the enemy could come, and that this piece of land impassable."[7] And they were right, too. These roads, as were in place at the time, in 1745 — the one inland to the Mira and the other north up to Baleine — did not assist the besiegers in getting ashore with their men, supplies and cannon. These roads, however, did assist in getting the English scouts back and forth to the far points where there was established outposts. It was thought these outposts were necessary to give the invaders ample notice if rescuing forces should come overland towards their back. This is something, incidently, which during the course of the siege both Pepperrell and Warren were continually concerned about.

And so we have the setting as the New Englanders scrambled over the sides of their anchored vessels and into smaller row boats. The coast around Louisbourg is rough and it is much to the credit of these New Englanders that they made their way ashore, especially since there is always swells coming in from the facing North Atlantic, no matter whether the wind is up or not. Through the surf and up and over the bouldery beaches came these enthusiastic men. They might have been amateur soldiers, but when it came to the handling of small boats, there was no group more expert. They came ashore in whale boats and dories; and within a period of eight to ten hours of their arrival, on the 30th of April, nearly 2,000 men gained the beach[8] at the Anse de la Cormorandiére, which today we recognize as the beach at Kennington Cove,[9] a position which is approximately three miles down shore of their objective.[10]

Behind the walls of Louisbourg there was much consternation: Governor Duchambon dawdled.

We now make mention of two French citizens of Louisbourg: Morpain and Boularderie.[11] Captain Morpain was a pugnacious 59 year old, a successful privateer who for years had worked out of Louisbourg; he was known and feared in the shipping circles of New England, the dreaded "Morepang." Boularderie was of the French aristocracy who had connections at the Court of Versailles. It is these two, once the magnitude of the English attack was realized, who urged Governor Duchambon to get out and fight the English on the beaches.

De la Boularderie said that, under cover of the woods, a force could advance within half a pistol-shot of the beach; that half of the garrison should be sent out to fall on the enemy, who would be in that confusion which always attends landings; that they would be chilled from exposure, and that they were, moreover, but poor creatures ('*misérables*'). Morpain recounted his exploits in 1707 [when last the French and English were fighting in Nova Scotia] and appealed to Du Chambon to give him leave to go out with those of the townspeople who were willing. Du Chambon, who had taken the view that he had no men to spare, at last gave way. Fifty civilian volunteers and twenty-four soldiers, the latter under Mesillac Duchambon, the Governor's son, the youngest officer of the garrison, set forth from the town with vague instructions and under uncertain command.[12]

So, there unfolded along the shore at Kennington Cove (as we know it today) "a short but smart engagement" between the French and the English. A Massachusetts man was to contemporaneously write up the event:

April 29th:
The Fleet sailed from Canso, with a fair Wind, and were off Chappearouge Point, about Eight of the Clock next Morning — Upon their Appearance, the Garrison made an Alarm to call in the Inhabitants from the Suburbs, and neighbouring Settlements — The Fleet anchored in Chappearouge Bay about 10 of the Clock, and the Signal was immediately given for landing the Troops — whilst the boats were getting ready — A party of the Enemy (about 200) shewed themselves on the Shore, marching towards the place where it was proposed to land our Troops. Upon which some Boats filled with men were ordered to make towards the Shore, as tho they would land, about a mile below the place designed for landing, which diverted the Enemy from proceeding further till they saw the Boats put back and row up the Bay, and by this Means some of the Troops landed and drew up on the Beach before the Enemy got to the place of their Landing — When about 100 of our men were on the Shore, part of them marched towards the Enemy, and Scouts were ordered to search the neighbouring Thickets — lest a large Body of the Enemy might have Sallied, and concealed themselves, in order to draw on our men too hastily — in the mean time the men continued landing with all the Dispatch possible, — The Enemy advancing along the Shore were soon met by our Men and after several Volleys exchanged, the Enemy fled, and we took — prisoners

and killed — more, without any Loss on our Side This Day, landed about 2,000 Men during which time the Enemy burnt all the Houses without the Walls on the West part of the Town — and Sank the Vessels in the Harbour. The Enemy began also immediately to secure the low Wall at the South East part of the Town by adding on the Top of the Wall a plank with pickets about — feet high and placing a range of pickets about [so many] feet within that Wall and planted a great Number of Swivel Guns upon the Wall next to the Harbour —

Our Massachusetts soldier continued to write in his journal:

May 1st
Landed the remainder of the Troops and began to encamp — and to get on shore some provisions and Stores. ... The landing of the provisions and Store (as well as the heavy Artillery) was attended with extreme Difficulty and Fatigue for want of a Harbour for the Vessels, the Surf running very high on the Beach almost continually, and oftentimes so that there was no landing — so that the Men were obliged to wade into the Water, to their Middles and often higher, for almost every thing they got on Shore which would other wise have been spoiled with the Salt water. — and were obliged when their Labour was over to lay on the Cold Ground in their Wet Clothes under no better Covering than some Boughs laid together — the nights exceeding cold and foggy — but no Signs of Discouragement or Complaint appeared in any of the Men who seemed resolved to surmount all Difficulties.[13]

The French effort to stop the landing was a case of too little, too late.[14] Certainly both Morpain and Boularderie gave the matter their best efforts, but to no good end. Boularderie was twice wounded and forced to surrender.[15] Morpain was also wounded, but found cover and was assisted in his escape by Georges, his 13 year old black slave.[16] After the passage of three days, Morpain and Georges found their way through the lines and back into Louisbourg.[17] The superior numbers who came up against the brave followers of Morpain and Boularderie soon prevailed and the inadequate French force sent to the beaches were dispersed.[18] Emboldened as they were with their preliminary success, the provincial troops advanced freely towards their objective. "In a few hours irregular groups of them emerged from the woods overlooking the town, in which their exultant cheering could be heard."[19]

Duchambon, in his report[20] to the authorities, let on that he had little advance knowledge. That, practically speaking, he had no knowledge at all until he saw a lot of ship activity off of the mouth of the harbor (April the 9th & 30th), and — can you believe — he wondered whether they might be French at the time? It was only when Duchambon saw a hundred sail in Gabarus Bay and the countryside infested with the enemy did he close the gates of the fort. This he did only after, as if it were good tactics, he gave orders to desert his only two strongholds outside of the main fort: the Grand Battery and the Lighthouse Battery. Further, with the reality of the calamity having finally penetrated into his distracted mind, Duchambon gave further orders to sink the ships in the harbor and to burn everything outside the walls that could be burned. Louisbourg was under siege.

Outside the walls of Louisbourg, that evening, April 30th, 1745, there was "Singing and Great Rejoicing" and the New Englanders were to sleep "in the open air" with dreams of a great victory ahead.[21]

Chapter 7

Annapolis Royal Spared &
A Spoiled Rescue Attemp

On May 1st (os[1]), 1745, New Englanders were before the French walls of Louisbourg, and were so, in considerable force. In addition, her sea lanes were completely cut off by Warren's fleet. The terror of war was to be brought home to the inhabitants at Louisbourg.

In this war, it was not the New Englanders who started the hostilities; it was those at Louisbourg. The first military strike was made by the French. In an event previously described, during May of 1744, a force of 357 French soldiers was carried in a flotilla of small boats to Canso to wage war on an English garrison which was unaware that war had even been declared. This French force had no problem taking the place, and its occupants as their prisoners. Canso was then burnt to the ground. Then we saw, within months of the Canso raid, where the French proceeded to invest the only other English stronghold in Acadia, Fort Anne at Annapolis Royal. During the course of the summer and fall of 1744 the French and their Indian allies had launched two separate attacks; but, due to bad luck and bad management, the French and their allies were not successful in the taking of Fort Anne and had to retire as the cold winds heralded the coming of another Acadian winter.

The retiring French forces had formed the intention of wintering over at Minas so as to get an early start in the spring (1745) in their offensive against Fort Anne; but the "neutral" Acadians upon seeing the retiring French attackers in their midst spoke plainly to the French commanders: the supplies and accommodations in Acadia were insufficient to maintain both the inhabitants and a wintering army. The French, I think somewhat surprisingly, took no issue with the Acadians and left the countryside and returned to winter over at Louisbourg.[2]

The defenders, after the last of the French besiegers retreated from the field, in October of 1744, were much relieved. The English at Annapolis Royal, however, yet had their work cut out for them. They wanted to bolster the neutrality of the Acadians; get badly needed supplies up from Boston; and, importantly, to rebuild their defenses at Fort Anne. From the con-temporary correspondence we may see that the commander at the English fort, Mascarene, was in communication with Governor Shirley and the Bostonians are seen to continue to take care of their hard pressed countrymen located at this protective northern post. Additional men and supplies were sailed up the coast to the relief of Annapolis Royal both during and after the sieges of 1744. As for the Acadians: Mascarene was to receive deputies from all areas, including those from Beaubassin. The deputies, who came in on their own, gave continued assurances that the Acadians, while unwilling to take up guns in support of the English, would not do so for the French (and by and large they did not). As for the dirt and wooden walls of Fort Ann: they were rebuilt with the help of Acadian labor. As Mascarene wrote:

> I had also prevailed with the Deputies of the Inhabitants of this river to furnish the Engineer the materials requisite for our repairs at the stated price, which, they seemed to undertake and perform cheerfully, and tho' the season was far advanced when the enemy totally left us, two Bastions have almost entirely been revested before the winter set in ... We have had no Enemy about us and the Garrison has been pretty easy ... The French Inhabitants have in general behaved well though it can not be surprizing the Enemy has creatures amongst them.[3]

While the English were fixing defenses at Annapolis Royal, at Louisbourg the French were making offensive plans. Communications were to pass between Quebec and Louisbourg. There was indeed to be a renewal of the effort to put all of Acadia under the *Fleur de Lis*. To achieve this, all that was necessary was to take Annapolis Royal. What was planned was to send out from Louisbourg an armed force similar in size and makeup to that force which it had sent out in 1744. At the same time Quebec would send down a number of soldiers which would meet up with those from Louisbourg somewhere on the peninsula — maybe Beaubassin, more likely Tatamagouche, or maybe Cobequid. What unfolded was that on January 15th, 1745, a detachment of about "three hundred troops, chiefly Canadians" under the command of the Marins (Paul and his son Joseph) was sent overland to the east. They traveled, as it seemed always French raiders and their Indian allies did in those days, in a line together, all covered in furs, on snowshoes, assisting their dogs in the pulling of sledges or toboggans over snow and ice, day after day. After weeks of such travel the Marins and their company of Canadians arrived in Acadia, and there they held up to await word from Louisbourg. Upon arrival the Martins had sent a messenger to Louisbourg advising that their Quebec contingent was in position and waiting to meet up with those from Louisbourg. The plan being that together, as a combined force, they then would advance south down the peninsula to attack Annapolis Royal. The Martins did not know of Louisbourg's impending peril; presumably the authorities at Louisbourg did. The messenger arrived at Louisbourg, but was put none the wiser. We now pick up the story as told by *The Anonymous Habitant*:

> The messenger whom M. Marin sent to us asked on his part for provisions and munitions of war. We should have sent back the same messenger to urge this officer to come to our help, but we were without forethought and were so far from such wisdom that steps were taken in the month of April to comply with his requests; we did not send provisions, however, for he let us know that he recovered some. [From the Acadians?] He was urgent in requesting powder and balls, and in granting his wishes, we made two irreparable mistakes. In the first place, we deprived ourselves of the help which this officer [Martin] was able to bring us; instead of explaining our situation, as we should have done, we gave him to understand that we were strong enough to defend ourselves. In the second place, already short of ammunition, especially powder, we further diminished our supply.[4]

Thus, the message received by the Marins was that they should proceed to Annapolis Royal and attack, even though he could expect no additional help from Louisbourg. The senior Marin (one can imagine with a Gallic shrug of his shoulders) turned and marched his forces off to Annapolis Royal. Within two weeks of the Marins putting Fort Anne under siege (May, 1745) another messenger came paddling down the Annapolis River; Louisbourg was under attack and the Quebec forces were now needed.[5] On May 24th, to the considerable relief of the English garrison at Annapolis Royal, the Marins and their forces packed up and got themselves going in the direction of Louisbourg.[6]

The Marin forces moved swiftly overland, likely getting assistance both from the Acadians and the MicMac. The Marins sent a message up the coast in a friendly French schooner, but she had the misfortune to be driven ashore just as she was coming about to go into Louisbourg harbor. The crew got away into the woods but the beached vessel was left to the English. Aboard was found the dispatch to Governor Duchambon from Lieutenant Colonel Marin. Marin was on the march with 1,300 men, his own and a strong contingent of Indian allies,[7] and would soon come up to a body of water, the Strait of Canso. Since the Strait needed crossing, Marin in this despatch (which fell into English hands) is seen asking the French governor to send as many small craft as possible down the coast so that the rescuing forces might be ferried over the Strait, and thus to be in a position to "thrust across Cape Breton Island to the relief of the Fortress."[8]

Thus, another piece of good luck for the New Englanders. The English knew that all that was needed was to lie in wait and ambush the French rescuers. Pepperrell, upon reading the intercepted message, immediately sent from Louisbourg to Canso the Rhode Island gun vessel, *Tartar* (Capt. Fones). You will remember the heroic effort at Canso when the *Tartar* and her crew had led the French man-of-war, the *Renommée*, away from the transports. This time, when Captain Fones arrived at Canso, he found a British warship and two small brigs, which, apparently, had just put in. Off they all went, this hunting flotilla, taking with them the Canso garrison. Clearing Chedabucto Bay, and sailing into the narrow channel of water which separates mainland Nova Scotia from Cape Breton, they headed northwest in a prevailing breeze to a point where St Georges Bay funnels into the Strait of Canso with lookouts at all the mastheads. They soon spotted, at a place called Passe du Fronsac, a swarm of canoes and boats. More good luck, the crossing had just begun! These little boats dotted the waters, more were being launched. It was short work for the English in their vessels. It was a matter of leveling their big guns and then to mow down small gunless vessels, a convoy of canoes loaded down with men and supplies. Needless to say, the French rescuers were scattered; no more was to be heard from them.[9]

In his report, filed with the French authorities after the fall of Louisbourg, Duchambon gave his understanding of what happened to Marin and his men in the Straights of Canso:

> Finally about three or four hundred of them embarked, some in a boat of approximately 25 tons, others in about one hundred canoes. As they were weathering a promontory in the bay, they were attacked by a privateer carrying fourteen cannon and the same number of stone-cannon pierriers. Our officer held off the attack vigorously, and just as he had gotten himself into a position to board the privateer, another one of equal strength came to its aid, and M. Marin was forced to give up and make for shore.

So it was, that the would-be-rescuers were disbursed before they got to their objective. There is evidence that some of them did get through to the outskirts of Louisbourg but not in sufficient numbers to make any difference to those behind the walls at Louisbourg.[10] With the Marins and their forces having been thus turned away, the promise of deliverance in which the people behind the walls at Louisbourg had placed so much stock, was broken. Within a couple of weeks of the disheartening news that the Marins had been defeated on the Straits of Canso, the French at Louisbourg, as we shall see, sent a white flag out into the field.[11]

Chapter 8

The Taking of The Royal Battery

Our scene shifts back to the bastions and bulwarks of Louisbourg and the amateur army which had landed in whale boats on a nearby shore. There then followed, as we have seen, "a short but smart engagement." The few brave Frenchmen who had met their attackers on the beach, other than those that were captured, fled to the safety behind their stone walls. The colonial troops then "filled the country." The French inhabitants who lived and worked within a mile or two of the walls of Louisbourg ran to the gates and did not apparently spend time gathering up their possessions.[1] The New Englanders were disorganized and undisciplined. Directly they found an empty French structure, they put it to the torch. The officers, when they finally caught up with their enthusiastic raiders, took them to task. This was not so much that they made certain French families homeless by their activities, but because many of these structures housed very valuable supplies which the invaders might well need before the event was over, such as sails and cables.[2]

The older and more experienced of the New Englanders (no less enthusiastic but possessed of an understanding that first things came first) continued to stick to the shores, or returned after taking a peek at this fabled fortress as supplies had to be landed and a camp set up.[3] This was to take time and some planning as there was considerable difficulty in landing guns and stores "for want of a harbour" and "the surf running very high" and the men "obliged to wade into the water to their middles and often higher."[4] By the 3rd, all the men meant to be ashore, were ashore. And, while there was yet some heavy work to do in getting the cannon off the ships and placed before the walls of Louisbourg, the feeling at this early point, was that — "We all seemed to of one heart and things are in a good posture."[5]

I now tell of an event that occurred just after the New Englanders landed and pushed to the outskirts of their objective. It was a very fortunate event, indeed; an event which was yet another piece of good luck for these amateurs who had "a tough nut to crack"; an event which made a critical difference in the capture of Louisbourg. The colonial invaders were to take the Royal Battery away from the French without a shot being fired. But before telling of that event we best remind ourselves of the physical positioning of the principal defenses of Louisbourg.

In describing the fortifications of Louisbourg in an earlier part of this work, it was pointed out that the defense of the town depended on two fortified gun batteries located beyond the reaches of the main fort, itself stuck on a rocky peninsula which acts as a lower jaw at the mouth of the harbor. This mouth stretches for about a mile to the upper jaw, Lighthouse Point. It is through this mouth that a ship must sail in order to get to the harbor side of the town. The outer edge of the peninsula, the eastern facing edge of Louisbourg, is impregnable having as it does a piece of Nova Scotian "iron bound coast," an eastern facing shore lined with a granite face and smashed continually with the breaking waters of the North Atlantic. These shore conditions extend out to the end of the peninsula on which Louisbourg is located, and beyond, in a submerged fashion, half way out into the harbor's mouth to an island located about midway between the enclosing jaws of the peninsula and Lighthouse Point. No ship can enter to the south of this island, between the island and the peninsula. She would be grounded and soon come to pieces from the action of the churning waters against the graveled granite just below the surface. The channel into the harbor was to the north of this small island, between it and Lighthouse Point. On this island the French built a small independent fort with cannon; the Island Battery, with thirty-six guns broadside to the narrow entrance.[6] A second independent fort was located on the shore of the harbor immediately opposite, northwest, situated like a uvula to the mouth of the harbor. Thus, it was, that any ship trying to get into

Louisbourg harbor would face a deadly cross-fire between the Island Battery and the shore battery.[7]

The shore battery to which we just referred, it needs to be pointed out, was not only located opposite the entrance of the harbor but also opposite, or nearly so, to the north-western edge of the town. Old Louisbourg, as has been stated, is located on a peninsula, the neck of which wore its heavily fortified walls. The town was within three walls. The fourth side, the north side of the peninsula, was where the docks were located. This side was comparatively exposed, as it must be, if it was to carry out its water borne trading activities. The shore battery was located about two miles along the curved shore of the harbor, but only about a mile across the harbor, in a straight line, just as a cannon ball would fly. This shore battery was very much the pride of the French engineers; it was called the Royal Battery. It was a very impressive stone structure complete with walls, towers, and twenty-eight 42-pounder cannon, mounted and pointed to the mouth of the harbour.[8] The French were just then (1744/45) in the process of carrying out improvements to the Battery's land-side walls; in preparation, they had leveled certain areas leaving openings which were vulnerable to attack. There was to this fortification, however, a serious geographical flaw. Inland of the Royal Battery there was higher ground which an invading enemy might easily command.[9]

Given the above description, one might now imagine the surprise of our colonial raiders, when the very next day after they land, a detachment sneaks up to take a look over the brow of the hill in behind the Grand Battery and find that it was deserted; the French had left it for them, guns and all. Well, these English colonials could not believe their luck. The small force which occupied the Royal Battery was headed up by Colonel William Vaughan; it was to be Vaughn's moment of glory.

One version (Downey) has it that Vaughan did it with twelve men. They had just finished, without any resistance, it would appear, torching "several large storehouses," likely somewhere between the fort and the Grand Battery. These storehouses were filled with combustible naval supplies (pitch, tar, cordage, and wood); it sent up a glorious signal. Being handy, the small group decided to have a peek at the Grand Battery — And, what to their surprise! No one was home! We quote from a journal kept by one of the New Englanders:

> This morning we had an alarm in the camp supposing there was a sally from the town against us we ran to meet them but found ourselves mistaken. I had a great mind to see the Grand Battery, so with five other of our company I went towards it and as I was a going, about thirty more fell in with us. We came in the back of a hill within long Musket shot and fired at the said fort and finding no Resistance I was Minded to go and did with about a dozen men setting a guard to the northward, should we be assaulted [when we saw] two Frenchmen whom we immediately took prisoners [along] with two women and a child. [We] then went in after some others to the said Grand fort and found it deserted.[10]

Fairfax Downey describes the event this way:

> The Battery was strangely silent. There was a lifeless look to it; no smoke from the chimneys, a soldier pointed out. But even the impetuous Vaughan was not going to be drawn into a trap with a rush to storm a fort of that size with thirteen men. He beckoned an expendable one of them, a Cape Cod Indian, gave him two lusty swigs from his silver flask of brandy and told him to take a look inside. The Indian slithered through the brush like a snake and up and over a low-leveled stretch of rampart. He vanished, reappeared, stood up and waved them forward.
>
> Muskets cocked — it might still be a trap — the colonials crawled through embrasures, squeezed past the big spiked 42s, and entered the deserted stronghold. Aside from themselves, the only living things in the fort were a forlorn woman, left behind in the haste of departure, and a puppy. Vaughan called over eighteen-year-old William Tufts of Massachusetts, borrowed his bright red coat, and had it hoisted up the bare flagstaff.

A message was sent to Pepperrell — sweet to all the colonials only just then trying to take up positions before the looming fortifications of Louisbourg; and sweetest of all to Vaughan — "May it please your Honour to be informed that by the grace of God and the courage of 13 men, I entered the Royal Battery about 9 o'clock, and am waiting for reinforcement and a flag."[11]

(Incidentally, the New Englanders had made up their own flag and brought it with them, a crude drawing of Lady Britannia sitting with banner and a union jack shield.)

Why did the French desert one of their prime defense positions. This decision, as more generally the defeat of the French at Louisbourg in 1745, can be laid at the feet of Governor Duchambon. The fact is: that as soon as the New Englanders arrived, Duchambon hauled everything in, turtle-like, and hunkered-down with his people behind the stone walls of Louisbourg. The governor did consult with his advisers, but the only discussion, somewhat heated, that was had was over whether the battery should be totally destroyed, or not. Étienne Verrier, the proud builder of the Royal Battery must have been very upset to see, so early in the conflict, the French give up the "Royal Battery," but he was totally distracted by the suggestion that it should be blown up, a suggestion to which he was "firmly opposed." Verrier won out, the governor did not insist, and Louisbourg suffered. "The battery would be abandoned but not destroyed, its guns would be spiked and its stores of foodstuffs and munitions evacuated to Louisbourg." The work was too hurriedly carried out; and, while steel rods were driven into the touch holes, the anxious soldiers neglected to smash "either trunnions or carriages" and left "virtually all the stores behind in their flight into Louisbourg."[12]

In short order, as we have seen, Vaughan and his small band entered this fortification of which the French were so proud and which the French believed they could reoccupy directly the New Englanders got tired and went back where they came from. Their pride was pricked when they spied from their ramparts, across the harbor, and instantly took note of the red "flag" flying from their Royal Battery. Soon they had "four boatloads of troops" being rowed across the bay; determined they were, to go back, retake, and make sure that their earlier spiking job was good enough. At this point, there were only a few New Englanders in the Royal Battery, however they had the upper hand as they occupied a fortified position which could hardly be taken by an approach from the harbor. The approaching barges were peppered with musket balls. There were more then just musket balls flying. The French boys at the main batteries located at both Louisbourg proper and at the island decided to join in and were lobbing cannon balls at the Royal Battery, which, as most fell short, only served in the colonial defense. Thus, the French proceeding in the boats were getting shot at from the front and the back. With the arrival of fresh New England troops, the meager French attempt to regain the Royal Battery came to an end; they beat a hasty retreat. The Royal Battery (also known as the Grand Battery) from this point on was to remain firmly in English hands.

By May 3rd, the armorers of the enterprising New Englanders, headed up by Major Seth Pomeroy, drilled out the spiked vents of three of the big guns at the Grand Battery. These enterprising men leveled these large guns, and, in time, had them doing the deadly work for which they were designed.[13] The inhabitants of Louisbourg were soon to feel the effect as deadly projectiles dropped directly into the town. As one resident of Louisbourg bewailed, "the enemy saluted us with our own cannon, and made a terrific fire, smashing everything within range."[14]

In time, most all of the big guns of the Royal battery were unspiked and made operational. Samuel Waldo, who was put in charge of the Grand Battery's guns, was certainly impressed with them, "as good pieces as we could desire." The problem was, "they devoured too much powder." Waldo feared he couldn't keep them going. Not, however, for lack of balls! The reader will recall that the optimistic New Englanders had brought large cannon balls along which would just fit these big French 42 pounders.[15] However, due to falling levels of gun powder,[16] the New Englanders could not keep up the intensity of the cannonading to any great extent; at any rate the most serious problem was that, "we are in great want of good gunners that have a disposition to be sober in the daytime."[17] Here Waldo puts his finger on the most difficult problem which faced the commanders of the New England forces, to which we will refer.

And so we see, that within three to four days of their arrival, the invading New Englanders were in full charge of all the ground beyond the walls of Louisbourg. They had with considerable ease, with thanks to a thoughtless move on the part of the French, captured 36 big guns which they could have never brought, landed and emplaced; and which, in turn, were used with terrifying effect on the French people harboring within their walls. So far, the English had much for which to be thankful and none in that age were embarrassed to get down on their knees under the direction of their religious ministers and offer to their maker their thanks.[18] So far, so good: but there was siege work ahead; and too, death and disappointment.

———————

Chapter 9

Siege Work

At Louisbourg, during the first week of May, 1745, there was a disuniformed collection of Englishmen in charge of the surrounding grounds. The initial success of these reveling invaders, achieved without any loss, had come about more to good luck than to good management. They had many detractors both at home and abroad; many, who would have bet good money (and would continue to do so, despite this initial success) that bunches of farmers and fishermen headed up by lawyers and merchants would not succeed at cracking this French military nut. The boys from New England may have been enthusiastic and excited; more so, now that they were before the walls, standing there back at a safe distance, their mouths agape, marveling at this medieval apparition. The next stage, however, the detractors might well have said, would require some real soldiering. There was no place in all of English North America that could compare to Louisbourg with its European style fortifications. Many of the young colonial boys must have been rudely started by their guffawing elders. There was work to be done; there was a siege to be gotten underway.

Behind the walls with the French governor, Duchambon, were 2,500; and out in the surrounding woods and bogs with the English general, Pepperrell[1] were 4,000.[2] A formal siege during the times of which we write was "a highly standardized process of advancing guns and men up to the walls in a series of parallel trenches connected by zigzag approaches." No one had illustrated this to the colonials. Indeed, they had originally thought that they could just run up to the walls, and, climbing over, surprise the French in their beds. This idea of a surprise attack was soon forgotten, especially after certain of the landing parties were forced to mix it up with Morpain and Boularderie. So, a siege it was to be. The colonials hauled their cannon off the ships, over the rocky beaches, and over impassible bogs (thought so by the French). Then, under the cover of night and fog, to set up their cannon and to start blasting their cannon balls against the fort. All of this activity of *les Bastonnais* was very much to the amazement of the French regulars who had come to expect a siege was an artistic event which took time to stage. This view of things mattered little to these enthusiastic raiders from New England. They had a French fort to take; they were fresh; and they were no strangers to weltering work and tricky terrain. On account of non-stop hard work, on the fifth day after the landing, "a battery was in position opposite the citadel at a distance of 1,550 yards, and then opened fire on the town."[3]

The English landed 34 guns and mortars and they were, at first "stood ranked on their wheeled carriages or platforms along the beach." One is going to have to go to Louisbourg to appreciate the challenge that then faced these New Englanders. Between the landing beach — which, as we have seen, was approximately three miles away — and the walls of Louisbourg, there was a Nova Scotian bog. Indeed, such a bog practically ringed the neck of the peninsula on which the fort was built. I would describe it as a thin lake with a bottomless bottom of mud all covered by a thick carpet of moss and low bush. The New Englanders, familiar with methods of moving large boulders in the business of clearing land back home, built 16 by 5 foot sleds (stone-boats) and loaded up a cannon on each. There were no horses,[4] no oxen: just men to move the great burden over the bog, the marsh, the swamp, the "miry barrier, the mud sucking trap." From a contemporaneous report prepared under the supervision of Pepperrell, we read:[5]

The transporting the cannon was with almost incredible labour and fatigue. For all of the roads over which they were drawn, saving here and there small patches of rocky hills, was a deep Morass, in which whilst the cannon were upon wheels, they several times sunk, so as to bury not only the carriages, but the whole body of the cannon likewise. Horses and oxen could not be employed in this service, but the whole was to be done by the men, themselves up to their knees in mud at the same time. ... They went on cheerfully without being discouraged or murmuring, and by the help of sledges of about sixteen feet in length, and five feet in width, and twelve inches thick they transported the cannon over these ways, which the French had always thought impassable for such heavy bodies; and was indeed impracticable by any people of less resolution and perseverance, or less experience in removing heavy weights; and besides this they had all the provisions, powder, shot and shells, that they daily made use of, to transport over the same ways, upon their backs.[6]

When reflecting on the trouble that the invading force took to get cannon in place, it is important to understand that cannon were absolutely necessary if fortifications are to be pierced and opened up for entry. One could just cut off supplies and wait for the effect of starvation to take hold; but such an approach was not an option to invaders camped on barren lands with freezing weather, ever, just months away. This much Pepperrell understood, advised as he was by a regular British naval officer, Peter Warren: the English had a chance for success, but only if immediate pressure was brought to bear on the population of Louisbourg and if such pressure was to be kept up in a relentless fashion.[7]

The pressure to which Warren referred and which he could not himself directly effect, was to keep up a steady cannonade of Louisbourg. The primary purpose, of course, would be to make a breech in the fortifications, but more generally to rain down missiles upon the heads of the besieged which it was hoped would cause the terrorization of the sheltering population which would release internal political forces leading to a capitulation. For this last purpose, the captured French Royal Battery was used to full advantage. At Louisbourg, what was needed, and what was planned for, was a battery or batteries positioned as near as was possible to their target. This target was the west gate, the principal entrance from the land side. There were three batteries set up: the "Eight Gun Battery," "Titcomb's Battery"[8] and "Sherburne's Battery"[9] (the latter sometimes during the course of the siege referred to as "The Advanced Battery"). These batteries were fascine batteries.[10] "Titcomb's" was to eventually consist of five of the 42 pounders which were hauled over from the Grand Battery and was located northeast, 800 yards from the West Gate and was operational by May 20th[11], after which date, it was booming away on target. On the 17th "Sherburne's" was raised 250 yards from the same gate; it mounted two 42 lb cannon which were laboriously hauled from the Royal Battery.[12] Though, as we will see, the New Englanders were to do considerable damage with these batteries that they had set up, they did at times, due to their inexperience, managed to do damage to themselves; this, because too many times they stuffed more powder down the barrels of the cannons they served than they could stand, once ignited. "We have split 3 cannon at the Grand Battery." So too, one of the cannons mounted at a fascine battery, "broke ... sorely wounding the chief gunner so that his leg was cut off."[13] Another example is given by Joseph Sherburne who was in charge of the Forward Battery, he wrote in his journal, "loaded the 42 pounder by some unskillful hand which split one and dismounted another blew up about 1½ barrels of powder killed two men and wounded two more."[14]

I should note, before passing on, that the besieging batteries were not constantly firing away, for, in respect to the land forces, there was a general shortage of powder. And, even when powder showed up behind the lines,[15] it had to be a tricky and risky business to get it up to the batteries.[16] Naval powder, for whatever reason, was not made available to the colonial batteries. My general impression, is: that while Warren and Pepperrell were to receive compliments for their cooperation with one another throughout, Warren would only send help, by way of men and/ or supplies, if such a step was to suit the objectives of the royal navy. The principal objective being to get ships into Louisbourg Harbor, so as to reduce Louisbourg with naval guns. And so, we do see where Warren did send men to assist in the attempt to silence the Island Battery; or, powder when a grand assault was planned just before Louisbourg's capitulation on the 16th of June (OS).[17] I think, though, that early on, Warren did send some of his experienced gunners to shore, for at least a period of time, in order to give some badly needed direction to the New Englanders who had little or no experience in the handling of big guns, and who were doing themselves grievous damage and injury due to their mismanagement and inexperience.

Not all New Englanders were involved, in any steady way, in the excessively arduous work of establishing batteries and serving them, indeed, most of them were not. A number were to be sent out to scout and keep an eye on the wide perimeter. As a general proposition, these men were undisciplined, untrained and totally disinterested in military procedure; a number were out for loot and a good time. Certainly most of them, it seems, were pouring rum into themselves, day and night. Further, there are numerous forthright references made in the journals about the plunder and destruction that went on.[18] Samuel Waldo, who, you will remember, was put in direct charge of the captured Grand Battery, observed that three fourths of those under his charge "are partly employed in speculation on the neighbouring hills and partly employed in ravaging the country."[19]

Plainly, both Pepperrell and Waldo were very much perturbed with all this pillaging, but it would appear there was not much they could do about it.[20] War is a harsh activity and the participants are usually in no position to give much regard to civilians who get in the way. This is so with a disciplined army; with irregular troops war is that much more of a scourge, as the unordered with their blood worked up go about combing and looting the countryside.[21] This activity slowed down as the pickings in the surrounding communities became slim. One, however, should not take away the impression that all the New Englanders were there just to loot the place. There were some very serious men at work who thoughtfully and carefully and with great dexterity and industry did all to advance the goal of taking Louisbourg, believing as they did that it was a threat to their country and their families.[22] Many men were to maim themselves as they hauled material to the lines and went about the business of erecting batteries. "These were pushed forward with a celerity which was possible only among a force made up of men, some with the dexterity of seafarers, others with that of woodsmen accustomed to handle mast timber from the stump in the forests of New Hampshire to its berth in the vessel."[23]

And so we see, by about May 20th, some twenty days after their landing, that the New Englanders had the siege of Louisbourg well and truly underway. The invaders were in charge of the entire countryside. They had set up their cannon in two separate batteries but a short distance from the West Gate and were battering it away. At the same time they were making full use of the Royal Battery approximately a mile across the harbor water, north of the city; lobbing missiles directly into the city. All of this was having considerable effect and the French were busy throwing up additional breastwork atop their walls and repositioning their cannon. And, if we were there, then — high on the walls — we would see to the east in the direction of the ocean and out of firing range, Warren's men-of-war "cruising off and on before the mouth of Louisbourg Harbour."[24]

———————

Chapter 10

Royal Naval Operations

We have seen where Warren left Antigua on March 13th, 1745, in his flag ship, *Superbe*, a large man-of-war (60 guns) in company with the *Mermaid* (40 guns) and the *Launceston* (40 guns). They arrived off Canso on April 23rd. Just at that time they were joined by a fourth, *Eltham* (44 guns) which had come up from Boston.[1] They did not spend any time at Canso but proceeded, all four, a further way up the coast in order to blockade Louisbourg.

The French, in choosing a location on the northeast coast of North America for their new stronghold, certainly chose right. Louisbourg has an inner harbor access to which can be denied to any sailing vessel, armed or otherwise. This was to be accomplished by placing cannon-fortresses at key positions found within this rock ensconced harbor. One should consider the harbor and the locations of the Royal Battery and the Island Battery. Once the French had fortified the place, during the 1730s, to sail into Louisbourg Harbor was to sail close by the mouths of well bunkered cannon. The French military engineers, some would argue the best of the age, in the building of the defenses at Louisbourg, had indeed taken full advantage of the coastal configurations of the place. While naval cannon could, soon enough, bring her occupants to their knees, its impenetrable harbor kept Louisbourg out of reach, as, naval ships would be ripped apart upon their entry. Warren's job, therefore, as he would have known, was to shut the place up by maintaining a blockade, he never had any reasonable expectation of getting into the harbor to use his naval cannon on Louisbourg.[2]

So, initially we see Warren with four British men-of-war standing off the mouth of Louisbourg Harbour.[3] With such a number to be effective they would have to keep sailing and stand in fairly close to the shores surrounding the mouth of

Louisbourg Harbor; so close, that on occasion the French gunners were tempted to get in a shot at them.[4] Rarely did these vessels go into Gabarus Bay, the handiest anchorage outside of Louisbourg Harbor. They would constantly have been sailing back and forth, no matter the weather[5] or sea condition; for a blockade was only effective if they were to keep at it. If a sail showed up on the horizon, in concert with the other blockading vessels, and ever mindful of keeping a continual cover on the mouth of the harbor, they would chase it down. This business would require the involvement of all available vessels. We see, however, on May 7th, or thereabouts, where the *Eltham* was detached and sent over the top end of Cape Breton Island to get at the settlement at St. Anns (Port Dauphin), there "to burn and destroy what they could of the enemy."[6] Because of the limited number of the ships in the fleet, and because they were not entirely devoted to the blockade, Warren, while achieving considerable success, did not shut down Louisbourg's harbor entirely. We see, that on May 13th, "A French snow from Bordeaux got in ..."[7] Warren wrote of this:

Sir,

I have received yours, and am extremely sorry to hear a snow is got in, when there are now out two men-of-war and eight colony cruisers, most of them to the eastward. As Mr Noble says many more may get in, I should have gone to sea before I received yours if it had been possible. I always thought the grand battery could have prevented a snow from getting in. I advised an English flag on the lighthouse, and am sure it would have a good effect, for, as I have often told you, if all the cruisers in Britain were here, vessels may escape them. I shall sail the moment I can with the *Launceston*, who has fitted her main yard that was broken.[8]

Warren Takes the *Vigilant*:

The role of Warren's fleet at Louisbourg, therefore, was to lock up Louisbourg's harbor. Its job, in this regard, was to be made easier and indeed the role was to change with the addition of more men-of-war. New arrivals, and a capture, as we shall see, were to eventually put eleven British war ships off Louisbourg though not all of them were in place until the first of June. These very impressive men-of-war carried near as many men as were on shore: "3,585 officers, seamen, and marines." And much more in the way of firepower: 554 naval cannon.[9]

France had not entirely forgotten Louisbourg, she knew that Canada's sentinel would require war provisions and to this end had dispatched the 64 gun, man-of-war, *Vigilant*, under the command of Alexandre Boisdescourt, Marquis de La Maisonfort.[10] She was to fall into Warren's snare. She made her appearance on May 19th (OS). She had a following wind which would have breezed her directly into the mouth of Louisbourg harbour.[11] However, as Maisonfort closed on Louisbourg he spied the *Mermaid*; it must have appeared to Maisonfort that she was sailing alone.[12] Slipping his spyglass into its case, the keen French naval officer made a bad decision — in spite of his orders that his primary objective was to get supplies into Louisbourg — he sailed down wind handy the shore and pass the mouth of the harbor with a view to coming up to the British man-of-war, the 40 gun, *Mermaid*.[13] A New York newspaper gave a contemporary account of the engagement:

> That on the 18th ult. the *Mermaid*, Capt. Douglas, a 40 gun ship, and the *Shirley-Galley*, Capt. Rouse, one of our cruizers, fell in with a French Man-of-war, and engaged her, the former broadside and broadside; and the latter being too small to lay along-side, and going well, annoyed her astern, or ahead, or on the quarter, as he could best; and as she proved a ship of force, they knowing how the Commodore got along side near enough to engage, when after 2 or 3 broadsides, she struck and asked for quarters, and was the next day secured; she is called the *Vigilant*, a new ship never at sea before, of 64 guns, and 560 men, and was commanded by the Marquis du Maisonfort ...[14]

Seth Pomeroy, witnessing the event from the shore, observed that the battle, "yard arm to yard arm," took place over a period of two hours. "The *Superbe*, the *Mermaid*, *Eltham*, *Massachusetts Frigate* and *Shirley* Galley were all in the engagement and at the taking of her ..."[15] At such odds, it is a wonder that the *Vigilant* fought on for better than two hours. Pomeroy reported that the British lost four men and the French 30 and many more wounded.[16]

As for the *Vigilant*: She was towed, with much panache, along the coast in front of the Frenchmen in the fort, so to taunt them; then into Gabarus Bay and put at anchor.[17] The French sailors were taken off as prisoners[18] and replaced with English sailors.[19] These sailors were first "employed about rigging and clearing the gun deck" and "fitting rigging." This work was to be carried out on the *Vigilant* over the next two weeks and by June the 4th she was sailing in company with her sisters as a commissioned English man-of-war, giving additional strength to Warren's fleet off Louisbourg. On the quarterdeck of this impressive 64-gun men-of-war sailing vessel, one would have seen Captain James Douglas, formally in command of the 40 gun *Mermaid*; the *Vigilant* was given to Douglas by Warren, as he was the one who "led her to me."[20]

The *Vigilant* was a handsome dividend[21] and all of those comprising of Warren's squadron must have been indeed very pleased with themselves; but the capture of the *Vigilant*, as valuable as she was in British hands, paid a larger dividend, that is, the eventual delivery of Louisbourg. Had the *Vigilant* gotten in it is doubtful whether Louisbourg would have been taken that season.[22] And so, like manna from heaven, valuable military stores fell into the hands of the English. The most valuable and most needed of the supplies aboard the *Vigilant* was that of gun powder, there was one thousand barrels of it. As well, taken off of her were twenty bronze cannons, these, together with the other captured provisions might will have extended Louisbourg's French life for a further four months. After that period of time the invaders, in the face of winter, would have had to retire from the field. The capture of the *Vigilant* also denied the Louisbourg garrison the reinforcement of three hundred soldiers which were aboard the *Vigilant*.[23]

Warren gets Reinforcement:

The capture of the *Vigilant* was accomplished through a coordinated effort of the fleet under Warren's command. The fleet at the time of *Vigilant's* capture on May 20th amounted to only four men-of-war. Just within a couple of days of the capture, over the southern horizon, came three more vessels. They were the *Princess Mary*, the *Hector* and the *Bien Aimé*. These additions to the fleet came up from Nantasket (Boston), presumably due to Warren's general order for all arriving British ships of war to report to him at Louisbourg. The first two[24] were to fit themselves in with the four that had been there since the first: the *Superbe*, the *Mermaid*, the *Launceston*, and the *Eltham*. Thus, by the 24th of May, there were six of these magnificent wind driven battleships blockading Louisbourg, seven when one counts in the *Vigilant*. These seven were to be joined by four more direct from England which reported to Warren on the 12th of June: the *Chester*, the *Sunderland*, the *Canterbury*, and the *Lark*.[25]

So it was, on June 12th, 1745, Commodore Peter Warren "commanded the largest British squadron in North American waters since 1711": Eleven men-of-war, including the captured *Vigilant*.[26] With such forces at his command, Warren was chafing at the bit. All that was necessary was to get close enough to Louisbourg so as to employ his more than 500 naval cannon. But that could come about only if he could make his way into Louisbourg Harbor. For that to happen, his fleet would have to sail by at close range to the Island Battery. If they were to try that, the British ships would suffer from the point blank punishment meted out by crack French crews who were manning well fortified and stationary gun emplacements; and who, were at the ready.

Chapter 11

The Island Battery

Fortress Louisbourg, as a short study of a map of the area will show (see page 210), is tucked in behind a rocky peninsula. No shot launched beyond the mouth of Louisbourg Harbor could reach her. And at sea, in the beyond, back and forth, prowled Warren's deadly squadron. To get close enough, the ships would have to thread themselves through a narrow passage which would put them in point blank range of French cannon, 24-pounders, all strategically placed so as to prevent the entrance of enemy vessels. It was not likely that Warren could sail his vessels through the passage abreast of one another. Even if the wind was right, these were close quarters and there were huge rocks about, ready to rip open even the stoutest of wooden hulls. As it turned out, half of Louisbourg's mighty harbor defenses were cut away by the French themselves when they determined to desert the Royal Battery at the very opening day of the siege. Thus, Warren would have little to worry about, if, he were to gain access to the inner harbor. What prevented this access, was, of course, the other half: the Island Battery. It had to be somehow captured and silenced, for, while it continued to be in French hands, any English ship that was to sail past would be pounded with the blasts of 31 cannon. For certain, as a first objective, the Island Battery had to be taken. Warren understood this early in the game.

Within three days of the troops landing, on May 3rd, Commodore Warren wrote out his plan in consultation with his captains and submitted it to General Pepperrell for his review and that of his officers.[1] The conclusion of the naval commanders was that "they can't advise going into the harbor with the ships, 'till the Island Battery is taken." This operation was not one in which the navy could be directly involved, but they would give "all the assistance in our power upon all occasions." The military installation to be taken was an island, thus long boats were to be used, "belonging to his Majesty's ships and the private ships of war, manned and armed."

Every seaman a musket, a pair of pistols, hand grenade, quick match and cutlass. Every marine, his musket, and bayonet. A box of spare musket and pistol cartridges in one of the boats of every ship, in proportion to the whole number of men sent by each particular ship; one or two days' provisions and a small keg of water in each boat, or in each longboat, one cask of water, the scaling-ladders in the whale boats; if in the night, lanterns, candles, tinderbox, steel, and a good knife in each man's pocket.

Warren's plan continued in a suggestive manner:

There should be two or three schooners with a surgeon on board of each to lie as near as possible to the battery ... to receive any men that may be wounded upon the attack, and his Majesty's ships and the country armed vessels should lie near as the weather will permit.

The plan allowed that it might be possible that after the island was successfully taken by the English, that the French may launch a counter attack from the mainland, from Louisbourg itself, and the English officers must be instantly ready in the event that should they see the French being successful in their counter attack, to spike the Island Battery cannons, and to that end carry spikes with them. The back up to spiking the cannon was to lift and throw the cannon over the walls. It was further suggested that about an hour or two before the intended attack that the troops ashore should make a separate attack on Louisbourg itself. Warren continued, "if not thought prudent effectually to do so," then to feign an attack against the town in several places in the hopes that the French will draw off some of their troops stationed at the Island Battery, if not, then to at least divert their attention. So too, Warren suggested that if he deemed conditions right that he just might, in all the confusion, run his ships through the passage. He gave specific instructions to his captains in the event that this contingency should materialize:

If any of the ships should be in danger of sinking by the enemy's shot, they should in that case run, or haul ashore as near the Grand Battery as possible (not in the way of the Battery's fire upon the town, nor in the line of direction of any of its cannon) in order to save their guns, arms, ammunition and provisions.

In going in, all the small vessels that have no great guns, should keep off the starboard side of the ships of war, and run in to the North-east harbour and land every man on the side of the Royal Battery in order to go round to join the general and the troops.

Warren continued to state in his plan warning that "The officer at the Grand battery should be directed to be very careful in firing at the enemy, that he does not hull any of our own ships that may lie between that battery and the town ..."

Warren concluded his written plan emphasizing the importance of getting such a plan executed as soon as possible:

The season of the year advancing apace that the enemy may expect provisions and succours from France, makes it highly necessary that we should take some vigorous measures, for the sudden reduction of Louisbourg ...[2]

Thus we see the written plans of Warren. These plans were written up and delivered to Pepperrell within three days of the colonials having landed on the beaches, May 3rd. On May the 7th, Warren went ashore in order to boost his plan.[3] After a Council of War, "A summons was sent into the town and an answer returned." Governor Duchambon's answer? The French in obedience to their king "would return no answer but from the mouth of their cannon.[4] The next day, on the 8th, the navy attempted to get the promised help ashore; but the sea conditions were such that they could not accomplish their mission, indeed, the conditions were such that boats were overturned and provisions lost.[5] The navy persisted and over the course of three days, from the 8th to the 10th, the needed material and men for the assault on the Island Battery was landed. All this activity did not go unnoticed by the French as they peeked and peered atop their walls in order to focus on these indistinct activities. Indeed, it was at this time that the French made one of their rare sallies, it seems, more to gather intelligence than to carry out any kind[6] of a surprise attack.[7] Within days of this sally, we see where Duchambon dispatched runners. As we have seen, there was a contingent of French troops that had come directly from Quebec and just at that time was putting Annapolis Royal under siege. On May 24th, the message had gotten through to the Marins: they and their fighting men were urgently needed at Louisbourg.

The Carry:

As we have seen from Warren's written plan to take the Island Battery, the Royal navy was prepared to give "all the assistance in our power upon all occasions." One of the contributions were to be small wooded boats, the kind that larger ships in normal times carried in considerable number, and at this time had been stacked up even in greater number in anticipation of the assault on Louisbourg, amphibious in part. So, there was no lack of boats; they were to be had. The difficulty was getting these small boats in place on the shores of the inner harbor without being brought under the guns of Louisbourg. Given the number of men that were eventually to be rowing about the inner harbor, at one point in time, I would guess that there had to be better than 50 of these small wooden boats shingled out on the beach at Gabarus Bay and marked for "the carryover." I say small — and they were, comparatively speaking — but still they were heavy wooden boats that had to be carried, not hauled. Carried over rough terrain along paths contemporaneously hewed through the bush and woods, away from the ever-threatening French guns. The place to which they determined to carry these boats was some three to four miles away, to the Royal Battery, a place where the New Englanders had become accustomed to gather, in broad view of their ultimate objective, Louisbourg, its steepled skyline being south from there about a mile across the interior waters. On the 10th of May, we see that the work of getting these smaller craft carried overland started and was to carry on to at least the 22nd, though not necessarily continuously.[8] On the 23rd there were enough boats in place so that a concerted attack on the Island Battery might be attempted.

The Lion And The Lily

In this part of the world, high on the northeastern seaboard, it is not uncommon for winter to get in its last licks during the month of May. As a review of the ships' logs will show,[9] the month of May at Louisbourg, in 1745, was one of those times when winter left the land protesting. On the 23rd of May we would have seen wet snow being driven by the cold winds up against the faces and knuckles of rowing men. About 800 of them under the cover of night had pushed off. A quarter of these men were seasoned sailors which Warren had sent to assist. This floating brigade was under the joint command of Colonel Noble and Colonel John Gorham. The weather (though generally throughout the siege very cooperative) was what brought this particular effort to an end. It was such that the men couldn't keep together[10] and the state of the turbulent waters leading up to the Island Battery proved too much. They rowed about most of the night and with the dawning of the morning they could be found pulling for the place from which they started, the Royal Battery.[11]

The news soon spread. The boys had a bad time of it. The Island Battery was still in the hands of the French. Warren was soon to hear. Likely he was in his cabin, the largest in the stern of the *Superbe*. "We shall have to get into that harbour. It is the only way we might assist in the taking of Louisbourg. We have a job! We have to dull the defences of the Island Battery." This was what was on the minds of Warren and his naval captains. "Was it not to be expected that reinforcements might arrive! From Quebec? From France? Gentlemen, time is not on our side?" "Is it not possible to do a front-on-attack and overwhelm the French that are nested on this island?" "Cannot these land officers get a rein on the colonial volunteers?" In turn, we might imagine the replies to these worrying complaints which were reported to Pepperrell, or to Waldo, or to Gorham. "The navy needed to exercise some patience. One can rely on New Englanders to get a tough job done; they will get this job done. The false start, you see, was due to the weather — the conditions need to be right."

A Ruinous Debacle:

The dimming moon was on the wane, the night was black and a mixed group gathered at the Grand Battery. Those gathered were determined, and between sips on their flasks had quite concluded that the right time had arrived. It was Sunday, the 26th of May; it was time to get the job done. About 400 had gathered and had volunteered on the enticement that they might have "any plunder and were permitted to choose their own leader."[12] They were "noisy, disorderly, and some riotously tipsy."[13] Each of these men had somebody that they liked to report to, but no one individual leader could seem to pull them all together.[14] The leaders knew perfectly well the principal difficulty. The difficulty in leading men in a military operation who hold democratic notions.[15] But there was little they could do at this stage and these eager New Englanders were all that were to be had, except for a number of amused sailors which Warren managed to send ashore.[16]

The Island Battery is — well, it is an island, and as such there is only one way to get there, by boat. The boats that the colonials had assembled were to be launched mostly from the less turbulent waters of the inner harbor, within a mile of their objective. Thus the reason for taking such pains to get all these small boats transported overland. However, boats were to be launched from more than one place. Some from the *Mermaid* which came in just beyond gun range of the French Batteries. These would come in from the sea and would be stealthily rowed into the mouth of the harbor. Another place, which provided a relatively short row, would be from the shores of the lighthouse point. Gorham's rangers, were to circle around the harbor overland, likely following the shoreline about three miles, and as planned, this group would meet others paddling or rowing the landing boats. One group headed north-easterly across the harbor from the Royal Battery, another came in from the *Mermaid*, north-westerly. Many of the paddlers, in order to come to a conjunction, would have had to come by, and thereby be practically under the noses of the French manning the island guns. These paddlers or rowers had to do their work quietly, not only for their own safety, but in order to preserve the very important element of surprise. The entire force was to meet at a point on the north-eastern shore of the harbor, at the Lighthouse Point just across from the Island Battery, a mini-castle in which two hundred French soldiers and thirty-nine French cannon were entrenched. There was a small beach on the northern side of the Island Battery on which the colonials might make their landing.[17]

The boats bearing the 400 men were pushed off and propelled towards their objective as the oars twisted in their muffled locks. Most had to be looking anxiously towards their objective, the Island Battery, dimly outlined in the south. Further on, in behind, a mile or so, the night lights of Louisbourg. Beyond that again, the diversionary blasts of the English batteries flashed in the southern sky.[18] There was little activity to be seen on the island. Closer and closer they came to the rocky shores of the island. It looked like they might get the first boats ashore before the French were to become aware of their presence and rush at the walls with their scaling ladders without hot lead coming at them. And then, just within a boat length or two of the shore, the French opened up with their deadly greetings.[19]

The French behind the fortifications of the Island Battery came instantly alive and showered piercing lead down through the men crowded together in packed boats about to land. Howls of French joy and shrieks of English agony went up into the black night all covered by the racket, smoke and smell of the exploding cannons and muskets. The raiding New Englanders who did get ashore, about two hundred ran for cover, a number ran to the foot of the walls to avoid the langrage shot[20] from the swivels and the cannon atop the walls. Seth Pomeroy wrote of it in his journal:

> The French being prepared with their cannon pointed down to strike the boats just before they came ashore loaded with chain and partridge shot: a

greatly number of men with small arms. As soon as our people came in sight: with all the fury and resolution possible they fired upon them and cut whole boat loads of them: but in spite of all their fire, four or five boat loads got on the island and engaged them for near an hour ...[21]

As many New Englanders died that dark night as did die since their arrival. Indeed, as many died of battle wounds within the interval of that bloody hour or two on the shore of that small island at the mouth of Louisbourg Harbor, as did during the entire period of the siege. There was no appreciation of the extent of their losses until morning. It was foggy. And there came drifting in from the direction of the Island Battery along the shores of the harbor lifeless junks of men. Bodies: some headless, some armless, some legless.[22] The count was sixty dead and the French had 116 new prisoners to deal with.[23]

On the 29th of May, at Louisbourg, the good spring weather had finally established itself, things were greening up and the lady slippers and trilliums which abound thereabouts were showing themselves. A number of the provincial sailing vessels were slowly swinging on their anchors as the reflections of the sun glittered on the surface of Gabarus Bay. Readily to be seen would have been the *Shirley*, John Rouse's vessel, with her 24 guns also picking up the sunlight. Some of her 150 men were aloft gathering in sail — when, suddenly, a crack was heard and seven men fell and three were killed in a moment.[24] Three more bodies are thus to be brought to the New England cemetery which had now been added to the countryside of Louisbourg. A cemetery, at which, on that day, May 29th, there were gathered hundreds of quiet and reflecting men; gathered to see more than 50 of their dead comrades committed to the freshly turned earth. A melancholy scene. For the first four weeks the English invaders were buoyant; they were in charge of the entire countryside; they had smelt success. On the 27th, Pepperrell, in surveying the rumbled remnants of the four hundred which had set out the night before, declared: "Now things looked something dark."[25]

There was a spell over the land as the boys from New England stood at that makeshift cemetery; there, on the 29th of May;

there, to bury their dead. The spell of a breezeless and beautiful June day; in the back ground could be seen Warren's men-of-war with their small boats out in front towing their respective mother ships off shore.[26] The men walked slowly back to their tents and their posts, giving off by their appearances the picture of sadness and depressed spirits; however, this picture could be seen to be gradually changing — just as was the background scenery — into a restlessness. See, there, a small breeze which just came up, zephyr like, to stir the trees; and there, in the near background, the anchored sail boats now beginning to give a gentle tuck at their rodes; and there, in the far background, the billowy white banks of fog ominously crawling along the horizon. When — Blam! Bang! — Blam! Bang! The New England Batteries came to life to spit out their revenge on the gates and walls of Louisbourg.

Chapter 12

The Bombardment

The abortive assault on the Island Battery on May 26th, sagged the spirits of the invaders which at the first were so high. A month had now passed and they had made little impression on the French behind their walls. The New Englanders were losing heart and many were sitting about, either lacking direction or unwilling to follow what little was forthcoming. Warren, stuck in the fog off the coast, was getting very short of patience, "For God's sake, let us do something, and not waste our time in indolence." Pepperrell, in his diplomatic manner, responded by reminding Warren:

... we have also kept out scouts to destroy any settlements of the enemy near us, and present a surprise in our camp ... that by the services aforesaid and the constant guards kept night and day round the camp, at our batteries, the army is very much fatigued, and sickness prevails among us, to that degree that we now have but about 2100 effective men, six hundred of which are gone in the quest of two bodies of French and Indians we are informed are gathering, one to the eastward, and the other to the westward.[1]

Their successful repulsive efforts at the Island Battery spurred the defenders into taking the initiative, which, with the exception of the time when Morpain and Boularderie went to the beaches to oppose the landing at the first of it, was generally lacking by the French during the 1745 siege. On May 27th, a French detachment in three shallops, with 12 days worth of supplies, set to sea and come to shore at Grand Lorembec (Lorraine). (It is to be remembered that the French at Louisbourg had the facility to move vessels onto and off their docks, incased as they were within the fortifications. Also, on account of their Island Battery, the French had control of the mouth of the harbor.) The objective of this French detachment was to retake Lighthouse Point, a position which the colonials then occupied. Lorembec is the next harbor up the coast, north of Louisbourg. The idea was for the French to land at Lorembec, which they could do in relative safety, circle back overland to the Lighthouse Point. They intended to surprise the English and take back the fortifications at the Lighthouse Point, a position which the French then realized was of considerable strategical importance; at a later point the English were to come to the same realization. On their way overland, just shortly after they had disembarked, the French party were happened upon by a larger English party led by Col. Noble.[2] Musket fire erupted: "The engagement lasted about four hours and the number of all that was killed of the English was eight about 15 wounded. Thirty of the French killed, 50 wounded; they got nothing by this bargain."[3] Retreating, the French and their Indian supporters, in total 120 men, went to Petit Lorembec (the next harbor up again at which were located sympathetic French fishermen) to see if they could get some boats so that they might make their way back to the fort. All at once, however, they found themselves facing "two or three hundred Englishmen." The French and the Indians scattered leaving their supplies behind,[4] heading inland and crossing the Miré River, a considerable distance away from Louisbourg.[5] Many of these Frenchmen were, in time, to be combed up and made prisoners.[6]

The Lighthouse Battery:

The ruinous debacle which the amphibious raid on the Island Battery had turned out to be was to confirm the thinking of many that the Island Battery was impervious to attack. Men could not get at it and neither could any of the cannon served by the English. There were three fascine batteries which the New Englanders had set up but they were located well away from the Island Battery doing their destructive work on the western ramparts of Louisbourg. The Royal Battery was just a little too far away to effect hits with any accuracy. Thus, the Island Battery was unreachable, at least, it seemed that way.

We have seen that Gorham and his rangers in connection with the amphibious raid on the Island Battery had made the Lighthouse Point their point of departure. Certainly by the 17th of May, Gorham had taken up a position at this point.[7] In scouting the countryside he had come upon the point and took an immediate liking to the position. It was defensible and from there he and his men could keep an eye on the entire harbor. It was here that he encamped his rangers, who, as a matter of practice were always kept off and away from the main encampment. There could be had from the point a fine view of the Island Battery. I suppose while admiring this view, it dawned on someone within the group that this place, the Lighthouse Point, would make "a hell of a good place to set up a gun battery"; from there, they could bring the Island Battery into range. All they needed to do was to get some cannon and set them up. This was easy said: difficult, however, to do. Cannon and their carriages are heavy and awkward things to move. To begin with, any available cannon to be had were located well to the west of Louisbourg. At such a distance, water transport was the only way; but not over the harbor, as the floating works would have to be brought under French guns. At any rate, the harbor side of the point was a sheer cliff. No — the cannon would have to be loaded well away from the French somewhere handy the original landing place on Gabarus Bay and then transported off shore, aways; then northeast; and then to land them at the first level beach to be found. From there, to muscle them overland, a haul through the woods, a mile or so, emerging from the land side of the Island Point. This was almost an impossible task. However, the New Englanders were to show, once again, how capable they were of hard work, ingenuity and perseverance: the job got done.

Pepperrell observed:

... two eighteen pounders mounted on the 11th of June and by the 14th four more sustained by three hundred and twenty men. (The difficulties were the transporting of the cannon in boats from Chappeaurouge Bay [Gabarus

Bay] to the eastward of the light house, the getting them up the bank of the shore, which was a steep craggy rock, the hauling them a mile and a quarter over an incredible bad way of hills and rocks and morasses.)[8]

Thus we see that by mid-June, a number of batteries were in place at Louisbourg; enough, such that the English could next lay hard siege to her. With the penetrating power of a continual cannonade, interest and passion will not long hold out. To the east of Louisbourg, as we have just seen, there was established a battery at the Lighthouse Point. To the north, the English had the Royal Battery at their command and hurling balls from it directly into the core of the city. To the west, were located three fascine batteries, one, the "Titcomb's Battery," was situated 800 yards from the West Gate; another, the "Sherburne's," 250 yards from it.

The matter was to come to an excruciating head for the French on the 14th of June. On that date, as explained by Governor Duchambon in his report, "the battery which the enemy had constructed at the lighthouse tower and which had seven cannon and a mortar began to fire on the harbour island with 18 pound balls and a 12 inch mortar ..." Before the English battery at the Lighthouse Point opened up, there was an airy calm which prevailed over the entire scene at Louisbourg. Apparently, for a number of days before the Lighthouse Battery was ready, the other established batteries, due to a shortage of powder, were quiet. Thus there was a lull on the surface of affairs. "The French had begun to creep a little out of their casemates and covers." In fact, Warren, mainly thanks to the capture of the *Vigilant*, had powder aplenty; it's just that at first he was reluctant to give much of it up to his colonial cousins. But now he recognized the importance of getting an adequate supply ashore. It took time to get the powder barrels slung off the ships, into small rowboats, onto the shore, and brought up to the batteries; but soon there was enough powder all around; the guns were again leveled and sighted on their targets. All hell was about to break lose, and on both sides everyone sensed it. Governor Shirley tells us of the events of 14th of June and of the few days following:

"... Orders were given for a general Discharge of all the Cannon from every Battery, at Twelve O'Clock, which was accordingly done, and follow'd by an incessant fire all the rest of the day.

... [The next day, the 15th:] When the Mortar began to play from the Lighthouse Battery upon Island Battery; out of 19 shells, 17 fell within the Fort, and one of them upon the Magazine, which, together with the Fire from the Cannon, to which the Enemy was very much exposed, they having but little to shelter them from the Shot that ranged quite through their Barracks, so terrified them, that many of them left the Fort, and run into the Water for Refuge."[9]

And from Duchambon's report:

... everyone was exhausted from much work and no sleep, and out of the 1,500 people which we had at the start of the siege, 50 had been killed, 95 had been too severely wounded to give further assistance, several had succumbed to utter exhaustion, and the ramparts which had only measured 5 by 5 feet at the beginning of the siege were all broken down by the 26th of June when the inhabitants of the town handed me a petition. ...

Finding myself in such a delicate situation, I informed M. Verrier, chief engineer, of the condition of the fortifications, and M. de Ste. Marie, captain in charge of artillery, of the status of our ammunition. Each man submitted a report to me; I then held a council of war which decided unanimously that, in view of the force of the enemy and the condition of our own fort, it would be better to capitulate.[10]

The author, C. Ochiltree Macdonald described the conditions which gave rise to the French capitulation:

The anniversary of the Accession of George II [celebrated by his subjects every June; by 1745, George II had been on the English throne for 18 years] ... was celebrated by a vigorous bombardment of the city from noon to nightfall; the French gunners were driven off the platform of the Island Battery; the cannon hastily brought up to strengthen the defences of the West Gate were silenced; bombs and red-hot shot poured steadily into the city; preparations were at length made for a general assault by land and sea. At this crisis, and after a gallant defence of 47 days — the Grand Battery being lost; the Island Battery, which the French esteemed the palladium of Louisbourg, almost annihilated by the Lighthouse Battery; the North East Battery being damaged and so exposed that the artillerymen could not stand to their guns; the Circular Battery ruined and all its guns but three dismounted; the harbour being, in short, disarmed of all its principal Batteries; the West Gate demolished, and the adjoining wall breached; the west flank of the King's Bastion almost ruined, and most of the guns mounted during the siege silenced; the houses and state buildings being demolished or damaged, the ammunition almost exhausted — extremely harassed by a long confinement in casemates and other covered holds, the city capitulated ...[11]

Chapter 13

The Capitulation

On the 14th of June, 1745, as we have seen, the matter of Louisbourg's situation was to come to an excruciating head for the French. All the English batteries, including the one at the Lighthouse Point, were ready. There was a lull on the surface of affairs immediately in and around Louisbourg; and, indeed, even the prowling men-of-war, who seem to be ever present at the mouth of the harbor since its investiture, had, ominously, disappeared; no where to be seen from the ramparts of Louisbourg. And the French could observe there were fewer men out in the clearings immediately around the fort. What was going on. Where are the ships and the men? What's next?

Warren's fleet, now consisting of numerous provincial vessels and eleven grand men-of-war, had not disappeared. They had come all together at anchor in Gabarus Bay in a position not to be seen from within the walls of the fortress. The crews were very busy, "clearing and barricading" their ships.[1] A determination had been made that the men-of-war would force an entry into the harbor and simply just take the punishment which the cannon of the Island Battery would mete out as they ran by it, broadside. Unneeded fittings and material, such as spare booms, which would normally be found on the decks of such ships, would just get in the way and turn into flesh tearing splinters as the Island Battery cannon balls crashed on through. So, all of it, was being winched up and lowered over the sides and unto waiting tenders and then sent ashore or unto anchored barges.[2] The sailors were also constructing landing platforms on their ships[3] so that marines could be put off under fire onto the docks of Louisbourg, once in. On shore, men were busy, many out of sight, combing the woods for moss which would be barged out to the waiting ships and which would then be stuffed into sacks and piled up as barricades and thus to lessen the effect of small shot. Further, the men ashore were gathering dry brush and piling it together with dry wood on the tops of three hills near the town, "to act as beacons for Commodore Warren."[4]

And, so, by the 15th of June everything was ready for a combined assault on Louisbourg. An all out effort was to be made by sea and by land. The army was called together: the Commodore had come ashore to address them. One of the soldiers wrote in his journal, "The whole army is called together to whom the commodore made an excellent speech." Warren told the men that he waits for nothing but a fair wind. If he were called upon he would lead the whole army to the walls and he would "cheerfully do it for he'd rather leave his body at Louisbourg than not take the city."[5]

Seth Pomeroy wrote in his diary:

A fair pleasant day [15th of June, 1745]: Commodore Warren came on shore our regiment with other regiments in the camp mustered in regimental order Commodore Warren made a fine speech to the army and marched through together with the general and some other gentlemen and agreed with the general and publicly with the whole army that as soon as the wind and weather should favour; he with all his ships should go into the harbour engage the Island Battery and the city: we upon the land with all our forces at the same time should engage them with all our artillery and scaling ladders.

And, in a letter to his wife, Pomeroy wrote further:

"He [Warren] has been on shore this day, and our army was mustered in regimental order. The Commodore, with the General and the other officers, marched through our ranks to view them. He made a fine speech to us, and very much encouraged the soldiers to go on and storm the city by escalating the walls, while he would go in with all his ships and engage them to the utmost of his power. This is to be done the first fair wind that blows."[6]

On June the 16th, 1745 (OS), on the anniversary of the Accession of George II, resounding over the waters and lands near Louisbourg, from noon to nightfall, pounding cannon could be heard. Bombs and red-hot shot poured steadily into the city and preparations had been made for a general assault by land and sea. Pepperrell described the moment and the effect:

The Grand Battery being in our possession, the Island Battery being so much annoyed by the Light House Battery, the North east battery so open to our Advanced battery, that it was not possible for the enemy to stand to their guns, all the guns in the [French] Circular Battery, except three, being dismounted, and the wall almost wholly broke down, the West Gate demolished, and a large breach in the wall adjoining, the west flank of the King's Bastion almost ruined, all the houses and other buildings almost tore to pieces, but one house in the town being left unhurt, and the enemy's stock of ammunition growing short.[7]

The conditions of the town were horrible.[8] Not only was the will of the French fighting man running low, so was the gun powder, as Pepperrell had alluded, there being but left only "thirty-seven kegs of powder, each of one hundred pounds."[9] As we have seen, the men-of-war were cleared for action and laying just off the shore ready to force the harbor and the land forces were ready to storm the breaches with scaling ladders and fascines.

The French gave in. Soon a flag of truce was seen raised above a small group of Frenchmen proceeding out of Louisbourg and up to the camp of the New England invaders.

We have a witness, the "First Anonymous Mass. Soldier":

So about sunset there came out a flag — from the town they requested there might be a cessation of arms for a while that they might call a Council to agree upon some terms whereby they may surrender the city into our hands, for so long as we fire so smartly they can't do any such thing.[10]

The messengers were sent back; they had until eight o'clock the following morning. Our next witness is Joseph Sherburne, a fifty-one year old who was in charge of one of the English batteries, he wrote as the appointed hour drew near:

... stock of full cartridges, shot in place, gunners quartered denied — matches lit ready but we hear their drums beat a parley and soon appeared a flag of truce which I receive half way between our battery and their walls which I conducted to the green hill and there delivered him to Colonel Richmond [and] so returned to my station at the advance battery.[11]

The citizens of Louisbourg, if not the soldiery, were thoroughly fed up. A people's petition had been presented to the French governor, Duchambon, praying they should be relieved of the terrors of a full scale assault. The French sent their flag bearer back out into the field, they would surrender the place on the provision that the French should be allowed their personal property. All the English officers (even down to the ensigns) were consulted and it was determined to accept these terms. Our "First Soldier" noted that "the wind was fair so that Commodore Warren's plan might well have been executed."

The Terms of Capitulation[12] included: that all the commissioned officers, their families and possessions would be let alone and left in their houses until "they can be conveniently transported to France," and that "if there be any persons in the town or garrison which shall desire may not be seen by us, shall be permitted to go off masked." There was one thing missing on which Duchambon had insisted and for which he intended to hold out: "Honours of War." The French wanted to march out of their fort "with arms, baggage, drums beating, and flags unfurled." Pepperrell and Warren consulted and they agreed, "the uncertainty of our affairs that depends so much on wind and weather make it necessary not to stick on trifles."[13] As for the French, they thought they had struck a good deal.[14]

Thus we would have seen, on the afternoon of the 17th of June 1745 General Pepperrell, at the head of his army, marching through the Dauphin gate into the town of Louisbourg. But I run a bit ahead of my story. For Pepperrell and his New Englanders were not the ones who took the keys from the French. It was Warren and his naval officers who did that; and who in turn went over to open the Gates for Pepperrell's waiting army.

We read from the log of the *Superbe* (Warren's flag ship) the entry of June the 17th, "Flag of truce came from Island Battery in order to capitulate. Sent Captain Durell ashore as hostage. At 5 A.M. sent marines and officers ashore to take possession of Island Battery. English colours hoisted." This was Philip Durell, the captain of the *Eltham*, and the *Eltham* log for the 17th reads, in part, "Ran into Louisbourg Harbour." Warren wrote up the hand-over in his contemporaneous report to his superiors:

> The 17th, I landed with Capt. James Macdonald. [I] sent him with twelve officers and 400 marines to take possession of Louisbourg and place proper guards. The governor having delivered me the keys of the town, magazines of powder and other warlike stores, which were immediately opened on that land side, the general and his troops marched into the town, of which we now have quiet possession.[15]

Now, there was something going on here! Could it have been that the Royal navy thought it should have the honor of first going in; or was it that the French military men were not prepared to deal with ragged colonials; or was it simply a question of logistics in that it was necessary, at first, for the victors to come in by water and land on the harbor front of Louisbourg. Without evidence, one historian's guess is as good as the next. What is clear, however, is that Warren was in first and it was Warren who opened the land-gate so to let in Pepperrell and his land forces. Is it not strange that Warren's officers were the first to take the keys and then for them to open up the gates? At any rate, it was only after this first little ceremony took place that we would have seen Pepperrell, at the head of his army, marching through the Dauphin gate into the town.[16]

M. Henry Baker, in an address given in the year of 1909, to the New Hampshire Society of Colonial Wars, was to say of the ceremony:

> The military etiquette of the occasion was punctiliously observed. Each army saluted the other. Then the French flag was saluted and lowered. As the lilies of France fluttered down the flag staff the cross of St. George arose over the citadel and was saluted by the guns of the army and navy and the cheers of the soldiers and sailors who had endured so much to secure the triumph and glory of the hour.

Our "Fourth Anonymous Mass. Soldier" was to write: "Looks like rain: in the morning the French flag was taken down ..." All the English batteries fired in celebration. "About three o'clock the Commodore came to anchor in the harbour and all our ships and all our small craft." James Gibson, one of Boston's leading merchants, who had come to Louisbourg as a "gentleman volunteer" was to write of his observations of the hand-over:

> Monday, 17. This day, the French flag was struck, and the English one hoisted up in its place at the island battery. We took possession early in the morning. We hoisted likewise the English flag at the Grand Battery, and our other new batteries; then fired our cannons and gave three huzzas. At two O'clock in the afternoon, Commodore Warren, with all the men-of-war, as also the prize man-of-war of sixty guns; (the *Vigilant*), our twenty-gun ships; likewise our snows, brigantines, privateers and transports, came all into Louisbourg harbour, which made a beautiful appearance.[17] When all were safely moored, they proceeded to fire on such a victorious and joyful occasion. About four o'clock in the afternoon, our land army marched to the south gate of the city, and entered the same, and so proceeded to the parade near the citadel; the French troops, at the same time, being all drawn up in a very regular order. Our army received the usual salutes from them, every part being performed with all the decency and decorum imaginable. And as the French were allowed to carry off their effects, so our guards took all the care they possibly could to prevent the common soldiers from pilfering and stealing, or otherwise giving them the least molestation.[18]

Those at Louisbourg at the time of its surrender, capable of bearing arms and who surrendered and were made prisoners, came to 2,000. The French, according the English, who were killed "within the walls" came to "about 300 besides numbers that died by being confined within the Casemates."[19] As for the English, who had twice the number of men at the walls: Shirley reported that during "the whole Siege, we had not more than 101 men killed by the enemy and all other accidents, and about 30 died of sickness."[20]

These numbers as provided by Shirley, however, should not be taken as an indication that the New Englanders had an easy time of it. Having left home in March, they had been all along up to the capitulation living in camps with very few conveniences. They kept up their spirits from when they first enlisted, with thoughts of filling their pockets once the French surrendered. Well, the time arrived and the French surrendered. These amateur soldiers now wanted to take what they had come for: the "Spoils of War"! The terms of the capitulation might have been satisfactory to the officers, but the question for the rank and file was, what was in it for them? History will show that robbing and molestation is the reward of the common soldier. The boys from New England had worked up quite a head of steam and allowing them to come into the walled city of Louisbourg was much the same as letting the fox loose in the chicken house. Not all the men could be kept under control. The French authorities complained and the English authorities agreed, but not much could be done about the problem.[21] The troops had to be brought in behind the sheltering walls, no matter that the French residents would thus be exposed to their pillaging ways; it was still feared that French and Indian reinforcements might, at any moment, come at them from the surrounding forests, just as there was a continuing fear that a large fleet of French war ships might also, at any moment, appear on the sea horizon.[22] The answer was to get the French citizenry out of the way; to get them transported as soon as possible; but that, as we shall see, was to take some time to arrange.

The day after Louisbourg's capitulation, on June 18, 1745, a schooner, under the command of Captain Bennet, got underway for Boston with a jubilant despatch for Governor Shirley. Bennet arrived in the middle of the night of July 3rd/4th and immediately sought out the governor to hand him Pepperrell's despatch.[23] The watch let him pass by, but, in the process, the officers of the watch got the news before any other person at Boston. At about four in the morning the watch finally let go with their information not able to hold it in any more. They were to alarm the town

by firing their guns and beating their drums, and before five, all the bells in the town began to ring, and continued ringing most of the day. ... the day was spent in firing of cannon, feasting and drinking of healths, and in preparing fireworks, etc. against the evening. ... in the evening the whole town appeared as it were in a blaze, almost every house being finely illuminated. In some of the principal streets were great variety of fire-works, and curious devices for the entertainment of the almost numberless spectators, and in the fields were several bonfires for the diversion of the less polite, besides a large one in the common, where was a tent erected, and plenty of good liquor for all that would drink. In a word, never before, upon any occasion, was observed so universal and unaffected a joy; nor was there ever so many persons of both sexes at one time walking about, as appeared that evening, the streets being as light as day, and the weather extremely pleasant.[24]

The news, of course, had to be gotten to England as soon as possible and to that end Captain Montague in the 40 gun *Mermaid* was despatched by Warren. An interesting side note to this can now be made: A second copy of the despatch[25] was placed in the hands of Capt. Geary. Geary was the Captain of the *Chester*. However, Warren did not want to lose the 50 gun ship *Chester*, so, he asked John Rous, Senior Provincial Naval officer, to do the honors and bring Capt. Geary to London in the *Shirley* (24 guns). That there was another vessel that was to race to London with the news was a development which bothered Capt. Montague, somewhat. (William Montague is described in history as having an "eccentric behaviour" such that it earned him the name "Mad Montague.") He was to make a special plea to Warren: "Sir, I am informed the schooner is to sail after me. I hope you will not do me so much injustice as to send her till at least ten days after my departure."[26]

London broke out into celebrations:

Salutes boomed from the batteries of the Tower; Cheapside and the Strand were brilliantly illuminated, and joy bells pealed. ... 'extraordinary rejoicings' loudly echoed the delight of the metropolis [to the countryside]; guns were fired from the finely illuminated church steeples, the house windows blazed with candles, the red glare of bonfires reddened the streets and shires, and barrels of beer were liberally distributed by the gentry to the shouting populace.[27]

The Reasons For The Fall Of Louisbourg, 1745:

Such as is the case in the making of all great historical events, the results (winning or losing) come about because of the effects of many events occurring over a period of time all interacting with one another. It is life — is it not! Some events are small at the happening and large in the result; others large in the happening, small in the result. Some predictable, some unpredictable, some as a result of nature, some of a group's making or even that of an individual. The outcome of the siege of Louisbourg in 1745 was the result of many factors and one can weave their own tapestry of events both minor and major. I have dealt with a number of these events and they are spread throughout this work. The three principal events which brought about the capitulation, I believe, are: the cooperation that existed between William Pepperrell and Peter Warren, the weather and the early desertion of the Royal Battery.[28]

Warren was plainly of the view that the conquest "could not have been acquired by the sea force without the land one, nor by the land one without the sea."[29] The personalities of William Pepperrell and Peter Warren were such that an extraordinary cooperation is to be observed between the two very different forces which they commanded; not only different because one was a sea force and the other a land force, but different because one was militia scratched up from a "rude population" of farmers, fishermen and traders; the other being, well — the British navy with all its successes and traditions, and its well known discipline. The fact of the matter is that land forces and naval forces, up to this time, had rarely only ever worked together in a common objective.[30]

The weather which plays so fateful a role in matters that require transport by sea, was clearly on the side of the New England raiders. It was such that not one single day was lost in the prosecution of the design. A resident of Louisbourg (*Habitant de Louisbourg*) a contemporary witness to the events wrote:

> The enemy appeared in March, a month usually extremely dangerous in a climate which seems to confound the seasons, for the spring, everywhere else so pleasant, there is frightful. The English, however, appeared to have enlisted Heaven in their interest. So long as the expedition lasted they enjoyed the most beautiful weather in the world, and this greatly favoured an enterprise against which were heavy odds that it would fail on account of the season. Contrary to what is usual there were no storms. Even the winds,

so unrestrained in those dreadful seas in the months of March, April and May, were to them always favourable; the fogs so thick and frequent in these months that ships are in danger of running upon the land without seeing it, disappeared earlier than usual, and gave place to a clear and serene sky; in a word, the enemy had always beautiful weather, as fine as they could desire.

The New Englanders, themselves, were to recognize the good weather factor. On June 26th the "First Anonymous Mass. Soldier" wrote:

> Clear & fair, this day, however, since the 18th it was foggy. Generally, in the 49 days of the siege, there was not so much as 24 hours of rain. A 'vast advantage' to the health of the besiegers and to using their artillery.

And, no sooner had the French given up, the weather changed. Seth Pomeroy:

> Continued foul weather. This is the fourth day sense it began and it is very remarkable that for the 47 days we have been on this island and in all this time not so much fowl weather by one half as there was now in one week which I look upon as a smile of Providence upon the army — For if there had been fowl weather as commonly there used to be here at this time in the year it would have rendered it exceedingly difficult, if not wholly frustrated the design, scattered the fleet, and sickened our army. ... Very remarkable that the enemy should give it up at the time it did. If they had not we must have made a bold attempt by scaling the walls; it seems it would have been fatal. ... remarkable thing the very next day after we had taken possession, — rain, fog, dark weather, eight or nine days together ..."

The taking of the Royal Battery by the New Englanders is something that I have dealt with in some detail at an earlier point in this part. That it should have been given up before the New Englanders had even arrived at the walls was for the French a tactical error. The French thought they had too few fighting men to defend both positions and thought it best to consolidate their numbers within the fort. It was further thought that the Island Battery alone would be enough to keep Warren's fleet out (and in this regard they may well have been correct). But the French never gave enough thought to what these enterprising New Englanders would do with these heavy guns at the Royal

Battery located as they were just opposite the town — a clear shot to the very innards of the city. The New Englanders used these big 42-pound cannons to considerable advantage, not only as the French had mounted them at the Royal Battery but also as the New Englanders had mounted them at the fascine batteries which they had industrially constructed but yards away from the western gate of Louisbourg. If only the French had taken the time to make sure these canon were fully disabled. The work was too hurriedly carried out; and, while iron rods were driven into the touch holes, the anxious soldiers neglected to smash "either trunnions or carriages" and left "virtually all the stores behind in their flight into Louisbourg."

The 1745 siege of Louisbourg had worked as sieges ought to work: the place was strangled. This French fortress was choked off from receiving supplies and men, of which the French were in bad need, even at the first of it. William Pepperrell effectively had locked them up; and, those who would have given aid, Peter Warren shut out.[31]

_____

Chapter 14

The English Garrison

Rev. Samuel Moody was a friend and neighbor of Pepperrell's, indeed he was related to Pepperrell's wife. Notwithstanding his advanced years, 70, Moody went off to Louisbourg with Pepperrell.[1] Moody was quite a character. Earlier on in life he had attended Harvard (1697) and it was there that he experienced a conversion; he became a minister of the Congregational Church. Shortly thereafter, he elected to go off to the western borders of the present day State of Maine, where he helped his parishioners fight the French inspired Indians. "Although he never failed in the performance of compassionate acts on behalf of the unfortunate, he nevertheless was a man of violent temper ..."; he was said to be "a powerful preacher."[2] Moody, it would seem, also had a taste for fighting, at least fighting "papists." He volunteered to be the chaplain to an earlier expedition to Nova Scotia, Colonel John March's 1707 campaign. Thirty-eight years later, in 1745, at Louisbourg, we would have seen Rev. Moody, once again; it gave the campaign "the character of a crusade."[3]

... when he [Moody] boarded the transport at Boston he seized an axe and exclaimed, 'The sword of the Lord and of Gideon,' predicting that Louisbourg would be taken and he would cut down the objects of papal worship. ... It is said that following the siege Moody did attack the alter and the images in the French church with his axe.[4]

The civil authorities sat reverently in the pews before the altar as Rev. Moody gave his fiery sermon in the axed chapel; Warren was undoubtedly there, likely next to Pepperrell and the other leaders of the expedition; all bedecked in their finest attire. Warren was particularly thoughtful as the old preacher raved on; he had thoughts of treasure on his mind, but I shall come to that shortly. Pepperrell had things on his mind, too. He and Shirley had promised the New Englanders that they could return home after

Louisbourg was taken. This was a rash promise, one that was to be repeated to the men on a number of occasions in the coming months as they showed their feelings, heightened, as they were, by the discomforts of Louisbourg and thoughts of their needy families back in New England. From the poor fighting soldier's viewpoint things were unfair. Here they were being told to be good and to take nothing; to continue to work and undo their siege work (filling up the trenches): and, at the same time, to see the officers, especially the naval officers, fill up their trunks with booty.[5]

The French Population Deported:

The first order of business for the victors was to expel the vanquished: Louisbourg had to be evacuated of its French population.[6] The French administrators and soldiers, by the terms of the capitulation, were to be transported back to France. As for the rest — just so many fifth-columnists — they had to go too, somewhere, anywhere; but away from Louisbourg as there was a continuing fear that a French military force might show up at any moment, either by land or by sea, or by both.

The 40-gun *Launceston* was stripped of all but two of her guns,[7] and extra cabins were built for the French officers and their families. As Warren reported, the *Launceston* "with some small transports belonging to the colonies, left Louisbourg on July 2nd (OS) to "carry to France about 1,500 men, women and children." Among the 1,500 was the "the governor, intendant, most of the chief officers and regular troops."[8] The *Lark* was to sail in company with this fleet headed out across the Atlantic and to continue on with them until they were well off shore, as Warren expressed it, "least they should presume to go to Canada, of which they seem to be very desirous."[9]

Another 400 French persons, less important types, were loaded on smaller auxiliary vessels and sent off, in the company of the *Hector* and the *Eltham* (Philip Durell, captain) to Boston. It was anticipated that the Boston authorities would then further see to their return to France.[10] Warren did not want the *Hector* and the *Eltham* to get too far away from Louisbourg, but felt obliged to employ them to convoy the "victualers" coming up from Boston.

And though approximately 1,900 French were thus transported, there was left 5,000 "peasants." Warren reported:

... I believe we have near 5,000 yet we shall not be able to transport this fall. Many of the peasants have offered to take the oath of allegiance to his Majesty. As they will be useful in getting in wood and other necessaries for the garrison, the general and I propose to tender the oath to such as we can not transport. We are determined by no means to let them remain here longer than until vessels can be procured to transport them. We see the ill effects of a thing of this nature at Annapolis, and till the French are transported from thence, or till we have possession of Canada, the colony of Nova Scotia will be continually alarmed.[11]

I do not believe Warren's estimate of 5,000 is an estimate of the number of those just to be found at Louisbourg; but, rather, the number of Frenchmen to be found throughout all of Île Royal and Île St. Jean (1,000). Warren in a despatch dated November 23rd makes reference to approximately 400 men, women and children who were required to move inside the fort, so to better keep an eye on them.[12] Whatever the number might be, and it could not have exceeded a couple of hundred, there was indeed a number of French who were to stay over that first winter with the New Englanders, and that number was to increase as Warren brought in his French prizes. A number of these new arrivals — and I am not sure of the holding facilities — were treated as prisoners. The English diarists (de Forest) made numerous references as to how English search parties were sent out to gather up escaped prisoners.[13]

Next in importance to evacuating the French was that of getting Louisbourg defenses back up and to eliminate the external offensive works which the New Englanders had built during the course of the siege. The fear which Warren and Pepperrell had right along, continued: Canadian land forces might appear from the west; from the east, a naval force from France. Within two weeks, by June the 28th, the sick and the stores were moved into the city.[14] Slowly, through the summer, Louisbourg was to arise, phenix like, back into its defensive posture, now in its English cycle. Where Frenchmen had lodged, now Englishmen did.[15] Debris was being cleared, holes patched and guns remounted. Outside of the walls, within weeks, siege trenches had been filled in and all provisions, munitions, and armament locked away securely within the walls. This was work for Pepperrell's soldiers; Warren had another kind of work for his sailors.

Warren's Prizes:

At the first of the year, when he was wintering over in the West Indies, a scene we described earlier, Warren had a chore convincing his captains that they should undertake a northern cruise. They were of the view that England would be better served if the ships of the fleet stuck to their regular routes which included a continuing presence in the West Indies. But Warren was the senior man and his orders were broad enough to allow him to take part of his fleet to Louisbourg to assist the New Englanders in their attack against Louisbourg. The success of this combined military operation fully vindicated him, and, as we will see, earned him a promotion to that of a Rear Admiral. However, Peter Warren was most unlikely to have adopted such a course without some ulterior purpose. This purpose we see unfold in a marvelous fashion within days after the capitulation of Louisbourg.

The French flag was left to fly over the ramparts of Louisbourg and the English men-of-war were to sport French colours.[16] And thus it was, that a number of French captains were in for a rude awakening as they made their run into the harbor of Louisbourg. One was the captain of the *Notre Dame de la Déliverance*. She no sooner laid out her ground tackle when to the amazement of her captain and crew she was boarded by an armed party of the British navy; they were immediately advised that they were now prisoners of war.[17] For months, Warren and his naval men continued to play their net, and, like so many deadly spiders, pounced on the unsuspecting French merchantmen.[18] Due to the system of prize money[19] in existence back in those days, Warren was to make his fortune at Louisbourg.[20]

The *Vigilant* was Warren's first prize that he took at Louisbourg; it had aboard 1,454 ounces of silver plate, 125 gallons of brandy, and 2,905 of wine.[21] The *Vigilant* was taken on May 19th. Prior to that on May the 2nd, the *Marie de grace* from Brest was taken.[22] After the capitulation of Louisbourg, Warren set his trap and a number of merchant vessels fell in, all carrying provisions for Louisbourg, which, while reaching their destination, were now to be consumed by Englishmen.[23] As important as these merchant vessels and their cargoes were, however, there was another species of merchantmen which Warren knew might show up in his net. The first of these was to show up on June the 23rd, the *Charmante*.

Louisbourg at this time was a rendezvous point for the East India Ships which were making there way back to France. They made their way there after many months at sea, sailing around Cape Horn and catching the prevailing winds up the eastern coast of the Americas. At Louisbourg they expected to be convoyed home with the protection of French men-of-war. The *Charmante* was the first of the "French India Ships" which Warren was to get his hands on. She came to him on June 23rd. She was a 500 ton vessel and had 28 guns and 99 men. The *Charmante* had in her holds, 100,200 pieces of eight.[24] The next "French India Ship" taken, "with little effort," during the later part of July, was the *Héron* (24 guns; 500 tons; 118 men) she had 250,847 lbs of pepper aboard.[25] But the richest catch of all, and, the one for which Peter Warren was to immeasurably increase his fame and fortune was *Notre Dame de la Délivrance* "with a cargo of bullion, cocoa, Peruvian wool and quinine." The *Chester* and the *Sunderland* brought her in. She was from "Lima in the South Seas, for which place she sailed from Cadiz; she apparently had been making her rounds since 1741; and, she was loaded. She had in her holds, 972,000 pieces of eight, 13,278 gold double doubloons, 291½ lbs. of virgin silver, 65½ lbs. in gold bars."[26]

The English navy, with its successful captures, brought great joy to all, even those on land, who, taking a moment out, and while leaning on their pickaxes and shovels, would witness a proud and patriotic moment and give out with a cheer as these captured French vessels were towed in. But there was to be nothing in it for the New Englanders. While they went about cleaning up Louisbourg, the navy boys were, — well, just cleaning up. It did not take long for some very serious unrest to spread among those on shore. "Hey! It was us that thought this business up. We came to Louisbourg and did the fighting. We're denied our right to plunder and pillage; hell, we have to stand guard and take care of the Frenchies and their stuff. Nothing in it for us; we just do the dirty work — hauling stuff around; repairing walls; cleaning out the shit; wrestling with cannon, getting them from here to there; and, nothing but slop for food and wet tents to crawl into.[27] And there — Look! These navy guys, these 'Brits' filling their pockets with gold. Now! — There's something wrong with this. And, besides we have families to get back to; and, there's a harvest to be gotten in. We were promised. We were ..."[28] Well, the mumbles and grumbles by September, as we will see, turned into loud and distinct signs of insubordination. These first signs of an uprising, however, subsided, as the troops were somewhat diluted with fresh men. On July, 5th, "There came in another transport of Men from New England." This was Col. John Choate with two companies of his 8th Mass. Reg't. Also, on July 13th, certain of the New England men were embarked on Choate's transports so to be returned to their homes; mostly, I suppose, the sick and those with the best excuses.

Governor Shirley's Arrival:

For the balance of July and for the month of August matters seem to have settled down. Good summer weather I am sure contributed to the ease. There was some fishing and hunting for the boys to do, and, more generally, there was expected work to be done.[29] Directly, Louisbourg had been taken, "orders had gone out to New England for the immediate supply of great quantities of window panes, pine and oak boards and planks, spikes and nails, bricks and mortar, and every sort of hand tool."[30] Supplies and fresh men came in; and everyone was flush with victory.

On August 16th, there was to be a timely distraction. Just at dusk, in came in the 40 gun man-of-war, *Hector*, which had made a special run down to Boston in order to carry His Excellency, Governor Shirley — and his Lady, the Commodore's Lady, and many other gentlemen, and women etc." And there she was, the *Hector* all bedecked out and gleaming in the setting sun, there with her equally bedecked sisters, there before the prize of Louisbourg, safely in her harbor. She was to stir early the following morning:

8 o'clock A.M.: His Excellency [Governor Shirley] came ashore who was received with great respect and great tokens of joy being saluted by the men-of-war, 17 cannon from *Superb* and 17 from the *Hector*. The whole army was called to attend upon his excellency while he was walking through the street up to his house; and as soon as he had set his feet upon Louisbourg the cannons in the city were discharged. With a great deal of drumming, trumpeting and other instruments of music was this day filled up. ...

... the whole army was called together and His Excellency made an excellent speech both to officers and soldiers but all insufficient to make 'em really willing and contented to tarry all winter. He gave the soldiers two hogsheads of rhum to drink his majesty's health. After which he with the General and sundry other gentlemen walked all round upon the wall of the city while the ensigns with their colours were placed at each angle of the wall and all the soldiers in proportion who fired valleys as they passed along.[31]

Another witness to the event reports that at the citadel "the General had delivered to him after a short speech in the presence of the commodore the keys of the fort. The Commodore made a speech in praise of the officers and soldiers."[32] And another, "A very pleasant day. This day His Excellency went to see the Grand Battery which fired seventeen cannon at his arrival ... and the same at his departure ..."[33]

September At Louisbourg:

Much of Louisbourg, though she was to wear her scars of the siege for months yet, was on her surface quite presentable, due, no doubt, to the preparations for a proper reception of Governor Shirley and the Ladies. On September the 13th a schooner came in with intelligence. Nothing was heard of the French squadron; the "Acadians were quiet."[34] Joseph Richardson was sent to Annapolis to give them information and to continue on and "cruize the Bay of Fundy for intelligence and return the latter end of the month."[35] On September 23rd, Capt. John Rous arrived in "19 days from England."[36] The news: England was all astir and celebrating the capture of Louisbourg, Warren was to be made Rear Admiral of the Blue and Pepperrell, a baronet. On September 24th, Colonel Gorham returned from Bay Vert, "every thing quiet at Nova Scotia."[37] On September, 30th: "Rous sailed upon a cruise to St. Lawrence River to get what intelligence he could."[38] The rumors of a French fleet from France, had been circulating since the New Englanders had first arrived in the spring.[39] In the following months there was no sign of this French fleet, then, in September, in came a vessel from Carolina loaded for London. She hauled into Louisbourg and delivered intelligence that she had fallen in, three weeks before, with a French squadron consisting of seven men-of-war.[40] This meeting occurred at sea "about 150 leagues to the eastward of Newfoundland banks." The French squadron was bound for Louisbourg, and, indeed, the French had captured this Carolina vessel. The French naval officers, however, released the vessel and directed her to go on her way to Louisbourg. This, presumably, to advise that there was a French naval force descending. The New Englanders now took a defensive position and there could now be seen English eyes peering out from the walls just as French eyes had been doing but three months earlier; an invasion fleet might anytime emerge, ghost-like, through the fog. Men on the ramparts seem to think they just spotted something, but, no. Fishing vessels come into harbor with reports that maybe they saw something? Everyone was on edge.[41]

In these northern parts, autumn is a time when all of nature stirs: all living matter — the land and the animals and men who live upon it — instinctively prepares itself for winter's assault. Men, more then than now, were aroused with their annual sense of unease: there was a harvest to be gotten in and things around the farm had to be put right. The New England men at Louisbourg in September of 1745, though far from home, were to feel this unease. The complaints, first registered in July, were now to be heard again. They had not signed on for garrison duty. They all wanted to go home; and, as the season advanced, despite promises, it seemed plain that no relief by way of regular British soldiers was going to be seen at Louisbourg, at least not that year. There was, by mid September, a "great tendency to general mutiny amongst the soldiers."[42] The authorities at Louisbourg — and during September at Louisbourg could be found Governor Shirley, General Pepperrell, and Admiral Warren[43] — they all knew that they had a serious problem on their hands. Louisbourg by feat of arms was captured for the King of England, but how was she to be held if there were no, or few men to hold her? First they would, as all administrators have done down through history, stage ceremonies. What was necessary was an outward rite or observance, solemn acts in accordance to prescribed form, all accompanied with appropriate solemnity. The military is very good at this. It was time to get the royal representatives back on display so as to promote a suitable amount of reverence and veneration. On the 17th of September, "The Governor and Commodore and their Ladies and other great men and ladies went to the Grand Battery and the Island Battery" and there was to be heard across the waters and echoing off the walls a 17 gun salute from each battery.[44] The pomp and ceremony had an immediate effect. Next, came the political promises. On September 18th there was a "Beat to arms" and speeches were made. The Governor made a speech to each regiment told them that he had sent to New York and Philadelphia for clothing, and that their wages should be eight pounds a month, and that, etc., etc.[45] The speech had a good effect. Afterwards, to the gathered throng, "the Governor and Commodore each gave 2 hogsheads of rum."[46] These celebrations, together with the increasing confidence that with the advancing season the French would not likely be launching a counter attack, put the attitude and spirit of the English garrison on a different plain. They were going to be there until spring and they might as well make the best of it.[47]

Sickness And Death At Louisbourg:

September turned into October and the countryside gave its blazing goodbye, then the weeds began to rot and the leaves began to fly. The men at first, it seems, ate well,[48] but as dull November took hold it must have been realized that they were short of supplies necessary to get them through the winter, now about to come down all around them. I am not at all clear why this shortage occured, it certainly made itself felt in a deadly fashion before spring.[49] Late in the summer or early fall of 1745, Mascarene had seen to the delivery of livestock; it immediately meant good eating, though I should think that most of it was salted down.[50] These fresh provisions from Acadia were but a mere supplement to the provisions that flowed into Louisbourg on account of Warren's activities. We have already dealt with Warren's prizes, the cargoes of which were shipped out to be sold with the proceeds used to fatten the bank accounts of the privileged. The record discloses that captured French ships had aboard: flour, butter, salt, pork (10 tons of it, presumably salted), vinegar, oil; and, too: soap, vinegar, oil and cloth; and kegs and kegs of brandy and wine. Given the dreadful events to be described, one can only but wonder what happened to all this stuff. And, remember too, that New England ships, along with men and building supplies, brought up food from Boston. Louisbourg itself, or rather its surrounding waters, would also give up a wealth of food in all manner of fish. We also see from the records that winter fuel was laid in.[51] Why was it that such a terrible winter was to be spent by these men from New England; within months, hundreds and hundreds were buried at Louisbourg.

Better than half of the garrison was to die, slowly from diseases exacerbated by exposure to the bitter elements of that winter, 1745/46. It was likely due to an epidemic that swept through the population at Louisbourg. Disease produced by causes which we now might only guess at. A lack of good food, or a lack of dry and warm accommodations might be high on the list; and the sick, especially where there is a preponderance of them, cannot fend for themselves. Warren and Pepperrell were to take honors and praise for their leadership, in the taking of Louisbourg; but can they take praise for seeing the men through the winter; they were both there, but their presence made little difference. Maybe there was nothing to be done about it. The right materials and the right provisions were needed to be brought in from England (impossible) and from New England (more likely.) These were hard times; these were times of war; these were times when privateers lurked about ready to capture a ship and take her provisions. And yet, I am not convinced that the tragedy of Louisbourg, not of the French, but of the English, might have been avoided and it is hard to believe it had much to do with lack of provisions.

As early as April, when the New Englanders landed at Canso, "Men begin to sicken."[52] We see that this trend continued throughout the first month of the siege.[53] With the better weather of the summer months one doesn't see much reference to sickness at Louisbourg. By September, it seems to take hold again.[54] As the fall of the year advanced, we see a real progression of disease and men start dropping like flies. A reading of Rev. Williams' diary, brings the deadly results out in stark relief. It shows the disorder, sickness and death that prevailed at Louisbourg, post-capitulation. It's as if the French knew and feared the forthcoming miseries, enough to hand over Louisbourg so that they (the French) could go home to the comforts of France and to leave the conquering heroes to the ravages of the diseases that were to take hold. Herein following, I set forth but a sampling of the entries of Rev. Williams' diary, entries, I should remind the reader, made before the worst of it was to arrive that dreadful winter:

July 26th:

I passed by the Commodore's he invited me in to drink — a dish of coffee — I saw the French merchant, and his daughter, that came from the Indies — who were gay and easy.

July 27th:

... vessels from New England with live stock as cattle — sheep — fowls — but I don't see how the poor people — are able to buy — I mean the soldiers who want such things very much.

July 29th:

... this afternoon there was an unhappy fray in the city — one of the captains of the men-of-war — caned a soldier who — struck the captain; again — a great tumult was occasioned — swords were drawn — but no life lost — but great uneasiness, is caused.

July 30th:

... a Court Martial, has been held — I know not what has been done — I wish there was more order.

August 10th:

... this day one Stanley the man that took the sheets from the dead corps [July 29th] was whipped at the parade, at the head of the army. 39 lashes were given to him.

August 29th:

Dined at [Ezekiel] Gilmans — with some French gentle folks — who were modest — and handsome — after diner visited Serg't Smead, and Mr. Dodgett — walked the walls — Joseph Crowell died this afternoon.

September 4th:

Visited Mr. [Samuel] Windslow — who is very sick, and prayed with him at his brothers [William], the commissary.

September 7th:

This day Mr. Samuel Windslow dies — as did one Tarbell ...

September 11th:

Went to the Generals — and found dear Mr. Bullman dead [Alexander Bullman, Pepperrell's personal physician] ... last night one Lt. Bullock ... died as did one Thomas ... and Captain Eastman's Negro, London, died this morning, thus the dead are multiplying. One of Captain Warner's men whose name was Procter died he had tended at the hospital. Yesterday one of Captain's Baglies men died ... One Sergeant Millet of Captain' Byles' company was buried — that died last night.

October 25th:

Went to dine with the Admiral again — afternoon — went and prayed — at the house where Captain John Baker lived — where they were very sick — attended — the citadel prayers — this day four men buried at the Grand Battery — Lt. Chaplins men and four more ...

November 10th:
... this day was buried — one Ebenezer Stevens and Amos Hovey both of Colonel Molton's company. And one, Mudget, of Captain Light's company of New Hampshire; and one, Slate, an Indian of Colonel Bradstreet's company — and a Lt. ... of Captain Goldthwait's company.[55]

Williams, himself, became sick. We see from one of his last entries in his Louisbourg Journal, where, on November 29th, 1745, he "went in chair — covered" aboard the Massachusetts frigate; so ill he was (a high fever) that he made no account of his voyage back to Boston.[56] But Williams was one of the lucky ones; he got out of Louisbourg, alive. By June, 1746, a great number of New Englanders, variously estimated between 400 and 2,000, were buried at Louisbourg.

The weather at Louisbourg, which turned wet just after the French gave up, also contributed to the increasing sickness; or, maybe I should say, not so much the weather but the inattentiveness of their leaders and of the colonial soldiers themselves to keep out the worst of it through proper clothing, footwear and shelter. Many of the men caught their first chill upon their arrival at Louisbourg. On wading, some up to their waists through the cold Atlantic waters at the end of April, they were then "obliged when their Labour was over to lay on the Cold Ground in their Wet Cloaths under no better Covering than some Boughs laid together — the nights exceeding cold and foggy ..."[57] As the month of May advanced we see other entries: "Very cold and has snowed for several hours together."[58] We read that on May 11th: "The variety of fatigues and the unwholesomeness of the climate with the poor accommodations, etc. — were hard for the men at last who were taken down in great numbers with fever and fluxes — so that at some times near 1,500 were uncapable of duty."[59] And Seth Pomeroy wrote in his diary on May 31st: "People many of them are ill — the reasons I think are plain and the ground is cold and wet the water much of it is in low marsh ground of a reddish colour and stagnated and the people no beds to lie on nor tents to keep out the fogs and dew. Too, our provisions is chiefly pork and bread without sauce, except a small matter of beans and pease. [The overall effect is to] set the people into fluxes."[60]

The diet of the common soldier was neglected, too. They were, it seems, left to generally fend for themselves.[61] And, as we might now all understand from our review: liquor flowed profusely. It's consumption, as is usually the case, if not controlled[62] — and there didn't seem to be any direction from the top in this regard — will do considerable harm to the body and the spirit of a man. Important personal duties were neglected and the gates for the entry of sickness and disease were thrown open. Governor Charles Knowles, on his arrival at Louisbourg in the spring of 1746 to take up his duties as its English governor found the place, as expressed in a letter to the Duke of Newcastle, in a "confused, dirty, beastly condition." Disparaging the New Englanders (a regular sort of thing to do for British officers) Knowles continued: "they not only pulled down an end of the house in which they lived to [use as fuel], but even buried their dead under the floors and did their filth in the other corners of the house, rather than go out of doors in the cold."

By the end of November, 1745, the number of New Englanders manning the garrison amounted to 2,000. A number had gone home, some replacements had come up.[63] Warren reported that of the 2,000 "near a third of them sick."[64] It was to get worse!

The wind blew and the snow piled up against the walls of the fort. From the chimneys, poking up from within, could be seen curls of smoke emanating from fires which now had to be continually tended.[65] If, at the time, you had examined the top of the walls carefully one might see some movement as blanketed men replaced those in the guard houses perched here and there. Off, on the other side of the frozen harbor, could be seen another ribbon of smoke coming from a single fire about which a small number of men in rags huddled in a barrack of miserable description within the white banked cannonless walls of the Royal Battery.[66] In the far background, at the northeast harbor, could be seen the *Chester* and the *Vigilant* now stationary and frozen in.[67] By January 18th, 1746, 400 of the 2,000 were buried in graveyards about Louisbourg and 1,100 were sick. There was no escape; there was nothing to be done for these dying men but to hang on, assisted only by their dreams of home and of an early spring.

Some 480 Provincial soldiers had died of disease through the winter; quadruple the toll of the battle.[68] As one said, "No survivor ever forgot the miseries of that dire winter in cold and clammy Louisbourg."[69] With the warming sun of March and April, winter was to lose it's grip on Louisbourg. It had been full of sick and starving men and the melting snows revealed Louisbourg to be a massive midden. Those who had survived the winter could not do much more then stand periodic guard; they waited; they prayed. What was necessary was for the ice to disappear from the harbor and the approaches: the sun did its business slowly. Men regularly mounted the walls and squinted at the sea horizon, "Is that a sail?"

Two regiments were to come from Gibraltar. It was intended that these regular British troops, should be transported directly to Louisbourg and so to relieve the weary New Englanders. It was initially promised that they would be there in the fall of the year. The delay in getting the escort and transport ships set at Gibraltar and, above all, because of the exigencies of ocean travel by wind driven ships, the British troops were delayed in their trip across the broad Atlantic. Not able to buck the autumn "northeasterlies," the transports put in at Virginia and New York, and there the Gibraltar troops wintered over. The following spring, on the 21st of April, 1746, troops, 1219 in number, were to disembark. They were of the 29th Foot (Fuller's) and the 56th Foot (Warburton's) under the command of Lt.-Col. Peregrine Thomas Hopson and Lt.-Col. John Horsman, respectively. In addition, somewhere near a 1,000 colonial volunteers raised back in Massachusetts by Pepperrell and Shirley, also arrived at this time. As of June 2nd, 1746 there were 2,524 at Louisbourg.[70]

Conclusions:

On July 4th, 1745, eleven transports carried Governor Duchambon and his French followers out of Louisbourg.

Duchambon had lost Louisbourg; this expensive edifice, built to serve the French king and his empire; this chessman, critical to the protection of the Laurentian throat of French North America. The English, with its powerful navy, could now cut French lines, both of supply and command; choke off New France, which by this time, the mid-eighteenth century, through her occupation of forts in the Ohio and Mississippi valleys, had extended her influence deep within the North American continent and stood as a French fence restricting the English from expanding into the broad west. Duchambon had some explaining to do.

Duchambon Filed His Report:

... I must tell His Majesty truthfully that all the enemy's batteries — mortar and cannon were firing constantly and had been since the day they were constructed. The same was true of the musket fire from the Francoeur battery. All the houses in the town were demolished, riddled with holes, and not fit for habitation. The flank of the Bastion du Roy was destroyed, as were the wooden embrasures which we had improvised.[71]

It would not seem, in the loss of Louisbourg, that the French authorities much took into account Duchambon's irresolution, for he "was exempted from surrendering the fortress on military grounds alone ..." It was thought that "the outcome of the siege was critically influenced by forces outside his control. Faults in fortification design, poor garrison morale, limited artillery and munitions, [and] the ministry of marine's failure to realize the full danger of an Anglo-American attack" until it was too late: these were the factors which accounted for the loss of Louisbourg to the Anglo-American forces.[72] The 65 year old Duchambon was simply pensioned off.

What happened to Shirley, Pepperrell and Warren? Well, Shirley returned to his gubernatorial duties (Massachusetts). In 1749, the British, taking advantage of his knowledge of America, appointed Shirley as their representative on the Boundaries Commission which meant that he was to spend time in France (it was there, Lady Frances having died in 1746, that Shirley married his landlord's young daughter, a Roman catholic, yet!). In 1753, he returned to his position as the Governor of Massachusetts, but did not last long; in 1756, he was recalled to England. Eventually, proving himself a bit of an embarrassment to everybody, he was shipped off to the Bahamas as its governor; he died there in 1771. As for Pepperrell, well he was knighted. Sir William retired to live the life of a gentlemen on his estate at Kittery (now, the State of Maine, close on to the border with New Hampshire). Pepperrell, for a generation of New Englanders, was the only real American military hero that they had ever known; until the American Revolution came along, which, of course, produced numerous heros and a foundation upon which the American military legend was built. Warren: On September 25th, he was made an Admiral of the Blue, the news of which was greeted by the saluting guns of his ships stationed in the harbor of Louisbourg. He was made the first governor of Cape Breton; but he did not want to stay, and soon, was with Shirley at Boston planing for its defense against a French attack which was expected to unfold in 1746. With the d'Anville disaster, which resulted in the scattering of dead and sick French soldiers on the shores of Chebucto (now Halifax), an event with which I shall deal in the next part, and the passing of the French scare of 1746, Warren sailed for England and was soon, once again, on active sea duty. He teamed up with his old boss Admiral George Anson; and the both of them went off to make history in the battle of Cape Finisterre (1747) (a place located off the northwestern corner of Spain). From it, Warren sailed home, once again a hero; he was made a knight companion of the Order of the Bath and promoted to a higher rank. With the coming of peace, in 1748, Warren turned his attention to politics and philanthropy. He died suddenly at Dublin and "buried in Ireland in the parish of his birth."

I end this piece with a quote from James Hannay: If such a deed — "a band of untrained artisans and husbandmen, commanded by a merchant, should capture a fortress that it had taken thirty years to build" was to have occurred in Greece 2,000 years ago, it would have been made "the theme of innumerable commentaries, the details ... would have been taught to the children in the schools generation after generation, great statesmen would have written pamphlets on the subject, and great poets would have wedded it to immortal verse." However, after a brief celebration, this victory, as a historical matter, was tossed aside as "a fluke." The English considered that Louisbourg was a worthless card, or so it seems, for they readily gave it back to the French in 1748, by the terms of the *Treaty of Aix-la-Chapelle*. The colonies were not to forget that the English authorities gave so little regard to their great feat of arms: they bled for the cause of Britain at Louisbourg and close on to 2,000 of their men died there; 28 years later they would bleed again in another cause, in the cause of freedom and the American Revolution, the roots of which can most certainly be traced back to the shores and bogs of Louisbourg.

a Fresh Water R. &c. Sackville Fort

3 . 4 . 5 6 6 6 6
7
5 . 4

B E D F O R D

B A Y

A PLAN of the
TOWN & HARBOUR
of HALIFAX in
NOVA SCOTIA

A Scale of 2 Miles

M. W. N

Sandwich River

This R. is Saltwater so far as 'tis Navigable

The Parade

C H I B U C T O   H A R B O U R

13
10

13
14

5

16 16

18

15

15 17

13 16

Georges I.

DARTMOUTH

H A L I F A X
T O W N

Sandwich P.

4 5
8
8

Cornwallis

10
5 6 9 7

12
14
15

Mouth of the HARBOUR

Part Five

The Intermission:

1746-1754

Chapter 1

Introduction

It will be recalled that during March of 1744 war broke out between France and England, *The War of The Austrian Succession.* For thirty years prior to that time there had been peace, one secured by *The Treaty of Utrecht,* 1713, which by its terms peninsular Nova Scotia was to be English and Cape Breton was to be French. In the intervening years, a fortress was built by the French on Cape Breton, one unequaled in all of English America. This was Louisbourg, the eastern citadel of New France. During these years, 1713 to 1744, the English held their peninsular part with but two ragged and forgotten garrisons: Canso and Annapolis Royal. Annapolis was then the English capital of Nova Scotia and situated at a well established civilian community of French farming inhabitants, the Acadians.

In May of 1744, before they were even aware that they were at war, the English were rudely awakened at Canso when a French force, dispatched from Louisbourg, suddenly arrived and overpowered the small English garrison. It was on this date that war between these two European powers, after a relatively peaceful thirty years, was to break out in Nova Scotia. Nova Scotia was no stranger to conflict; she was born to conflict. Many of the senior French and Indian fighters, who now took to the field in 1744 with their sons, knew of these old conflicts and feelings of hatred for the English which had continued to burn deeply in their souls.

During these days, an English civilian population was practically non-existent in Nova Scotia. During the 17th century Nova Scotia was settled, and exclusively so, by the French. The French settlers which came over beginning in the mid-century came to be known as Acadians. The Acadian families prospered, grew, and expanded their territory throughout the farming lands of peninsular Nova Scotia, being, for the most part, those lands which had been washed by the waters of the Bay of Fundy: from Port Royal, to Minas, to Cobequid and around to Beaubassin. The Acadians were to remain, by and large, neutral in the French/ English conflict during these years. The natives, the MicMac, whose population was small and spread out, were united under their French missionaries and ready, in most engagements, to help their French friends.[1]

In addition to the taking of Canso and to a number of French raids on Annapolis Royal[2] the major engagement during the *War of the Austrian Succession* was that at Louisbourg, when, much to the surprise of many, an army of New Englanders with the help of the British navy took the place in 1745, the First Siege of Louisbourg, an engagement which I have treated in some detail in our last part.

We will, in this part, deal with the major concluding events of the *War of the Austrian Succession* which unfolded in Nova Scotia, being: the d'Anville's Armada (1746) and the Massacre at Grand Pré (1747). Then we shall see how the *War of the Austrian Succession* came to an end with the signing, in Europe, of the *Treaty of Aix-la-Chapelle* in 1748. By its terms, Louisbourg was returned to the French; and how, in the result, Halifax was founded in 1749.

With the conclusion of the war, one would have thought that this period of time which we are about to review, between 1748 and 1756, would have been years of peace. However, all that the *Treaty of Aix-la-Chapelle* was to accomplish was to return things back to the *status quo anti*. The questions in North America, in respect to territorial rights, had not been resolved: they just became more pressing: matters continued to seethe.[3] Historians have expressed the view that the *Treaty of Aix-la-Chapelle* was less a treaty of peace then a treaty of truce. War, this time a decisive one, was to break out in 1756, *The Seven Years War*. This part of my history deals not only with those events of 1747 through to 1749, as outlined in the previous paragraph, but also those events occurring in Nova Scotia leading up to *The Seven Years War*: Fights at the Isthmus of Chignecto (1750-54), The

Burning of Beaubassin (1755) and The Taking of Beauséjour (1755). Thus we deal with the events in that period between the wars, 1748 and 1756: the intermission.

Before we start into describing the events of this part, let me remind you of the dreadful situation which had existed in Louisbourg during the winter of 1745/1746. Hundreds of New Englanders had died due to sickness and starvation. They were relieved with replacements in April of 1746, both by regular British troops and new colonial volunteers. These British troops were the first sizable group of English regulars yet to come — Nova Scotia was to see many, many more in the next fifteen years. On the news that Louisbourg had capitulated, the English authorities had sent out orders to Gibraltar to board a couple of the regiments located there onto transports and to send them to America. A considerable amount of time was to pass before the transports were rounded up in England and then sent with their escorts over to Gibraltar; and then more time to provision and embark the troops. So too, on account of bad weather, the crossing was delayed. The best they could do was to make it to Virginia and New York. At these places they wintered over, renewing their trip in the early spring. These "Gibraltar troops" were of the 29th Foot (Fuller's) and the 56th Foot (Warburton's) under the command of Lieutenant Colonel Peregrine Thomas Hopson and Lieutenant Colonel John Horsman, respectively. In addition, somewhere near a 1,000 New colonial volunteers, which Pepperrell and Shirley had raised back in Massachusetts, were sent up to Louisbourg. Thus, as of spring, 1746, there were 2,524 fresh troops at Louisbourg. The British navy, which played a critical role in its capture in the previous year, was also to be found at Louisbourg, and, in considerable force. To begin with, there was the *Dover* (44 guns) and the *Torrington* (44 guns) which had convoyed the Gibraltar regiments up from New England during April. Then, on the 9th of May, Vice-Admiral Townsend arrived from Antigua in the *Pembroke* (60 guns), with the *Kingston* (60 guns) and *Kinsale* (44 guns). These were, on the 23rd of May, to be joined by the *Norwich* (50 guns) and the *Canterbury*

(60 guns). Both of these last mentioned men-of-war came in directly from England. Aboard the *Canterbury* would have been found Commodore Knowles who succeeded Admiral Peter Warren as the governor of Louisbourg.[4] The royal navy, with their seven men-of-war, would have doubled the manpower at Louisbourg, manpower that was badly needed during this critical period. Both Knowles, Townsend, and their men focused exclusively on getting Louisbourg ready for the expected onslaught, such that on October 13th, Townsend reported that "very little remains to be done at Louisbourg. It is now in a much better state of defence than ever it was."[5]

Other than Louisbourg, Annapolis Royal, during these years, was the only other fortified place in Nova Scotia and, as such, the theater in which conflicts between the English (as defenders) and the French (as attackers) were played out. Pretty Annapolis Royal was the scene of more battles through the years than any other contested place in North America.[6] Mascarene, who had come in with the invading British forces in 1710 to take the place, continued to be in charge. It is Mascarene whom we are to thank for holding Annapolis Royal and keeping the French population, the Acadians, generally quiet and neutral throughout the succeeding and lonely years between 1710-1745. In 1746, Mascarene and his forces came close, however, to being totally overpowered by a massive French invasion fleet; but the forces of fortune (good for the English and bad for the French) was to keep Annapolis Royal, English; and, it is to this day, peculiarly so.

———————

Chapter 2

The d'Anville Armada (1746)

The Grand Plan:
   The French, totally exasperated by the loss of Louisbourg, set out in 1746 to put the matter back to right. There was to be a lesson taught to those who thought they could interfere with the might of France. The teacher was to be Admiral Jean-Batiste, De Roye de la Rochefoucauld, Duc d'Anville, a French aristocrat, in his thirty-seventh year, a man "worthy to be loved and born to command."[1] He carried "the French king's commission to retake and dismantle Louisbourg, effect a junction with the army of Bay Verte,[2] and expel the British from Nova Scotia, consign Boston to flames, ravage New England, and waste the British West Indies."[3] Alas, this powerful French Armada, was to suffer every disaster known to the seafarer: all, at the hands of nature.

The Fleet:
   The fleet consisted of 20 warships, 32 transports and 21 smaller auxiliary vessels.[4] On the transports were 3,000 veteran troops[5] which, when added to the naval hands of 10,000, made for a grand total of 13,000 men.[6] In addition, four more large warships under Conflans,[7] which at this time were cruising the West Indies, were ordered to join up with d'Anville at their gathering place, the harbor of Chebucto, present day Halifax.
   This military force, short possibly of the Spanish conquistadors of a previous century, was, I believe, the largest ever to venture into American waters up to 1746. The plan germinated in the minds of the French military men when first they received news that Louisbourg, thought impregnable to the sallies of New Englanders, was taken. Louisbourg could not be left in the hands of the English. For, what then would be next? Quebec? Was Canada and 150 years of French development in North America now at risk? What was needed, if France's world

reputation was to be maintained, was to launch such a strong force, that, in quick order: Louisbourg would be retaken; then Annapolis Royal; and then to sail down and bombard both Boston and New York. From there, these ambitious Frenchmen would travel down into the West Indies and take certain of the English plantations. Such a force must be massive so to accomplish these objectives in one season, so massive that sustained resistance to it would be impossible, so massive that these English colonists would think long and hard before attempting any further attacks on New France.

Throughout the late fall of 1745 and through the winter and the spring of 1746, this massive French armada was formed. The French countryside was combed; military stores and men were being concentrated in the ports. Though it was soon to be obvious to all, including the English, that the French were getting ready to make a large amphibious attack,[8] only a few at the top of the military hierarchy knew that it was intended that this attack was to be on the English northeastern coast of North America, beginning with a recapture of Louisbourg.

The Delay:

Advance scouting ships, two of them, at different times, set sail for Nova Scotia early in April. I think it had been expected that d'Anville and his fleet would follow within weeks of that, but delay after delay was to be experienced. All it took was for one contractor not to make his promised date and the missed material or supplies would cause the entire project to shift this way and then that. Ships at the last minute were condemned. Men and cargoes had to be shifted; then yet, another missed date. More despatches from Paris, more delays. Another contractor fails in a delivery, or is short, or delivers the wrong material. More problems. Troops are put on board and then taken off again as another delay was announced. Time, precious time considering the difficulties of a late Atlantic crossing, melted away. Finally, on May 22nd, this very impressive French fleet gets under way and departs Brest. Head winds are encountered and the fleet determines to put in and wait for more favorable winds. They make their way into another French port south of Brest, Rochelle. More despatches are sent and received. Certain men are taken off the vessels; others put on. The ships are topped up again with water and supplies. More time passes. More despatches. On June the 20th, the fleet got under way a second time and cleared Rochelle. The men on board were already tired and beginning to be sick, and this even before the coast of France faded from view over their sterns, as the seventy plus seagoing sailing vessels made their way westward into the great expanse of the Atlantic ocean.

Canadian Forces Gather:

The Quebec authorities had received despatches and knew that there was to be a great fleet of French ships and would make Chebucto at some point during the summer. Land forces were to be sent down from Quebec to coordinate activities between the French allies the MicMac and the local French population, the Acadians. Fresh supplies and pilots were to be ready at Chebucto to assist the French sailors and soldiers who would need help after their long trans-Atlantic voyage. At some point during the summer, about 150 of de Ramezay's[9] men were in place at Chebucto scanning the sea horizon for French ships.[10] On June 7th, 1746, the first of two advance ships of the d'Anville expedition arrived.

The Advance Ships:

The two advance ships were the *l'Aurore*, having left Brest on the 9th of April, and the *le Castor* which had gotten away about three weeks later.[11] By June these two vessels were at Chebucto, and, by turns, were patrolling the seas nearby. For weeks they did this hoping to discover the large French fleet, however, no French ships were to be seen. By August the captains of these French men-of-war, I suppose, concluded that the expedition had been called off. It was now getting to be too late to carry out the plans. Something has happened! But, what? On August 12th these two advance vessels departed and shaped up their courses for France. They were to arrive at Brest on the 22nd of September.[12]

Rumors:

In the meantime, the English knew the French, because of their activity throughout the winter were up to something. It was war; attacks were to be expected. Was it to be at some point along the English coast. Maybe a landing in Scotland. Maybe in America. With the capitulation of Louisbourg during the summer of 1745, it was thought that the French would likely make a try at getting it back. So too, they may attack other centers. The rumors were flying amongst the British colonists. The people were fearful — the British fleet not being in American waters — that the French would open up with their big seagoing guns and pour down fire and destruction on seaport after seaport along the New England coast; and, each time, to come ashore and have their way. As imaginations ran wild, both at Boston and New York, there was panic in the streets and prayers in churches. No one knew exactly when, or exactly how; but the French would not let the events of the previous year at Louisbourg go unrevenged.

It was a summer of rumors. Indeed, French men-of-war were active off the coast of Nova Scotia during the summer. But — What was their strength? — Their plans? The first information of any substance that a French fleet might descend on Louisbourg was contained in a despatch which Admiral Townsend received at Louisbourg on the 5th of July. The despatch arrived in a ship which had been detached from a British squadron cruising off of Brest. The following day a message was written and sent to Boston:[13] there was "certain advice that a strong squadron of the enemy's men-of-war, frigates and fire ships with transports (on board which are a great number of troops) actually sailed from Brest 22 May, designed for Great Britain, Ireland or Louisbourg."[14]

The American poet, Longfellow, expressed the feelings:

A fleet with flags arrayed
Sailed from the Port of Brest
And the Admiral's ship displayed
The signal: "Steer southwest."
For this Admiral d'Anville
Had sworn by cross and crown
To ravage with fire and steel
Our helpless Boston Town.

There were rumors in the street,
In the houses there was fear
Of the coming of the fleet,
And the danger hovering near.
And while from mouth to mouth
Spread the tidings of dismay,
I stood in the Old South
Saying humbly: "Let us pray!"

"Oh Lord! we would not advise;
But if in they Providence
A tempest should arise
To drive the French Fleet hence,
And scatter it far and wide,
Or sink it in the sea,
We should be satisfied,
and thine the glory be ....

The Crossing:

As it turned out: the prayers of the frighten New Englanders were answered. The French expedition of 1746 was a calamitous failure from beginning to end. The main fleet, as we have seen after extensive delays through the spring, finally got underway on June 22nd. No sooner did they clear the shore, indeed while yet in the Bay of Biscay — another problem literally blew in. A gale struck. Like all storms, this one in the Bay of Biscay eventually subsided. Suffering from storm damage and seasick men, the French officers might have determined to run back into a French port. To do so would cause further delay. The officers determined to press on sail and keep to their westward course, sailing over the broad Atlantic, fixing their positions as they went. Never could they steer a straight course; the winds dictated which way they would go; zig sagging this way and that. Worse yet, were the times that there was no way to be had at all, the entire French fleet still in the water, as lines and sails flapped to the rhythm of the rolling seas with not a breath of air to move them along. Weeks passed. Catch a breeze, here; catch a breeze, there. More weeks went by. The men were sick; the drinking water putrid; the biscuit buggy; and the contents of the brine barrels gray, smelly and sour. Men began to die and their bodies were then stitched into canvas, together with a cannon ball, and the resultant white bag slipped into the deep. Over it went; and, the corpse inside, some would say, in a better state than those, who, with vacant eyes, watched the daily ceremony. More weeks went by and finally their destination was near as the thin line of Sable Island was spotted. Then, suddenly, another more dreadful storm hit the fleet and scattered it.[15]

The Arrival At Chebucto:

This long crossing and two Atlantic storms wrecked both men and ships. The men, so full of spirit but three months earlier, at least those who had not been relieved by death, were now exhausted, diseased and infested — and, were soon to be faced with the shores of an American wilderness.[16] On September 10th, "three ships of the line and a few transports,"[17] after having been upon the dreadful sea for three months, limped into Chebucto (Halifax), its intended assembly point. The men were sick and dying; indeed, their leader, d'Anville, succumbed from the disease which was now sweeping the fleet; he died within six days of having come into Chebucto.[18]

Vice-Admiral d'Estournelle,[19] the second in command, arrived with "four more ships of the line" on the very day that d'Anville died. There then followed a sad scene which was played out on a little grassy island in the harbor (Georges Island in Halifax Harbor, or, as known by the French, Île Racket). One can just imagine a small group of down trodden French naval officers (d'Estournelle and La Jonquière among them) being rowed by a ragged and sick crew of French seamen, with the remains of their shrouded leader, to the shore of this little island in the middle of a huge bleak wilderness.[20] This business being done, the officers gathered in the main cabin of the *Trident*, in order to determine their course of action. The date was September the 31st and there was a nip in the air and the fall breezes announced to the experienced northern sailors that not too much time remained to carry out water born operations.

The Regrouping:

At the Council of war being held aboard the *Trident*, d'Estournelle recommended that the expedition be abandoned. Not all of the fleet had come in, and, missing with them, were the necessary stores and war materials; further, 2,500 men had already died.[21] Jonquière, the third in command, and, it seems, the only experienced naval officer with any gumption, was opposed to just giving up; at least, he urged, Annapolis might be taken. D'Estournelle was taken back with this opposition. D'Estournelle also now had the news that the expected help from Quebec, had, but days before, returned to Quebec.[22] D'Estournelle was heard to exclaim, over and over again, "All is lost; it's impossible."[23] He suddenly left the meeting. Angered and bewildered he went to his cabin and left the officers at the table wondering what his final decision might be. At some point through the night groans were heard emanating from d'Estournelle's cabin and a call soon brought certain of the officers to the cabin door. They torn the door down, and there they found d'Estournelle, there on the wooden floor of his cabin in a pool of blood: d'Estournelle had thrown himself upon his sword.

Jonquière Takes Command:

With d'Estournelle's attempted suicide and resignation, Jonquière found himself in the lead. This dynamic officer (if only he had been put in charge in the first place) faced a huge challenge. He recognized that whatever the next step might be he had to regroup. "There were still forty-two vessels left, of which thirty were ships, but the strength of the land forces had dwindled away to one thousand efficient men." The first order of business was to revive the men. He brought most of the vessels well into Chebucto and anchored them along the shore of the basin (Bedford Basin, near Birch Cove) and saw to the disembarkment of the suffering men. The sick were to be isolated and taken care of, to the extent possible. Certain of the large transports were made over to hospital ships. Shore camps were organized. All of this was to take time, but the steps were unavoidable if the French forces were to get themselves up and out of Chebucto, no matter what their next objective might be. Maybe, just maybe, they could get a small force assembled out of the mess so as to attack Annapolis. Through the balance of September and on into October those Frenchmen that could, were to carry out Jonquière's commands. Food was to be brought in overland by way of a long establish route.[24] These desperate Frenchmen were being served by their compatriots, the Acadians. The Acadian communities (Minas and Piziquid) were but 30 to 40 miles distant. So we would have seen oxen and men hauling carts of food, recently harvested, and driving animals along the broadened road from Minas to Chebucto (Windsor to Halifax).[25]

The tables had been overturned; and now it was to be the French who were to feel vulnerable. On October 22nd, a New England prize was taken by a French man-of war cruising off Chebucto. Aboard this prize was found a despatch from Shirley to Knowles advising that the English admiral, Lestock, with a fleet of 18 men-of-war, was due to arrive off the Nova Scotian coast, any day. This was cause of much concern. Also, at about the same time, an English schooner with a flag of truce came into Chebucto from Louisbourg with 40 French prisoners aboard. Intelligence was thereby gained that Louisbourg had a strengthened garrison of 2,000 regular soldiers and six British men-of-war. La Jonquière, in addition, was to receive a third

piece of discouraging news: de Ramezay and his Canadians
— who by then had been laying siege since the first week of
October — were having no noticeable success; for, Annapolis
Royal had been strengthened and had over a 1,000 men under
arms.[26] The decision was made to get clear of Chebucto. The
fleet would sail no matter their condition; and the Acadians and
MicMac who had been with the French at Chebucto were to be
sent overland to assist at Annapolis Royal.[27]

On October 12th, Jonquière's fleet was pared down. Certain
of the ships of the fleet were condemned, and, together with a
number of English prizes, were run ashore and burnt in Bedford
Basin.[28] La Jonquière "also distributed at least four English
prizes, including a 16-gun snow, to Acadians and Indians to carry
provisions to Canadians at Beaubassin." The assisting Acadians
were told by Bigot to return to their farms and then to cart and
drive fresh supplies (livestock) to Annapolis Royal to feed the
men of the fleet, who, it was intended, would make their way
there by sea.

The Final Push:

On October 13th (NS), "five weeks less a day" since it had
hauled into Chebucto, the French fleet, or what was left of it,
being 42 vessels, close to only half the number that had left
France, made its way out of Chebucto. Aboard these vessels
the French had about "1,000 efficient soldiers," out of the 3,000
which had embarked at France. Their intended destination,
now, was Annapolis Royal. The French Canadian force under
de Ramezay, which amounted to possibly 1,000, was, just as
Jonquière was clearing Chebucto, setting up camp about two
miles above Annapolis Royal.[29] The plan was that Jonquière
would sail into Annapolis Basin with his sea born forces and
meet up with the Canadians. The combined force would then
attack the English fort at Annapolis Royal. It was thought that
Annapolis must surely fall, even with this reduced French force.
To insure the safe arrival of every vessel, a large number of the
French inhabitants who were familiar with Annapolis Basin, had

come over from Minas to pilot the ships.[30] But, this doomed French expedition was yet to suffer another disaster. Off Cape Sable, just before the fleet was to make its turn into the Bay of Fundy, another storm came crashing into the fleet. After it had subsided, the scattered fleet was gathered in; and Jonquière made his final assessment. The threat still existed of the English fleet under Admiral Lestock coming upon them. Further, there was additional information coming to them from the runners on shore that Annapolis Royal had received even more help from Boston by way of men and ships.[31] A decision was made. The French would abandon the planned attack on Annapolis; the Acadian pilots were to be landed; and the fleet was to bear back to France.

The *Sirène*:

Earlier we had seen where two advance ships, *l'Aurore* and *le Castor*, had made Chebucto during June and then spent weeks patrolling the seas nearby looking for the French fleet. Sure that the plans had been changed, they left Chebucto on August 12th; on the 22nd of September they hauled into Brest. An interesting side story can now be told. The captain of the *le Castor* was Lieutenant chevalier de Saliés. As he jumped to the dock at Brest he was immediately greeted by his superiors. What news of the North American expedition? This question together with other questions were but answered with questions. No one knew what had become of d'Anville's fleet. Though de Saliés had just completed a six week voyage, he was given a fresh crew and a new ship, *Sirène* (30 guns) and ordered to make his way back across the Atlantic with dispatches for d'Anville. De Saliés returned to Chebucto, and, in record time, too; pulling in there on the 27th of October (OS), just one day after the fleet had left for Annapolis Royal. La Jonquière had left a message on shore for any French ship that should come into Chebucto to join the fleet by proceeding to Annapolis Royal; and that, de Saliés did. De Saliés sailed right on by the fleet, missing it, possibly because the ships were sheltering in one of the many bays of the area, getting water and tightening things back down to ready themselves for their trip back across the Atlantic. In any event, de Saliés got himself into the Bay of Fundy. He did not however proceed into Annapolis Basin, for, his intelligence was that there were three English gun ships in the Basin; he dared not venture in by himself. On November the 4th, having given up on meeting up with the fleet at Annapolis, de Saliés sailed the *Sirène* out of the Bay of Fundy and after casting about and looking for the fleet came to anchor at Port Maltois (Port Medway). During this period he came into contact with the French allies and was informed that the main fleet had left off and was making its way back to France.[32] On November 20th, the *Sirène* pulled her anchors and departed for France.[33]

The English Reaction:

The English had expected that the French might make a descent on Louisbourg during 1746; and, as we have seen, the first indication that this was likely to occur was the receipt of an official English despatch at Louisbourg during July. Within days of d'Anville's arrival, in September, the English were to know of it. A French prize was brought into Louisbourg, and, with a little persuasion, her captain was to tell the story. He had sailed from Rochelle on June 22nd (NS) in the company of "70 sail of ships, men-of-war and transports under the command of the Duc d'Anville, with 8,000 troops on board. Fourteen ships were of the line, from 50 to 70 guns. He left them on 15 July in the latitude of 44° 22'."[34] Also, a Marblehead fishing vessel was to come into Louisbourg, aboard her was a Frenchman which the Marblehead fishermen had rescued. This Frenchman had been cast away on Sable Island on September 3rd (OS). His story was that he had been on one of the ships in d'Anville's fleet which was separated by a "hard gale of wind." He knew nothing of the plans but he did know that the French "were very sickly and had buried a great many men." And yet, another report came into Louisbourg from a captain that "fell in with three sail of large ships about 40 leagues to the westward of a place called Jeddore."

The continuing intelligence, which flowed into both Louisbourg and Annapolis as October passed, showed that the French were sticking to Chebucto. Was it that they were going to mount an overland attack against Annapolis Royal? Were they going to winter over? The local English commanders prepared for the worst.[35]

The fear initially was that this mighty French armada would take Louisbourg, then take Annapolis Royal and then proceed down the coast and bombard Boston and New York. As time passed and summer wore on, this fear was to become less and less. Only during the first part of September was there to be any positive proof of the French presence on the shores of Nova Scotia. The news included reports that the French expedition was in serious difficulty because of sickness and storm damage. Thus, fears were to subside further, to the point, as September passed, that the people of Boston started to relax. More time passed. Louisbourg started to rest easier;[36] fears at Annapolis Royal, however, continued.[37] Warren reported, in a letter dated 24th October (OS), that an "express" had just arrived in from Annapolis Royal and the report, is, that "all was well there, that not one of the enemy's ships had appeared, but that the French and Indians ... were still about the garrison. I do not hear that they had any cannon or had much molested them. As the French fleet sailed on the 13th from Chebucto and had not got to Annapolis by the 20th (nor any of them seen by the vessel from thence), it strengthened my former opinion that they will not venture to go in there."[38] Shortly after, November 4th, 1746 (NS), Ramezay's forces, which had been besieging Annapolis Royal, broke camp and retreated up the valley as the first licks of winter were felt. The French threat to Nova Scotia, at least for 1746, was over.

Contemporary Wrap Ups:

And now what remains, is to give a few contemporary wrap ups.

Admiral Townsend, who was anxious to leave Louisbourg with his British fleet so to return home before winter would sock him in, on October 24th, concluded:

> ... the enemy are retired from Chebucto. They have not appeared in these parts. If you [Warren and Shirley] have heard nothing of them at Boston nor from Annapolis Royal, I shall take it for granted we shall hear no more of them in these parts this year. If we may depend upon the intelligence we have received, they are gone off in a miserable, shattered condition, having lost their *duc* and a great many men, a very considerable number remaining sick. Soon after they put out of Chebucto, they were overtaken by a violent gale of wind, [in referring to one of his own ships which had been caught out in it] which sprung the ship's mainmast and bowsprit and broke her fore yard. She was in such imminent danger that they [the English crew] were obliged to throw over four of her guns, by which we may judge the enemy suffered not a little.[39]

Mascarene, the closest English commander to the scene, has given us his intelligence of the events, gathered at the time and reported to Warren and Shirley in a despatch to them dated at Annapolis Royal, 26th October:

> I have acquainted you before of the French admiral duc d'Anville being dead with grief, soon after his arrival at Chebucto with a small part of his fleet, on his believing the rest either lost or scattered as not to reinstate... the intended projects. His death is confirmed. [In] addition, on the arrival of the rest of the fleet in that harbour, in a council held by the several commanders great divisions arose. The person who was appointed by the court of France next in command fell distracted and stabbed himself, but, his wound not being mortal, and coming to himself, was made to sign a declaration that he judged himself not capable of undertaking the command of the fleet. This command fell on M. La Jonquiere, *a chef d'escadre*.
>
> All relations agree that their fleet was extremely sickly. Besides the men thrown overboard at sea (which is said to be above 1,000) they buried above 1,500 at Chebucto, and sent 500 sick in six ships to France. They set out however from Chebucto on Monday the 13th instant for this place, as will appear by what follows. Coming abreast of Cape Sable [they] were met by a violent [northeast] gale of wind, which I think was on the 17th. When [they] again came together (except two ships missing) they came to a resolution not to prosecute their intended course hither, but to bear away for the West Indies. In consequence, having given two vessels to some inhabitants of Minas

whom they had taken [as pilots from here] to send them home and [tell] the Canadians that they were not to expect the fleet, they sailed away from this coast.

The Canadians received this intelligence on the 23rd and began to march away that same evening. The next morning two of the deputies of this river came to acquaint me with it. Their several scattered parties had begun to draw off early that morning and marched after their leaders up the river, on their return to Minas. I stopped the deputies and sent for Col. Gorham to take 200 men and follow the enemy, which was immediately executed.[40]

Edward How gave his version:

The best intelligence I can learn of the motions of the French fleet is as follows. They grew very sickly soon after they set out from France. They had 2,000 men die in the passage, besides a 50 gun ship foundered at sea and one lost on Sable Island. They dropped into Chebucto in small numbers until at last they all met together there, to the number of thirty-five men-of-war and transports. They found there two Canada frigates, who had been there all summer and had taken many prizes — amongst which was a ship that carried down a chaise and horses for Gov. Knowles. They say they had sent 200 English prisoners to Canada. The duc d'Anville died of grief soon after his arrival. There were two competitors for the command after his death, which occasioned a great quarrel between them and great disturbance among the whole fleet. [They] lay in Chebucto until the 13th instant [October], at which time they sent an officer express to advise the commander in chief of their troops here, whose name is de Ramezay, that he might expect them very soon. They buried 1,800 men whilst they lay at Chebucto. Some time before they set out, they sent six ships to France with their sick men.

On the 17th they were off Cape Sable, where they met with a northeast storm which dispersed them for a while. On the 19th, they all met again, except two. As they had Minas pilots on board, they put them on board [two] schooners and sent them home with a letter to M. de Ramezay, to acquaint him that they were put away through sickness to the West Indies, and that he might make the best of his way home, which he punctually obeyed ...[41]

And, so it was — but, only a single solidary French warship, *la Sirène*, was to come close to one of the prescribed destinations. A fleet of 70 ships had carried proud Frenchmen bent on a military mission to recover Louisbourg and revenge France by bombarding New England. This was the last of it, as *la Sirène* showed her stern and sailed over the eastern horizon; and, as her top sails disappeared, so did the last traces of the French threat of 1746. The mission had come to an ignoble end: not a shot was fired at the English.[42]

On December 5th, 1746, five commissioned merchantmen came into Chebucto Harbor laden with supplies that had long since been gathered up at Quebec as part of its contribution to the grand effort.[43] There they were, lying at Chebucto, with 570 tons of supplies; but, — no French fleet, — no grand army. All that could be seen on the deserted shores are ragged camps; deserted; blown in the wind; and, maybe, a few lingering natives to tell the sad story.[44]

———————

Chapter 3

Battle At Grand Pré (1747)

The Setting:

In June of 1746 we have seen where the French forces had mustered here and abroad. In the previous chapter we read of the trials and tribulations of the French naval forces under d'Anville. In order to assist the d'Anville expedition, the French authorities at Quebec had sent Ramezay[1] to Chignecto with "six hundred Canadians, and was joined there by three hundred Malicites, under Lieutenant St. Pierre, and a large body of MicMacs, under Marin."[2] Arriving during the month of June, they set up camp and waited at the isthmus intending to assist in the attacks on Louisbourg and on Annapolis Royal in concert with the French navy.

The Canadian forces spent the summer waiting at the isthmus, well positioned as they were to either spring to Louisbourg or to Annapolis Royal depending on the orders that should come. At Baie Verte, supplies continued to flow in from Quebec by shuttling sailing vessels. D'Anville's fleet, expected at Chebucto (the Halifax of today), due to its string of disasters, did not arrive until September. Thus the summer months of July and August were idled away by Ramezay's forces. As for the English at Louisbourg and Annapolis Royal, they too idled away their time, in fearful anticipation.

It will be remembered that the scattered French naval forces were regrouped such that, it was thought, that they might get at least one lick in at the British. Jonquière had intended to sail around from Chebucto to Annapolis Royal and then to bombard and take the place; but alas, due to yet another storm which was to severely knock the French fleet, the plans to attack Annapolis Royal were abandoned. In connection with this attack Jonquière had ordered the Ramezay forces, then divided between Chebucto and the isthmus to converge on Annapolis Royal. At some point in October all of this was put in motion and Ramezay and his limited Canadian forces appeared before Annapolis Royal. Not much could be done until the French naval forces and their cannon were to arrive; again, Ramezay waited, having pitched his camp about two miles above the English fort near the banks of the Annapolis River. On November 4th, 1746 (NS), having received the news that the French navy had sailed for France, the Canadian forces broke camp and traveled eastward up the valley towards Minas. It was determined that this French force would winter over in Acadia. They might well have, but the pleading Acadians[3] convinced them to move on; and so they returned back to places they had inhabited since June, at the Isthmus of Chignecto, there to set up their winter camp and make plans.[4]

The presence of d'Anville's fleet in Nova Scotian waters had given the people of New England quite a fright. Due to the threat, New England had significantly reenforced their outpost at Annapolis Royal. During September, Shirley sent approximately 300 soldiers up from Boston, thus raising the number of men under arms to about 1,000 at that garrison, a level which it had not seen for a number of years.[5] With the French fleet having departed North American waters in late fall, the French threat of 1746, disappeared. The English knew that the French would be back; so, the governor at Massachusetts, William Shirley, set his new plans for Nova Scotia, in motion.[6]

The English March:

Shirley's plans included sending a force immediately up from Boston. The force consisted of approximately 500 "Massachusetts men" under Colonel Arthur Noble. In the late fall this force[7] sailed into Annapolis Basin and called by at the fort. Not much time passed in exchanging courtesies. The force, it was determined, should go to Minas, particularly that part of it known as Grand Pré, a place that might be considered the middle point of Acadia. It was from Grand Pré that an English fort might be set up, a place from which operations might be launched for an early spring offensive against the French at the isthmus.[8] Part of the forces

(100 men under Charles Morris) marched down the valley to get to Grand Pré, some 70 miles distant, I would say a good two day march over a fairly well established roadway. It had been determined that the rest of the English forces with the heavier equipment would sail the distance from Annapolis Royal, down the Bay of Fundy and then into the Minas Basin. There was no thought that by sending vessels down, that time would be saved; as, in those days, the time spent in sailing ships varied depending on the wind and tide experienced. This was December in the Bay of Fundy and it could not have been expected that any great time would be made by sailing. The vessels would have had to buck head winds; and, so too, they had to buck the reversing tides of the Fundy, the fastest and the highest in the world. The land loving men on the sailing vessels, at one point, became nervous and they were put ashore at the "French Cross" (Morden), on the other side of the north mountains; they would simply meet the sailors and their vessels at Grand Pré, when ever they got there. Thus, on Christmas eve of 1746, we would have seen a couple of hundred New Englanders being put ashore; they were to make their way from there, best they could. This second group, while they might have originally thought that they were to have the easier time of it, had a tough eight day march, "without paths or guides," through the winter snow, over the Aylesford mountain and along unmarked sidehills, northeast, down the valley, until, finally, they met the south banks of the River Gaspereau, and there to find their comrades; who, most likely, were by then well settled in at Grand Pré. It was now January; the ground would most likely have been frozen and covered with the snows of winter.[9]

The New Englanders had brought along with them building materials and supplies in order to build two block houses for their defense. These materials and supplies were aboard the vessels, which, while they had some difficulties bucking the tides and the storms of the season, eventually did arrive.[10] So, in the background, there would have been seen these two English trading vessels, there in the midstream of the Gaspereau, battened down for the winter. Colonel Noble and his men soon came to terms with the local French Acadians, who, though not pleased, moved themselves around so that some twenty odd houses were taken over by these armed Englishmen. One was quite a large building made of stone,[11] the rest made of wood; all, were more or less in a row overlooking the marsh, Grand Pré, which the Acadians had through the use of dikes, turned what was once a flooded and silt laded flat, into superior pasture land. Noble might have made the decision to unload the boats and build the defenses, as hard as that might have been given the winter weather — he did not. The New Englanders went directly into winter quarters thinking they were completely safe for a couple of months after which better weather would allow them to free up their ships and supplies. The intelligence was that the French army was 150 miles away at the isthmus snugged in for the winter. In between, was nought but a frozen and pathless forest.[12] And so, the New Englanders settled in for a long winter's sleep.

The French March:

Now, by whatever means, while at his camp at the isthmus, Ramezay came to know during the course of January, 1747, that English forces had very recently gone into winter quarters at Grand Pré.[13] Ramezay had been at the place but two months earlier when he and his Canadians were on their way back from an abortive attempt in the late fall of 1746 to take Annapolis Royal. When he came through, all that could be seen at Grand Pré was a population[14] of Acadians who had pleaded with them (the French soldiers) to keep moving on through. The intelligence that first reached Chignecto, was that there were two or three hundred New Englanders that had arrived in late December at Grand Pré. This first report did not take into account that there was an English force of equal size on its way. This second group, as we have seen, had taken a different route and was to arrive around a week after the first group had reached Grand Pré. Ramezay certainly reckoned that the force reported to him, was larger than his and if the French were to wait for the spring for the English to attack them at the isthmus, then they were likely to be in for a bad time of it, as any such attack might be supported by additional sea-borne forces. The best chance was to march overland and engage the English as soon as possible, and, hope to catch the English napping. Thus the decision was struck to attack and to do so in the dead of an Acadian winter. The French, it should be observed, had a penchant for winter raids — the history books are peppered with them.[15]

Ramezay was feeling the effects of his 1746 exertions and determined not to lead his men on this arduous winter trek.[16] In any event, Ramezay had a very capable officer to lead the attack, Nicholas Antoine Coulon de Villiers. There were also among this French force at the isthmus a number of other able lieutenants; in all, possibly the best collection that New France was ever to see. Under Villiers were Chevalier Louis-François Chapt De Louis La Corne (1703-1761), second in command; Major Daniel Hyacinthe Marie Liénard Beaujeu (1711-55), the diarist of the mission[17]; and, Charles des Champs de Boishébert, an ensign and nephew of Ramezay's who at this time was but nineteen years of age and who was to fight bravely on for the cause of France in North America straight through to the end, in 1763. These were but a few of the *noblesse* of New France[18] who tramped along through the winter snows with their native friends; intent, as they were, to teach the *Bastonnais* a lesson.

So it was, that on January 23rd, 1747, we would have seen a couple of hundred[19] snow-shoed Canadians hauling their sledges[20] across the Isthmus of Chignecto. They first made their way on a traveled track from Beaubassin, on the western side of the isthmus to the head waters of Baie Verte, on the eastern side. There, likely more men[21] and supplies were folded into the larger group. Then they followed along[22] the shore of that body of water we now know as the Northumberland Strait — from Tignish to Tatamagouche, arriving on the 26th. At Tatamagouche these fur and snow covered soldiers were to replenish at the small French community there located. Next these Frenchmen turned inland, their next way-point being Cobequid (Truro). This next way was a well traveled, and indeed the principal road into the central lands of Acadia over which for many years cattle had been driven, destined for the French population at Louisbourg. A smaller party was sent forward in order to block roadways and to prevent the news of their march from traveling further into the Acadian heartland and thus to warn the New Englanders. These determined French travelers, in order to reach Cobequid, followed up the frozen French River to its head waters, then up and over the Cobequid Mountains to the head waters of the Chiganois River whose frozen ribbon traced the route to the eastern extremity of the Minas Basin. The Canadians reached the shores of the Minas Basin and the first of a number of Acadian villages located there, on January 31st, Nijaganiche.[23] At Nijaganiche they reprovisioned. They were expected; and fresh supplies had been assembled by Acadians friendly to the cause. The following day they carried east to the next village, Cobequid; more provisions were there available for the troops. Now they were coming closer to their objective, but immediately ahead, was one of their principal obstructions, the Shubenacadie River. It was to be reached by going a dozen miles west of Cobequid, through another community which the English in later years were to call Old Barns. The Shubenacadie is one of the larger rivers of Nova Scotia (none of which are of continental proportions) and it is open during the winter at its mouth and inland for several miles due to the fast rising Fundy tides that sweep in twice daily. There, on the eastern banks of the Shubenacadie, Villiers and his followers stopped. Could they get enough canoes together? Would they risk a crossing? After conferring amongst themselves and certain of the knowing locals, a determination was made to carry on up the eastern banks 25 miles, or so, until they reached the frozen and crossable upper reaches of the Shubenacadie. The nineteen year old, Ensign Boishébert, a noted boat handler, with ten of his men, volunteered to make the hazardous run across the mouth of the Shubenacadie.[24] It was important to the mission to get someone over so as to stop up the road to Piziquid (Windsor). Boishébert and his men were to travel along aways and then to stop and wait for the larger group which would take the longer, less riskier route. The crossing of Villiers forces was to take place just above where the Stewiacke River joined the Shubenacadie. This was Indian territory, one of the principal homes of the native MicMacs.

Where the Stewiacke spills into the Shubenacadie, there was then, and there is yet today, a community of MicMac. Le Loutre had established his mission there. These native people were naturally suspicious and could prove to be dangerous to any vulnerable group; however, due to careful French grooming, most all of the natives of North America, including those of the MicMac, were reasonably well disposed to the French. Our Canadian winter travelers, assisted on their way by their friends, were soon plodding towards the head waters of the Kennetcook which they reached on February the 7th. There they met up with Boishébert who reported that no one had passed him, so to give the English advance notice of the approaching French force.[25] Then down the frozen course of the Kennetcook to Piziquid (Windsor), the only major Acadian habitation between Cobequid and its objective and but 20 miles away from the mouth of the Gaspereau where the English were lounging the winter away.

Approaching Piziquid had to be done with some caution, as, it might be there that the first English soldiers could be encountered. Slowly, the advance scouts proceeded until the first Acadians houses came into view. The occupants confirmed that there were no Englishmen about at Piziquid and that they had all nested together at Grand Pré. The Acadians at Piziquid, just as it seems all Acadians along the tortuous winter route, were ready to lend assistance. At Piziquid, it is reported, "for the first time leaving Beaubassin, the French slept under a roof, with guards stationed on all the roads."[26] By noon the next day, which I believe would have been on the 9th of February, the French were on the move again, now but only a few miles from their objective. A winter's snow storm had started; indeed, from all accounts it turned into a blizzard. This condition made it difficult for the French to travel, but it covered their approaches, beautifully. We might then have seen, in his sleepy quarters at Grand Pré, an English officer, who: firsts steals a peek through a snow plastered window; then, yawns; then, meanders across a stone walled room, stepping lightly to avoid several sleeping men; then, over to stoke the fire; then to ladle out another mug of a mulled concoction in a pot hanging nearby; and, then to slump down, so to continued his dreamy existence.

The Prelude:

In anticipation of the coming battle, the French forces paused half way between Piziquid and Grand Pré. There, on the banks of a small intervening river, Villiers divided his men into ten squads. The 300, or so, were grouped off, as follows: seven of 25 each[27]; one of 50 (headed by Villiers); one of 40 (de la Corne, second to Villiers), and another of 21 (Lotbinière). They then proceeded, carefully through the driving snow. It was in the afternoon of the 9th. They halted, once again. They wanted to come on their targets under the additional cover of night. The men remained quiet and still; they became numb with the cold; night gradually fell. Lights in the not too far distance flickered, these were Acadian home fires along the Gaspereau. They moved forward; they stopped. One of the squads, however, continued its cautious approach.

The first house was that occupied by the Melançon family. Inside there was signs of a crowd; music and voices — why there was a party going on. One of the Melançon girls had been married and a reception for family and friends was taking place. It was dark; and a couple of our French travelers, dressed in leather and furs, all dusted with snow except that part of their beards where their steamy breaths were adding to tiny balls of ice; these desperate looking men, peered through one of two glass windows. Inside, the light made by lamps and a fire coming from an open hearth revealed people: men, women and some older children; all were making merry. No Englishmen were to be seen. These French soldiers went back to the group waiting in the shadows. Shortly, a delegation went up to the door, their muskets at the ready, Villiers in the lead. Archibald MacMechan described the scene:

> It was Melançon's house where a wedding feast was in progress. The sudden apparition of such a force, in mid-winter, in a tempest, without a word of warning, as if it had dropped from the clouds, was a portent and a terror. At the sight of the armed men, their snow-powdered clothing, their gaunt, unshaven, cold-pinched faces, the music and dancing ceased on the instant.[28]

After the realization that a great armed force of Frenchmen had arrived in the territory, the initial shock was replaced with considerable excitement. The French officers warned the people to quiet down, that the last thing they wanted was to put the English on notice of their arrival. Now, Melançon's house was one of a number of French Acadian homes along the eastern banks of the Gaspereau River. They were spread apart from one another with farming lands in between. Villiers and his officers were soon to be put into the picture. The entire English force was located on the western side, that is to say, the other side of the Gaspereau River, somewhat beyond its mouth on a ridge over looking a delta (Grand Pré) which had been diked off by the farming Acadians. The houses along the ridge were comparatively close to one another. The English had completely taken over the 24 houses along this ridge putting the regular occupants out of possession. One, a large one, was made of stone, likely a communal structure used as a mill or for storage.[29] This the English determined to use as their winter headquarters. Details, of all of this, were given by the inhabitants to the French officers.

The column of French soldiers had reached the Melançon house at about 9 o'clock in the evening of February 9th. Within a short period of time the French forces, moving in the platoons which had been made up earlier in the day were gathered around roaring fires in several of the nearby houses. There they warmed themselves and dried out and made ready their powder horns and musket and then carefully wrapped them so that they may be kept dry until the critical moment should arrive. Zédore Gould, as an old timer, many years later, who had been with the French raiders that night recounted that "the Melançon girls handed round black bread, and cheese and hard cider, a satisfying ration for exhausted men. Two hogsheads of cider laid down in the fall were emptied that night." More and more detail was comprehended by the French officers as certain of the Acadians spoke freely; others, however, held back, wondering what all of this might lead to.

Each French platoon had two houses allotted to it.[30] At the appointed time, they would creep up and attack: two-thirty in the early morning, a favorite attack time for the French.

As the appointed hour drew near, the French priest conducted an abbreviated mass and blessed the men. Then, expertly led[31] each platoon positioned itself in the snow before one of their two targets. The winds continued to howl and the snow swirled about; it was dark; the houses before them cast out through their small windows and threshold slits, an eerie light.

The Battle:

The blinding snow, which while generally favoring them, had the effect of confusing certain of the French and their Acadian guides. Not each platoon ended up in front of their assigned house. Villiers, for example, who had the strongest and most numerous platoon, and who was going to attack the Stone House, somehow, ended up in front of the house which Lotbinière's smaller platoon was to attack. It was too late, especially in a blinding snow storm, to sort things out: the house before them, was the house they were going to attack. Villiers held up for a bit; he and his officers considered their position. The interior was lit and they could make out some movement inside. While so observing, suddenly, the door was thrown open, and there was an Englishman silhouetted against the square of light where the door had been. The Frenchmen in unison dropped into the snow banks. "Who goes there?" Nothing but sounds of the storm, it well masked the breathing of the 50 Frenchmen but 30 paces away, all face down in the snow. The English guard peered out into the swirling snow and the dark night beyond. He turned, then turned again, and with a facial expression to indicate he was just hearing the "bumps of a stormy night," he went inside and closed the door behind him. The French stood once again, and crept closer; then the door swung open for a second time, more abruptly than the first. And a yell went out, "Turn out!" The interior of the house was all a stir as men jumped for their arms and accoutrements. Villiers hesitated. Beaujeu who was by his side whispered loudly, "This is it!" Villiers ran to the door with sword in hand and three shots from the guards rang out: the French saw their leader go down. "Before the guard could reload, the French were upon them, and, in six or seven minutes, they were masters of the first post. Twenty-one of the *Bastonnais* lay dead, and three were prisoners."[32]

Villiers and one of his junior officers (Lusignan) were badly wounded.[33] They were put on sleds and sent back to the Gaspereau houses from whence they had just come; where the surgeon, Jus, had set up to do his work. Villiers' platoon then fell under the command of Beaujeu, our diarist. Just after Villiers' platoon took this first house, which took but minutes, up trundled, according to plan, Lotbinière's squad. The two forces combined; and, with the first blow in, they went off to join the thickening fray. The night filled up with flashes and reports, some near, some further away. "The alarm was now general throughout Grand Pré. The crackle of musketry, the war-whoops of the Indians, the crash of axes on wooden doors sounded above the winter storm. Doomed men routed from their deepest sleep to encounter in a daze, the hostile faces and deadly weapons. Their end was speedy; resistance was impossible."[34]

Not all the English occupied houses folded as simply as the first. Many of the occupants had the notice of distant musket fire. The Stone House, seemingly remained free of attack during the first and critical period time of the battle. It was to become the last, for that matter, the only bastion of the English: many made a run for it. The stone walls would not only stop musket balls, but they would not burn.[35] Three hundred and fifty men crowded into it. It "had five small cannon, two of which were four pounders, and three were swivels; but these were probably not in position, as it does not appear that any use was made of them. There was no ammunition except what the men had in their powder horns and bullet-pouches ..."[36]

It was thought by the French that the English commander and his officers would be found in the Stone House. It was Noble's headquarters, so normally they would be there. However, not this evening. Noble had decided to spend the night with a few of his fellows in a wooden house a few hundred feet to the west of his stone headquarters.[37] Early in the fight la Corne's platoon came up to Noble's house and an axe was put to the door. "Noble sprang from his bed in his shirt, seized sword and pistol and rushed at his foes. He received two flesh wounds. The French offered him quarter, as his soldier servant testified, but he would not heed. A musket bullet through the brain stretched him dead."[38] La Corne's men stepped over Noble's bloody body and dealt as mean a blow to a number of other resisting Englishmen, including the commander's brother, Ensign Francis Noble, shot dead. Edward How who was in this house with the Noble brothers was badly wounded in the mellay such that he was to lose the use of his left arm. The few left standing were soon to throw their hands up in the air; and, with that, what was Noble's headquarters turned into that of la Corne's, who, because Villiers was put out of action, was now in command of the entire French force.

The noise of the battle started to settle down. The houses which the French took[39] were now under their command and the others were ready to be easily taken, as, the majority of the New Englanders, notwithstanding the confusion, managed to get themselves to their principal place of protection. The Stone House quickly filled up with an English crowd. Visibility continued to be bad and both the French and the English could not make out whether the men moving about were friend or foe.[40] The snow laid deep and there was great difficulty getting about. The only real fighting that took place at Grand Pré was that within the houses which the French had succeeded in entering.

When things had settled down some, a decision was made by the French to tramp down to the shore, which they were to do at about sunrise. They, of course, were interested in securing the two English vessels and their contents for themselves. An English guard of but ten men had been posted at some old ruins of a fort, *Vieux Logis*, located near the shore. It is not surprising to see that upon four French platoons arriving, the place immediately carried.[41] With the capture of *Vieux Logis*, the French had consolidated their position. If the New Englanders were to be reinforced, they would be able to cut the whole, off from their supplies, indeed, preparations were made to set the two English vessels aflame directly there was any danger of the French forces being overwhelmed. Two of the four platoons (de la Colombiè and Boishébert) were left at *Vieux Logis* the other two joined la Corne.

As February 10th reached its half way point, the situation was this: the French had control of two places, the wooden house a few hundred feet to the west of the Stone House (the English) and *Vieux Logis* located near the shore a mile or so to the east. Nobody could move within a musket shot of these two houses. In any event, movement in the snow which was high up around a man's waist was very difficult. Generally though, the French had command of the area extending beyond. Of the 300 or so French that had started in: 22 were dead or wounded[42] and about 50 had run off[43]; la Corne did not have enough to storm the Stone House[44] and it could not be burnt down. As for the English: Benjamin Goldthwaite, who had taken over with the death of Noble, tried to organize the crowd in the Stone House, best he could. Upwards to 75 English officers and men were killed, 60 were wounded, and 69 were made prisoners.[45] Goldthwaite likely fell quiet on occasion, to think, I suppose, what might have been: if only, they had erected the blockhouses which had been brought with them, framed and ready to go; if only, the pickets had been put up; if only, the powder, ball and cannon had been brought off the vessels and set up; if only, the food provisions had been taken off the vessels and stored in such a fashion so that they could be gotten at in the event of a siege. Only if — only if — only if —.

The 10th wore on; night fell; and, then daybreak of the 11th came. Both sides were dug in. Nothing was happening, though the occasional musket shot would have been heard. More time passed; and still nothing was happening. If the French would not make a run at the Stone House, then, Goldthwaite determined, the New Englanders would storm the French, after all, it appeared they had the French outnumbered. So, on the morning of the 11th, some 200 Englishmen spilled forth from their hideout with the intentions of storming the French: it aborted almost directly it began. The light snow was up high around their waists; they could not use their weapons; for that matter, they could hardly move.[46] The English hastily returned to the safety of their stronghold.

Stalemate! The soldiers of each side were safely bolted into their respective houses, overhead a *Fleur de lis* on the one and a Union Jack on the other, both whipped in the wind driven snow. Movement for each seemed impossible.

We have seen where Edward How had been with Noble and was badly wounded. His left arm continued to bleed. Edward How could speak French and he conversed with his captors. The French officers, especially in those days, were ever the gentleman; at any rate, they liked How. How expressed the view that he would bleed to death if he didn't get medical attention. The French surgeon, Jus, was back at Gaspereau attending to the wounded, one of whom was Villiers, their commander. How said that he would like the English surgeon to come over under a white flag to attend him. After some consultation between one another the French sent Joseph Marin over with a white flag. Marin remained in the Stone House as a hostage while the English surgeon came over and treated How. While Marin was with the English, discussion was to eventually came around as to how the thing might be ended. Could they not agree to an armistice without submitting entirely to one another? Then we would have seen one Englishmen go over to the French; and, then, a Frenchman go over to the English. At some point a despatch was sent back to Gaspereau to see what the wounded Villiers had to say. The message came back that Villiers was in a world of hurt and that la Corne and his officers would have to work things out for themselves. The French — though they would not let on to the English — were very near the breaking point. "Three days of marching on empty stomachs, with all the hard fighting at the end, made the convened council-of-war ready enough to meet the *Bastonnais* half way."[47]

The shooting was, by agreement, to stop until 9 o'clock the following morning; each were to say put. It was hoped that terms might be in the meantime worked out. In the morning of the 12th, the French observed a number of Englishmen out, towards the brook. "Why! — those Englishmen were just using the truce so to round up some provisions." Certain of the French were ready to start back to fighting, right-a-way; but cooler heads prevailed. An English officer, Prebble, arrived at the French house with an interpreter and explained they were out to get water, they were in need of water — that's all. Thereupon Prebble pulled out pen and paper and sat down and wrote out three terms: first, the prisoners of war and two captured vessels be restored; second, all plunder be given back; third, the English be free to proceed to Annapolis Royal, with honors of war, a pound of powder and ball per man, and six days rations in their haversacks, leaving all artillery, munitions of war, provisions and supplies to the victors. La Corne did not accept these terms. First off, he was still uncertain that he had the authority to deal with the English in such a fashion, so, he sent another runner back to Villiers. The message received back was somewhat the same as was sent up earlier. Whatever la Corne and his officers worked out was going to be OK with Villiers. The French refused to give the vessels back, nor the prisoners of war.[48] As for the pillage, the French said there was none except that which was carried off by the Indians and they were long gone. The honors of war were granted.

A condition was set (quite normal in those days) that the English, while being allowed to return to Annapolis Royal, could not bear arms up the Bay for six months. The English were in no condition or in any mood to bargain further: the deal was struck. With considerable ceremony the articles were written up and all the officers of both sides signed them. They then broke out a bottle or two, to toast and congratulate one another.

The Aftermath:

The first order of business was to bury the dead. The snow was cleared and the ground, likely with considerable difficulty, was opened up.[49] Depending on who you want to believe (the French or the English) there was between 80 to 150 men to be buried.

The grave of the New Englanders was dug near the road which now [c.1930] runs north to Grand Pré station. The Nobel brothers were buried by themselves between two apple trees; the Canadians accorded full military honours, and fired the customary volleys over their grave.[50]

After the solemn business of burying the dead, all were busy packing provisions for the departing Englishmen who were to march out for Annapolis Royal. The French had agreed to allow the New Englanders to spread out, as they were packed like sardines in the Stone House, 350 of them. But the English did not want to take the time to move, what they wanted to do was to just pack up and go. The evening before they trudged out, however, there was to be a most peculiar gathering of the French and the English.

There was good feelings running between them, though they had been bloody enemies but hours before. The evidence of it appeared directly the parties signed the articles of capitulation. Clearly the English were very impressed by these Frenchmen who had made an unbelievable march in the middle of winter and so to spring a surprise attack. That evening the English officers delivered a formally written invitation to the French officers "requesting the honour of their company to dinner, in order to make their acquaintance over a bowl of punch (*en buvant le ponche*)." The invitation was accepted with as much courtesy as was extended by it.

We are left to the devices of our imagination to paint in the scene as the French officers came up to the Stone House to be greeted by their English hosts. Each group would have spent some time trying to put their respective uniforms in order: cleaned, polished and brushed as best they could. There was no sparkle, and bits and pieces were missing or stitched. These men had just come through the trenches of war; but this was the age of gentlemanly manners and gentlemanly presentation — there had to be quite a conversion in looks.

No doubt the Canadians came as a body, shaved and spruced up, wigs in order, with their weather-worn uniforms and accoutrements made as smart as possible. No doubt the New Englanders met them as a body, and there were formal presentations, with graceful French reverences and less courtly English bows. If hosts and guests were imperfectly acquainted with each other's speech, good will on both sides brought mutual understanding.[51]

The meal proceeded; the fare was simple. The local Acadians must have been prevailed upon to supply certain of that which came to the table. Likely too, there were a few special jars that were retrieved from the two vessels. La Corne and Goldthwaite sat at the two ends of the table and the other officers in between. It had to be a strange dinner party. The French with their extreme courtesies; the English holding back at first then respectfully quizzing their guests. How did you manage such a feat? What route did you take? Broken English was exchanged for broken French and all along the punch was ladled out. At some point during all of this, so MacMechan reported, all the deputies of the surrounding Acadian communities arrived at the Stone House, and, no doubt, were invited to partake of the punch. This was a scene to be painted; the French in their blues; the English in their reds; the Acadians in their homespuns.

The next day was Valentines Day. Despite the merrymaking of the previous evening there was to be an official leave taking. The New Englanders came marching out of the Stone House two by two, haversacks and snowshoes slung over their backs, muskets at the shoulders, to march along a lane made by two blue-coated hedges of French soldiers with shouldered arms; drums beating and colors flying. These winter clad New Englanders tramped through Grand Pré and kept right on going down a snow laden road, headed out, they were, for the English fort at Annapolis Royal, sixty frost bitten miles away, each carrying in their hearts a sad tale of Acadia. As for the French: well, they stood proud. As Parkman was to describe, the overland trek and the resultant Battle at Grand Pré was to become "one of the most gallant exploits in French-Canadian annuals."[52]

In spite of their victory, the French military did not stay at Grand Pré, indeed, within months, they removed themselves from Acadia altogether. La Corne knew he could not throw his forces onto the local Acadians for their support; they had gone through quite enough. Besides, they were in no position to fortify Grand Pré and for sure the English would be back in the spring.[53] La Corne was to lead his men (many being sick and wounded) out of Grand Pré nine days after the English had left and within two weeks, on March the 8th, 1747, they were back at Beaubasin.[54] As for Ramezay, who there waited for the return of his forces, and who came to Acadia in June of 1746 with his French Canadian forces in order to put an end to the English presence in Acadia — well, he was ordered to return with all of his forces to Quebec, as the fear now was that the English would strike at the heart of New France, therefore, Acadia and the Acadians would have to fend for themselves.[55] In the fall of 1749, New France was to finally get its promised leader, one of dash and daring, la Jonquière. He was to hear that the English had in that year established a new citadel at Chebucto and named it, Halifax. This caused Jonquière, directly he heard the news, to send Chevalier la Corne with a strong detachment to hold Chignecto, build a fort and prevent the English from going beyond the Missaguash River.

Chapter 4

The Founding Of Halifax (1749)

Introduction:

It was a gross and mannerly age. Though dead by a dozen years, or so, hung as common criminals before great galleries of English spectators, Dick Turpin (1705-39) and Jack Sheppard (1702-24) by the middle of the 18th century had been made into popular heroes. All travelers of the day knew of the risks of bouncing along ill kept roads and so invariably carried pistols to be used, if necessary, against highwaymen. "Beau" Nash reigned over the gaming-tables of Bath; the ostrich plumes of great ladies and the peacock feathers of the courtesans were matched by the young lords with their velvet suits and embroidered ruffles. In dress the two sexes were never more alike. Men dressed with great flair whether going to a dance or going into battle in their "three-cornered hats, powdered perukes, embroidered coats, and lace ruffles"; their valets would serve them ices in the battle field.

The English and the French courts were coming to terms with one another with a view to putting an end to their most recent squabble which historians have labeled *The War of the Austrian Succession*; it had its start in 1744. In March of 1748 the congress of Aix-la-Chapelle was opened and discussion began between France on the one hand; and, England and Holland on the other. A general peace was accomplished with the signing of a treaty on October 18th, 1748. "England had gained nothing in the long struggle, though she had, thanks to successes at sea and in the colonies, suffered no great losses. Only the national debt had considerably increased."[1]

The population of the British colonies, spread along the coast of eastern North America, was 1,200,000. Thus, at 55,000, the French population at Quebec (Canada) was dwarfed; Massachusetts alone had a population of 188,000.[2] It is a marvel, when one comes to think of it, that the French in America lasted as long as they did during times of war, a state, incidently, that existed between England and France more times than not. Any calculations as to the strengths of the opposing sides, of course, would have to include the fact that the French had long since swung over most all of the native populations to their cause.[3] So too, figuring large in the calculation, is the fact that those of New England and those of New France lived under entirely different political regimes.

While those to the south, beginning with Virginia, had a different set of beliefs and social organization based on the old aristocratic structure, those English colonies to the north were more populous or democratic. The social structure of New England was a reflection of the beliefs and character of their founding fathers, the Puritans.Their piety, their intolerance, their simplicity of life, their pedantry, their love of equality: these Puritan qualities created a natural acceptance of the democratic institutions, institutions which had evolved in England, and which the common Englishman brought with him to his new home in America. Thus it was, that the English along the eastern coast of America, each of them, pursued their own interests with minimal intervention from government authority. This Lockian system accounted for a phenomenal growth in both population and commercial activity. However, such a system posed a distinct problem in times of war. To gather people together for a long and trying war, especially one which is to be conducted in foreign parts, is a difficult problem where people are used to the freedom of making their own choices. On the other hand, in a system where the people are subservient, as they were in New France[4]; where the people, as a matter of course, have been indoctrinated, and where they were in perpetual harness and ready to go; then the state, a totalitarian state, is ready to throw its military force at just about anything that comes along, within a season. The fact is that New France was ever ready to pursue the objective of keeping the western fur routes to itself and thus it was necessary to hold the English in check. As for the English: well, they would be content with their share of furs, but what they really needed, as the burgeoning population pushed west up against the Appalachian ridge, was more living room and the valleys beyond, such as maybe found in Ohio, beckoned. The French were nervous. It was necessary to see the extent of the English incursions, to stop them, to divert them, to keep them busy in an another direction.

An officer by the name of Céloron de Bienville was dispatched by La Galissonnière to the valley of the Ohio in order to properly stake France's claim. He concluded after traveling thousands of miles by canoe and overland that the native tribes are becoming increasingly more disposed towards the English and their trading goods. More to our story, is that La Galissonnière at the same time and for the same reasons sent to Acadia, in the early part of 1749, a 22 year old by the name of Charles des Champs de Boishébert, a determined and brave young officer, who, we had seen in the previous chapter, was a participant in the Battle at Grand Pré two years earlier. Boishébert went "out with eighty soldiers and militia. From Quebec they went on snowshoes (all the way) to Hocpaak, a French settlement, dragging their supplies and baggage with incredible exertions."[5] We shall come to Boishébert and his activities at the Isthmus in a future chapter. In this chapter, we will deal with the English and the founding of Halifax.

The Choice of Chebucto:

Chebucto,[6] the Halifax of today, had long been used by the French, and longer still by the MicMac. Brouillan[7] had put into the place in 1701 and "took the opportunity to visit this fort"; from there he traveled overland so to arrive at the French community of Les Mines (Grand Pré). One need only a little familiarity with the geography of Nova Scotia to realize that Chebucto had to be a starting or ending place for those who wanted to cut across the long peninsula of Nova Scotia at one of its narrowest spots. For the migratory Indians, Chebucto was indeed the terminus as they paddled along the water way of the natural Shubenacadie water system; inland to their wintering places and out again in the summer to their traditional fishing grounds along the Atlantic shores.

Chebucto was identified[8] by the British, as early as 1715, as a good harbor for "all occasions ... and being most convenient for trade and fortification."[9] Indeed, a nobleman, Sir Alexander Cairnes, in 1717, was ready to build a fort and do some trading at Chebucto, but the board kept rethinking the plans and Sir Alexander became discouraged. And so, the years passed. About fifteen years later, the idea to build a new English center in Nova Scotia was to come to the forefront, again. In 1732, a captain of an English vessel brought to the Admiralty's attention the excellent possibilities of Chebucto Harbor. Not anything was done about it then, but thereafter, it was standard practice for visiting British naval captains to recommend to the board that a settlement be made, "either of LaHave or Chebucto Harbour."[10]

Up to 1745 there was but two places in all of Nova Scotia which might be labeled an English port: Annapolis Royal and Canso. A third was added with Louisbourg's capture in 1745. A certain English naval officer,[11] however, was to sour everyone on Louisbourg. Besides, by the *Treaty of Aix-la-Chapelle* (1748) George II gave Louisbourg back to the French king. Though I have not been able to put my hands on any official accounts as to why Annapolis Royal was passed over, I can only imagine it did not suit the English to build up that place, because, well, it was too far out of the way of the main Atlantic routes, and too far from Louisbourg, a place which the English wanted to keep an eye on. Further, there was the tides and currents of the Bay of Fundy and the resultant difficulties to shoot the passages in order to make it to Annapolis Royal. As for Canso: well, I'll let Admiral Warren explain:

The form and situation of the islands of Canso seems calculated by nature for the use of the fishery and nothing else, for which reason a small fortification there for the protection of the fishery would be necessary. And as the barrenness of that soil, and that adjacent, renders it incapable of any other improvement, I apprehended a settlement made in one of the best ports on the south side of Nova Scotia, where the soil is good and proper for agriculture as well as fishing, and as near Canso as such port may be found, would be of great advantage to the fishery. Port LaHave and Chebucto the former about fifty, the latter about forty leagues to the eastward of Canso, would be the properest place for such settlement, but especially Port LaHave, the soil being [the better] though both [are] fine harbours. In the present situation, the French, by their missionaries and the presents the crown makes annually of powder and shot, and triannually [of] a new gun to each Indian fit to bear arms, has so riveted them to their interest that they will not suffer an Englishman to settle or cure fish in any of the ports on the south side [of] Nova Scotia. In all which ports there are a few Indians; one of them has a commission from the governor of Canada or Cape Breton to command a particular district, and generally bears the title of captain of the fort to which they belong."[12]

And so discussion amongst those in official circles continued, until, in 1747, the decision was made:

A civil government [should] be forthwith established in Nova Scotia, and encouragement given to Protestant settlers by granting them small portions of land without quit rent or other charge for a number of years. ...

The security of Nova Scotia and the frontiers of the neighbouring colonies very much depends on the friendship of the Indians, to which nothing can conduce so much as making them presents. ...

A strong fort, fit to contain a garrison of 500 men, [should] be built in the harbour of Chebucto, to be mounted with 6 or 9 pounders. A blockhouse fit to contain 100 men [should] be built at Canso, mounted with some large cannon. ...

That the communication between Canada and that province be wholly cut off by blockhouses erected on the passes, or [by] other proper methods.

That the new fort, which at the commencement of the war was ordered to be built at Annapolis, be not built there at all, but that a strong fort be built at Chebucto, sufficient to contain a garrison of 500 men at least. Upon this fortification being finished and garrisoned, it is presumed the garrison at Annapolis may be reduced to the number of 100 or 150 men. ...

That presents, not exceeding the value of 500 [pounds], be sent for the Indians in those parts, to be used in such manner as shall be thought proper by the commander in chief.

That a fort be built at Canso sufficient to contain 100 men.[13]

The Founding of Halifax:

And, so it was, Chebucto was chosen, the very same place at which d'Anville and his men came to so much grief. Having left England May 13th, the lead ship, a fast sloop of war, the *Sphinx* (20 guns) came into view off the coast of Nova Scotia on the 14th of June, 1749 (OS). Edward Cornwallis,[14] the English officer in charge, was aboard, together with his various lieutenants and advisors. Not having any experienced pilots aboard, the vessel sailed back and forth until a friendly vessel come along. On the 20th, the *Sphinx* fell in with a sloop from Boston bound for Louisbourg; this Boston vessel had a pilot aboard and the way to Chebucto was soon pointed out. It was Governor Cornwallis' intention to proceed to Annapolis, but "the wind not serving the Bay of Fundy, and the officers assuring him that in case of foggy weather setting in they might be a long time in getting to Annapolis, he concluded on proceeding at once to Chebucto, rather than risk the possibility of being separated for any length of time from the fleet [which was still making its way across the broad Atlantic]. He also felt, that by so doing, he would save the Governor of Louisbourg [Hopson] the bad and long navigation to Annapolis ..."[15]

So, on June 21st, the *Sphinx* cast her anchor in Halifax Harbor; and for a time, she was the only vessel that would have been seen off the wild shore above which Halifax was to be built. A number of days passed before the transports[16] showed up (13 of them had left England with Cornwallis). Within a day of his arrival, Cornwallis penned his first report to the authorities at London. In part, it read:

> The coasts are as rich as ever they have been represented; we caught fish every day since we came ... The harbour itself is full of fish of all kinds. All the officers agree the harbour [Halifax] is the finest they have seen. The country is one continued wood; no clear spot is to be seen or heard of.

The arriving English were well aware that a very large French military force had made an encampment, but within the past three years. The English had expected a clearing or two, but none were to be seen which led them to believe the French in 1746 must have "encamped their men on the beach." Also, because of the "continued wood" it was "with difficulty one is able to make his way anywhere." Cornwallis continued,

> I have seen few brooks, nor as yet have found the navigable river that has been talked of. There are a few French families on the east side of the bay, about three leagues off. Some have been on board.[17]

By the first of July, the last of the 13 transports[18] rounded up and cast their anchors out into the waters of Chebucto Harbor. Two thousand, five hundred and seventy six English settlers[19] had by then arrived; and, Halifax was founded.[20] They were headed up by a smart set of army and naval officers.

One of Cornwallis' first acts upon arrival was to dispatch a courier overland to Annapolis Royal. He also sent, the next day, a sloop, *Fair Lady*. It was necessary to advise Mascarene so that arrangements might be made for the transfer of power. (If any man is to deserve the name "father of Nova Scotia," it would be Mascarene. By this time, 1749, he had given 39 years of service to Nova Scotia.) Cornwallis penned a letter to Mascarene: he had come and wished to call the most prominent Englishmen of the province and form a council. It was expected that Cornwallis would have put into Annapolis Royal upon arrival from England, but circumstances prevented him from running down to this old capital of Acadia. Mascarene received his message on June 26th; and, on the very next day, the 27th, he ordered Captain Jonathan Davis with his 70 ton schooner, the *Warren*, and another owned by John Gorham, to sail around to the newly arrived and sea weary settlers with fresh provisions. On July 12th Mascarene "his council, together with Gorham's Rangers (60 of them) and part of his garrison" arrived at Halifax.

Within days, during the early part of July, a settlement was started at the south eastern point of the peninsula on which Halifax (city proper) now sits. Thus what is a park today, Point Pleasant, was where the settlers first envisioned their new community to be. But it was soon realized that a town at the point would be a bad setup since ships could not pull up close to the shore due to shoaling waters. Thus a better place was struck upon, midway along the eastern side of the peninsula,[21] "with a bold anchorage close to the shore." Charles Morris, an experienced surveyor from New England, was employed to lay out the land lots.

The town was laid out in squares or blocks of 320 by 120 feet deep, the streets being 55 feet in width. Each block contained 16 town lots, forty feet front by sixty deep, and the whole was afterwards into five divisions or wards, called Callendar's, Galland's, Ewer's, Collier's and Foreman's divisions, after the names of the persons who were appointed captains of Militia, each ward being large enough to supply one company.[22]

The structures went up in quick order, especially since "frames and other materials" were brought up from Boston. By the 27th of July, Cornwallis reported on his new settlement:

It has all the conveniences I could wish except a fresh water river. Nothing is easier than to build wharves; one is already finished for ships of 200 tons [which would exclude any of the ships that came in from England]. I have constantly employed all the carpenters I could get from Annapolis and the ships here to build log houses for stores. I have likewise offered the French at Minas considerable wages to work, and they have promised to send fifty men to remain until October. As there was not one clear yard of clear ground you will imagine our difficulty and what we have here to do; however, they have already cleared about twelve acres, and I hope to begin my house in two days; I have a small frame and pickets ready.[23]

A settler wrote home in July:

Our work goes on briskly, and the method of employing the people in ships' companies has a good effect, and as the Governor is preparing to lay out the lots of land, we shall soon have a very convenient and pleasant town built, which is to be called Halifax. There are already several wharves built, and one gentleman is erecting a saw mill; public store houses are also building, and grains of various sorts have been sown. We have received constant supplies of plank and timber for building, and fresh stock and rum in great quantities, 20 schooners frequently coming in one day.[24] We also have a hundred cows and some sheep, brought down to us by land, by the French at Minas, which is about 30 miles distant from the bottom of the bay, and to which we propose to cut a road. The French Deputies who came to make submission have promised to send us 50 men for the purpose, and to assist us as far as they are able; we have received the like promise, and friendship and assistance from the Indians, the chief having been with the Governor for that purpose. In short, everything is in a very prosperous way.[25]

It was during July, too, that the newly minted colony at Halifax was joined by the English garrison which had sailed down with their possessions from Louisbourg, that place having been handed over to the French. On August 8th lots were drawn so that each family[26] was to have their own plot of land being 40' on the street with a 60' depth. From that point onwards a particular family's attention was directed to their own plot of land, to such an extent that it was difficult to get them going on any larger communal work, such as building a picket fence around the entire complex. As Cornwallis wrote, "There was no persuading them to do it." So, council voted to pay money to the men who worked on the defenses, "1s. 6d. per day."

And so, on this wild shore, land was cleared and structures of a new community went up: houses, a church,[27] warehouses, wharves — a new town, the first English town in Nova Scotia, came into being. In addition to the physical structures, with two or three thousand people living in close proximity, a civil government[28] was put in place. On July 14th (Friday), Cornwallis gathered his advisors around him and formed his first council and had its first meeting.[29] This first council deliberated on board the spacious *Beaufort*, one of the transports anchored just off the shore in Halifax Harbour.[30]

The broader plans called for a number of English settlements with the central one to be at Halifax. The places considered, were: Minas, Whitehead, Baie Verte and LaHave.[31] Because of the activities of French priest, Abbé Le Loutre and his followers, these plans were frustrated. In the first few years, only Lunenburg was settled (1753) and a road from a small military post at the head of Bedford Basin was to be cut through the woods thirty miles, or so, to Minas Basin where another small military post was built. I shall come to the details of this expansion in due course.

Everything turned on the settlers. It was the settlers who were to do the primary work of building the new town. Unfortunately, those[32] that had been recruited in England to come over with Cornwallis were less than satisfactory. Only those who were trying to escape their circumstances, usually debt ridden circumstances, would ship out for the new world. Few came with any particular commercial plan in mind (though some figured it out quick enough on arrival). The promise that was made was for free land and the tools to work it, and supplies to keep them going for the first year. Most of those that signed up were from the low end of the city streets or discarded military men[33] who never worked with an axe or a pick in their entire lives. Cornwallis was to become very unhappy. On July, 24th, 1749, he wrote the authorities:

> The number of settlers men, women, and children is 1400 but I beg leave to observe to your Lordship that amongst these the number of industrious active men proper to undertake and carry on a new settlement is very small — of soldiers there is only 100 — of tradesmen, sailors and other able and willing to work not above 200 more — the rest are poor idle worthless vagabonds that embraced the opportunity to get provisions for one year without labour, or Sailors that only wanted a passage to New England. ... Many of the settlers are without shoes, stockings or shirts ...[34]

The authorities back at London, of course, understood, that to broadcast Cornwallis' sentiments would do no good; better that some encouragement should be given. And so, Lord Halifax was to write of the community named after him:

> No garden stuff or corn had been yet put in the ground, but that they had carrots and turnips very cheap from Annapolis Royal. That there were hares, partridges, wild pigeons and geese in the different seasons, that they had some hogs and cows enough. That a brewhouse was erecting to brew spruce for the settlement and that in the meantime molasses was delivered to the people to brew for themselves that their beer was exceeding good and wholesome and fit to drink in two days. ... It consisted of about 400 houses, built of wood and covered with shingles and chimneys of brick or stone dug up there. .... That the road to Minas lately made was a very fine one, twenty feet wide, and had five bridges on it. ... the people were in good health and very industrious and

their numbers increased by 7 or 800 familys from New England ... That 300 houses were already tenantable, 400 covered in, and the frames for 700 up, that there was plenty of provisions two days in a week.[35]

If all had depended on those settlers that had come out with Cornwallis, then, it is likely that Halifax might have fizzled out; and might have, except for two groups of people that came in and buttressed the population. I turn to Thomas Beamish Akins:

> After the evacuation of Louisbourg the population received a considerable accession; a number of the English inhabitants came with Governor Hopson and became settlers, and many from New England[36] were daily arriving, and upwards of 1000 more from the old provinces had expressed themselves desirous of joining the settlement before winter. The Governor therefore gave orders to all vessels in the government service to give them free passage. The New England people soon formed the basis of the resident population, and are the ancestors of many of the present inhabitants. They were better settlers than the old discharged soldiers and sailors who came on the fleet; most of them died or left the country during the first three or four years, leaving, however, the most industrious and respectable among them as permanent settlers. Many settlers and traders came out for the purpose of making money; these people infested the settlement in great numbers, and gave Mr. Cornwallis and his successors much trouble and annoyance, in demoralizing the people by the illicit sale of bad liquors, and in other ways retarding the progress of the country.[37]

The expectations of the new settler and the actuality of what he or she faced upon coming ashore in these first years; were to be quite different things. Most of them were determined within a season or two to make their way to the more hospitable English colonies to be found south along the American seaboard, where there was promised "cultivated lands, Rivers with Fish and Woods with Fowl ... No ... Wild Indians to fight or disaffected French to keep in awe ..." These promises are to be contrasted with the reality of Nova Scotia in 1749 and 1750:

> Desolate Lands, and unfrequented Shores. ... not an English Inhabitant nor a Rood of Land on our Possession throughout the whole County ... Here there was no trade, nor scarcely any ships seen, except their annual ones, that came like Spanish galleons in the season, with salt beef and clothing for

the troops, and ordinance stores — they had no communication, nor useful intercourse with the Indians, and their valuable trade in furs and sables was entirely engrossed by the French through the province who carried it all to Canada ...[38]

That those who arrived with Cornwallis, looking out upon "Desolate Lands, and unfrequented Shores," wanted to take the first boat out and make a get away — should come as no surprise to anyone. Indeed, I surmise, a great number did surreptitiously slip away, as visiting vessels from New England returned to their home ports with paying passengers aboard. Cornwallis on his arrival had but a 100 soldiers with him and was thus limited as to what he might do to enforce his ordinances. The best people, the able and the willing, of which there were precious few to begin with, were deserting Cornwallis for greener pastures. Those in charge of the new colony of Halifax were therefore to be doubly pleased when Colonel Hopson, the retiring governor of Louisbourg, sailed into Halifax Harbor on July 25th. He had with him, on a number of transports, two British regiments with provisions and military stores.[39] The military presence was thus to be given a considerable boast and much better control was to be had. Also, there came in from Louisbourg civilians that were well used to colony life and ready to fill many of the needs of the new colony at Halifax.

Chapter 5

The Return Of Louisbourg (1749)

On October 18th, 1748, the *Treaty of Aix-la-Chapelle* was signed and with it came the return of Louisbourg. The giving back of Louisbourg to the French brought on feelings of intense anger and indignation in the colonists of New England; its capture had come about as the result of the blood and sweat of their sons.[1] Louisbourg's return was as a result of a trade made at the treaty table. In exchange: France was to give back Madras and other Indian territories, and to abandon her support it had given to the Scottish rebels, and to dismantle the fortifications at Dunkirk. These were all very great concessions on the part of France — what was Louisbourg but a far off piece of territory of no great consequence. Thus it was that Louisbourg became a small chip in an international "peace" making deal.[2] And so, in the bargain, the colonial governors, who had spent much and gained much upon its capture, were to lose Louisbourg.[3]

So, that's it — Louisbourg was to be returned.[4] On July 12th, 1749, Charles Des Herbiers de La Ralière (1700-1752), the new French governor, sailed into Louisbourg Harbor with 20 transports[5] which had the new French garrison and large quantities of military supplies aboard, escorted by two 80-gun French war ships. As the vessels proceeded slowly into the harbor, cannons echoed from shore to shore as the ground batteries returned the blank shots of the French Men'O'War. Those aboard — 500 troops, plus many returned civilians — came ashore to take Louisbourg back and to raise the French flag over her ramparts, once again. The transfer went smoothly:

> The opportune arrival of Cornwallis at Halifax set free British transports which came to Louisbourg. They were supplemented by French Ships, and so effectively were the arrangements made and carried out, that on the 23rd of July Des Herbiers marched into the town, and received its keys from Hopson. The French flag replaced that of England over the citadel and batteries. Hopson received a certificate that the transfer was complete and satisfactory, and the English forces and people withdrew to Halifax.[6]

It was plain, now, in this second era, 1749-58, that the French authorities were intent not to commit the same errors which had brought the mighty fortress down and into the hands of Englishmen in 1745. After the fort had been taken over and put on a regular footing, in 1751, Jean Louis, Comte de Raymond (c.1702-1771) was appointed as Louisbourg's governor. Raymond was a military man, and this was the first time that Louisbourg was to see an army officer as its governor, prior to Raymond they all had been naval. With his appointment, just so that everyone was to know the importance which the French authorities attached to the position, came a promotion. Raymond was made a Major-General and his aids were to be high ranking military officers. "There was to be a girding of the loins in the bureaux of the French Admiralty, when Louisbourg was again under its care. ... the raising of the garrison until it approached in number that of Canada, showed that a high value was set on Louisbourg and its security."[7]

Louisbourg has been, by times, portrayed by the authors as poor and as rich. The descriptions range from the early springs[8] when the French colony would be diseased and starving, having suffered through an ill provisioned winter, to a time, in season, as a port rich in trade. I suspect the tough times generally occurred earlier on in her history, but by the second French occupation Louisbourg, no doubt, exhibited the attributes of a busy seaport, bustling in trade.[9]

Louisbourg was thus an important commercial centre as well as the greatest military stronghold on the northern coasts, and 'ships of all nations' rode at anchor in her ample port. In 1751, 150 English vessels traded there, and the commerce of the city was increasing so rapidly that 30 Boston ships could sometimes be counted in the port.

An English traveler who visited the city found 30 sail of English ships loading and discharging there; 20 vessels from France lay at the quays, discharging wines, oils, cambrics, linens, silks, velvets, and, 'in short, an assortment of all the manufacturers of France'; and others arrived almost daily from the West Indies laden with rum, sugar, molasses, coffee, cotton, indigo and cocoa. These commodities were purchased on a large scale by the New England and other 'Colonial' merchants for the British 'Colonial' markets as far south as South Carolina. Most of them were paid for in good silver dollars; and as the trifling commodities the British traders could sell were chiefly lumber, the balance of trade was greatly in favour of France.

Louisbourg was also the emporium of a fishing industry, which competed with the fishing industry of New England, employed fully 2,281 vessels, manned by 15,138 men, and is stated to have supported an export of 974,700 quintals of fish per annum.[10]

C. Ochiltree Macdonald illustrates his point by setting forth a table of the French fishing villages (tributary to Louisbourg) giving forth in separate columns the number of larger and smaller vessels found in each village. It is an interesting exercise to run down the list with a map in hand. Macdonald lists twenty villages beginning with Egmont Bay (Bay St. Lawrence?) and working itself along the northern and eastern shores of Cape Breton until one arrives "in places in Straits of Canso." After Louisbourg, with 600 hundred sailing vessels (300 of then "decked"), came Ingonish with 245 "shallops" and Main-à-dieu with 190. The outer exposed harbors had just the smaller sailing vessels the larger decked vessels were to only be found in the more secure harbors found at the end of deep waters which ran inland for aways, such as St Anne's. The total count for this area of Cape Breton, including Louisbourg, was 726 "decked vessels" and 1,555 shallops.[11]

Of course, Louisbourg had always been a refuge and haven for those who preyed on English shipping, with the hand-back, she eagerly clutched at this role once again. Clearly this might be expected during times of war[12]: 1744-48 and 1756-63. But, the years in between were almost as bad. There were always desperate men who ran armed vessels, and whose sole aim was to plunder any under-gunned or under-manned vessel that should come into range.[13] Those who had relieved an English vessel of its cargo could always put into Louisbourg and find there helpful people who were ready, able and willing, to look the other way, to falsify papers and generally to play booty.[14]

Chapter 6

Foreign Protestants (1750-2)

England's desire was to have the inhabitants of Nova Scotia loyal to it. The difficulty was that the inhabitants were French. These Acadians had come over directly from France in the mid-seventeenth century and grew to a sizable population, one that had spread from its starting point at Port Royal to the fertile and ancient flood plains as surrounded their communities of Minas, Cobequid and Beaubassin. The Acadian population was somewhat less than 2,000 at the time the English wrested Port Royal away from the French in 1710. For 39 years thereafter, Acadia became a forgotten country. The French sent in no help except for a few ministering priests who the English believed (with good reason) were French agents. The English changed the name of Port Royal to Annapolis Royal and put in place a small garrison both there and at the other end of the peninsula, Canso. Except for one or two at Annapolis Royal, there were no English families in Nova Scotia. In the meantime, during the years 1710 to 1749, there was continued growth in the Acadian population, such that by the mid-eighteenth century there were to be 10,000 Acadians. All of them possessing a distinct French tongue, French culture and French religion. The proper conclusion of history is that these Acadians, at least not in any great numbers or to any great degree, did not go against their English overlords at Annapolis Royal. However, though the English tried, over and over, to get them to do it, the Acadians would not swear unconditional allegiance to the English crown. They would promise not to take up arms against the English but they were not prepared to take up arms against Frenchmen (invasive military men from Quebec). Fundamentally, what the Acadians wanted was to simply be left alone, so to farm their lands and raise their families — two things they were very good at.

The worry of the English, was, that the Acadians in a time of war would turn into "Fifth Columnists." It was a worry which caused them to take extreme measures in 1755, but as of 1749, it was thought that all that might be necessary was to dilute the French population by putting in amongst them, or to match them community by community, inhabitants that would be loyal to the English crown. Those of a culture different than that of the French. It was not essential that they be English speaking; it was essential that they be of the Protestant religion. Englishmen would do just find. The first of them came over with Cornwallis in 1749. This group, some 2,500 of them, proved to be a sad lot. Only but a few of them were cut out for the pioneering life, especially a pioneering life that included cold winters and butchering Indians. The problem was that there was an easy back door to any mobile Englishman who came to the barren shores of Nova Scotia; with a little money or work, he could grab the first New England schooner going south. It struck the English authorities, that if they could not muster a shipload of suitable immigrants in England, then, they might be able to do so in central or northern Europe where there then existed, due to centuries of war, a population which was naturally inclined to dislike the French, one, which was primarily of the Protestant faith. What was necessary was to find these willing and suitable immigrants and in this regard they thought to hire an agent who was familiar with the territory and could carry out an effective recruiting campaign.

John Dick was hired to be the official agent of the British government on the continent. Dick's job was to round up and convince people who wished to take passage to America to do so on one of his chartered ships and settle in Nova Scotia. Terms were to be worked out as between the British government (the Board of Trade) and Dick for his work. Terms were also worked out between Dick and his passengers whereby the cost of their passage would be financed and paid back in Nova Scotia where they were guaranteed work ("public work at Halifax"). Into the bargain, the new settler would get "free land," provisions and implements, and victualing for the first year. The authorities in England emphasized with the recruiters that what was wanted were "young single men."[1] The thought was that old men, women and children[2] would not be able to contribute much to the work required in the building of a new colony; indeed, they would just be a drain. In fact, as Cornwallis was soon to observe, this was a bad policy. Single men were entirely too mobile.[3] Women and children may have been a drain on the colony, but, by and large, it was only the married men who stuck around to do the work.

There was in these times a great competition for immigrants. America was is need of people. The governors of the English colonies also had their recruiting agents in Europe. Competition was keen, but it certainly seems that John Dick had the best deal for those willing to go to the northern part of the American eastern seaboard, Nova Scotia. Those who wished to go to the more southern colonies were obliged, generally to pay their own way, though government help on the other side was near as generous as it was to be for those who took passage to Nova Scotia. Dick's competitors were keen to fill up their own vessels which were headed to Pennsylvania or Georgia. These recruiters were ready to turn people off on the idea of going to Nova Scotia. Thus stories were spread. Nova Scotia was, "a barren land, good for nobody but fishermen" and where the unprotected settler would be "in constant danger from French and Indians." And if that were not enough, there were those "vicious rattlesnakes."[4] Another pamphleteer was to give no comfort or credit when he wrote at London: "Many unfortunate people died of cold the first winter after their settlement. This indeed, may be imputed to the want of houses, which only such as could build were able to obtain; and to see the vast flakes of snow lying about the tents of those who had been accustomed to warm fires about Newcastle and London, was enough to move the heart of stone ..."[5] In fact, the winters at Halifax as far as northern winters go are quite mild, and, the evidence is that it was not the cold that knocked off so many of the English settlers in that first year, but rather disease and sickness due, most likely, to the bad habits of this first lot of settlers.

The plan, which had turned into Cornwallis' orders, was that he should get himself and his people established at Halifax and use it as a working base from which would be sent the settlers to a number of points throughout Nova Scotia for its "Englishification." This proved to be a multi-faceted problem. The Indian threat obliged the settlers to huddle together in one protected place, Halifax.[6] With the arrival of the immigrant ships during 1751, Cornwallis was to acquaint his superiors that he had enough. They were proving to be more of a hinderance than of help. Costs were going up and a year's worth of free victuals was not going to see the typical immigrant family through to the point when it might be considered self-sustaining. While Nova Scotia did have good farm lands (as were then, by and large, occupied by the Acadians) the part which the British had chosen to settle, along the Atlantic coast, was rock strewn and barren.[7] If all the settler could do was to line up for another handout, then what was the use of more? "I should advise the not sending more till affairs change."[8] The wheels of bureaucracy, if they grind at all, grind slowly. That proposition is as true today as it was during the days under review.[9] The bureaucracy problem back then was considerably delayed and complicated because of the great amounts of time required for sailing ships to get authoritative messages back and forth across the Atlantic. The directions or orders made in one year could not be implemented until the next. In December, 1751, the Board of Trade, upset as it was with the increasing costs of the new settlement at Halifax, and, in view of Cornwallis' comments, advised John Dick that his services were not required for 1752. John Dick was not a man to be put off that easily. He traveled to London in January of 1753 and made his case. He had already incurred great expense in getting things lined up for the forthcoming shipping season; he had numerous would-be-settlers on his hands who had sold their possessions in anticipation of the British promises. If the British were to pull their plans so abruptly, then, it would not be so easy to get things started in another year. In the end, Dick was to win out and the project was to be kept going for yet another year.

Dick was to ship another 1000 souls or so to Nova Scotia during 1752; to be added to the 4000 that had come in during the years 1749-51.

While at Halifax the "Foreign Protestants" were treated as people in transit. The lots at the core of Halifax, those inside the stockade had been granted to the original English settlers. Further, it would appear that the newly arrived New Englanders were allowed to settle where they pleased including on choice lots in downtown Halifax. However, the Palatine[10] Settlers were set up but in a temporary fashion. Since these foreigners were to be "out-settled," there was no sense in taking any great trouble with them until they were properly relocated. Once this was done, then they would be given their lots of land, tools, building materials, and alike. In the meantime they camped, and they waited. Two places were set up for them. The one at Dartmouth in the fall of 1750; the other was to at the head of the Northwest Arm, later to be called Dutch (Deutsche, German) Village.[11] A number of the single men, it would seem, were immediately housed on Georges Island in Halifax Harbor. This meant they could be put to work on a daily basis with its fortifications, at the same time, they were kept together with their only escape being into the woods after a swim to the main land.[12]

None of these poor people piling up at Halifax could make a living there. Farming, for the reasons stated, was out of the question, and it would be years before Halifax — with all the attending commercial opportunities — was to become a military entrepôt, that, indeed it was to become. Cornwallis and his council might have gotten matters in hand except the problem got worse and grew in accordance with a progression of immigrant ships which sailed into Halifax Harbor during the years 1750-1752. Thousands of fearful and ill kept German/Swiss immigrants hung in and around the protected position at Halifax. Provision or victualing lists were long and getting longer as one immigrant ship came in after another. Cornwallis took the heat. It was determined by those back in London that he was a good soldier but a poor bookkeeper. As for Cornwallis: he prayed to be relieved, and his prayers were answered.

It will be recalled that Peregrine Thomas Hopson, a British army officer of good reputation, had come over to Louisbourg with the "Gibraltar troops" to relieve the English garrison at Louisbourg during 1746. He was to continue on there with the English forces during its occupation, 1745-49; indeed, in 1747, he took over as the English governor at Louisbourg. In July of 1749, after the hand back to the French, Hopson led the English garrison that had been at Louisbourg to Halifax, there to meet the newly arrived Cornwallis. Hopson, it seems, his work done, had returned to England; however, in the early part of 1752, Hopson was chosen to go and replace Cornwallis.

Hopson took over from Cornwallis in August. What was before him was a town full of needy settlers. Hopson's immediate challenge was to get these immigrants settled and functioning on their own. Just at this time, on August 21st, the *Pearl* arrived. She had left Rotterdam on June the 6th. Two hundred and twelve persons were waiting to come ashore: they were sick and tired. The report delivered to Hopson was that 39 had died at sea. This high mortality together with the general condition of those aboard led Hopson to fear a contagious disease. The order went out to leave these immigrants aboard; they were not to disembark until his health officer was satisfied that it was safe to let these new arrivals loose into the existing population at Halifax. So, there was the *Pearl* lying at anchor; and those aboard, lean and bedraggled, looking out with their darkened and sunken eyes at their nearby and long desired goal. Little could be done except to put some fresh water and food aboard: they would just have to wait. Besides there was no extra accommodations ashore. Things take time. When finally they came ashore they could hardly move. Some were sent off to the hospital, others, as charity cases, were to be nursed back to health by adoptive families. Then September came, and, on the 6th, a pair of immigrant ships come limping into the harbor: the *Sally* and the *Gale*.

The *Sally* and the *Gale* had apparently met up at sea, as, they had left Rotterdam at different times, though but only days from one another, the *Sally* on the 30th of May and the *Gale* on the 6th of June. They had long and stormy passages. An illness of some kind had swept through them and carried off an unusually large number of the passengers just as had happened on the *Pearl*. On the *Sally*, 40 had died; on the *Gale*, 29. Hopson's action was the same as that he had taken when faced with the same sort of problem a few weeks back. This time they were to remain in the stream for three weeks. So, with winter's start expected within eight to ten weeks, the colony was faced with yet more mouths to feed, with more people to house, more sick to take care of. And, in this setting, on October 16th, 1752, Hopson wrote the Lords of trade: "... among the number of these settlers which Mr. Dick has sent this year there were many, very many poor old decrepid creatures both men and women who were objects fitter to have been kept in almshouses than to be sent over here as settlers to work for their bread."[13] Hopson continued, and observed that a number of the settlers that had arrived at Halifax during September of 1752 "could not stir off the beach" and that within days "fourteen orphans belonging to these settlers were taken in the Orphan house."

Much of the ocean passage for these immigrants was to be made while confined to the lower deck. There was no choice in that — as we are here dealing with the age of sail and the top deck was an operating deck with every square inch of it needed for line handling seamen. Certainly, when there was no breeze, then a number of the passengers would be allowed to take the air on deck in a prescribed place, one group at a time. Such a situation (families living closely together confined by the wooden bulkheads and decks all around), to mention nothing about the discomfort of it, was unhealthy. However, compared to the transports that plied the oceans in those days, the conditions aboard Dick's vessels, I should say, were not that bad. The British government sent artificers over to Rotterdam from England in order to fit ventilators so that the air between decks was refreshed. The English authorities carried out inspections before they cleared port, and, indeed, the ships from Rotterdam that Dick had sent were to call in at either Gosport or Cowes for a further inspection[14] before setting out on their trans-Atlantic voyage. Generally, the inspectors found that conditions were good with generous margins of safety in respect to water supply. Still the typical ocean voyage of the day was long, very long; and poor diet and tedium was the rule. So too, storms were bound to come up which would have had the effect of striking terror into the souls of the seaborne settlers.[15]

John Dick's involvement with Nova Scotia in the sending of the Palatine ships (ten of them) during the years 1750-52 was to end with the arrival of the *Sally* and the *Gale*, in September. The controversy of John Dick's role in bringing about the suffering of these Protestant settlers started back then, and has, through the writings of the historians, continued ever since. With such charges as laid by Governor Hopson[16] the British government was bound to carry out an investigation. The complaints were sent to Dick and he did an admirable job of refutation, such that, no other than Lord Halifax was to conclude that Dick had "perfectly acquitted himself." The ships which brought the setters to Halifax in the mid-18th century were but a small number of a larger number which had brought thousands of settlers to the more popular English colonies lying south of Nova Scotia. The fact of the matter is that a trans-Atlantic voyage in those days of sail was a risky affair; it was expected that a certain number of the passengers would die. The success of any voyage in those days was gaged by the mortality rate.[17] You could make it across the Atlantic in as little as 30 days (a rare event), but if the winds and weather were against you, four months might pass before land was sighted. Provision and fit out the transports as you will, a long time at sea meant misery for all and death to some. The water in the casks turned putrid and the hard biscuit wormy; people became sick; and there was nothing to be done about it. The evidence is that the British authorities and John Dick,[18] whether out of compassion or commercial expediency, took all the precautions that could be taken back then. Ventilators, a new contrivance, with the exception of one, were built into each of the transports hired by Dick. The between deck spaces, were as commodious as any. Indeed, Dick went beyond that which he had to do to accommodate the immigrants.[19]

Overall, Winthrop Bell, in his authoritative book on the subject, was to conclude[20] that "Dick's emigrants were decidedly less crowded than almost any others in the 'Palatine trade' of the period ..." That the passengers of Heyliger's vessels[21] (those on the *Alderney* and the *Nancy* which came over in 1750) and those of Dick's (those on the ten that arrived during 1750-53) "fared much better in the way of provisions on the voyage than did the great majority of 'Palatine' emigrants." As for the food: salted meat, dried peas and hard biscuit, while it would not have satisfied a modern dietician, was as of good a quality as might be had, a fact sworn to by the passengers, themselves.[22] That some of the food and the water turned bad — well, that was not John Dick's fault, but rather, and proportionately so, of the great amount of time required to cross the Atlantic ocean. Those that came to America as a result of the "Palatine Trade" suffered as did any who came by way of the passenger ship of the age. Those who stepped ashore at Halifax during these early years did indeed suffer from the misfortunes of their passage, and did so "due to the hazards of the sea and not to anything that could be charged against human agency."[23]

Chapter 7

The Indian Threat (1749-58)

The MicMac[1] got on with the French in a much better manner than they ever did with the English. I suppose the primary reason is that for the first century of European settlement, during the 1600s, there were to be no other settled white men in MicMac territory other than that of the French. What the MicMac knew of the English is what they learned from their friends the French — and, make no mistake, the French had nothing good to say about the English. So, throughout the course of several generations, the MicMac were to become firmly entrenched in their hatred of the English. Another reason is that the French temperament was much better suited to that of the MicMac. The French, much to their credit and benefit, met their native friends at their level and learned the way of the woods: the English were much too stiff and direct and did not believe the Indians could teach them a thing. The French went to the natives and feasted with them and gave them presents. With the coming of the English, especially as of 1749, the English would issued summonses to the MicMac to come to the English and then proceeded to dictate terms. Another important reason as to why the French and the MicMac got along as well as they did, is, that they put themselves, in time, in a position to claim a common religious bond. The fact is that the French saw to the conversion of the MicMac to Catholicism, in wholesale lots; and then proceeded to control them through the missionaries who lived among them, full time. These missionaries were to gain control over the MicMac, to the extent that anyone ever could, through the old-fashioned prescription of fire and brimstone.

With the traditional attachment of the Indians for the French, it was not difficult for the missionaries to gain great influence over them. Indeed, they became the most important political agents of the French officials in holding

the allegiance of the Indians and in inciting and encouraging them in their
ruthless attacks on frontier houses and villages, frequently being present in
person during the massacres which took place. ...

Among the many priests who performed devoted services in Canada
during three hundred years, only a very small number have had similar
records, and it must, therefore, be concluded that the natures of these few men
were warped and their spiritual development completely dwarfed by political
and material considerations and by certain unrestrained natural instincts and
passions. Their policy was to keep the Indians ferocious savages ...[2]

The Indians were treated like children, and like parents, the
white men awarded the Indians for good deeds and punished
them for bad: except the French preferred the former approach,
the English the latter. The French made a point of gathering
their Indian friends together once a year and gave them gifts of
powder, lead, flints, and axes. The English were quick to single
out wrongdoing Indians and then to proceed to give to each a
dose of English justice, which, in those days, was harsh and
humiliating. The French treated the Indians as sovereign allies;
they lived among them and traded with them. Not so the English!
The English treated the Indians like so many land squatters.

The result of this treatment, upon their settlement in Acadia,
was that for a fifty year period, 1710-60, the English were forced to
live within fort walls and to proceed beyond only in the presence
of an armed guard. As an early 18th century English governor
at Annapolis Royal, Lawrence Armstrong (1664-1739) wrote, the
English were subject to "the daily insults and cruel massacres of
the Indians, who are supported and clandestinely encouraged by
the French" and who make annual gifts to the Indians "of arms,
powder and ball."[3]

That the French were ready to lend a hand to the Indians —
no doubt, but, in the process, it served the international aims and
purposes of France. It is clear that the French used the native Amer-
icans to make the English settler's life on the Atlantic seaboard,
one of constant worry. It was a matter of French policy. The
following quote is from the official instructions from France to the
Governors of Île Royale and of Canada, dated August 29th, 1749:

As it is impossible to openly oppose them [the English], for they are within their rights in making in Acadia such settlements as they see fit, as long as they do not pass its boundaries, there remains for us only to bring against them as many indirect obstacles as can be done without compromising ourselves, and to take steps to protect ourselves against plans which the English can consider through the success of these settlements.

The only method we can employ to bring into existence these obstacles is to make the savages of Acadia and its borders feel how much it is to their advantage to prevent the English fortifying themselves, to bind them to oppose it openly, and to excite the Acadians to support the Indians in their opposition (to the English) in so far as they can do without discovery. The missionaries of both have instructions and are agreeable to act in accordance with these views. ...

Our savages have taken a number of English scalps, their terror of these natives is unequaled, they are so frightened that they dare not leave the towns or forts without detachments, with the protection of these they go out for what is absolutely needed.[4]

Now, to come away from our general comments on the topic, we shall talk of the impact of the Indian threat on the English settlers who came in considerable numbers to Nova Scotia, beginning in 1749 with the founding of Halifax. This Indian Threat existed in 1749 and continued through to 1758.

In the years leading up to the English settlement at Halifax, Admiral Peter Warren wrote, both in 1739 and then again in 1747, of the Indians of Nova Scotia, the MicMac:

In the present situation, the French, by their missionaries and the presents the crown makes annually of powder and shot, and triannually [of] a new gun to each Indian fit to bear arms, has so riveted them to their interest that they will not suffer an Englishman to settle or cure fish in any of the ports on the south side [of] Nova Scotia. In all which ports there are a few Indians; one of them has a commission from the governor of Canada or Cape Breton to command a particular district, and generally bears the title of captain of the fort to which they belong. ...

The security of Nova Scotia and the frontiers of the neighbouring colonies very much depends on the friendship of the Indians, to which nothing can conduce so much as making them presents. ...

That presents, not exceeding the value of £500, be sent for the Indians in those parts, to be used in such manner as shall be thought proper by the commander in chief.

That a fort be built at Canso sufficient to contain 100 men.[5]

Though it was the intention of the English upon establishing their new headquarters at Halifax to pacify the Indians — it being the most practical solution to a long standing problem[6] — they knew it would take time and effort to do so.[7] The English were working against the French, who, as we have seen, were past experts[8] when it came to winning the native people over. Halifax, until the situation improved, was to be a stockaded community. These stockades, as events were to prove, were needed.

Edward Cornwallis, obedient to his orders to pacify the Indians, within a couple of weeks of his arrival to found Halifax, on July 9th, 1749, sent Edward How to the Saint John River.[9] How made two trips; the first with John Rous and the second with John Gorham. The efforts were aimed at winning over the Malecites.[10] On his second trip he took presents to the Indians including 1,000 bushels of corn and 500 bushels of wheat. These efforts lead to a treaty being signed.[11] On August 15th, the Indians, a delegation of them having come to Halifax, signed a confirmation and ratification of the previous treaties entered into both in the years 1725 (December) and 1727 (July). The ceremony was concluded upon the deck of the *Beaufort* while she rode at anchor in the harbor. The Saint John Indians and the population at Halifax entertained one another: the befeathered and red faced Indians signed, while in the back ground a 17 gun salute boomed out: it was a ceremony that impressed all and sundry.[12]

The First Attack At Dartmouth:

All of this pomp and ceremony was for naught: On September 30th (OS), a group of men were out cutting wood to supply a mill operated by a Major Gilman in Dartmouth, a place just over the harbor from Halifax. I quote Thomas Beamish Akins: "Six of his [Gilman's] men had been sent out to cut wood without arms. The Indians laid in ambush, killed four and carried off one, and the other escaped and gave the alarm, and a detachment of rangers was sent after the savages, who having overtaken them, cut off the heads of two Indians and scalped one."[13] It is reported[14] that an Acadian by the name of Joseph Broussard ("Beausoleil") led the natives in their attack at Dartmouth.[15] Next day the council determined to let loose the brave-hearted men among them, of which there were only a few, in declaring a bounty ("as is the custom of America") of ten gold guineas for every Indian taken or destroyed.[16] This decision came as a result of an emergency Sunday meeting held aboard the *Beaufort* the day after the butchery in Dartmouth. "Within three days Captain Clapman raised a company of seventy volunteers, though only fifty were needed. They scoured the forest, but apparently without result. It does not appear that any ranger ever claimed a scalp bounty at Halifax."[17]

Thereafter, and for a ten year period,

> Nova Scotia lay under the continual terror of Indian warfare. Fear brooded over the land. There was no calculating where or when the deadly blow would fall. The thick set spruces gave no sign of warning. Stealthy forms glided through the forest by secret trails, or passed along the net-work of waterways in noiseless canoes; savage eyes watched the ways of the careless white man. And then muskets spoke suddenly from green boughs, or war-whoops shattered the night; and there were piteous scalped corpses to bury, or friends to mourn, who had vanished with their captors. There are trackings of rangers and skirmishes with war parties, exchange of shots without result.[18]

Reference has already been made to the attack at Gilman's saw-mill on the Dartmouth side of the Halifax Harbor. There was an earlier attack in 1749. Lieutenant Joseph Gorham (John's brother) had departed Halifax on the *Wren* to accompany a party which was going to Canso to cut hay. At Canso the party was surprised by Indians, who capture the vessel, took twenty prisoners and carried them off to Louisbourg (they were almost immediately released). Akins reported that during this incident "three English and seven Indians were killed."[19] The killing continued into 1750. In October of that year, a group of about eight men went out "to take their diversion; and as they were fowling, they were attacked by the Indians, who took the whole prisoners; scalped ... [one] with a large knife, which they wear for that purpose, and threw him into the sea ..."[20]

The brutal killing continued on into 1751. At Dartmouth on March 26th, "A little baby was found lying by its father and mother," wrote a settler, "all three scalped. The whole town was a scene of butchery, some having their hands cut off, some their bellies ripped open, and others their brains dashed out."[21] Then on May 13th, the largest Indian attack to ever be staged in the area was carried out. A group of about 130 Indians and Acadians (likely led by "Beausoleil"), after a frustrating attack on Fort Lawrence, formed up at the Isthmus of Chignecto. They likely made their way down to Tatamagouche, then over the Cobequids to the Acadian community of Cobequid (known as Truro these days), and then down the Shubenacadie water system[22] to arrive at the back door of the lightly protected community of Dartmouth. John Wilson: "A little before four in the morning; they all at once appeared, fired through the windows and doors, and killed fifteen persons, including women and children; wounded seven, three of whom died in the hospital; six men were carried away, and never heard of since."[23] It was a calm night and "the cries of the settlers, and whoop of the Indians were distinctly heard" across the harbor at Halifax by their fellow settlers.[24] As a result of this particular attack, Sylvanus Cobb was employed to round up some men (he sailed to Boston to do so) in order to go after the perpetrators; with the incentive of £10 for every Indian scalp and £50 for Le Loutre's. In fact, Cobb was not successful in raising any men and the "hunt" was called off.[25]

Also, in 1751, near the neck of the peninsular on which Halifax was built, and where there was a series of blockhouses that had been constructed, another attack was carried out. "The North Blockhouse was once surprised by Indians when the guard was drinking and playing cards, and the men were killed. Near the South Blockhouse, Indians attacked workmen at a saw-mill on the stream flowing out of Chocolate Lake, and killed one or two of them. The casualties were buried by the guard, but the savages returned in an effort to obtain the scalps."[26]

There was apparently a hiatus during 1752. It has been put down to Hopson's enlightened governorship. Peregrine Thomas Hopson took over from Edward Cornwallis in the summer of 1752.[27] Hopson was obliged to give up his position due to health problems in the fall of 1753 at which time Charles Lawrence took over. However, the fact that the Indians were quiet during this period could equally be — and I wish to take nothing away from Hopson as an administrator — and more likely due, to the fact that Abbé Le Loutre was out of the country for most of this period.[28] In June of 1753, we see bloody murder, once again. This time it was seven English sailors: six were killed by Indians at Musquodoboit. The seventh, Anthony Casteel was taken as a prisoner. Casteel, after being led on a long circuitous route via the Isthmus of Chignecto, was traded off by the Indians at Louisbourg two months later; and, shortly thereafter, he found his way back to the English establishment at Halifax.[29]

As the last of the war years passed, the Indian threat became less and less. I note that in the spring of 1756, a wood gathering party out of Fort Monckton at Baie Verte (it being formally the French fort, Fort Gasperaux, which was captured by the English in 1755) was surprised by Indians, "nine of them are scalped." This attack was but only one, there were others at the isthmus as were reported by Webster. It caused the English commandant at Fort Cumberland (formally Fort Beauséjour which the English renamed upon its capture in 1755), Col. Scott, to proclaim a bounty for Indian scalps. Further, he wrote his superior at Halifax, Charles Lawrence, and suggested that similar bounties for certain of the Acadians be declared, as, "they now act in conjunction with the Indians."[30]

The new settlers at Lunenburg, which were settled by the English in 1753, were in for a particularly hard time of it through the balance of the war years. In May of 1756, four people (a two year old included) were killed and scalped.[31] In August, Indians descended on the Lay family's farm and caught the members of this family and visiting neighbors (the Hatts): killed them all.[32] On an island in Mahone Bay, now Covey Island, where the Payzant family lived, Louis Payzant was murdered and scalped, so too, a small boy, a servant and her infant.[33] In March 1758, a similar incident to that just described happened once again. It took place not too far away from the scene of the 1756 tragedy. A young farmer, his wife and their two children (aged four and two years), were killed and scalped. And again at Lunenburg, in 1759, on the 22nd March (Holy Week): "Indians scalped Oxner and his wife and heir."[34]

Incidently, no similar attacks on the French communities within Nova Scotia were carried out, at least there is no historical accounts of it. However, when French officialdom, as was represented by the priests in their midst, wanted to impress the Acadians they warned they were ready to play their Indian card and would do so if the Acadians did not fall into line. For example, during January, 1750, at Beaubassin, on the church steps, in the presence of their own priests, Abbé Le Loutre, with Indians at his back, threatened death to any Acadian who should travel to trade with the English.[35] Francis Parkman gives an accounting:

> This priest [Le Loutre] urged the people of Les Mines, Port Royal, and other places, to come and join the French, and promised to all, in the name of the governor, to settle and support them for three years, and even indemnify them for any losses they might incur; threatening if they did not do as he advised, to abandon them, deprive them of their priests, have their wives and children carried off, and their property laid waste by the Indians.[36]

A concluding word on the MicMac: though it seems plain they could not have chosen to be at the side of any other, in the great French/English conflict over North America, the MicMac had simply chosen the wrong side. With the end of the *Seven Years War* and the *Treaty Of Paris*, in 1763, France, by force of arms, had permanently lost her power in North America. The MicMac were thus left with but memories of their friends the French, and left, too, to carry the burden of vanquished rivals. Victory had given to the English the right of Dominion over the MicMac people. One hope only was to remain to them, the only hope of the vanquished — the hope: that in their resignation that their new masters would treat them with understanding and compassion.

Chapter 8

The Settlement Of Lunenburg
(1753-4)

The new arrivals were piling up and were proving to be a problem.
Winthrop Bell[1]:

> Those people had been drawn to Nova Scotia by the offer of lands and implements and the rest of it; and the original idea of an initial one year's free victualing had been to tide them over until they could begin to producing something on their promised lands. The government had been unable to perform its side of the bargain by placing them on land where they could even make a beginning toward self-sufficiency. Halifax being the sort of place it was, the government was then under moral obligation to see to it that some means of support was available to the foreigners until it could fulfil its own principal undertakings to them.[2]

This was not just a local problem. The question for the English authorities at London, who were obliged to turn to parliament for yet more funds, particularly pressing during the winter of 1752/53, was — Why was it taking so long to get the new English settlements established in Nova Scotia? It was now going on four years since Edward Cornwallis with 2,600 settlers was sent out in order to establish a stronger English presence in Nova Scotia, a presence which was to start with the founding of a new capital for Nova Scotia, Halifax in 1749. In the succeeding years, through to 1752, many more settlers arrived which had the effect of doubling the population at Halifax; these events we have dealt with in a previous chapter. It was the intention of the English, as we have seen, at government expense[3] to establish Protestant settlements throughout Nova Scotia in order to offset the French Catholic population, which had been the only European population in Nova Scotia for quite some period of time. (The Acadian farmers had established themselves in the province 110 years earlier.) In addition to a major English fort and settlement at Chebucto (Halifax), settlements were to be established in outlying areas. Considered among the areas were: Minas, Whitehead, Baie Verte and LaHave.[4]

What had happened, was, that the French through their allies were able to effectively keep the English settlers pinned down at Halifax. The settlers, except those that had arrived earlier and who had received lots of land and were expected to stay on at Halifax, were temporarily put up and maintained at government expense. It was not intended that this situation, the victualing of the settlers, should go on beyond a year; but Cornwallis could not move them into their intended settlements. The Board of Trade, the administrating authority in London, not quite understanding the depth and extent of the problem, was to put considerable pressure on Cornwallis to bring an end to the expense. Cornwallis knew that to move the "Foreign Protestants" beyond the protection of the Halifax garrison would mean certain butchery. He had to keep them at Halifax. The infertile lands in and around Halifax could not be worked so to support the numbers that were located there; and, at any rate, their labor was required to build up the necessary defenses. With every ship from England there were to be official letters demanding explanations from Cornwallis; and with every ship departing for England, together with the demanded explanations, there was to be petitions for more money and supplies. Cornwallis found himself to be in an impossible position; he was neither able to satisfy the settlers who looked to him for the delivery of promises made, nor was he able to satisfy his superiors in England to cut the expense and get on with the settlement plans. He pleaded to be relieved of his position, and the Lords in London thought it best to bring him home and to put someone in place that could get the job done in Nova Scotia and who understood the necessity of maintaining proper books of account.

Hopson Arrives:

On August 3rd, 1752, Cornwallis, disillusioned and wearied of "his financial responsibilities and of the reiterated and detailed instructions to economize," was grateful to hand over the reins of governorship to his replacement, Colonel Pergrine Thomas Hopson.[5] It will be remembered that Hopson had been the English governor of Louisbourg for the greater period of time that it was under the English flag, 1745-49. His duties done, he had left America for England, likely with the fall sailing of 1749, but only after he had overseen the removal of the troops and stores from Louisbourg to Halifax. Hopson, the authorities fully appreciating his experiences at both Louisbourg and at Halifax, still the colonel of the 29th Foot, was appointed to go and to take over from Cornwallis. Before leaving England, it is noted[6] that he had two "long conferences" with the Board of Trade; one on the 21st of April and another on the 6th of May. Undoubtedly, it was impressed upon Hopson, that he had to out-settle the bulk of the people on the "victualing lists" at Halifax. How it was to be done and where they were to be located — well, that was to be a matter for Hopson to decide; but, to get them on their own lands and to get them self-sufficient within a year of them being moved to their new settlement, was, paramount.

Governor Hopson's plan may have been to get the crowded settlers at Halifax out-settled as soon as possible; but it was a plan that could not be implemented late in the year. The opportune time would be early in the spring so as to have as much time as possible, to: clear land, put crops in, and erect shelters. All of this to be done before, as was expected in these northern latitudes, the winter snows flew. His arrival at Halifax during August of 1752, meant that Hopson could not direct that a move be made that year. The balance of the year would be used to fix up the conditions at Halifax. The situation was bad due to the crowding of the settlers, and became extreme with the arrival of yet more settlers during August and September. These new arrivals were exhausted as a result of their long transatlantic voyage; they had to be housed and fed; and the sick taken care of. So too, Hopson was to immediately have his hands full because of civil unrest at Halifax. There was conflict between the newcomers from England and the newcomers (who didn't think themselves to be

so new) from New England.[7] Thus, it was, that Hopson was
to be a very busy man[8] through to the end of 1752. During the
winter of 1752/53, however, Governor Hopson and his Council
had the chance to perfect the plans to relocate the German/Swiss
settlers.

   Hopson was sympathetic to Cornwallis. He was to immediately recognize the huge problems which were faced in
bringing to fruition the 1748/49 plans of establishing a number of
"English" settlements throughout Nova Scotia. We have dealt, in
previous chapters, and in some detail, with the Indian threat and
the resultant pile-up of settlers at Halifax. But there were other
practical problems of getting the penniless settlers out into the
countryside and onto their own lands. Hopson wrote of them,
"whenever they are sent out, so far from nine months' provisions
being sufficient for the purpose till they get rightly settled and
have raised something of their own to be able to subsist upon
... a further supply of fifteen months more will be absolutely
necessary to be allowed them." And further, "provisions, arms,
tools, implements for clearing and cultivating the land materials
necessary for building their habitations."[9] Thus was Hopson
to advise the Board in London by a letter dated at Halifax in
December of 1752, to which he attached "a list of the estimated
requirements." Hopson also wanted authority to go to Boston
and charter vessels so that the immigrants might be transported
by water to their new lands, a place somewhere along the eastern
seaboard of Nova Scotia, a place which in the fall of 1752 had yet
to be selected. By April of 1753, by which time matters ought to
have been underway, Hopson had not heard from his superiors
in London. Was he to get the requested supplies, or not? He met
with his Council and wanted them to approve a course of action
which he was willing to take without getting the final word from
London. He would immediately go to Boston to secure, on his
signature, "a sufficient number of blockhouses, magazines,
frames for storehouses and materials necessary for the settlers
habitations ... " In addition he would, on his authority, hire
sufficient vessels for transports.[10]

The Choice of Mirliguesch:

That getting the excess people out of Halifax and into a community of their own was on the top of the new governor's agenda, is disclosed in the minutes of the governing Council dated August 10th, 1752. During this meeting, called shortly after Hopson's arrival, there was discussion as to what place might be best for a new settlement beyond Halifax. For some reason, which escapes me, and I find it curious, there was no discussion that led to any significant movement of the new arrivals to the farming lands in the western part of the province which we now refer to as the Annapolis Vally — in and around the Acadians: Annapolis Royal and Minas. I made note in an earlier chapter of this work where the governor of Massachusetts, a colony which oversaw Nova Scotia for many years, William Shirley (1694-1771) had sent Charles Morris (1711-81) up in 1748 to survey the Acadian lands in order to see how newcomers might be best fitted in and around the existing Acadian population. It ought to have been plain to everyone, from Hopson on down, that if what was wanted was to employ the newcomers as farmers (being from central Europe, they certainly had no experience in making a living from the sea) then the place for them was to be on lands known to be productive. The point is that the eastern seaboard of Nova Scotia was not the place to establish a farming community. Oh! Well, there were small patches of good land here and there; but most all of the eastern side of Nova Scotia is barren and rocky. But the question is — Why this reluctance to move the newcomers in amongst the Acadians? I suppose, it was thought that they, the German/Swiss, would most likely be absorbed by the Acadians and become more French then English. Another important consideration, given the recent experiences with Indian raids, was that any new community should be in close communication with Halifax. Communication in those days meant traveling in order to deliver a message. Travel by sea, as uncertain as it was by times, was preferable to traveling through virgin forest the veils of which hide Indians. At any rate, during the Council meeting of August 10th, 1752, the only places under discussion were those along the Atlantic side of the province within a hundred miles or so of Halifax. It was intended that surveys should be carried out of the Chezzetcook area to the east and the LaHave area to the west. The harbors in these two areas had at times been occupied by the French, and, indeed, there was yet to be found scattered French families in these places. To locate in an area that had been cleared and where salt marshes were nearby would be important. Time would be saved in clearing the land, and, the hay that grew naturally in the salt marshes could be harvested for the animals located both in the new community and that at Halifax. Most importantly, given the experiences that those at Halifax and Dartmouth had with Indian raids, whatever place that should be chosen, should be one that could be defended; it should be a peninsula. Thus the place to be chosen would be one on the Atlantic, within (under normal conditions) a day's sail from Halifax, having a harbor to the west of a rising land head, with deep water just off the beach, a place which, at least in part, had been in the past cleared of large trees, which had salt marshes nearby; and which could easily be defended, a peninsula. Mirliguesch, or Lunenburg as it was to be called, qualified on all counts.

With the coming of the spring, further surveys were to be carried out of those areas which were thought to be appropriate for the settlement of the German/Swiss. In particular, the *Albany* (Capt. John Rous[11]) was sent down to Mirliguesch with a contingent of rangers under Captain Lewis. They left Halifax on the April 23rd and by May 1st they were back at Halifax. Hopson, after taking into account the observations of Rous and Lewis, then made up his mind.[12] Mirliguesch was the place at which to make the new settlement; its name was to be Lunenburg; and the chosen people together with the necessary supplies were to be sent down under a strong guard to establish the new town as soon as the Boston ships were in place at Halifax to receive them.

The Move to Mirliguesch:

The ships which the governor had arranged drifted into Halifax Harbor during the month of May. Their cargoes were shifted and sorted. Supplies were needed for the new endeavor; and, so too, after a long winter, supplies were needed at Halifax. The month of May at Halifax was a busy month, the usable docks were stacked with such things as lumber, live stock, bricks, hay, etc. Red jacketed officers hovered about with their lists directing men to put this there, and that there. Loads of material were brought into the warehouses at Halifax; lighters brought material back and forth to the anchored transports. Invariably, mixups occurred; and, material on a recheck after loading were unloaded and reloaded once again. Then things seemed to have been sorted out and things quieted down. Notices went up. The listed settlers were called to a meeting at the Halifax Parade on Monday, 21st May at 7 a.m., "there to draw lots of land."[13] Such an announcement was sure to cause a complete turnout. Final counts could then be made and directions given.

In the meantime, rumors had come to Governor Hopson that there were upwards of 300 hundred hostile Indians gathered in and around Piziquid (Windsor) biding their time until they get word that the settlers had left Halifax to go and build a second "English" settlement. This had to spark some hot discussions between Hopson and his advisors. To send the settlers away from Halifax in the face of a threatened attack — well, they could not do that, could they. "But, the plans are set." It has been four years since the British sailed into Halifax and the intention was that they were going to spread out. The Indian raids were fresh in everyone's mind. "Why, just two years back, at Dartmouth, innocent settlers, women and children included, were butchered." But had not treaties just been signed, the one last fall and the other just earlier this year? And, the settlers, was there not strong military support being sent down with them? And, blockhouses — they were framed up and ready to be put in place, only within a matter of days of their arrival. The decision was made!

"We shall go! — And, be the wiser for this intelligence."
However, Hopson determined to attempt a ruse. He would send
a false message that he knew would fall into the enemy's hands.
"I have sent letters by them [couriers] calculated to fall into the
hands of the Indians, acquainting the officer [at Fort Edward,
Piziquid] that I have sent a large party to Cobequid [Truro] to
see how the Indians are disposed, and that I had deterred the
expedition [to Lunenburg] until their return."[14]

The settlers came to Lunenburg in two waves, with the greater
number coming down on the second run. The first run carried
642 of the 1,453 settlers which were to eventually disembark at
Lunenburg.[15] It was thought to be more important to get the
military men and their armaments and supplies including the
pre-framed block houses on the ground, first.

I now turn to Winthrop Bell to tell us of this first wave which
set out from Halifax on the early morning of Tuesday, 29th of
May, 1753:

> Protection of the first expedition was entrusted to H.M. frigate *Albany*,
> Captain John Rous; and she was to remain in the harbour at Lunenburg to
> guard the site with her guns until land defences could be built. She served
> also as a floating headquarters for Lawrence. The rangers were carried in
> the armed sloop *Ulysses*, Jeremiah Rogers, master, and the detachments
> from the regiments in the chartered New England sloop *Rainbow*, 98 tons,
> Wm. Montgomery, master. Two or three vessels already in provincial service
> (armed sloop *York*, Sylvanus Cobb, master; schooner *Bulkeley*, Cox, master;
> and the Halifax "pilot boat") were employed in the work. And settlers,
> baggage, utensils, supplies, and provisions were distributed among the ...
> hired New England vessels ...[16]

Bell then set forth a list of the transport vessels[17]:

NAME OF VESSEL	SIZE	NAME OF MASTER
Bedford	95(tons)	Benjamin Donnel
Endeavour	93	Richard Trivett
Swan	90	John Waite
Speedwell	90	John Horner
Industry	90	George Goodwin
Mary	90	Andrew Denning

Victory	90	John Roddick
Industry	88	John Bristoll
Dolphin	81	Samuel Hodgkins
Endeavour	80	Josiah Stover
Medford	80	William Nichols
Three Friends	75	John Simpson
Speedwell	64	Isaac Martin
Sally	60	Daniel Stickney

The Departure:

On Tuesday, May 29th, 1753, the settlers "mustered that were appointed for the first embarkation."[18] The settlers, on the 29th, were placed with their "baggage" aboard,[19] apparently while along side, in turn, and then put to anchor in the stream of the harbor. It took time to assemble the fleet which consisted of upwards to 20 sailing vessels. In advance of the settlers, 92 regular troops and 66 rangers were put aboard the armed vessels, the *Rainbow* and the *Ulysses*.[20] While the fleet was ready to sail, by the 30th, and, while indeed they paraded up the harbor that day, they eventually had to seek shelter and came to anchor not far from where they left, just in behind a sand spit on an island which is at the entrance of Halifax harbor (today McNabs, then called Cornwallis' Island). First off there were a couple of stragglers for which they had to wait. Once they were all gathered in, the wind became foul and the weather thick.[21] They would have to wait for the right wind, one that is out of the north in order to clear the Sambro ledges to the south of them and then to point southwest on an easy reach of a few hours down to Lunenburg. They waited; and they waited. For better than a week, they waited. Though the weather was generally fair, the wind continued to came out of the south. Smaller vessels were kept running back and forth to the Halifax docks but a couple of miles away in order to keep the water and foodstuffs topped up.[22] The people were getting uneasy and a number were becoming seasick.[23]

Finally, on the early morning of the 7th, it was perceived that the wind, though light, was beginning to become fair, a signal boomed out for the ships of the fleet to weigh their anchors.

No sooner their anchors were lifted, the winds died. But there was a sea breeze off shore if only they could clear the land. The naval ships lowered their deck boats and got their rowing crews busy. Off Sambro there was wind, however, while headway was made by the leaders, certain of the vessels lagged far behind. Lawrence wrote in his journal, "... the *Albany* [Lawrence's ship] shortened sail, and made a signal for the headmost and weathermost vessels to come under her quarter, in order to better keep company. At 8 in the evening the wind came to the northward, and we laid our course. All the vessels, except the *Ulysses*, being in their stations." So, it was a night's sail: and, "the wind continued fair at N.E., and the weather clear and fine. It made an easy sail all night."[24] We can but imagine a star studded night, and within hours the land which they sought was lit in the warm morning sun as it came up over the eastern sea horizon. It was June 8th, 1753.

The Arrival:

Governor Hopson was to put his most experienced man in charge of the mission, Lieutenant-Colonel Charles Lawrence. Reporting to Lawrence was Captain Patrick Sutherland. Lawrence knew what was to be the first order of business: it was to see to the defences.[25] Within the first 24 hours the frames for the first block house were floated ashore from the ships at anchor in the harbor, landing them at high tide on the shores of the future town. These frames were hauled up about a half mile to a steep rise to a place where they were to be erected. Also, within this first day a crowd of blade swinging men were turned loose and soon there was a cleared strip across the neck of the peninsula to the northwest of the present day town, in line with the blockhouse.[26] So too, on this first day, some of the lumber for the buildings to be erected was off loaded and rafted ashore; it was piled up and put under guard.[27] In respect to the founding of Lunenburg, historians are indeed fortunate in that Lawrence's accounting[28] of the events have come down to us. I herein next set forth Lawrence's entries of June the 8th (Friday) and the 9th, 1753, whole:

Friday 8th.

From 8 o'clock last night, (when we were abreast Samborough Island,) the wind continued fair at N.E., and ye weather clear & fine. Made an easy sail all night. At 3 this morning ye Commodore fired a Gun, to call off some of ye Vessels that were too near ye Shore. Between 4 & five we were abreast of Cross Island. At 7 came to an anchor in ye harbour in Merliguash, most of ye Vessels being 2 leagues astern. In coming in ye sloop *Victory*, Capt. Rodick, tailed upon a rock on ye larboard side of ye harbour. The Commodore sent boats to her assistance, and had an answer from her that she had received no damage, & as ye tide was making would be off presently. The last of ye Vessels came to an anchor at ½ an hour after 9. At 10, ye vessels being all in their berths, made a signal for all masters to come on board. Gave them orders to prepare their boats & make a disposition for landing. At 11 ordered ye Regulars & militia and Rangers on shore, directing them to wait on ye beach, till I disembarked with ye Settlers fit to bear Arms. When the settlers got on shore, ordered the Rangers to march along, near ye beach, with Captain Morris to ye head of Harbour: ordered Capt. Sutherland with ye regulars to take ye middle of ye Hill — Marched myself (Major Lawrence) with the Militia along ye top of ye Hill; and all assembled at ye head of ye harbour. Then reconnoitred, making what remarks we could for a future disposition of ye troops. Then fixed with Capt. Morris, ye Surveyor, the situation of the Town, and also of ye blockhouses for the defence of it; which — This being done in about the Space of 4 hours, we then marched back again, and at 4 o'clock in ye afternoon reembarked ye troops & settlers, it being too late, to encamp, to any advantage, before night. At 5 in ye evening called on board ye Captain of ye militia to consult what number of settlers might be had from each vessel to go to Work at 3 o'clock ye next morning. They agreed on 120, observing that it would be very difficult to prevail with them to work more than every other day. Gave them orders to have provisions dressed before night for ye next Day, that no time might be lost. Whereon they acquainted me, that ye week's provision served on Monday last was quite out — (expended) and that if I would allow another week to be served, they could with ye help of their pease (which have not hitherto been served) & ye abundance of herbs on shore, easily afford to have it deducted out of their future issues. Sent for ye Storekeeper, & ordered it accordingly; Directing him to charge it as extra provisions, to be hereafter accounted for. Then fixed with ye Captains to have 120 men on shore at 3 o'clock the next morning; in order to carry up ye blockhouses, But to take with them their arms; and to lodge them under ye care of a party of Rangers to be posted at ye foot of ye hill for that purpose. Then sent for Capt. Sutherland, and agreed on the following disposition of ye troops for ye next morning, Viz. The regulars & Rangers to be landed at day break. A Serjeant & 9 men of ye Rangers to be detached to ye Summit of ye Hill to ye South East. An officer & 20 Rangers to remain at the landing place.

A corporal's guard to be posted at ye head of ye Harbour, on ye fresh water brook: The body of ye regulars with ye remainder of ye Rangers to march up to, & take post on ye Spot where ye upper block house is to stand., By his disposition the extremities of ye cleared land being well guarded ye Settlers may pass & repass, & do ye labour required of them in as much safety, as our numbers can afford. At 6 o'clock ordered Capt. Joseph Rouse with ye Gondula's & boats to get out ye Blockhouses & have them towed up to ye proper landing places. — The gondulas were filled with ye timbers & ye remainder made into rafts by half past 9 at night, and ye whole towed up at high water which was about 2 in ye morning. The lumber vessels were ordered up ye Harbour for ye more convenient landing ye lumber, & the Sloop *York* was ordered to follow to Cover them & ye blockhouses.

Saturday 9th.

Between 3 & 4 o'clock this morning, the Regulars, Rangers, & Settlers landed according to ye disposition made last night. The Settlers carried up on their Shoulders the timbers of one blockhouse, (the distance being near half a mile) by 10 in ye morning, during which time ye carpenters set up nearly ye first story. Then ye people broke off for Breakfast, and as they had worked with great willingness & so as to make extraordinary despatch, they were allowed a dram each for their encouragement, which their officers & overseers were all desirous they should have, conceiving it would be most usefully bestowed.

Then ordered the tents on shore, and directed that they should be pitched at ye foot of ye hill, that being ye most convenient place for encampment so as at once to cover ye Settlers, stores & baggage, an to secure them against any attempt from the Enemy.

The settlers growing very impatient to get on shore, have landed their wives & children without my knowledge, and seem so disposed to range about, that I am but too apprehensive of some mischief.

The lumber being now rafted, it is ordered to be landed at high water which will be at 2; when we shall endeavour to raise sheds with it; shall land ye remainder of ye settlers and their baggage, and so be prepared (if possible) to dispatch 5 or 6 Vessels for Halifax some time to Morrow.

From 11 till two ye settlers continued to work and to make great dispatch, so as by that hour to get up ye whole of ye timbers and other materials for the Blockhouses. Then broke off for an hour & dined, After which ye settlers were employed till night in opening a large avenue from ye Blockhouses to ye Water side at ye back of ye hill, which, When they had completed, they may be fairly said to have done a most extraordinary day's work, especially as it has rained hard for ye greatest part of ye day.

After this removed ye troops from ye Blockhouses to their encampment at ye foot of ye hill, leaving proper guards at such posts as tended most to secure ye environs of ye Hill. Then appointed a picket of 50 men out of ye Militia to be left on shore to Strengthen ye Camp.

Being unable to land the whole of ye Settlers and their baggage this night, as was proposed in the morning, I reembarked all that were on shore except ye 50 for ye picket.

(N.B. [Dr. Brown adds:] A day of this nature comprizes ye exertions & toil of several weeks in a settled country. Few people ever witnessed a scene of greater bustle. The whole is well describe in ye Journal of Lawrence.)

We see from the subsequent entries where, on the 10th of June, the vessels[29] picked to return to Halifax, in order to ferry the balance of the settlers down to Lunenburg, were cleared and made ready for sailing. Lawrence dispatched part of the fleet on the 10th. They made good time and were away again from Halifax on the 15th of June, arriving safely at Lunenburg on the 17th.

I have already set forth in a previous footnote the difficulties Lawrence was having keeping the supplies together, particularly the lumber needed for building. It became urgent that the town lots be assigned to the settlers as soon as possible, so that the supplies could be distributed and the settlers would expend their time and efforts in improving their own property rather than wondering about and causing Lawrence more trouble. As we saw there was a lot draw at Halifax; but it would be a number of days before the surveyors, Charles Morris included, had the lots marked on the ground. On Tuesday, the 19th of June, 1753, the settlers were put into possession of their town lots. For the purposes of defense, a tight town surrounded with pickets and strategically placed blockhouses was what was to be built. But, it was farming to which the settlers intended to turn, so, garden lots outside of the protective defenses of the town were eventually to be given to each settler. Such a division of land, however, would take time, and, in the meantime, there was much to do in getting the town and its defenses set up. Getting gardens in, during this first summer, was not the priority, and, at any rate, it was guaranteed that the settlers would be fed[30] until the expected crops of 1754 were to come in.[31]

A Land of Timber and Fish:

Thus, a beachhead was established. The weather was wet, however, in spite of it, the work went ahead. The settlers were less than cooperative[32] with the authorities; nevertheless, the town's defenses went up. The Indians, as was feared, did not attack; had they, the whole project would have been brought to an end and the settlers forced back to Halifax. Everybody's spirits were raised upon the completion of both the blockhouses and a line of pickets. There was now time for everyone to look about. Lawrence was to report to the governor on June the 10th: "The more we look around us the more promising our prospect appears. We have fine land, fine timber, fine fish, & great abundance."[33]

Lawrence realized early that there was a need for support which was to extend much beyond the nurturing stage of those first few summer months. Knowing that Hopson was to sail for England at the end of the summer he made a compassionate plea in writing to Hopson knowing it would be passed on by Hopson to the Board of Trade. Lawrence wrote:

The people in general are extremely necessitous and I may say without at all aggravating the circumstances, in real want of common conveniences and necessaries of life. Victuals above all things they are in absolute want of and as I observed in a former letter being unable to subsist for seven days on an allowance sufficient for four or five only. They sell off weekly what little matters they have to enable them to keep life and soul together. ... We cannot build houses, make gardens, cut timber and take fish at the same time even tho: we had craft and tackling. Now that the people are barefooted and have neither money to buy more shoes, leather to make them of nor the time to make them in. What are they to do ... They were sent here not to be starved and beggar'd but to be cherished and supported, it will be then possible to guide and govern them. ... I dare not discontinue paying them twelve pence for their labour [on the public works] till I have your liberty to increase their allowance of provisions. Was I to strike off the twelve pences to day we should loose one hundred and fifty families before tomorrow ...[34]

And then again, in August:

Absurd & outrageous as these people are in their dispositions [they expected to get paid for government work, notwithstanding they owed the government for their passage] I must yet do them the justice to observe that they are indefatigable when labouring for themselves. Most of them are well under cover. All of them have gardens, & many of them good framed houses. They have cut on the whole a considerable quantity of hay. They are acquainted with the country for 10 miles round; and the more they know of it the better they seem to like it ...[35]

Lawrence was due to take his leave of Lunenburg at the end of the summer, as he was to take over the governorship duties back at Halifax.[36] When Lawrence handed over responsibilities to his second in command, Capt. Sutherland, Lunenburg was in a good state. Doctor Brown:

The most important part of the work [in respect to the settlement of Lunenburg] was now happily concluded. A town was planned and built — a new stroke was added to the uncultivated coasts of North America. A discontented people were daily becoming more quiet and the views of government began to be accomplished.[37]

The Hoffman Insurrection:

It is appropriate to conclude my chapter on the founding of Lunenburg by giving a brief outline of "The Hoffman Insurrection"; it is, indeed, also an appropriate ending to an earlier chapter "Foreign Protestants By the Shipload" (1750-52). "The Hoffman Insurrection," a rebellion, lasted but a few days, and, was ended in mid-December, 1753, when Monckton with a body of regular troops was send down from Halifax at the request of the local commander (Sutherland). This show of extra force and Monckton's promise to get to the bottom of things, and his immediate investigations, was enough to quell the rebellion. Before getting into the facts of the Lunenburg rebellion which came about within months of its settlement, best we get to the roots of the problem which had its beginnings with the arrival of the Swiss/German immigrants at Halifax during the years 1750-52.

These Protestant Foreigners, these Germans, had not been treated on their arrival in Nova Scotia as well as they thought they ought to have been. They complained about their conditions in letters back home and were to present formal petitions to government. After all the suitable curtesies ("Government's judicious foresight and fatherly care") and recognizing the very good reason why they were not immediately put on their farm lands (the "wild enemy") they proceeded to point out "that on our arrival we had not time given us to recover ourselves from fatigues of such a tedious passage we were unused to, but immediately forced to hard labour with no other than salt provisions except once two pounds fresh beef each." High prices and ill treatment had reduced them to a "sad deplorable condition" and that because of it they were reduced to beg for provisions. They also, in this petition, made known that the best lands in Halifax and in Dartmouth "is chiefly given off to the New Englanders" who but refer to the German/Swiss as the "Dam Dutch Rascals"; and, as the petitioners asserted, the New Englanders did nothing to improve their lands.[38]

These problems of the new arrivals to which we have referred were never adequately addressed and so they continued to stew or seethe even after they were relocated on their allotted lands at Lunenburg. Much was promised to them and they all felt short changed. They became very suspicious that the undelivered supplies and provisions had in fact been sent from England but had been diverted to the use of others — they became convinced of it. Rumors spread; and — whether the stories were accurate or embroidered has little to do with how these hard pressed foreigners felt about the matter — just like the winter snows that then started, rumors flew from one family to another as the dull days of November and early December of 1753 cast their spell. They were living in miserable little shacks with a questionable supply of fire wood (as to whether it would last the season) and victuals from government stores: salted meat, hardtack and dried peas. Guards had to be mounted because of the continuing threat of an Indian attack. They would like to cut more wood for themselves and begin clearing more land; but they were forced into the public work of cutting pickets for the ever growing fence between themselves and the promising lands beyond.

The rumor that set everyone off in the new community was that there existed a letter whom one, Jean Pettrequin, a fellow settler, had, and which had been written by a person in the know, back in Germany or England, to the effect that there were abundant supplies which the local government had been directed to disburse. Finally there was some tangible proof of some skulduggery, that is to say that certain officials (whoever they may be) were fattening themselves up at the expense of the poor settlers at Lunenburg. A mob of men grabbed Pettrequin and threaten him with dire consequences if he didn't cough up the incriminating letter. The local commander, Captain Patrick Sutherland, having heard of this, immediately, with the justice of peace, Sebastian Zouberbuhler, went to Pettrequin's aid and soon saw to his release. A short time thereafter, the mob grabbed Pettrequin again and this second time locked him up in one of the blockhouses. Pettrequin, now fearing for his life blurted out that while he had the letter it was seized by Zouberbuhler. Well, there it is, so the mob thought — Zouberbuhler is one of them and the letter would have been destroyed. Now the mob was after Zouberbuhler, who, upon seeing the mob coming, headed for another of the blockhouses and held up there with a number of Captain Sutherland's soldiers.[39] It was then that Sutherland sent a message off to Halifax for help.[40] Help came in the form of two ships with regular troops under the command of Lieutenant-Colonel Robert Monckton. Order was soon restored and Monckton called the actors to account each being interviewed. Pettrequin, likely under considerable pressure, "'fessed up." He didn't really ever see a letter, but rather John Hoffman told him of it, "he, he actually read from a letter held in his hand." Hoffman then encouraged Pettrequin to spread the word. Now, Hoffman, as I write elsewhere, was holding a grudge which had stimulated his zeal. He had been a justice of the peace at Halifax, but, because of a residency problem, he was replaced by Sebastian Zouberbuhler. So, Monckton determined Hoffman was the instigator of the problem and promptly put him under arrest and brought him to Halifax and imprisoned on Georges

Island while he waited for his trial. Afterwards: Hoffman was tried, convicted and sentenced to a fine of £100 and two years imprisonment.[41]

Conclusion:

And now I conclude my accounting of the founding of Lunenburg. I fear that between the difficulties that Lawrence experienced in getting the settlers to work for no pay in the building of the public works and the insurrection a few months later, might lead one to think badly of the German/Swiss that came to the shores of Nova Scotia during the years of 1750-53. This was the third (counting the Englishmen with Cornwallis is 1749 as the second) wave of Europeans that were to come to settle Nova Scotia. The first of course which had come more than a hundred years earlier was the French wave (the Acadians). The Lunenburgers had good reason to be upset with the authorities in the first few years, but they soon settled in and were to form a strong base of people with a distinct character: hardworking, no nonsense and independent people. It is this character that for years best described, more generally, Nova Scotians; it is certainly the character that describes the Lunenburgers of these days who descended from those first settlers of 1750-53. Their hard, sensible, and industrious ways were evident even in 1754 by Lawrence, who, at the best of times, was a hard man to please. He wrote of them as being,

almost incredibly industrious and have already this year planted 700 bushels of potatoes, they have also sown some flax seed they brought with them from Germany which comes up very well and will furnish them with a sufficient quantity of seed that they propose to make use of as soon as they have properly prepared the land for it. The people have cleared and cultivated their town and garden lots, and have made some progress on their farm lots to which they seem greatly attached; they have now in the ground about 200 bushels of oats a great quantity of turnip seed and some barley. They have cut a vast quantity of timber staves and hoops and built a great number of boats and canoes.[42]

Chapter 9

English Fortification (1749-54)

The English Forts:

The European habitation in Nova Scotia, prior to the coming of Cornwallis in 1749, was simply this: with the exception of a few English families at Annapolis Royal and a few more who resided on a seasonal basis at Canso, the only inhabitants of the province were French, the Acadians. There may have been 10,000 Acadians, most all of them farmers. They occupied the farming lands located around their first settlement at Port Royal (these days known as Annapolis Royal) in the early 1600s. Through the years they spread and occupied the best farming lands in all of Nova Scotia. These lands included the Annapolis Valley to the shores of Minas Basin and from there to the upper reaches of the Bay of Fundy to the Isthmus of Chignecto. Lesser populations of Acadians (fishers, traders and fur trappers) also existed in the Cape Sable area to the south of peninsular Nova Scotia on the hard shores of the Atlantic Ocean. Acadians were eventually to be found along the shores of a strait which we now know as the Strait of Northumberland (e.g., Tatamagouche).[1] English garrisons, as mentioned, were to be found only at Annapolis Royal and at Canso. There was no permanent French military presence on peninsular Nova Scotia, as the French had granted at the end of one of its wars with England, in 1713, that this part of Nova Scotia was thereafter English territory.

The year 1748, especially in comparison to the four years previous to that, was relatively quiet in Nova Scotia. It was indeed the year that *The War of the Austrian Succession* was brought to an end with the signing of the *Treaty of Aix-la-Chapelle*. However the treaty was not signed until October and during that summer Mascarene wrote the deputies at Mines and severely reprimanded the Acadians for the "aid and comfort" they had given the enemy. Twelve of the Acadians were proscribed as being guilty of treason. Notices of rewards for their capture were posted both in Acadia and at Boston. On the first of June the *Mahon* and two armed schooners (the *Anson*, Capt. John Beare; and the *Warren*, 70 tons, Captain Jonathan Davis) came to Annapolis with stores for the garrison. Another vessel, "laden with merchandise" came up to Minas (Grand Pré) during the summer, there, to sell the merchandise and to use the proceeds to pay "those persons who had supplied provisions to Colonel Noble's troops ..."[2] In the autumn of 1748, several vessels loaded with warlike stores came to Annapolis from Louisbourg, which, because of the English success in 1745, was then in English hands. We see too, where John Gorham came up from New England to dislodge the French on the St. John River; he treated with them, but the few that were there continued to remain. With the closing of the season, the *Anson* and the *Warren* returned to Boston with retiring troops aboard.

And so, we come to 1749, a year during which, though they had internationally recognized claims to it since 1713, the English, finally, laid a better hold on Nova Scotia. Plans to fortify Nova Scotia were to be implemented pretty much as was suggested in 1747 by the English admiral in charge at the time, Peter Warren. Warren wrote[3] the Duke of Newcastle on January 17th, 1747, and recommended a "strong fort, fit to contain a garrison of 500 men, [should] be built in the harbour of Chebucto [Halifax], to be mounted with 6 or 9 pounders. A blockhouse fit to contain 100 men [should] be built at Canso, mounted with some large cannon." Warren also recommended that "communication between Canada and that province be wholly cut off by blockhouses erected on the passes ..." The primary pass in respect to the communication with the Acadian population would of course be at Chignecto. These new forts were to be built in lieu of shoring up the fortifications at Annapolis, indeed, it was thought that once the new forts were built and garrisoned, that "Annapolis may be reduced to the number of 100 or 150 men." It was not just Warren who wrote Newcastle, Governor Shirley also did.[4] The same sort of recommendations: "... a strong blockhouse there [Minas] with a garrison of 150 men ... another blockhouse there [Chignecto] equally necessary ... these two with a fort and a garrison at Chebucto [Halifax] of 300 men at least, and the continuance of a garrison of 300 at Annapolis Royal as it is at present, with a strong blockhouse at Canso garrisoned with 100 men ..."[5] Shirley also recommended the extended use of "rangers," two companies of them in addition to that of Gorham's[6] which had demonstrated their usefulness, each of 50 Indians, one to be posted at Minas and the other at Chignecto. It was also recommended that truck houses be established at these two places. These truck houses would supply "the Indians with all necessaries in exchange for furs, and proper presents [to be] made to them in the manner which the French use to keep them in their interest." Also Shirley recommended to Newcastle that there be two armed sloops with a tender to be constantly employed in the Bay of Fundy and around as far as Cape Sable, so too, "one of his Majesty's Frigates be employed for the protection of the fishery at Canso" and which might run up to Bay Verte on occasion.

These plans were adopted, and, during June of 1749, an auspicious beginning was made with the founding of Halifax. Two stockaded forts were soon completed, including one known as Fort George located close to the top of what was to become known as Citadel Hill. Before the first winter arrived, there "had been completed, and a rough barricade of felled trees, logs" which had been carried around the settlement.[7] A year passed, however, before Halifax was adequately fortified with the first rough barricade being replaced, by July of 1750, with a picketed line, or palisade. Then, in 1750, the English turned their attention to Georges Island, which, by 27th November, 1750, had seven heavy guns in place with a palisade around them. To complete the picture at Halifax, I make but reference to a series of fortifications, the Peninsular Blockhouses, including the Peninsular Road, which were built in the ensuing years across the narrowest part of the Halifax peninsula, from the head of the Northwest Arm to Bedford Basin; thus, closing the back door to attack.[8]

Thus it was that Halifax became the principal fortified place of the English in Nova Scotia and was to remain so. However, in keeping with the larger plan, other small forts were to be built in strategic places throughout Nova Scotia. On September 11th, 1749, Edward How, having returned from the Saint John River where he treated with the Indians at that place, was sent up the Basin (Bedford Basin, the body of water leading inland from the ocean, north-west of Halifax), there, to construct Fort Sackville. This was a natural outpost to the new community at Halifax. "It over looked the Sackville River, a water route used by the Indians in their travels to and from the interior parts of the Province, and commanded also the road to Minas which was cut through the woods some years earlier by the French in order to facilitate the shipment of provisions and livestock to Louisbourg."[9]

On July 12th, 1749, Mascarene and five of his councilors came up to Halifax from Annapolis Royal (which up to then had been the capital of Nova Scotia), in order to officially hand over power to the newly arrived governor, Edward Cornwallis.[10] Cornwallis instructed Mascarene to return to Annapolis Royal and send a detachment from Annapolis Royal to Minas. On August 24th, 1749, Mascarene (at the age of 65 years, I should remind the reader) left Halifax together with "a captain, three Subalterns and hundred men." They marched overland taking, which by then, was a well established route to Annapolis Royal. On arrival, Mascarene sorted out his men under him and sent a detachment of men to Minas under Captain John Handfield. By November of 1749 there was, at Minas, a British military presence which included "a picketed fort containing a blockhouse."[11]

The French At The Isthmus:

We have seen where, in 1747, the French had a substantial force under Jean-Baptiste Ramezay at the Isthmus of Chignecto, indeed it was from their base at the isthmus that they were able to launch a successful attack against the New Englanders in their winter quarters at Grand Pré. After the French victory at The Battle at Grand Pré the French trekked back to their position at the isthmus. Shortly thereafter Ramezay, under newly received orders, pulled out his entire force and returned to Quebec. Thus, by the end of the summer of 1747, there was not much of a French military presence in any part of Acadia.

In October of 1748, in Europe, the *Treaty of Aix-la-Chapelle* was signed by England and France bringing *The War of the Austrian Succession* to an end. By it, Acadia was confirmed to be English territory, as it had been since an earlier treaty signed in 1713. The parties, however, were not of the same mind as to where the Acadian territory ended and Canadian territory started. The English were of the view that Acadia included that which we now know as the Canadian province of New Brunswick: France did not, but rather was of the view that the "ancient limits" of Acadia meant that English territorial claims were limited to peninsular Nova Scotia. The *Treaty of Aix-la-Chapelle* may have brought the war to an end, but the controversy as to what lands constituted Acadian was to continue — as we shall see.

In the early part of 1749 the administrator of New France, Galissonnière[12], was determined in the wake of the new peace to flex the power of France by bolstering the French presence in the valleys of the Mississippi and the Ohio. He decided to do likewise on the western edges of Acadia. Boishébert[13] was chosen to go to Acadia. He went "out with eighty soldiers and militia. From Quebec they went on snowshoes (all the way) to Hocpaak, a French settlement, dragging their supplies and baggage with incredible exertions."[14] In the fall of 1749, New France was to finally get its promised military leader, one of dash and daring, la Jonquière.[15] Directly he arrived he approved of Galissonnière's earlier moves and took steps to increase the military strength at the borders of Acadia. La Jonquière sent Chevalier la Corne[16] with a detachment of regulars supported by Canadian militia, with instructions to hold Chignecto and prevent the English from going beyond the Missaguash[17]; thus it was that Fort Beauséjour on the northern bank of the Missaguash River came into being.

Directly he arrived at the isthmus in the fall of 1749, at the western end, La Corne commenced the construction of Fort Beauséjour. At the other end at Baie Verte, about 15 to 20 miles away to the northeast, Fort Gaspereau was built.[18] Earlier in the year, as we have seen, Galissonnière had sent Boishébert to the Saint John. Boishébert was to build a fort, of sorts, at its mouth. Boishébert did not stick exclusively to the Saint John but traveled about attempting to garner support for the French flag in these western parts of Acadia. Traveling by canoe, a favorite mode of transportation for this 22 year old, he went to "the different settlements of this country disguised, sometimes as a sailor, sometimes as an Acadian habitant ..."[19] Thus, by the time La Corne arrived, in the fall of 1749, Boishébert had paved the way to a considerable extent. La Corne was Boishébert's senior by 24 years, but La Corne had to be very much impressed by this young French officer; they had served together in Acadia during the years, 1746-47.

It is to be emphasized that it was not so much that the French military from Quebec were positioning themselves to recapture peninsular Nova Scotia, as at this time, 1748-1755, they were not officially at war with the English, but more because the French were anxious to assert their territorial rights to Canada (as they perceived her boundaries to be); and thus to protect its route for communications and supply from Quebec to Louisbourg. The French, however, had strong connections to native populations, and encouraged their allies to keep the war up against the English, particularly in light of the new English settlement at Halifax. Though numerous treaties had been signed,[20] the native Indians (it would appear more so the Malicites than the MicMac) kept up considerable pressure on the English, pressure which proved to be successful in hindering English settlement. The attacks, however, went beyond just those against innocent settlers. For example, there was the attack on November 27th, 1749, "A party of about three hundred MicMac and St. John Indians"[21] assisted by "eleven of the French inhabitants of Piziquid" attacked the English troops at Minas that were stationed there under Captain

Handfield. They caught Lieutenant Hamilton and eighteen men unawares and held them as prisoners. The natives prowled around the fortifications for about seven days and then disappeared into the woods. The Indians turned over the prisoners (including the one they took at the Dartmouth saw mill) to the French soldiers at the Tantramar River at the Isthmus; eventually these captives turned up in Quebec where there were ransomed back to the English.

The Battle at St Croix River (1750):

Given that there was "eleven of the French inhabitants of Piziquid" involved in the attack on the English troops at Minas, Cornwallis determined to send John Gorham and 60 of his Rangers to hunt the rebels down.[22] At this time there was a small fort at Minas under the command of Captain Handfield, but there was nothing at Piziquid. Cornwallis' orders to Gorham was "to take the properest post you can to dispose of your company to the best advantage, till you can erect a block house, for your security."[23] Gorham and his men, who were at Fort Sackville (near Halifax), upon the first signs of spring made their way overland. After two days of travel, at about mid-March, 1750, they came to the St Croix River. It was there that they were to meet up with a large number of Indians and a battle broke out. "A saw mill and two houses on the Halifax side of the river were commandeered, and for three days, Gorham fought a defensive action. As soon as the superior numerical advantage of the Indians became apparent, a messenger was sent post haste back to Fort Sackville for reinforcements. He made the 28 mile trip through the woods in eight hours."[24] British regulars, hauling two field pieces, came to Gorham's aid and on their arrival the Indians melted back into the woods; the group proceed to Piziquid without suffering from any further attack on the way.

Lawrence At Chignecto (April,1750):

We have seen that the latest war between the English and the French was brought to an end by the *Treaty of*

Aix-la-Chapelle, 1748. One of its terms was that the English were
to hand back Fortress Louisbourg, together with all of Île Royale
(Cape Breton) and of Île St. Jean (Prince Edward Islands). In
these circumstances, the English were of the view that the
French should understand that no lands, other than these islands
at the mouth of the St. Lawrence, were to be considered French
territory. The English knew that the French, notwithstanding
their agreement, would proceed to push their southern limits far
to the south of the St. Lawrence. A few weeks after Cornwallis
arrived at Halifax, he received instructions from the Lords of
Trade, among the lines of which, we read: "And as there is great
reason to apprehend that the French may dispute the right of the
Crown of Great Britain to these territories, we further earnestly
recommend to you to have a watchful eye to the security thereof
and upon the proceedings of the French." Thus, during April
of 1750, with the beachhead at Halifax having been fairly well
established, Governor Cornwallis put Major Charles Lawrence
under orders to establish himself and his troops at Chignecto.

> As there is reason to believe to apprehend that there is a detachment of
> French forces at Chignecto or thereabouts, and that they have erected a fort,
> in that case, you are to endeavour to erase it, as it is an open violation of
> treaties subsisting between the crowns of England and France.[25]

Having left Halifax on the 5th April with 300 men under
his command, Lawrence made his way down the basin to Fort
Sackville[26] and from there he struck out overland on a well
established route to Piziquid. We can but only imagine the men
in their red military jackets trudging along a woods path, one
wide enough to allow the hauling of a cart or gun carriage.
The land had yet to come fully awake from its northern winter,
though spring was showing its long awaited signs. Within a
couple of days the bivouacking troops were to arrive at the land
of the French Acadian inhabitants. John Salusbury had been sent
along. He wrote in his journal:

April 7th:

Arrived that night at the five houses on the river St. Croix. Before we got there — at about five miles distance [Stillwater] came down a very long descent to the River Ardois — from the hill to the River Ardois, ... The vale deep and narrow and the assent perpendicular almost in some places ... in the vale the largest pines I ever saw ... in going near two mile [Ellershouse] we ascend into excellent gravel land clear ... Half a mile [St. Croix] further on the descent then into a good meadow land — where the St. Croix falls in* — we crossed that river over a new bridge made by Gorham after his late action here. On a fine rising ground good land above the meadows the houses are — even this land looks mineral tho' the surface is so good.[27]

In light of the fact that Gorham had been ambushed by an Indian force but a few weeks earlier, the men, following along in the same tracks, proceeded cautiously.[28] On April 8th they arrived at the English "camp on the Piziquid River":

April 8th:

... now every little village in each particular district is called after the name of the clan and these are many. We marched ... for three hours ... then we opened on a fine champion [plain] — with scattering houses. ... and this continued to the very banks of the river of Piziquid. This river carry's a great deal of water and the tide rises near sixty foot. At low water [tide] we waded through this river for the channel is wide ... about a half mile further we found St Loe encamped near a neat French chapel.[29]

This was, as Salusbury observed, "excellent land." On Monday, April 9th, Lawrence's troops arrived at Grand Pré ("a large marsh, diked in and plowed"[30]). Unlike the Piziquid River through which they could wade at low tide, at the Gaspereau the troops had to be ferried across the short distance in canoes. They proceeded down the west side, "two miles," until they reached "the stone house[31] on the Grand Pré" where Captain John Handfield was situated in "a picketed fort containing a blockhouse."[32] There, round about Grand Pré, Lawrence's men were to pass a few days. With the addition of Gorham's Rangers, which had joined in at Piziquid and certain of the men under Handfield, Lawrence now had some four hundred men under him, and, the plan was to sail the rest of the distance to Beaubassin. The ships, of course, there being none regularly stationed at Minas, had come around from Halifax. The fleet, under Captain John Rouse, had left Halifax on April 5th, the same day that the troops had set out on their overland march. It was to be a long voyage around, for 10 days were to pass; but, finally, on Sunday (Easter Sunday), April 15th, "Rouse arrived with the *Dove* and Phillips schooners."[33] They did not depart for the isthmus right away, for there was some difficulty with the inhabitants at Grand Pré. Apparently, the British had relieved a number of the locals of their arms and gave them to Gorham's Mohawks (rangers) as they had lost theirs. Thirty muskets were taken with promises that they would replace them. This move did not go over very well with the Acadians, and, for awhile there, it looked like that Lawrence would have to leave most of his men right there at Minas in order to quell a fomenting revolt. However, by whatever means[34] things were settled down and most of Lawrence's troops boarded the six waiting transports and got underway away on April 18th with the gun ship *Albany* in escort.[35]

From Minas, the Isthmus of Chignecto might well be made on an overnight run, given fair winds and good tides. But fair winds and good tides are not something to be expected with any regularity in the waters of the Fundy. The fleet leaving the mouth of the Gaspereau at seven in the evening had a good start and managed its way out of the Minas Basin and through the choke point between Cape Split and Rams Head on the Parrsboro shore (as we know it today), and must have done so mostly in the dark on an outgoing tide. The tide or wind, likely both, then turned against the fleet and it tucked under Spencers Island in weather that John Salusbury described as "squaly with foggs." Within a day, the fleet was able to start out again and soon cleared Cape Chignecto; but the winds and tides again turned against them so they clawed their way into the sheltering waters beyond the mouth of Apple River. I should say that during these two days of sailing, smoke signals were observed first to the north of them and then to the east of them; their arrival at Chignecto was being heralded to the knowing French in the most ancient of ways.[36] Again the winds and tide turned and the ships of the fleet pulled in their riding rodes, and, clearing their anchorage, ran along the south eastern shores of Chignecto Bay and then into Beaubassin (Cumberland Basin). Ahead, was their objective; and ahead they could see yet more smoke; it was thick and seemed to curl away into the sky from several places to the east — Why! The French community of Beaubassin, their intended disembarkation point, was, was — in flames.[37]

Chevalier la Corne was ready for the descending Englishmen. And while he may have not positioned his regulars south of the Missaguash, his allies apparently did and had struck upon a scorched earth policy. Le Loutre who was now headquartered nearby having determined that the people at Beaubassin, a community south of the Missaguash, should not live under direct English supervision set fire with his own hand, the parish church.[38] His red and white adherents then went about systematically burning down this Acadian village which forced the occupying Acadians to relocate beyond the Missaguash River out of peninsular Nova Scotia into a territory that was calculated, by the French, to be French.

The day was "chill and windy with heavy showers" as the six transports and their escort rounded up and dropped their anchors. If the element of surprise was what was needed to get everyone ashore safely — well, such an element was lost. As John Salusbury wrote in his journal, "we found the enemy ready to receive us in all form. La Corne in his picketed fort so large as must have been the work of time." There was, ready to meet the four hundred men aboard the English transports, a great number of armed Frenchmen and their allies. The French knew the terrain; the English did not. A quick survey of the area convinced, at least Salusbury, that La Corne,

> had made his dispositions in a soldier like manner — manned well the dyke on which he fixed his flag, that was equal to any entrenchment. With Indians had his own corps in reserve on the wind mill hill with a wood on his left and a river on his right, at a distance of a quarter of a mile from his picketed ground ... the asylum for all the rebel inhabitants. Now we had

nothing but small arms nor a possibility of getting our cannon or shells to dislodge them. We might have fought but could never have made a proper impression — in his circumstances and ours.

Lawrence, however, was not one to be easily deterred; he wished to take a closer look at the situation. He sent the *York* (Cobb's vessel) closer to the action, further up in the Basin which we now know as Cumberland Basin and just opposite the shore where the remains of the houses lay a-smoldering, a detachment under Captain Bartelle was sent ashore (Gorham and Clapham were in this shore party). This reconnoitering party was to return to the ship that evening on the 21st. Though the intelligence that Lawrence then had was not of the kind that would give him much encouragement of success, nonetheless, the next morning, Sunday morning, he was successful at getting all of his 400 men ashore. The weather had been wet however conditions improved somewhat. The landing which was south of the Missaguash was not resisted by the French. However, it was plain to Lawrence as he lined up his troops that a crossing of the River to his north would be met with resistance from the French. "Whilst we were forming the troops a large white flag was waved several times by two peasants [Acadians] and afterward planted on a strong dyke with a small creek in front of it." Thinking it was a flag of truce, Lawrence sent a company of men over and they returned with the message that the flag was being planted as a "spot as being the boundary of the French king's territories." Lawrence also "observed that the dyke aforementioned was entirely lined with Indians from the sea at one end of it to a thick wood that flanked it on the other." Soon another flag was to appear and it became clear that La Corne wished a parley.

I went to meet him in company with Captain Bartelle and Captain Scott, and on joining put to him all such questions as I thought were proper on the occasion, and such as I thought might contribute to the finding out his strength and the knowledge of his designs and intentions. Amongst other questions I demanded to know by whose orders he was there within His Majesty's undoubted limits, committing such unheard of outrages; he replied by M. Jonquière's who had directed him likewise to take possession of Ceppodie,

St. John's River, Memramcooke, Pitcodiak and all that country up to the river on our right, as being the property of the French king, or at least that he was to keep it and must defend it, till the boundaries should be settled by commissioners appointed for that purpose. I asked him where were the inhabitants; he said dispersed about in their territories, Where were the deputies? There were none. Who had burnt Beaubassin which he confessed belonged to the king of Great Britain. He said the Indians who claimed it as there own. By whose instructions? He knew nothing of that. Where was the villain Loutre? With his Indians ...[39]

Well, there it was, as was perfectly plain to Lawrence: la Corne had a dyke "on his front, the sea to his right, an eminence with picketed ground to his rear, and a wood on his left." This was considered by Lawrence and his captains, together with the wet weather (not a good situation in the days when battles were fought with black powder that was required, several times during the course of such battles, to be loaded into the muzzles of muskets). And too, there was the fact that the Missaguash River for some distance inland could not be crossed but with boats. As if this wasn't all bad enough: Lawrence was badly outnumbered. As against his four hundred there was, he calculated, a 1,000 against him. There was a mass of Indians; La Corne's detachment of regulars from Quebec; and, who knows how many "rebel inhabitants of all the different parts of the province." The English forces, understandably, retired to their waiting transports. That night, further discussions were had between the English officers. Lawrence concluded, in his report of the event, as follows:

The next morning had the opinion of Captain Rouse [the commander of the fleet] and the principal officers upon that affair which were all in the negative; on the contrary they thought it much more for His Majesty's service to repair with the utmost despatch to Minas lest in the interim great mischief should be committed in that part of the province, which they rather apprehended from our ill success at Chignecto and the bad disposition of the Minas inhabitants at the time we sailed from thence. We therefore resolved to repair directly thither ...

And so, Lawrence and his 400 retired and returned to the Minas area. The English would have had a bad time of it, if, in

April of 1750, they had tried to establish themselves at Chignecto: there would be another day. Plainly, too, Lawrence was concerned about the worsening situation that he had observed earlier in the month as he marched through Piziquid and Grand Pré. The troops were needed at these nearer places. The worry was that these Minas Acadians might leave the province and join the French. After all, that's exactly what the Chignecto Acadians had gone and done. If, as was surely considered, there existed in the neighborhood a strong English military presence, then the Minas Acadians might be prevented from "carrying off their effects."[40]

By the 26th of April, retracing their outward course, including layovers near Apple River and in behind Spencers Island, Lawrence and his men were back at Grand Pré. After disembarkation, the transports sailed back to Halifax while the troops were marched overland. The exercise would do them good, but in addition there was work to be done at Piziquid. Lawrence employed his forces to build a well positioned fort on the eastern side (Windsor) of the Piziquid, Fort Edward. By July the 22nd, Lawrence was back at Halifax.[41]

Lawrence's Second Descent (September, 1750):

On August the 13th, the English military force at Halifax was considerably strengthened. Six transports, having departed Ireland earlier in the year, hauled into Halifax Harbor. Aboard was a full regiment, Laschelles', "all in health."[42] We see on Friday, the 17th, at Halifax, there were "great preparations for the expedition, Rouse, the *Fair Lady* and several transports sailed for the Bay of Fundy." On the 19th, the weather being "warm, clear and fine, ... the troops under Lawrence went up in shallops to Fort Sackville." Lawrence, newly appointed to Lieutenant-Colonel, then went overland with his troops. He had under his command a significantly larger force than he had on the first descent made earlier in the year.

To limit the time that the troops would have to spend on transports and in order to keep them well exercised, the approch was to march them up to a debarkation point reasonably handy their objective. As it had been that spring, the embarkation was to take place at Grand Pré and their objective, of course, was Chignecto. The fleet, as we have seen, was assembled and provisioned at Halifax and then sent around. Captain Rous in the sloop, *Albany* was in charge of the fleet. There was in total, "seventeen small vessels and about seven hundred men." This time, Lawrence was meaning to take firm control of the isthmus, above which the French had established, as we have seen, a strong presence.

I am not in a position to give as much detail on Lawrence's second descent on Chignecto as I was on the first one made two months earlier. The leaders on both sides were the same, the principal difference is that Lawrence arrived with more men, substantially more as one might discern from the fact that a greater number of transports were used in September *versus* April. So too, Lawrence knew this second time what he was up against and undoubtedly brought some field pieces with him. Also, there seemed to be two valuable additions, "armed sloops," the *Anson* and the *Warren* which Edward How had chartered to the English. What we know is that this much strengthened fleet sailed from Minas on August the 31st and arrived at the isthmus on September 3rd. Lawrence, Rous and Gorham went in the *Anson* to reconnoitre the shore and pick out a landing place. A landing was made. Le Loutre and his followers were there, just as they had been that spring. He and his men "had thrown up a breastwork along the shore and manned it with his Indians and his painted and befeathered Acadians." The English forces apparently got themselves ashore, and after a "sharp skirmish,"[43] the Le Loutre forces retired north, behind the river Missaguash. What remained of the Acadian habitations in the area was torched: "the Indians and their Acadian allies set the houses and barns on fire, and laid waste the whole district, leaving the inhabitants [at least those remaining after the spring conflagration] no choice but to seek food and shelter with the French."[44] Lawrence did not cross the Missaguash. He was satisfied to dig in on the south side of it, effectively letting La Corne have his way that the French were to remain to the north of it, the English to the south of it.

On an elevation, a short distance south of the Missaguash, Lawrence then commenced the erection of a picketed fort.[45] It was built up, in time, and was to have block-houses incorporated into its structure. We shall come to a better description of Fort Lawrence when we tell of the momentous events of 1755 in the next part of this history. Sufficient to write at this place, that through the years 1750 to 1755 Fort Lawrence was garrisoned by a few hundred English soldiers. And, across the Missaguash River, within easy sight was its opposite pawn, Fort Beauséjour, garrisoned by an equal number of French soldiers. No major battle was to unfold, after all, this was a time of "peace." Parlaying parties would come forth, and exchanges would be made on one side or the other of the Missaguash. The exchanges might be that of prisoners who had the misfortune of straying into the wrong territory, or it may be a keg of wine or a special food which one commander thought the other might like for his table. However, this was a time of unease, for while the parties were not at war: ancient hates continued to seethe.

It is in this atmosphere, on September the 6th (NS), 1750, an "atrocious act of treachery" was to take place. Francis Parkman described this event:

One morning, at about eight o'clock, the inmates of Fort Lawrence saw what seemed an officer from Beauséjour, carrying a flag, and followed by several men in uniform, wading through the sea of grass that stretched beyond the Missaguash. When the tide was out, this river was but an ugly trench of reddish mud gashed across the face of the marsh, with a thread of half-fluid slime lazily crawling along the bottom; but at high tide it was filled to the brim with an opaque torrent that would have overflowed, but for the dikes thrown up to confine it. Behind the dike on the farther bank stood the seeming officer, waving his flag in sign that he desired a parley. He was in reality no officer, but one of Le Loutre's Indians in disguise, Étienne Le Bâtard, or, as others say, the great chief, Jean-Baptiste Cope. Howe, carrying a white flag and accompanied by a few officers and men, went towards the river to hear what he had to say. As they drew near, his looks and language excited their suspicion. But it was too late; for a number of Indians, who had hidden behind the dike during the night, fired upon Howe across the stream, and mortally wounded him. ...[46]

Edward How was "an intelligent and agreeable person."[47] He ably represented the English claims to Nova Scotia; but, in so doing, he proceeded with "the greatest of fidelity and care." He was forever mindful that minds, faculties, and manners differed, not only from one race to another, but from one man to another. How, on the day of his death, was doing what he did best, as the *DCB* describes, he went out under "a flag of truce ... to secure the release of some English prisoners." This was a regular event for Edward How, as he proceeded out to parley with what he thought was a fellow officer, a French officer, when, but in a brief and for him a last moment, he saw, but not to hear, arise from the cover of the dyke and the tall marsh grass in between, a line of men; and then, along the line, puffs of white smoke. Treacherous men sent their messengers into his chest. And so, we end this part with the scene of Edward How: slain, lying in the deep grass that lines the Missaguash River; there, splayed on his back, lifeless and still, his tunic of homespun serge ripped apart by a score of leaden blunt balls, and his bright red blood oozing its last.

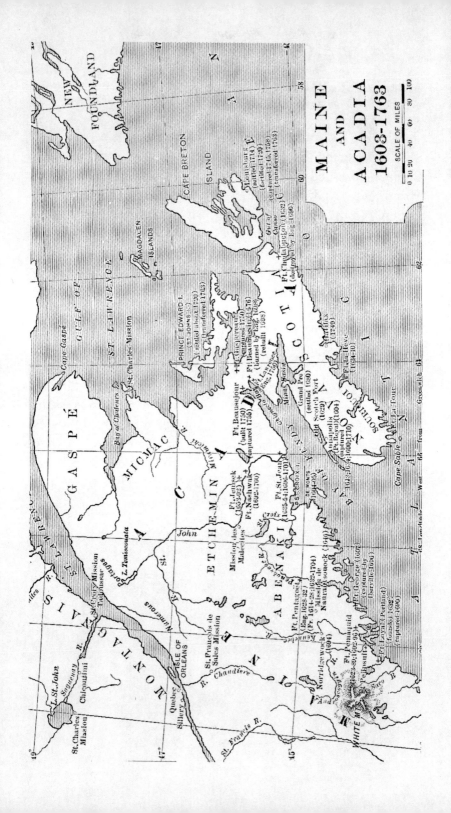

MAINE
AND
ACADIA
1603–1763

SCALE OF MILES
0 10 20   40   60   80   100

NEW FOUNDLAND

GULF OF ST. LAWRENCE

CAPE BRETON
ISLAND

Louisburg
(settled 1714)
(fortified 1720)
(captured 1745, 1758)
(transferred 1763)

Gut of Canso

Ft. Chedabucto (1682)
(destroyed by Eng.1690)

MAGDALEN ISLANDS

Cape Gaspé

GASPÉ

MICMAC

Bay of Chaleurs

St. Charles Mission

PRINCE EDWARD I.
(ST. JOHN'S)
(settled about 1720)
(transferred 1763)

Ft. Gaspereau
(burned 1750)

Ft. Beausejour
(built 1750)
(captured 1755)

Ft. Lawrence
(Eng.1750)

Minas Basin

Grand Pré

(settled 1680)
Old Scotch Fort
(1629)

Annapolis
(Pt. Royal) (1604)
captured
1613;1654;1690;1710

Port Royal

Halifax
(1749)

Pt. de la Hève
(1634–30)

Ft. la Tour

NOVA SCOTIA

LOUIS

BOURG

Cape Sable I.

ETCHEMIN

L. Temiscouata

St. Croix Mission

R. Madawaska

St. John R.

Numerous

MONTAGNAIS

R. St. John
Quebec
L. St. John
R. Saguenay
Chicoutimi
St. Charles Mission
Sillery

ISLE OF ORLEANS
St. François de Sales Mission

R. Chaudiere

St. Francis R.

Ft. Jemseg
(1659–70)

Mission des Malecites

Ft. Nashwak
(1692–1700)

Ft. Jemseg

St. Croix

Ft. St. Jean
1635–54;1696–1701

ST. CROIX R.
DE MONTS
(1604–05)

BAY OF FUNDY

ABENAKI

Penobscot R.

Ft. Pentagoet
(Eng. 1628–32)
(Fr. 1614–28;1635–1701)

Kennebec R.

Norridgewock
Mission de
Naurantsouck (1649)

Ft. George (1607)
(captured by
Iberville 1696)

Ft. Pemaquid
1625–89;1692–96
(captured 1632)
(captured 1640)

Pejepscot

Ft. Loyal (Portland)
(captured 1690)

Androscoggin R.

Saco R.

WHITE MTS.

Part Six

The Deportation of the Acadians:

1755

Chapter 1

The Setting: 1755

In 1744, England and France had gone to war. It was known as *The War of the Austrian Succession*. Immediately the French governor at Louisbourg got word of this — and, I dare say before the English were to know that a state of war existed — he sent off 400 armed men to capture Canso; this was in May of 1744. Then, at Annapolis Royal, on September 7th, 1744, Fort Anne was invested. Troops and supplies from Massachusetts were hustled into place and the French forces from Louisbourg were obliged with the coming of winter to retreat to the warmth and comfort of Louisbourg. This French activity of 1744 only served to raise the ire and scorn of the New Englanders. Close on to 4,000 men were raised to go on the attack. Together with a strong fleet of English men-of-war, Louisbourg was put under siege in 1745 — and, much to everyone's surprise, this mighty French fortress, one which could not be equaled in all of North America: capitulated. The taking of Louisbourg was a huge blow to French prestige. In 1746, a large amphibious force was assembled in France. This attack force, under Duc d'Anville, was, however, attended by calamity after calamity; and, as a consequence, it was to never get a shot off at any of its intended targets: the English, at Louisbourg, at Annapolis Royal and at Boston: it proved to be the most disastrous naval expedition, ever.

With increasing war debts, matched with increasing difficulties to raise more funds, both the English and the French courts saw the advantages of putting an end to the war. In March of 1748 the *Congress of Aix-la-Chapelle* was opened and discussions began. The internal examinations carried by both parties, necessary for such discussions, were to bring to light to the respective policy makers, like never before, the territorial situation as existed in North America. Thus, the peace making process, paradoxically, while ending one war (as one so often sees in the history of wars) was to plant the seed for the next.

One of the consequences of the *Congress of Aix-la-Chapelle*, the intended one, was that a peace treaty was signed on October 18th, 1748. Generally, there was to be a return to the state of affairs as existed before the war, *status quo ante*. (Thus we saw in 1749, the return of Louisbourg to the French.) In order to get signatures on paper (as is so often done, and, almost as often with dire consequences) certain terms — in this case the territorial boundaries in America — are left vague. It was hoped, that with the striking of a boundary commission composed of statesmen from both England and France, discussions would ensue which would result in a resolution, particularly as to the boundaries of "Ancient Acadia": boundaries which the English sought to expand and the French sought to limit. No resolution was to come about by these discussions; it was, as we will see, to come about only through the force of arms.[1]

France and England, in 1755, differed widely in their military and naval strengths. France had only half the navy of England's, on the other hand, France had ten times the number of men under arms. France's superiority in numbers of men would not, however, be of much help to them in a war across a sea which was covered with British naval guns. Leadership was lacking in both countries.[2] In all of this, it is to be kept in mind, that at this time, England was not, in comparison to France, Spain or Germany, a big European power. She was "a small state, which had obtained abnormal influence only by commercial and mercantile alertness, by a well-ordered financial system, and by means of a well-equipped fleet."[3] The population levels of France and Britain (including Scotland and Ireland) stood out in stark contrast: Britain, nine million; France, 21 million. Each year with her climate and soil, France renewed her riches; England had to make do with what she had, and agriculturally it was much, much less. Louis XIV proved to be England's greatest ally as he went about draining France of her resources in order to support his corrupt court.

In North America the English speaking settlers had an overwhelming superiority in terms of numbers[4]; but because of the decentralized political state of the New Englanders, and the resulting difficulty in getting a sufficient number of people to agree on any one point, the French, given its political structure (feudalism), and notwithstanding its significantly smaller population, continued to hold a superior military position.

The American territorial claims as were made by both the English and the French were rooted deep along the St. Lawrence (the French) and along the American seaboard (the English). The real race was for the lands to the west of the Appalachians and south of the Great Lakes as is first represented by the Ohio valley. In July of 1754, this competition for the interior of North America was to erupt beyond the main ridge of the Alleghenies, at a spot known to history as the Great Meadows. It was there that an English scouting group headed up by a young Virginian by the name of George Washington was to get itself involved in a shootout between it and a French military detachment which was just then roaming the same territory. Though Washington and his forces put up a brave fight, they were decisively thrown out of the land which the French claimed for themselves. As historians seem to agree, it was this obscure skirmish in Ohio, the first in a series of events, which led to a declaration of war in 1756. An analysis of the proximate causes of *The Seven Years War* is not within the scope of my work, but sufficient for our purposes to say that it had mostly to do with European politics. Agreements were entered into between Austria and England in a common defense against Prussia and France. England was primarily concerned with the protection of the King of England's old home and regular summer retreat, the German state of Hanover; it was in danger of being marched over by Prussian troops. This house of cards was to come tumbling down when France, in June of 1756, peremptorily took an island in the Mediterranean for itself, the Island of Minorca. As for the events as did unfold in Nova Scotia, in 1755: they were triggered by the French asserting they owned all of the land north of the Isthmus of Chignecto. The fact that the French laid claim to the upper half of Acadia, together with the even more galling assertion that they owned the vast interior of North America, so to limited England to a strip of land on the eastern seaboard, — were facts which revolted the leadership in England. If, in 1755, England could not, as a practical matter, get their troops over to America to defeat these French claims, then they could, considering England's superior power at sea, limit at least the ability of France to get their troops over.

By the first of April, the English cabinet authorized the sending of a naval squadron to America with instructions to "fall upon any French ships of war that shall be attempting to land troops in Nova Scotia or to go to Cape Breton or through the St. Lawrence to Quebec."[5] The intelligence was that the French were going to build up their military presence in America. The aim was to catch the French fleet in a net of British war ships. Admiral Boscawen was put in charge, and, having received his orders, got his fleet of fourteen ships underway, reasonably promptly. After the fleet left, the English admiralty determined to boost Boscawen's American bound naval force, even further. About three weeks after the departure of the main fleet, Admiral Holburne was sent out with seven more ships. Thus there was, by the end of May, 1755, a British war fleet cruising between the southern coast of Newfoundland and the northern coast of Cape Breton. Such a large British war fleet,[6] up to this point in time, had been rarely seen to be operating in American waters; it foreshadowed the English policy which was to be struck by the English prime minister, William Pitt, when it came time to fight *The Seven Years War* (1756-1763), that is to fight it, not on the ancient battle fields of Europe, but in America.

The French also made their preparations. After a considerable delay a French fleet left Brest on May 3rd, 1755. Aboard were six battalions of French soldiers: *La Reine, Bourgogne, Languedoc, Guienne, Artois*, and *Béarn*; 3,000 men in all. The French troops were under the command of a German veteran by the name of Baron Dieskau (1701-1767). Admiral de la Motte was in charge of the fleet. De la Motte had been dispatched with provisions for the French colonies in North America, its first call being Louisbourg.

On June 15th, 1755, just a day before the French were to surrender Beauséjour, the subject of our next following chapters, Boscawen fell in with four, French, sail-of-the-line. These French vessels, in a gale of wind, had parted from the French fleet of 43. After a chase which lasted 48 hours the British ran three of the stragglers down: the *Alcide* (64 gun, Captain Hocquart[7]), the *Lys* (64 gun) and the *Dauphin*.[8] When the British ship *Dunkirk* (64 gun, Captain Richard Howe) came alongside the *Alcide*, the French captain called out through his hailing trumpet enquiring if France and England were at war: they were not, but the reply was as if they were. Whatever it was that the British captain uttered in reply, it was drowned by a fire belching, metal hurling, broadside of British cannon in unison.[9] The scene on the open deck of the *Alcide* was immediately changed from dozens of gawking whole soldiers into bloody parts mixed with smashed and splintered wood; the whole being under and surrounded with a smokey pall, with crying and moaning sounds, and echoes and re-echoes coming through the fog that blended sea and air together.[10]

Chapter 2

The Taking Of Fort Beauséjour

Beyond The Isthmus, Disputed Territory:

The problem is traceable back to 1713 and the *Treaty of Utrecht*, when Louis XIV, desperate to see that a French Prince take the Spanish throne, made a bad deal. France was to give away to England, three sections of her holdings in North America: Hudson Bay, Newfoundland and Acadia. The twelfth article of the treaty provided that "all Nova Scotia, or Acadia, comprehended within its ancient boundaries, as also the City of Port Royal, now called Annapolis" was to be given over to the English. Lawyers know that a poor choice of words can get parties to an agreement into years of expensive and frustrating litigation. The words "ancient boundaries" as contained in the *Treaty of Utrecht*, were to cause the French and the English much difficulty. The English claimed, in their opening position, that Acadia included all the territory east of a line from the mouth of the Kennebec to Quebec, including the whole south shore of the St. Lawrence, Gaspé, the Island of St. John, and Cape Breton. All the lands lying east of the St. Lawrence was a convenient and easily understood dividing line, but one that was hardly accepted by those Frenchmen who had a long and deep connection to the lands now claimed by the English. Their position was fully reflected in the Charlevoix report. Pierre Charlevoix was a Jesuit priest (clerics played political roles back in those days) who earlier in the century gave his government a commissioned report in respect to the dispute that had arisen between France and England in respect to the southeastern boundaries of Quebec. Charlevoix, true to his French king, maintained that the English had only received peninsular Nova Scotia.

And so it was, though a peace treaty had been entered into by each during the autumn of 1748, the French and English held a different view as to who "owned" the territory which these days we know as New Brunswick. The French said it was Canadian territory; the English said it was Acadian, and as such, English territory. Each side was fully confident of its rights to occupy and control that land just north of the neck (isthmus) of peninsular Nova Scotia.

During the winter of 1748/1749, the French established a presence at the isthmus. This initial and small force was added to in the autumn of 1749 when a strong detachment of Canadians, regulars and Indians, were sent down from Quebec with the express orders to prevent any Englishman coming into the territory north of the Missaguash River at the Isthmus of Chignecto. It might be speculated[1] that the construction of Fort Beauséjour was commenced, at that time. Certainly, Pointe Beauséjour, considering the immediate area, was the best place for a fort; it had been spotted as a good place just a year before by the British. Charles Morris,[2] in 1749, reported: "On this marsh also within a quarter of a mile of the basin is a fine hill or island in an oval form near sixty feet in height, more than a quarter of mile long, and about half that width, the foot of which this river passes by, on which a noble fortress might be erected for the protection of the country; the marshes surrounding it for a mile distance except toward the basin, would render it impregnable and large ships cannot approach within half a mile, and that only upon the top of high water, and in great danger by the rapidity of the tide and their grounding in two hours."[3]

While the English thought to build their fort at that position as was described by Charles Morris; they were too late; the French had beat them to the punch. We have seen in an earlier part where Governor Cornwallis sent Major Charles Lawrence and 400 troops up from the newly found English capital, Halifax, to establish themselves at Chignecto, in April of 1750. They were cowed by the French presence and returned from whence they came. In September of the same year the English were successful at installing themselves at the isthmus, and built for themselves a fort, just opposite Fort Beauséjour, to the south of Missaguash

River. Fort Lawrence, named after its builder, thus came into being. The English thus were to leave the French to hold the land they claimed. The English, however, continued to maintain that the French were occupying English territory. An uneasy peace continued through the years 1750-1754 as each side peered at the other through their pickets across the Missaguash.

Fort Beauséjour: Its Disposition:

At such a position — a hill, as the Englishman Charles Morris was to determine, "in an oval form near sixty feet in height, more than a quarter of a mile long, and about half that width" at the foot of which, to the south, was a river, and to west the sea — "a noble fortress might be erected." In the fall of 1749, Chevalier la Corne doubtlessly had come to the same conclusion as to where the best location might be for a fort. His regulars and the Canadian militia soon set to work and the beginnings of Fort Beauséjour on the northern bank of the Missaguash River came into being. In the spring of 1751 orders came from Quebec to expand and improve Fort Beauséjour, and, to build another fort at the eastern end of the isthmus, at Baie Verte, about 15 to 20 miles away, it was to be the smaller of the two, Fort Gaspereau. In August of 1751, Fort Beauséjour began to take on substantial proportions when Franquet, a French officer, an engineer, paid a visit to Fort Beauséjour and "instructed St. Ours, the commander, as to the proper mode of making it defensible."[4]

Through its short lived existence under the French flag, the years 1750-55, Beauséjour was one of those plague-spots of official corruption which dotted the whole surface of New France. The place was under the command of Duchambon de Vergor, "a dull man of no education, of stuttering speech, unpleasing countenance, and doubtful character."[5] He owed his place to the notorious intendant, François Bigot.

The Prelude To The Attack:

The French actions in the Ohio valley and at the Isthmus of Chignecto were to bring the colonial governors of New England together. The competition hitherto between them, kept them apart. The governors, especially those of the north, were to be of one mind: the French, for their incursions, were to be repelled and chastised. It was time to put an end to the French pretensions. Surely a population of 1.2 million English speaking people need not put up with the outlandish claims of 60 thousand Frenchmen. They had to be put in their place; no matter whether mother England could send help, or not. It was on April 14th, 1755, when certain governors of the British colonies (Dinwiddie of Virginia; Dobbs, North Carolina; Morris, Pennsylvania; Sharpe, Maryland; Delancy, New York; and Shirley, Massachusetts) met at Alexandria on the Potomac (known in history as the *Council at Alexandria*). The French were to be attacked, notwithstanding that the two countries were not at war, at four points at once: the general (Braddock) and his regulars were to attack Fort Duquesne (Pittsburgh); Shirley against Fort Niagara; Colonel William Johnson, Crown Point; and Colonel Monckton, Acadia.[6]

So, keeping within the scope of this history, I take up that expedition of 1755 under Colonel Robert Monckton, being but one (and as it turned out, the only successful one) of the four which had been authorized by the English royal governors at the *Council at Alexandria*. Notwithstanding that the two countries, France and Britain, as already emphasized, were not at war,[7] Monckton received orders to attack and take Fort Beauséjour. Though he was to have some "regulars" with him, the force was principally made up of two thousand colonial men, "provincials." These men were eventually mustered at Boston and were formed up in two battalions; one under John Winslow and the other under George Scott. These New Englanders were to be transported up the coast in "sloops and schooners," though there was to be some delay as they were obliged to wait for a shipment of muskets coming from England.[8]

The French could account for 1,400 fighting men on or near the isthmus, and another 250 on the Saint John. Behind the walls of Fort Beauséjour there were but 160 regulars supplemented by 300 hundred civilians, Acadians.[9] By 1755, indeed by 1750, the

Acadian population in and around Fort Beauséjour mainly lived north of the Missaguash River away from the lands to the south, which the French granted was English territory. The principal settlement of the Acadians at the isthmus had been, historically, in this southern part: Beaubassin. During 1750, in anticipation of the arrival of English forces, the Acadians were forced out of their homes by an incendiary crowd of Indians led by Le Loutre. Seemingly all the buildings, including the Acadian church,[10] were torched in one grand conflagration. By 1755, there was not much to be seen south of the Missaguash except Fort Lawrence which had grown over the five years of its existence.[11] Seen around Fort Lawrence would have been a number of tightly drawn abodes of those who favored the English cause, such as traders; few if any would have been Acadians. The Acadians, then, were on the "French side" of the isthmus, spread out along the banks of the Shepody, Petitcodiac and Memramcook rivers, rivers located northwest of the Missaguash. Further, at both of the French forts, Fort Beauséjour and Fort Gaspereau, or rather clinging around their outsides would have been found all manner of abodes occupied by the sheltering Acadians, the balance of those who had once made their living to the south of the Missaguash and who then depended on the French at the fort for their subsistence.[12] Further, there would have been found numerous Indians (French allies) who were quite at home in their temporary skin and bark homes pitched around the French forts. Imagine for yourself the scene: fires smoking, dogs yapping, children alternatively crying and laughing; Indian women working at various projects such as chewing and sewing skins and stirring pots; Indian men sitting about with their white clay pipes, most silent while one of their number expounds on the bravery of one party or another who had in the past had been on a hunt or was part of a war party. Days and seasons passed and the forts opposite one another on the Missaguash took on the look of permanent fixtures with the occupants of each not much bothered by the presence of the other fort across the muddy marsh river as is the Missaguash.

After the parties took up their respective fortified positions at the Isthmus of Chignecto in 1750 no direct military conflict was to be observed between the French and the English in Acadia. Parties of men, from one side or the other, under the appropriate flags would sally forth from their fort and stride over the marsh towards the opposite fort with a definite purpose in mind. There were trades to be made.[13] The trades would be worked out and included food, wood and other needed supplies. Men were often part of the trade. The Indians, who were at war with the English, would bring those that they had captured in their raids and be paid ransoms by the French, who in turn would recover their expenses by trading them back to the English at the isthmus. The times were long for the soldiers at the isthmus garrisons;[14] one season would blend into the next; the years 1750 through to 1753 simply passed away, one much like the other. The year 1754 was much the same too. It was in August of that year that news was received at Fort Beauséjour that a new governor, Drucour, had just arrived with his family at Louisbourg. In September, we see where Lawrence was expressing his concern that Acadian produce was going to the French at both Louisbourg and Beauséjour; and further, that there was free and uninterrupted trade between these two French strongholds in Acadia (*via* Baie Verte). The settlement at Halifax was, by 1754, five years old and was a well established and well fortified English position. There was also now an "English" establishment at Lunenburg, by then, one year old. During October, the first Chief Justice of Nova Scotia was appointed, Jonathan Belcher; so too, during October, Charles Lawrence was officially sworn in as lieutenant-governor. At Fort Edward, located at Piziquid (the Windsor of today) Captain Alexander Murray reported that the local habitants had refused to bring in firewood and timber for fort repairs. It was determined that Abbé Daubin, their priest was behind this trouble. First summoned, and then arrested, Daubin and five Acadians are brought to Halifax under guard and sent back to Piziquid with orders to supply the required wood.[15] That winter, 1754/55, Smallpox got in among the population at

Louisbourg and in the result unusually large numbers died. And, at Fort Beauséjour, — well, Dr. Webster writes:

> The winter of 1754-55 was quite peaceful in Acadia, and, at the Fort, there was no knowledge of any definite preparations being made against the French. It was known, of course, that the fortifications at Halifax were being rapidly advanced, that military activities were reported in New England and that merchant vessels were being collected in their ports, and, also, that a French ship with supplies and munitions from Louisbourg to the King's post at the mouth of the river St. John had been captured.[16]

Chapter 3

The Attack & The Aftermath

The attack force consisted of approximately 2,000 provincials, which, as we have seen, were gathered together at Boston. The operation was under Colonel Robert Monckton.[1] The troops were divided into two battalions; one headed up by Colonel John Winslow[2] and the other by Colonel George Scott.[3] On May 23rd, 1755, the English forces sailed from Boston. "Forty sloops and schooners" were escorted in convoy by three small frigates; the *Success*, the *Mermaid*, and the *Siren*. The fleet was under the command of Captain John Rous.[4] It arrived at Annapolis Royal on the 25th, "forty-one sail." "Here the expedition was joined by three transports from Halifax under convoy of the *Vulture*, Sloop -of-War, with a detachment of Artillery under the command of Capt. Broome, Mr. Bruce, Chief Engineer and others, the fleet sailed on June 1st, at 8 a.m. ..." The armada pushed up to the head of the Bay and before sunset the same day were anchored within nine miles of their objective.

Winslow wrote in his journal:

June 1st:
> Sailed from Annapolis Royal on board his majesty's ship *Success*, John Rouse, Esq., Commander the whole fleet consisting of forty one sail. Got out of the Gut at eight and stood up the Bay, the wind blew fresh. Passed by the Isle of Holt, Cape Chignecto, anchored about sun setting, about five miles distance from Fort Lawrence ...[5]

The commander at Beauséjour at the time, to whom we have already referred, was Louis du Port Chambon, Sieur de Vergor.[6] The intelligence of a build up at Boston and the fleet's arrival at Annapolis Royal doubtlessly was patched through to Vergor. Given the slowness of the age, Vergor would not have had much lead time to fix up the defenses of Fort Beauséjour.[7] Upon the English armada making its appearance in the basin, the fears of the French were considerably heightened: the descent of such a force could mean only one thing. A call went out to the able bodied Acadian men in the district to come into the fort for its defense; approximately 300 responded. At the time the English commenced its attack, Fort Beauséjour had "twenty-one cannon and a mortar, and it was manned by one hundred and sixty-five officers and soldiers of the regulars ..."[8]

We have had preserved for us a contemporaneous French accounting of events. Jacau de Fiedmont,[9] a French officer who was behind the walls of Beauséjour at the time, wrote:

> April — It was known, however, that their coast-guards had captured and taken to Chebucto a French ship, which had been loaded with munitions and food — supplies at Louisbourg for the King's post on the Saint John River. We also learned about this time, that great preparations for war were being made throughout New England, and that all merchant ships had been held in their respective ports; even those which habitually brought provisions to their fort in this neighborhood, early in April, were being detained until June 1st. The confidence that peace would continue was so deeply impressed on the minds of those who lived in the district, that none of these reasons sufficed to awaken the slightest alarm, and we continued to enjoy a sense of security as perfect as though we were residing in the centre of Paris.
>
> On June 2nd we realized our mistake. At 5 o'clock in the morning a settler who lived at Cape Maringouin, in the Bay of Fundy, about 2 leagues from Point Beauséjour, came to warn M. de Vergor du Chambon, Commandant of the Fort, that an English fleet of about forty vessels, laden with men, had sailed into the cove on the inner side of the Cape, and was there awaiting the turn of the tide to enter Beaubassin. The commandant, who could no longer doubt the intentions of the English, dispatched couriers to Quebec, the Saint John River, Louisbourg and the Island of St. John to solicit aid. The inhabitants from rivers dependent on this post, and from the surrounding country, were summoned to the Fort, raising to about six hundred the number of men under orders to take up arms and fire on the English whenever they should attempt to set foot in the King's domain, or to make an attack on our fort.
>
> At 5:30 in the afternoon, the enemy's fleet composed of 37 sail made its appearance; three frigates, a snow, and two other vessels, equipped for fighting, which served as an escort, anchored at the entrance to Beaubassin; the transports were run aground close to Fort Lawrence, the English post, 1,450 fathoms from our own. The troops landed at about 6:30 in the evening and the great majority of them passed the night under arms.[10]

The English forces landed at a place which the French did not dispute was British territory, just to the south of the Missaguash River and below the English fort. Soon thereafter there were 2,000 men camped in two lines of evenly spaced tents in the field below Fort Lawrence.[11]

It was the early morning of June 4th: the British tents were struck and the troops lined up in marching order.[12] Following along in the tracks of this army was a train of "four short brass field guns, 6 pounders."[13] The progress was slow as the army made its way east through the marsh grass, along the south bank of the Missaguash River.[14] Their initial objective was to get across the river and then proceed west along the north side in order to lay siege to the French fort. They thought it best to cross over at a place on the river called Pont-ô-Buot, a place where there was a bridge; or, rather, where a bridge had been, as not unexpectedly the French had destroyed it. The English engineers were simply going to throw another one up; they had brought the materials along for the job. This position was several miles east of Beauséjour. It was an attack point which the French had anticipated and had built there a block-house.[15] Monckton reported: "Upon our beginning to lay the bridge the enemy behind the works that lined the woods gave us a fire and the Indian Cry, they likewise fired some swivel guns from a log house."[16] Between the British line and the French fort on the northern side of the river there was, seemingly, an entire French Acadian village. Most of it likely came in to being after the Acadians were forced to flee Beaubassin five years earlier. There was at least 60 buildings and a church which were directly to the east of the French fort. These structures, it was calculated by the French would be used to some advantage by the advancing British troops; so, the French put the torch to every one of them before the British were to get into position.[17]

A contemporaneous French version of the events just above recited, as given by Fiedmont, is, as follows:

Their artillery fire was directed especially at the emplacements of the four swivel-guns [mounted at the blockhouse at Pont-ô-Buot] which were ineffective and moreover, badly served; they were soon put out of commission. The Indians immediately abandoned the entrenchment and took up a position on a height beyond range of the cannon; nor, with two or three exceptions, did the settlers linger long before retreating into the woods; only a few soldiers remained in the entrenchment with the officers. M. de Baralon saved the swivel-guns, which were taken into the woods on a cart and sunk in a bog; he ordered the guard-house, storehouse and the buildings in the neighbourhood to be set on fire. ...

Orders were given to bring to the fort all the provisions which were in the storehouses and dwellings in the neighborhood, and to set fire to the buildings. Some cattle were also brought inside the palisades. Only a few men were engaged on the works, and a very small quantity of fascines and other material was collected, because the settlers were making use of their carts to save their portable property. ...

On the 5th, the settlers of Buot bridge and those who had been at the barricades and had remained in the woods since the action, joined forces and came to the fort. They reported that to establish their communication with Fort Lawrence, the enemy were constructing a bridge across the river opposite their camp. These men asked the Commandant's permission to fight in their own way.

By the evening[18] of the 5th the English were encamped on the north side of the Missaguash some five miles from Fort Beauséjour. We can see from Winslow's journal that the English were to take the next couple of days to clear the land for their camp, build defenses around it and bring up supplies. Many of the war materials were brought up in Cobb's vessel[19] up the Missaguash, right under the noses of the French.[20] A bridge, lower down the Missaguash, was built in order to have easier access to Fort Lawrence. "By the 7th all the tents were pitched." On June the 8th, Monckton sent out his engineers to reconnoitre and to determine the best emplacements for the siege cannon. On the 10th a number of the soldiers were employed making a road through the marsh in order that they might move their heavy cannons and munitions into place.[21] A site for the cannons was chosen, it being up a rise above and to the north of the French fort. The French attempted to defend this place, but Scott with 500 men took control. During this skirmish "Engineer Tonge was badly wounded. Major Preble slightly. One private was killed and four wounded but not seriously. In the evening, Colonel Scott and his force broke ground for the entrenchments. The fort fired several cannon shots at them."[22]

Thus, the English had seized the high ground to the north of the fort. Amongst their preparations was the opening up of the siege trenches to within 700 feet of the walls of the French fort. The men creeped ever closer within the protection of their trenches which teams of sappers had dug under the cover of night while their fellow infantrymen lay on their bellies ahead of them ready to return fire. The trenches were only started on the 12th and once advanced, a "13 inch mortar" was moved along under cover, ever closer, and closer. On the 16th, this mortar was to do its work, very well; though the English did not know it. The English likely thought they had weeks, maybe months of work ahead; when, on the 16th, out of the gates came a group of French officers under a flag of truce. The English were surprised to learn that the French wished to capitulate.[23]

What the English did not know at the time was that the French defenders were a very dishearten group. As previously mentioned there was behind the walls of Fort Beauséjour but 160 regulars. This force was supplemented, it is estimated, by 300 hundred Acadians[24] which had been recruited from the local population, but only with much difficulty. The work during these days was not just happening outside but also inside the walls as the French went about trying to improve their defenses from within. The Acadians became increasingly more difficult as the time wore on and as the English came closer and closer.[25] They knew what might well happen to them if the English were to succeed in their attack. The French commander, Vergor, promised them that reinforcements were on their way.[26] This hope was shattered, when, on June 14th, French couriers managed to get into the fort with a message from Louisbourg that it feared for itself, in that an attack may be launched by the English against them; indeed, ships of Boscawen's fleet were cruising its mouth: Louisbourg could not afford to send help: Fort Beauséjour was on her own. From this point onward the Acadians started to desert their posts,[27] slipping over the walls and off into the woods to join their families which they had placed well away from the scene when the matter first started to unfold.

So what transpired inside the fort on the 16th of June, was this: as Le Loutre and Vergor sat in one of two "bomb-proof" shelters within the fort, a great explosion was heard from the other; an explosive shell hurled into the fort by the British rolled into the open door way and, going off, killed seven French officers in one terrible explosion.[28] The effect was immediate. A white flag was sent out; and, whether it was by jigs, or tricks, or quirks — Vergor knew he was beaten; he intended, by that evening, to have the British officers over for supper.

Thus it was, that on June 16th, 1755, the French surrendered Fort Beauséjour to the English. Terms were worked out with the usual back and forth. Ultimately it boiled down to the French being allowed to march out with their bags and guns, their flags flying and their drums beating: they retired with honor and allowed to go to Louisbourg with the transport being laid on by the victor. Another condition was that there should be no retribution against the Acadians found behind the walls.

As to what then happened, we turn to our French eye witness, Jacau de Fiedmont:

> The English took possession of the Fort at 7:30 in the evening on the fourth day after they had opened their trench. Their troops passed the night under arms, and did not touch any of the merchandise or the King's property which, because all the buildings had been destroyed, were scattered about the fort; when, however, they saw that our own people were pillaging, the English officers could no longer restrain their men. They did, however, safeguard a portion of it. Our garrison marched out the following day to embark on the transport vessels for Louisbourg.

So, what conclusions might a historian make as to the reasons for the fall of Fort Beauséjour?

The French at Beauséjour did not have their hearts into the business of defending their position at the isthmus; they were lacking effective leadership; they were daunted by the numbers of the advancing English; and, the Acadians which had initially been pressed into service, as the battle wore on, became more interested in escaping than in fighting. With the word on the 14th that they could expect no support from Louisbourg; well, the faith in their ability to hold off the English, melted. What precipitated an immediate motion to surrender, was, however, a lucky shot from one of the English cannons. Sure, the French might of held out for a little longer, the fate of Fort Beauséjour, however, was sealed directly 2,500 English soldiers took their position before it. The feeling of the time, as expressed by Jacau de Fiedmont, was that the capitulation was necessary: "in view of the impossibility of receiving assistance, ... the weakness of the garrison, the insecurity of the casemates, especially the powder magazine ..."[29] Louis-Léonard, Sieur de Courville, the royal notary for Acadia who was stationed at Fort Beauséjour at the time, wrote the following criticism:

It was not necessary to remain in the Fort and await the enemy, especially as the Fort was overcrowded with a greater number than it was ever intended to hold. He [Vergor] could have camped in full view of the enemy, where he could observe and, at the same time, break up their plans: he could have disputed their crossing of the river Beaubassin [Missaguash]; he could have harassed them without cessation due to his advantageous position. He should have been able, without actually launching an attack, to have forced Colonel Monckton to adopt an aggressive policy before the Fort became actually besieged. And in this interval, he would have obtained aid from Canada.[30]

I should say, in conclusion to this chapter, that in all the confusion Le Loutre made good his escape. Traveling initially in the disguise of an Acadian woman, he managed to get himself overland to the Saint John and from there to Quebec. Incidently, it is seen from a directive from Monckton to Winslow, that Winslow, when he went to demand the surrender of Fort Gaspereau, that he was to see if he could locate Le Loutre's chest, as Monckton had intelligence that it was stored with the priest at Baie Verte. Winslow was to use his "utmost endeavor to get his chest and take particular care of it as it will clear up and open many dark scenes to us."[31] If such a chest existed it was not found, as the priests located at Baie Verte had slipped over into French territory by boat, to Île St. Jean (Prince Edward Island). At Quebec, we see where neither the civil nor the ecclesiastical authorities, for their own good reasons (he was neither fish nor fowl) were to give Le Loutre much time; so, soon thereafter, he was on a ship bound for France; he was never to return to America. It was with the fall of Fort Beauséjour that Le Loutre's reign of terror in Acadia, came, finally, to an end.

The Aftermath:

It was more than a hill with a fort on top of it, an entire territory was taken by the British when they took Fort Beauséjour. It was the linch-pin, and with its surrender, all of those parts north of the isthmus slipped out of French control. However, to cinch the victory, it was necessary to take two subsidiary forts; one to the west and another to the east.

Colonel Winslow, on June 18th, was sent with 500 men[32] to take Fort Gaspereau situated 12 miles on the other side of the isthmus. From Winslow's Journal we learn that he left Fort Beauséjour at 11 o'clock of the morning of June 18th., and:

Stopped at two by the side of a brook, refreshed ourselves and set forward. Came to Missaguash River at about three mile of the Bay Vert where the French had a fine bridge across; but now demolished, which retarded us some time til we could lay a new one which we accomplished & marched on all the way. A good cart road though wet. The land for the most part very good til we came near the bay where it grew worse. Past through the village at Bay of Verte. Arrived at the fort about sunset. Immediately entered and took possession. Monsr. Vilray commands with about thirty regulars and some artificers ...

As would be expected, the next day Winslow took an inventory, which, makes for interesting reading:

4 cannon, 7 barrels of powder, one hundred weight musket balls, 8 hhds molasses, 3 barrels of pease, 6 barrels of flower, 230 barrels of pork, 3 barrels of tallow, 10 galls lamp oil, 9 doz. of cod lines, 1300 iron shot and about 50 cartridges.

Winslow then proceeded to give a bit of a description of Fort Gaspereau, and its condition:

> I take [it] to be one hundred and eighty foot square with four bad blockhouses one at each corner. A ditch partly dug. No ramparts nor glasses nor an extraordinary palisade. A large storehouse but not tight nor [having a] floor. Neither is there one building in the whole, tenantable, Everything miserable to the last degree. ... We must be supplied with bread ... also ... camp kettles as I find no kind of vessels to dress their provisions ... I ... am told by the inhabitants that ... the garrison fetch their water at a large distance in carts.

With such a description it will be no surprise that Winslow became, "persuaded it will be best to quit it. For it is situated so near the water that it must fall to the first attack that is made that way."

After securing the fort, Winslow then sent 200 men to comb the village of Bay Verte. "This village," Winslow reported, "contains about twenty-five houses, a chapel and priest's house, well furnished. And the inhabitants of this village live in better form and more after the English manner than any I have seen in this province. And have an open communication with the Island of St. John & the inhabitants of Cape Breton, whom they furnish with lumber, Indian goods etc.; and from whom they receive all the conveniences of life in return."

We know that it was Winslow's view that Fort Gaspereau was useless and should be abandoned, however, that was not Monckton's view. Monckton sent over a fresh detachment of 200 men under the command of Captain Thomas Speakman. He delivered orders for Winslow to return to Fort Cumberland, which Winslow did on the 23rd.[33]

The French fort at the Saint John proved to be more difficult. Captain Rous, glad now to have some activity, sailed down the Bay to deal with the French at the Saint John River. He left on June the 23rd, in company with the transports loaded with the French soldiers who were being returned to Louisbourg. On June 30th, Rous in three 20 gun ships[34] and a sloop arrived off of the mouth of Saint John. Directly the French became aware of their presence, they "burst their cannon, blew up their magazine, and fled up river."[35]

The garrisons of both Fort Beauséjour and of Fort Gaspereau were shipped off, by the way of the Bay of Fundy, to Louisbourg.[36] The Acadians who were found behind the walls of Beauséjour (they claimed that the French officers gave them little choice) were forgiven and released.

In July, Winslow, while still at the isthmus, had occasion to write Governor Lawrence who continued to be at Halifax throughout this period. Winslow observed that though the English forces had put an end to the French "pretensions," both at the isthmus and at the Saint John River, the province was still left with the "neutrals" and "their brethren the Indians." Their submission to the English had been only "low and mean." They were, as Winslow further observed, not to be trusted. And that they could never be good. Winslow doesn't suggest to his superior what course of action might be taken, but wonders — now that the principal object has been met — as to what "our future operations" might be? Almost as a separate thought, Winslow then advises that his New England troops be "not kept in a state of indolence."[37]

The most significant impact of Monckton's victory at the isthmus, was this: the success, that is to say the early success in subduing the French at the isthmus, allowed Governor Lawrence, almost immediately, to carry out a plan which while it had been brewing for a considerable period of time, could not be carried out for lack of resources. At the isthmus there was approximately 2,500 paid-for troops. Their job was done by the end of June. Lawrence had another job for them.

Chapter 4

Introduction
To The Dispersal Of The Acadians

Due to superior note keeping of the English officer in charge at that place, the general view is that the deportation took place at one time (1755) and only at one place, Grand Pré. It in fact took place over a period of time which stretches back to 1745 and continued on through to the end of the war in 1763. Certainly, it was in 1755 that the greatest number of Acadians were to lose their homes and native lands; but there were other times to which we will make reference. The principal deportation points were, of course, all of the then established Acadian communities: Annapolis Royal, Grand Pré, Piziquid (today, the town of Windsor) and Fort Beauséjour (near the town of Amherst). During the succeeding years of the war, further deportations were to take place in other French communities located in Yarmouth County, in Cape Breton, in Prince Edward Island, along the shores of northeastern New Brunswick and up around the Gaspé coast (as all these places are known today).

The emotion of the event, as it unfolded at Grand Pré, was captured by Longfellow in his poem "Evangeline."[1] Such efficiency! Imagine the scene, one of the most pitiful scenes in history, possibly to the strains of "Romeo and Juliet" as rendered by either Tchaikovsky or Prokofiev, as these resolute players went through their parts in this real life drama, more sorrowful then any passion play that can possibly be imagined. Reluctant English soldiers went about dutifully and methodically, and while giving as much comfort as they can to the dispossessed, proceeded to carry out their military orders. Picture the scene: The hardwood trees were just beginning to dress themselves in their colorful autumn coats and transport ships with sails a'bellowing were on the water. In the fields curious cattle looked on as wooden buildings all about were being licked up by the flames. So too, there in the foreground, were the Acadian men, women and children, looking on in anguish to see everything that they and their forbearers had built-up, twirl away skyward in great smoky columns; their anguish worsening as they wondered what was to become of themselves.

Sad to think of what these Acadians had gone through due to British army orders. Those who gave them, as Professor Brebner wrote, "had no adequate conception of the transformation of pleasant farms, green meadows, comely orchards, and primitive homesteads, into a barren waste scarred by fire and destruction. ... To the authorities in England the expulsion of the Acadians was merely an incident in one small campaign in a bitter, dangerous, and expensive war, something already accomplished and therefore beyond useful discussion."[2]

What must be kept in mind as we go about considering this matter is that up to that time and ever since to these days — many people are dispossessed in times of war. Refugees run in advance of invading armies and occupying armies root out all those who might give aid and comfort to the enemy. France and England during the years under review, for all practical purposes, were at war; and war is the "son of hell, ... the artificial plague of man, a time when the vials of the Apocalypse are poured forth and shaken over countries ... a time of slaughter, famine, beggary, infamy, slavery, despair." War, as was described by Macaulay, has always been this way and I fear it will always be. The object of a combatant at war is to bring it to an end by winning it. In order to win a war a country must put everything aside that will not serve the objective. Many policies which would be adopted and promoted in times of peace are of no account during a time of war. I again quote Macaulay:

> To carry the spirit of peace into war is a weak and cruel policy. When an extreme case calls for that remedy which is in its own nature most violent, and which, in such cases, is a remedy only because it is violent, it is idle to think of mitigating and diluting. Languid war can do nothing which negotiation

or submission will do better: and to act on any other principle is, not to save blood and money, but to squander them.[3]

Purging territory, which a country claims as its own, of all except its own citizens, is a step which did not start with the events in Acadia, in 1755. Indeed, France was an old hand at it. For example, in 1666, the French captured the Island of St. Christopher's in the West Indies; they deported the English population, about 2,500 in number, and, kept all their property. The event was considered sufficiently glorious enough for France to warrant the striking of a commemorative medal. Closer to the situation which was to present itself to the British in Acadia 66 years later, was that when in 1689 Frontenac laid plans down to capture Albany and New York. The instructions he received from his ministers were, that, after the conquest, the Catholics might be allowed to remain, on taking the oath of allegiance, but that as regards all others: "Men, women and children — his Majesty deems it proper that they should be put out of the colony and sent to New England, Pennsylvania and other such quarters as shall be considered expedient, either by land or sea, together or in divisions all according as he shall find will best serve their dispersion and prevent them by reunion affording enemies an opportunity to get up expeditions against that colony."[4]

The events herein described will be entirely new to some of those who read these pages; and to others, those who have read of the events or have had some accounting of it told to them, much of the detail will be new. Any person who but reads of the deportation of the Acadians in isolation without considering the larger contemporaneous events which unfolded, and which are wrapped up in the single expression, *The Seven Years War*, will have deprived themselves of a very rich piece of history, a history which mightily impacted in political divisions and population variations of an Europeanized America.

Chapter 5

The Plan:
A Long Time In The Making

Way before they staked out their respective claims in North America, beginning in the early 17th century, as any reader of European history will know, the French and the English were long time enemies. Very old wounds were to break out as they jostled one another in the wilds of North America. The English claims were rooted in the discoveries of Cabot (1497); the French in Cartier (1534). A European hunger for fish and furs drove mariners and traders, of both countries, to the northern eastern shores of North America. Small wooden sailing vessels made their way out over the broad Atlantic in the spring of the year and with the early autumn westerlies returned to the docks of Europe, their holds filled with product: the ivory and hides of the walrus; the long horn of the narwhal, the down of eider ducks; the skins of the beaver, the otter, the fisher, the martin, the mink, the muskrat and the bear (brown, black and white); and, of course, bundles of dried fish and barrels of pickled fish. These early European venturers likely got on with one another, just as traders usually do. As a practical matter, however, no European settlement of North America was to take place for many, many years.

I have already told of the first settlement in Acadia. It was, putting aside the Spanish in Florida, the first permanent settlement of Europeans in all of North America. Port Royal was founded in 1605. The English made their way into Chesapeake Bay and up the Powhatatan River and there they founded Jamestown, "the first vital germ of English colonization on the continent." And so, the first two European pieces were set down on the political game board of North America: Port Royal and Jamestown. These first European communities had hardly a chance to jell when —

no matter that there existed practically 500 miles of wilderness between them — the English were of the view that there were "rights" to be enforced. By 1613, the French had made three establishments in the greater area of Acadia: Mount Desert, St. Croix and Port Royal. Samuel Argall, with lawless violence, ransacked and plundered all three; he thought Acadia was "effectually blotted out." Thus it was, that the first shots in America were exchanged between these ancient European enemies, between the English and French, in Acadia. These bloody exchanges — of which Acadia was to have more than its share — kept up for over a century and a half and continually shook the struggling communities of North America until accounts were permanently settled with the conclusion of *The Seven Years War* and the loss to France of her North American colonies in 1763.

These bloody exchanges, to which I have referred, have been dealt with in some detail in previous chapters. These exchanges — and, a reader of this history is bound to be struck by the fact — those that were to take place on Acadian soil, were not so much between the English and the Acadians, as much as it was between the English and the French military sent down from Quebec. Acadia was a whipping-boy. The English knew who the real culprits were: the French at Quebec. The French, ensconced as they were in their northern fortress at Quebec, however, were difficult to get at because of the natural elements of geography and climate.[1]

Thus, Acadia, in its nearness to New England, was to pay for the sins of Quebec. It is not that the Acadians were virtuous: they were not. Their allegiance was to the French king; outwardly, when the French troops were around; inwardly, when the English troops were around. But at all times the Acadians were interested in making their own way in the world; they were a people who devoted themselves to their church, to their families and to their farms. Good fortune had thrown them up onto some of the most fertile lands to be found in North America, and, they made the most of it. They established their farms on the ancient flood plains of the Bay of Fundy. Like farmers everywhere they did not live close together in villages; there would be a farm here with more than one habitation to house the different generations of one branch of the family; another farm a mile or two away, and another beyond. In time, each of the river valleys of Acadia were to become loosely occupied as families worked the soil and raised their animals to sustain themselves. There were Acadian trading centers, ports of call, though only a very view. Port Royal was the most well known. Then there were the more tightly packed communities to be found at the mouth of the Gaspereau River (Grand Pré) and at Beaubassin (Isthmus of Chignecto). At these places would have been found Acadian traders and Acadian mariners, but not very many. These individuals had among them, as does any group, those who would take advantage of various situations as might come along. When the English were not in control, Port Royal became a harborage to French cruisers and a place from which hostile Indians drew supplies. More generally, New Englanders were upset when they heard stories of English fishing boats being taken by French and Indian marauders off the coast of Acadia. Though New Englanders had better reasons to flatten Quebec (a most daunting military project), they had reasons sufficient enough to conquer Acadia.

Thus, an English force under Francis Nicholson sailed up the coast from Boston in 1710 and entered the basin, of what was then known as Port Royal, a French holding. Port Royal was captured and the English renamed it Annapolis Royal and that is its name today. It was to be the only English post in all of Nova Scotia except for a small garrison that was to be found, at times, at Canso. We see directly the English took Port Royal, they made plans to deport the Acadians.[2] We see in a Board of Trade report,[3] filed in 1721, where there was a recommendation to carry out a "survey of the location, trade, and structure of government" of each of the colonies from Nova Scotia to South Carolina, so as to have "a catalog of the resources which those colonies could muster against the French." This report was commissioned because of a general concern which the English had of French expansion in North America. In this report, South Carolina, New York and Nova Scotia were identified as frontier colonies, and Nova Scotia was to receive special attention. The Board wanted four regiments to be stationed in Nova Scotia; and further, wanted the Acadians evicted and in turn to transport the English inhabitants of Newfoundland to occupy the agricultural lands of Acadia.

Thus the thought of getting rid of the Acadians was not new. It was a thought first expressed not too long after the capture of Port Royal, and it was a thought that was expressed numerous times as the 18th century wore on. However, the government in England did not pursue the matter, not so much that they didn't have the heart to load people up on transports and replant them elsewhere — it is just that they never saw to the business of providing the means to do so. Acadia, or more particularly Annapolis Royal, was a very small and forgotten post and as such got very little in the way of support, this despite the numerous pleas over the years. The French inhabitants just a few miles beyond the walls of Fort Anne at Annapolis Royal and from there throughout all of Acadia, did pretty much as they pleased being bothered by no authority, English or French; and under that situation, I might add, prospered — if one might measure prosperity by population growth.

With the success of the English in the taking of Louisbourg in 1745, serious thought was once again given to the job of clearing the Acadians out of Nova Scotia. The English admiral, Peter Warren, raised the topic in a letter to the authorities just two days after Louisbourg had capitulated:

We shall find great difficulty and expense in transporting the prisoners to France, agreeable to the capitulation. They insisted much upon going to Canada and letting as many of the peasants reside here as should desire it. As this is the key to all the French settlements on this continent, and to Canada in particular, which his Majesty may think proper to reduce to his obedience, we would by no means agree to it. We have an example of the ill consequence of the French being among us at Annapolis, and it is worthy of the ministry to consider whether those people should not be transplanted to some other colony, and have an equivalent in such manner as his Majesty shall think proper.[4]

And then again on July 4th, Warren wrote:

> ... I believe we have near 5,000 yet we shall not be able to transport this fall. Many of the peasants have offered to take the oath of allegiance to his Majesty. As they will be useful in getting in wood and other necessaries for the garrison, the general and I propose to tender the oath to such as we can not transport. We are determined by no means to let them remain here longer than until vessels can be procured to transport them. We see the ill effects of a thing of this nature at Annapolis, and till the French are transported from thence, or till we have possession of Canada, the colony of Nova Scotia will be continually alarmed.[5]

So it was with the capitulation of Louisbourg in 1745 that a number of French peasants were distributed by the English amongst their colonies to the south, though it would not appear many and mostly only those in and around Louisbourg. However, Warren was to write forebodingly, "that while such a number of French are suffered to remain in [Nova Scotia], with a very little mixture of English (if any at all) except the garrison, it will ever be a thorn in our side. ... by intermixing them in some of the remotest of our colonies from the French, a great advantage would thereby accrue to our country, and the expense of so many garrisons would be taken off. That of Annapolis Royal might be transplanted to strengthen this or Newfoundland, for it would be useless there."[6]

Warren continued with this theme in a letter to Newcastle written at Louisbourg on October 3rd, 1745. Warren was advising how he was unable to immediately transport the inhabitants of Île St Jean (about a 1,000) he expressed the hope to be able to do so the "next spring as we see ill consequences in Nova Scotia that attend keeping any of them in our territories. Indeed it would be a good thing if those now at Annapolis could be removed ..."[7]

Though there was to be some deportations immediately after the capture of Louisbourg and an intention to keep the program going into the following year; it does not seem, from the record, any such further deportations were to take place until that fateful year of 1755. Indeed we see, in 1748, an alternate plan was considered. Leave the French Acadians in place but dilute their influence by bringing in English or Protestant settlers to be located in amongst the Acadians. That summer with *The War of The Austrian Succession* having come to an end, Governor Shirley of Massachusetts sent one of his lieutenants, Captain Morris, up from Boston to Nova Scotia to do a feasibility survey in respect this settlement. Captain Morris concluded in his report:

> Another advantage will arise, that the Protestants will be intermixt with the present Inhabitants, and consequently an Intercourse of Trade and Intermarriages, whereby in Time they will come to have one Common Interest & mutually send out Colonies to settle the Inland Countrys.[8]

Nothing was to come of Morris' plans. To work, it would have been necessary to swamp the Acadian lands with great quantities of English immigrants. While quite a number were brought over by the English during the years 1749-52, they were not of sufficient numbers, and it was feared that if they were placed down among the Acadians, it would be them and not the Acadians that would be diluted. Besides, the English, in regards to their settlement plans, beginning in 1749, were thwarted by "The Indian Threat."

So it was, that more than forty years were to pass and the English never were to have a sufficient presence in the province to effectively deal with the intransigency of the Acadians. During the first part of the 1750s the English finally started in on fortifying Nova Scotia. In July of 1755, with the surrender of Fort Beauséjour, there were to be better than 2,000 English troops laying about at Chignecto. With a full scale war about to break out, the English now had the means to finally, and once and for all, deal with these potential "fifth columnists": the Acadians.

Chapter 6

The Oath

Towards the close of the last chapter, reference was made to the intransigency of the Acadians. I refer to their steadfast refusal to take an absolute oath of allegiance to the British crown. Now, an oath is a solemn or formal appeal to God, in witness of the truth of a statement, or the binding character of a promise or undertaking. It is an act which is proceeded with less thought in these modern days than it did in days past. The taking of an oath, for the Acadians, being the religious people that they were, was indeed a very solemn piece of business; hell and damnation was held in the balance.

We now shall trace the record from 1710 to 1755 in regard to the numerous British requests made of the Acadians for such an oath of allegiance; and their continuing refusal to give such an oath. Over this single issue: the Acadians were to loose their hereditary lands in Acadia.

Acadia, being the earliest European settlement in America, has the longest history. It is, too, an extraordinary one. The people from a very early period suffered from the neglect of France, internal strife by rival proprietors and frequent harryings at the hands of the English. It is, throughout its entirety, a history of conflict, an ancient one carried over from Europe. We see it, immediately these two rival countries, France and England, set up their first settlements in America. In 1613, Captain Samuel Argall sailed out of Virginia in the fourteen gun *Treasurer*, up to the Jesuit colony at Mount Desert and destroyed it, and then went on to do the same at St. Croix and at Port Royal. In later years there is the example of the raids carried out by Benjamin Church in 1696 and then again in 1704. Thus, the French Acadians had good reason to always be concerned that the English could, at any time, appear off their shores — intent to do them harm.

Queen Anne's Promise, 1713:

In 1710, during the course of *The War of the Spanish Succession* or *Queen Anne's War*, the British captured Port Royal. Three years later the war was brought to an end by the *Treaty of Utrecht*, and, by its terms, France granted that the English should keep Acadia. Among the exchanges was that the Acadians would be allowed their religion and to stay on their lands, if they wished; provided, however, that they make themselves subject to the English crown. These agreements were inked in 1713, at a time when the entire Acadian population was not much more than 2,000. If the Acadians chose not to submit to English sovereignty, that is to say not to take an oath of loyalty, then, it was agreed that they had but a year to remove themselves from the territory.[1]

Though France had given up her claims to Acadia, she did retain the islands at the mouth of the St Lawrence. It was on one of these islands that she determined to set up a new capital. And so, in 1713, Louisbourg was founded on Cape Breton (newly renamed on this occasion by the French to Île Royale). Recognizing the benefit to them of having the Acadians come and settle on Île Royale, the French determined to send a delegation to Port Royal (Annapolis Royal). Thus, it was, during 1714 that two French vessels arrived off Annapolis Royal and the French officers aboard begged leave from the English governor, Francis Nicholson, to allow a representative of the French king, under the supervision of the English Governor, of course, to assemble and address the Acadians throughout the land. Nicholson allowed that the Acadians might be so assembled. The first of these assemblies was to be at Annapolis Royal; where, representing the population thereabouts of 916, there stood 169 French Acadian men. The French military officers from Louisbourg headed by La Ronde Denys and their English counterparts from the local garrison then each took their turns and addressed the assembly. McLennan, a noted historian of the period describes what took place.

They encircled the officers in the square, and heard read to them Nicholson's order for the meeting and the Queen's letter, both of which were translated for them, and the latter formally compared with La Ronde's copy. Then, invited by Nicholson, La Ronde made his propositions. If his letters indicate his oratorical style he was a fervid speaker, careless of grammar, and not altogether accurate as to facts. He, on this occasion, went beyond his instructions in the promises he made to the Acadians. He spoke of the goodwill of the King who would furnish to them vessels for their transport, provisions for a year to those who needed them, freedom from duties on all their trade for ten years, and added a promise which was of great importance to them, for the Acadians disliked the land system of Canada, that there would be no seignories, but that they would hold their lands direct from the King. Nicholson added that he was ready to receive any complaints of bad treatment.[2]

After the headmen at Annapolis River valley were so addressed, the French and British officers traveled to the Minas area where a similar meeting or meetings transpired. The population of Beaubassin and the other settlements about the Isthmus of Chignecto, however, were not visited by La Ronde, though undoubtedly the word was patched through to them that any arrangement made would have an equal application to them. La Ronde's mission was successful. With a few exceptions all the people he saw agreed to go to Île Royale. No obstacle was put in their way, and the outcome would seem to have depended entirely on the French authorities carrying out the promises which had been made on their behalf. I should say that the principal promise was that ships would be sent for their transport.

It was going to be almost an impossibility for the Acadians to make their way to Cape Breton with their essential possessions without sea going vessels being made available. The British never felt obliged to go through the expense and trouble to arrange for transport; and while the French promised to do so, they never saw to it. As it turned out, through the years, 1710-1749, only but a few Acadians were to find their way to the French territories (and when they did, they did so entirely at their own expense). The vast majority, for whatever reason,[3] preferred to stay on the lands which they had worked for generations. Thus, the transfer of the Acadians to Cape Breton, so ardently hoped for, at first, did not take place, and the likelihood of it taking place decreased with the passing years.

Philipps' Compromise, 1729/30:

With the death of George I, it being the custom to request such things upon the ascension of a new sovereign, the English asked the Acadians to take an oath of loyalty to the new sovereign. Therefore, during September of 1727, word having been received of the death of the English king, a detachment of soldiers from Annapolis Royal were sent forth to proclaim George II "throughout the province and invite the habitants and Indians to take the oaths."[4] The Acadians made it known that they would give no absolute oath; but that they would give a conditional one if they were allowed to have their priests reside among them and that they would not be obliged to bear arms during a time of war. This position was unacceptable to the British. The Acadian deputies were summoned to appear before the Council at Annapolis Royal. The deputies were advised of the governor's displeasure, and, in an effort to send out some kind of a message, they were clapped into irons and marched off to jail.[5]

It would not appear that the deputies were imprisoned for long, and within a matter of weeks calm was once again restored to Acadia. In the autumn of 1729, a new tack of a more amiable and conciliatory nature was taken by the English. We see where Abbé Bréslay was approved to take up his position as the parish priest at Annapolis Royal. This led to good feelings all around and shortly thereafter, undoubtedly through the intervention of Abbé Bréslay, an oath of allegiance was to be secured.[6] The following year, with the breakup of winter, a detachment under the orders of Governor Richard Philipps traveled throughout Acadia proffering the same oath as had been administered at Annapolis Royal the previous year. Except for "six scattering families on the eastern coast" whom he had intended to visit at a later point, Philipps was successful in getting all Acadians (every man, age 16 years and upwards) to sign. He acknowledged, as the Board had subsequently pointed out to him, that the wording of the oath might have been "stronger." Incidently, the total Acadian population estimated by Philipps in 1730 was 4,000.

The Acadian oath (1729/30) as was secured by Governor Philipps was unconditional, at least on paper it was.[7] It seems, however, that the Acadians were talked into signing the oath on the basis of "verbal promises" made. They were told at the time that they would be exempt from the necessity of bearing arms in the event of a conflict with the French. This compromise — and it seems there was not much doubt that it was made — was to haunt the masters of Nova Scotia for the next 25 years and contribute significantly to the tragic developments that were to culminate with the deportation of 1755.

The parties — the English (really just a few English soldiers at Annapolis Royal) and the Acadians — thereafter, were to enter into a long period of relative stability, reflective of the relatively peaceful relationship that existed between France and England through the years 1713-44. No doubt, though, the general faithfulness and peaceful disposition of the Acadians in these intervening years were much to the credit of one man: Paul Mascarene and his careful cultivation of the English/Acadian relationship.[8] This period of time in Nova Scotia is one which is dealt with in some detail in Part 3 of this work, and, in particular, I direct the reader's attention to the chapter, Annapolis Royal (1720-39). Beyond 1739, in the five years leading up to war, the English became increasingly more nervous about their position in Acadia. Acadians and their English governors were becoming more and more impressed with the French military presence which had blossomed into the stone fortifications at Louisbourg. All the English had was a little garrison at Annapolis Royal, there were no English settlers from one end of Acadia to the other. How was it expected to keep thousands of French Acadians in line, especially with Louisbourg looming in the distance and with the French priests in their midst spreading subversive messages. War did break out in 1744, and it was the New Englanders that saved Acadia for the English during that War, which by 1748 had come to an uneasy end. Everyone seemed to know that the following period — that between the end of the *War of the Austrian Succession* and the beginning of *The Seven Years War*, that is to say between 1748 *to* 1756 — was but an eight year intermission in the hostilities. The English at the beginning of this intermission, in 1748, finally came to grips with the problem of Acadia, being that it was an undermanned and undersettled territory. It will be recalled that it was in Part 5 where we took up the dramatic steps which England took to establish her presence in Nova Scotia with the establishment of Halifax in 1749, and, thereafter, the general fortification of Nova Scotia.

Renewed Pressure, Cornwallis, 1749:

Cornwallis' first order of business upon the fleet anchoring in Chebucto Harbor (Halifax) in 1749, was to get a message off to Mascarene. He and five of his councilors, having traveled up from Annapolis Royal, presented themselves to Cornwallis on July 12th. Mascarene in the next few weeks (he returned to Annapolis Royal in August) recounted the history of the Acadians especially up from the time the British took Port Royal some thirty-nine years earlier. No better person could be found to brief Cornwallis. Mascarene had been there with General Francis Nicholson when Acadia was captured in 1710, and his official duties had kept him there ever since.[9] In his French accented English, Mascarene filled Cornwallis in on the nature and character of the Acadians. Mascarene was of the view that the best that could be expected of them, in the event of war with France, was that they would be neutral; the worst is that they would assist any invading French military force with supplies and even with fighting men. Cornwallis was to conclude then that he would set about to immediately get these Acadians to sign an unconditional oath, and there was to be no shilly-shally about it. At Halifax: the English had a settlement like none they ever had before, with thousands of settlers loyal to the English crown now on the ground. With the addition of the troops that came down from the vacated Louisbourg garrison, the English had an even stronger military presence at Halifax than what it had been when first it had started. Cornwallis summoned the Acadians. Within days a small delegation traveled overland to pay their respects. They had walked the fifty miles which separated Halifax from the eastern edges of their homelands (St Croix River) and which marked, going westward, the beginning of a string of fertile valleys of which the Acadian lands consisted. There were three of them: Jean Melanson of Canard River, Claude LeBlanc of Grand Pré and Phillipe Melancon of Piziquid.[10] Cornwallis, in the airs of his aristocratic background, figured it was time to remind these presumptuous, homespun clad Frenchmen of a few things. He told them that it was only out of pity for their situation and their inexperience in the affairs of government that he condescended to reason with them, "otherwise, the question would not be of reasoning, but of commanding and being obeyed."[11] The exchange that next took place was recorded in the minutes:

> The Deputys being asked if they had any thing to offer from their several Departments answered, they were only sent to pay their Respects to His Excellency & to know what was to be their Condition henceforth, & particularly — whether they should still be allowed their Priests — His Excellency assured them they should always have them provided that no Priest should officiate within the Province without a License first obtained of His Excellency — Copys of His Majesty's Declaration, & of the Oath were given to the Deputys to issue to the Inhabitants, & they were commanded to return within a forthnight & to report the Resolutions of their several Departments — They were also ordered to send to the other French Settlements to let them know His Excellency desired to see their Deputys as soon as possible.[12]

In keeping with this order, ten men from the Acadian districts arrived at Halifax on the 29th of July, 1749. On the 31st, all of them boarded small boats at a roughly hewed wharf at the base of the new community and were then rowed out to the transport ship, *Beaufort*. (The *Beaufort* was serving, and was to continue to serve throughout Cornwallis' first summer as his headquarters.) A meeting of the Council had been convened and the Acadian

Deputies were to present themselves. The men were: Alexander Herbert, Annapolis; Joseph Dugad, Annapolis; Claude LeBlanc, Grand Pré; Jean Melancon, River Canard; Baptiste Gaillard, Piziquid; Pierre Landry, Piziquid; Pierre Gotran, Cobequid; Pierre Doucet, Chignecto; Francois Bourg, Chignecto; and, Alexander Brossart, Chippodie. Out of the small boats and onto the deck they went. After being kept on the deck for a period of time, a signal was relayed from the companionway. The men were then escorted into a crowded chamber below decks. There, before them were a number of earnest looking Englishmen, there at a table with assistants of varying kinds hovering in the background. Among the seated were: Colonel Edward Cornwallis, Colonel Peregrine Thomas Hopson, Colonel Jean Paul Mascarene, Lieutenant Colonel John Horseman, and Major Charles Lawrence — military men, all. So, too, at the table was John Gorham, a New Englander who headed up an Indian fighting unit known as Gorham's Rangers. For the most part, these inquisitors were finely dressed, and, stood out in contrast to the standing men in their homespuns.

The meeting had begun before the ten Acadians had been called into the chamber. There was some preliminary business, including the swearing in of a new man, one who was to play a central role in the stirring events that were to unfold over the next ten years in Nova Scotia, Major Charles Lawrence. We assume that Lawrence came down with the Louisbourg troops, newly arrived at Halifax under the command of Colonel Hopson. Hopson, himself was but on his way through; that autumn he sailed for England. The 65 year old Mascarene had just handed the reigns of power over to Cornwallis. Mascarene had a knowing and tired look about him: the rest were all newcomers to the territory. Mascarene, who as a young man fled his homeland in France as a persecuted Protestant, a Huguenot, knew these French deputies; knew their families and their ways; and knew what might be expected of them.

When a general inquiry was made of the deputies as to whether those whom they represented intended to sign the oath as has been demanded of them: Jean Melancon stepped forward. What was wanted, one and all, were reassurances that they should be able to carry on with their priests and their religion. Doubtlessly there was some impatience by the English spokesman which was immediately displayed: "Yes, yes, — your religion and your priests ... practice your religion, whatever you like; and as for your priests: they need but register themselves with the governor's office." "But," with a quick look at a parchment on the desk before him, "this business of you not wanting to bear arms in a time of war — well, as British citizens, which you all are to become upon swearing and signing the oath, you *must* come to the aid of your country when called upon." Then impatient observation broke out into peremptory demand, as was written in the minutes:

> [Your people must] take the Oath of Allegiance as offered them, for His Majesty would allow none to possess lands in His territory whose allegiance and assistance in case of need could not be depended upon. And that such as should behave as true subjects ought to do will be supported encouraged and protected equally with the rest of His Majesty's subjects.[13]

The deputies were told to return to their communities and tell everyone that they had until October the 26th: and, this would be the last day allowed to them to sign such an oath. Offices for the purposes of taking these oaths would be set up at both ends of the main Acadian valley, at Halifax and at Annapolis Royal; and the inhabitants (males above age 16 years) could go to either place and the oath would be administered and recorded.

On the 6th of September, a Council Meeting was once again convened on Board the *Beaufort*. Hopson had by this time apparently returned to England; Mascarene was now at Annapolis Royal in semi-retirement; and John Gorham was off at the Saint John cementing into place the recent treaty the English had entered into with the Malecites. The other council members, as we would have seen on 29th of July, were present. Governor Cornwallis was presiding. The French deputies are again to be seen entering the chamber. A long roll of parchment was produced by the deputies at the bottom of which were row upon row of signatures, "Xs," mostly. It was produced by the French Deputies and supported by oral presentations in broken English and translated French. The Acadians were thankful for all the British have done for them, however, "we are in great peril from the savage nations. Should we sign an unconditional oath as requested — we shall assuredly become the victims of their barbarous cruelty."[14] It is for this reason, they explained, that they are resolved not to take the oath unless they were exempted from taking up arms. Indeed, as they further explained, they have already taken such an oath, years ago, when Richard Philipps was governor, and it was understood by those that signed that they and their heirs were bound by it. "If your Excellency is not disposed to grant us what we take the liberty of asking, we are resolved, every one of us, to leave the country." The spokesman went silent; everyone in the room was still. Then the deputy spoke once again, as if an afterthought, — "We beg to know from your Excellency whether his Majesty has annulled the oath given to us by General Philipps." The chamber, again fell silent.[15]

Cornwallis drew himself into an upright posture. A moment, no doubt was spent eyeing those he was about to address:

We have cause to be much astonished at your conduct. This is the third time that you have come here from your departments, and you do nothing but repeat the same story without the least change. To-day you present us a letter signed by a thousand persons, in which you declare openly that you will be the subjects of His Britannic Majesty, only on such and such conditions. It appears to me that you think yourselves independent of any government; and you wish to treat with the King as if you were so. ...

Gentlemen, you allow yourselves to be led away by people who find it to their interest to lead you astray. They have made you imagine it is only your oath which binds you to the English. They deceive you. It is not the oath which a King administers to his subjects that makes them subjects. The oath supposes that they are so already. The oath is nothing but a very sacred bond of the fidelity of those who take it. It is only out of pity to your situations, and to your inexperience in the affairs of government, that we condescend to reason with you; otherwise, Gentlemen, the question would not be reasoning, but commanding and being obeyed. ...

Gentlemen, you have been for more than thirty-four years past, the subjects of the king of Great Britain, and you have had the full enjoyment of your possessions and your religion.

Show now that you are grateful for these favors, and ready to serve your king when your services are required. ...[16]

Thus, Cornwallis voiced his disappointment, but he did not threaten them any further, nor did he say that anything was about to happen to them. It is plain that the Acadian resolve, not to sign the requested oath, impressed Cornwallis and his Council. He expressed his thoughts in a letter written five days later: "As I am sure they will not leave their Habitations this season, when the letter was read to the Council in their presence, I made them answer without changing any thing of my former Declaration, or saying one word about it. My view is to make them as useful as possible to His Majesty while they do stay. ... They went home in good humour promising great things."[17] The fact is that when faced with the reality of it, at least at this time, the English knew that they needed the Acadians to be working the lands: there were English soldiers and settlers at Halifax that needed to be fed. At the conclusion of his address to the Acadians aboard the *Beaufort* on 6th of September, Cornwallis was to end on an up-note: "We are going to send a detachment of His Majesty's troops to Minas to establish themselves there[18] — for your protection against the Indians. We hope you shall assist them. They will pay for every thing that you supply to them with ready money.[19] I expect, and hope that you will manage to let me have here in ten days, fifty of your men, in order to assist me in building houses for the settlers that have arrived with me. These men will be paid in ready money and be fed on the king's provisions."[20]

Before the worst part of winter set in, the Acadians did come overland to assist the English newcomers. On December 23rd, 1749, Salusbury wrote into his diary: "The French come down with cattle. Some of them engage again in the works." And, the 29th, "Provisions in plenty from Minas." And so, the winter passed with the English and the French in relative harmony. In the spring there came to Halifax a further delegation of Acadians.

This time there were four deputies: Jacques Teriot from Grand Pré; Francois Granger from the River Canard; Batiste Galerne and John Andre from Piziquid. They presented a petition to the governor for permission to "evacuate the province and carry off their effects." This must have come as somewhat of a surprise to Cornwallis as he had done nothing to press them on the signing the oath since their refusal to do so the previous fall. He did know however that the French military had established a presence at the Isthmus of Chignecto and undoubtedly had heard rumors that the Acadians at the isthmus were crossing over into French territory. Now, it seemed that the Acadians located in other centers, ones closer to Halifax, were intending on doing the same. They declared they were not going to put their crops into the ground and would spend the summer moving their people and animals over the Cobequid mountains and beyond, all in order to pass into French territory. The councilors spoke pleadingly to the deputies. "You are listening to the wrong people; your priests are leading you astray; you would be better off to stay on the lands and to be under the benevolent rule of the British" — as we might have heard them say and as were written in the minutes:

> For once more my friends, you are the subjects of the king of Great Britain, and not of France. It is true that you refused to take the oath of allegiance to our king last autumn ...
>
> I informed you then that neither your situation nor your duties as subjects were at all changed by that act. It was at that time that you were indebted to us for not having made you leave the country even during winter.
>
> But after having passed the winter in the province and commenced to prepare the lands in the spring, it is ridiculous to come and tell me that you will not sow having resolved to withdraw. My friends, you must go and sow your lands.[21]

Now, what was concluded as a result of this meeting — I cannot say. It might be supposed that the deputies returned without getting the requested permission for the Acadians of their districts to leave. There then must have followed some late night meetings in the Acadian cottages throughout the Minas and Piziquid areas. The vote, if there was such a thing, had to split. The majority determined to stay on and to continue to work their lands. A large number, however, the records disclose, took their leave of the province and fled to the French held territories beyond peninsular Nova Scotia. Justice Patterson was to write of this:

> From 1750, till the year of the Expulsion the threats and inducements of the French agents [Abbé Le Loutre being the principal one] were having their effect and the Acadians in large numbers left the colony, and Cobequid in common with the other places suffered a loss in population. Some went to Cape Breton, St. John River, and to the Isthmus, but the largest number went via Tatamagouche to St. John's Island [Prince Edward Island]. In August 1750, it was reported from Port La Joye (Charlottetown) that the Acadians were arriving daily and that there were seven hundred persons on rations.[22] But they did not go willingly. The Governor of Isle St. Jean, himself writing of the inhabitants of Cobequid said, 'they leave their homes with great regret and they began to move their luggage only when the savages compelled them.' This is cogent evidence that coercive methods were being used by the French, quite impervious to the suffering they were inflicting upon those of their race and religion. Many reached the Island in a state of virtual starvation and their condition there was little better.[23]

On the 25th of May, 1750, the Council at Halifax was faced with a similarly written petition presented by those Acadians along the Annapolis River. The Minutes show that the council members were very suspicious. These petitions were not in words chosen by the Acadians; why, it was rare to find even one among them that could even write out their own name! They were asked about the contents of the petition and the two deputies (Charles Pregian and Jacques Michel) "seemed not to understand the petition themselves and being asked when where and by whom the petition was wrote, they could not and would not make an answer."[24]

A response to the Annapolis petition was worked out and read to the deputies by Governor Cornwallis:

> My friends, the moment that you declared your desire to leave and submit yourselves to another government, our determination was to hinder nobody

from following what he imagined to be his interest. We know that a forced service is worth nothing and that a subject compelled to be so against his will, is not very far from being an enemy.

We frankly confess, however, that your determination to leave us gives us pain. We are well aware of your industry and your temperance, and that you are not addicted to any vice or debauchery. This province is your country; you or your fathers have cultivated it; naturally you ought yourselves to enjoy the fruits of your labour.

You possess the only cultivated lands in the province; they produce grain and nourish cattle sufficient for the whole colony.

I know that the troops put you to some inconvenience at present, as your custom is to leave the houses where they are. It is a matter of necessity which you must endure for some time. That will pass away and you will find it to your advantage. In the meantime you can rely upon our word, that as soon as tranquillity is reestablished in the province, we shall give passports to all those who shall ask for them. We have already given you to understand, that no government permits those who withdraw from it to carry with them their effects.[25]

Though there was an attempt, as we have now seen, with the arrival of Cornwallis in 1749 to bring the Acadians to the British heel, matters after the spring of 1750 pretty much returned to what they had been. Though there were fewer of them on account of the outflow during the years 1749-51, the majority of the Acadians remained and went on working their family farms as they had done for generations. Putting aside the events at the Isthmus of Chignecto, not much changed in the Acadian lands, except that at Piziquid and Grand Pré, there was located English forts: Fort Edward and *Vieux Logis*[26]. The fort at Annapolis Royal, Fort Anne, continued to be manned by English soldiers as it had since 1710. Halifax, which for the Acadians was an out-of-the-way place, developed into an impressive capital in the wilderness. It became, mainly due to the Indian threat, well fortified; and, possessing a superb harbor with no tidal problems (unlike the Bay of Fundy), was fast becoming an important British terminus for ocean going vessels. The Acadian community at the isthmus, Beaubassin, a fertile place at which Acadians had started putting down their roots as far back as 1676 — in 1750, disappeared. Most all of the French structures, being led by the French priest,

Le Loutre, were burnt by the Indians and the population driven over the border into territory which these days we know as New Brunswick. The English territory at the Isthmus of Chignecto, as of 1750, had no Acadian population. There, at the isthmus, the French military (not the Acadians) had drawn a line, as was represented by the Missaguash River; the French were to remain to the north of it, the English to the south of it. There, too, at the isthmus in 1750 the opposing sides built their forts: Fort Beauséjour and Fort Lawrence. On a review of this period, 1750-54, it seems plain that the English concentrated their limited resources in the fortification of Nova Scotia and generally made no demands on the Acadians; and, in particular, the taking of the Oath of Allegiance.

Governor Cornwallis was unhappy with his post, he wanted to get back to his aristocratic life in England and the many entreaties made by him and his influential friends back home were to eventually bring him relief. Colonel Peregrine Thomas Hopson was appointed governor. We referred earlier to Hopson when we mentioned he had been in Halifax briefly during the summer of 1749 and then had returned to England. Hopson came back to Halifax in 1752 in order to take over from Cornwallis. He had been the last English governor at Louisbourg before it was returned back to the French in 1749. It is reported that Hopson was a "mild and peaceable" officer and was well respected by has own people and by the French. He was equally respected by the Indians, and, within four months of his arrival at Halifax, had concluded a treaty with them. It was Hopson, incidently, who finally dealt with the burdensome problem of an over collection of "English" settlers at Halifax: he saw to the establishment of Lunenburg. He had no time or inclination to stir up the Acadians by making any demands upon them; indeed, he made it a policy to deal with them as if they were British citizens.

You [Hopson's subordinate officers] are to look on the French Inhabitants in the same light with the rest of His Majesty's Subjects, as to the protection of the laws of the government, for which reason nothing is to be taken from them in force, or any price set upon their goods but what they themselves agree to; and if at any time the Inhabitants should obstinately refuse to comply with what his Majesty's service may require of them. You are not to redress yourself by military force, or in any unlawful manner, but to lay the case before the Governor and wait his orders thereon. You are to cause the following orders to be stuck up in the most public part of the fort, both in English and French:

1. The provisions or any commodities that the inhabitants of the country shall bring to the fort to sell, are not to be taken from them at any fixed price, but to be paid for according to a free agreement made between them and the purchasers.

2. No officer, non-commissioned officer, or soldier, shall presume to insult or otherwise abuse any of the Inhabitants of the country, who are upon all occasions to be treated as His Majesty's, and to whom the laws of the country are open, to protect as well as to punish.

At the season of laying in fuel for the fort, you are to signify to the Inhabitants by their Deputies, that it is his Excellency's pleasure they lay in the quantity of wood that you require, and when they have complied, you are to give them certificates specifying what quantity they have furnished, which will entitle them to payment at Halifax.[27]

Due to his health, in November of 1753, Nova Scotia lost Governor Hopson (he had serious eye problems). The scene was then set for Charles Lawrence[28] to step forward. He was, with the departure of Hopson, the most senior man in the province.[29] Lawrence had been in the province since at least 1749 and during the course of the time leading up to his appointment as the chief administrator of the province, in 1753, had had a number of direct dealings with the Acadians. The record[30] gives us some indication that he was not liked by the Acadians; thus, it is likely, that his appointment was greeted, in the Acadian way, with a knowing look and a silent nod of the head as the one told the other; and in the background, we might have seen, perched on an Acadian tree, there high overlooking the scene, an omen-bearing bird, such as a ball-headed eagle or a wise old owl.

Lawrence was to take no precipitous steps in the first period of his administration, mainly, I think, because he was not so sure of his power. Hopson, or another favorite of the Lords of Trade, may well show up and announce that Lawrence was to reassume his secondary position; he was after all just holding things down until he heard from England. Lawrence did hear from England; and, to his great gratification, he was to receive papers on October 6th, 1754, direct from England: Charles Lawrence was to be the Lieutenant-Governor of Nova Scotia. On October 21st, amidst pomp and ceremony, Lawrence was officially sworn in at Halifax by Jonathan Belcher, who, by the way, and at the same time as Lawrence, was to learn of his appointment as the first Chief Justice of Nova Scotia. Winter was soon to close in, and those in Nova Scotia, whether English, French or Indian, would stick close to their respective home fires. In the spring, however, we see Lawrence writing his commander at Piziquid. Monckton's forces had just sailed from Boston and the plans were now set to attack the French garrison at Fort Beauséjour. Lawrence wanted to give a stern warning to the Acadians; whom, he, as a careful military man, only ever considered were but a dangerous threat at the backs of the English.

I [Lawrence] desire you [Captain Murray at Piziquid] would, at this time also, acquaint the Deputies that their Happiness and future welfare depends very much on their present behaviour, & that they may be assured, if any Inhabitant either old or Young should offer to go to Beauséjour, or to take arms or induce others to commit any Act of Hostility upon the English, or to make any Declaration in favour of the French, they will be treated as Rebels, their Estates and Families undergo immediate Military Execution, and their persons if apprehended shall suffer the utmost Rigour of the Law, and every severity that I can inflict; and on the other Hand such Inhabitants as behave like English Subjects, shall enjoy English Liberty & Protection.[31]

Chapter 7

The Deportation Orders

Clear the whole country of bad subjects ... and disperse them among ... the colonies upon the continent of America. ... Collect them up by any means. ... Send them off to Philadelphia, New York, Connecticut and to Boston.

Thus it was — with this order of Governor Lawrence's, dated August 11th, 1755 — an entire people were yanked off their lands like so many weeds; a consigned cargo, to be herded and prodded onto wooden sailing vessels. The fate of these people was then to be in the hands of ship captains for weeks, months in some instances; many were to die and slipped into watery graves; and those that survived were then placed in the hands of foreign governors who took them to be but a great nuisance and a great burden. How did it ever come to this! We have in our previous chapter, reviewed the forty-five year relationship of the French Acadians and their English masters. The deportation of the Acadians, while considered at times, was never to be a plan that was set. Even with the dawn of the new year, 1755, where we last left off: no such plan existed. Yet, before the year was out, the Acadians were banished from their ancestral lands; their homes and much of their possessions — burnt; their livestock killed or only to die unattended during the ensuing winter.

Among the ambitious plans made by the English at the Council at Alexandria during April of 1755, none are to be found in respect to the removal of the Acadians. The Acadian deportation took place as an afterthought and as a result of orders taken at the local level. What was planned by the English royal governors at Alexandria was that there should be a pre-emptive strike against the French, notwithstanding that the two countries were not then at war with one another, at four different points in North America carried out at the same time. The one that concerns us is that which was made by Colonel Robert

Monckton against Fort Beauséjour. What is very significant to the subsequent events of 1755 — very significant, indeed — is, not just that the English defeated the French and took their fort at Fort Beauséjour but they managed to do so within a matter of a couple of weeks.

Governor Lawrence was not to directly involve himself in the attack on Fort Beauséjour. At first, one will wonder why he didn't travel up to Chignecto and get in on the action? Lawrence, after all, was an English military officer, and, indeed, Monckton's superior. It was not unusual that a royal governor should lead troops into battle. Governor Shirley of Massachusetts, for example, was leading the companion attack in 1755 against Fort Niagara; and, as we will see, Lawrence himself was with General Amherst during the Second Siege of Louisbourg in 1758. While it might be expected that Lawrence was at Halifax so he could perfect his plans to deport the Acadians (I think not); the fact is that Halifax was an important place which was vulnerable to French attack. Further, some very important naval officers from England were calling by at Halifax, and, it was likely thought that they should receive the personal attention of the governor, himself. I refer to Admiral Boscawen, who, with his fleet of twenty-one ships of war, was cruising off the coast trying to nab French war ships. These English vessels and their officers and men were in and out of Halifax harbor throughout the spring and summer; indeed, at one point captured French men-of-war, the *Alcide* and the *Lys*, were brought into Halifax together with a sizable number of French prisoners.

Lawrence, by May 25th, would have been advised that the transports with the New England troops were about to leave Boston and that it would be but a matter of days before Monckton with his forces of about 2500 men would be at the gates of Fort Beauséjour. Lawrence was fearful that fighting men from Acadia might head to the isthmus with a view to assisting the French. Thus we see, where, on May 25th, Lawrence wrote one of his key commanders, Captain Murray at Piziquid.

I desire you would, at this time also, acquaint the Deputies that their Happiness and future welfare depends very much on their present behaviour, & that they may be assured, if any Inhabitant either old or Young should offer to go to Beauséjour, or to take arms or induce others to commit any Act of Hostility upon the English, or to make any Declaration in favour of the French, they will be treated as Rebels, their Estates and Families undergo immediate Military Execution, and their persons if apprehended shall suffer the utmost Rigour of the Law, and every severity that I can inflict; and on the other Hand such Inhabitants as behave like English Subjects, shall enjoy English Liberty & Protection.[1]

Piziquid, being but 50 miles from it, was one of the closest Acadian communities to Halifax which since 1749 was the English seat of government in Nova Scotia. Fort Edward was located at Piziquid, situated on a rise with a commanding view of the Piziquid Valley.[2] Any significant movement of the French Acadians would likely be spotted from the ramparts at Fort Edward. Captain Alexander Murray,[3] the forty year old Scot in charge at that time, kept a careful eye on the local population and was taking steps to enforce the governor's order. No food was to be moved about on account of the corn embargo.[4] Further, he denied the Acadians the use of their boats, so necessary in those days for communication and for fishing. And further, he required the Acadians to hand in their arms, which, of course, the Acadians needed for their protection and the hunting of game.

These actions of Captain Murray were to cause consternation among the French inhabitants. Meetings were held which led to the preparation of a petition. The petition was addressed to Governor Lawrence, dated at Minas, June 10th, 1755, from all the inhabitants and signed by 25 of them. It was worded in a formal and respectful manner and requesting that they be restored to "the same liberty that we enjoyed formerly, giving us the use of our canoes, either to transport our provisions from one river to the other, or for the purpose of fishing; thereby providing for our livelihood." As for the guns: an order, according to this petition, had been posted at Fort Edward on June the 4th requiring that all guns be carried to the fort. The inhabitants explained that their guns are needed to protect their stock from wild animals. And that: "It is not the gun which an inhabitant possesses, that will induce him to revolt, nor the privation of the same gun that will make him more faithful; but his conscience alone must induce him to maintain his oath." These pleas, as were contained in the petition, and as were sent down to Halifax, were received by Lawrence at about the same time as the news that the French at Fort Beauséjour had surrendered to Monckton.[5] This news from the isthmus, pleasant as it was, undoubtedly surprised Lawrence: in such a speedy time was Monckton able to accomplish his objective! And so, at just about this point, a few days before or a few days after, into Lawrence's hands comes this, this petition from the Acadians listing their grievances; it was but, as far as Lawrence was concerned, just another example of the presumptuousness of the Acadians.

Not much time was to lapse before Governor Lawrence sent a courier overland to Fort Edward. The message to Captain Murray was that he should round up the people who signed the petition and they should be sent to Halifax to see him, as he had a few words for them.[6] At Piziquid, ten of the 25 signatories pleaded sickness, the other fifteen were packed off to Halifax. On July 3rd, Lawrence sat with his Council[7] and the fifteen Acadian deputies were paraded before Council in their chambers at the Governor's House. I set out, next following, extracts from the minutes[8] of that meeting:

The Deputies were then called in and the Names of the Subscribers to the Memorial read over, and such of them as were present, ordered to Answer to their Names, which they did to the number of fifteen, the others being Sick, after which the Memorial itself was again read, and they were severely reprimanded for their Audacity in Subscribing and Presenting so impertinent a Paper, but in Compassion to their Weakness and Ignorance of the Nature of our Constitution, especially in Matters of Government, and as the Memorialists had presented a subsequent one, and had shewn an Appearance of Concern for their past behaviour therein, and had then presented themselves before the Council with great Submission and Repentance, The Council informed them they were still ready to treat them with Lenity ...

That they had not only furnished the Enemy with Provisions and Ammunition, but had refused to supply the Inhabitants, or Government, with

Provisions, and when they did Supply, they have exacted three times the Price for which they were sold at other Markets. That they had been indolent and Idle on their Lands, had neglected Husbandry, and the Cultivation of the Soil, and had been of no use to the Province either in Husbandry, Trade or Fishery, but had been rather an Obstruction to the King's Intentions in the Settlement. ... All His Majesty's Subjects are protected in the Enjoyment of every Liberty, while they continue Loyal and faithfull to the Crown, and when they become false and disloyal they forfeit that Protection. ...

That they wanted their Canoes for carrying Provisions to the Enemy, and not for their own use or the Fishery, That by a Law of this Province. All Persons are restrained from carrying Provisions from one Port to another, and every Vessel, Canoe or Bark found with Provisions is forfeited, and a Penalty is inflicted on the Owners. ...

That Guns are no part of their Goods, as they have no Right to keep Arms. By the Laws of England, All Roman Catholicks are restrained from having Arms, and they are Subject to Penalties if Arms are found in their Houses. ...

They were then informed that a very fair Opportunity now presented itself to them to Manifest the reality of their Obedience to the Government by immediately taking the Oath of Allegiance in the Common Form before the Council. Their Reply to this Proposal was, That they were not come prepared to resolve the Council on that head. They were then told that they very well knew for these Six Years past, the same thing had been often proposed to them and had been as often evaded ...

They then desired to leave to retire to consult among themselves, which they were permitted to do, when after near an hour's Recess, They returned with the same Answer, That they could not consent to take the Oath as prescribed without consulting the General Body, but that they were ready to take it as they had done before.... the Council [could not] accept their taking the Oath in any other way than as all other His Majesty's Subjects were obliged by Law to do when called upon, and that it was now expected they should do so, which they still declining, they were allowed till the next Morning at Ten of the Clock to come to a Resolution.

So, the meeting adjourned and reconvened the following day, the 5th. The Acadian deputies were once again brought before the Council. Now that they had a night to sleep on it — had they changed their minds? No! "They declared they could not consent to take the oath in the form required without consulting the body."[9] With this, the Council responded that it was these Acadians who stood before them that they addressed, and the oath was to be signed, then and there; and, if they did not do so, they could not be considered as British citizens; but rather considered as subjects of the King of France and would be treated as such. They were then ordered out of the room while Council considered what might be done. In a short space of time, while waiting in the halls, it dawned on the deputies that the bitter end had come; and the English now had a prescription in mind for their refusals. The waiting deputies were ordered to return from the halls and paraded once again back into the Council Chambers. Hardly had they assembled in the room, when they (the deputies) declared they had changed their minds and would now sign an unconditional oath. Silence — it was, as if, they were not heard. Then the spokesman, we might imagine, looked up from his desk, from his papers, plume in hand and after a pregnant pause, spoke:

... there was no reason to hope their proposed compliance proceeded from an honest mind, and could be esteemed only the effect of compulsion and force, and is contrary [to law] ... whereby persons who have once refused to take the oaths cannot be afterwards permitted to take them, but are considered as Popish Recusants; therefore they would not now be indulged with such permission, and they were thereupon ordered into confinement.[10]

As to what occurred next is determinable from a despatch that Lawrence had sent off to The Lords of Trade. It is dated at Halifax, 18th July, 1755:

... they [the deputies] were ordered to be kept prisoners at Georges Island, where they were immediately conducted. They have since earnestly desired to be admitted to take the oath, but have not been admitted, nor will any answer be given them until we see how the rest of the inhabitants are disposed.

I have ordered new deputies to be elected, and sent hither immediately, and am determined to bring the Inhabitants to a compliance, or rid the province of such perfidious subjects.[11]

At this time there was at Halifax two admirals: Edward Boscawen and Savage Mostyn. I referred earlier to the fact that Boscawen's fleet of twenty-one ships of war were then operating in the area. Letters (dated the 14th), with the approval of Council, had been delivered to both of the admirals who were then, apparently, resting themselves at Halifax. Lawrence invited them to attend the meetings of Council in order to discuss the security of the province.[12] The first Council meeting in which the admirals were in attendance was held on the 15th. It was at this meeting, as the minutes disclose, that a decision was taken to retain the 2,000 troops (militia from New England) then at the isthmus of Chignecto[13] and that the transports "should be immediately discharged to avoid unnecessary expense." I might observe, that this last decision, to discharge the transport ships, is consistent with keeping the troops; it is not, however, consistent with any discussion to transport the Acadians. The Council and the admirals — and, the minutes of the 15th reflect this — were continuing to wait on word from the population, in general, whether they intended to take the oath, or not.

On Friday, the 25th, another meeting of Council was convened. In attendance, were the admirals, and, so too, was John Rous having just come in from rooting the French out at the Saint John. At this meeting (25th), yet another petition from the Acadians of the Annapolis River was presented. This time it was signed by 207 French Acadians. The Acadian deputies from the Annapolis River area had come to present the petition in person. The substance of their position, was, that while they would deliver up their guns, they were resolved not to take any kind of a new oath; and that, "if it was the [English] king's intentions to force them to quit their lands, they hoped that they should be allowed a convenient time for their departure." Was this a bluff? It could have been: for there was now a forty year plus history where the Acadians independently (though always respectfully) determined that they would sign no absolute oath; and the British never were seen to force the issue. Or, were the Acadians genuinely ready to leave the fertile Acadian valleys that they had occupied for generations and cast themselves into an uncertain future? No matter what the Acadians thought of it, the British, this time around, intended to force their hand. I quote from the minutes of this meeting held on the 25th of July:

They were then told that they must now resolve either to Take the Oath without any Reserve or else to quit their Lands, for that Affairs were now at such a Crisis in America that no delay could be admitted, that the French had obliged us to Take up Arms in our Defence against their Encroachments, and it was unknown what Steps they might take further, for which Reason if they (the Inhabitants) would not become Subjects to all Intents and purposes, they could not be suffered to remain in the Country. Upon which they said they were determined One and All, rather to quit their Lands than to Take any other Oath than what they had done before. The Council then told them that they ought very seriously to consider the Consequences of their Refusal, That if they once refused the Oath, they would never after be permitted to Take it, but would infallibly loose their Possessions; That the Council were unwilling to hurry them into a Determination upon an Affair of so much Consequence to them, and therefore they should be allowed till next Monday at Ten of the Clock in the forenoon to reconsider the matter and form their Resolution; when their final Answer would be expected.[14]

Monday, July the 28th, arrived. This is a day to be remembered: by all Acadians, since, and for a long time yet to come. A number of them were now at Halifax. In addition to the deputies that had arrived earlier and who had assembled before Council the Friday just passed, there were those who had newly arrived, apparently over the weekend, from the Piziquid and Minas areas. The original Piziquid and Minas deputies, as we have seen, had been imprisoned on July the 5th, and, from what I can see, were still waiting out their time on an island within easy view of Halifax. These Acadians, the cream of their communities, were there to speak for their people. Persistent, they were, as was reflected in two new petitions; one signed at Piziquid on July 22nd, by one hundred and three Acadian head-men; and, another, at Minas, signed by two hundred and three. Same message — They would sign no new oath. "We will never prove so fickle as to take an oath which changes, ever so little, the conditions and the privileges obtained for us by our sovereigns and our fathers in the past."[15]

The rest and balance of the Acadian deputies were then sent off to Georges Island; prisoners, all.[16]

The minds of the Council members had been made up. If they were to receive such refusals at this deadline meeting of

July 28th, then they would transport the Acadians out of the province. They had earlier consulted with Jonathan Belcher, in his capacity as the Chief Justice of Nova Scotia (never mind, that, as a Councilor, he was in on the decision). He dutifully prepared a report (it was dated the very day, the 28th of July, 1755) one that the Council felt they needed to support the steps they were about to take. What was necessary, was to dress their decision up so it would appear less than the dastardly outrage that indeed it was. This judicial report, this judicial decision, recounted the history of the relationship of the Acadians and their English masters since the *Treaty of Utrecht* (1713); and concluded, as a matter of law, that in the interests of His Majesty, as Chief Justice Belcher was to advise in his judgment "that all the French inhabitants may be removed from the Province."[17]

[I should say, at this point, that no request was made of the Board of Trade (the principal colonial authority at London) for authority to deport the Acadians. It is not for me to speculate what the Board of Trade might have said of the plan if it had been set before them. Certainly after the event they gave it very little notice, mainly, I suppose, because in the succeeding years England was very busy fighting a war.[18] Earlier, on March 4th of 1754, the Lords Of Trade did write Lawrence: "The more we consider this point the more nice and difficult it appears to us; for, as on the one hand great caution ought to be used to avoid giving any alarm, and creating such a diffidence in their minds as might induce them to quit the province, and by their numbers add strength to the French settlements, so on the other hand we should be equally cautious of creating an improper and false confidence in them, that by a perseverance in refusing to take the Oath of Allegiance, they may gradually work out in their own way a right to their lands, and to the benefit & protection of the law, which they are not entitled to but on that condition."[19] To which, on August 1st, 1754, Lawrence replied: "They have not for a long time brought anything to our markets, but, on the other hand, have carried everything to the French and Indians, whom they have always assisted with provisions, quarters and intelligence; and, indeed, while they remain without taking the oath of allegiance (which they never will do till they are forced), and have incendiary French priests among them, there is no hope of their amendment. As they possess the best and largest tracts of land in the Province, it cannot be settled while they remain in this situation, and though I would be very far from attempting such a step without your lordships' approbation, yet I cannot help being of the opinion that it would be much better, if they refused the oath, that they were away."[20]]

In any event, it is clear, that the decision to deport the Acadians was one that was taken at the local level (Governor Lawrence and his Council). Even if he felt he had to clear the intended deportation with England — there was no time for it in these days of sail. Here was an opportunity to be seized upon. The Acadians boldly refused to take an oath of loyalty. Nothing new. They had done this in the past, and with no consequences. The difference this time, was that Lawrence had 2,000 troops who were but a couple of days away, who had been contracted at Boston for a year's service; and who now had not much to do since the capitulation of Fort Beauséjour on June 16th, 1755.

The meeting of Council on July 28th was all but over when the Acadian men were led away as prisoners. After the clamor of the exited Acadians faded away, the Council then made their fateful decision and recorded it into the minutes:

After mature Consideration, it was unanimously Agreed That, to prevent as much as possible their Attempting to return and molest the Settlers that may be set down on their Lands, it would be most proper to send them to be distributed amongst the several Colonies on the Continent, and that a sufficient Number of Vessels should be hired with all possible Expedition for that purpose.[21]

In a letter dated the 31st of July, Monckton was advised of the decision, and it continued:

In the mean time, it will be necessary to keep this measure as secret as possible, as well to prevent their attempting to escape, as to carry off their cattle &c.; and the better to effect this you will endeavour to fall upon some stratagem to get the men, both young and old (especially the heads of families) into your power and detain them till the transports shall arrive, so as that they may be ready to be shipped off; for when this is done it is not much to be feared that the women and children will attempt to go away and carry off the cattle. But least they should, it will not only be very proper to secure all their Shallops, Boats, Canoes and every other vessel you can lay your hands upon; But also to send out parties to all suspected roads and places from time to time, that they may be thereby intercepted. As their whole stock of Cattle and Corn is forfeited to the Crown by their rebellion, and must be secured & apply'd towards a reimbursement of the expense the government will be at in transporting them out of the Country, care must be had that nobody make any bargain for purchasing them under any colour or pretence whatever; if they do the sale will be void, for the inhabitants have now (since the order in Council) no property in them, nor will they be allowed to carry away the least thing but their ready money and household furniture.

The officers commanding the Fort at Piziquid and the Garrison of Annapolis Royal have nearly the same orders in relation to the interior Inhabitants.[22]

Thus the wheels were set in motion; and, on August 11th, Lawrence gave directions to the commandants at the garrisons at Annapolis, Chignecto, Piziquid, Minas and Cobequid, which directions included the following:

... you will give each of the masters their sailing orders in writing to proceed according to the above destination, and upon their arrival immediately to wait on the Governor or Commander-in-chief of the provinces to which they are bound with the said letters, and to make all possible despatch in debarking their passengers, and obtaining certificates thereof agreeable to the form aforesaid; and you will in these orders make it a particular injunction to the said masters to be as careful and watchful as possible during the whole course of the passage, to prevent the passengers making any attempt to seize upon the vessels, by allowing only a small number to be upon the decks at one time, and all other necessary precautions to prevent the bad consequences of such attempts; and that they be particularly careful that the inhabitants carry no arms, nor other offensive weapons on board with them at their embarkation, and also that they see the provisions regularly issued to the people agreeable to the allowance proportioned in Mr. George Saul's instructions.

You will use all the means necessary for collecting the people together, so as to get them on board. If you find that fair means will not do it with them, you must proceed by the most vigorous measures possible, not only in compelling them to embark, but in depriving those who escape of all means of shelter or support, by burning their houses and destroying everything that may afford them the means of subsistence in the country.[23]

Chapter 8

Winslow's Departure
For Grand Pré

At the end of May, 1755, 2,000 troops from New England, mustered at Boston, sailed up the coast and were to came ashore at the Isthmus of Chignecto, there to combine with a a number of British regulars who, for the most part, had been stationed at nearby Fort Lawrence. From there the combined English force, on June the 2nd, marched on Fort Beauséjour. The French fort capitulated on the 16th of June. With the surrender of the subsidiary French fort, Fort Gaspereau, on the 18th and with the routing of the French at the Saint John on 30th, all of the northern parts of Acadia, before the month of June was out, were brought under English control.

The English forces at Chignecto consisted of two battalions of men which were raised up out of the civilian population in New England for up to one year's service in Nova Scotia. One battalion was under Colonel George Scott and the other under Colonel John Winslow, with the combined force under Colonel Robert Monckton. It was not expected that the French would have given up their fort in such short order. The English troops were in sufficient number, and so equipped and supplied, that they were ready for a longish siege. However, as it turned out, by mid-June, the primary objective, the taking of Fort Beauséjour, was achieved. For the balance of the month of June the troops were kept relatively busy putting Fort Beauséjour back into shape, filling in the siege trenches, and consolidating their hold by taking the subsidiary forts at the Gaspereau and at the Saint John. The month of July arrived and with it a question which came to the minds of all the English soldiers, officers and men alike. What's next?

An army of men must be kept busy and generally can be if there is good supervision and an objective which is plainly placed before them. The supervision of the troops at Chignecto was good enough, but there was, as a practical matter, nothing much for the 2,500 men to do. John Thomas, a surgeon's mate, one of the men who came in with the English forces to Chignecto kept a diary. On the 5th of July, we see where he wrote, "This evening there is a great disturbance in camp among the people by reason of their not having their allowance of rum. Several were committed to [the guard house] for words tending to mutiny."[1] Numerous references were made to trouble in the English camp at the isthmus as the summer of 1755 wore on.[2] Time and time again, court martials were held and whippings handed out. At one point we see Winslow reminding his captains: "Whereas divers men from the camp straggle about without orders and in danger themselves. Lievt Colo Winslow acquaints both officers and soldiers that there is a standing order that the roll should be called three times a day in the presence of an officer of each company & expects that order to be strictly obeyed."[3]

Colonel Monckton was a regular army officer, and, like all regular army officers, had little regard for the average colonial soldier. Why, such an individual came right off the farm! Can it be expected, that, in a week or two, he can be turned into a real soldier. This lot at Chignecto, was, to Monckton, all too typical. Monckton was not only upset with their behavior but also with their appearance. In his orders of July 7th, as promulgated by his adjutant, we see: "Col Monckton desires the officers [Winslow and Scott] commanding the two New England battalions take care that their captains provide their men with shirts and other necessarys who having observed many of them who have not changed their shirts since their first putting them on at Boston [six weeks back]. Likewise many of them he has taken notice are in great want of shoes & stockings."[4] Monckton's view of the New England officer was not much better. Though these militia officers had standing in their respective communities and some wealth due to their activities, oft as not as merchants, they were still but rustic colonials. What did they know of military matters: they but pretend they know. There was of course the incident of August 14th which illustrates the point perfectly. Colonel Winslow had been then appointed by Governor Lawrence to take his battalion, at least in part, to Minas and superintend the deportation of the Acadians at that place. Winslow was doing his march pass in front of Fort Cumberland (as the English had renamed Fort Beauséjour) when Monckton sent his adjutant, his assistant, Mr. Moncrieffe, to advise Winslow that it was not appropriate to be marching along with his standard unfurled, or some other such problem with the standard, as it didn't appear to suit Monckton's view of proper military protocol. Another example, was where, just after the French had signed the articles of capitulation, Winslow wrote Monckton the next day advising he "should be glad of the favor of a copy of the capitulation that I [Winslow] may send it to my Col., Governor Shirley who doubtless will expect it from me." To which Monckton in a rather imperious manner replied, "I shall despatch the vessel to Boston. You will be pleased therefore to send me your letters, and, as through my hands the terms of capitulation ought to be sent. You will be so good as to refer Governor Shirley to me on that head."[5]

The following day Winslow wrote Monckton, just before he sailed, explaining that he found it surprising that "my colours being struck yesterday" in that Winslow took it that the colors went with "the commanding officer." And that, it sure looked odd that the conquered French should be allowed to march away with their colors flying "and that we who assisted to conquer them were not permitted." Monckton wasted no time in writing back the same day saying he couldn't see any grounds for Winslow to get upset. Monckton was the commanding officer and no colors were to be removed without the commanding officer's permission. At any rate the colors were to remain where the largest part of the regiment was to be; and Winslow had simply taken off a small detachment. The fact of the matter is, as Winslow was to confide in his journal, his men were off on several different posts and he had the largest contingent with him.[6]

The relationship between Winslow and Monckton, as between the 52 year old colonial gentleman and the 29 year old army field officer from England to whom Winslow was obliged to report, was, to say the least, strained.[7] These feelings of superiority which were generally to be found among all of the regular English military officers that came to America goaded the English colonial leaders so badly that by 1776, they had had it with their English cousins and opted for declaring themselves independent. I should say, that this difficulty as existed between colonial militia and regular army officers from the continent was not peculiar to the English, the same kind of problem existed with the French in North America.

Winslow, though he gave little notice of it, must have wanted to get out from under Monckton's command as soon as possible. He wrote Governor Lawrence at Halifax, arranging to get his letter to him directly rather than through Monckton.[8] Lawrence and Winslow had never met and Winslow knew that Monckton was Lawrence's man, so, Winslow chose his words carefully. He thus managed to bring himself to Governor Lawrence's attention in a timely fashion, so that, when the orders went up to Monckton to send a detachment down to Minas to see to the rounding up of the Acadians at that place, Lawrence was to personally ask for Winslow.[9]

It took a couple of days for a determination as to how large the Minas detachment should be and of whom it should consist. During this time, on August 12th, word of General Braddock's defeat at Fort Duquesne (Pittsburgh) was received at Chignecto.[10] This news, that the general with most all of his army had been killed or wounded due to a trap laid by the French and their allies while on their way to attack a French fort (near present day Pittsburgh), had to have a very depressive effect on all of the officers and troops in Nova Scotia, and would make them all the more wary in their dealings with the French and their allies in Nova Scotia. In any event, on August the 15th, Winslow's detachment of men and officers went aboard three vessels in order to proceed to Piziquid: the sloop, *York*; the schooner, *Grayhound*; and the schooner, *Warren*. Three hundred and thirteen men were to go aboard: Winslow and three captains (Nathan Adams, Humphrey Hobbs & Phinias Osgood), 6 lieutenants, 4 ensigns, 15 sergeants, 12 corporals, 6 drummers and 264 privates.[11]

John Winslow, on leaving Beauséjour, due to his run-in with Monckton, and due too, to the news of General Braddock's defeat, as Francis Parkman wrote, was "ruffled in spirit."[12] He sailed southwest to just out of the mouth of Chignecto Bay and then sharply southeast around Cape Chignecto and into the second and largest arm of the Bay of Fundy. The vessels held their course southeast while skirting Advocate Bay and around Cape d'Or, then, northeast-east with Cape Split at their bows. Things would have been timed for a slack tide so that the whirling waters of Cape Split might be avoided. Clearing this spectacular head of land, where the north mountain range of Nova Scotia drops off to the sea, Winslow's vessels carried on in, into Minas Basin, a body of water protecting the mariner from all sides. It was mid August and the land was heavy with bounty; indeed the Acadians were in the fields taking in the grains needed for the winter. The entire land was ripe and full, and the short northern growing season was soon to be at an end.[13]

Chapter 9

Winslow's Arrival
At Grand Pré

A Short History of Minas:

The Bay of Fundy splits itself against a rock like a carrot piercing itself into ill-cultivated ground; the rock in this case is Cape Chignecto, which sends the fast rising tides of water of the bay of Fundy left and right of the Cobequid Mountains. The cleavage of the Fundy results in two separate bodies of tidal water; the one continuing northeast as the true extension of the larger bay, the Bay of Fundy; and the other which fits its way, twice a day, through a pincered channel and into Minas Basin which runs directly east. The northeast extension of the Bay of Fundy is known as Chignecto Bay, and it splits itself again on Cape Maringouin into two smaller tidal basins, Shepody Bay and Cumberland Basin (which in the days under review was known as Beaubassin). The eastern extension of the Bay of Fundy is known as Minas Basin; it is isoscelar like with its base to the west and its apex to the east; its sides run fifty miles or so, and its base is twenty. It was on the south-western shoulder of Minas Basin that the greatest Acadian population was to occur: below the sheltering highland of Blomidon, areas flooded by their respective rivers: Pereaux, Habitant, Canard, St. Antoine (Cornwallis, these days) and the Gaspereau. This area was populated by the Acadians for a very good reason. They contain flood plains which have been silted up by the high tides of the Fundy system for centuries, and centuries. No back breaking clearing of the land was much required and the soil with a minimum of toil yielded its produce in great abundance, year after year. These are the legendary Acadian lands which we simply know as Minas.

As to who determined that the area should be named Minas is a question not answered by our histories. What we do know, is, that Minas was a name struck because it was thought, by the earlier French explorers, that there existed on the shores of Minas Basin sought-after metals and that mines existed in these southern parts of Acadia. The area was first explored by Poutrincourt during August of 1612. To these early French explorers it was, no doubt, virgin territory, though there had to be communities of MicMac who occupied the key fishing places at the mouths of the rivers flowing into the basin.

The territory is located between two rivers, at the delta formed between the St. Antoine and the Gaspereau and upon which we now focus: the fabled, Grand Pré. Grand Pré was first settled in 1680. Two of the founders, "proceeding independently of each other,"[1] were Pierre Theriault and Pierre Melanson. Soon the inner southern banks of the Minas Basin, up its creeks, away from easy access by English vessels, were to be found the families headed by Jean Theriault, Martin Aucoin, Philippe Pinet, and Francois Lapierre.[2]

Just within a few years of it first being settled an important event was to occur at Minas, for that matter, for all of Acadia. A pastoral visit was paid during the years, 1685-6, by Jacques de Meules, the Intendant at Canada who was traveling together with the bishop.[3] The principal historical significance of this event is that Meulles caused a census to be conducted. The result showed that the total population of Acadia, in the year 1686, was only 885 persons, of which, 592 were at Port Royal, 127 at Beaubassin, and but 57 at Minas.[4] I quote from an earlier part of this history:

> Prior to 1686 there was not much of a settlement to be found at Minas, this because of the uncertainty of title. As is the case today, no one is interested in settling in and improving lands if there is a risk of being displaced by another with a better right to title. Two influential Acadians, Bellisle (LeBorgne) and Beaubassin (Michael Leneuf de la Valliè), were at odds with one another, both asserting seigniorial rights to the lands at Minas. Thus, there was to be found only 57 people at Minas (1686 census); none at Piziquid (Windsor) or Cobequid (Truro). Hitherto, this land dispute held development back.

Intendant Meulles, being on site, brought the dispute to an end by giving the nod to Belleisle, who was then to be the seignior at both Port Royal and Minas; there was, therefore and thereafter, to be a significant transfer of population from Port Royal to the Minas area. At this time, too, Cobequid (present day Truro) Matthieu Martin (b.1636), a life long bachelor, having received one of the few signeuries ever given out in old Acadia, planted a settlement on the River Wecobequitk (Cobequid, the present day Truro).[5]

The population at Minas was to immediately pick up, such that by 1689 it was 164, compared to that of 57 reported in 1686. This growth was at the expense of Port Royal which went from 592 to 461. There was to be an impressive growth of the population in the Minas area (excluding Cobequid) through the next twenty years such that by 1707, at 577, it had the largest number of Acadians of all the Acadian areas. England and France were at peace (one of their longest stretches). Acadia was English territory so the French had no direct say in Acadian affairs, and, as for the English, well — they had but a small garrison at Annapolis Royal. Thus being bothered little by authority (the great unlearned lesson) the Acadians prospered for most of the first half of the 18th century with family and church taking precedence over all matters. Their loving ways led naturally to large families. During the years, 1710 to 1750, the Acadian population ballooned out: it went from 1,500 to 10,000. And while exact numbers for the Minas area are not available, we might guess that on the eve of the deportation, in 1755, there had to be around 3,000 Acadians in the western parts of the Minas Basin area.[6]

Winslow's Arrival at Grand Pré:

It was on August 16th that an English detachment of soldiers under Colonel John Winslow, consisting of 313 men and officers,[7] departed Chignecto. They had been embarked on three sailing vessels: the sloop, *York*; the schooner, *Grayhound*; and the schooner, *Warren*. They were under Governor Lawrence's orders to set up camp in the Minas area; and there, to carry out their mission: by fair means or foul.[8] Their task: to bring the Acadians together and ready them for their removal out of the province.

The sail down from Chignecto was to cover a distance of approximately a hundred miles. And even if the tides and the winds could be worked to advantage the trip would normally exceed a day. They came to anchor and laid over on the night of the 17th. On August the 18th the three vessels "stood up the River Piziquid to Fort Piziquid at which we arrived at eleven o'clock in the forenoon."[9] Winslow and certain of his officers would have disembarked, but I imagine the men for the most part would have stayed aboard the vessels until it was determined how they should be disposed. As Winslow proceeded along the shore and up the hill to Fort Edward, he was to perceive that things at Piziquid presented a "fine pleasant situation."[10] Acting under Cornwallis' orders, Fort Edward had been built by Lawrence during the summer of 1750 and doubtlessly was expanded and improved upon in the course of the following five years such that it was much more than the block house which we may yet see there today.

At Fort Edward, Winslow "waited on Capt Murray and dined with him & the gents." It was during this time that Winslow was given Lawrence's letter of instructions which Murray was holding for him. In this letter Winslow read that the inhabitants were to be kept in the dark. "Suffer as little as possible any communication between the inhabitants and the soldiers and between the former and Mr. Mauger's people.[11] And above all things keep from their knowledge the news relating to General Braddock."[12] Further, Winslow is to learn that Lawrence desires that Winslow is to quarter his troops at Mines around the church at Grand Pré.

Winslow was not to spend much time at Piziquid, though long enough to exchange pleasantries with Captain Murray and to start a letter to Governor Lawrence. In this letter, Winslow explained that he had but eight days of provisions which neither included butter nor molasses for brewing and that he would trust to Lawrence's "fatherly care for our future supply, which I hope will come seasonably." Further, he suggested that more of his men be sent to him from Chignecto so that he might be able to better carry out the job that is before him. "One thing I would just hint that is that the body of the regiment is and may be encamped under the cannon of the garrison at Chignecto and that the party with me are in open country have neither cannon nor any protection ..." Specifically he thinks that "the whole or part Gorham's Rangers could be spared for our assistance," as they are familiar with the country in and around Minas, and, Winslow and his New Englanders were not.

On the next day, the 19th, we would have seen Winslow and his detachment, on the first tide, slip over to Grand Pré, but a dozen miles from Fort Edward. He entered the River Gaspereau and landed his forces. Winslow and his men were in anticipation that "it is likely shall soon have our hands full of disagreeable business to remove people from their ancient habitations." He took up his quarters "between the Church and the Chapel yard, having the priest house[13] for my own accommodation and the church for a place of arms."[14] On the 21st, we see from his diary, where he "gave orders for picketing in our encampment." This he had intended to do the moment he had arrived, "a line of pickets from the church to the church yard."[15]

One of the first things Winslow did upon his arrival at Grand Pré on the 19th, was to break out his writing material. He added to the letter to Governor Lawrence which he had started the day before at Fort Edward, he wrote: "Arrived at Grand Pré and have viewed the situation and pleased with the place proposed by your excellency for our reception (the church). Shall secure the party; run a line of pickets ..." A second letter was then written up and directed to Captain Handfield at Annapolis Royal.[16] In this letter, Winslow explained that while he had received powder and ball from Captain Murray at Fort Edward, he was in need of flints as his men have only those that are in their flintlocks. "Should be glad you would by Capt Adams send me 600 that are good and I will either replace them, or send an order to discharge your store of them, I am etc."[17] Then a third piece of paper parchment was drawn out, upon which, Winslow wrote out the first of his orders to the local inhabitants:

To: The Deputies & Principal Inhabitants Of The Several Districts Of Grand Pré River Habitants River Aux Canard.
You are hereby required to appear at my headquatres of incampment at the mass house at Grand Pere at nine of ye clock tomorrow morning.
Hereof fail not, on your peril.
Given under my hand at Grand Pré, the 19th of August, 1755.

The following day, on the 20th, "several deputies & principals met as was yesterday directed." Winslow simply explained that he was sent "to take command of the place." He further explained that he had little in the way of provisions but he expected to receive "supplies by water." In the meantime he would like to be supplied by them. "They agreed & said that they would collect means together so as to furnish me at Saturday & continue to grant me supplies til such time as I was otherways relieved." Further, we see from Winslow's journal, where, on his second day, on the 20th, he "marked out the ground for our encampment." Winslow and his staff then moved into certain of the enclosed houses near the Acadian church, making the whole of the complex their headquarters.

On the 21st, as mentioned, Winslow "gave orders for picketing in our encampment to prevent our being surprised & broke ground on the southerly side next to the plain of Grand Pré. Worked very briskly. All hands employed, some fetching pickets, others in digging, clearing away rubbish, etc. Patrol: Johnson."[18]

So, Winslow's objective of setting up a camp at the center of one of the major Acadian communities, Grand Pré, was, by the 21st of August, well under way.[19] When Winslow arrived at Grand Pré in 1755 it consisted of a cluster of rustic wooden homes on rising ground south of a flat plain which the Acadians had captured from the sea through the use of dykes. These Acadians, all related to one degree or another, farmed this rich plain that stretched away to the north, towards another rise which was once an island. The Acadians had built and expanded upon dykes leading away from the mainland to each end of the island. Their homes were not on this plain, I repeat, but on the rising lands (thus to be free of potential floods) to the south and north of it. In the background, beyond the dykes, beyond the ensconced green, east and west, will be seen, at low tide, masses of red mud which cover the long shores everywhere in the Fundy system. Beyond again, to the north and east, is the blue of the Minas Basin water; and beyond that, to the north is Cape Blomidon, its red cliffs pincering off the western extremity of Minas basin; and then as one's eyes scan to the northeast, well over the blue waters and very much in the distance, a line of hills marking the Cobequid range which shelters and closes in the fifty mile long northern shore line of the Minas Basin.

Grand Pré is a flat delta extended by manmade dykes. To the west of it is the mouth of the Rivière St. Antoine (renamed by the English the Cornwallis River). To the east of it is the mouth of the Gaspereau River. These two rivers arise in the west and flood out into the Minas Basin. At low tide the rivers discharge themselves right out into the capturing basin. On the high tide, the world's highest tide (20 feet plus), the sea water of the Minas Basin reverse matters and run up the rivers for a number of miles with considerable force, at first; a most strange occurrence for those who first lay their eyes on these wonderful rivers of Minas Basin. Of the two river systems, the St. Antoine (Cornwallis) is larger than the Gaspereau, both in length and breath. While running pretty much parallel, and but only a few miles from one another, the St. Antoine and the Gaspereau flow along two distinct river valleys being separated by a rise of high ground. If one travels up the Rivière-des-Mines, as the St. Antoine (Cornwallis) was alternately called by the original French inhabitants, one will be traveling along the central core of the larger valley which today we label the Annapolis Valley. Going east on easy ground, within twenty miles, the St. Antoine peters out and a few miles beyond that one picks up the head waters of the Annapolis River (which in the earlier days was called by the French La Rivière Du Dauphin) which flows west and empties at the western end of the Annapolis Valley where at its mouth is the old capital of Acadia, Port Royal, renamed Annapolis Royal by the English on its capture in 1710. The valley is but five to seven miles wide, and runs northeast a distance of sixty miles connecting up Annapolis Royal in the west to Grand Pré in the east; and, all along, one will see lands which are among the most fertile in all of northeastern America. The highland to the north-west, is known as the North Mountains, a range which blocks the cold north winds and which hides the ocean waters of the Fundy Bay lying beyond. This northern range abruptly comes to an end at a spectacular bluff, Cape Blomidon. Below it, the series of rivers to which we previously referred: the Pereaux, the Habitant, the Canard, the St. Antoine and the Gaspereau: on the banks of them all, would have been found Acadian Inhabitants. And between the last two, the St. Antoine and the Gaspereau, is found Grand Pré: the spring from which the spiritual soul of all Acadians come. In August of 1755 it was a place where the English colonel, John Winslow, commanded his men to erect their tents and surround themselves with pickets and from which place went out English orders for the inhabitants of these rivers to gather together, as, there was to be an important message to be read to them.

Chapter 10

Preparations At Grand Pré

Within days of his arrival, on the 19th of August, Colonel John Winslow had situated himself fairly well at Grand Pré. On the 23rd, he wrote Captain Murray at Piziquid, Fort Edward, some 12 miles away, requesting nails and a lock; also, in the letter we see where Winslow gives a picture of his situation: "there is a small house within the pickets of which I have made the captains [three of them] quartres. One thing I still lack is a guard room, and have a frame up and partly enclosed and old boards sufficient to cover it."[1] Winslow's force, consisting of 313 men and officers, had been detached from the larger force of 2,500 men, which, as we have seen, had assembled themselves at Chignecto earlier in the year. Three days after Winslow arrived, he gave orders for a work party of forty men to unload the three vessels which had brought Winslow and his men over from Chignecto. We would have seen these vessels just at the west bank of the Gaspereau River, likely propped up, and, high and dry at low tide. One half of this work party was to attend to the unloading and the other half to the stowing of the provisions in the church which had been cleared of all of its usual ecclesiastic accoutrements. In the meantime, the other work of securing the camp, such as picketing, continued.[2]

There is every indication that Winslow was liked by his men even though he was strict, as I suppose every good officer must be. On the 26th of August, with the men now pretty much settled in, he was to forbid the playing of cards, for fear, "that they neglect their duty and get an idle habit." Further, on August 28th, he ordered:

Whereas playing of quoites[3] within the camp tends to brake the sword [sod?] and spoil the encampment. Those gentlemen and soldiers who have a liking to that exercise on the north side or in the rear of the pickets and as it is observed that the soldiers are not so exact as could be wished in regard to cleanliness in the camp leaving cabbage leaves, pea pods, etc., among their tents which in a little time become noisome. Therefore ordered that every person within the line take care to throw out all their cast provisions, greens, etc., not used, without the pickets in the front of the camp and not less than thirty feet from the gate on the left hand. For fatigue [work party] four men from each company to assist the well diggers and one sergeant or corporal to each command. Patrol — Newberry.[4]

It is plain, that if Colonel Winslow didn't want his men hanging about and falling into "idle habits" it would be best to employ them in the business for which they were sent; the rounding up and the placing of the inhabitants upon the transports. These transports had to come in from distant parts. In the meantime, Winslow and his fellow officer at Fort Edward, Captain Murray, did not want to take any steps that would alarm the Acadians. They would like to numb these people with surprise, and, while in such a state, carry out this "disagreeable business." They did not intend to take any precipitous steps until the transports arrived. In the meantime, the unsuspecting Acadians went about taking care of themselves and their farms, and, in particular, bringing in their field crops.[5] The Acadians did not know what it was that the English had in store for them. The officers swore one another and their respective men to secrecy: there was to be no alarm until the trap was fully set and the springs ready to be sprung. The Acadians far out numbered their would be captors and no opportunity or time was to be given to the Acadians for fear they might organize themselves and prove to be a problem. The English wanted to handle the Acadians, when the right moment came, like so many sheep to be herded up and put into their floating stalls.

On August 30th, three transports came in from Boston: the *Mary*, the *Endeavour* and the *Industry*.[6] These were the first of a sizable number of sailing vessels which Governor Lawrence had arranged to come up from Boston under government charter. These first three, that had came into Winslow's area, Minas basin, had been dispatched by Chas. Apthorp & Son (Thomas Hancock) on August the 21st. The Acadians at Grand Pré were now to see three sailing vessels in the stream at the mouth of the Gaspereau. Their leaders, to the extent they had any — the best of them had been taken away from their people and imprisoned on Georges Island at Halifax earlier that summer — must have at this point begun to put things together. All these English soldiers? These large sailing vessels? What's up?[7] They were to be kept wondering for a number of days, yet.

During the first week in September two more transports came in: the *Elizabeth* on the 4th and the *Leynord* on the 6th. Winslow's work, in conjunction with Murray at Piziquid, could now start in earnest. The arrival of these last two was to put a plan that had been struck by Murray and Winslow on a better footing. On the evening of August 29th, as is disclosed in Winslow's journal, Murray had made his way over from Fort Edward at Piziquid to pay a visit to his more senior officer and to coordinate plans.[8] Murray stayed only as long as it took to hand over the latest dispatches from Governor Lawrence and to settle on a date on which they would both take the first step. A note of this first meeting was recorded in Winslow's journal, as follows:

> I consulted methods for removing the whole [of the] inhabitants ... and [Winslow and Murray] agreed that it would be most convenient to sight [command] all the male inhabitants ... to assemble at the church in this place [Grand Pré] on the 5th of September next to hear the King's Orders, and that at the same time Capt. Murray to collect the inhabitants of Piziquid, and villages adjacent to Fort Edward for the same purpose ...

After Murray had left, Winslow assembled his three captains (Adams, Hobbs and Osgood) and brought them up to date; and, consistent with the plan to keep the Acadians in the dark, he swore them to secrecy. It was important to the English plan that they should not alarm the Acadians. As Winslow wrote, "after taking an oath of secrecy from them laid before them my instructions and papers and also of the proposed agreements made between Capt. Murray and myself of which they unanimously approved." Just as this meeting was being held, or shortly thereafter, on August the 30th, the first of the three transport vessels, to which I earlier made reference, having come up from Boston, hoved into view.

September of 1755 arrived. These were to be busy days. As for the Acadians: they, not knowing of the English plans, were very much involved in the harvesting of their crops. As for the English: they secretly went about making preparations for the deportation. One difficulty was that Winslow and his New Englanders were not familiar with the country. On arrival, Winslow wondered in a letter to Governor Lawrence if "the whole or part Gorham's Rangers could be spared for our assistance." Despite the request, no one was sent up from Halifax, presumably because all their men were needed to man their own defenses; so, Winslow turned to Captain Murray at Fort Edward. The two had met, as we have seen, on August the 29th, likely at that time Winslow made a request of Captain Murray to send a party of his regulars who had been stationed in the area for some time. Winslow, it would appear agreed to exchange some of his own New Englanders for the regulars sent over from Fort Edward. On September the 1st or the 2nd, similar detachments of soldiers headed out; one from Grand Pré, the other from Fort Edward to meet at the "foarding place."[9] Murray sent one Lieutenant, one sergeant, one corporal and 30 private men.[10]

A date had been picked, yet, there were still details to be worked out in respect to the coordinated action against the Acadians. It was intended that another visit between Winslow and Murray should take place. When Murray heard the news at Fort Edward that the first three transports had arrived, indeed, just hours after he had left Grand Pré, he wrote a message to Winslow: "I hear some vessels are arrived at Mines which I suppose are the transports, if so, I think the sooner we strike the stroke the better, therefore, will be glad to see you here as soon as conveniently you can."[11] One of the details to be worked out was the form of the order to be directed to the Acadians. Murray had a draft ready for Winslow's review.

(It should be pointed out, at this juncture, that Captain Murray had taken into his confidence, a 33 year old Swiss civilian, a Protestant who spoke French, Isaac Deschamps. Deschamps was in charge of the truck-house owned by an entrepreneur at Halifax, one, Joshua Mauger. This truck-house — a store-house for trading with both the Acadians and the Indians — was located at Piziquid, if not within the confines of the fort then likely very handy to it. Murray had brought Deschamps into the loop and apprised him of the plans; it was, after all, necessary to have someone translate the English orders into French.[12])

On September 2nd, Winslow set out with a small contingent in the "whale boat for Fort Edward ... to consult with capt. Murray in this critical conjuncture." Winslow left early in the morning and was soon inside the picketed fort at Piziquid. There he and Murray were to settle on the wording of the following citation:

TO The Inhabitants of the district of Grand Pré, Mines River, Cannard, etc, as well ancient as young men & lades:

Whereas his Excellency [etc., etc] proposed lately ... and has ordered us to communicate ... his Majesty's intentions ... such as they have been given him.

I therefore order and strictly enjoin by these presents to all the inhabitants as well of the above districts as of all the other districts. Both old men and young men, as well as all the lads of ten years of age, to attend at the church in Grand Pré on Friday, the fifth instant, at three of the clock in the afternoon, that we may impart what we are ordered to communicate to them; declaring that no excuse will be admitted on any pretence whatsoever, on pain of forfeiting goods and chattels in default.

GIVEN at Grand Pré the Second of September in the 29th year of His Majesty's reign, A.D. 1755.

Before the morning was out, Winslow and his small party were sailing back to Grand Pré. He had in his pouch a good copy of the citation translated into French. He arrived at his camp at two o'clock in the afternoon. Winslow was to immediately call for his officers: copies of the citation were to go out, to be posted in all conspicuous places so as to come to the attention of all the inhabitants. Captain Adams and party went off to the communities of Habitants River (the Canning area) and Canard River, in particular to the center of the Acadian life in that area, the Church of St. Joseph at Canard. Adams reported back, "that it was a fine country full of inhabitants, a beautiful church & abundance of goods of the world. Provisions of all kinds in great plenty."[13] By the next day Captain Adams' party had returned, and, another party under Captain Hobbs (with one sub officer, two sergeants, two corporals and 50 private men) paid a visit to the nearby villages, making reference in particular to "the Village Melanson on the River Gaspereau." The message was spread: Acadian men, old and young, without arms,[14] were to come to the church at Grand Pré to hear of the English King's intentions.

Right along, in all of this, and in the back ground, we would have seen the Acadians, peaceful and spread out on their many farms in their river valleys. The great anguish, as we shall soon see, was to wash over them like a great sudden flood. In the meantime, they, like all farmers in the northern part of the continents when hints of cold weather are blown in with the first of the autumn breezes, had crops to get in. As for the English soldiers situated thereabouts: their tensions were rising as their nerves were being slowly stretched and strained. It was necessary, in view of the coming piece of work, for Winslow to keep his men steady. The men were required to stay in camp and not to go beyond the pickets unless on official duty.[15] On September the 4th, the day before all the Acadian men were to report to the church, the soldiers were required to appear on parade, so that, "their arms and ammunition be examined into as also that an inquiry be made what number of powder horns there be." Captain Murray at his desk in Fort Edward writes to his fellow officer, Winslow, but twelve miles away at Grand Pré, and to be delivered that day:

Dear Sir,
Yesterday I received a letter from Annapolis which you will get from [a runner] ... whom I have sent to look after some horses for the governor [Lawrence wanted some Acadian horses sent down to him at Halifax].

I was out yesterday at the villages [in and around Piziquid]. All the people were quiet and very busy at their harvest. If this day keeps fair all will be in ... their barns. I hope tomorrow will crown all our wishes. I am most truly with great esteem ...

Your most obedient Servant

A. Murray

On His Majesty's Service To Colo Winslow commanding his Majesty's Troops at Grand Pré.

At his quarters at Grand Pré, Winslow wrote out further orders for the day, September 4th, "The guard to be relieved tomorrow ... one hundred men strong with one captain, two subalterns, four sergeants, four corporals & two drums." Winslow emphasized that none, "neither regulars nor irregulars [are to] stir out of their lines tomorrow. ... The companys to be supplied with powder and ball at eight of the clock to morrow morning." These orders are reflected in Winslow's journal, the final line for that day being, "A fine day and the inhabitants very busy about their harvest ..."

We can imagine John Winslow closing his journal. It is late in the evening and we may have caught him looking out one of the few small windows of the Acadian cottage which he had turned into his residence but a couple of weeks back. Off in the yards there would have been a few camp fires. Then, likely, he found his long white pipe and filled its bowl from a leather pouch which he had retrieved from a shelf. He stoops to the fire place, and from its embers brings a burning taper to the pipe bowl. After assuring himself that it is lit he ambles over to the open door of the cottage and looks out. The sky is clear. The smoke curls away from his white, long handled pipe. After a couple of puffs he returns the pipe to its holder on a nearby table. A glance to his cot; then, another glance out the door. Nothing to be done now. A good sleep would serve him well for a busy day will soon be dawning.

———————

Chapter 11

Grand Pré (Part 1)

On September the 15th Winslow verified a count of the local Acadians. He was to incorporate this count into a reporting letter which he sent along to Governor Lawrence at Halifax.[1] This report has come down to us and shows the total number of Acadians with which Winslow was to deal, to be — 2,793 people. The document set forth the names of all the males in the area, Minas (excluding Piziquid) through which run the rivers: Pereaux, Habitant, Canard, St. Antoine (Cornwallis, these days) and the Gaspereau. On it, run the names, page after page. The more common surnames to be found are: Aucoin, Boudrot, Comeau, Dupuis, Granger, Hebert, Landry, LeBlanc, Melanson, and Terriot. Listed are the names of 483 men. From it, we can see that there were in these districts: 387 married women, 527 sons, 576 daughters and 820 "old & infirmed." A count of the live-stock was also set out: 1,131 bullocks, 1,422 cows, 1,959 young cattle, 7,210 sheep, 3,827 hogs and 419 horses.[2]

Prior to getting the Acadian count, on September 2nd, a citation had gone out to all the Acadian Habitants of the Minas area. All men, both old and young, including "lads of ten years of age" were ordered, to attend at the church in Grand Pré on Friday, September the 5th, at three of the clock in the afternoon, so that, they might hear of the English king's intentions; and that no excuse will be admitted if they should not appear as ordered, "on pain of forfeiting goods and chattels in default."

The idea of course was up to this point, to leave the unsuspecting Acadian farmers in their fields so to get as much of the harvest in as was possible; though, as the British knew, not for the benefit of the Acadians. The plan called for taking the well exercised Acadian men into custody before they had too much time to think about things. Their guns had been taken away from them earlier that summer by order of Captain Murray, the commander at nearby Fort Edward (Piziquid, the Windsor of today) Thus, it was hoped that the scheme would come off without shedding blood, nonetheless, extra powder and ball were served out to the men, and they were ordered to "lye upon their arms."

They came in: in all, 418 of them. Men and boys from all of the surrounding villages. They all had the same solemn expressions; and dressed, much alike, in rough woolen clothes spun by their women. Some may have arrived the day before, to be put up for the night by their relatives in the Grand Pré area.[3] Some traveled directly from their homes varying at distances of up to several miles away. They had time, as the appointed hour was not until 3 o'clock in the afternoon. Likely, just after noon a crowd around the pickets of the English camp began to thickened up. They were to be let in, so as to assemble within the church which was now at the center of the English camp. Best, I am sure the English thought, to leave the Acadians outside of the pickets until it was near the appointed hour.

Winslow had ordered a table to be set up in the middle of the Church. At the desk sat, amply backed with armed men in their red coats, the bewigged 53 year old commander with "double chin, smooth forehead, arched eyebrows, close powdered wig, and round, rubicund face; and there, now at 3 o'clock, there is a congregation of peasants, simply clad, tanned faces, anxious and intent. A motion was made for quiet. Colonel John Winslow, dressed and groomed for the occasioned, with a number of pieces of parchment before him and one in hand, then, spoke:

Gentlemen,

I have received from His Excellency, Governor Lawrence, royal instructions which I have in my hand. You have been ordered to come here together to hear his Majesty's final decision as to what is to become of the French inhabitants of this his Province of Nova Scotia. His majesty, for almost half a century, has extended more indulgences to the inhabitants of this province than to any of his subjects in any other part of his dominions. What use you have made of them, you yourself best know.

The duty I am now upon, though necessary, is very disagreeable to my nature and temper, as I know it must be grievous to you.

But it is not my business to make observations on his majesty's commands, but rather it is my duty to obey them; and, therefore, without hesitation, I shall read to you His Majesty's instructions and commands, to wit,

That your lands and tenements, cattle and live-stock of all kinds are forfeited to the Crown, together with all your other effects, except money and household goods, and that you yourselves are to be removed from this his province."

"That you will now shortly be removed from the province is certain and without appeal. However, through his majesty's goodness, I am directed to allow you the liberty of carrying with you your money and as much of your household goods as you can take without overloading the vessels you go in. I shall do everything in my power that all these goods be secured to you, and that you be not molested in carrying them away, and also that whole families shall go in the same vessel; so that this removal, which I am sensible must give you a great deal of trouble, may be made as easy as His Majesty's service will admit; and I hope that in whatever part of the world your lot may fall, you may be faithful subjects, and a peaceable and happy people.

I must also inform you that it is His Majesty's pleasure that you remain in security under the inspection and direction of the troops that I have the honour to command.[4]

And thus, almost as an afterthought, the corralled Acadian men were all declared to be prisoners and as such to be detained under guard. The English soldiers stepped forward with guns cocked and flash-pans at the ready. It was as if lightning had struck the audience. Winslow promptly took his leave of the church and proceeded out and over to his quarters at the priest's house. He was, however, unable to elude pleading French elders who managed to follow him. "Our families must be told of what is happening." Winslow then consulted with his red suited officers and it was "arranged that the Acadians should choose twenty of their number each day to revisit their homes, the rest being answerable for their return." The situation, in respect to the Acadian men, as of September 5th, 1755, was that their church was their prison. Additional arrangements were also made so as to allow for family visits; a compassionate move no doubt, but one that was to relieve the English from the trouble and the expense of seeing to their prisoners. Thereafter, during daylight hours, there was to be a steady stream of Acadian women and children who were allowed to come into the church yard. They came to see to their captured husbands, fathers and brothers; they brought baskets of food; and generally to do what they could do to keep their men well.[5]

I shall come to describe this in greater detail under the "Deportation at Chignecto"; but, what should be generally known of the Chignecto deportation, was that the Acadians at Chignecto were to resist the English as they did in no other place. The Acadians at Chignecto, being for most of its history located well away from English soldiers, were the most independent of all Acadians. There, too, at Chignecto, could be found regular French military officers, such as Boishébert, who, despite the fall of Fort Beauséjour, were able to keep pressure on the English and generally lead the resistance. One example of this was, where, on August 28th, an English officer, Major Frye, together with 200 New Englanders had been sent to destroy the villages of "Chipody, Memweamcook & Pitcondiack" and to bring in the inhabitants of those areas. Frye was surprised by a number of Acadians and in the ensuing fight Frye had 24 of his men killed.[6] By September the 5th, it is likely that this news of the troubles at the isthmus would have come to Winslow's attention; and it undoubtedly unnerved him. The fact is that Winslow had under his charge near 500 Acadian men; and he had but 300 British soldiers to control them.[7]

As for Grand Pré, due to smart moves at first, Winslow was to lessen the risk of injury to himself and his men. Straight away, on his arrival at Grand Pré on the 19th of August, he picketed in his camp. Every move was carefully coordinated with his fellow commander at Piziquid, Captain Murray. On the 5th of September, in Machiavellian fashion,[8] both Murray and Winslow locked up the Acadian men and effectively disabled the communities. The best thing, of course, for the English, was to get all the Acadians aboard the transports and clear them out and away. But, a considerable time was to pass before this was to be accomplished. The delay, due to the late arrival of the transports ships, was not only long and painful to the distressed Acadians;

but, so too, to the anxious English officers. It was, incidently, not just the seeming inability to get a sufficient number of transport vessels to Minas, but also the general need for supplies for the English soldiers and for the growing number of people being brought under their charge. Winslow's pleas to Colonel Monckton at Chignecto were completely ignored; and those made directly to Governor Lawrence were eventually to be responded to but only after an interminable delay.

Winslow was persuaded that "the government has not provided sufficient vessels." Further, he was of the view that what was to come was to come from Chignecto where Monckton was in charge. And further, Winslow was persuaded, that it was Monckton who was responsible for the delay — though, officer like, Winslow made no direct statements to that effect.[9] On August 31st, Winslow despatched an officer in the "large whale boat" with despatches that had come up from Halifax and a letter from himself to Monckton: "I apprehend you have directions to supply us with ammunition of which we stand in present need ... let not flints & cartridges be forgotten ... [also] molasses." Within the week a vessel came in from Chignecto. The requested supplies were aboard, together with 50 men. This was done, clearly on Governor Lawrence's orders, not because of any direct request made by Winslow. There was a letter delivered to Winslow by Monckton's commissary; it is telling that there was, at this time, no note from Monckton himself.

Winslow and Murray waited. They both had prisoners now under guard. What was needed were the transports in sufficient number to carry the inhabitants off. But where were they? They had five, but three times that number would be needed. Though apprehensive, due to the reported difficulties at Chignecto, Winslow experienced no trouble with his Acadians. On September the 8th Captain Murray was to write from Fort Edward: "I ... am extremely pleased that things are so clever at Grand Pré and that the poor devils are so resigned. Here [Piziquid] they are more patient than I could have expected for people in their circumstances, and, which still surprises me more, is the indifference of the women who really seem quite unconcerned."[10]

The correspondence between Murray and Winslow show the differences between the characters of the two. Winslow, though conscious of his duty, was compassionate in the manner in which he carried it out. This conclusion is supported by all of his actions and is readily spotted in his writings, for example, in writing Murray on September 5th, "Things are now very heavy on my heart." Another example is to be had in his letter to Hinshelwood at Halifax, dated September 29th, 1755, "it hurts me to hear their weeping & waling and nashing of teeth, I am in hopes our affairs will soon put on another face and we get transports and I [am] rid of the worst piece of service ever I was in." Murray, on the other hand, treated the Acadians as a sub-species: "you know our soldiers hate them and if they can find a pretense to kill them, they will ... I long much to see the poor wretches embarked and our affair a little settled and then I will do myself the pleasure of meeting you and drinking your good voyage."[11]

I mentioned that Winslow experienced no trouble with his Acadians, and, generally, throughout all of this, that seemed to have been the case; though, there were a couple of times when he was obliged to tangle with his prisoners. The first time was to occur on September the 10th. Early on that day, there was a disturbance of which we have no details. This was to bring home once again to Winslow's mind the danger of keeping 500 men prisoners when all he had was but 300 men to do the job. He hardly had enough men to act as around-the-clock guards. Then, there was the business of sending out patrols to the surrounding areas to see if indeed all the Acadian men had responded to the order to come in, to verify counts and to check on the families. And, so too, at any given time there was a detachment of men out on courier service, either to Fort Edward, or Annapolis Royal, or off in the whale boat to Chignecto. As we have seen, the transport vessels that Governor Lawrence had arranged to come up from Boston had begun to arrive on August the 30th, three of them arrived: the *Mary*, the *Endeavour* and the *Industry*.

The number was to come up to five, when, the *Elizabeth* came in on the 4th and the *Leynord* on the 6th. Now, when his concern about the trouble in camp was combined with the observation that he had five empty transports hanging on their rodes just at the mouth of the Gaspereau, a switch was thrown in Winslow's head. Why! He would — he would use these five vessels as floating prisons. These transports couldn't swallow up all the Acadian men that he had by then imprisoned; but, if he could get a couple of hundred of them onto the vessels, then, that would relieve his situation considerably.

Winslow called his officers together and informed them of his plans which he wished to carry out without delay on that day, the 10th. He would put fifty French men on each of the five transports. The youngest and strongest would be chosen. To bolster the crew of the vessels he would put aboard six soldiers on each. An armed vessel, the *Warren* (Capt. Adams) was also at the mouth of the Gaspereau River and it could act as a shepherd. The five transports and the *Warren* once loaded would then drop down into deeper water. The trick would be to get these men embarked.

At Grand Pré there was a sixty-five year old Acadian by the name of François Landry. He had a farm at la rivière des Habitants and had come, in response to the English order, to the church at Grand Pré with his sons, only to be captured there along with all the rest of the Acadian adult men. He was to become the spokesman for his fellows; this, mainly, I suppose, because he could speak English.[12] Winslow sent for Landry on the morning of the 10th and he was soon standing before Winslow, likely with cap in hand. Winslow "told him the time was come for part of the inhabitants to embark and that the number concluded for this day was 250 and that we should begin with the young men and desired he would inform his brethren of it." Landry was, as Winslow explained, "greatly surprised." Winslow responded, "it must be done." Landry was to get the Acadian men lined up in the yard six deep with the young men to the left. Winslow then told Landry that there was not much time as the transports would be pulled up at high tide — they had but an hour to get themselves ready. Now, it seems clear that Winslow did not tell Landry that he was taking this step for security reasons, seemingly not wanting to give the Acadians any idea that they, the English, were at all concerned about their position; for, every one in the camp and soon the women outside the camp came to the idea that the men were to be shipped away as a separate lot.[13] This belief on the part of the Acadians was to cause quite a scene.

All of Winslow's men, I would say a couple of hundred, were lined up with guns at the ready.[14] The Acadians were assembled. The young Acadian men, as had been directed were to the left; they were separated out and a count was made: 141 of them. Captain Adams, with eighty men, was ordered to put them under guard and march them to the vessels. These young men were ordered to march. They were all possessed with the idea that they were to be torn from their families and sent away at once; and they all, in great excitement, refused to obey the marching order. These men did not want to be separated from their fathers who were then just opposite them and on the right. These young men continued to assert they would not move without their fathers. They responded in unison — No, No, they would not move. Winslow wanted most of all to avoid blood shed, and knew that he must take the matter firmly into his hands for the sake of his own men and that of the prisoners. He dramatically stepped up and with firm resolve rudely grabbed a young French demonstrator. "I do not understand the word, "No" in the face of the king's command and shoved him with great force in the direction of the path they were to take. "There would be no parleys or delays." Winslow called out to his line of soldiers to advance with fixed bayonets. The young man picked himself up and started to move down the path, fearfully looking back over his shoulder; the rest followed, albeit slowly. They went off, as Winslow wrote in his diary, "praying, singing, and crying." The families of these men were stationed, it seems on route, one that extended for a mile and a half from the church to the bank of the river mouth. The women were inconsolable, thinking, as they did, that these dearly loved young men were to be taken away from them. They were there at stations, along the route, "in great lamentation, upon their knees, praying" with unallayed grief stamped on their faces.[15]

Soon, there followed the second lot under the escort of 80 men and Captain Osgood. The married men followed along, and, as Winslow was to put it, "the ice being broken," they did so without incident. The second group amounted to 89 men, so with the 141 young men, the English had successfully embarked 230 Acadian men aboard the five transports.[16]

Maintaining the 250 men aboard the vessels might have proven to be a problem for the English, but a simple solution was struck upon; Winslow was to allow the Acadian women who were ashore to take care of their men aboard the ships. He would "permit them to have their familys and friends provide for them their victuals and dress it and send it on board." To accomplish this, the transports would move up once a day on the high tide near the shore, and — well, Winslow explained:

> I ordered all the boats to attend on the top of every tide that should happen in the day time to receive such provisions as should be brought by the women and children for those on board their respective vessels, and that a French man come in every boat to receive and see that the provisions be delivered to each person to whom it was sent and to permit as many French people to go on board to see their friends as their several boats could carry.

Though 230 men were imprisoned on the transports, there was still left on shore, within the pickets, close on to 200 men to guard; Winslow still had his hands full. In addition to guard duty, men were needed to send out on daily patrols. So too, Winslow determined to assign certain of his men to go and assist the Acadian women and children, where needed, in order to get the crops in. These activities required all of the supervisory talent that Winslow and his three captains could muster, as, being but part time soldiers (in large part, militia from New England) there was a tendency on the part of some of the men to get out beyond the officers' sight and harass the locals.[17] Like most occupying armies, there were those among Winslow's detachment who thought that the people and their goods were there for the taking. Winslow, however, kept command over his men. Orders of the day (September 13th): "That all officers and soldiers provide them selves with water before sun set for that no party or person will be admitted out after calling the roll on any account whatever, as many bad things have been done lately, in the night ... to the distress [of] the French inhabitants in this neighbourhood and in the day when the company wants water a sergeant or corporal to go with the party who are not to suffer the men to intermeddle with the French or their effects."

On September 15th, a detachment under Captain Lewis was to arrive overland from Halifax. He had with him despatches for Captain Murray and for Colonel Winslow. He also had with him the deputies that had been held as prisoners at Halifax since early in the summer; they had been sent up so that they "may go off with their families." This newly arrived group under Lewis was to be strengthened by taking detachments from both Murray and Winslow, as was ordered, in order that Lewis might be in a position to be sent off to Cobequid. Further, Lawrence ordered Winslow to send a detachment down through the long valley to assist Major Handfield at Annapolis Royal.[18] Further, by his despatches received on the 15th, Lawrence ordered Captain Murray "to send [Piziquid to Halifax] a party twice a week to acquaint the Lieut. Governor how everything goes."

On the 17th, Winslow wrote a long report to Governor Lawrence. In this report Winslow was to observe that the Acadians "were greatly struck" by the steps that he had taken (loading their men aboard the five transports on the 10th) and was to express his belief that "they [the Acadians] did not believe then nor to this day do I imagine that they are actually to be removed." He advised how he lets twenty men off the vessels, ten for each district of Grand Pré and Canards, in order for them to check on their families and to assist in the running of the mills so that all might be fed. The men to go were picked by the Acadians themselves and required to return in twenty-four hours, when the next twenty could immediately go for the next twenty-four hours. This system seemed to work very well. Winslow then informed the governor of his disappointment that the greater number of the transports have yet to arrive, nor has the provision ship arrived which was meant to supply the transports. He heard that "Mr. Saul and the fleet" had arrived at Chignecto on August the 20th, "What's detained them I cannot tell." He then explained how he has employed "Fifty men a day for four days past to gather in the harvest to whom I ventured to promise pay, and the French women & boys assisted with their cattle to get in to the adjacent barns." The harvest, Winslow identified as oats and wheat. He would have proceeded to start killing the cattle, except for the fact that these Acadians yet considered the cattle to be their property; he would wait until the Acadians have been shipped out.[19] In any event, he has no salt for pickling purposes, "don't know where to find a peck of it in the country. Should be glad of a supply."[20] Winslow continued, "Bread is the most essential thing we want for although we are surrounded with wheat yet can't obtain one bushel of meal as the streams that carry the water mills are low." The windmills, which apparently the Acadians had, as Winslow observed, grind slowly, and ground no more than that could be, and which apparently was, immediately consumed by the inhabitants. As for the party to be sent to Cobequid: it was to go off the next day, the 18th and was, in addition to Captain Lewis, to consist of 4 lieutenants, 5 sergeants, 4 corporals and 100 privates. This contingent was made up of an equal number of men from the Grand Pré camp and from Fort Edward, consistent with Lawrence's orders. Winslow then advised, however, that he was obliged to send up to Captain Murray at Fort Edward, in order to fill up his depleted ranks, an officer (Ensign Gay), a sergeant, a corporal and 30 privates. So too, he had formed a party to go to the assistance of Major Handfield at Annapolis Royal: an officer (Lieutenant Peabody), two sergeants, a corporal and 35 privates. The Annapolis deputies, 27 of them, part of a larger group that had come up with Lewis from Halifax on the 15th were to go along with the detachment headed for Annapolis Royal.[21]

Then, Winslow, so as to fully make his point, explained how he has thirty of his men stationed on the transports, another thirty out gathering up cattle so that they can be sent to Halifax so to provision the royal navy, and, has ten men sick. He concluded, "so that in fact I have only in my camp 158 non commissioned officers and private men to guard nearly twice their number, besides doing other duty, which makes things extremely heavy and I am not quite so easy in my present circumstances as I wish to be."

On September the 19th, Winslow wrote Monckton: "Have upwards to 500 French men which with their families amount to 2,000 persons. Have parties at Cobequid, Fort Edward, Annapolis and for collecting of cattle etc. ... Should be glad Mr. Saul might be hurried with transports this way." Plainly, Winslow was of the view that his compliment of transports would come from Chignecto; but none were to come to Winslow's assistance from that quarter. Mr. Saul, a provisioner from Halifax with important connections, was indeed, by then, at Chignecto with two supply ships. Saul was victualing the Chignecto Transports that had gone directly to Chignecto, and had arrived there on August the 21st, seven of them. At the same time he wrote Monckton, Winslow wrote a couple of letters[22] to his officers and friends at Chignecto. To Major Jedidiah Preble, he wrote: "I have two Frenchmen to an Englishman, which I never could have kept had it not been for my precaution of picketing in my camp. I am really distressed for want of men, when I can't [help] but think you abound. Provisions I am also obliged to conjure for. And what detains Mr. Saul and the transports with you ... we really live well for eating but no bung save honest flipe ..."[23]

The days passed and Winslow's position deteriorated. The weather turned bad. Winslow was worried about the men who are imprisoned on the transports. In fine weather they can be supplied by their own families by boats; but when the weather is foul, then the transports are obliged to hang on their anchor rodes; and the people on board go without their food. In bad weather, some of the women folk try to get food out to their men.

There was one incident, where, apparently, a small boat capsized and all were tossed into the water, with the result that one woman was in danger of death.[24] On the 23rd, Winslow sent off another message to Handfield at Annapolis: "Encumbered with many things, I steal a moment to let you know that we are all [but holding on] ... taking care of today and letting tomorrow take care of itself. We have not had the least intelligence from any quarter ... expected ere this to have been strengthened from Chignecto, but now despair of that or of transports from that quarter." On the 25th he wrote Murray advising that he had heard that there were some French strangers in the next valley or two, away (River Habitant). He believed they have come down from the Chignecto area to encourage the Acadians in the Minas area to take a stand. He wrote, "I am extremely weak in men & some of the French say they will be prisoners but a little longer." Murray replied on the 26th, "I am amazed what can keep the transports & Saul. Surely our friend (Monckton) at Chignecto is willing to give us as much of our old neighbours company (reenforcements) as he can. I sincerely wish no accident has happened to them."

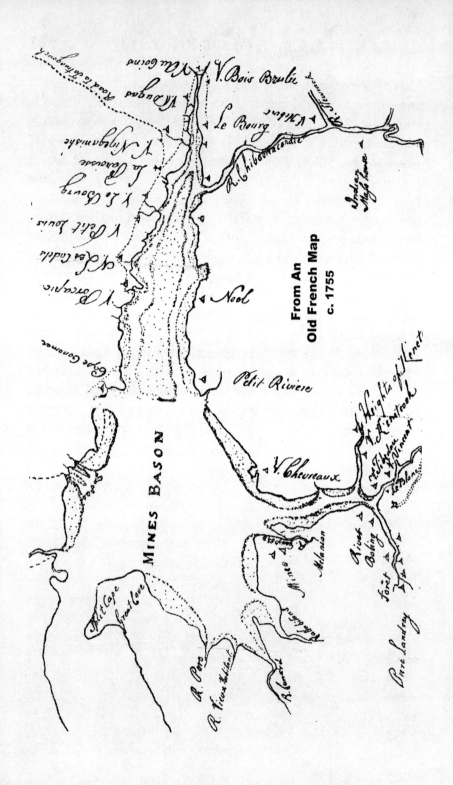

From An
Old French Map
c. 1755

Chapter 12

Grand Pré (Part 2)

On the 26th of September, in Minas Basin, sailed three newly arrived ships. Two were the provision vessels which Winslow had long expected: the *Halifax* (snow, John Taggert, master) and the *Ulysses* (sloop, Captain Rogers). The third, was a British naval vessel, HMS *Nightengale* (Captain Digges). Thomas Saul was aboard the *Halifax* and was proceeding under Governor Lawrence's instructions.[1] The *Halifax* had provisions for the transports, which, it was expected, would be lined up and waiting at Minas. However, as we have seen, there were but only five, and, three times that number was needed. The *Ulysses*, while at one point at Chignecto, had come in from the capital of Halifax, having taken aboard there, on September the 13th, provisions for "four weeks for Colo Winslow's detachment at Mines, 400 men."[2] The *Halifax*, being a snow, was a substantial vessel, I suppose it had to be, as it was to provision all of the expected transports vessels at Grand Pré, Piziquid and at Annapolis Royal. The provisioning of the vessels at Chignecto had been completed and Grand Pré was Saul's second stop. It was likely that details were given to Winslow by Saul as to the happenings at Chignecto; further, Saul had aboard letters for him from Chignecto. Only then, after some discussion with Saul — as one might conclude on an over all view and analysis of the correspondence — did Winslow come to the conclusion that he ought not, as he had right along, to expect that the needed transports would be coming from Chignecto[3]; though, he continued to hope that a couple might yet come from that quarter. Saul wanted to know what he was to do after he "victualed" the *five* transport vessels. "Where were the others?" How long was it expected that he should have to wait, as, there were transports at Annapolis Royal that were waiting on him? Chiming in would have been Captain Dudley Digges of His Majesty War Vessel, *Nightengale*. He had been detached from Admiral Boscawen's fleet, the bulk of which was then, I suppose, at Halifax. We can just hear this naval captain, "Yes! Yes! I must be moving along. We have fair winds. These transports — from where did you say they were coming? When?" These were questions that Winslow could not answer. For two days, it would appear, there were discussions between Winslow, Digges, and Saul; then Winslow, at least together with Digges, took the whale boat and sailed off to Piziquid, but 12 miles away, to consult with Captain Murray at Fort Edward. A plan had been struck which would necessitate an immediate application to the governor at Halifax, a plan that might yet save the situation.

On returning to his quarters at Grand Pré, Winslow went to his desk and drew out his writing material:

Grand Pre Camp, September 29th 1755
May It Please Your Excellency,
    I am Favored with yours of the 23 Instant, and am Greatly Pleased that my Proceedings have Met with your Excellencys approbation and it would have Doubled that Pleasure Could I inform your Excellency of the Arrival of the Transportes (you were So Good as to Mention) from Chignecto, but alas in that Pointe we Fail and are Entirely Disappointed, as Capt Taggert arrived on the 26th with Mr. Saul & the Provisions and Information that there is not more Vessels than will take the People they have, and that no Dependance Can be had of relief from that Quarter, I have also a Letter from Colo Monckton, in answer to one I wrote him Desiering to Know what Vessels Might be Depended on, and Sent in a whale Boate from this with your Excellencys Dispatches, but in return he does Not so as much Mention anything about the Transportes, have Duly Considered these things and yesterday Morning went up with a whale Boat to Forte Edward to Consult with Captain Murray on These affairs, when it was by us Determined That as Major Handfield Could Not begin his Embarkation of the Inhabitants of the River of Annapolis, til he had a Large Detachment from me as he Informed Me by the return of the Party Sent to convey the Deputys, who belonged to that River, and my officer in Passing up and Down the River Says, that all the men Left their Habitation on his approach.
    And Such a Detachment in our apprehension in our Present Situation Cannot be Spared, and that the Transportes Intended for the removing the People there are & will be Idle, Concluded it Proper to Propose to your Excellency, wither or not, it would be best that these Transportes now at Annapolis Joyne us as Soon as Possible and we Go Through with Shipping

the Inhabitants here and at Piziquid & that Others Might be provided to replace those already there while we were a Going through this party of Duty, which when over I Should be able to Send a Sufficient Force to assist Major Handfield, or if your Excellency thought Necessary the whole Party might be ordered to his assistance, your Excellency will Give me Directions in those Points, for as matters now are, the Season Growing Every Day worse and we Gaine Nothing Forward for want of Vessels am Greatly Mortifyed that we Loose Time. I have advise from Capt Lewis of the 25th Instant, that the Inhabitants of Cobequid have Entirely Deserted that Country and that he began to Burn and lay waste on the 23rd and Intended to Finish as This Day. The Boat that Brought this Express Brought one of our Party who had the Misfortune to be Shott Through his Shoulders by a Brother Sentry when on Post taking him to be an Enemy. The Vessel that Carryed Capt Lewis party was Drove out from Cobequid Bay and arrived here this morning without a Boate & Left the party Destitute (& by whom I have this Verbal Intelligence) I have ordered her to Depart for that Place as Soon as the Tide will admit having a Good Deal of Concern for that Party.[4]

... We have Received Six Hhds Molasses from Mr. Winslow [a relative who served as a commissary Chignecto] ... I have Certain Intelligence that partys of the French Do Pass & repass across from Shepody Side over to ours & that they hold rendezvouses &c about the River Pero. As Soon as Capt Lewis returns Shall Make a Thorough Visit to that part and the old River Habitant where are Villages I have but Lately heard of and none of their Inhabitants Come in.

We are Not as yet able to Do anything in Getting out ye Grain Nor Like too til we have God rid of our French Friends ...

Capt Diggs arrived here on the 26th Instant in his Majestys Ship the *Nightengale* and Expected our People were Embarked & Informed Me that he Could remain but a Short time wither the Vessels were ready or Not, but however was Soo Good as to go up with me to Capt Murray and acquaint with the Scheme Proposed and will waite the return of this Express, wither he writes the admiral or Not I Don't Know your Excellency is Best Judge what is necessary to be Done on that account.

The French are Constantly plying me with Petitions & remonstrances with which I Shante Trouble your Excellency but with one which they So Importunate with me to Send that I Could Not put them off.

Here is one Colo Donnal an old Trader in this part recommended to me by My Friend Sir Willm Pepperell, that Says he has a Quantity of Indian Corne and Some Goods that he Imported into this Place, and the Property of them never altered, and desiers permission to take them off. I have Told him nothing Can be Done but by you Excellencys Immediate orders which I Shall waite.

Our People in Camp Suffer as their Camps are very thin & do Not Protect them from the rain or Could and Can't but apprehend their Health is in Danger, which moves me more Pressingly to alter our Situation and that as Soon as May be. Here is one jean dine [sic?] whose Parents were English and he Borne in New Yorke and is Very Serviceable here and would be Glad to remain (has Marryd a French wife). I Told him I would acquaint your Excellency & believe he would be of Service to Settlers that may Come as he has a Perfect Knowledge of the Country. Have now on Board the Transportes, 330 men.

Am with the Greatest regards your Excellencys Most Dutifull Most obedient & Humble

Servt.

John Winslow.

On his Majtys Service To His Excellency Chas Lawrence Esq Lievt Govr & Commandr in

Chief of his Majtys Province of Nova Scotia &c.[5]

On the same day, the 29th, Winslow dispatched Ensign Fasett with 30 men to travel overland *via* Fort Edward to Halifax. Time was now clearly running out, and if the governor didn't direct the transports now lying at Annapolis Royal up to Minas, then, all the work at Minas will have been for naught. Murray and Winslow waited. These were the days when messages were physically delivered in person and a considerable period of time might elapse before an exchange was completed; Halifax was two days away on foot. Winslow and Murray continued to wait and commiserate. On the 30th, Murray came down to Grand Pré and was to return that evening.

On October 4th, Ensign Fasett and his party came in from Halifax. He had with him a packet from Governor Lawrence, it contained a letter for Winslow and another for Major Handfield at Annapolis Royal. Lawrence had finally come to the realization, "we will fall short of transports." (He obviously had been of the view that Monckton at the isthmus would have enough left over to send down to Winslow.) He was in full agreement with the suggestion made in Winslow's letter of the 29th that all the transports at Annapolis Royal should be relocated to Minas, so that, those Acadians at that place might be taken off at once.

As for Handfield, Lawrence would "send him transports from hence [Halifax] in a few days[6] to replace those we take from him. Therefore you will please to hurry away the major's letter with all speed to prevent his shipping any of the people there and that you may have the vessels, as soon as possible." Winslow was to immediately act, and, within half an hour of Ensign Fasett and his party coming in, organized another party of 30 men under Lieutenant Fitch and sent them out, overland to Annapolis Royal. Fitch's detachment would have taken two days to get to Annapolis Royal. Handfield didn't waste much time implementing the orders; for, on October 10th, seven transports arrived at Grand Pré. The vessels were: the *Hannah*, the *Dolphin*, the *Three Friends*, the *Ranger*, the *Swan*, the *Sarah & Molly*, and the *Prosperous*.

They finally had their vessels; thus the deed could be done. On the 10th of October, the mouth of the Gaspereau was bristling with sails. Earlier, though, with the message having come up from Governor Lawrence on the 4th, both Murray and Winslow knew that they could start taking positive steps in the loading process. They had, it will be recalled, five vessels that had long been waiting in the stream: the *Mary*, the *Endeavour*, the *Industry*, the *Elizabeth*, and the *Leynord*. In addition, the *Neptune* was at the mouth of the Piziquid and had been there since August the 31st. With the exception of the *Elizabeth* and the *Neptune*, which it would appear were kept clear in order to transport troops, as was the case for Captain Lewis' detachment which went to Chignecto, the ships had been used, as we have seen, as floating prisons for the Acadian men which had been isolated during the early part of September. There was to be a juggle, now that the loading of the families was to commence. Each transport was to take full sets of families from one or two villages immediately adjacent.[7] I suspect that the *Mary*, *Endeavour* and the *Industry* were to continue to act as prison ships while the other transports were loaded, with the prison population being thinned as the men joined up with their respective families.

The *Elizabeth* and the *Leynord* were cleared and made ready to receive the first families from Grand Pré. Notices had gone out to the selected families to bring themselves and what of their personal possessions they could carry to the embarkation point. They were to meet on the 7th, but rainy weather delayed the embarkation of these first two vessels to the 8th. In the meantime the news that it was now to really happen, that they were to be put on vessels and sent away from their lands, swarmed from family to family. The men, too, were to get the news from the family members who came aboard the prison ships as they had been allowed to do right along. A certain group of young men, about 24 of them, in the confusion of a rain storm, on the 7th, managed to make good an escape. According to an account given by Winslow, they had gotten away from two of the "prison ships" by disguising themselves as women. (It was a regular daily event for Acadian women to go back and forth to the vessels with baskets of food for their menfolk.) They got ashore and were on the loose for a number of days. Winslow was to launch an immediate investigation: he wanted to know how these men got loose. He was to determine that the escape took place mainly through the instigation of one Francis Hebert, "either the contriver or abetter." Hebert, I believe, was one of the prisoners aboard the *Leynord*, presumably, one of the two vessels from which the young men had made their escape. Winslow was to pull Francis Hebert off the vessel together with "his effects shipt." Winslow then ordered that he should be brought to his (Hebert's) house, there, at Grand Pré. Herbert was then ordered to put all of his goods inside of his house. He then was made to stand there in front of his house, together, presumably, with a gathered crowd so that they might all witness the next event. The house was torched by the English together with all of Hebert's "effects." Then Winslow made pronouncement for all the spectators to hear, if "these men did not surrender themselves in two days, I should serve all their friends in the same manner."

Winslow's drastic measure was not to have the intended effect, at least, not for a number of days. The young Acadian men made their escape on the 7th of October, and, we see that by the 12th they were still on the loose. These were busy days for Winslow's men: a sufficient number of transports were now at Grand Pré, and that meant getting provisions and people back and forth from ship to shore; it meant getting parties of his men out to the various villages and arranging which families should go on which transports. So, there wasn't much time to go chasing run-a-ways. On the 12th however there was an encounter. I quote from Winslow's journal: "Our parties reconnoitering the country fell in with one of the French deserters, who endeavoured to make his escape on horse back. They hailed him and fired over him, but he persisted in riding off when one of our men shot him dead off his horse." Apparently, this same party Winslow had sent out met more of the deserters, and, "fired upon them, but they made their escape into the woods." These incidents on the 12th, it seems, drove the English soldiers into thinking that it was open season on any Frenchman that seem to be out of place. The problem was serious enough, such that Winslow had to restrain his men. For example, on the 13th we see this entry: "Morning Orders: Whereas orders some time since was given directing that no soldier stir out of the pickets without order saving for water and that only with a non-commissioned officer, which lately have been violated and the French inhabitants thereby injured, this is therefore to remind the soldiers of this camp of the former orders and to require strict obedience to them." It seems that a number of the ordinary soldiers were of the view that since the Acadians were going to be obliged to leave most everything behind; well, that must mean that Acadian property was free for the taking. And, it was not just the soldiers which managed to get beyond the pickets, so too the seaman — of which, as of October the 10th, there were quite a number — were coming off of the waiting transports and escort vessels and giving the Acadians unnecessary trouble. On the 13th, Winslow gives further orders: "Whereas complaint has been made to me by the French inhabitants ...

as people who come after cattle etc. ... no seaman without the master of the vessel, being with him, or an order in writing from the master showing their business, be allowed to pass higher than the Dutchman's house nor on the other side of the River Gaspereau, nor any Englishman, or Dutchman[8] stir from their quarters without orders, that an end maybe put to distressing these distressed people ..." As for the escaped Acadians: in the middle of all of this, they all came in, it seems in a peaceful manner. How this was accomplished — is not something the record shows; except that there was a promise that these young men would not be punished, and that they would all be allowed to go aboard the transports to join with their respective families with nothing more to be said about it.[9]

So it was, that the loading of the Acadian families started on October 8th, 1755. The *Elizabeth* and the *Leynord* were the first to be loaded and received 80 families from the Grand Pré region. The Acadians embarked, as Winslow was to describe in his journal, "very sullenly and unwillingly, the women in great distress carrying off their children in their arms. Others carrying their decrepit parents in their carts and all their goods. Moving in great confusion and [it] appears as a scene of woe and distress." With these two ships loaded, Winslow had no choice but to hold up for the other vessels which he had faith would be up from Annapolis Royal within a few days. In the meantime he continued to get the people on the shore sorted out in anticipation of their embarkation. So too, the men aboard the "prison ships" were being ferried about so that they may be re-assigned to their particular transport ship with their families when the right moment was to come. Captain Digges of the HMS *Nightengale* continued to complain to Winslow, as he did in his letter sent ashore on the 10th: "With great impatience I waited for these sloops from Annapolis but there is no sign of appearance, I should be glad to hear when you really expect them, we had a fair wind yesterday & the day before, what detains them." He then asked to borrow Winslow's shallop so that he can replenish his water[10]; further, he would be grateful if Winslow "could send me some yeast for bread which you were so kind to promise me the other day." Also this very English naval captain was to remind Winslow of his "promise concerning a little fresh meat, for my people, two bullocks will be of great service."[11]

No sooner had Captain Digges registered his complaint to Winslow about the non-appearance of "these sloops from Annapolis," then, on the same day, the 10th of October, seven sailing vessels, to which we have referred above, hoved into view off the shore at Grand Pré; and, it can be imagined, much to everyone's relief. Finally, after weeks of delay, Winslow had enough transports to just about do the job that he had been sent to do, seven weeks back.

The English at Grand Pré, now had their work cut out for them. The entire fleet of transports were to be, all at once — provisioned, loaded with Acadian families and made ready for sea. Three of the new arrivals[12] were designated to be sent up to Murray at Piziquid.[13] Winslow was left with nine, four of which (the *Mary*, the *Industry*, the *Indeavour* and the *Prosperous*), on October the 19th, were sent along the coast a few miles away to Pointe-des-Boudrot. There, 677 persons, being the inhabitants of Rivière-aux-Canards and Rivière-des-Habitants, were embarked.[14]

I should say, too, at about this time, to add to the gathering fleet at the mouth of the Gaspereau, there was to come in, within a day or two of the 13th, the Chignecto transports. Monckton had sent them over to rendezvous. They had aboard, 1,652 Acadians which had been embarked at Beaubassin.[15]

Things were now quickly coming to their conclusion. On the 20th of October, the four transports that had been loaded at Piziquid dropped down the basin to join the other vessels which were still being loaded at Grand Pré. They had sailed from Piziquid with over a 1,000 Acadians aboard. The provision ship, *Halifax*, accompanied them and Murray was aboard. It seems, then, that there was some juggling of the people as between the fourteen Minas transports, which, by then, had collected up in the one spot; such, that the four transports that came in from Piziquid were to have their numbers reduced. I think these British officers, particularly Winslow, were very conscious of the problems of over crowding and were doing all they could do to relieve the problem. One of the steps taken was to press into service a trading vessel, which, having come up from New England, was just then at Minas. This vessel was the *Seaflower*. The *Seaflower* took up a number of the Piziquid Acadians, which Winslow could plainly see, were crowded on those vessels which Murray had loaded up.

A good recap of the above events which were to unfold after the seven transports came in from Annapolis Royal on October the 10th, can be found in a contemporaneous letter which Winslow had sent to Governor Lawrence:

> After the arrival of the seven sail from Annapolis, three of them, after victualing, I sent forward to Captain Murray at Fort Edward. The others remained at Minas, and after two days to fill water and take on board wood, we began to embark the inhabitants & shipt the whole at Grand Pré & River Gaspereau. And, to expedite this affair, sent Capt Adams with half of my party to encamp between the River Canard & Inhabitant at a place called Boudrot Point, where the whole inhabitants of those rivers and all Larure Habitants [?] & Peron were ordered to be & in compliance of those orders actually came with their whole families & effects and having been given orders to the transports that had the inhabitants of Grand Pré etc. on board on the 18th. On the 19th went to Boudrot Point to dispatch those collected there ..."

Winslow continued in his written report:

> On the 21st was completed & the transports fell down under convoy of Captain Adams [I believe this to be Captain Abraham Adams of the *Warren*] to the *Nightengale*, Captain Diggs [the man-of-war which Admiral Boscawen had sent up from Halifax and which arrived at Grand Pré on September the 27th, whose captain was most anxious to get underway]. And although I put in more than two to a ton, and the people greatly crowded,[16] yet remains on my hands for want of transports the whole villages of Antoine & Landry & some of Cannard amounting to 98 families & upwards of six hundred souls, all of which I have removed from Boudrot Point to Grand Pré, where I have at present set them down in houses nearest the camp and permit them to be with their families upon their word of being at any call ready to embark and answering to their names upon the roll call at sun set in the camp.[17]

So it was, that we would have seen, on October 27th, 1755, a fleet of twenty-four sailing vessels making their way out of the

Minas Basin on an ebbing tide. Of the 21 transports, fourteen carried Acadians from Minas and seven from Chignecto. There were three armed vessels which escorted the fleet.[18] Of the seven transports from Chignecto there were 1,652 Acadians aboard; the five from Piziquid, 1,062; the five from Grand Pré, 826; and the four from Rivers Canard and Habitant, 677. Thus, on that day, a grand total of 4,217 Acadians were borne out of the Minas Basin, away, from their native lands.[19]

With most all of the Acadians gone and those that were left, five to six hundred, compressed into their cousins' homes in the Grand Pré area, the English could proceed with the execution of the final part of their plan without being bothered by "weeping & waling" Acadians. Detachments spread out into the Acadian countryside; and, then, proceeded to torch every standing structure they came upon. Close up, there was the crackle and heat of raging fires; and, in the nearby fields, animals,[20] some on the scurry, others looking on over their shoulders, seemingly wondering; and, in the distance, all about, stretching everywhere, twirling white plumes reach into the blue. Within two weeks, excluding those at Grand Pré, 698 wooden structures went up in smoke.[21]

With his work all but done Winslow broke up his forces,[22] and, leaving Grand Pré, set out for Halifax by foot on November 13th.[23] He left behind Capt. Phineas Osgood together with 130 men.[24] Winslow had seen to the deportation of 1,510, but yet left, as the noted historian Placide Gaudet figured, were 732 Acadians.[25] By November the 29th we see that Winslow was at Halifax and was writing the commander at Minas. He expressed the hope that there will be no further "delay in putting a finishing stroke to the removal of our friends, the French."[26] In December, Osgood, with four more transports having been found, cleared out the last of the Acadians. He then burnt the remainder of the wooden structures at Grand Pré and departed overland for Halifax, leaving, no evidence of the Acadian occupation except the blackened ruins of stone foundations.

Chapter 13

Piziquid & Annapolis

The Deportation at Piziquid:

To a large degree the events at Piziquid have already been dealt with, as was necessary, when we reviewed in the last couple of chapters the Acadian deportation at Grand Pré. Piziquid is but the northeastern area of the larger territory of which it forms part: Minas. The deportation of the inhabitants of River Gaspereau and Grand Pré, and of Rivers Canard and Habitant, was directly superintended by Colonel John Winslow. Piziquid — which, then had the only English fort in the Minas area — was under the direct command of Captain Alexander Murray. Thus, it is, that many of the particulars — to the extent we know them[1] — have already been dealt with in these pages; I but use this section to give additional background and to fill in some of that material peculiar to Piziquid and to which I have yet to refer.

In 1680, we have seen, the Minas area was first settled by a few Acadian families that came up from Port Royal. Due to very close family connections, communications were kept up between Port Royal and the new communities at Minas. No doubt other young members of the Port Royal families decided to make the move to the fertile creeks which abound in the Minas area, the furthest ones of which would have been found in Piziquid. It was during the last of the concluding years of the 17th century and the beginning years of the 18th that the number of French inhabitants in the area significantly increased. A census of all the Acadian parishes, in 1714, show a count of 1,259 souls. The greatest concentration of Acadians was then to be found at Port Royal, it had 210 families. This is to be compared to River Habitants with 24 families; "River of Old Habitation", 5 families; River Canard, 10 families; River Gaspereau, one family (the Gautreaux family); Piziquid, 53 families; Cobequid, 22 families; and Beaubassin, 60 families.

We know little of the events that occurred in Minas in the 70 year period after the Acadians had first established themselves there. Relatively speaking, for Acadia, these were years of peace. The only records we have available to us for this period were those that were kept at Annapolis Royal, mostly minutes of Council. The Acadians, themselves (and it is for this reason that the story of Acadia, must, of necessity, be so one sided) did not keep records, as, but only the exceptional Acadian could write.[2] What we can conclude, is that for the first half of the 18th century these Acadian families prospered. They were seasonal farmers who raised cattle and sheep, and children, lots of children. Their success could be primarily contributed to the rich alluvial soils to be found thereabouts. They learned how to cut productive lands out of the salt marshes surrounding the lower reaches of the rivers that drained into Minas Basin; this they did by building earthen dykes. During these years, as a practical matter, there was no one to bother them: they depended but upon themselves and their extended families: they prospered: and they multiplied.

The fortunes of the French in North America, and for those in Acadia in particular, were to take an ominous turn, when, in 1744, *The War of the Austrian Succession* broke out. It was to end with a "treaty." [The *Treaty of Aix-la-Chapelle* (1748), as history was to show, was more of a truce then a treaty.] Both sides soon were to realize that the last war had not solved a thing and both were building up their defenses in anticipation of another. It was then that Acadia, an English possession long neglected, was to get a significant boast with the founding of Halifax in 1749 and within a couple of years of that, the fortification of peninsular Nova Scotia. With war looming and the English fearing that the Acadian population represented a potential "fifth column," there was to be renewed pressure put on the Acadians to get them to swear absolute allegiance to the British crown, something that they steadfastly maintained they would not do. Life for the Acadian farmer, beginning in 1749, was never to be the same again; and, in 1755, their way of life, as they had long known it, came abruptly to an end.

As part of the larger English plan to fortify Nova Scotia, which occurred within a couple of months of Cornwallis' arrival at Halifax in 1749, Captain John Handfield, an officer who had long been at Annapolis Royal, was ordered up with a detachment of soldiers to establish themselves at Minas. By November there was in place "a picketed fort containing a blockhouse."[3] Also, Captain St. Loe with a detachment was positioned on the western side of the Piziquid River (Falmouth). Fort Edward, on the western side (present day Windsor) was not built until the summer of 1750. Charles Lawrence, then being under the orders of Governor Cornwallis, was to personally oversee the construction using materials that were originally meant to be used in the construction of the intended fort at Chignecto. (As we have seen, Lawrence's first descent on Chignecto, in April of that year, was unsuccessful. It was to be in the fall of 1750, after Lawrence's successful second descent, that Fort Lawrence at the isthmus was built.)

During the first part of April, 1750, Lawrence and about three hundred military men moved themselves through Piziquid in order to get to Captain Handfield's fort (likely positioned on the high ground overlooking Grand Pré). Lawrence's objective was to get to the Isthmus of Chignecto in order to block the French military, which, it was rumored, had built themselves a new fort, Fort Beauséjour. These English troop movements, both in 1749 and in 1750, were to trigger discussion amongst the Acadian farmers in the area. Big trouble was brewing and they likely thought they were going to be caught in the middle of an armed conflict. So too, Indians, sworn allies of the French were making their presence felt; led, as they were, by black robed agents of the French, the most active of them at this time being Le Loutre. These Acadians, who wanted nothing but to be left alone felt seriously threatened by all sides. Thus, we see, that in April of 1750, "deputies arrive at Halifax from River Canard, Grand Pré and Piziquid, asking for leave to evacuate the Province, and to carry off their effects." They also, as James Hannay pointed out, "announced their determination not to sow their fields."

Cornwallis at this time, "replied in a most kind and conciliatory strain." If it was Indians these Acadians were concerned
about, and it seems little doubt they were, then he would see to
their protection. In March of 1751: Cornwallis strengthened the
English positions at both Piziquid (Fort Edward) and, at Minas
(*Vieux Logis*). It should be noted that a number of Acadians
(among them your compiler's ancestors), at this time, 1749-
51, did in fact depart; no matter whether they had the leave of
anyone to do so, or not. They were to feel, I am sure, that they
would be safer by getting themselves into French territory such
as Île St Jean (Prince Edward Island), Île Royale (Cape Breton)
and/or beyond the isthmus at Chignecto (New Brunswick). And
while a number of Minas Acadians left, the greater number of
them determined to continue farming their ancient lands, hoping
for the best.

As the fateful year of 1755 approached, things did not get
better. At Piziquid, matters were on a bad footing. It is not
because the inhabitants were not grateful for the facility of the
English fort, Fort Edward as it likely did have the intended
effect of keeping the Indians at bay; and too, there was now
a trading post located within the fort, or possibly just outside.
(In 1754, we would have found Isaac Deschamps, afterwards
the Chief Justice of Nova Scotia, working as a clerk in Joshua
Mauger's store at Piziquid.) On balance though, especially
with the arrival of a new English commander at Fort Edward,
Captain Alexander Murray, there was to be increasing trouble.
In the autumn of 1754, Murray reported that "the local habitants
had refused to bring in firewood and timber for Fort repairs.
It was determined that Abbé Daubin, their priest, was behind
this trouble. First summoned and then arrested, Daubin and five
Acadians are brought to Halifax under guard and sent back to
Piziquid with orders to supply the required wood."[4] In another
piece of correspondence, this time to his wife who lived in the
relatively safe confines of the fortifications at Halifax, dated
April 10th, 1755, we see where Murray wrote, "I have not been
off the Hill (Fort) since you went away excepting" a small trip to
buy some "skins" and another time to "dine with the Indians."[5]

While Murray was "dining with the Indians," the great historical pendulum in the form of English armies had commenced its swing. In its great arc it sliced away from the French their fort at the isthmus, Fort Beauséjour. The success of Monckton and his forces in the taking of Fort Beauséjour in June of 1755 gave the English the momentum to take a step they had long contemplated. And so it was, that the pendulum, with its great weight, dislodged the bulk of the Acadian population and sent them off, reeling, to foreign ports, away from their beloved Acadia.

Lawrence had a concern for the English forces which he expected would arrive at Chignecto during the latter part of May. His concern was that the French forces at Fort Beauséjour would be bolstered by men and supplies from the Minas area. On May 25th, he wrote Murray at Piziquid.

> I desire you would, at this time also, acquaint the Deputies that their Happiness and future welfare depends very much on their present behaviour, & that they may be assured, if any Inhabitant either old or Young should offer to go to Beauséjour, or to take arms or induce others to commit any Act of Hostility upon the English, or to make any Declaration in favour of the French, they will be treated as Rebels, their Estates and Families undergo immediate Military Execution, and their persons if apprehended shall suffer the utmost Rigour of the Law, and every severity that I can inflict; and on the other Hand such Inhabitants as behave like English Subjects, shall enjoy English Liberty & Protection.[6]

In June Captain Murray in obedience of this order took steps, on the representation that he is to enforce the corn embargo, and denied the Acadians the use of their boats; and further, he required the Acadians in the area of Minas to hand in their arms. As it was, on June the 16th, the French were to surrender their fort at Beauséjour, and, shortly thereafter, the English under Monckton were to take command of the entire area at the Isthmus of Chignecto. As the summer wore on, Governor Lawrence was to realize the opportunity that then presented itself. With a surplus of troops at the isthmus and with the Acadians having been effectively disarmed; he could, once and for all, deal with the vexing problem of having Frenchmen in his backyard. On the 28th of July, the governing Council at Halifax, resolved to send the Acadians out of the province, "to be distributed amongst the several colonies on the continent, and that a sufficient number of vessels should be hired with all possible expedition for that purpose." The wheels were thus put in motion. After effecting the necessary communications (a slow process in the mid 18th century) Winslow, who had been with Monckton at the isthmus, was despatched with about three hundred men to supervise the removal of the Acadians in the Minas area. He was to do this in conjunction with the commander at Piziquid, Captain Murray.

We have given details of the Grand Pré roundup of the Acadians and the confrontation at the church on September the 5th. The same thing was to occur at Piziquid except the Acadians came to Fort Edward. Details are missing, as Murray's journal, if he kept one, has not come down to us. We do know, however, that 183 men came into Fort Edward and were there imprisoned.[7] (This is to be compared to the 418 which Winslow had captured.) Murray's object was the same as that of Winslow's at Grand Pré, and Murray succeeded equally as well, if not better. The sequence of events was much the same as those that were to unfold at Grand Pré as has been dealt with, beginning with the surprise capture of the men on September the 5th. After a long and exasperating wait for the transports, finally on October 10th, a number of these transports came into Minas Basin from Annapolis Royal. Of these, three (the *Three Friends*, *Dolphin* and the *Ranger*), within a couple of days, were sent over to Piziquid, there to join the *Neptune*. These four transports were to be loaded. Then, on October the 20th, they dropped down the basin to join the other vessels at Grand Pré. On October the 27th, 1755, as we have seen, a full fleet of 24 vessels sailed out of Minas Basin. While there was yet left 500 or so Acadians at Grand Pré (shipped in December), as for the rest of Minas, and in particular the Piziquid valley, the territory, as of the end of October, 1755, was emptied of its Acadian inhabitants.[8]

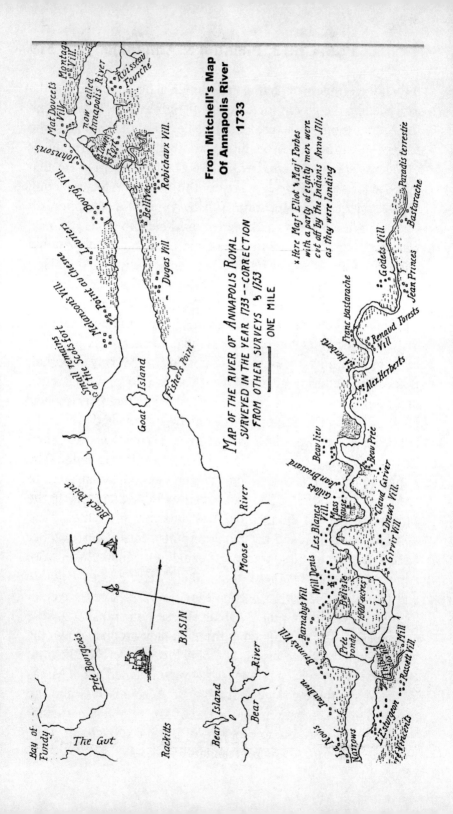

From Mitchell's Map
Of Annapolis River
1733

Map of the river of Annapolis Royal
surveyed in the year 1733 – correction
from other surveys & 1753

— ONE MILE —

x Here Majr Eliot & Majr Forbes
with a party of eighty men were
cut off by the Indians Anno 1711.
as they were landing

Bay of Fundy

The Gut

Prée Bourgeois

Black Point

BASIN

Rackitts

Bear Island

Bear River

Moose River

River

Small remains of the Scots fort

Melansons Vill.

Point au Lanniers

Bourg's Vill.

Johnsons

Mat Dovcets Vill.

Montage Vill.

now called Annapolis River

Town 1696

Ruisseau Fourche

Belliveo

Robichavx Vill.

Dugas Vill.

Goat Island

Fisher's Point

Beau lieu

Gillods

Jean Brussard

Mass House

Beau Pree

Franc bastarache

A Herberts

Alex Herberts

Renaud Forests Vill.

Godets Vill.

Paradis terrestre

Bastarache

Jean Princes

Claud Garver

Drews Vill.

Garver Vill.

Belisle

160 acres

Tribodo

Mill

Rossett Vill.

L'Esturgeon

S.t Vincents

Prée yonde

Will Denis

Les Blancs Vill.

Barnaby's Vill.

Jean Bruns

Bruns Vill.

Ft. Nauns

Narrows

The Deportation at Annapolis Royal:

We are not able to go into the details of the deportation at Annapolis Royal as we did of those at Grand Pré. This is not because the events were not as dramatic; they undoubtedly were, if not more so; it's just that we have no journals like that of Winslow's to which we might turn.

Annapolis Royal is the seat and forever the capital of Acadia. It was known during the times when the French flag flew over it, as Port Royal. Its history is intimately wrapped up in the larger History of Nova Scotia being most prominent during its earlier parts.

The French Acadian population at Annapolis Royal, particularly in the early part of the 18th century, did not experience the same growth rate as was experienced in other parts of Acadia. The families there were as prolific as ever, it's just that there was to be an outflow of young Acadians. This was as a result of a combination of two forces. The easily dyked land along the Annapolis River was becoming more scarce and certain members of the large Acadian families spread their wings and relocated to the western shores of the Minas Basin. From there, secondary waves carried along up the Minas Basin towards its eastern extremity, Cobequid. Others proceeded from Port Royal by boat to what was to be the most promising lands as found at the Isthmus of Chignecto, there to establish Beaubassin. The second force which drove the Acadians away from their ancestral seat was the near presence of a garrison of English soldiers. In 1710, the British flag was to permanently fly over the ramparts of Fort Anne. Prior to that time, as a regular occurrence, during the 17th century, New England raiders would come up and cause havoc; this in response to the French raids (initiated at Quebec) on the frontier towns of New England.

In 1755, at Annapolis, a 55 year old regular British officer, Major John Handfield,[9] was in charge. Handfield was just one of those lonely British army officers, who during the 1720s, 1730s and 1740s, during times of peace, were charged with the duty to keep safe the English king's territory of Nova Scotia. I have dealt with this era in an earlier part of this work, sufficient to say here at this place that John Handfield (unlike Winslow at Grand Pré and Murray at Piziquid) had a long connection with Annapolis Royal and a close relationship with the French inhabitants along the Annapolis River. At some point, I'm not sure when, as did other officers of the garrison, Handfield married one of the local French girls. He married one of the Winniett girls, Élizabeth (b.1713). With the arrival of Cornwallis and the general strengthening of the British presence in Acadia in 1749, Handfield was sent up in the fall of the year from Annapolis Royal with 100 men to establish a stronghold at Minas. He did not stay there long and was soon back at his command at Annapolis Royal, which is where we find him as the momentous events of 1755 were to unfold.

In the business of corralling the French in preparation for their deportation, Handfield was not as skillful as Winslow. It could be that the lie of the ground was different. More likely, it was that he could not be as calculating as his fellow officers were at Grand Pré and at Piziquid, simply because he was dealing, not with strangers, but with friends and family. When Handfield did make his play, the Acadians knew fully what was up and many of the men made their escape into the Acadian woods.[10] We see where Handfield, on August 31st, wrote Winslow asking for help. It seems Handfield had sent out a party up the river and found the various villages "destitute of all the male heads of families who are entered into the woods having taken their bedding, etc., with them, therefore I am to desire you to send me a reinforcement of men so soon as you can possibly spare them that may enforce me to bring them to reason." The next day, September 1st, another letter with the same plea was sent up from Handfield to Winslow.[11] It is interesting to note that not only was Handfield calling on Winslow for help, who himself thought he had too few soldiers to do the job, but Captain Murray at Piziquid within the next few days was to make a similar request of Winslow.[12]

Ever so conscious of his exposure — not being within a fort but rather camped in a church yard surrounded by a picket fence — and, the fact that he had too few soldiers to guard too many prisoners, Winslow was not anxious to send any of his men over to either Handfield or Murray: after all, did they not have the men which were assigned to them, and, a regular fort in which they might defend themselves and more easily confine their Acadian prisoners? Governor Lawrence, who continued throughout to stick to Halifax and supervise matters from there, knew of the needs of Murray and of Handfield; and, knew too, of the precarious position in which Winslow found himself. Lawrence had, as Winslow plainly suggested, more men that might be called upon at the isthmus. Sure it was, that Monckton needed a substantial number in order to garrison three forts (Fort Lawrence, and the captured French forts of Beauséjour and Gaspereau); but, after all, he had two thousand men, 700 of which were suppose to be under Winslow's orders, anyway. Monckton was most likely of the view that he needed the men he had and was likely reluctant to leave any of them go. Lawrence, it seems, intervened and did a re-balancing of the forces. I am not aware of the numbers, but it would appear that Lawrence ordered a hundred up from Halifax and another hundred down from Chignecto to strengthen Winslow. These movements were to take place during the first part of September. In a letter dated September 11th and received by him on the 15th, Winslow was ordered to send a detachment down through the long valley to assist Major Handfield at Annapolis Royal and on route, down the Annapolis River, to visit the Acadian communities and force the Acadian men to march with them to Annapolis Royal, advising the families to follow along with their possessions. Almost without exception, I should add, the men along the river managed to run off before the detachment come into their respective settlements: this was an experience unlike that which occurred in the Minas area.

The situation at Annapolis Royal, was that Major Handfield had seven transport vessels that had come in and were waiting in the stream off of Annapolis Royal: the *Hannah*, the *Dolphin*, the *Three Friends*, the *Ranger*, the *Swan*, the *Sarah & Molly*, and the *Prosperous*. The captains of these vessels had orders to report to Handfield at Annapolis Royal, and that they did. Now, it is recognized that Handfield had more difficulty than Winslow in getting his Acadians captured and lined up for deportation; but, in any event, he was in no position to start the embarkation process until the vessels were victualed and made ready for sea. For this he was obliged to wait, for, as we have seen, the victualing vessels under Thomas Saul were to first supply the transports at Chignecto then they were to proceed to Minas and then to Annapolis Royal, the last stop on Saul's list. Though running late, Saul arrived with his supply ships at Grand Pré on September 26th to victual the transports that he had expected would be there, and waiting. The problem was that Winslow was short of vessels, he had a few, but hardly enough. It was soon realized that unless Winslow was to get his vessels, the deportation process for both Annapolis and Minas would not proceed. So, at the suggestion of Winslow, Lawrence ordered that all the transports at Annapolis Royal should be relocated to Minas, so that the Acadians at that place might be taken off at once. As for Handfield, Lawrence would "send him transports from hence [Halifax] in a few days to replace those we take from him."[13] Winslow was to receive the governor's letter dated the 1st of October on the 4th, it having come overland, express from Halifax in the same packet as contained a letter for Major Handfield at Annapolis Royal. Within half an hour of it coming into his hands Winslow sent a party of 30 men under Lieutenant Fitch overland to Annapolis Royal.

Handfield lost no time in getting his seven vessels sent up the Fundy. They all came into the Minas Basin and reported to Winslow on the 10th of October. Matters then progressed at Minas and within 17 days the vessels were victualed and loaded with Acadians. During this time, 10 vessels came down from Chignecto to rendezvous; and, a fleet of twenty-one transports and three escorts proceeded out of the Bay of Fundy on October the 27th to carry their worried passengers to strange lands and new destinies. At Annapolis Royal — and this is the point — on October 6th, or thereabouts, Major Handfield was in the same situation which Winslow had been in for weeks: shipless. Transports, however, as promised, were to be sent up from Halifax; and while I have not determined exactly when these additional transports were to finally arrive, we do know they did, as a fleet departed Annapolis Royal on December the 8th — loaded with the Acadians of Annapolis. To achieve this goal, Handfield received additional help which Winslow had sent down at the first of November, Winslow's work at Grand Pré by then having been done.

It is to be remembered that Handfield was to oversee the deportation of the Acadians which occupied a sizable territory, mainly along the banks of the Annapolis River which had its beginnings more then half way to Minas. The plan, pretty much from the start, was that once Winslow had seen to his Acadians at Minas, he would send a sizable detachment towards the fort at Annapolis beating all of the Acadians into the waiting arms of Handfield and his men. Winslow sent a force of about 100 men to Annapolis: "On the third of November detached, per orders, Captains Adams and Hobbs, 3 subs and 90 non-commission officers and privates to assist Major Handfield to collect the inhabitants of Annapolis Royal."

Captain Nathan Adams shortly after his arrival at Annapolis, on November 10th wrote Winslow:

Honoured, Sir,
We arrived safe here Friday last [November 7th] afternoon. The way being so extremely bad, we were obliged to lodge two nights in the woods. Our party's all well. The transports are not yet arrived. Capt. Shirley[?] in his majesty's ship sailed Saturday last. Capt. Taggert [the *Halifax*, Saul's provision ship] is in this port, but Adams [Captain Adams of the *Warren*; there is a footnote, "Nov. 11th, went for Halifax] is not heard of. Nor likewise the fleet [the 24 vessels, 21 of which were transports that had left Minas Basin on the 27th of October]. Capt. Gorham embarks this day for Chignecto in a schooner just arrived from Boston ...
Your most obedient servant to command.

Unlike what had happened at Piziquid and at Grand Pré, Handfield did not, it would appear, round up the men on false pretenses and then pounce on them and hold them as prisoners until they could be embarked upon the transports with their families. He let each go their own way in exchange for a promise that they would report in with their families when the transports were ready to receive them. This approach did not work as well as that which was used by Winslow and Murray, as Murray was to observe to Winslow:

I ... am extremely pleased that things are so clever at Grand Pré and that the poor devils are so resigned. Here [Piziquid] they are more patient than I could have expected for people in their circumstances, and, which still surprises me more, is the indifference of the women who really seem quite unconcerned.

When I think of those at Annapolis, I applaud our thoughts of summoning them in. I am afraid there will be some lives lost before they are all gotten together, you know our soldiers hate them and if they can find a pretense to kill them, they will."

Due to lack of details of the deportation at Annapolis Royal, we can but only speculate on how matters proceeded. We know of the emotional difficulties which Winslow, the officer in charge at Grand Pré, had experienced and to which we have already referred. As to the rest of the English officers throughout Acadia: well, we can, on the whole, but only imagine what their reactions were to the carrying out their orders to round up and to transport the French Acadians, this, this "very disagreeable business." But this business could not have been any more disagreeable than it was to Major John Handfield, the English officer in charge at Annapolis Royal. What unfolded at Annapolis Royal is a story of great drama, and that great tale has yet to be told. There, there is Handfield married to a French Acadian, Elizabeth Winniett, the grand daughter of Pierre Maisonnat, "Baptiste," the famous French privateer. And there, there is Elizabeth's mother, Baptiste's daughter, Marie-Madeleine[14] — she was the sister to Alexandre Bourg, one of the French deputies who had been appointed to see over his French brethren at Minas and beyond. Imagine! If you will, as this English officer, this commander of the British forces throughout the territory, went about his duties — went about the business of loading his wife's close relatives onto the transports. Handfield knew most all of the senior members of this Acadian community as individuals; I imagine most all, by first names. Many of these Acadians had helped the British in their establishment at Annapolis Royal for many years. Take, for example, Louis Robichaux (1704-1780): Robichaux was a merchant at Annapolis Royal and the British troops were his best customers. He, in 1730, as did a large number of Acadians, took an unconditional oath to be "completely loyal" to George the II. During May and June of 1744, when Robichaux and the British knew an attack was imminent, he and his family employed themselves repairing the fortifications at Annapolis Royal. Because of his affiliation he "was twice plundered of his household goods and cattle and twice taken prisoner by the French. Each time they managed to escape."[15] The loyalty of those of the Robichaux family didn't help them much when the orders came down to deport all Acadians. The best that Handfield could do was to give the Robichaux family a choice as to where they wanted to go. They choose Boston and lived in the area until the American Revolution, when, loyal as they always were to the British crown, they moved to Quebec, where, in 1780, Louis Robichaux died of the scourge of the age, smallpox.

A total of 1,664 Acadians were deported from Annapolis Royal. "We have embarked 1,664 on board 2 ships, 3 snows & one Brigantine who sailed from Goat Island and the *Baltimore*, sloop of war was their convoy. It is generally judged about 300 of the inhabitants of the head of this river are gone into the woods and the remainder sent off to the great mortification of some of our friends." And, as a footnote, our contemporary witness, adds in his letter of December 8th, 1755, "This morning at 5, the fleet sailed out of the basin with a fair wind."

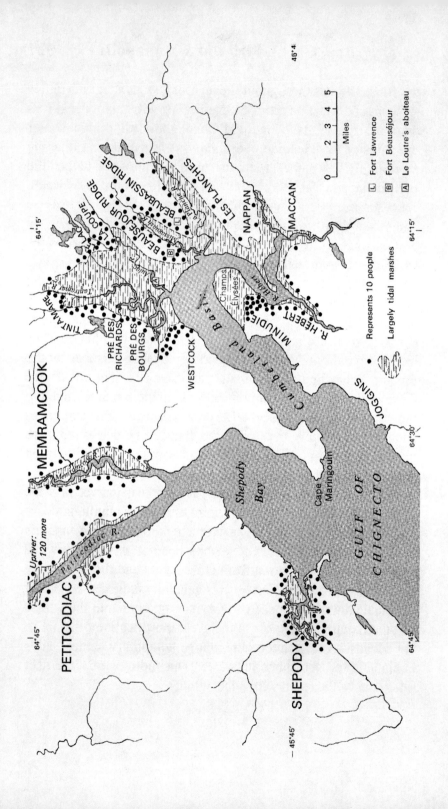

Chapter 14

Chignecto & Cobequid

In 1672, Frontenac granted a large piece of land to Michael Le Neuf sieur de La Valliere de Beaubassin (1640-1705, the elder). It was at a neck of land, the Isthmus of Chignecto, upon which hangs the almost-an-island of Nova Scotia. It was to become known as the Beaubassin seigneury.[1] In 1672, five families, having all come up from Port Royal, were located there at the isthmus.[2] The census of 1714 shows that there was 60 families.[3] In 1750, Beaubassin consisted of 140 houses and its population was more than a thousand souls.

The Acadians at Beaubassin, like most, throughout all of Acadia, were farmers making their living from the land.[4] They lived pretty much undisturbed through the years except for the occasional English privateer who would arrive and cause havoc.[5] There was no government intervention (either French or English); the people went about facing their own communal challenges and solving their own communal problems, usually through inter-family cooperation, and, where necessary, turning to an elder or two for a judgment. With the *Treaty of Utrecht* (1713), all of Acadia was to be a prize of war. Acadia then came under the command of the English governor located at Annapolis Royal, as Port Royal was then and thereafter to be known. But the territory was large, and, except for the inhabitants on their farms around the lower reaches of the Annapolis River, the presence of a small garrison of soldiers at Annapolis Royal made little difference to the average Acadian. Of the Acadian districts — Annapolis Royal, Minas, Cobequid and Chignecto — it was Chignecto that gave the most difficulty to the English; this, because it was the furthest from the English fort at Annapolis Royal.[6]

The years succeeding the *Treaty of Utrecht* through to 1744, consisting of thirty years of peace, were relatively uneventful in Acadia. The French population in Acadia increased and spread

The English presence in the province was pretty much restricted to their capital at Annapolis Royal, and, then, pretty much only within the confines of Fort Anne. The English took no steps to strengthen their position. There was to be, however, a relatively rapid change in the state of affairs, when, in Europe, the French and the English mutually declared war on one another. *The War of the Austrian Succession*, or in the simpler American nomenclature, "King George's War," invited the combatants to make raids on their respective positions at Canso, Annapolis Royal and at Louisbourg. Except for those in the immediate vicinity of the fort at Annapolis Royal, and once at Grand Pré, these battles during these years, 1744-47, had little impact on the Acadian population, but the looming clouds must have bothered them greatly. These battles were brought to an end in 1748 when the English and the French courts came to terms. The *Treaty of Aix-la-Chapelle* was signed on October 18th, 1748. In Acadia things were to be *status quo ante*. The *Treaty of Aix-la-Chapelle*, to historians, was more of a truce than a treaty. Both the English and the French knew immediately they received word that hostilities were to cease, that there was to be another war: things were still unsettled. One of these things, especially as far as the French at Quebec were concerned, was the definition of the Acadian border. They did not dispute that Acadia, since 1713, was English territory; but they were of the view that Acadia, by its "ancient limits," did not go beyond the Isthmus of Chignecto. Acadia, as the French at Quebec saw it, was but just peninsular Nova Scotia and all the land to the north and west (which would include the present day state of Maine and the Province of New Brunswick) was part of Canada, that is, French territory. Needless to say, the English were of a different view.

The intervening years between the two wars, 1748-56, were to be busy ones for both the English and the French soldiery. The English, after almost forty years of neglect, determined to fortify Nova Scotia. As for the French at Quebec, they decided to gate the English in, at the isthmus. At each end of the 12 mile long choke-point the French built two forts: Fort Beauséjour and

Fort Gaspereau. These fortifications were well begun by 1750. The French authorities then obliged all of the French inhabitants in the area to move north in behind the line which the French had determined should be the Missaguash River. The principal place for the Acadians thereabouts had long been Beaubassin which was a village south of the Missaguash. The French, to encourage the Acadians who must have been most reluctant to move off their lands and to relocate themselves to the north, resorted to a simple expedient: the French agent Le Loutre and his Indian friends torched the community.

The English plans to fortify Nova Scotia, to which we have referred, included building a fort at the isthmus were thwarted; the French outmaneuvered them. In April of 1750, Lawrence, who was then under the orders of Governor Cornwallis, made his first descent but was obliged to retreat. In the fall of that year Lawrence made his second descent with a stronger force and established himself on the south bank of the Missaguash, there to build, pawn-like, Fort Lawrence. The English continued to deny that the French from Quebec had any right to establish themselves in the area, but the English were in no position to force the issue. For five years the English and the French stared at one another over their respective ramparts.

We are thus brought to the momentous events of 1755. The English colonial governors, at the Council at Alexandria (never mind that the two countries were then not at war with one another) determined to put the "presumptuous French" in their place by launching a number of preemptive attacks, from Ohio to Acadia, all at once. The initiative with which we are concerned is that which constituted an attack on Fort Beauséjour, one which, unlike the others carried out by the English in 1755, was entirely successful. Colonel Robert Monckton led a force of 2,500 men against the French soldiers at the isthmus. On June 16th, 1755, Fort Beauséjour was surrendered to the English, and, in the result, all the territory we now know as New Brunswick was to come under English control. On June 18th, Colonel John Winslow (at this point in time at the isthmus and under the command of

Monckton) was sent with 500 men to take Fort Gaspereau situated 12 miles on the other side of the isthmus. Winslow and his men, by sunset, had finished their march and carried on right into the fort where the French commander was waiting to surrender his sword. The cleanup included transporting the French troops out of the area and up to Louisbourg.[7] On June 30th, Captain Rous in three 20-gun ships and a sloop arrived off of the mouth of Saint John. Directly the French became aware of their presence, they "burst their cannon, blew up their magazine, and fled up river."

Though the Acadians played a role in the defense of Fort Beauséjour,[8] they were generally forgiven by the English, if, for no other reason, then it was one of the terms of the capitulation. Within days of the end of the fighting, and "in consequence of the orders of the English general, a large number of the settlers came to-day, bringing their arms with them; these they laid down."[9] They were allowed to return to their farms, and, I suppose they thought life would go on as usual. Likely too, Monckton and his officers thought they would not need to take any further steps in respect to the Acadians. Certainly they recognized the importance to the English troops to have some farmers in the area. On June 21st, five days after the fighting stopped, the Acadians were coming to the English camp, there to sell "eggs, milk, fowls and strawberries," and, as John Clarence Webster observed, "doubtless did a good business."[10]

And, that was it. The English had accomplished their objective of removing the French military from the Isthmus of Chignecto. This had been done so, in fine style, and in short order. What remained, during the summer of 1755, was for them: to fill up the siege trenches, clean out the two captured French Forts and rebuild their defenses. Assuming the Acadians returned to their farms and settled down — and it would appear they did just that — there was not much to do but to sort out the numbers needed for three English garrisons (Fort Lawrence, Fort Beauséjour and Fort Gaspereau). Of the 2,500 English troops then at the isthmus, 2,200 had come up from Boston at the end of May for the specific purpose of attacking Fort Beauséjour. For the most part they were colonial militia-men and they all expected to return to their homes by the end of the season; until then, until the autumn of 1755, they were generally available for whatever duty Governor Lawrence at Halifax should assign. The Council at Halifax, on July 28th, came to a decision which would keep them all very busy for the next few months.

> After mature Consideration, it was unanimously Agreed That, to prevent as much as possible their Attempting to return and molest the Settlers that may be set down on their Lands, it would be most proper to send them [the French inhabitants of Nova Scotia] to be distributed amongst the several Colonies on the Continent, and that a sufficient Number of Vessels should be hired with all possible Expedition for that purpose.[11]

In a letter dated the 31st of July, Monckton was advised of the decision, and in part included:

> In the mean time, it will be necessary to keep this measure as secret as possible, as well to prevent their attempting to escape, as to carry off their cattle &c.; and the better to effect this you will endeavour to fall upon some stratagem to get the men, both young and old (especially the heads of families) into your power and detain them till the transports shall arrive, so as that they may be ready to be shipped off; for when this is done it is not much to be feared that the women and children will attempt to go away and carry off the cattle. But least they should, it will not only be very proper to secure all their Shallops, Boats, Canoes and every other vessel you can lay your hands upon; But also to send out parties to all suspected roads and places from time to time, that they may be thereby intercepted. As their whole stock of Cattle and Corn is forfeited to the Crown by their rebellion, and must be secured & apply'd towards a reimbursement of the expense the government will be at in transporting them out of the Country, care must be had that nobody make any bargain for purchasing them under any colour or pretence whatever; if they do the sale will be void, for the inhabitants have now (since the order in Council) no property in them, nor will they be allowed to carry away the least thing but their ready money and household furniture.
> The offers commanding the Fort at Piziquid and the Garrison of Annapolis Royal have nearly the same orders in relation to the interior Inhabitants.[12]

By his journal entry of August 5th, we see where Monckton received orders from Lawrence "in relation to the sending off the French Inhabitants."[13] On the 10th, the "inhabitants of the neighboring villages mustered in considerable but not so many as expected; upon which they were ordered to tarry all night under the guns of the garrison ..." On the 11th, Monckton proclaimed at Fort Cumberland (as Fort Beauséjour was to be called) to "all officers and soldiers, all settlers, followers and retainers to the camp" that "all oxen, horses, cows, sheep, and all cattle what soever which were the property of the French inhabitants are become forfeited to his Majesty."[14] Following, immediately after this, on the 11th of August, with very little ceremony, the gathered French Acadian men, 400 of them, were declared to be "rebels" and promptly locked up.[15] (This was a pattern — gather them up on false pretenses, then pounce — that was followed by Winslow when he went over to Grand Pré at the end of the month.)

Within a couple of days of the Acadian men being locked up, Monckton's force was reduced by 313 men. Three vessels: the sloop, *York*; the schooner, *Grayhound*; and the schooner, *Warren* (with Winslow's detachment aboard) set sail on August the 16th for Grand Pré. This would still have left approximately 2,000 men under Monckton's command at the isthmus.[16] After Winslow's departure, there would have been considerable movement as the English troops redistributed themselves nearer the forts.[17] It seems, too, immediately Monckton had received his orders, he despatched squads of men to comb the countryside so to bring in more of the Acadian men, and in the process torch any Acadian structure they should come upon.[18] It was during the course of one of these forays, which purpose was to spread ruin and desolation in the Acadian lands at the isthmus, that the Acadians were to rear up and show their teeth.[19]

On August the 28th, Monckton despatched from Fort Cumberland Major Frye with a party of 200 men. They boarded vessels "to go to Sheperday & take what French they could & burn their villages there & at Petcojak."[20] It is doubtful that Major Frye was to see many Acadians as he and his troops first set about their business: the Acadians, so it was thought, had run off. That there were no Acadians about, meant for easy work.

And so, they started in and burnt 253 buildings. Instead of keeping his 200 men together, which he apparently had been told to do, Frye broke his forces down into smaller groups so as to more efficiently carry out the work at hand. One of these detached parties, while industrially going about their incendiary duties were surprised, when, about 300 French and Indians came bounding out of the nearby woods. They were led by a French officer, Boishébert. They came howling down upon their enemies with guns blazing. Frye's force, before gaining the safety of the transports, which were anchored just off the shore, was badly beaten and a sizable number of the English were "killed, wounded, or taken."[21]

In a letter dated September 5th, a New Englander, Major Jedediah Preble wrote his friend and colonel, John Winslow who then was at Grand Pré:

> It is with grief that I inform you that on the 2nd Inst. Majr Frye being at Shipodia where he was ordered to burn the buildings and bring off the women and children the number of which was only twenty-three which he had sent aboard and burned 253 buildings and had sent 50 men ashore to burn the mass house and some other buildings which was the last they had to do. When about 300 French and Indians came suddenly on them: killed Doctr March, shot Lievt Billings through the body and through the arm, and killed or took 22 and wounded six more. They retreated to the dykes and Major Frye landed with what men he could get on shore and made a stand. But their numbers being superior to ours were first to retreat.[22]

Overall, we can see, and as is represented by Major Frye's sad experience, the English were not very successful at bringing in the Acadians from the outlying areas. They did, however, as a result of their preemptive move on August 11th, have about 400 prisoners, Acadian men, locked up at both Fort Cumberland and Fort Lawrence. These were added to, as the scouring English parties brought in additional prisoners.[23] Basically, it was thought, and this was to generally turn out to be the case, if they had the fathers and the older sons, the families would not be far off and could be easily gathered up by the English soldiers when the time came to load up the transports. Unlike the experience at Grand Pré and Piziquid where there was to be a long delay waiting for the transports, at Chignecto, the transports arrived in good time; they had arrived on the 21st of August.[24] The embarkation by September 10th had commenced.[25] As the vessels were not to leave with their human cargo until October 13th,[26] it seems, that a number of the Acadians were to be on the transports for weeks before they set sail. Though the vessels would act as reasonably good prisons, maintaining those aboard had to be troublesome. Supplies would have had to have been ferried out; and, the work and trouble would have been proportionate to the level of the on-board population.[27]

With the browning of the fields and with the hardwoods turning in their summer greens for autumn colors, it was becoming plain that the English could not continue to wait, hoping that more Acadians might be brought in. In any event, as the ripening October days passed, the English were to calculate that they had more than enough Acadians to fill up the waiting transports. It was time to finish the job. The transports were to be victualed, wooded and watered; and the Acadian families embarked. On October the 9th, the 24-gun frigate, *Success*, came into the basin at Chignecto. She had come up from Halifax. Her captain, John Rous, was obliged by Governor Lawrence's orders to hurry the job along — time was passing.[28] With this impetus, the pace quickened, for, we see, that on October the 11th, "The last party of French prisoners were sent on board the vessel in order to be sent out of the province." On October the 13th, John Thomas further reported, "Capt Rouse sailed this morning with the fleet consisting of 10 sail under his command. They carried nine hundred & sixty French prisoners with them bound to South Carolina & George."[29]

And thus it was done at the Isthmus of Chignecto. The population thereabouts was depleted. There were those that were sent off on the transports; and there were those (likely a greater number) which fled the area. Many of those which fled, did so up the north-eastern coast of present day New Brunswick. The winter of 1755/56 was to be a miserable winter as these Acadian families trekked through the wilderness. Farther and farther they went and farther again to make sure they were clear of the red coats; to camp out in the cold and to see the little ones and the old ones and the sick ones, die on the frozen shores of the Miramachi. In any event, by November of 1755, there were to be precious few Acadians to be found at the isthmus. The English had complete control of the area and three forts from which to command. Monckton picked the men that were to garrison these three forts; and then in November he and an undetermined number of his army, through the cold winds and bare hardwoods, made their way to Halifax.[30]

The Destruction Of Cobequid:

This note on Cobequid, is but a supplement to the material that I have already set out in connection with my treatment of the deportation at Grand Pré.

The seigneury of Cobequid[31] covered a much wider territory which we today define as Truro. It stretched out to include Noel, Stewiacke, Tatamagouche and Five Islands. The Acadians were to first come to Cobequid, when, in 1689, Matthieu Martin[32] came up from Port Royal and going to the far eastern extremity of Minas Basin planted a settlement on the banks of River Wecobequitk (Salmon River) near the present day town of Truro.[33] Its population, as did most of the Acadian centers, had an impressive growth. It was, indeed, the last stop for many of the Acadians who were looking for good lands in the Minas area upon which to settle. For instance, there was the Benoist family, which, in 1708, came to Cobequid to settle. As was usually the case, this was an extended family which made the move. There was 65 year old Martin Benoist, and his son of 27 years and his son's young family. They had all struck out from Port Royal for the Minas Basin area. Pisiquid was their first stop. But, it would appear, by then, by 1708, the best lands had already been claimed at Pisiquid; so the family struck out for Cobequid. By 1714, there were 22 families located in the Cobequid area.[34] During the next six years a number of other families were to arrive, as we see

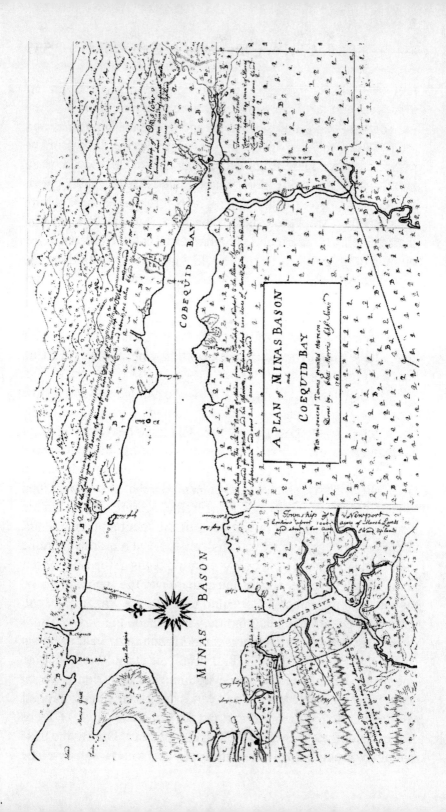

A PLAN of MINAS BASON and COEQUID BAY

With the several Towns granted thereon.

Done by John Morris Chf Surv.
1761

that by 1720, there were 50 French families at Cobequid.[35] By 1748, the count at Cobequid stood at 800 persons.

It should be noted that Cobequid, though not as far away from the English fort at Annapolis Royal as were the French communities at Chignecto, was, nonetheless, in those days of slow travel, one of the more remote Acadian centers; and, as such, the Acadians of Cobequid were more independent then most. So too, the Cobequid Acadians were close to an Indian mission located where the Stewiacke meets the Shubenacadie; and which had been run for many years by Le Loutre. The close proximity of Le Loutre and his native friends (the sworn allies of the French crown) meant that the Acadians of Cobequid dare not ever get too friendly with the English. We see, for example during January, 1750, at Cobequid, on the church steps, in the presence of their priests, Le Loutre, with Indians at his back, threatened death to any Acadian who should travel to trade with the English.[36]

In 1755, unlike the centers at Annapolis Royal, Grand Pré, Piziquid and Chignecto, there was no English force encamped at Cobequid. In order to carry out the deportation orders of Governor Lawrence, detachments were sent in from other commands. In August, Monckton sent two independent detachments overland from Chignecto. The one, consisting of 150 men under Captain Thomas Lewis; and the other, of 100 men under Abijah Willard. We know little of Captain Lewis' route and just exactly what he was to achieve in this particular excursion. Lewis was, however, to head up a second expedition in September which originated at Minas, one which we know more about, and to which I shall shortly refer. Willard kept a journal.[37]

Willard and his 100 men left Fort Cumberland on August the 6th. They had two French guides with them. Their route to Cobequid first started by going up the Maccan River. Heading due south and after a three day trip the men popped out on the shores of the Minas Basin, at a place which we now know as Moose River. On Sunday, August 10th, they came to the French village Portapique, where stands today an English village of the same name. They carried on through, "east about seven miles to the house of an old Frenchman, where the whole party was lodged and kindly supplied with milk and butter."[38] By the next day, August 11th, they had made it to the parish church at Cobequid. At this church they were to meet one of the officers who had been with the Lewis detachment. (Lewis' larger force had left Fort Cumberland a day before Willard's and apparently had taken the clockwise route — along the shores of the Northumberland Strait to Tatamagouche and then overland to Cobequid.) After resting awhile, during which time "the French brought in good beef and mutton," Lewis' group then made their way over the Cobequid range by going up the Chiganois (or possibly the North River) and then to take the French River down to Tatamagouche. On route they were to meet Captain Lewis, who, apparently had just been at Tatamagouche. At the meeting Lewis was to hand Willard "sealed orders" at which Willard expressed much surprise. He was commanded "to proceed and burn all the French houses on the way to Tatamagouche and on the Northumberland."

Soon Willard was at Tatamagouche; and, this old French community and another by the name of Remsheg (known today as Wallace) were systematically destroyed. Frank Harris Patterson, a Supreme Court Judge and noted historian, wrote about what next followed:

About noon of August 16th, Captain Lewis returned from Remsheg where he had captured three families and burnt several houses. Willard with some of his men then crossed the Tatamagouche River and burnt twelve buildings, one of which was a store house filled with rum, molasses, sugar, wine and iron works. Here they also destroyed the Chapel. The men first took so much rum as they had bottles to carry, and then set fire to the buildings. They also destroyed all the vessels and canoes, including a sloop of seventy tons and a schooner of thirty tons, loaded with cattle, sheep and hogs for Louisbourg.[39]

Willard and his men burnt every French structure they came upon. He then drew his men up in a body and marched off forcing the French men to come with them. Their women, who willingly gave freshly baked bread to the arriving soldiers but a day or two ago, were "left lamenting bitterly" as their men were marched off, who knows — if ever to be seen again? Left behind were their women and children; left behind to fend for themselves.

By the 19th — the Willard and Lewis detachments by then apparently having combined themselves into a force of approximately 250 men — the New Englanders were back over the Cobequids. After crossing both the North and the Salmon Rivers, they proceeded to the eastern bank of the Shubenacadie River. Here, in this area, they came upon "several hamlets of French families" where Willard was to find "the finest of French farms" and "large orchards of apples." The English, acting under orders to bring in "only the deputies," proceeded to their houses, the location of which were presumably well known. Willard was "kindly treated" at each of these homes. He did not destroy anything in this area of Cobequid, his orders being only to destroy the villages found at Tatamagouche and Remsheg — this, so as "to prevent the shipping of the Acadian cattle and produce to Louisbourg."[40] The Cobequid villages along the Minas Basin were not touched, for fear that any such act would serve to tip the Acadians of the English plans before their forces were fully in place at Piziquid and Grand Pré. The New Englanders then made their way back to the north shore of the basin and proceeded west and then cut north so to pick up the headwaters of the Maccan River. They arrived back at Fort Cumberland, traveling in different groups, on August the 25th and the 26th.

As for Captain Lewis: he was to come and pay another visit to Cobequid during the month of September. Whether he peeled off for Halifax mid-August when on the Shubenacadie River, but 40 miles from Halifax and on a well established water route (the Shubenacadie system), or whether he took a vessel from the isthmus after reporting in with Willard, I do not know. What we do know, is that on September 15th, a detachment under Captain Lewis was to arrive at Fort Edward (Piziquid) overland from Halifax. He had men with him and despatches for Captain Murray and for Colonel Winslow. Among these despatches were orders from Governor Lawrence at Halifax that a force be mounted to go to Cobequid and to ferry the Acadians found there to the embarkation points at either Grand Pré or Piziquid, and, to burn the place out upon leaving. This force was to be put together and made up from the existing forces then at Fort Edward and Grand Pré and that which had come up from Halifax with Captain Lewis. Lawrence emphasized the importance and the urgency of such a mission. Lewis, in Governor Lawrence's opinion, was the best officer to lead this force, he having been "lately there and being perfectly well acquainted with the situation."[41]

I have already dealt with Captain Lewis' second expedition to Cobequid in that part where I dealt with the deportation at Grand Pré. So, I need not say much more about it at this place, other than to say: not an Acadian at Cobequid, all those that Lewis had seen but a few weeks early, was to be found — every village and every structure was empty. These Acadians had evidently caught wind of what had happened at Tatamagouche and Remsheg, or what at that time was happening at Piziquid and Grand Pré — and, they fled. Though there is no record of it, it is safe to assume that these Acadians, one and all, during the last part of August or the first part of September, trekked bag and baggage over the well tread paths through the Cobequid range to come to Tatamagouche. And there, somehow, to find boats so as to get themselves to what was still then French territory, Île St Jean — these days, the Canadian province of Prince Edward Island. Though not finding any inhabitants, Lewis did achieve his secondary objective, and, from the 23rd to the 29th of September, "laid waste the country with fire."[42]

The Voyages

When sorrows come, they come not single spies - But in battalions.
— Shaks.: *Hamlet.*

As we have seen, on October 27th, 1755, a fleet of twenty-four sailing vessels sailed from the Minas Basin. It consisted of 21 transports escorted by three armed vessels.[1] Aboard the transports were 4,217 Acadians who were deported away from their native lands at Minas and Chignecto. I quote from William A. Calnek's history:

> We cannot follow the wretched and heart-broken exiles in their dispersion, nor recount the deaths on the way, nor speculate on the deaths from diseases, contracted in crowded holds of vessels, where no sanitary or even decent arrangements could be provided or were attempted; the deaths from hardships and privations afterwards, and the lingering and in some cases life-long agony of separated members of a family inquiring and searching for each other throughout the continent, among an alien people for the most part unsympathetic or indifferent; and the almost interminable journeys of detached groups, wholly destitute, seeking to make their way to some place of rest among people congenial in language and religion, or disposed to extend sympathy and charity to a robbed and ruined people.

The story of these "wretched and heart-broken" people making their way to some place of rest, is a story, if it could be told, that would extend over generations. The wave of misery which was to first flood over them while assembled in their churches at Acadia as the deportation orders were read out rebounded as they were herded on underprovisioned and overcrowded transports. The misery rebounded when sea storms hit their wooden sailing vessels and rebounded as they were delivered into English communities who thought them pests. Their delivery to the English colonies was but the beginning of another phase of the extirpation of these innocent people: they were to face years of poverty and deprivation. Only their children and their children's children were to find a "place of rest among people congenial in language and religion." Only with the passing of the 18th century did these Acadians find peace once again and did so in such diverse areas of the world as Louisiana in the United States and Belle-Isle-en-Mer in France.

Sea Storm:

From different quarters of the historical record we see that the fleet, which bore the Acadians, and which left Minas Basin on October the 27th, was struck by a "a furious gale." It would seem that this storm sweep the fleet even before they were able to clear the Bay of Fundy. A storm at sea is frightening enough for seasoned sailors; it must have been a frightening event for the 4,000 or so Acadians, a body of people which included the young, the old and the infirmed. These people were farmers and some of the adult men might have had some experience with row boats; none would have had any sea experience, at all. What is it like to be at sea in a storm, let us turn to Joseph Conrad:

'A gale is a gale, Mr. Jukes. ... There's just so much dirty weather knocking about the world, and the proper thing is to go through it ...'

It was something formidable and swift, like the sudden smashing of a vile of wrath. It seemed to explode all round the ship with an overpowering concussion and a rush of great waters, as if an immense dam had been blown up to windward. In an instant the men lost touch of each other. This is the disintegrating power of a great wind: it isolates one from one's kind. An earthquake, a landslip, an avalanche, overtake a man incidently, as it were — without passion. A furious gale attacks him like a personal enemy, tries to grasp his limbs, fastens upon his mind, seeks to rout his very spirit out of him. ...

The motion of the ship was extravagant. Her lurches had an appalling helplessness: she pitched as if taking a header into the void, and seemed to find a wall to hit every time. ... The gale howled and scuffed about gigantically in the darkness, as though the entire world were one black gully. ...

And, in describing the results of the storm Conrad proceeded in his inimitable way to describe the vessel as having been ...

looted by the storm with a senseless, destructive fury: trysails torn out of the extra gaskets, double lashed awnings blown away, bridge sweep clean, weather cloths burst, rails twisted, lightscreens smashed — and two of the boats had gone already. They had gone unheard and unseen, melting, as it were, in the shock and smother of the wave.[2]

By November 5th, the fleet, at least in part, limped into Boston seeking shelter. We see from the records where the authorities ordered an enquiry on that date. This led to on board inspections. Certain of the vessels seem to have more of their share of "sickly" passengers, others, such as the *Neptune*, with 209 aboard, were found to be "healthy but about 40 lie upon the deck." More generally there is a comment: "The vessels in general are too much crowded; their allowance of provisions short ... too small a quantity ... to carry them to the ports they are bound to especially at this season of the year; and their water very bad."[3]

It is necessary to follow up with the findings of the unnamed inspector at Boston, *viz.*, "The vessels in general are too much crowded; their allowance of provisions short."

Ill-Provisioned:

Thomas Saul, who was in charge of the government stores at Halifax, needed to gather all he could in order to provision the Acadians for their sea voyage. I believe, from what I have read, that he did his best, but he had only so much to work with.[4] Saul, proceeding under Governor Lawrence's written instructions given at Halifax on August 11th, sailed to each of the embarkation points in the Bay of Fundy and laid in provisions so that the vessels could stay at sea for 20 to 30 days. The instructions read, "You are to victual every person for thirty days bound to the southward of Philadelphia and those that shall be disembarked at Philadelphia or to the northward thereof shall be victualed each person for twenty days ..." Each transport was to be supplied with food so that each person aboard for a seven day period was to have "Five pounds of French flower,[5] Two pounds of bread, and one pound of beef." Still, it is curious that when the sea storm tossed vessels made their way into Boston Harbor on November 6th, but ten days after they left Acadia, that our inspector should comment, "their allowance of provisions short." What was it? Did they eat too much in the first few days? Or, is it that provisions were sweep overboard during the storm?

Crowded:

As for the transport vessels being crowded: well, plainly they were. The officers in charge at Minas were aware that they were loading on more people then they ought to. John Winslow at Grand Pré knew of the problem: "And although I put in more than two to a ton[6] and the people greatly crowded ..." And while Winslow pushed the limits, he was, at least, aware of them; and, indeed, he determined not to attempt to ship all of his Grand Pré Acadians. He kept back about 600 of them and they were not shipped out until that December. On the other hand, the indelicate officer at Fort Edward, Alexander Murray, wanted to get every Acadian in his district, Piziquid, off of his hands, no matter the consequences: "Even then with [four vessels at Piziquid] ... they [the Acadians] will be stowed in bulk but if I have no more vessels I will put them aboard let the consequences be what it will."[7] On these Piziquid transports, Murray originally squeezed "920 people ... children included." These vessels were not to be loaded to a greater extent then "two to the ton"; the four vessels amounted to 246 tons; thus, there should have been loaded no more than 500 people, yet, twice the number were loaded. Winslow and Murray were to relieve this situation, somewhat by finding another vessel, which just happened to be in the area, the *Seaflower*, such that the 920 people were spread out over five vessels with an additional hundred from other areas, so that the five sailed on October 27th with 1062 aboard; still, seemingly, seriously overcrowded.

It should not be concluded, notwithstanding Longfellow's fanciful poem, that any great number of Acadian family members were to be separated from one another; though, I am sure some were. The loading did not go on at a leisurely pace. The transports, at least at Minas, arrived very late. As Captain Murray at Fort Edward wrote, "the weather is bad ... [further] I am afraid the governor will think us dilatory."

Brook Watson[8] who as a young man was at Chignecto during 1755, wrote Dr. Brown from London in 1791:

> In September I was directed to proceed with a party of Provincials to the Baie Verte, then considerable and flourishing settlement, there to wait further orders, which I received on the following days, to collect and send to Beausejour, for embarkation, all the women and the children to be found in that district, and, on leaving the town, to fire it; this painful task performed, I was afterwards employed in victualing the transports for their reception; the season was now far advanced before the embarkation took place, which caused much hurry, and I fear some families were divided and sent to different parts of the globe, notwithstanding all possible care was taken to prevent it.[9]

The Disembarkation Of The Acadians: Massachusetts:

Of the 21 transports that sailed on October 27th, there was only the one that was to disembark her Acadians at Boston, that was the *Seaflower*. She carried 206 persons which had lived in the Grand Pré and Piziquid areas. The likelihood is that she was one of a number of transports that had, by November 5th, limped into Boston seeking shelter. The others — Massachusetts not being their intended destination — were sent on their way. If it was to be only 206 Acadians to be thrown on the citizens of Massachusetts, why, then, that would not have been so bad; but approximately 680 more Acadians were to step onto the docks in the month of December. These were the 323 aboard the *Helena* which had departed Annapolis Royal on December 8th; the 236 aboard the *Swallow* which had departed Minas Basin on December 13th; and the 120 aboard the *Race Horse* which had departed Minas Basin on December 20th. The Acadians aboard the *Swallow* and the *Race Horse* were from "villages of Antoine & Landry & some of Cannard."[10]

We can see that by December 18th, the authorities at Boston were scrambling to take care of the Acadians that were dumped on their doorstep. Lieutenant-governor Phips, on this date is seen writing Governor Lawrence, "we have received a number of the inhabitants of Nova Scotia sent hither by your order who arrived here when the winter season was so far advanced, that they could do but little for their support."[11] Phips then proceeded to ask Lawrence who is to pay for all this expense. The people of Massachusetts, of course, did lend a hand to the Acadians. They were spread out, thus to occupy a number of villages. The money spent that winter to transport them, to feed them, to cloth them came by order of the people's assembly, and the people's assembly wanted the crown to pay.[12] It seems there was to be a bit of a scrap between the two arms of government over this affair. Governor Shirley, of course, supported his fellow governor in dealing with a long standing problem which Shirley knew had existed in Nova Scotia. He wrote the Massachusetts legislature: "I believe Governor Lawrence had no apprehensions that it would occasion any considerable charge to this province, or that it would be a disagreeable thing to have those people sent here: I am sorry that it is likely to prove so burdensome. I have it not in my power to support them at the charge of the crown ..."

Connecticut:

It is interesting to note that of all the colonies, it was only Connecticut that had made some arrangements and preparations in advance to receive the deported Acadians. The Connecticut legislature passed a resolution in October, before, it seems, the transports had even left Acadia. The rest of the English colonies claimed that they had no notice and "complained they had not been apprized of the intention of Lawrence to quarter on them a body of the Acadians." However, of the 21 transports that departed Minas Basin on October 27th, not one came into Connecticut? It was to be December, with the later sailings, before Connecticut was to get her share of Acadians. In came the *Dove* with 114 Acadians aboard; she had left Minas Basin on December 13th. Another 558 were also suppose[13] to have arrived at Connecticut; 278 on the *Edward* and another 280 on the *Two Sisters*; they had both departed Annapolis Royal on December the 8th.

New York:

It is reported that one vessel was to deliver her Acadians to New York. It was the *Experiment* which had sailed from Annapolis Royal with 200 Acadians aboard. I do note that the agents for the *Experiment*, Apthorp & Hancock, billed the crown for the use of the vessel up until May 27th, 1756.[14]

Maryland:

Four of the transports of the October 27th fleet were to arrive at Annapolis, the last of them on November 30th. Now, it should normally have taken but a few days to sail down the coast from Minas Basin, so, given that they took better then a month to get to their destination, one might presume that these vessels were storm-stayed in some port (maybe Boston) for a period of time. The four vessels were: *Ranger, Dolphin, Elizabeth* and *Leopard.* The *Ranger* (263) and the *Dolphin* (230) had Piziquid Acadians aboard; the *Elizabeth* (186) and the *Leopard* (178) also had Piziquid Acadians aboard.[15]

From *The Maryland Gazette*, December 4, 1755, we see the following:

Sunday last (Nov. 30) arrived here the last of the vessels from Nova Scotia with French neutrals for this place, which make four within this fortnight who have brought upwards of 900 of them. As the poor people have been deprived of their settlements in Nova Scotia, and sent here for some political reason bare and destitute. Christian charity, nay common humanity, calls on every one according to their ability to lend their assistance and help to these objects of compassion.[16]

Pennsylvania:

One of the escort vessels of the October 27th fleet was the Royal navy ship, *Nightengale*. It was intended that this ship should carry on down as far as Philadelphia. Presumably the *Nightengale* kept her charges together, as, on December 8th, three of the transports arrived at Philadelphia: *Three Friends* (156, ex Piziquid), *Swan* (168, ex Grand Pré) and *Hannah* (140, ex Grand Pré).

Arthur G. Doughty (Dominion Archivist), in his work, *The Acadian Exiles* was to write of the Acadians who arrived at Philadelphia:

> The vessels touched Delaware on November 20, when it was discovered that there were several cases of smallpox on board, and the masters were ordered to leave the shore. They were not permitted to land at Philadelphia until the 10th of December. Many of the exiles died during the winter, and were buried in the cemetery of the poor which now [1916] forms a part of Washington Park, Philadelphia. The survivors were lodged in a poor quarter of the town, in 'neutral huts,' as their mean dwellings were termed.
>
> The Acadians had arrived at Philadelphia in a most deplorable condition. One of the Quakers who visited the boats while they were in quarantine reported that they were without shirts and socks and were sadly in need of bed-clothing.[17]

Georgia:

The 400 Acadians that came down to Georgia from Chignecto aboard the *Jolly Phillip* (120) and *Prince Frederick* (280), it seems, made immediate plans to make their way back to their beloved lands. In quoting Stevens' *History of Georgia*, Placide Gaudet writes that the 400 Acadians had arrived in two vessels that December and "were distributed in small parties about the province, and maintained at the public expense until spring, when, by leave of the Governor, they built themselves a number of rude boats, and in March most of them left for South Carolina; two hundred, in ten boats, going off at one time, indulging the hope that they might thus work their way along to their native and beloved Acadie."

Virginia:

I quote from a letter dated February 21st, 1756, from Governor Dinwiddie of Virginia to Governor Morris of Pennsylvania:

> We have 1,140 Neutrals from Nova Scotia, which gives great uneasiness to our people, we have recd them & now maintain them by my order and the Councils; but whether the Assembly will be prevailed on to make some provision for them is very uncertain; & I complain of Gov. Lawrence's not giving us some previous notice of their coming that we might be prepar'd to receive them. ...

These "neutrals" arrived at Virginia on seven transports: *Neptune* (207, ex Piziquid), *Sarah & Molly* (154, ex Grand Pré), *Endeavour* (166, ex Canard & Habitant Rivers), *Industry* (177, ex Canard & Habitant Rivers), *Mary* (182, ex Canard & Habitant Rivers), *Prosperous* (152, ex Canard & Habitant Rivers) and *Ranger* (112, ex Minas Basin).[18]

South Carolina:

Two of the transports were to make their way down as far as South Carolina. The *Endeavour*[19] which had originated at Chignecto and carried 121 Acadians and was part of the 21 transports which had sailed from Minas Basin on October 27th; and the *Hopson* which sailed from Annapolis Royal on December the 8th with 342 Acadians aboard. Since the *Endeavour* likely was delayed by a storm, it is likely that if the two did not arrive together then they were not far from one another.

England & France:

Virginia and South Carolina were not too much impressed with having hundreds of people thrust upon them, to be maintained, for, God knows how long! On the 8th of July we see that the Board of Trade Lords wrote Lawrence advising him that he is mistaken if he thinks that all the Acadians were received by the colonies south of Nova Scotia for "several hundred of them... from Virginia, and several from South Carolina" have arrived in England having been directed there and that they are being maintained by "the commissioners for sick and hurt Seamen."[20]

The Acadians that arrived in England were treated substantially as prisoners, spread out among the ports of Liverpool, Southampton, Bristol and Penyrn. There, they stayed for the duration of the war. In 1763, they, together with additional numbers that had been deported in 1758 from Île St. Jean and Île Royale, were sent to St. Malo and Morlaix. In 1765, 78 families, with the assistance of Abbé Le Loutre who had returned to France, were given lands at Belle-en-Mer.[21] Late in 1762 a report had been prepared by the authorities in advance of the arrangements made to get them over to France. From this report we may determine that the number of Acadians then in England, in 1762, spread about at the above named places, totaled 866, this was a substantial reduction in the number that had arrived in England during the war years.

The *Pembroke* Mutiny:

I cannot conclude this chapter and not make a reference to the story of the *Pembroke*. She was an Acadian transport, the only one it seems, to have experienced a mutiny. Such an eventually was one that was certainly contemplated by the English; and they attempted to guard against it, as we see from the orders given to the transport captains: "You are to take care that no arms or offensive weapons are on board with your passengers, and to be as careful and watchful as possible during the whole course of your voyage to prevent the passengers from making an attempt to seize your vessel by allowing only a small number to be on the deck at a time and using all other necessary precautions to prevent the bad consequences of such an attempt ..."[22]

The *Pembroke* had sailed from Annapolis Royal, presumably with the other six or seven Annapolis Royal transports. They had set sail on December 8th, 1755. I don't know whether the fleet, like that which had departed Minas Basin, earlier, on October 27th, was under armed escort, or not. Further, I am not sure of the size of the transport crews, likely not a great number. There was 232 Acadians aboard the *Pembroke*, and of that number, there was 33 men, 37 women, 70 sons, 92 daughters. Her crew was either overpowered by the Acadian passengers; or, maybe, she was caught in a storm and headed into the harbor of Saint John; or, maybe, she was taken by a privateer.[23] In any event, Boishébert, a French officer who was one of the few heros of Acadia, was there, at Saint John. Boishébert took the distressed Acadians under his wing and led them into the inner parts of present day New Brunswick. Thus, it is, that countless numbers of French Acadians in New Brunswick might well be able to trace their ancestral roots to the "33 men, 37 women, 70 sons, 92 daughters" of the *Pembroke*.[24]

Chapter 16

Cape Sable & Later Deportations

War makes the victor stupid and the vanquished vengeful.[1]
— Nietzsche.

The destruction of Acadia and the dispersal of her people did not end with the closing of the year. Certainly the territories of Annapolis Royal and Minas, as a practical matter, were cleared of French inhabitants during 1755, but thousands of Acadians yet remained in the wider territory that today we might define as lying within the Canadian provinces of Nova Scotia, New Brunswick and Prince Edward Island. The 1755 operation was to clear away the Acadians from the heart of Acadia, the Annapolis Valley, an area which was strategically important to the new English capital of Halifax. There remained thousands more who had fled to Île St. Jean, Île Royale and up the north shore of present day New Brunswick. Further, there were the French fishermen which had long made their living along that part of present day Quebec which we describe as the Gaspé coast.

The year 1755 marked but a beginning of the English persecution of a people, which was to continue, really, for the next eight years until the full defeat of the French in North America and the peace of 1763. The largest deportation, aside from that which occurred in 1755, was that which was carried out just after the final fall of Louisbourg in 1758. The telling of these subsequent deportations will have to wait until we come to our next part. However, I must now make mention of the deportation at Cape Sable, an area which in the early days of Acadia was known as Pobomcoup, today it is known as Yarmouth. The efforts to remove the Acadians at Cape Sable in 1756 was but an extension of the 1755 operation. The experience the English had with the Cape Sable Acadians was quite different than the experiences had at Annapolis Royal, Minas and Piziquid; the experience was more like that had at Cobequid.

The first serious French effort to colonize Acadia was the de Razilly settlement of 1632. It is likely from this time or shortly thereafter that one of de Razilly's lieutenants, La Tour, was to establish his outpost at Sable Island.[2] Thereafter, I imagine, the presence of French families might have always been discovered.[3] In 1654, one, Philippe Mius d'Entremont (b.1601), received from his commander, LaTour, an exclusive grant of land, the signeurie of Popomcoup, at Cape Sable. Another signeurie, during 1706, was granted to Jean-Chrysotome Loppinot at Cape Forchu (Yarmouth).[4] I am unable to comment on the Acadian population levels at Cape Sable through the years. I imagine that the growth, though not as great as the agricultural areas[5] such as Minas and Chignecto was nonetheless steady through the years, such that, by 1756, it consisted of a thousand or two.

In May of 1755, as we have seen, better than 2,000 troops from New England had come to Nova Scotia in order to attack Fort Beauséjour at the Isthmus of Chignecto. With the fall of that French fort, a certain part of that force from New England was detached under John Winslow in order to see to the deportation of the Acadians at Minas. The deportation of the Acadians was to take place at three of the major Acadian population centers: Annapolis Royal, Minas and Chignecto. In the process other Acadian centers were visited by English troops including those located along the northern shores of Nova Scotia where lies, as we call it today, the Northumberland Strait. Because of limited resources, however, not all Acadian settlements were to suffer the effect of Lawrence's orders of 1755. The significant Acadian settlement at Cape Sable was one. Governor Lawrence was of the view that the French at Cape Sable might be dealt with — their possessions destroyed and their persons deported — in the spring of 1756.

The government of Nova Scotia was under an obligation to return the New England troops back to their homes; they being only militiamen and hired but for a year's term. A large part of them had retired into winter quarters at Halifax, a significant number of them across the harbor from Halifax at Dartmouth. One of the senior officers of this New England force was one, Major Prebble. It was arranged that he and a large contingent of the New England soldiers were to be transported back to New England directly with the spring breakup. It was determined, that, on route, this force was to call by at Cape Sable and the adjacent harbors. "Seize as many of the said inhabitants as possible ... You are at all events to burn & destroy the houses ... & carry their utensils & cattle of all kinds, and make a distribution of them to the troops under your command as a reward for the performance of this service, & to destroy such things as cannot conveniently be carried off."[6] Major Prebble paid a call on these communities, and while he and his men, in regards to Acadian property, undoubtedly burned what they couldn't carry off; they were not very successful at taking Acadians to Boston. Prebble and his men, I am sure, were anxious to get back home to Boston and likely were not interested in spending too much time chasing Acadians at Cape Sable.

The Acadians at Cape Sable, who Major Prebble tried to round up, resisted and fought a guerilla war for two years, but eventually had to give it up. In September of 1758 a petition signed by Joseph Landry was presented to Governor Lawrence. They, 40 Acadian families consisting of 150 souls, were in very poor circumstances and yet another winter was coming on. Accordingly, Lawrence despatched "armed vessels to Cape Sable, where they took on board one hundred and fifty-two persons, men, women and children, and when they arrived here [Halifax], I ordered them to be landed at Georges Island, as being the place of the most security." There, as far as I can tell, these poor people were to remain prisoners. Lawrence, in 1759, was successful in getting Admiral Saunders, who had just then returned with certain of his vessels from their success at Quebec, to free up one of his transports, upon which, 151 Acadians embarked for a trip to England under convoy of the HMS *Sutherland*.[7]

I have already made reference to the deportation which took place in 1758. Jeffrey Amherst and his forces took Louisbourg in 1758, and, with that, the plan to rid the countryside of Acadians was prosecuted with renewed vigor as the British descended down upon port after port: in Île Royale (Cape Breton Island), Île St Jean (Prince Edward Island) and up along the French shore of present day New Brunswick. During the months of August and September of 1758, British forces, borne by naval ships, under the command of James Wolfe, spread terror in all of the French villages right up to the Gaspé coast.[8] It had been determined that it was too late in the year to launch an assault on Quebec itself, and that the forces then assembled at Louisbourg would be best employed to level all these French establishments so as to secure an entry into the St. Lawrence planned for the following year.[9]

It was during these incursions of 1758 that 3,540 French inhabitants were to be taken off of Île St. Jean (Prince Edward Island) and deported. Thus, those Acadians which had avoided the deportation of 1755 by trekking to Île St Jean and Île Royale[10] mostly through the years 1749-1752 were to suffer pretty much the same fate as their cousins, three years later. According to Placide Gaudet, a pre-eminent Acadian authority, these harried people "were transported to France in 1758, where some remained and others came to Louisiana about the year 1784."[11] It would not appear that the destination for these poor people was to be New England: not after the complaints received on account of the 1755 influx. No, the Île St Jean Acadians were, by and large, destined for a trans-Atlantic voyage. While there are hardly any accounts of this 1758 deportation, Arthur G. Doughty (Dominion Archivist) did make this reference to it:

Now, on the fall of Louisbourg in 1758, some of the British transports which had brought out troops from Cork to Halifax were ordered to Île St. Jean to carry the Acadians and French to France. The largest of these transports was the *Duke William*; another was named the *Violet*. Some of the Acadians made good their escape, but many were dragged on board the vessels. On the *Duke William* was a missionary priest, and before the vessels sailed he was called upon to perform numerous marriages, for the single men had learned that if they landed unmarried in France they would be forced to perform military service, for which they had no inclination. Nine transports sailed in consort, but were soon caught in a violent tempest and scattered. On December 10 the *Duke William* came upon the *Violet* in a sinking condition; and notwithstanding all efforts at rescue, the *Violet* went down with nearly four hundred souls. Meanwhile the *Duke William* herself had sprung a leak. For a time she was kept afloat by empty casks in the hold, but presently it became evident that the ship was doomed. The long-boat was put out and filled to capacity. And scarcely had the boat cleared when an explosion occurred and the *Duke William* went down, taking three hundred persons to a watery grave. The long-boat finally reached Penzance with twenty-seven of the castaways. The other vessels probably found some French port.[12]

Brook Watson (to whom I referred in a note of the previous chapter, and who as a young man was at Chignecto during 1755) wrote Dr. Brown from London in 1791:

... many of the transports having on board were ordered to France, about thirteen hundred perished by ship wreck on the voyage, those who arrived, France would not receive; they were landed at Southampton and other ports where, taking the smallpox, they were carried off in great numbers. Of those who went to the French West India Isles the greater part died for want of food, a famine at that time prevailed in the island, the people could not support them, the Governor-General said that they were not French subjects.[13]

Chapter 17

The Wanderings
Of The Acadians

During the deportations of 1755, in total, around 6,000 Acadians were shipped out of the province. It might be estimated that close to twice that number constituted the Acadian population at its peak, in 1749. A couple of thousand, through the years 1749-53, fearing the worst, fled into the French territories that then existed: Île St. Jean (Prince Edward Island) and Île Royale (Cape Breton). The Acadians that did not get caught up in the English net, in 1755, may have amounted to three or four thousand.[1] The bulk of those made their way out of the province: the Chignecto Acadians either to Île St. Jean or up the coast of northern New Brunswick (as we know it today); and, the Cobequid Acadians, likely to Île St. Jean and Île Royale. Certain of the Acadians, those in the areas of Cape Sable and the Annapolis River, having avoided the English, retreated to the woods, whence they waged, for several years, guerilla warfare. By the end of 1755, however, the Acadian strength in Nova Scotia was certainly broken, for all time. The Acadians which were transported in 1755, were distributed down along the eastern coast of North America, beginning with Massachusetts. They arrived unannounced. Further it was expected by Governor Lawrence that these foreign strangers should be accommodated. There was absolutely no word received as to who was to bear all the expense involved in keeping these people. Needless to say, the governing councils in the English colonies were not too impressed with these events.

Though not very much is known of them, it is for sure that the sufferings of the Acadians who had been dumped on foreign shores were great. However, those who were left behind were to put up with their own sufferings. Acadians, through the years of *The Seven Years War*, 1756-1763, and for many years thereafter, were to be driven from pillar to post. My ancestors did not, apparently, fall in with the English: they managed to first evade them by making their way to the then French territory of Île Royale (Cape Breton). Sixty-two year old Jean-Baptiste Landry with three of his sons (38 year old Jean-Baptiste, 35 year old Joseph and 27 year old Alexis) with a battery of 15 children made there way from Piziquid (St. Croix) to Île Royale during August, 1751. They apparently intended to put roots down at Riviêre dux Habitants (near St. Peter's); but they did not stay long at that place. Members of this family, it would appear were subsequently to make their way to Île St. Jean being listed there in 1752, then others at Chédabuctou (Halifax) around 1763, and then at St. Pierre & Miquelon in 1767. One of these Landrys, Pierre, by 1766, was located at Miquelon, and by 1766 at Chezzetcook.²

But only a few Acadians were ever to make their way back to their native land.³ Those who did, certainly did not head directly into any part Nova Scotian territory being watched by the English; and none, indeed, that I can see, were ever to return to their old homesteads. A year after the war came to an end, in 1764, instructions were received to permit the Acadians to settle back into the province and hold lands upon taking the customary oaths. The lands, however, that they were permitted to occupy, were not to be the rich lands which they and their forefathers had once worked.⁴ The land grants given to the Acadians were generally located in the extremities of the province: in the Cape Breton and Yarmouth areas, which are known more for fishing than for farming.

Directly the Acadians disembarked at the various ports of the English colonies, they attempted to carry out plans to get back to their beloved "Acadie." We see that in July of 1756, within months of their deportation that a number of them were retained at Boston. These intrepid Acadians had "procured small vessels and embarked on board them in order to return by coasting from colony to colony, and that several of them are actually on their way." Lawrence urged his fellow governors to "stop them and to destroy the vessels."⁵ A number of the governors, especially the ones to the south, were not only disinterested in stopping the Acadians; but, indeed, encouraged the Acadians to keep moving along.[6] Whether any of these deported Acadians in their small boats were to carry themselves all the way back to Acadia, is questionable. We have heard the stories how some, if not by boat, then by foot, made their way through the territories we today know as the State of Maine and the Province of New Brunswick.[7] That they then got themselves around the English forts at Chignecto and then over the Cobequid range, so to come to the heart of Acadia at Minas — well, I doubt if any made it. What if they had made it back? They would have found nothing but burned-out ruins! And, by 1760, the returning Acadians would have found English people. English people protected by English soldiers. English people who had taken over the farm lands of Acadia.

Lawrence, at whose feet the decision to deport the Acadian population must be laid, died during October of 1760. It took a couple of years before the British government sent an official replacement over to Nova Scotia, in the meantime Jonathan Belcher[8] administered the government, and, the anti-Acadian policy continued. This is not surprising since *The Seven Years War* between the French and the English continued. While there was not to be much action in Acadia after 1758; still, there were scares. For example, during April of 1762, news was heard at Halifax that St. John's, Newfoundland had been attacked and captured by the French.[9] The worry was that Halifax would be the next target of the French. There followed extensive work on the Halifax fortifications, such that batteries were added to those already in existence on Georges Island, more were erected at Point Pleasant and near the Dockyard, the walls of the eastern redoubt at Dartmouth were repaired, and a boom of "timber and iron" was established near the mouth of the Northwest Arm.[10] The English were far too concerned about their own safety to give any thought to displaced Frenchmen; indeed, in 1762, the "French Neutral prisoners" were collected up and lodged (likely at Fort Edward), and, French fisherman were denied any right to set to sea.

The war, of course, came to an end in 1763; so too in that year Nova Scotia was to receive its new governor, Montague Wilmot.[11] In respect to the Acadians, Wilmot seemed to adopt the prevailing opinion of the English then residing in Nova Scotia. As he wrote in 1764: "They are most inflexibly devoted to France and the Romish Religion, and being much connected with the Indians by intermarriages, their power and disposition to be mischievous is more to be dreaded."[12] Wilmot enclosed a return letter bearing the date of 22nd March, 1764, setting forth the number of "families of French Acadians still remaining in the different parts of the province." I set out, the return, in part, next following:

	Families	Persons
Halifax and the Environs,[13]	232	1,056
King's County, Fort Edward,[14]	77	227
Annapolis Royal,	23	91
Fort Cumberland,	73	388
TOTAL	405	1,762

It is not likely, as mentioned earlier, that many, if any, of the deported Acadians were to make it back to Nova Scotia; certainly not within the years immediately following 1755. The numbers of them in the province through these years, indeed, support the proposition that even more of them, with the encouragement of the government, were to leave the province. We see that Governor Wilmot had reported a count of 1,800, or so, at the beginning of 1764; however by the end of the year there was but left only about 1,200. Wilmot wrote:

[Because] no reasonable proposals being able to overcome their zeal for the French and aversion to the English government, many of them soon resolved to leave this Province; and having hired Vessels at their own expense, six hundred persons including women and children, departed within these three weeks for the French West Indies ...[15]

Governor Wilmot,[16] who comes across to me as a terrible sort of person, seem to be of the view that this was good riddance to bad foreign rubbish. "Thus my Lord, we are in the way of being relieved from these people who have been the bane of the Province, and the terror of its settlement. ... their settlement in the West Indies removes them far from us, and as that climate is mortal to the natives of the northern countries, the French will not be likely to gain any considerable advantage from them.[17]

Not everyone shared Wilmot's view of things. General Amherst, for example, thought, as of 1761, that the further expulsion of the Acadians served no purpose: "If the removal of the Acadians still remaining in the province [for security reasons, then] ... I should be the first to advise their expulsion; but as under the new circumstances of that valuable and flourishing province, I do not see that it can have any thing to fear or apprehend from those Acadians, but on the contrary that great advantages might be reapt in employing them properly ..."[18]

The low point for the Acadian population in the province appears to have been reached during the years, 1764-1767. The count of as of 1767 was made at 1,265; and it broke down as follows: 271 at Cape Breton, 197 at Canso, 200 at Halifax and 140 at Windsor.[19] In 1768, we see the first upturn. In that year, steps were being taken to settle Acadians in "Cape Breton under the protection of temporary licenses."[20] Governor Wilmot died in 1766, and with his death the appointment of Michael Francklin[21] as the lieutenant-governor came about. There then was to be a refreshing change in the official attitude towards the Acadians. This attitude is reflected in a letter which in part I next set out. The letter was one that Michael Francklin wrote to Isaac Deschamps.[22] It was written at Halifax and dated June 1st, 1768. Francklin was writing in response to an earlier letter which Deschamps sent advising that many of the Acadians in the Windsor area have "at length come to a sense of their duty to the King, by taking the Oaths of Allegiance."

And you may ... give them from me the fullest assurances that I totally disclaim and disavow any intentions to make use of them as forces to be employed out of this province, and that such report could only have risen from weak or evil-minded people, and you may still further assure them, that they will be treated at all times with the same degree of indulgence and protection with His Majesty's other subjects. And to this you may also add that the government has not the least design either to molest or disturb them on account of their religion.[23]

Calnek did an analysis of the census of 1768-70. He observed, of the total population of Annapolis Royal (513) there were 445 protestants and 68 Roman Catholics. Of the total: 370 were of American birth; 40, English; 8, Scotch; 20, Irish; and 67, Acadian. There were 99 families and the people were "almost wholly devoted to agriculture pursuits." "Of mills," Calnek continued, "there were eight — four saw and four grist mills. Of vessels there were two schooners and nineteen fishing boats." Parts of Calnek's analysis was likely applicable to the entire province, but the people in the communities along the eastern coast of the province would have involved themselves in fishing; at Halifax, though some would have made their living at fishing, most would have been traders making a living off the military presence.

In July 1768, "a warrant of survey was issued to 44 Acadian families for lands at St. Mary's, in the County of Annapolis. They were from Windsor and Annapolis."[24] In later years the County of Annapolis was divided into two counties, Annapolis and Digby. Yet today, one of the largest concentrations of Acadians in the province can be found along the shores of St. Mary's Bay. These lands, however, were infertile and barren when compared to the valley lands which the Acadians had occupied, and which were then being preserved for English settlers: thank you very much.

Thus the re-settlement of the Acadians within the province of Nova Scotia began in 1768 and continued through the 1770s. It was the settlement of the Acadians then to be found in the province, not, by and large, Acadians that came back into the province (as mentioned, I am of the belief that few of the deported Acadians were ever to return).[25] By 1774, most of the Acadians then to be found in the province were either in the Digby and Yarmouth areas (the south end of peninsular Nova Scotia) or in Cape Breton (the south end).[26] The total population in Nova Scotia was estimated by Governor Legge in 1774 at "17,000 exclusive of the French Acadians, who may amount to about 1,300."[27]

The year 1774 was a significant year for all French inhabitants, whether in Acadia or in Quebec. All of Canada was governed by the British and had been since 1760. In the next dozen years the English leaders in London became increasingly more focused on their administrative problems in the English colonies along the eastern seaboard. The problems took a dramatic turn in 1773 when certain rebels in Boston threw a tea party. One thing became certain: the English could not deal with the unrest in the colonies and with the French problem in Canada all at the same time. Thus in October of 1774, the *Quebec Act* brought Canada under the control of Great Britain's parliament. Prior to that time, things happened by royal proclamation. The *Quebec Act* greatly extended the boundaries of the province of Quebec. It also provided that Roman Catholics (which was to have great significance for the Acadians then residing in Nova Scotia) should no longer be obliged to take the test oath,[28] but only the oath of allegiance. Thus, as a consequence of the *Quebec Act*, the Roman Catholic population of Canada were relived of their cruel disabilities before people of the same belief in Great Britain and Ireland.[29]

Chapter 18

The Summation

We did, in my opinion most inhumanly, and upon pretences that in the eye of an honest man are not worth a farthing, root out this poor, innocent, deserving people, whom our utter inability to govern or to reconcile gave us no sort of right to extirpate.[1]

— Edmund Burke

Governor Lawrence received no instructions from England to deport the Acadian population out of the province of Nova Scotia. After the deed was done, and only after, was he to write his masters at London advising them, in a somewhat incidental manner, that he had taken steps to put the province in a more secure position. Lawrence reasoned that the removal of French inhabitants of Acadia

... furnishes us with a large quantity of good land ready for immediate cultivation, renders it difficult for the Indians who cannot as formerly be supplied with provisions and intelligence, to make incursions upon our settlers, and I believe the French will not now be so sanguine in their hopes to possessing a province that they have hitherto looked upon as ready peopled for them the moment they would get the better of the English.[2]

And, the Lords Of Trade responded:

Whitehall, March 25th, 1756.

We look upon a War between us and France to be inevitable, and from the best judgment we are able to form of the views and the designs of the enemy. We are inclined to believe a great part of their force will be exerted to distress and annoy us in North America.

We have laid that part of your letter which relates to the removal of the French Inhabitants, and the Steps you took in the Execution of this Measure, before His Majesty's Secretary of State; and as you represent it to have been indispensably necessary for the Security and Protection of the Province in the present critical situation of our affairs, We doubt not but that your Conduct herein will meet with His Majesty's Approbation.[3]

As a result of the French attack on Minorca, on May 17th, 1756, England declared war on France. Thereafter, there was no time for the English or French leaders to give even the merest thought to the ancient inhabitants of Acadia which had been flung on the eastern shores of English North America. *The Seven Years War* ensued which ended in 1763 with the *Treaty Of Paris*. The French claims to North America, as a practical matter, were, by this war, utterly defeated.[4] The reconstruction of what had been French territory, then, was to take all of the attention of the English administrators. Within a dozen years the cauldron known as the thirteen colonies — long had it been heating up — boiled over: the English then had their hands full with the American Revolution. In the 1780s, Canada and Nova Scotia was to receive a flood of loyalists from the English colonies to the south. With all of these events, few people gave much thought to the trials and tribulations of the Acadians; and certainly no historian was to take up the subject (with the exception of Brown[5]) until many, many years had passed and all of the actors had long since retired from the stage.

The question: Are the British to be faulted for what they did to the Acadians? Let us accept that what occurred was cruel; it was, however, not unusual. It must be remembered that the French did to the English years earlier when 2,500 English persons were expelled from St. Kitts, an island in the Antilles group, rich in tobacco and sugar. The possession of the island was taken by both the French and the English in 1626 and each took half. With *The Second Anglo-Dutch War* spreading to North America both the French governor and the English governor plotted against one another with a view to taking St. Kitts over for their respective countries: the French won out. There then followed the expulsion of the English from St. Kitts, which the French celebrated by the striking of a metal. Then there was the French treatment of the Huguenots — no, the French could not from their glass houses throw any stones at the English over the deportation of the Acadians; nor, from what I can see, did they ever attempt to do so.

It was a sad scene, one that is difficult to equal in all of history, but those that were inflicted with the cruel punishment of being ripped from their homes cannot be said to have been pure in respect to their dealings with the English. They had long traded with the enemy and some of them took up arms against the English. It seems plain that they aided and abetted the French soldiers and joined the Indians in their raids against the English.[6] James Hannay, a most respected writer of Nova Scotian history, concluded "that very few people, who follow the story to the end, will be prepared to say that it was not a necessary measure of self preservation on the part of the English authorities in Nova Scotia."[7]

Their neutrality, however, did not present them from aiding the French to the utmost of their power and throwing every possible embarrassment in the way of the English. It did not prevent many of them from joining with the Indians in attacks on the garrison at Annapolis and on other English fortified posts in Acadia. It did not prevent them from carrying their cattle and grain to Louisbourg, Beauséjour and the River St. John, instead of to Halifax and Annapolis, when England and France were at war. It did not prevent them from maintaining a constant correspondence with the enemies of England, or from acting the part of spies on the English, and keeping Vergor at Beauséjour informed of the exact state of their garrisons from time to time. It did not prevent them from being on friendly terms with the savages, who beset the English so closely that an English settler could scarcely venture beyond his barn, or an English soldier beyond musket shot of his fort for fear of being killed and scalped.[8]

The neutrality of the Acadians, was, it should be said, self proclaimed. However, by international law[9] they had no right to such a claim. With France having given up their claims to Acadia by the terms of *Treaty of Utrecht* in 1713, the Acadians had no choice but to swear allegiance to the British crown, or leave. They were asked again and again to take an absolute oath; but they were steadfast in their refusal. The criticism to be leveled at the English is that they should have acted by deporting those who did not swear allegiance at a much earlier stage, in 1715 or 1716. The English did not act; this because they never had sufficient forces in Nova Scotia to act; they had but only a small garrison of soldiers at Annapolis Royal. The Acadians ignored the English and got away with it for forty odd years.

Though the act against the Acadians in 1755 was swift and sure it was one that was contemplated for many years, the deportation of the Acadians having been first proposed in 1720. The history is clear, that up to 1755, the English treated the French inhabitants in Nova Scotia with tolerance. The English military, being as a practical matter the only English people in Nova Scotia up to 1749, depended on the Acadians for food and fuel. The official government policy was to pay for whatever they received from the Acadians at prices determined by the Acadians. The fact of the matter is, that through the 45 year period leading up to 1755, the English treated the French inhabitants in a manner that impressed the French military officers at Louisbourg to a considerable degree. Francis Parkman gave a contemporary view of just such a French officer, who, from Louisbourg was writing to the court at Versailles:

> The fear that the Acadians have of the Indians is the controlling motive which makes them side with the French. The English, having in view the conquest of Canada, wished to give the French of that colony, in their conduct towards the Acadians, a striking example of the mildness of their government. Without raising the fortune of any of the inhabitants, they have supplied them for more than thirty-five years with the necessaries of life, often on credit and with an excess of confidence, without troubling their debtors, without pressing them, without wishing to force them to pay. They have left them an appearance of liberty so excessive that they have not intervened in their disputes or even punished their crimes. They have allowed them to refuse with insolence certain moderate rents payable in grain and lawfully due. They have passed over in silence the contemptuous refusal of the Acadians to take titles from them for the new lands which they chose to occupy.[10]

The historians who tell of the 1755 deportation are generally consistent in not seriously faulting the English, though there are other slants.[11] Professor Brebner, in his book, *New England's Outpost*, stated the facts in less than a paragraph:

... over six thousand peaceful farming people were by force and stratagem rounded up and hurriedly placed on transports and distributed from Massachusetts to South Carolina; of how others took refuge in the forests of what are now New Brunswick, Prince Edward Island, and Quebec, or made their way to Quebec City, the Ohio Valley, and Louisiana; of how some of them who escaped the first seizure only to be made captives in the terrible guerilla campaign of the succeeding years were sent to France and England or allowed to join the French in St. Pierre and Miquelon or the West Indies; or of how many lost their lives from starvation, exposure, ship-wreck, and the hazards of war. It was a cruel, pitiless affair. Everything was subordinated to the determination to make the expulsion as thorough as possible.[12]

What brought about this "cruel and pitiless affair"? Brebner summed it up: "... a number of forces of enduring weight and consistently determined character were woven together through many years to bring about the Acadian tragedy. Neglect, expediency, ignorance, the rivalries of empires and religions, eagerness for economic advantage, inertia ..."[13] The events of 1755 in Nova Scotia, as Brebner further pointed out, provide an excellent illustration of how the impersonal relations of nations mixed in with geography create imponderable forces, which in turn put into motion colossal human consequences.

John Clarence Webster:

These people loved their homes and their life in Acadia They learned too late that they had been mere pawns in the game of high politics directed from Quebec. Many of them had been cajoled and terrorized, mainly through the machinations of priests like Le Loutre, to sacrifice their homes and possessions for the nebulous promises of the French authorities, which were never realized, and which only precipitated the entire Acadian people into a morass of prolonged sorrows and miseries.[14]

In his paper read before the Nova Scotia Historical Society in 1886, the year in which he was elected to its presidency, Sir. Adams G. Archibald said this:

If there were cruelty in the sentence of deportation, surely the men of their own race and creed, who rendered that proceeding inevitable, are the persons to whom blame should attach. ...

But there cannot be a question that the Government and its subordinates were most anxious to do what had to be done, (which, at best, was admittedly a very painful necessity), with as much consideration and humanity as the case permitted.

One consolation we certainly derive from the perusal of the voluminous papers touching this subject to be found among our archives, and that is, the evidence they afford of the unceasing efforts of the British authorities, continued without intermission for the long period of forty years, to induce the Acadians to become good citizens and loyal subjects. ...

Instead, therefore, of imputing the calamity which befell these people, to the cruelty of the English authorities,we ought rather to charge it on the men who rendered it inevitable. The true authors of the tragic event, were the French Governors at Quebec and Louisbourg, and their agents, lay and clerical, in the Province. They created the necessity, the British only met it. They played with cruel skill on the ignorance, credulity and superstition, as well as on the generous affections, of the poor Acadians, and if that followed, which could not but follow, under such circumstances, surely they ought to bear the blame whose intrigues and instigations brought about a natural and inevitable result. The Acadians may therefore say with truth, that if they suffered calamity beyond the common lot of humanity, they owe it to men of their own race and creed-pretended friends, but real enemies.[15]

In conclusion, it should be said that historically, as sad as an event as it is was, the deportation of the Acadians in 1755 was but a minor part in the great military operations of that year: at Fort Duquesne (Pittsburgh), at Fort Niagara, at Crown Point, and Fort Beauséjour; and one that was hardly noticeable in the even greater military events that followed along and are summed up in the expression, *The Seven Years War.*

Any person who examines the removal of the Acadians during these years, and views the particulars in isolation and measures the effect by the standards of today will come to curse those who were responsible. What is required is a knowledge of the general situation which prevailed in the fifty years preceding this sorry event. The point needs to be clearly made: the English, though imminently practical people, were never known as cruel conquerors. They took great pains, and it is evident as one reads through all of the correspondence of the time, to treat the Acadians fairly. For example, there is the time that Vetch ordered his officers upon going into an Acadian village to not molest and not to kill any domestic animals. If soldiers needed food then a foul (versus an egg laying hen) might be killed, but, before the British soldiers left the community to continue on their rounds, the farmer was to be reimbursed. The English in their act of deporting the Acadians, though in the military balance of things considered to be a good idea, was an act which was to hurt Nova Scotia, a hurt that was to extend through many of the years which succeeded the event. The Acadian lands were of little use to the English without a people such as the Acadians to be on them and to be working them.

On April 10th, 1749, John Salusbury, who was with Lawrence when a company of English troops made their way through the Grand Pré area, wrote this in his journal:

> Every [British military] proceeding is extremely critical for the inhabitants [Acadian] are on the balance now either to go or stay, and that is of great consequence to us, for if they go they will greatly reinforce the French, which is the great design of leLoutre. If they stay, though they are not hearty in our interest, they are not actually against us — which they must be if they quit the province and truly they are a great body of people.[16]

That the deportation of the Acadians came about because of an overly zealous military man who was at the time in charge, and who at the same time found himself quite unexpectedly with the means, surplus troops, so to carry out his will; well — as an explanation, this is just too simple. It is history's conclusion, that *The Seven Years War* was to have greater results on the history of the world and brought greater triumphs to England then any other war.[17] No one knew this at the beginning of it, nor can anyone lay out the exact formula for such an English success. Anyone of us might point to an ingredient, many ingredients, and I shall attempt to do so in my next part; but one ingredient that will make the list for sure, is this: key military officers take precautions, which, a couple of hundred years later, as we sit in our comfortable arm chairs, we might describe as being cruel.

— End of volume I